Royal Commission on the National Health Service

Chairman: Sir Alec Merrison

REPORT

Presented to Parliament by Command of Her Majesty
July 1979

London
HER MAJESTY'S STATIONERY OFFICE
£8.00 net

Cmnd 7615

The estimated total expenditure of the Commission is (£918,000) of which (£71,180) represents the estimated cost of printing and publishing the report. This figure includes the cost of certain common services provided for all occupants of the building in which the Commission's offices were located.

ISBN 0 10 176150 3

The Royal Warrant

ELIZABETH R.

ELIZABETH THE SECOND, by the Grace of God of the United Kingdom of Great Britain and Northern Ireland and of Our other Realms and Territories QUEEN, Head of the Commonwealth, Defender of the Faith, to Our Trusty and Well-beloved

Sir Alexander Walter Merrison, Knight;

Sir Thomas Brown, Knight;

Sir Simpson Stevenson, Knight;

Lady Sherman;

Ivor Ralph Campbell Batchelor, Esquire, Commander of Our Most Excellent Order of the British Empire;

Audrey Mary Prime, Officer of Our Most Excellent Order of the British Empire;

Christopher John Wells, Esquire, Officer of Our Most Excellent Order of the British Empire, upon whom has been conferred the Territorial Efficiency Decoration;

Paul Anthony Bramley, Esquire;

Cecil Montacute Clothier, Esquire, One of Our Counsel learned in the Law;

Ann Clwyd;

Peter Roy Albert Jacques, Esquire;

Jean Kennedy McFarlane;

Kathleen Brenda Richards;

Cyril Taylor, Esquire;

Frank Reeson Welsh, Esquire;

Alan Harold Williams, Esquire;

Greeting!

WHEREAS We have deemed it expedient that a Commission should forthwith issue to consider in the interests both of the patients and of those who work in the National Health Service the best use and management of the financial and manpower resources of the National Health Service:

AND WHEREAS We have also deemed it expedient that the Commission should consider in the interests both of the patients and of those who work in the parallel services in Northern Ireland the best use and management of the financial and manpower resources of those services:

NOW KNOW YE that We, reposing great trust and confidence in your knowledge and ability, have authorised and appointed and do by these Presents authorise and appoint you the said Sir Alexander Walter Merrison (Chairman); Sir Thomas Brown; Sir Simpson Stevenson; Lady Sherman; Ivor Ralph Campbell Batchelor; Audrey Mary Prime; Christopher John Wells; Paul Anthony Bramley; Cecil Montacute Clothier; Ann Clwyd; Peter Roy Albert Jacques; Jean Kennedy McFarlane; Kathleen Brenda Richards; Cyril Taylor; Frank Reeson Welsh and Alan Harold Williams to be our Commissioners for the purposes of the said inquiry:

iii

AND for the better effecting the purposes of this Our Commission do by these Presents give and grant unto you, or any four or more of you, full power to call before you such persons as you shall judge likely to afford you any information upon the subject of this Our Commission; to call for information in writing; and also to call for, have access to and examine all such books, documents, registers and records as may afford you the fullest information on the subject and to inquire of and concerning the premises by all lawful ways and means whatsoever:

AND We do by these Presents authorise and empower you, or any of you, to visit and personally inspect such places as you may deem it expedient so to inspect for the more effectual carrying out of the purposes aforesaid:

AND We do by these Presents will and ordain that this Our Commission shall continue in full force and virtue, and that you, Our said Commissioners, or any four or more of you, may from time to time proceed in the execution thereof, and of every matter and thing therein contained, although the same be not continued from time to time by adjournment:

AND We do further ordain that you, or any four or more of you, have liberty to report your proceedings under this Our Commission from time to time if you shall judge it expedient to do so:

AND Our further will and pleasure is that you do, with as little delay as possible, report to Us your opinion upon the matters herein submitted for your consideration.

GIVEN at Our Court at Saint James's the nineteenth day of May 1976;

In the Twenty-fifth year of Our Reign.

By Her Majesty's Command.

Roy Jenkins

Note: Professor Alan Harold Williams resigned from the Commission on 31.8.78. Mr C M Clothier QC resigned from the Commission to take up the appointment of Parliamentary Commissioner for Administration and Health Service Commissioner on 3.1.79.

To the Queen's Most Excellent Majesty

MAY IT PLEASE YOUR MAJESTY

We, the undersigned Commissioners, having been appointed by Royal Warrant on 19 May 1976 to consider in the interests both of the patients and of those who work in the National Health Service the best use and management of the financial and manpower resources of the National Health Service and the parallel services in Northern Ireland

Humbly submit to Your Majesty the following Report.

Table of Contents

List of Tables

Figures

Chapter 1 Introduction

1.1   We were appointed with these terms of reference:–

"To consider in the interests both of the patients and of those who work in the National Health Service the best use and management of the financial and manpower resources of the National Health Service."

Our remit covered England, Scotland, Wales and the parallel services in Northern Ireland.

1.2   The Royal Warrant was issued on 19 May 1976 and there have been 35 meetings of the Commission, including five conferences lasting two or more days. Much of our work was done in sub-committees which between them held 83 meetings. In addition we visited each of the four constituent parts of the United Kingdom at least once, and took oral evidence in Edinburgh, Cardiff and Belfast as well as in London. Groups of us visited and held discussions with officials and individuals in Canada and the USA; West Germany; France and Holland; Sweden and Denmark; Yugoslavia and the USSR.

1.3   We received 2,460 written evidence submissions and held 58 oral evidence sessions. In addition we met and spoke informally to about 2,800 individuals during the course of our work and visits in the UK and abroad.

The background to our appointment

1.4   We were appointed at a time when there was widespread concern about the NHS. There had been a complete reorganisation of the service throughout the UK in 1973 and 1974 which few had greeted as an unqualified success. The NHS had suffered a number of industrial disputes accompanied in some cases by at least a partial withdrawal of labour by ambulancemen, some ancillary staff, and hospital doctors and dentists. The then government's decision to phase out private beds from NHS hospitals was being heatedly debated in the NHS, and was itself the occasion for some of the industrial action mentioned. In addition to all this, the NHS could not shelter from the country's chill economic climate in the mid-1970s, so that although it suffered no real financial cut-back it was denied the growth which it had come to expect to help it meet the rising demands made upon it. In Northern Ireland there were continuing strains arising from civil and political disorder.

1.5   There were less pressing, but nonetheless important, reasons why a general inquiry into the use of resources in the NHS was timely. Despite the

1

close attention which had been given to the administration of the service; the three Royal Commissions[1] and the large number of committees which had reported on aspects of it since 1948, the NHS had been considered as a whole only by the Guillebaud Committee[2] and that Committee had not covered, as our terms of reference require us to, the health services in Northern Ireland. Largely because of this we have used the broad scope of our terms of reference to the full.

Our approach

1.6   It would have been possible to have interpreted our terms of reference in a narrow financial and administrative context and written a straightforward technical report along these lines, but it would have been wrong to do so. The NHS is an institution which enables human beings to offer care, and sometimes cure, to others in need of it. It is a vast institution, with all the administrative consequences which follow from this, and the people who staff it must never be overlooked or the quality of their humane commitment undervalued; they are the foundation on which all else is built.

1.7   Our work has been informed throughout by the idea that the NHS is a *service to patients*. Necessarily, a good part of our report deals with such topics as the details of NHS administration and the careers of nurses, to give two examples of matters which affect some of those who work in the service but are likely to be of little immediate interest or concern to patients. While the efficient use of resources or the morale of NHS workers cannot be neglected – indeed, we regard them as of central importance – it must not be forgotten that the purpose of the NHS is the care and comfort of patients, and we should want our report to be judged against those criteria. We urge those whose business it is to decide which of our recommendations should be implemented to be mindful of this.

1.8   Our first act was to invite views about which of the problems of the NHS we should examine. Having considered over 1,000 replies we published "The Task of the Commission"[3] in October 1976, which listed topics to be considered and was intended as a guide to those submitting evidence. We remarked in that publication that what was in the interests of those who worked in the NHS would also generally be in the interests of the patients but, where those interests conflicted, the interests of the patient must be paramount. That is not a view from which we would wish to retreat.

1.9   With these points in mind we have spent a great deal of our time, at the beginning of our inquiry and subsequently, considering how the patient actually gets service. It seemed to us most important to understand matters of

[1]*Report of the Royal Commission on the Law relating to Mental Illness and Mental Deficiency 1954-57,* (Cmnd 169), London, HMSO, 1957; *Royal Commission on Doctors' and Dentists' Remuneration 1957-60,* (Cmnd 939), London, HMSO, 1960; *Royal Commission on Medical Education 1965-68 Report,* (Cmnd 3569), London, HMSO, 1968.

[2]*Report of the Committee of Enquiry into the Cost of the National Health Service,* (Cmd 9663), London, HMSO, 1956.

[3]Royal Commission on the NHS, *The Task of the Commission,* London, HMSO, 1976.

this kind before we began to inquire into questions of administration and finance. We remarked in The Task of the Commission that "large organisations are most efficient when problems are solved and decisions taken at the lowest effective point."[1] Nothing we have learned in our inquiry would lead us to modify this view.

1.10   We have said already that we have thought it right to see our inquiry as something more than an accounting exercise. We should say too that we certainly would not be the right people to conduct such an exercise and we have felt it right to play to our strength, which we see as the wide experience we possess collectively in NHS matters and matters which affect the NHS. Naturally, we have not been able to consider all aspects of the service in detail nor give some the attention that might have been expected. The one common experience we share is that we have all been patients and have personal reasons for being thankful for the NHS, and all of us have experienced some of its frustrations.

1.11   There is one more important point to be made about the nature of our work, and that is that the measurement of "health" and of the effectiveness of health care are at best uncertain sciences. A good deal of the evidence presented to us, and a good deal of our own work, might be termed anecdotal or subjective. We have not regarded it as less instructive or valuable on that account and, indeed, given the difficulties of quantitative work in this field and the infinite variety of human behaviour, it is hard to see that we could have done otherwise.

1.12   We felt that it was vital for us to talk to as many people in the UK and abroad[2] as we possibly could, given the limitations on our time. We have been met everywhere with friendliness and candour and we should like now to place on record our deep gratitude to those who have given so generously of their time and thought. Perhaps the pleasantest of our duties is to thank our Secretary, David de Peyer, his two Assistant Secretaries, Roy Cunningham and Alan Gilbert, and all those in the Royal Commission Secretariat who have worked so devotedly for us. We are all too conscious of the burden we have put upon them and of the skill, energy and friendliness they have shown in carrying it. As Commissioners we shall take with us the happiest memories of the way we have been served in the last three years.[3]

1.13   There were many areas of our inquiry where we considered we could benefit from commissioned research. We decided to concentrate on a few main areas which we considered crucial and to call for work which could be completed within our time scale. We accordingly commissioned:

(a) a study of the working of the reorganised NHS, primarily aimed at establishing the truth of the frequent allegations of delays resulting from NHS reorganisation, undertaken for us by Professor Maurice Kogan and

---

[1] *Ibid* p2

[2] Appendix A lists organisations and individuals who have given written and oral evidence and those who have helped in other ways. Appendix B lists visits made in the UK and abroad.

[3] Appendix C lists the names of the Commissioners and of the full-time Secretariat.

a team of researchers at Brunel University (published as *The Working of the NHS* Research Paper Number 1, London, HMSO in June 1978);

(b) a study of the local administration of NHS finance, intended to help us tackle that part of our terms of reference which refers to the "best use and management of the financial ... resources" of the NHS, undertaken under the supervision of Professor John Perrin of Warwick University (published as *The Management of Finance in the NHS* Research Paper Number 2, London, HMSO July 1978);

(c) a commentary on the health departments' resource allocation arrangements prepared by Professor Rudolf Klein of Bath University and Mr Martin Buxton of the Policy Studies Institute (published as *Allocating Health Resources, A commentary on the Report of the Resource Allocation Working Party* Research Paper Number 3, London, HMSO August 1978);

(d) a report on medical manpower forecasting prepared by Mr Alan Maynard and Mr Arthur Walker of York University (published as *Doctor Manpower 1975-2000: alternative forecasts and their resource implications* Research Paper Number 4, London, HMSO September 1978);

(e) a study by the Social Survey Division of the Office of Population Censuses and Surveys of patient attitudes towards hospital services which complemented one already commissioned by the Department of Health and Social Security on access to primary health care services (published as *Patients' attitudes to the Hospital Service* Research Paper Number 5, London, HMSO January 1979);

(f) jointly with the National Consumer Council a survey of problems of certain groups in gaining access to primary care services (published as *Access to Primary Care* Research Paper Number 6, London, HMSO February 1979).

We published these papers to get the reactions of others to them, and because we were sure they would be of value to many of our readers. We have profited too from other work carried out for us by a number of people outside our own secretariat. Some of them are referred to in the text of this report.

1.14   The 21 chapters of our report that follow are arranged in five parts:

a general view of the nation's health and health care;
the NHS and the patient;
the NHS and its workers;
the NHS and other institutions;
management and finance of the NHS;

followed by conclusions and recommendations.

1.15   Since "How well are we doing?" is a question which exercises the minds of everyone, the first part of our report, formed of the three chapters which follow this introduction, gives our assessment of the NHS and its strengths and weaknesses at present.

1.16   Throughout the report the four parts of the UK are dealt with

1.16 Throughout the report the four parts of the UK are dealt with together. Wherever possible we have made what we say apply to each part of the UK, but the wide range of circumstances which exist in them may mean that on occasions what we say is not of universal application. Where important differences between the countries exist they are commented on in the relevant chapters, and Appendix D gives details.

Part I   A Perspective of the Nation's Health and Health Care

We could not carry out the task defined in our terms of reference without considering what were the objectives of the NHS, what they should be and how far the NHS does and may succeed in reaching them. We therefore started by asking what as individuals we could reasonably expect of society in helping us maintain our health and caring for us when we were sick. We found no simple, unique answer to this question. But whatever answer is offered will define the nature of the health service we want and its objectives. It is therefore a question which, whether we are patients, providers or policy makers, we all should keep before us.

It is important also to understand from the outset that good health depends on much more than a good health service. No health system can be looked at in isolation from the society it serves or the way that that society chooses to behave.

In Chapter 2, the first chapter of this section of the report, we put forward our view of what the objectives of the NHS should be; there and elsewhere we discuss how well it achieves those objectives and how it might be helped to do better in the future. In the succeeding chapter we make some estimate of how well the NHS is performing compared with what it has been able to do in the past and with what other countries have achieved. In the last chapter of this introductory section we discuss some of the failings of the NHS which have been put to us.

Chapter 2   Objectives of the NHS

2.1   The idea that a community of any size should undertake the major responsibility for the health of its members – a national health service – is of comparatively recent origin and one certainly not accepted everywhere. Setting objectives for such a service is no easy matter.

2.2   Health itself is not a precise or simple concept. In practice the state of health of individuals ranges from the ideal through different degrees of illness and disability to the brink of death. Judgments often have to be made about accepting a level of health which is far from the ideal, and what is acceptable will vary from one individual to another, from one health worker to another, and even from one part of the country to another. We are therefore dealing with many different concepts of health, and the functions of the NHS should reflect this. It should be concerned with more than the treatment of disease, important though that is, but deal also with disease prevention and with helping people to achieve the wider benefits of good health.

2.3   As the general level of health in a community improves, the concern for mere survival diminishes and more attention can be paid to the quality of life. As the killing diseases of early and middle life are conquered and we live longer, the demands for the care that helps us to cope with the degenerative diseases and disabilities which will inevitably affect us all in later life must increase. It is a wry comment on the way of life in developed countries that we now pay more attention to the diseases of affluence than we do those of deprivation.

2.4   The principles and objectives of the NHS are defined, very broadly, in the duty laid by Parliament on health ministers to provide a National Health Service. Section 1 of the National Health Service Act 1977[1] recalls the words of the 1946 Act which created the NHS in England and Wales and declares:

"It is the Secretary of State's duty to continue the promotion in England and Wales of a comprehensive health service designed to secure improvement –

(a) in the physical and mental health of the people of those countries, and

(b) in the prevention, diagnosis and treatment of illness,

---

[1]There is similar provision in the separate legislation for Scotland and Northern Ireland. Most of the legislation on the NHS was consolidated for England and Wales in the National Health Service Act 1977 and for Scotland in the National Health Service (Scotland) Act 1978. All subsequent references to NHS legislation refer to these Acts except where otherwise stated. The main provisions about health services in Northern Ireland are contained in the Health and Personal Social Services (Northern Ireland) Order 1972.

and for that purpose to provide or secure the effective provision of services in accordance with this Act."

2.5   The absence of detailed and publicly declared principles and objectives for the NHS reflects to some degree the continuing political debate about the service. Politicians and public alike are agreed on the desirability of a national health service in broadly its present form, but agreement often stops there. Instead of principles there are policies which change according to the priorities of the government of the day and the particular interests of the ministers concerned. We have therefore written down what we believe the objectives of the NHS should be.

2.6   We believe that the NHS should:

encourage and assist individuals to remain healthy;

provide equality of entitlement to health services;

provide a broad range of services of a high standard;

provide equality of access to these services;

provide a service free at the time of use;

satisfy the reasonable expectations of its users;

remain a national service responsive to local needs.

We are well aware that some of these objectives lack precision and some are controversial. They are further discussed later in our report. We are aware too that some are unattainable, but that does not make them less important as objectives.

Encouraging and assisting individuals to remain healthy

2.7   We consider it legitimate and positively desirable to devote public resources to the maintenance and promotion of personal as well as public health, not only by the constraints of law but also by offering exhortation, education and incentives. The NHS cannot cover the whole field. Though protracted unemployment and poor social conditions may impair the quality of life and health, it is the responsibility of other organs of government to promote employment and to care for the environment. The encouragement and advancement of good personal health is vitally important and we discuss the part the NHS has to play in Chapter 5. It is a proper objective of the NHS to keep the individual in good health.

Equality of entitlement

2.8   We consider, like the framers of the original legislation, that the NHS should be available without restriction by age, social class, sex, race or religion to all people living in the UK.[1] We are in no doubt that one of the most

[1]We propose no change in policy towards providing treatment to non-residents of the UK. It is right that those who fall ill while they are in this country should continue to receive treatment under the NHS but that unless there is a reciprocal agreement with a particular country a charge should be made if treatment is specifically sought in the UK.

significant achievements of the NHS has been to free people from fear of being unable to afford treatment for acute or chronic illness, but we regret that they must often wait too long for such treatment.

A broad range of services of a high standard

2.9   This is perhaps the most difficult matter we have to discuss and it is at the heart of our terms of reference. We deal with it more fully in Part II of the report, but our definition of this objective includes health promotion, disease prevention, cure, care and after care. The NHS was, from the first, designed to be a comprehensive service. The 1944 White Paper said:

> "The proposed service must be 'comprehensive' in two senses – first, that it is available to all people and, second, that it covers all necessary forms of health care."[1]

The impossibility of meeting all demands for health services was not anticipated. Medical, nursing and therapeutic techniques have been developed to levels of sophistication and expense which were not foreseen when the NHS was introduced.

2.10   Standards of cure and care within a given level of resources are in practice largely in the hands of the health professions. They are nevertheless of the greatest concern to the patient. The aim must always be to raise standards in areas where there are deficiencies, but not at the expense of places where services are already good. The NHS has achieved much. It should remain an objective of a national health service to see that it has an active role in disseminating high standards. Sir George Godber, Chief Medical Officer at the Department of Health and Social Security 1960–73, puts the point thus:

> "The burden upon the NHS is that of generalization from the example of the best and the result of having such a national service should be the more rapid development of improved services available to all."[2]

Equality of access

2.11   It is unrealistic to suppose that people in all parts of the United Kingdom can have equal ease of access to all services of an identical standard. Access to the highest standard of care will be limited by the numbers of those who can provide such care. There are parts of the country which are better or worse provided with services than others. We draw attention, for example, to the special problems of rural areas and declining urban areas in Chapter 7. Nonetheless, a fundamental purpose of a national service must be equality of provision so far as this can be achieved without an unacceptable sacrifice of standards. We deal with the financial aspects of this objective in Chapter 21.

---

[1]*A National Health Service*, (Cmd 6502), London, HMSO, 1944, page 9.

[2]Godber, Sir George, *Change in Medicine*, The Nuffield Provincial Hospitals Trust, 1975, page 101.

A service free at the time of use

2.12   Charges for services within the NHS have always been a matter of controversy, and have led on occasion to the resignation of ministers. We discuss charges in Chapter 21, but there are three points to be made here. First, the purpose of charges may be to raise revenue, or discourage the frivolous use of the service, or both. Second, charges may be made for a service which, though provided by or through the NHS, is not *essential* to the care or treatment of patients – for example, amenity beds in NHS hospitals. Third, in any consideration of charges, it is important to stress that "free at the time of use" is quite different from "free". We do not have a free health service; we have a service to which all taxpayers, employees and employers contribute, regardless of the use they make of it. The effect of this is that those members of the community who do not require extensive use of the NHS help to pay for the care of those who do. It is worth remembering that about 60% of the total expenditure of the NHS goes on children, the old, the disabled, the mentally ill and the mentally handicapped.

Satisfying reasonable expectations

2.13   This objective can be considered from the point of view of the individual patient, or more generally. Most patients lack the technical knowledge to make informed judgments about diagnosis and treatment. Ignorance may as easily be a reason for a patient being satisfied with his treatment as for his being dissatisfied. One aspect of care on which he will be reliable, however, is whether he has been humanely treated. While doctors are properly deferred to as experts on the technical aspects of medicine, options, when they exist, should be carefully explained and wherever feasible the choice of treatment left to the patient and his relatives. Maximum freedom of choice seems to us an important aspect of this objective although we recognise that there may sometimes be practical limitations on complete freedom of choice for patients. A patient, or potential patient, who is capable of deciding for himself, should be free to:

> consult a doctor, dentist, or other health professional;
>
> change his practitioner;
>
> choose a particular hospital or unit with the help of his general practitioner; and
>
> refuse treatment or advice except where the health or safety of others would be endangered.

2.14   More generally, it is important for any health service to carry its users with it, given that it can never satisfy all the demands made upon it. It is misleading to pretend that the NHS can meet all expectations. Hard choices have to be made. It is a prime duty of those concerned in the provision of health care to make it clear to the rest of us what we can reasonably expect.

A national service responsive to local needs

2.15   Health services meet different situations in different parts of the

11

country. The range, speed of development and pattern of service delivery will need to vary. Some services can best be provided on a national or regional basis; specialised treatment may require complicated equipment and a higher degree of expertise than can be provided in every community. But if inflexibility is to be avoided, health authorities should implement national policy in the context of their particular geographical and demographic constraints. We discuss the implications of this for the structure of the NHS in Chapters 19 and 20.

Conclusions

2.16   The objectives set out above do not always lead in the same direction: for example, the provision of health services of high standard may conflict with equality of access. Because each objective will be costly to pursue and resources are limited, the community will continually face the problem of choice between one objective and another and between different ways of achieving those objectives. But, after all reservations have been made, we consider that the NHS needs to operate within a general framework and the objectives which we set down here have guided our thinking in the chapters which follow.

2.17   The financial resources available to the NHS are finite. We show in Chapter 21 that real expenditure on health services has increased significantly since 1948. Although we naturally hope that resources will continue to be made available on a generous scale, it would be unrealistic to suppose that the fortunes of the NHS can be insulated from those of the nation. We have the highest regard for what has been attempted and accomplished in the NHS – which means by those who work in it. We hope that the recommendations we make will improve the NHS further.

Chapter 3   How good the Service is now

3.1   In the evidence submitted to us we found a complete spectrum of descriptions of the present state of the NHS ranging from "the envy of the world" to its being "on the point of collapse". We hope we shall not be judged to be mere trimmers if we declare immediately that our judgment lies between these extremes. It should occasion no surprise that views on the health service differ so widely. The giving and receiving of health care is necessarily a sensitive and emotional subject. It would be expecting too much from both patients and the providers of health care that they should be able to distance themselves from the subject, nor would it be desirable. Relationships between patients and those providing care necessarily carry emotional overtones, and it is as much the duty of any health service worker to comment honestly upon the failings he sees as it is to promote good practice.

3.2   In the preceding chapter we put forward objectives for the NHS and discussed them briefly. In this chapter we attempt to give an impression – and it can be little more than that – of how successful the UK has been in meeting those objectives and how well it compares with other nations, some richer some poorer, in caring for the health of its citizens. We consider the NHS from three different points of view – the patient who makes use of it, the statistician seeking objective measurements of performance, and the worker who provides it.

The Patient's View

3.3   The NHS is a service for "consumers" and any discussion of its performance must start with the views of the patients it is intended to serve. Patients may not have the expertise to make technical judgments about the treatment they receive but they are in a unique position to comment on the results of the treatment.

3.4   We thought it essential to have as clear an idea as possible of what the users of the service considered its strengths and weaknesses. We commissioned a national survey of patients' attitudes to hospital services[1], and we had access to one of patients' attitudes to primary care[2], both undertaken by the Office of Population Censuses and Surveys (OPCS). We discuss the results in more detail in other chapters. The hospital survey indicated that over 80% of in-patients thought that the service they received was good or very good, but 7%

---

[1]Gregory, Janet. *Patients' attitudes to the Hospital Services*, Royal Commission on the NHS, Research Paper Number 5, London, HMSO, 1978.

[2]Office of Population Censuses and Surveys, *Access to Primary Care*, (to be published).

said that if they had to go back into hospital they would definitely not want to go into the same hospital again.

3.5   We complemented the OPCS primary care survey with a study of services for children and old people in two markedly different communities in London and Cumbria[1], and we were also able to use the results of a study of access to primary health care in the Western Isles[2]. These surveys showed that though there were criticisms of particular aspects of primary care, patients were generally satisfied with the service they received. Simpson's study concluded that:

> "On the whole, while always capable of improvement, the NHS did provide an accessible primary care service which was generally appreciated by its users."[3]

Access to services

3.6   One of the objectives we referred to in Chapter 2 was equality of access to health services. It is a mark of a successful health service that it is available equally to all potential users. We concern ourselves here with geographical and social equality of access. We deal with the question of priorities between particular patient groups in the NHS in Chapter 6.

Geographical equality

3.7   It is not difficult to show that some parts of the UK are better served than others in terms of expenditure on health services and numbers of staff. Tables 3.1 and 3.2 give some crude comparisons. The figures make no allowance for differences in demand or need for health services, nor for differences in the cost of delivering health care. The age patterns of populations differ; a relatively elderly population will need fewer maternity services but may make heavier demands on acute and community health services. The stock of hospital buildings will be of better quality in some places than in others. Teaching and research responsibilities vary.

3.8   Commonly used measures of health are infant mortality rates, perinatal mortality rates and standardised mortality ratios.[4] Table 3.3 shows that there are geographical variations in these measures of health as well as in health service resources. Tables 3.1, 3.2 and 3.3 show that the relationship between health service resources and the health of the population served, as measured by mortality rates, is far from simple and that judgments about the effectiveness and efficiency of health services must make allowance for other influences on health. Nevertheless, it is clear that striking differences in

---

[1]Simpson, Robin. *Access to Primary Care*, Royal Commission on the NHS, Research Paper Number 6, London, HMSO, 1979.

[2]Scottish Consumer Council, *Island Health Care*, Institute of Medical Sociology Occasional Paper Number 3, Aberdeen, 1978.

[3]Simpson, Robin. *Op cit*, paragraph 7.49.

[4]See footnote 1 to Table 3.3.

effectiveness and efficiency of health services must make allowance for other influences on health. Nevertheless, it is clear that striking differences in resource provision remain within each of the four parts of the UK and between them.

TABLE 3.1

Distribution of Health Expenditure: UK 1976/1977

£ per capita

	Hospital services expenditure	Community health and family practitioner services expenditure	Total expenditure[1]
ENGLAND	61.76	28.31	104.88
Northern	56.19	28.42	100.13
Yorkshire	56.86	27.42	97.44
Trent	50.49	26.67	93.80
East Anglia	53.83	26.94	95.22
NW Thames	74.91	33.21	122.38
NE Thames	76.35	25.95	117.00
SE Thames	73.61	29.28	118.17
SW Thames	67.00	28.67	112.73
Wessex	52.44	28.15	94.00
Oxford	53.18	28.23	96.09
South Western	57.87	30.50	103.33
West Midlands	52.65	26.96	91.52
Mersey	62.16	27.92	107.16
North Western	57.63	28.88	100.46
WALES	61.50	31.21	107.39
SCOTLAND	78.10	30.00	127.10
N IRELAND	83.07	33.67	138.67
UNITED KINGDOM	63.84	28.76	107.98

Source: compiled from Central Statistical Office, *Regional Statistics*, 14, HMSO, 1979.

Note: [1] Includes "headquarters administration", "other services" and capital expenditure not shown separately.

TABLE 3.2
Distribution of Health Manpower: UK 1977

Per 10,000[1]
population

	General medical practitioners[2]	Hospital doctors (wte)[3][4]	General dental practitioners	Nurses and midwives (wte)[3]
ENGLAND	4.84	6.13	2.55	73.5
Northern	4.55	6.24	1.84	71.4
Yorkshire	4.70	5.62	2.18	73.6
Trent	4.54	5.14	1.88	66.1
East Anglia	4.85	5.71	2.20	65.6
NW Thames	5.48	7.84	4.01	75.4
NE Thames	5.10	7.40	2.77	76.6
SE Thames	5.01	6.85	2.91	80.5
SW Thames	5.17	6.25	3.61	76.5
Wessex	4.98	5.45	2.72	68.5
Oxford	4.73	6.04	2.51	62.3
South Western	5.17	5.32	2.97	74.7
West Midlands	4.56	5.45	2.10	67.9
Mersey	4.60	6.13	2.44	80.6
North Western	4.55	6.59	2.12	75.0
WALES	5.05	5.96	2.09	79.0
SCOTLAND	5.98	9.19	2.33	102.2
N IRELAND	5.56	7.84	2.27	98.6
UNITED KINGDOM	4.98	6.45	2.50	77.1

Source: health departments' statistics (see notes to Appendix E).

Notes: [1] Figures will differ from those in Table 3.8 because of differences in dates and definition. Table 3.8, for example, refers only to fully trained nurses, thus excluding auxiliaries included in this table.

[2] Throughout the report figures for general medical practitioners include restricted and unrestricted principals, assistants and trainees except where otherwise stated.

[3] Whole time equivalents.

[4] Figures for English regions are for 1978

16

TABLE 3.3
Mortality Rates: UK 1977[1]

	Infant mortality rate	Perinatal mortality rate	Standardised mortality ratio[2]	
			M	F
ENGLAND	13.7	16.9	99	99
Northern	14.9	19.1	111	109
Yorkshire	15.5	18.1	105	105
Trent	13.9	16.7	103	102
East Anglia	11.2	13.0	89	96
NW Thames	11.8	14.8	89	90
NE Thames	14.0	16.1	94	92
SE Thames	13.1	16.8	95	92
SW Thames	11.6	14.6	90	95
Wessex	13.1	15.5	92	92
Oxford	12.7	15.0	90	96
South Western	12.5	16.2	93	97
West Midlands	15.0	19.4	103	103
Mersey	14.4	18.8	110	109
North Western	14.8	18.5	113	111
WALES	13.5	17.9	108	106
SCOTLAND	16.1	18.3	112	109
N IRELAND	17.2	21.1	112	115

Source: Office of Population Censuses and Surveys.

Notes: [1] The infant mortality rate is the number of deaths under one year of age per 1,000 live births; the perinatal mortality rate is the number of deaths occurring after the 28th week of pregnancy or during the first week of life per 1,000 total births; and the standardised mortality ratio (SMR) compares the number of deaths actually occurring in an area with those which would be expected if national mortality rates by age and sex were applicable to the population of that area.

[2] England, English regions and Wales based on England and Wales=100. Scotland and Northern Ireland based on UK=100.

3.9   Inequality in the distribution of NHS resources has always been with us. As the Resource Allocation Working Party (RAWP) put it:

> "The methods used to distribute financial resources to the NHS have, since its inception, tended to reflect the inertia built into the system by history. They have tended to increment the historic basis for the supply of real resources (e.g. facilities and manpower); and, by responding comparatively slowly and marginally to changes in demography and morbidity, have also tended to perpetuate the historic situation."[1]

As NHS resources have increased since 1948 inequalities have been reduced, though, as we have seen, some remain large. In England RAWP was established by the Department of Health and Social Security (DHSS) to

---

[1]Department of Health and Social Security, *Sharing Resources for Health in England: Report of the Resource Allocation Working Party*, London, HMSO, 1976, paragraph 1.2.

investigate and reduce imbalances in the distribution of resources. The Working Party proposed a formula for the fairer allocation of funds between the English regions, and comparable exercises have been undertaken in Scotland, Wales and Northern Ireland.[1] Whatever their failings, these exercises represent attempts to achieve a fairer distribution of resources for the NHS.

TABLE 3.4

Male Standardised Mortality Ratios by Social Class: England and Wales 1921–23/1970–72

Social Class	1921–23 (age 20–64)	1930–32 (age 20–64)	1949–53 (age 20–64)	1959–63 (age 15–64)	1970–72 (age 15–64)
I Professional occupations	82	90	86	76	77
II Managerial and lower professional occupations	94	94	92	81	81
III Skilled occupations	95	97	101	100	104
IV Partly skilled occupations	101	102	104	103	113
V Unskilled occupations	125	111	118	143	137

Source: Brotherston, Sir John. "Inequality: is it inevitable?" in Carter C.O. and Peel, J. (editors). *Equalities and Inequalities in Health*, London, Academic Press, 1976, Table 8.1.

Social equality

3.10 The opening paragraph of the 1944 White Paper said that the Government:

> "want to ensure that in future every man and woman and child can rely on getting all the advice and treatment and care which they may need in matters of personal health; that what they get shall be the best medical and other facilities available; that their getting these shall not depend on whether they can pay for them, or any other factor irrelevant to the real need."[2]

There is plenty of evidence to show that there are still striking differences in mortality and morbidity between social classes as defined by the Registrars General. Table 3.4 shows male standardised mortality ratios by social class in England and Wales between 1921/23 and 1970/72, and Table 3.5 some measures of morbidity by social class. Nor does the evidence suggest that social inequalities in health have decreased since the establishment of the NHS. The position of those in social classes IV and V appears to have worsened relative to those in social classes I and II, though it should be remembered that all social classes are healthier than they were thirty years

---

[1] Scottish Home and Health Department, *Scottish Health Authorities Revenue Equalisation*, Edinburgh, HMSO, 1977.
Welsh Office, *Report of the Steering Committee on Resource Allocation*, 1977.
Department of Health and Social Services (Northern Ireland), *Proposals for the Allocation of Revenue Resources*, 1978.

[2] *A National Health Service*, (Cmd 6502), London, HMSO, 1944.

ago and the proportion of the population in social classes IV and V has fallen. There is also evidence that the higher socio-economic groups receive relatively more of the expenditure on the NHS.[1]

TABLE 3.5

Persons Reporting Chronic Health Problems by Sex and Socio-Economic Group: Great Britain 1977

percentage

	Males	Females
Professional	49	61
Employers and managers	53	68
Intermediate and junior non-manual	54	67
Skilled manual and own account non-professional	58	71
Semi-skilled manual and personal service	60	75
Unskilled manual	65	79
Total	56	70

Source: OPCS, *The General Household Survey 1977*, London, HMSO, 1979, Table 6.21.

3.11 There are a number of possible reasons for this inequality, not all of which have much to do with the NHS itself. Sir John Brotherston, Professor of Community Medicine at Edinburgh University and former Chief Medical Officer to the Scottish Home and Health Department, has suggested that amongst the factors which may play a part in the poorer health of social classes IV and V is a tendency for those most in need of health services to gravitate towards the lower end of the social scale, the biological effects of deprivation, and the influence of intelligence and education in making the best use of preventive and curative services. He also points out that the NHS is a "self-help" system, reacting to individual demands but not actively seeking out those most in need of its services.[2]

Conclusion

3.12 Despite the general level of satisfaction with the NHS it is evident that patients find defects in some services. Even simple analyses of the way NHS resources are distributed in the UK and of various crude measures of health show that there is significant geographical and social inequity. Resource and mortality or morbidity statistics do not reveal many of the more specific concerns of patients, such as waiting times for orthopaedic out-patient

[1]Titmuss, R M, *Commitment to Welfare*, London, Allen and Unwin, 1968. Le Grand, Julian, "The distribution of public expenditure: the case of health care", *Economica*, 1978, Vol 45, pages 125-142.

[2]Brotherston, Sir John, "Inequality: is it inevitable?" in Carter CO and Peel J (editors), *Equalities and Inequalities in Health*, London, Academic Press, 1976, page 97.

appointments, or for some other forms of surgery, or anxieties about the availability of adequate services or facilities for the management of illness in the old and infirm. We consider some of these concerns later in this report. Nor do statistics reflect the many intangible qualities which patients rightly expect from the health service. Humanity, consideration and courtesy are important in any public service, but especially so in the health service. They cannot easily be measured but should not therefore be ignored. Many patients will judge the health service by these qualities.

Statistical Comparisons

3.13 It is common practice when discussing the merits of the NHS to compare the amount spent on it with amounts spent in other countries, or to cite particular mortality statistics – perinatal mortality is often used – to demonstrate the success or otherwise of the NHS. Handled carefully, this kind of exercise can be useful, but it may also be misleading.

Measuring health

3.14 In Chapter 2 we pointed out that health is not a precise or simple concept. There are some further caveats to be entered. To begin with, measuring the health of a nation should not be confused with measuring the performance of its health service. The fact that over eight million teeth had to be extracted in Great Britain in 1977 has more to do with the way we live, and more importantly the way our children live, than the competence of our dentists or the efficiency of our dental services. Such examples can be multiplied endlessly. Even when health care is available and used properly it can make only a contribution, albeit a vital one, to a nation's health; and even the most cursory examination of the past shows clearly enough that improved nutrition, hygiene and drainage have had greater effects than many dramatic cures for specific ills. We say more about this in Chapter 5.

3.15 The lack of a clear and commonly accepted definition of health creates problems for attempts to assess the efficiency of a health service by measuring the health of a population or by making historical or international comparisons. Such morbidity data as are available may be unreliable, though they may nonetheless be useful in indicating the size of a health problem or highlighting a particular service deficiency. A few diseases are "notifiable" to health authorities, but do not provide a guide to the general health of the population: an increase in whooping cough, for example, may be balanced by a decrease in some other non-notifiable complaint. Hospital statistics give information about numbers of patients treated in hospital, and about numbers waiting to be treated, but variations in these figures may be due as much to facilities available, either in hospitals themselves or in the community, and to the costs to patients of using the service, as to differences in the health of the population. The number of working days per worker lost through certified sickness cannot be relied on as an accurate indicator of health. The lack of satisfactory morbidity statistics is a real handicap in distributing resources and directing effort effectively.

3.16   Because of the difficulty of measuring morbidity, comparative studies of health usually stick to mortality though even here there are difficulties with the reliability and comparability of the data. Advances in medicine may improve perinatal mortality figures by preserving the lives of severely handi-capped babies who would otherwise have died at birth but whose prospects of survival for more than a few years, or of having anything like a normal life, are small. Mortality figures in any case say nothing about the quality of life: the benefits of chiropody and hip replacements will not show up in the statistics but may make the difference between immobility and self-sufficiency for many old people. Quality of life becomes increasingly important as the possibilities develop of extending life for people who would in the past have died from their illnesses or injuries, and as people live longer and the chronic conditions of old age become more common.

Assessing health services

3.17   These substantial reservations must be kept firmly in mind when making historical or international comparisons. Table 3.6 shows changes in mortality rates since 1948, and Table 3.7 shows changes in life expectancy between 1950 and 1977. The question arises how far these improvements can be attributed to the NHS. In one sense it is impossible to answer because there is no way of knowing what would have happened if the NHS had not been introduced in 1948. It is likely that mortality rates would have fallen, as they have in comparable countries, whatever the organisation of health services.

TABLE 3.6
Mortality Rates: England and Wales 1948–1977

	1948	1977	% Change 1948–1977
Perinatal mortality	38.5	17.0	55.84
Infant mortality	34.0	13.8	59.41
Mortality[1]			
Age 35–44 M	3.15	2.01	36.19
F	2.45	1.41	42.45
Age 45–54 M	8.24	6.81	17.35
F	5.33	4.09	23.26
Age 55–64 M	21.60	18.77	13.10
F	12.20	9.87	19.10

Source: Office of Population Censuses and Surveys.

Note: [1] The mortality rate is the number of deaths in that age range per 1,000 population in that age range.

21

TABLE 3.7
Life Expectancy at Age 1 Year: UK 1950–1977

	Sex	1950–52	1961–63	1973–75	1975–77	% Change 1950–52 to 1975–77
England and Wales	M	67.7	68.6	69.8	70.0	3.4
	F	72.4	74.3	75.7	76.0	5.0
Scotland	M	66.2	66.7	67.9	68.2	3.0
	F	69.9	72.5	74.2	74.4	6.5
N Ireland	M	67.5	69.0	67.6	67.9	0.6
	F	70.3	74.1	71.1	74.1	5.4

Source: Office of Population Censuses and Surveys.

3.18   Because of the difficulty of measuring the "outcome" of health services, the extent to which health has improved, a good deal of effort has gone into measuring "input", numbers of doctors, nurses and other workers as well as supplies and buildings. Table 3.8 compares health care resources and measurements of outcome for the UK with a number of other developed countries for 1974, the latest date for which comparable information is readily available. The proportion of gross domestic product (GDP) in the UK devoted to the NHS rose from 5.3% in 1974 to 5.6% in 1977, but this trend is likely to have been followed by most if not all of the other countries listed. The table shows that the UK was spending less in relation both to its population and to its national income than most, though not all, of the other countries listed. In terms of medical and nursing staff employed the UK was doing rather better than the differences in per capita expenditure might lead one to expect. There is little doubt that this was largely because of the relatively lower costs and salaries in the NHS compared to many of the other countries.[1]

3.19   The UK was also performing relatively poorly in 1974 in terms of the three indicators of health – life expectancy and perinatal and maternal mortality – shown in Table 3.8. Figures 3.1 and 3.2, which plot two of the "input" measures (per capita health expenditure and doctors per 10,000 population) against one of the outcome measures (perinatal mortality) are illustrations of the difficulties in making international comparisons. Figure 3.1 shows that the general trend is for countries with a high per capita expenditure on health to have a relatively low perinatal mortality rate, although Japan and the USA diverge from this pattern. Figure 3.2 shows a more unexpected pattern; a high ratio of doctors to patients is associated with a relatively high perinatal mortality rate. A number of workers have examined this anomaly,

[1]Organisation for Economic Co-operation and Development, *Public Expenditure on Health*, Paris, 1977, Tables 9.24, 25.

TABLE 3.8

Health Service Resources and Results: International Comparisons 1974 or Near Date[1]

Country	Per capita total expenditure on health US $[2]	% Trend GDP[3]	Doctors (per 10,000 1974)	Nurses (per 10,000 1974)	Life expectancy at age 1 M	Life expectancy at age 1 F	Perinatal mortality (per 1,000 live births)	Maternal mortality (per 100,000 births)
Australia	308	6.5	13.9	54.1	68.5	75.4	22.4	11.3
Canada	408	6.8	16.6	57.8	69.7	77.0	17.7	10.8
Finland	265	5.8	13.3	46.0	66.8	75.5	17.1	10.6
France	352	6.9	13.9	23.7	69.5	77.1	18.8	24.0
Italy	191	6.0	19.9	7.8	70.0	76.0	29.6	42.4
Japan	166	4.0	11.6	16.1	70.8	76.0	18.0	38.3
Netherlands	312	7.3	14.9	22.5	71.2	76.9	16.4	10.3
Norway	270	5.6	16.5	46.4	71.4	77.7	16.8	3.3
Sweden	416	7.3	16.2	58.6	72.0	77.4	14.1	2.7
USA	491	7.4	16.5	40.4	68.0	75.6	24.8	15.2
W Germany	336	6.7	19.4	27.6	68.6	74.9	23.2	45.9
England and Wales	212	5.2	13.1	33.7	69.5	75.6	21.3	13.0
Scotland			16.1	45.6	67.7	74.0	22.7	21.5
N Ireland			15.3	36.6	67.0	73.6	25.9	17.1

Sources: Organisation for Economic Co-operation and Development, *Public Expenditure on Health*, Paris, 1977, Table 1.

McKinsey & Co, *International Comparisons of Health Needs and Health Services* 1978.

Irving B Kravis, Alan W Heston and Robert Summers, "Real GDP per capita for more than one hundred countries", *Economic Journal*, June 1978, Table 4.

Notes: [1] There are a number of caveats concerning the figures in this table. Details are given in the sources listed.

[2] The column is indicative rather than definitive: it has been derived by multiplying per cent of *trend* GDP spent on health care by *actual* GDP adjusted for purchasing power differences.

[3] Trend GDP is used to avoid the influence of cyclical business fluctuations on the level of output, which could distort the measured share of health expenditure in that output. For details see OECD, *Public Expenditure on Health*, Paris, 1977, page 9.

but have found no convincing explanation,[1] and it would be a mistake to accept either proposition at its face value. First, no single mortality statistic or group of statistics can summarise the health of a nation. Second, the scatter of points in the figures does not permit sweeping conclusions from such grossly simplified data. For example, Table 3.8 shows that in 1974 West Germany and the USA had much larger national incomes and per capita health expenditure than England and Wales but were performing worse in terms of perinatal and

[1]See Cochrane A L, St Leger A S and Moore F "Health Service 'input' and mortality 'output' in developed countries", *Journal of Epidemiology and Community Health*, 1978, 32, pages 200-205.

maternal mortality, and no better on life expectancy. On the other hand, Canada, Sweden and the Netherlands were all spending more per capita on health and had better life expectancy, perinatal and maternal mortality figures than the UK.

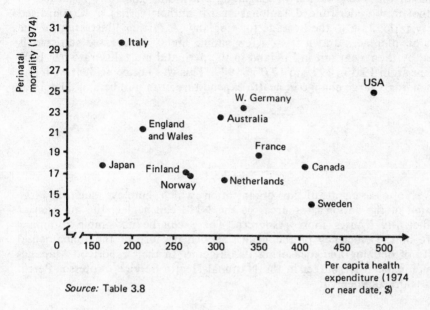

Figure 3.1: PER CAPITA HEALTH EXPENDITURE AND PERINATAL MORTALITY

Source: Table 3.8

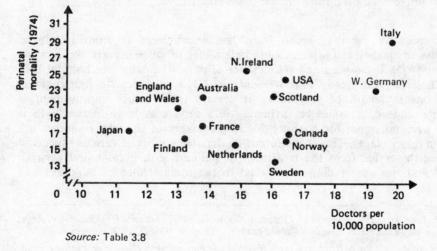

Figure 3.2: DOCTORS PER 10,000 POPULATION AND PERINATAL MORTALITY

Source: Table 3.8

3.20   Similar problems of interpretation are suggested by an examination of the distribution of NHS resources within the UK. Tables 3.2 and 3.3 showed that in 1977 Scotland, with 50% more hospital doctors and about 40% more nurses and midwives per 10,000 population than England, nonetheless had a comparatively lower life expectancy and a higher infant mortality rate. On the other hand, the Trent region in England, which was generally regarded as being the most under-funded regional health authority, has a standardised mortality ratio close to the average for England. A further illustration of the dangers of inferences drawn from a few simple highly aggregated statistics is provided by the recent fall in England in the perinatal mortality rate per 1000 live births from 19.3 in 1975 to 17.0 in 1977. This was not coincident with any correspondingly large change in health expenditure or in numbers of doctors or nurses.

Efficiency

3.21   No assessment of an organisation which employs such a large proportion of the nation's resources as the NHS can neglect the question of how efficiently it uses those resources. There can be no simple summary measure of the efficiency of the health service because of the fundamental difficulty of defining and measuring its outcome. In their report on Management of Financial Resources in the National Health Service, Professor Perrin and his team commented:

> "It is difficult to know with any certainty the effects of medical treatment, so it is difficult to compare the results of different kinds of treatment, and to judge which treatment is the more efficient."[1]

Lower resource use may result from greater efficiency or from a reduced quantity or quality of output. Crude indications of efficiency are the average length of stay in hospital and the number of patients treated per hospital bed, and these suggest steady improvements in NHS efficiency, though regional variations in length of stay make it certain that further improvement is possible. Indeed, it would be surprising in a service as large as the NHS if there were not room for considerable improvement in the way resources are used in many places. This is reinforced by detailed studies of various aspects of the health service from the treatment of patients with hernias and varicose veins[2] and the use of diagnostic tests[3] to the maintenance of buildings and grounds.[4]

---

[1]Perrin, John. et al, *Management of Financial Resources in the National Health Service*, Royal Commission on the NHS, Research Paper Number 2, London, HMSO, 1978, paragraph B7.3.

[2]Waller, Jane et al, *Early Discharge from Hospital for Patients with Hernias or Varicose Veins. Report of a Randomised Controlled Trial*, London, HMSO, 1978.

[3]Sherwood, T, "Resources and decisions in clinical radiology." *Journal of Epidemiology and Community Health*, March 1979, Vol 33, pages 59-65.

[4]Department of Health and Social Security, *The Way Forward*, London, HMSO, 1977, Appendix III.

Health Workers' Views

3.22   Health workers are critical of the NHS. They are involved with it daily and are in the best position to see defects and departures from the ideal. Most patients use the NHS only occasionally and are generally appreciative of the treatment they receive, but those who man the service know where improved practices and techniques cannot be achieved because of limited resources or unco-operative attitudes. It is natural and desirable that they should wish to provide better services: unless there is ambition the NHS will not improve. However, if patients give too rosy a picture of the state of the NHS, health workers paint one that is too gloomy. We consider some common complaints about the NHS, most of which were made by its workers, in the next chapter.

Our Verdict on the Present

3.23   Our own approach to the assessment of the NHS as a national service has been to look as carefully as we can at the mass of statistical data, which does not lead in a single consistent direction, and also to see for ourselves how the services in this country and elsewhere are working. In the course of our work we have seen things we have liked and admired, and things we have not liked at all. But our general view is that we need not feel ashamed of our health service and that there are many aspects of it of which we can be justly proud.

3.24   As we have seen in this chapter, social and geographical inequalities in health and health care remain. The NHS by itself cannot overcome this problem, but it must remain a cause for concern, and an area in which the performance of the NHS can be improved. There are problems in measuring efficiency in health care, but apart from improvements which may be achieved through the use of more resources, we are convinced that the NHS can provide a better service by making better use of the resources now available to it.

Chapter 4   What Others Say

4.1   In this chapter we outline some of the main themes which emerged from our evidence and add some comments of our own. We return to the questions raised here in later chapters, where they are discussed in greater detail.

4.2   Most of our evidence[1] came from people who work in the NHS, and much of it was critical. This did not surprise us since those who work in the NHS have the greatest direct interest in how it works and the strongest views on methods of improving it. We would have been concerned by an apathetic silence, but we were surprised not to hear more from individual users of the service. We hope their views were adequately represented in the evidence we received from community health councils, other bodies representing patients and in the surveys of patient attitudes referred to elsewhere in our report.

Failures

NHS reorganisation has not worked

4.3   Many of those submitting evidence referred to what they saw as the debilitating effects of NHS reorganisation, even though the structural changes that were introduced in 1973 in Northern Ireland and in 1974 in England, Scotland and Wales should have directly affected relatively few NHS workers. But clearly changes in administrative structure have repercussions far beyond the structure itself – a consideration we bear in mind when formulating our views on the merits of further change. It is important to distinguish between the structural changes which were the result of reorganisation, and other processes which became apparent at roughly the same time.

4.4   Some of the changes that affected the NHS in the early 1970s were external to the service, others were developments within it. The main ones were:

> *shortage of funds* – almost since its inception there had been a slow but steady growth in the resources available to the NHS. More money in real terms could be spent each year on staff, buildings and equipment. By 1974 it was clear that these rates of growth would not be sustained and schemes for improving the service had to be cut back or postponed. We

---

[1] Of the 2,460 written submissions received, 1,640 were from organisations in or concerned with the NHS and 820 were from individuals. Of the 820 individuals nearly half were workers or ex-workers in the NHS.

28

deal with general questions relating to the funding of the NHS in Chapter 21;

worsening industrial relations – NHS workers at all levels are now prepared to risk the well-being of patients by disrupting or withdrawing services. This has contributed to longer hospital waiting lists and probably lowered morale. We say more about this in Chapter 12;

the changing status of the medical profession – the status and influence of doctors has been eroded in recent years. Their authority has been challenged by the rise in influence of other NHS professions, and there has been a narrowing of pay differentials between them and the less well paid workers in the health service. We discuss various matters relating to doctors in Chapters 7 and 14;

the position of nurses – nurses have acquired more influence in the management of the NHS partly due to the restructuring of the profession after the Salmon and Mayston Reports[1] and partly due to their increased participation in management through reorganisation. We discuss various matters relating to nurses in Chapters 7 and 13;

the pay beds argument – the then government's decision to phase out pay beds from NHS hospitals was announced at a time when hospital consultants were already under pressure. The pay beds issue was also the occasion for industrial action to be taken by ancillary and other workers for motives which were not directly connected with their conditions of service. We deal with pay beds in Chapter 18;

local government reorganisation – health and local government reorganisation took effect at the same time in England and in Wales and Northern Ireland. In Scotland local government reorganisation occurred roughly a year after health services were reorganised. In Northern Ireland an important innovation was bringing health and personal social services together under the same authorities. We discuss the relationship between the NHS and local authorities in Chapter 16.

4.5 The unification of the three parts of the NHS under single health authorities was generally supported before reorganisation was introduced. There were arguments about the means of achieving it, but the principle of unification was not seriously disputed. Indeed, the desirability of unification had been part of the conventional wisdom for many years. The difficulties of introducing the new arrangements were undoubtedly underestimated, and one important part of it, the NHS planning system, was not launched until two years after the transfer of staff and responsibilities had taken place. One commentator offered us the following advice:

"It will probably be at least a decade before its [ie the 1974 reorganisa-

---

[1]Ministry of Health, Scottish Home and Health Department, *Report on the Committee on Senior Nursing Staff Structure*, London, HMSO, 1966. Department of Health and Social Security, Scottish Home and Health Department and Welsh Office, *Report of the Working Party on Management Structure in the Local Authority Nursing Service*, London, HMSO, 1969.

tion's] advantages and faults can be properly determined. For the moment perhaps one of the more significant contributions the Royal Commission on the National Health Service may be able to make is to encourage both the public not to make unrealistic demands for, and of, health care and also individuals working in the NHS not to have unrealistic expectations regarding the speed and manner in which the service's problems can be resolved."[1]

NHS has too many tiers

4.6   The most common complaint in evidence about the reorganisation of the NHS was that it added an extra and unnecessary tier or management level. Many people suggested to us that this had resulted in delays in decision making, buck-passing, excessive quantities of administrators and paper, duplication of work, too much consultation and too many meetings, and a lack of effective accountability at local level. The most popular solution suggested in England was abolition of the area health authority (AHA) but some people thought that the regional tier was unnecessary. Outside England, the function of the management team at district level was sometimes criticised.

4.7   The AHA in England and Wales (health board in Scotland and health and social services board in N. Ireland) is often seen as the new tier, probably because before reorganisation there was no level in the hospital service which corresponded to it. The case for these authorities is founded on the interdependence of the NHS and local government in providing an integrated service to patients: for example, they provide medical advice to the matching local authority and the local authority provides social work services to the NHS. The overlapping functions are recognised in the common boundaries of most health and local authorities, and by local authority appointments to health authority membership. The pros and cons of these arrangements are dealt with in Chapter 16.

4.8   The case for the Regional Health Authority (RHA) is based largely on management needs. The White Paper on NHS Reorganisation in England said that regional health authorities were needed because:

> "a central Department operating from London could not hope to exercise effective and prompt general supervision over area authorities whose numbers will be six times those of their counterparts in Scotland and eleven times those in Wales".[2]

RHAs also provide a number of services which are organised above area level, major building schemes, ambulances, blood transfusion and strategic planning, for example. However, common services like these do not require a regional tier. Regional health authorities do not exist outside England, but the Common Services Agency in Scotland provides ambulances, blood transfusion and other

[1]Taylor, David, *The Reorganised NHS*, Office of Health Economics, Paper No 58, Luton, White Crescent Press Ltd, 1977, page 33.
[2]*National Health Service Reorganisation: England*, (Cmnd 5055), London, HMSO, 1972, paragraph 31.

services for the health boards without exercising the monitoring role of RHAs in England, and similar agencies exist in Wales and Northern Ireland.

4.9 Reorganisation introduced new health authorities with unfamiliar roles and since reorganisation defects in the NHS have become apparent. But it does not follow that the one caused the other. Still less does it follow that abolishing one management level will produce an efficient service. We return to this theme in Chapters 19 and 20.

Too many administrators

4.10 There were allegations in our evidence about the swollen number of administrators, their poor quality and the diversion of clinical staff to administrative duties. Some of these were strongly worded. Mr A J N Phair wrote:

"Bureaucracy used to be a term to define the most efficient office procedures now in the NHS it can only be used in its perjorative sense of red tape, buck passing and considerable inexcusable delays which is partly caused by administrators shying away from their responsibilities and receding into the management structure cocoon".

Nurse administrators

4.11 The implementation of the Salmon Committee's recommendations on grading is often alleged to have "resulted in efficient Ward Sisters being promoted into administrative positions where their clinical expertise is unused, even though they may have none of the attributes of a good administrator", as the British Hospital Doctors Federation told us. The argument was not that ward sisters should not be promoted, but that they should not be promoted away from caring for patients. On the other hand nursing organisations tended to support the Salmon structure and the improvement in status for nurses which it and the introduction of consensus management have brought. We make some suggestions about the nurses' clinical career structure in Chapter 13.

4.12 While these complaints cannot be ignored, the figures do not support the view that the Salmon structure has markedly increased numbers of nurses in the grades above ward sister. In fact the proportion of nurses in these administrative grades has fallen over the period as Table 4.1 shows. There was a similar trend in Northern Ireland but precisely comparable figures are not available. No doubt these figures do not tell the whole story but, taking the UK as a whole, there seems little basis for the complaint contained in evidence from the BMA that "the Salmon Report [removed] from the clinical sphere, to the administrative one, an army of the best and most capable nurses".

TABLE 4.1
Hospital Nursing Staff: Great Britain 1966–1977

Whole-time equivalent

Year	All Nursing Staff	Administrative Grades (grade 7 and above)	Administrative Grades as % of all nursing staff
1966	252,211	11,768	4.7
1971	287,751	11,511	4.0
1973	311,497	11,228	3.6
1975	346,208	11,226	3.2
1977[1]	379,699	13,822	3.6

Source: Health departments' statistics.

Note: [1] Includes midwives.

Administrators[1]

4.13   The number of administrative and clerical staff employed in the NHS has increased substantially in recent years. In England in 1977 the equivalent of 99,000 administrative and clerical staff were employed, an increase of 21,892 (28%) on the numbers of equivalent staff employed in the health service and by local authorities in 1973. Slightly higher increases occurred in other parts of the UK. One explanation is that most of the increase stems from new jobs created by the reorganisation of the NHS: over 600 staff have been employed to service CHCs, for example. Some of the increase is due to expansion and developments which would have occurred anyway, particularly in clerical and secretarial staff supporting doctors and other NHS professionals and in personnel and other management services of the NHS, but some is undoubtledy due to new posts created by reorganisation. Detailed figures are not available before 1977 but are now being collected.

4.14   Many people assume that administrators are too remote from patients to have any substantial effect on their recovery and are at best a necessary evil, so that any increase in their numbers is to be deplored. But the assumption is not necessarily correct: the introduction of ward clerks and appointments and records clerks has enabled nursing staff to be released from clerical work, and the increase in their numbers may have contributed to the fall in the proportion of nurse administrators referred to above. The employment of more receptionists/clerks in general practice has improved communication between GPs and hospital services; and better management of services may lead to savings. Finally, it is unfair to criticise the number of administrators unless a standard can be applied. We are aware of no research which could enable the "right" number of administrators to be established.

---

[1]The term is used to refer to staff covered by the Administrative and Clerical Whitley Council. These range from regional administrators to clerical and typing grades, and include such workers as catering, laundry, and domestic service managers.

4.15   Administrators have tended to be blamed for a lot of what has gone wrong in the NHS since reorganisation. As one assistant sector administrator in the South of England put it:

"The worst affected is the Administrator, who has been as usual the scapegoat for all the Service's ills. Indeed the majority of overspending is blamed on the Administrator, and all proposed cut-backs in the Service refer to administration."

The Institute of Health Service Administrators pointed to the difficulties that administrators in the NHS have had to cope with since reorganisation, and drew attention to the discussions about further changes which might occur as a result of devolution, local amalgamations of health districts, and our own work. They told us that "The debilitating effect that uncertainty about the future has on morale cannot be too strongly stressed." We have formed an encouraging view of how well many administrators have coped with the real difficulties caused by reorganisation and change, and we would reject criticism of them as a group. There is, however, much that can be done to make their work more effective, including improving standards of recruitment.

Slow decision taking

4.16   We were told about difficulties in getting decisions taken quickly since reorganisation. Various reasons were suggested, including unclear areas of responsibility, consensus management and the consultation it apparently requires, the advisory committee structure, and the lack of administrators of sufficient seniority and calibre at hospital level.

4.17   Delays in decision making in the NHS seemed to us to be an important criticism of the reorganised service and we therefore commissioned Professor Maurice Kogan to undertake a study for us.[1] His report, "The Working of the National Health Service", was published in June 1978. Its findings, though to some degree impressionistic, were consistent with what we had been told in evidence. Complaints came mainly from those at operational level in hospitals. Those people working in the community health services may have been less affected, and paragraph 13.17 of the report comments:

"Especially in community services, nurses and doctors seemed to have little contact with the administrative structure, and did not feel hindered in carrying out their functions through lack of decision making. The units within which they worked were small and independent, and decisions about work were almost wholly taken by staff based within the unit."

The report also makes the important point:

"It is not possible to say whether in fact decision making does take longer now than before reorganisation, but it is true that staff strongly think it

---

[1] This study was carried out in some health authorities in England, Scotland, Wales and Northern Ireland. Altogether over 500 NHS personnel were interviewed at region, area and district level. The sample was not randomly selected and the authors of the study did not claim that it was representative in the statistical sense.

does, and this colours their perceptions and feelings about the structure. Without structural modifications, the decision making process may improve when planning has become a more established and certian activity, and as staff gain in familiarity and skill in working the system. Some of the problems discussed above are related to the structure, but others are inherent in the health service." (Paragraph 13.25)

These issues are discussed more fully in Chapter 20.

Money being wasted

4.18   Our terms of reference required us to consider "the best use and management of the financial" resources of the NHS. We deal with financial matters mainly in Chapter 21. We commissioned and published a report prepared by Professor John Perrin of Warwick University and his team, on the management of financial resources in the National Health Service.

4.19   In an organisation the size of the NHS it is not difficult to find places where money might be saved. Suggestions put to us ranged from smaller helpings of food for patients in hospital to the cost effectiveness of preventive medicine.[1] But it is important to distinguish between complaints of waste founded on different judgments about what the NHS should spend its money on, and those alleging inefficient use of funds. Professor Perrin's study showed that while the system of financial management was probably adequate as a means of checking irregularities or improprieties it did little to ensure that resouces were efficiently and effectively used.[2]

Staff morale

4.20   We were also required to consider "the interests ... of those who work in the National Health Service". We would in any case have had to consider seriously the allegations in our evidence that morale amongst health service workers was low and what the causes of this might be. We go into these questions in more depth in Chapter 12, but we say immediately that although there is reason for concern we do not believe that the NHS is on the point of collapse because of low morale, as many of our witnesses would have us believe.

4.21   "Morale" is a vague term, and it is not easy, therefore, to demonstrate convincingly that it is low or high, falling or rising. Professor Kogan's report suggested that staff equated morale "with a general state of content or discontent which might relate more to general feelings about the NHS than the feelings of satisfaction with their jobs or working context".[3] There are

[1]One interesting proposal put to us was the partial but systematic extraction of children's teeth. This would save money on later dental repair. We felt that it might be dangerous to generalise this suggestion too widely.

[2]Perrin, John et al, *Management of Financial Resources in the National Health Service,* Royal Commission on the National Health Service, Research Paper Number 2, London, HMSO, 1978, paragraph E1.2.

[3]Kogan, Maurice et al, *The Working of the National Health Service,* Royal Commission on the National Health Service, Research Paper Number 1, London, HMSO, 1978, paragraph 14.1.

certainly sound reasons for discontent amongst health service workers, but they are not necessarily the same reasons in all cases.

4.22 One factor which should not be overlooked is what the Rt. Hon. Enoch Powell MP (Minister of Health from 1960 to 1963) has called "a vested interest in denigration". Writing before reorganisation he put his point this way:

> "One of the most striking features of the National Health Service is the continual, deafening chorus of complaint which rises day and night from every part of it, a chorus only interrupted when someone suggests that a different system altogether might be preferable, which would involve the money coming from some less (literally) palpable source. The universal Exchequer financing of the service endows everyone providing as well as using it with a vested interest in denigrating it, so that it presents what must be the unique spectacle of an undertaking that is run down by everyone engaged in it."[1]

It is not true that criticism of the service is unjustified, but it is certainly true, in our view, that some of the problems of the NHS and those who work in it are exaggerated. This is true of morale also. The Mid Glamorgan AHA pointed out:

> "What is apparent is that if the leaders of the service and the media continue to state that such a situation [i.e. low morale] exists staff will generally come to believe it."

A "sickness service"

4.23 A common criticism is that the NHS is a "sickness" rather than a "health" service. Critics point to what they see as an imbalance between what is spent on preventing ill health, health promotion and long-term care and what is spent on the treatment of disease. Some people assume that if large sums were spent on prevention it would make curing unnecessary in most cases, and, as well as saving money, would keep us all much healthier. We think this too simple a view, and we go into the subject and the question of priorities in the next two chapters.

Remedies

The NHS should get more money

4.24 Easily the most popular remedy for the failings of the NHS, especially and understandably with those working in it, was that much more money should be made available. The Labour Party in their evidence to us said:

---

[1]Powell, J Enoch, *A New Look at Medicine and Politics,* First Edition, London, Pitman Medical, 1966, page 16.

"The national health service and the personal social services are under-financed and have always been under-financed compared with other comparable services."

There is also the feeling that a higher proportion of the gross national product ought to be spent on health services. The BMA in their evidence said that "An insufficient share of total national resources has hitherto been allocated to the health services". We have more to say on this subject in Chapter 21, but it is important to remember the almost unlimited capacity of health services to absorb resources.

Alternative methods of financing the NHS

4.25 Various ways of raising money for the NHS have been suggested. At present about 90% of the cost of the NHS is raised from taxation, the balance coming from National Health Insurance contributions and charges of various kinds. It was argued to us that if only people knew how much it cost they would be more careful in using the NHS. Popular suggestions for raising or supplementing funds for the NHS put to us included; a lottery or some other method of voluntary fund raising; extending the present charges for NHS services and an insurance based scheme funding the whole or part of the NHS. The first two are usually seen as means of supplementing central funding rather than replacing it.

4.26 Those who support the idea of a lottery to help fund the NHS argue that large sums are spent on football pools, horse racing, etc, and that the profits might just as well be used in a good cause. They argue that people would like to contribute to the NHS if they knew that they were paying specifically for that purpose. A lottery seems a painless way of raising money, and there is the example of the Irish Hospital Sweep Stake available. We were also told that patients would gladly pay for some NHS goods and services, for example by making a contribution towards hospital "hotel" expenses, on the grounds that it costs something to live at home which is saved when meals and accomodation are free in hospital. Some patients are already "charged" for their stay in hospital; long-stay patients receiving pensions or social security benefits have these reduced after their eighth week in hospital, for example. The main alternative to financing the NHS out of central taxation is to do so through a health insurance scheme on the model of Western Europe or North America. We say more about these suggestions in Chapter 21.

The NHS should be taken out of politics

4.27 Underlying most proposals for alternative methods of raising money for the NHS is the assumption that government control and parsimony can somehow be avoided by an "independent" source of income – a lottery mechanism which delivers money without government strings attached, charges which add to funds automatically without government interference, or an insurance system outside the government fiscal institutions. The BMA, for example, referred in evidence to "the need to maintain a fund for health care separate from central Government funds". This is one facet of the popular

36

proposal that the NHS should be "taken out of politics". Another is the feeling that the NHS should be above party political squabbles which may lead to changes in the priorities given to client groups within the NHS or to "political" decisions being made, such as that to phase out pay beds from NHS hospitals. On the same theme, some people consider that lay appointments to health authorities ought to be apolitical.

4.28   A solution often proposed is an independent health commission or board. It is said that such a body might act as a buffer between the government and the NHS, determine the money needed by the service on objective and non-political criteria, and undertake strategic planning and other functions required at national level. The role of the health departments would be modified accordingly. The analogy most often drawn is with the BBC or the nationalised industries. The pros and cons of a health commission are discussed in Chapter 19.

Integrating health and personal social services

4.29   NHS reorganisation in Great Britain was intended to integrate the hospital, family practitioner and local authority health services under the new health authorities, but laid responsibility for providing social work support on local authorities. The importance of collaboration between health and local authorities was constantly stressed to us, and some of those who sent us evidence proposed that the two services should be integrated in some way. The main suggestions were that the NHS should be run by local government, or that relevant social service provision – home helps, residential homes and social workers – be provided by the NHS. We deal with these matters in Chapter 16.

Further NHS reorganisation

4.30   Despite the dislocation and expense of the recent reorganisation, many of those giving evidence to us suggested further structural changes. They felt that the structure had to be got right now even if this meant further upheaval. We have already referred to proposals to drop a tier and to integrate the NHS and personal social services under one authority. After the upheavals of reorganisation the willingness of some staff to contemplate further major structural change shows an impressive commitment to the welfare of the service, as well as considerable frustration with existing arrangements. The 1974 reorganisation produced:

an immense amount of administrative work in preparation for the new machinery;

disruption of ordinary work, both before and after reorganisation caused by the need to prepare for and implement the changes;

the breakdown of well established formal and informal networks;

the loss of experienced staff through early retirement and resignation;

the stresses and strains on some staff of having to compete for new jobs.

We were very conscious of these effects when considering further structural change. This is reflected in proposals we make in the chapters that follow.

37

Part II   Services to Patients

In this part of the report we discuss those aspects of the NHS which most directly affect the individual.

We start with a chapter on maintaining good health because this affects fundamentally the provision of NHS services. We then deal with priorities in the NHS, medical and nursing services in the community, pharmaceutical, chiropody, and ophthalmic services, with dentistry, with hospital services, with hospital/community relationships and, finally, the consumer's voice in the NHS. This is perhaps the most important part of our report.

We have found it useful – and we think our readers will too – to identify four categories or gradations of care. They are:

the care which a healthy person will exercise for himself so that he remains healthy;

the self-care which the slightly ill person will exercise which may involve medication and treatment;

the care provided by the person's family and by the health and personal social services outside hospital;

the care which can be provided only in hospital or other residential institution.

These are not wholly distinct categories and will merge into each other. A patient should be able to move easily between them as his need for care becomes greater or as he improves. Most of us spend most of our lives, if we are fortunate, in the first category; but, again, most of us at some time will need to call upon the care offered in other categories. Whatever our needs, administrative barriers should not be created which prevent our being cared for in an effective and convenient way.

There are considerable differences in the balance of hospital and community health care between the four parts of the UK and the regions within England. While this balance should so far as possible be determined locally, it is a proper function of the health departments to stimulate and support research into the effectiveness of alternative patterns of health care delivery and to propagate the findings of this research to health authorities. The balance between hospital and community care is important. So too is the determination of priorities and the ability of the public to influence them. In what follows we examine ways in which these issues are resolved at present and look forward to new approaches which may prove effective in the future.

It is clear from our evidence that whilst there is general appreciation and satisfaction with services provided by the NHS certain aspects do cause concern. For example, criticisms were made of waiting times for appointments in hospital out-patient departments; of GP deputising services and GP receptionists; of closures of pharmacies, particularly in rural areas; and of the lack of emergency dental services and confusion about dental charges. All these criticisms are dealt with in greater detail in the following chapters.

Chapter 5 Good Health

5.1 Although the promotion of "a comprehensive health service designed to secure improvement . . . in the prevention"[1] of illness is one of the duties laid on health ministers by the NHS Acts, only a small proportion of NHS resources is devoted to prevention. The NHS has always been primarily a "treating" service. The curative and caring services make the essential contribution to the alleviation of suffering and always will, but we regret that more emphasis has not been placed in the past on the preventive role of the NHS. This must change if there are to be substantial improvements in health in the future. We received a great deal of evidence to support this view, and in Chapter 2 we stated as our first objective for the NHS that it should aim to encourage and assist individuals to remain healthy. In this chapter we examine ways in which this objective may be achieved.

Prevention

5.2 Prevention of ill health has been classified as primary, secondary or tertiary. Primary prevention is taking measures to prevent disease or injury occurring, immunisation, good obstetric care and discouraging smoking for example. Secondary prevention measures are concerned with identifying and treating ill health promptly, for example through screening patients at risk. Tertiary prevention is concerned with mitigating the effects of illness or disease which has already occurred and includes rehabilitation and continuing care such as the care and after care of diabetics and terminal care. Health services are for the most part concerned with the second and third categories. In this chapter we deal mainly with primary and, to a lesser extent, secondary prevention.

5.3 To put into perspective what may be accomplished by the NHS, it must be understood that many of the main improvements in the health of the nation have come not from advances in medical treatment but from public health measures, better nutrition and improvements in the economic, social and natural environments. As the Health Education Council's evidence pointed out:

"The three main components of successful health promotion over the last 100 years were achieved by regulatory procedures affecting the environment, specific programmes addressed to pregnant women, infants and school children, and the general improvement in the level of nutrition."

The provision of a clean water supply, an efficient sewerage system and better

---

[1]*National Health Service Act 1977*, Section 1 (1).

standards of food hygiene in the nineteenth century virtually eliminated cholera and greatly reduced enteric fever which until then had been endemic in the UK. Medical advances made little impact on mortality rates until the introduction of immunisation and the sulpha drugs in the 1930s, and the antibiotics in the 1940s. Since then mortality has declined at a slower rate – although for particular age and sex groups, infants and women between the ages of 35 and 44 for example, the fall has been much sharper. Curative and caring services and related research contribute a great deal to individual treatment and their importance must not be under-rated, but on the basis of past experience a substantial improvement in national and community health is more likely to be achieved by preventive measures.

5.4   We make the point, not to belittle what the NHS has achieved, but to put it in perspective. Mortality statistics do not tell us much about the state of health of the existing population, or the quality of life of the old or chronic sick. The introduction of effective vaccines for polio in the 1950s made only a small difference to the mortality statistics since not many people died from polio, but led to a big reduction in the incidence of disablement in the population. Important though the acute services are for the individual, dramatic improvements in the general health of the nation or in mortality will not be achieved by simply spending more and more money on curative medicine. We have therefore considered the case for putting more money and effort into preventive medicine.

5.5   The most obviously preventable conditions are those which can be attributed directly to the way we live. Smoking is an important contributory factor in lung cancer, bronchitis and coronary heart disease, but in 1976 46% of adult men and 38% of adult women smoked cigarettes.[1] Road accidents account for about 6,500 deaths in Britain each year. The White Paper "Prevention and Health" points out that "deaths and serious injuries to front seat occupants of cars involved in road accidents could almost be halved" if front seat passengers wore seat belts at all times.[2] Excess blood alcohol contributes massively to road accidents, and alcoholism to other accidents and to social problems. The wrong kinds of food encourages obesity and dental decay. Nutrition influences both health and disease and an increasing interest in diet amongst the general public indicates that educational efforts are likely to be rewarding. Society's concern about nutrition may be seen in the provision of school meals. Reduction in smoking and alcohol related illness, the prevention of road accidents and mitigating their results, improved nutritional policies, should be the prime targets for prevention. But there are other factors which are outside the control of the individual, and we comment on environmental and occupational health considerations below.

5.6   The first problem of preventing ill-health is lack of detailed and precise knowledge of the causes of many diseases, and therefore of the best means of preventing them. Obviously there is no difficulty of this kind about, for example, the link between smoking and lung cancer – where Britain has particularly high death rates. This is an exceptional case, and in heart disease,

---

[1]Office of Population Censuses and Surveys, Social Survey Division, *The General Household Survey. 1976,* London, HMSO, 1978, Table 2.62, page 84.

[2]*Prevention and Health* (Cmnd 7047), London, HMSO, 1977, paragraph 189.

for example, there is no such certainty. Risk factors such as smoking, obesity, lack of exercise and high blood fat levels have been identified. The role of diet in heart disease is particularly contentious and similar uncertainties exist about other killing diseases.

5.7 There is also a lack of established fact on which some other preventive measures, particularly screening, might be based. It is a widely held view that early diagnosis and treatment of a disease improves the prospects of cure. Some of those giving evidence to us argued that mass screening – even an annual check-up for everyone in the country – would be desirable and effective in enabling disease to be identified and treated early. There are two important points to be made here. First, it would be quite impracticable to provide regular screening even for major diseases for the whole population; second, there is no evidence that unselective screening of this kind would produce useful results. While screening is not the universal panacea that some people believe, there is a place for it where high risk groups can be identified and treated effectively at acceptable cost. The use of age and sex registers in general practice can make a contribution to screening and health visitors have an important role to play in the developmental screening of children and the elderly. One programme which has been shown to be effective is the screening of "at risk" pregnant women for foetal abnormalities. The continued expansion of pre-natal screening and genetic counselling with the support of therapeutic abortion facilities could do much to reduce the number of handicapped children born each year. We recommend the expansion of *proven* screening programmes.

5.8 The second problem raised by preventive measures is personal freedom. To what lengths should society go, to force each one of us to do things which are good for him? In a free society it is unlikely that we shall be compelled to take exercise or to eat things which are good rather than bad for us except by social pressure. But society can choose to fine those who do not wear seat belts in cars, to fluoridate all drinking water (discussed more fully in Chapter 9), and to tax cigarettes and alcohol punitively. Opponents of such measures argue that they are an unwarrantable intrusion on the freedom of the individual.

5.9 This is a well understood and extensively argued ethical problem, but it is difficult to find common examples of individual action which affect only the individual. There are few of us who could kill ourselves whether by motor-car or by cigarettes without affecting others. On another level, there is the cost to society of medical treatment. A great deal of regulation of society exists already and is accepted as necessary: on the road it includes, for example, a requirement that people should not drive with more than a certain amount of alcohol in their bloodstream and a host of other regulations designed to protect road users. A balance has to be struck between extending measures of this kind, which benefit the health of the nation, and interfering unreasonably with the liberty of the individual. Yet if the health of the nation is to improve we have little doubt that society should be prepared to be considerably less self-indulgent, and the government to take a stronger line, on restricting activities, like smoking, which are known to be harmful. The William Temple Foundation, in its evidence to us, commented on this aspect of community responsibility for health:

"Although the responsibility and potential for each individual to influence

43

his own level of health should not be undervalued, this approach ignores the important perspective that should be part of a community diagnosis. This would include consideration of *society's responsibility* for preventing illness amongst its members. It would appear unhelpful to encourage people as individuals to stop smoking, over-indulging in the 'wrong' foods, and leading stressful sedentary lives, when there are evidently so many strong influences encouraging, or even ensuring, that people continue to do these harmful things."

5.10　The third problem is putting prevention into practice. We discuss health education, environmental health measures and occupational health services below, but there is a general point to be made about costs first.

5.11　Preventive services will not necessarily reduce NHS costs. Some preventive measures are expensive in themselves and some, for example screening programmes, may increase current demand on the NHS if more cases requiring treatment are discovered. Future costs may also rise if prevention increases life expectancy without a significant reduction in individual morbidity. Calculation of the balance between present and future costs is extremely difficult. But the effects of prevention on NHS costs is only one of the factors to be taken into account when preventive measures are evaluated. The benefits of prevention will include the improved health of the population and reduction in those costs of ill-health which fall outside the NHS.

5.12　There are some preventive measures which certainly do or could reduce NHS costs. Vaccination and immunisation programmes are obvious examples. There has been a disconcerting fall in recent years in the number of children being immunised and efforts must be made to regain the previous high levels. The economic benefits of preventing illness amongst the working population must not be forgotten. The annual cost of treating smoking-related diseases in England and Wales was estimated in the recent report of the Expenditure Committee at about £85m at 1977 prices and the number of premature deaths at between 50,000 and 80,000 each year.[1] The Department of Environment has estimated that in 1977 road traffic accidents cost the NHS about £44m and imposed considerable costs elsewhere in the economy in loss of output and property damage. We recommend that the wearing of seat belts should be made compulsory for drivers and front seat passengers in motor vehicles.

Health Education

5.13　A great deal of evidence was sent to us urging that more effort and money should be spent on health education. The Health Education Council for England, Wales and Northern Ireland received £3m in 1977/78.[2] It is difficult

---

[1]First Report from the Expenditure Committee, *Preventive Medicine,* Vol 1, London, HMSO, 1977, paragraph 144.

[2]The Scottish Health Education Unit, a Division of the Common Services Agency, received about £1m in 1977/78. It was set up at the same time as the Health Education Council and co-operates closely with it. In addition, the Scottish Council for Health Education has a number of training functions in this field.

to calculate the additional value of work undertaken, for example by health professionals and teachers as part of their normal duties, but it is certain that the amount of money devoted to health education represents a very small proportion of the total health and education budgets.

5.14   The aim of health educators is to inform people about risks to health and to increase understanding of factors which will promote good health. Information will not of itself make people lead healthier lives and needs to be reinforced by the example and advice of government, teachers, and health professionals. To change attitudes and behaviour is difficult and although health education has led, for example, to some reduction in the number of smokers there is no clear evidence that without legislation or political commitment, it can improve health on its own. This is not necessarily a reason for limiting expenditure on health education but is an argument for not relying too heavily on it as the saviour of the nation's health. Existing ways of encouraging people to lead healthier lives are not well developed. We recommend the continued expansion of health education but some of the increased resources must be spent on developing more effective methods and on monitoring and validating existing and new techniques.

5.15   It is likely to be easier to promote healthy habits at an early age than to change established attitudes and behaviour. We would particularly welcome a considerable strengthening of health education in schools, with teachers, health education officers and health professionals playing a much fuller part than they do at the moment. Health visitors are particularly important in this respect because they are specifically trained to promote health education, but all those who teach health education need to be trained to communicate information about healthy living. Too few in-service training opportunities exist at present. We were not impressed by the account we received of existing arrangements in schools from the main authorities concerned. We recommend that they should examine seriously their efforts in this field.

5.16   While health visitors and environmental health officers have for long had a clearly established role in the promotion of health, other health professionals, for example, doctors, dentists, pharmacists and nurses, all have an important part to play. They may be able to advise people at times when, because of personal or family circumstances of illness, they are particularly receptive to advice, and it is important that they encourage patients' self-help activities. We should like to see health education given greater emphasis in the training and continuing education of health professionals.

5.17   The operational responsibility for health education lies with the area medical officer who plans health education programmes with the assistance of specialist health education staff. But many health authorities have been slow to appoint area health education officers and six areas in England have no health education officers at all. One of the reasons for lack of progress has been a shortage of able, qualified staff, and we were encouraged to hear that the Health Education Council and the Scottish health education bodies are working to meet some of the training gaps. It does not necessarily follow, of course, that because a health authority has no health education officers it makes no health education effort, but health education should be emphasised in the forward planning of health authorities and we so recommend.

5.18   Voluntary bodies have often shown the way to future provision of services by health and other statutory agencies. It is clear that they have also a great deal to offer in promoting self-care and in providing care and support for groups of people suffering from particular illnesses and diseases. We say more about this important role of voluntary bodies and volunteers in Chapter 11.

5.19   Intelligent self-medication and care can undoubtedly reduce demands on health services, and it is essential that society accepts the need for appropriate self-care. However, there are wide variations in individuals' abilities to care for themselves, and excessive emphasis on self-care could mean that patients were discouraged from using NHS services when they needed them. That would be contrary to a number of the objectives of the NHS which we suggested in Chapter 2. Valuable work is or can be done by health professionals, especially pharmacists, in enabling people to treat themselves.

5.20   The growing interest of the health departments in health education has been show recently by several useful publications, including "Reducing the Risk: Safer Pregnancy and Child Birth" and "Eating for Health". We hope that this impetus will not be lost and that further high quality publications will be forthcoming. Another important function of the health departments is to bring pressure on other government agencies. The Expenditure Committee's Report on Preventive Medicine pointed out that:

"Decisions which may affect health are taken in a number of government departments other than the DHSS; such matters as transport planning, food pricing policies and housing are particularly clear examples of this and fluoridation has implications for the Department of the Environment."[1]

5.21   Radio and television could have a great deal to offer by providing information to individuals and families about ways to improve and keep their health. For example, it has proved difficult to reach people in social classes IV and V using the more conventional methods of health education. There are welcome signs of collaboration between the Health Education Council and the television companies. However, there is no doubt that television and radio, certainly in their commercial forms, do a great deal of harm by promoting excessive consumption of alcohol, tobacco and sweets, for example – which, except in moderation, are bad for us. As the Society of Community Medicine pointed out to us when commenting on the failure of health education to persuade more than a minority of individuals to alter their way of life:

"the effects of the present cultural backcloth outweigh the influence of health education effort. It follows that the cultural weave and woof as exemplified by plays, films, books, advertising material, etc., must contain strands of positive health".

No health education programme will make much impression on the public unless it is forcefully presented and widely disseminated. The most effective

[1]*First Report from the Expenditure Committee, Op cit,* paragraph 47.

medium is undoubtedly television. The high cost of using it should be reflected in the funds made available to the Health Education Council and the corresponding bodies in Scotland. We recommend that they are increased for this purpose.

Environmental Health

5.22   As we have already pointed out, it is through public and environmental health measures that the greatest advances in preventing ill-health have been made. NHS reorganisation did not include the transfer of environmental health services to the NHS, and responsibility for preventing the spread of communicable diseases, food hygiene, port health, public health aspects of environmental services and the enforcement of requirements about conditions at work places, remains with district level local authorities.[1] There were few complaints in our evidence that this had caused problems, although the difficulties of co-operating closely with medical staff employed by health authorities may be similar to those experienced by other local authority services, outlined in Chapter 16.

5.23   Although it is clear that the levels of the most serious killing and crippling diseases, for example heart and lung diseases, are largely affected by individual behaviour, there remain many other areas where government action could help to improve our environment. Restrictions on smoking in public places and a more vigorous policy on noise pollution are examples. Local authorities should also ensure that sufficient resources are made available to environmental health services to allow them to maintain their previous high standards. The Society of Community Medicine pointed out that:

"Despite many advances in improvements of environmental control, especially in the more traditional sectors, ie, water and air, there is little evidence that the physical environment continues to improve; rather the reverse with the environment being continually and subtly degraded."

5.24   Community physicians have a particularly important part to play in environmental health and health education. Their role and future is discussed more fully in Chapter 14 but some comments are appropriate here. At reorganisation the identifiable responsibility that the medical officer of health (MOH) had for a defined population disappeared. The community physician who discharges these responsibilities is less in the public eye than the old MOH, and some of the impetus for the development of services may have been lost. This is not to suggest that the clock should be turned back to before 1974, but to indicate that this is an area of health service activity which must be kept under review.

Occupational Health and Safety

5.25   Occupational health is concerned with "the reactions of workpeople to their working environment, and the prevention of ill-health arising from

---

[1]Responsibility for conditions at work is shared for example in England and Wales with the Health and Safety Executive.

working conditions".[1] To this definition others would add that it should also be concerned with the effects of ill-health on work. Except for its own employees the NHS does not carry responsibility for the prevention and control of health hazards at work. The 1974 Health and Safety at Work Act provides a legislative framework for maintaining and improving health and safety, with the onus on the employer "to ensure, so far as is reasonably practicable, the health, safety and welfare at work of all his employees".[2] The Health and Safety Commission (HSC) and its operational arm, the Health and Safety Executive (HSE), are responsible for promoting and enforcing higher health and safety standards. The Act applies to nearly all employees but, as Crown employers, the NHS is immune from the enforcement provisions. The Health and Safety Commission have asked the government to remove that immunity so that NHS employees receive the full protection of the Act. We support this request. Occupational health for NHS workers is discussed in Chapter 12.

5.26   Our evidence on occupational health concentrated on the relationship between the NHS and occupational health services, some of it recommending that the NHS should establish a comprehensive occupational health service. It was not always clear what was meant by this and there are a number of possible alternatives to the present situation. The first is for the NHS to become responsible for the occupational medicine aspects of occupational health. Doctors employed in occupational health would be taken into the NHS, their closer contact with the main stream of medicine would be ensured and there would be less duplication of activities by the two services. The NHS could provide a service obviously independent of the possible biases of individual employers; and it could do so on repayment.

5.27   The second possibility would be for the NHS to be made responsible for all health aspects of occupational health, leaving the safety and welfare responsibilities where they are. Unless the Health and Safety at Work Act were revoked such a move would lead to the duplication of the tasks of the HSC and HSE, since new bodies with similar responsibilities would need to be established.

5.28   The third approach would be to transfer overall responsibility for health, safety and welfare from the Department of Employment to the DHSS and NHS. It is far from certain that this would lead to the required integration or to a comprehensive service.

5.29   This is a complicated subject, but it seems to us that the bodies established by the Health and Safety at Work Act should be allowed to continue to develop. While there are obvious links and overlap with the NHS in the health aspects of their work, the safety aspects demand special expertise and knowledge from a variety of professions not all of whom have much connection with the NHS. Doubtless there are deficiencies in the services provided under the 1974 Act at present, but we do not think these would be remedied by a large scale reorganisation. Probably the right way forward is to

---

[1]*Safety and Health at Work*, Report of the Committee 1970-72, (Cmnd 5034), London, HMSO, 1972, paragraph 356.

[2]*Health and Safety at Work Act 1974*, London, HMSO, 1974, Section 2(1).

strengthen the Health and Safety Commission and Executive and to foster the development of links with the NHS. Even if industries and firms provide their own occupational health services there will inevitably be overlap with the NHS; and they are unlikely in the main to be able to carry out the epidemiological studies and the monitoring of health trends which depend on research. Consideration should therefore be given to the NHS providing, in each region and based on a university department of occupational, social or community medicine, a consultant in occupational medicine.

5.30 We asked one of our members to discuss in greater detail the issues raised here and his paper is reproduced at Appendix F.

Conclusions and Recommendations

5.31 Preventive measures are by no means the exclusive responsibility of the NHS. Nonetheless, in our view a significant improvement in the health of the people of the UK can come through prevention. There are major areas where government action could produce rapid and certain results: a much tougher attitude towards smoking, towards preventing road accidents and mitigating their results, a clear commitment to fluoridation and a programme to combat alcoholism, are among the more obvious examples.

5.32 This must be matched by other measures. More emphasis should be put on health education and on the development and monitoring of its techniques. There is room for greater involvement of GPs and other health professionals, and better in-service training for teachers in health education. The imaginative use of radio and television will be important. Much more can be done to emphasise the positive virtues of health and the risks of an unhealthy life style, and this should include environmental and occupational hazards as well as personal behaviour. It is important that local authorities should not let 'standards of environmental health slip. The NHS needs to face its responsibilities in prevention.

5.33 Occupational health and safety is not a responsibility of the NHS at present though some evidence we received suggested it should become so. This is a complicated field, and one which in many respects has little to do with the central functions of the NHS.

5.34 We recommend that:

(a) *proven* screening programmes should be expanded (paragraph 5.7);

(b) the wearing of seat belts should be made compulsory for drivers and front seat passengers in motor vehicles (paragraph 5.12);

(c) health education should be expanded, but some of the increased resources must be spent on developing more effective methods and on monitoring and validating existing and new techniques (paragraph 5.14);

(d) education authorities should examine seriously existing arrangements for health education in schools (paragraph 5.15);

(e) health education should be emphasised in the forward planning of health authorities (paragraph 5.17);

(f) funds for the Health Education Council and the corresponding bodies in Scotland should be increased to allow them to make more use of television (paragraph 5.21).

Chapter 6 Priorities

6.1   We emphasised in Chapter 2 that the demand for health care is always likely to outstrip supply and that the capacity of health services to absorb resources is almost unlimited. Choices have therefore to be made about the use of available funds and priorities have to be set. The more pressure there is on resources, the more important it is to get the priorities clear; and the more difficult the choices are, the more important it is, in our view, that the ways in which they are reached are generally known and susceptible to public influence. In this chapter we consider how priorities are set in the NHS, and go on to discuss some of the current preferences.

6.2   The DHSS Consultative Document on priorities for health and personal social services in England[1] begins by saying:

> "This Consultative Document is a new departure. It is the first time an attempt has been made to establish rational and systematic priorities throughout the health and personal social services."[2]

The Hospital Plans of 1962[3] were an attempt to control services in accordance with a national strategy but they concentrated almost entirely on capital expenditure. In the late 1960s a series of reports drew attention to the neglect of long stay hospital services. White Papers about services for the mentally handicapped and the mentally ill in the early 1970s set out strategies for the development of health and personal social services for these groups.[4] They paved the way for the comprehensive approach in the priorities document which each health department has published since NHS reorganisation.[5] These differ slightly in detail but the broad emphasis in each is the same.

---

[1]Department of Health and Social Security, *Priorities for Health and Personal Social Services in England. A Consultative Document*, London, HMSO, 1976.

[2]Although this is true for England, the Northern Ireland Department of Health and Social Services had already published a similar document (see footnote 5 below).

[3]*A Hospital Plan for England and Wales*, (Cmd 1604), London, HMSO, 1962.
Hospital Plan for Scotland, (Cmd 1602), Edinburgh, HMSO, 1962.

[4]*Better Services for the Mentally Handicapped*, (Cmd 4683), London, HMSO, 1971.
Better Services for the Mentally Ill, (Cmd 6233), London, HMSO, 1975.

[5]Department of Health and Social Services (Northern Ireland), *Strategy for the Development of Health and Personal Social Services in Northern Ireland*, Belfast, HMSO, 1976.
Department of Health and Social Security, *Priorities for Health and Personal Social Services in England – A Consultative Document*, London, HMSO, 1976.
Scottish Home and Health Department, *The Health Service in Scotland. The Way Ahead*, Edinburgh, HMSO, 1976.
Welsh Office, *Proposed All Wales Policies and Priorities for the Planning and Provision of Health and Personal Social Services from 1976/77 to 1979/80. A Consultative Document*, Welsh Office, 1976.
Department of Health and Social Security, *Priorities in the Health and Social Services. The Way Forward*, London, HMSO, 1977.

Setting priorities

6.3 Unfortunately there is no universally acceptable method of apportioning the limited health resources available to the NHS between different possible users and services. One might hope to be able to proceed on the basis of statistical, epidemiological and economic data, and quantified measures of need. Attempts have been made to measure "need", for example by employing indices of mortality and morbidity or use of health service resources.[1] The development of such indices may help to clarify possible ways of using scarce resources, but is unlikely to lead to any agreed formula for allocating resources to different services. Cost effectiveness studies, of which there are few, may assist the choice between different ways of delivering particular services, but they help little when the choice is between services delivering different kinds of care. Attempts to quantify gains in cost effectiveness terms are likely to be of only limited assistance because so many of the data are uncertain or fragmentary. But it is nevertheless important to use what tools are available in reaching national decisions.

6.4 The absence of objective criteria for settling health priorities means that decisions are for the most part a matter of judgment. NHS funds are provided annually by Parliament following consideration of the public expenditure White Paper which sets out the government's views on the competing claims of different public expenditure programmes. Ministers and MPs are vulnerable to lobbying from various quarters and may consider that, for example, education services should be improved while health services are held back. They may be subject to the influences of the many national pressure groups and to pressures from their own constituents for a new hospital or health centre. The health professions in general, and doctors in particular, play a full part in this process. Ultimately it is Parliament that decides, but health ministers – and especially the Secretary of State for Social Services – probably have more influence than any other individuals on determining priorities in the NHS. A Secretary of State is subject to pressure groups, but is in a position to rule between them. His own preferences and judgment will therefore be important.

6.5 Health ministers are advised by their professional and administrative staff, and have access to professional advice from outside the health departments. Some of this advice will come from epidemiologists, medical statisticians and community physicians, and will reflect their concern for the needs of populations and communities rather than individual patients. This may be resented by clinicians who have had to deal with the daily pressures of caring for individual patients and who may have very different views on needs and priorities. Those who have to take a wider view will seem to be less sensitive to individual need; while those concerned with patients must concentrate on their individual requirements. The tensions will be particularly marked where a reduction in resources for a group of patients is proposed.

---

[1]For example; Black, D A K, and Pole, J D, "Priorities in Biomedical Research: Indices of Burden", *British Journal of Preventive and Social Medicine,* 1975, 29, page 222–227, and Culyer, A J, "Need, values and health status measurements" in Culyer, A J, and Wright, K J, *Economic Aspects of Health Services,* London, Martin Robertson, 1978.

6.6   In deciding priorities, ministers must also consider the influence that health services have on other services and vice-versa. Some services provided by local authorities are necessary to the NHS, and the availability of, for example, social services and suitable housing may be the determining factor. The personal social services are particularly important when arrangements are being made to transfer patients from hospital to their own homes or elsewhere in the community, or for helping them to remain in the community and be treated at home.

6.7   We have some comments on the way NHS priorities are determined. First, we believe it is important that the lay public should be involved in the process. The discussion should not be left solely to health professionals and administrators, though we recognise that policies and priorities must be realistic and reflect what can be achieved, and must therefore take account of the views of professional and management staff in the NHS on their feasibility and likely consequences. The media have an important role here: without informed discussion in newspapers, radio and television there is a risk that decisions at national level will not be exposed to public debate at all. We welcome the way in which, since reorganisation, the health departments have encouraged public discussion of priorities in the NHS, and believe that this approach should be developed. We recommend that more of the professional advice on which policies and priorities are based should be made public. This would strengthen the authority of the advice issued and lead to its readier acceptance in the field as well as promoting public discussion.

6.8   Second, much of the criticism of centrally determined priorities has been directed at the lack of clear guidance on the resource consequences of priorities. Guidance on priorities must take resource considerations into account. As the Rt Hon Dr David Owen MP, a former Minister of State at the DHSS, put it:

"We must be prepared to say, if we want priority for one sector, where the money should come from."[1]

This is particularly important when resources are tight and it is not possible to fund improvements in priority services from a general increase in allocations. Unfortunately Dr Owen's wise advice has not always been followed.

6.9   Third, a frequent criticism of the way in which priorities are determined is that too many decisions are taken at national level and that there is insufficient local influence. There are arguments both ways here. Some factors can be effectively considered only at national level. It is an important function of the health departments to both influence and take into account developments and policies in government departments and other agencies outside the NHS which may affect health. A report by the Central Policy Review Staff pointed out that central government is "plural" and "joint behaviour is the exception rather than the rule". It recommended that further steps should be taken inside central government "to reduce inter-service boundaries in the area of social

[1]Owen, David, *In Sickness and in Health,* London, Quartet Books, 1976, page 113.

policies."[1] We agree with this approach. Government, and in particular ministers, are also sensitive to public opinion and national political pressures in a way in which health authorities are not. Some pressure groups, including those representing important patient groups, operate effectively only at a national level. A more local determination of priorities might not be in the interests of these groups. Finally, the initiative in launching major policies in areas such as prevention can come only from central government.

6.10   Nevertheless, there are considerable advantages in encouraging local participation in setting priorities. Central government cannot know local requirements in any detail; and for historical and other reasons needs and the current levels of provision vary considerably from place to place. The two main advantages of allowing decisions on priorities to be taken locally are that it encourages a greater pride in the local service and sense of commitment to it, and stimulates experiment in methods of provision. The health departments have no monopoly of wisdom, nor are we dealing with a field which presents itself in terms of simple, logical answers to logically stated problems. While there are some aspects of policy making which can sensibly be undertaken only by the health departments, and the broad framework of priorities should be centrally determined at the level where political accountability lies, there is considerable scope for leaving more detailed discussion and decision on priorities to local level. With the increased public participation at the operational level of the NHS which we recommend in Chapter 20 the case for allowing priorities to be determined at that level will be strengthened.

Implementing priorities

Difficulties

6.11   It may take a long time to achieve changes in the pattern of expenditure on different priority groups in the NHS. There are several reasons for this, but the most important is that the vast bulk of the funds available to the NHS are committed to services already in existence even before Parliament has voted them. Moreover, in practice:

> "for hospital and community health services current expenditure needs to grow at about 1 per cent a year merely to allow for demographic change and to make some provision for the spread of improved medical techniques without detriment to standards in other parts of the service."[2]

When resources available to the NHS are rising slowly a government is probably doing well if it can divert as much as one per cent of NHS funds in any one year to the development of priority services.

6.12   In the implementation of priorities some patient groups and their services are going to gain, and others to lose. The lower the expansion rate of

[1] *Relations between Central Government and Local Authorities,* Report by the Central Policy Review Staff, London, HMSO, 1977, paragraphs 5.4 and 14.2.

[2] *The Government's Expenditure Plans 1979–80 to 1982–83,* (Cmnd 7439), London, HMSO, 1979, page 143.

the service as a whole, the more acute the problem. Major breakthroughs in the cure of disease are rare; and it is therefore usually only population changes (for example, a decline in the birth rate) which give real scope for the contraction of services. Proposals to reduce a service will be opposed by those who wish to improve it and claim that they must retain their threatened resources to enable them to do so. The NHS employs a large number of workers, many of them specialised. More than marginal changes in the priority given to different services would mean moving, training and retraining staff. Resistance to such change is usually intense.

6.13   A further difficulty about implementing nationally determined priorities lies in allowing for specific local factors. Local pressures may conflict with national priorities, and there may be strong ties of loyalty to particular services or institutions. Diversion of funds from one district or area to another required by national priorities may be sternly resisted by those responsible for managing the health service locally, as well as by staff and the local community.

The planning system

6.14   The main mechanism for implementing the government's priorities in the NHS is the planning system. Ministers and health authorities need a framework within which choices can be made in the full knowledge of the possibilities available and any wider consequences of them. The planning process is designed to provide this framework.

6.15   In England a systematic planning process was introduced in the DHSS in 1974, and the NHS planning system and a system of social services planning were initiated in 1976. The planning process in the field is set in motion each year with the issue of guidance from the Secretary of State on policies and priorities and on the resource assumptions within which planning should proceed. The initial guidance was published as a consultative document, and the whole process is seen as consultative rather than directive. The health authorities' responses are contained in the documents submitted to the DHSS, and these are taken into account by the Secretary of State in his regular reviews of planning guidance. The planning system also enables the consistency of health authorities' plans with national policies to be checked, and the development of services to be assessed. Planning guidance is flexible in two senses; it is subject to review over time, and it is considered by field authorities in the light of local circumstances. Substantial divergence from the national pattern may be justified in particular circumstances, and indeed may result in a better use of available resources. But the reasons for it may merit exploration, and that may lead to review of the national guidance itself.

6.16   In conjunction with the planning system the DHSS has developed a programme budget approach as a means of costing policies for services development across the board. Expenditure can be allocated to broad patient and client groups, and can show the trends in spending on the groups identified. Health and personal social services expenditure in England by programme for the period 1975/76 to 1977/78 is shown in Table E1 in Appendix E (comparable figures are not available for earlier years). Too much weight should not be given to these figures, but they suggest that over the last three years the pattern of expenditure by health authorities has been broadly consistent with the current DHSS priorities.

6.17　We agree with the Expenditure Committee that:

"the expenditure planning and priority-setting of DHSS should be synchronised so as to enable Parliament to examine the relationship between the two"[1]

but even after listening to careful explanation by representatives of the DHSS about the way in which the needs of particular priority groups are taken into account in the allocation of resources to health authorities, we remain mystified. We are bold enough to think that this is because there is some cloudiness in the Department's thinking about these matters, which are as important as anything in the Department's care.

6.18　Broadly comparable planning arrangements tailored to local needs have been developed in Wales. The health authorities prepare annually operational plans covering a four year period and strategic plans looking ten years ahead, which are then reviewed by the Welsh Office and taken into account in planning guidance and resource allocation. In addition the Welsh Office allocates provision for all-Wales services and retains responsibility for the long-term all-Wales capital programme. In Northern Ireland a similar planning system has been developed for both health and personal social services. The health and social services boards prepare annually detailed comprehensive plans for the development of services covering the following five years, with general proposals for a further five years. These plans are then considered by the Department of Health and Social Services (Northern Ireland), and an overall plan, which is reviewed and up-dated annually is prepared.

6.19　Arrangements for planning differ in Scotland where at reorganisation the Scottish Health Services Planning Council was established with representatives of the health boards, the universities and the Scottish Home and Health Department. In addition there are national consultative committees for the main health professions which tender advice to the Secretary of State through the Planning Council. The Council has played a major part in the development of priorities for the health service in Scotland and has set up a number of multi-disciplinary programme planning groups which have reported on services for particular patient and client groups. The Chairman of the Council, Professor EM McGirr, told us that:

"Health planning in Scotland is built into the central decision-making process to a significant extent. On the other hand, the way the planning council and the national consultative committees have been constituted also ensures that central planning is not over centralised."

---

[1]*Ninth Report from the Expenditure Committee Session 1976/77, Chapter V: Spending on the Health and Personal Social Services,* London, HMSO, 1977, page lvi.

Earmarked allocations

6.20 A more direct method of implementing national priorities, is to earmark part of the funds allocated to authorities for use in particular services. In the period 1971–76 additional capital allocations totalling more than £44 million were made to health authorities in England to be spent on mental handicap, mental illness and geriatric services, though with little noticeable effect on the overall proportion of capital expenditure devoted to services for those three groups. Currently health authorities in England are receiving funds specifically allocated for the development of regional secure units, but these funds have sometimes been diverted to other purposes. While earmarking within the general allocation can influence the pattern of expenditure it evidently cannot ensure that funds are used for the purposes intended. A variation is to make additional funds available outside the normal allocation for use on specific projects, such as capital funds for the development of health centres. These funds are separately administered and cannot be diverted to other uses, but may not be fully taken up. In the same way, capital and revenue funds in England and Wales allocated for projects undertaken in collaboration with local authorities, although a part of health authorities' normal allocations, cannot be used for other purposes.

6.21 A disadvantage of earmarked allocations is that they reduce the discretion of health authorities to tailor their policies and priorities to local needs within the framework of national policy guidelines (the philosophy of the planning system), and undermine the influence of the individual health authorities. On the other hand it may be that a substantial shift of resources to the "Cinderella" services cannot otherwise be achieved.

6.22 Priorities are generally expressed in a way which makes their implementation difficult to measure. Over time, progress can be checked through centrally collected statistics: activity and staffing statistics and financial returns. The development of the planning systems should mean that the health departments are better able to monitor the implementation of priorities, but it is too early yet to know whether these hopes are being realised and expenditure is leading to the achievement of desired outcomes.

Information

6.23 Good information is of prime importance for planning purposes. In Chapter 21 we refer to some of the defects in existing arrangements for collecting statistical and other information in the NHS. We are therefore pleased to note that the DHSS has recently undertaken a study of information requirements of the health services, and a consultative document was circulated in the NHS in February this year.[1] The document proposes a joint NHS/DHSS Steering Group "to provide a permanent forum for considering information matters". We support this approach, and suggest that other government departments and local authorities, who both contribute to, and make use of, information relevant to the NHS, should be involved.

---

[1]HN (79) 21, *Information requirements of the health services.*

Current priorities

6.24   Current NHS priorities are services for the elderly, the mentally ill, the mentally handicapped and children. Community services are also being developed, along with services for some smaller groups of patients whose needs have in the past been neglected. There is considerable overlap between the four main patient groups currently being given priority. The major problem of mental illness is now the dementias of old people, and it is therefore impossible to plan services for the old and the mentally ill separately. The mentally handicapped may also be mentally ill and this is one of the commoner reasons for their continued stay in hospital. Children may be mentally handicapped or become mentally ill. "Programme planning" of services has therefore not only to be comprehensive for each patient group but has also commonly to be "joint" in that it involves more than one provider of services and must take into account the needs which more than one of these groups have in common.

6.25   Children apart, the priority groups have other features in common. The resources devoted to their care by the health authorities have been less than those allocated to other patient groups, while the services for them have had persistent recruiting difficulties and have been staffed by a high proportion of men and women from overseas. In recent years these men and women, trained and untrained, have given invaluable service in psychiatric and geriatric hospitals; but the quality of the care which they can provide is limited by deficiencies in communication, because they come from cultures with different assumptions and conventions and have often an imperfect command of English. Where understanding, diagnosis and treatment all depend upon ease of communication, and where abnormalities of attitude and behaviour of a subtle kind may be of great significance, staff from overseas may be at a serious disadvantage and patients may suffer in consequence.

Community care

6.26   For all the priority groups the present policy of the health departments is that wherever possible, care should be provided in the community rather than in institutions. First, it is said that care in the community is generally preferred by most patients, providing they can be assured that their needs are being adequately met, and that they should be admitted to hospital only when they require those forms of treatment and care which cannot effectively be provided in their homes. Second, it is argued that care in the community will relieve pressure on the hospital services and may be cheaper. There are, however, a number of difficulties about comparing the costs of treating or caring for patients in hospitals and at home. The degree of dependency of patients may vary, the quality of treatment and care may be different and is difficult to measure, the outcome or effectiveness of the treatment is hard to assess, and treatment at home may impose heavy burdens on relatives and neighbours. More research is required into the relative costs and effectiveness of hospital and community provision for conditions where there is an option about the place of treatment.

6.27   Community care is provided primarily by families or neighbours, with the support of the health and personal social services. Its expansion requires additional facilities, such as health centres, day hospitals and day centres, which involve capital expenditure. The main requirement, however, is additional staff: GPs, district nurses, health visitors, home helps, chiropodists, midwives and others. Expenditure on community health services is a relatively small proportion of total NHS expenditure, but adjustment of the pattern of care will inevitably be slow unless additional resources are made available to both NHS and local authority services. Some of the other difficulties have already been mentioned: for example, it may take time to recruit or retrain staff with the necessary professional skills. Community care is especially dependent on co-operation between health and personal social services, but (except in Northern Ireland) two separate authorities must be prepared to work together and agree to give priority to this aspect of their functions, rather than to other pressing local needs, if the necessary change in emphasis is to be achieved. Other services have an important influence on community care; for example in Great Britain nearly 30% of local authorities' new house building is devoted to housing designed for old people and a number of new cash benefits have been introduced in recent years to ease the burden on relatives or others caring for elderly or disabled people at home.

6.28   Teamwork is of central importance in community care. A patient may need the support and services of several different workers, who may be employed by health authorities or local authorities, or who may be independent contractors. Effective teamwork is much easier where there is regular contact between all those involved. The increased number of health centres has done much to facilitate effective teamwork, and this is discussed more fully in Chapter 7.

6.29   The extent to which there has been a switch in emphasis from hospital treatment to care in the community in recent years is difficult to measure. One indication would be the number of in-patient treatments in relation to the number of out-patient or day patient treatments or day hospital attendances. This is set out for three patient and client groups in Table 6.1, which suggests that for the elderly, the mentally ill and the mentally handicapped there has been some development of care in the community. The hospital population for these groups over the same period is shown in Table 6.2. In spite of an increasingly elderly population, the number of patients in geriatric departments has remained constant and the number of patients in mental illness and mental handicap hospitals and units has declined. However, in the case of the elderly these figures could reflect a failure to provide adequate in-patient accommodation as much as a deliberate attempt to provide services in the community.

6.30   A better measure of the extent to which there has been a switch from hospital to community care might be the number of staff employed in the community in relation to the numbers of staff employed in hospital. The figures in Table 6.3 describe a complex situation but do not indicate a greater increase of staff in the community.

TABLE 6.1

Patients Receiving In-Patient, Out-Patient or Day Patient Treatment: Great Britain 1970–1976

Thousands

	1970	1973	1976	% change over period
Geriatrics[1] discharges and deaths	201	220	259	28.9
out-patient and day case attendances	149	189	244	63.8
day hospital attendances[2]	580	838	1,172	102.1
Mental Illness discharges and deaths	212	217	219	3.3
out-patient and day case attendances	1,748	1,880	1,877	7.4
Mental Handicap discharges and deaths	15	18	19	26.7
out-patient and day case attendances	16	26	28	75.0

Source: compiled from health departments' statistics.

Notes: [1] Includes younger disabled.
[2] England only.

TABLE 6.2

Hospital Population; Daily Occupied Beds: Great Britain 1970–1976

Thousands

	1970	1973	1976	% change over period
Geriatrics[1]	65	65	65	0
Mental Illness	131	117	105	−19.8
Mental Handicap	64	61	58	−9.4

Source: compiled from health departments' statistics.

Note: [1] Includes younger disabled.

60

TABLE 6.3

Staff Employed in Community Care and in Hospitals: Great Britain 1974–77

Whole-time equivalents

	1974	1977	% Change over period
COMMUNITY CARE STAFF			
District Nurses	12,428	14,929	20.1
Health Visitors	9,861	10,248	3.9
Social Workers	24,414	28,317[1,2]	16.0
Home Helps	53,860	56,687	5.2
General Medical Practitioners (numbers)	25,844	26,810	3.7
HOSPITAL STAFF			
Hospital nursing and midwifery staff	333,592	369,983	10.9
Hospital medical staff	31,486	36,293	15.2

Sources: compiled from health departments' statistics.

Notes: [1] Scottish figure is for 1978.

[2] English figure is provisional.

6.31   We have not been able to reach a firm judgment about whether the present balance between community and hospital care is correct. The pattern of health services varies in different parts of the country, and probably both reflects and conditions local needs and preferences. We think it right that the emphasis should be on the development of community services. Although in some places it may be possible to transfer resources from the acute hospital services, in general those services are already severely constrained, and often in need of improvement. It follows therefore that the development of community care requires additional resources and at a time when the resources available to the NHS and to local authorities are growing slowly, progress will necessarily be restricted. We say more about the relationship between hospital and community care in Chapter 10.

Services for the elderly

6.32   Meeting the health needs of the elderly is one of the major problems facing the NHS. The higher age groups are increasing both in absolute numbers and as a proportion of the total population, and Table 6.4 shows that this is particularly marked for those aged 75 and over and 85 and over. At the same time the number of women in the 45–60 age group who provide the main source of support for old people in the community, will fall in the next decade. Expenditure per head on health services is almost six times as much for people aged 75 and over as for people aged 16 to 64.[1] They also make heavy demands on the support provided by the local authorities, particularly in personal social services and housing. The health departments are well aware of the problems created by the increasing number of old people. The DHSS and the Welsh

[1] *The Government's Expenditure Plans 1979-80 to 1982-83*, (Cmnd 7439), London, HMSO, 1979, page 143.

Office published "A Happier Old Age: a discussion on elderly people in our society" in 1978, and this is to be followed by a White Paper on services for the elderly this year. The needs of the elderly in Scotland are being considered by a Programme Planning Group set up jointly by the Scottish Health Services Planning Council and the Scottish Advisory Council on Social Work. A review of the needs of the elderly is also being carried out in Northern Ireland.

TABLE 6.4

Projected Elderly Population: UK 1976–1996

	Persons aged 75 and over		Persons aged 85 and over	
	Numbers (thousands)	% of total population	Numbers (thousands)	% of total population
1976	2,842	5.07	520	0.93
1986	3,407	5.96	612	1.07
1996	3,498	5.91	740	1.25

Source: Office of Population Censuses and Surveys, *Population Projections 1974–2014*, London, HMSO, 1976.

6.33 Services for the elderly demonstrate very clearly the requirements for community care already discussed. Everything possible should be done to assist old people to remain independent, healthy and in their own homes. It is important to detect stress and practical problems, and to ward off breakdown, for example by regular visiting of those who are identified through GP case registers as being at risk, by providing physical aids or adapted or sheltered housing, and by assistance from home helps, chiropodists, or meals on wheels. Planned short-term admissions to residential care play an increasing part in helping the elderly remain in their own homes or with relatives. The supporting role of relatives is of great importance and their needs for relief from time to time must be met. Voluntary bodies and volunteers can often help in numerous understanding ways.[1] Where there is illness the full resources of the primary care team have often to be deployed, and a heavy load of work and responsibility falls on the district nurses and the home help services. Day centres are helpful, and day hospitals have been widely developed: their place in a comprehensive service urgently requires critical evaluation and this is being studied by the DHSS. When independence at home is no longer possible, care in a nursing home or local authority residential home may be appropriate.

6.34 Illness in old age commonly has both physical and mental aspects. A deterioration in an old person's faculties may or may not be accompanied by disturbances of behaviour, and may or may not be due to or worsened by physical illness. Detailed assessment is often necessary and the skill of geriatricians, psychiatrists, nurses and social workers may be jointly called upon. We recommend that all professions concerned with the care of the elderly should receive more training in understanding their needs.

6.35 Many elderly patients admitted to district general hospitals do not

[1]Personal Social Services Research Unit, University of Kent, *Kent Community Care Project: an interim report*, 1979.

need the technology which that type of hospital can provide. They frequently remain in hospital long after any investigations or active treatment have been completed because they are not fit to go home and there is nowhere else for them to go. Residential homes cannot care for those who are physically very dependent and need nursing care, or whose behaviour is more than mildly disturbed.

6.36   In any plans for the care of infirm old people in the NHS nurses must play the most important part: they are the only category of caring staff essential when active treatment is no longer possible. Recruiting and retaining these nurses will present an increasing problem. Many nurses, like others in the health professions, do not want to look after mentally disturbed old people. Commenting on the DHSS Consultative Document "Priorities for Health and Personal Social Services in England" the Royal College of Nursing noted that:

"those engaged in this work tend to be regarded as having opted for a less demanding branch of nursing"

by their nursing colleagues. They may be so regarded but it is grossly unfair: it is one of the most demanding branches of nursing, calling for personal qualities and skills of a high order, and it should be so rewarded. The Royal College of Nursing also noted that;

"the Joint Board of Clinical Nursing Studies has produced some excellent courses in this speciality, but the take-up has been very disappointing."[1]

6.37   Since the burden of care will fall predominantly on nursing staffs, they should have a major influence in determining the conditions under which they will work. We were impressed by some of the arrangements we saw for the care of the elderly during our overseas visits, and particularly by the nursing homes in Denmark. There, old people needing long term care were normally accommodated in single rooms for which they were expected to provide their own furniture, and were encouraged to maintain a social life and be as active physically as they were able. Unfortunately large numbers of old people are too frail to be able to achieve even such a moderate degree of independence. We recommend that further experiments in different ways of meeting the needs of elderly and other patients requiring long-term care should be undertaken urgently.

6.38   Geriatricians do not deal comprehensively with the health and sickness problems of this age group, even if one excludes surgical cases. Where mental illness or dementia is the dominant feature of the old person's state, as it often is, the geriatrician may take the view that a psychiatrist should look after him. The geriatrician is basically a physician, and most physicians working in hospitals now have to care for a great many old people. In view of the considerable difficulties of recruitment into the specialty, and the fact that the majority of those recently appointed to consultant posts are doctors from

[1]Royal College of Nursing, *Comments on the Consultative Document. Priorities for Health and Personal Social Services in England,* 1976, page 13.

overseas,[1] doubts have been expressed whether geriatric medicine can be a viable specialty. Whether or not it should be considered a specialty, it is certain that not all elderly disabled people can be cared for by specialist geriatricians: there are not, and will not, be enough of them. The care of the old is inescapably part of the mainstream of medicine, the daily responsibility now of physicians, psychiatrists and surgeons, and it must remain so.

6.39   We consider that there is a place for specialisation in the care and treatment of the illnesses of old age, but that this should usually be a part-time commitment, the doctor being a physician or psychiatrist with a "special interest" in geriatrics. This is an approach which has the support both of the Royal College of Physicians of London[2] and the Royal College of Psychiatrists. Such a specialist interest can be fostered in postgraduate training programmes and built into contracts of service. It is a more flexible, and for many a more attractive category than whole-time specialisation. There has, we think, been too much emphasis on the latter by some of the leaders in this field.

6.40   Nevertheless, some doctors will continue to wish to give all their attention and energies to this field of work and this should also be welcomed. Some pioneering physicians and psychiatrists have devoted themselves to geriatrics and have contributed outstandingly to knowledge and to improved standards of investigation and care. These are the people who lead and develop services. They may also wish to pursue this field of work in an academic setting: important advances have been made in university departments of geriatric medicine. There is a paucity of such research, but the limiting factor is the lack of talented research workers rather than the amount of money potentially available.

Services for the mentally ill

6.41   In the detection and treatment of psychiatric illness the largest and most important role is played by general practitioners. A survey of general practices in London showed that 14% of the patients had "consulted at least once during the survey year for a condition diagnosed as largely or entirely psychiatric".[3] Similar findings have been reported in other surveys. Most patients with these conditions are treated by GPs themselves: fewer than five per cent are referred to psychiatrists. Yet most GPs consider themselves inadequately trained and equipped to deal with these problems. It is therefore of prime importance that the competence of the primary care team should be strengthened in this respect. It is an aspect of care with which the public already show some dissatisfaction by their complaints of GPs not having time to listen to them. It is impossible to do justice to psychiatric problems within the present average consultation time of six minutes.[4] GP trainees can now

---

[1]In 1978 in England and Wales, 84.6% of registrars in geriatrics were born overseas. In 1977/78, 54% of appointees to consultant posts in England were born overseas.

[2]Royal College of Physicians of London, *Report of the Working Party on Medical Care of the Elderly*, 1977, page 10.

[3]Shepherd, M, Cooper, B, Brown, A C, and Kalton, G W, *Psychiatric Illness in General Practice*, London, Oxford University Press, 1966.

[4]Buchan, I C, and Richardson, I M, "Time study of consultations in general practice", *Scottish Health Service Studies No. 27*, Edinburgh, SHHD, 1973.

spend part of their three years' vocational training in gaining psychiatric experience. It is to be hoped that many will do so, but it will be necessary also to review the content of continuing education in general practice, the place of psychologists in the primary care team, and the possible training of other members of the team in techniques of counselling.

6.42   In many places the psychiatric services have long embraced hospital and community elements, and in the community both the NHS and the social services departments of local authorities make major contributions. The NHS provides mental hospitals and the psychiatric units in district general hospitals (DGHs), day hospitals, out-patient clinics, supervised hostels and community psychiatric nursing services; and the local authority provides hostels, group homes, supervised lodgings, sheltered workshops and social casework of many kinds.

6.43   Psychiatry is a shortage specialty. Though there has been a considerable expansion of the specialty in the last decade its staffing levels do not match the demands made upon it. Recruitment has recently fallen off: there are consultant posts unfilled and recruitment to the training grades has been deficient in both quantity and quality. Until the quality of recruitment improves it would be unwise to promote expansion of the specialty.

6.44   There are problems with the provision of hospital services for the mentally ill. The development of psychiatric units in DGHs in itself desirable, has had the effect of leaving to the large specialist mental hospitals the incurable, the behaviourally disturbed, the old and demented. The policy of running down these institutions has undermined the morale of their staff. Nevertheless they can provide facilities and a therapeutic environment of a kind which cannot be provided by a psychiatric unit in a DGH. We discuss their problems in Chapter 10.

Services for the mentally handicapped

6.45   It is an accident of history that the NHS has such a large responsibility for the mentally handicapped. Medical and nursing staffs have had to look after those whom society and other disciplines have rejected. Recently the situation has changed; the education of the mentally handicapped has become the responsibility of the education departments of local authorities, and their social services departments have been more active in providing training centres, hostels and residential homes. But the community provision is still far less than it should be, except in the case of children where a higher proportion of the hospital population has recently been discharged to community care. Most mentally handicapped people need no more medical attention than the average person. Some require intensive attention from psychiatric, medical and other specialties, as well as skilled nursing, and in-patient treatment and care in hospital may be imperative.

6.46   The general strategy for the development of these services was set out in the White Paper "Better Services for the Mentally Handicapped" in 1971,[1]

---

[1]*Better Services for the Mentally Handicapped,* (Cmnd 4683), London, HMSO, 1971.

and has general assent. A National Development Group for the Mentally Handicapped and a Development Team have been instituted in England and Wales. Prevention of mental handicap is of prime importance, research in this has been adequately supported and progress has recently been made.

6.47 Many people working in these services would like to see them comprehensive, specialist and distinct. Others consider that their isolation has been a major problem, and overcoming this professional, social and geographical isolation appears to be the key to their improvement. Those who hold the first view get little or no support from the facts of the present situation. Staffing presents a major problem and looks like getting worse. Recruitment of doctors is poor both in quantity and quality. Many trained nurses are approaching retirement age, there is a high proportion of untrained staff and high staff turnover. About 25 per cent of the teachers are reported to be without professional qualifications, and still more are without specialist training in teaching the severely mentally handicapped. There is a serious shortage of clinical psychologists, who have an essential contribution to make in diagnosis and treatment. The fact that several enquiries have had to be set up in England and Wales and have reported adversely on the conditions they have found in hospitals for the mentally handicapped shows that, whether or not it is carrying too extensive a responsibility, the NHS is, in certain places at least, failing badly to fulfil its obligations.

6.48 As in the case of the medical specialty of geriatrics, we consider that there is a place for the full-time wholly committted specialist but much greater scope for appointments shared with other specialties. Specialists in child and adult psychiatry and paediatrics have a most important part to play in the care of the mentally handicapped, particularly in supporting those nurses, residential staff and families who have the responsibility for full time care. Every effort should be made to encourage this by funding joint appointments. This development has been resisted by some of the longer established, whole-time specialists in mental handicap, but we consider this short-sighted and ultimately self-defeating. Similarly, the barriers between mental handicap and the other branches of nursing should be taken down. Many who would not be prepared to make this their life's work might be prepared to work for a time, or work part-time, in this most challenging field.

6.49 The Jay Commitee reported recently on mental handicap nursing and care.[1] The report makes important recommendations on the training of residential care staff and the management of residential units, whether in hospital or local authority accommodation. Consultation on the report has only just begun, and we have not had time to consider its recommendations in detail.

Services for children

6.50 A range of services for children is provided under the NHS – general medical services and complementary primary health care including the health

---

[1]*Report of the Committee of Enquiry into Mental Handicap Nursing and Care* (Cmnd 7468), London, HMSO, 1979.

visiting service, community health services and child health clinics, school health services, and hospital paediatric services. In 1974 the reorganisation of the NHS brought all these services together for the first time under the new health authorities. At the same time "the provision made for health services for children up to and through school life [and] the use made of these services by children and their parents" were being considered by the Court Committee which reported in 1976.[1] An implication of the reorganisation of the NHS, which is elaborated in the Court Report, is that there should be much closer co-operation and integration of the various health services for children. While the government have not accepted some of the Committee's detailed recommendations which were aimed at creating an integrated child health service, we urge that they continue to bear that objective in mind.

6.51   One problem in the field of child health services to which the Court Committee drew particular attention was the continuing comparatively high rate of perinatal mortality in the UK. The figures in some geographical areas and the higher rates in social classes IV and V are disturbing. Against this background the health departments have advocated the concentration of maternity facilities in a smaller number of properly equipped and staffed maternity units, which will normally be situated in district general hospitals. They have urged that more special care "baby cots" should be provided where there are shortages. It is also necessary to improve the health and related services (including genetic counselling) available to women during pregnancy, and their take-up of these services.

6.52   The Court Committee identified health surveillance as one of the main functions of the child health services. By this they meant evaluation of the child's state of health and pattern of growth, monitoring development, providing advice and support for parents and arranging further examination or treatment where necessary, providing an effective immunisation programme and health education. At present these functions are carried out at different times and in different places by different people. Some general medical practitioners hold regular child development clinics for their patients and health visitors undertake routine child development surveillance of the normal population. Often there is little liaison with the community child health services. It is important that co-ordinated programmes of child health surveillance should be developed, and especially that efforts should be made to ensure that all children are covered.

6.53   The Court Committee examined the school health service and identified a number of problems:

>   restricted ability to meet the needs of school children caused by the nature, organisation and concentration on regular medical examinations;
>
>   failure to meet the needs of adolescents directly by advising parents and teachers rather than the teenagers themselves;
>
>   failure to give adequate attention to health education;

---

[1] *Fit for the Future: Report of the Committee on the Child Health Services,* (Cmnd 6684), London, HMSO, 1976.

the isolation of school health staff from relevant specialist services and problems of effective communications between GPs and school doctors.

The Committee thought that every school should have a nominated doctor and nurse with appropriate training and sufficient time to get to know their schools well. They would be responsible for all aspects of health within the school and for liaising with other NHS services. The Committee emphasised the importance of the school nurse as "the representative of health in the everyday life of the school" and recommended the appointment of full-time nurses to large secondary schools. The government rejected the proposal for specialist professional grades in school health, but accepted the principle of a better and more integrated service, and more research and experimentation with providing school health services.

6.54 We agree with the general approach of the Court Committee's recommendations though not with their proposals for new categories of staff. Routine school health care seems to be a logical extension of the responsibilities of the primary health care teams; and it would be valuable if post-graduate educational programmes could enable some GPs to obtain the training needed for them to develop a special interest in paediatrics. To focus attention on, and bring help to, particularly vulnerable families and children at risk will call for close collaboration between general practitioners, health visitors and social workers.

Some other services

6.55 In Chapter 10 we comment on the rehabilitation services. We found it convenient to consider briefly at this point service for the deaf, and for the blind and partially sighted.

Services for the deaf

6.56 There are perhaps two and one half million people in the UK with a degree of hearing loss that constitutes a social handicap. The DHSS estimate that about 120,000 children under the age of 16 may be experiencing difficulty in hearing at any one time, including those with temporary conditions. Despite these large figures we received very little evidence about services for the deaf.

6.57 Services for adult patients with hearing problems are based on hospital ear, nose and throat departments. Children may be treated in hospital or in clinics. Some with hearing impairments require surgery: those who do not are often helped by the provision of a hearing aid, normally supplied free of charge. The early detection of hearing impairment in young children is important, because if it is not detected it can cause serious damage to the child's intellectual, emotional and social development. Health authorities aim to screen all children for hearing impairment in the first year of life and again shortly before or after entering school, as part of the routine child development surveillance undertaken by health visitors.

6.58 We were pleased to learn of a number of promising developments in services for the deaf. The medical Royal Colleges agreed in 1975 to the creation of a new specialty of audiological medicine concerned with the medical and rehabilitative aspects of deafness. Increasing numbers of scientific and technical supporting staff are becoming available. There have also been improvements in hearing aids, and hearing aids centres are being established by health authorities. The needs of the elderly deaf are often seriously neglected and the NHS and local authorities should collaborate to ensure an improvement in this position.

Services for the blind and partially sighted

6.59 The great majority of eye problems are dealt with by the general ophthalmic services which we discuss in Chapter 8. The problems reported in our evidence were mainly to do with obtaining spectacles.

6.60 In general, services for the blind and partially sighted are well developed in the United Kingdom. A particular point on which we would like to comment here is the availability of low vision aids which enable blind and partially sighted people to retain their mobility and independence. These aids include simple magnifiers; individual multi-lensed optical devices to assist close work; distance telescopes to help with the identification of bus numbers, road signs, etc; and even closed circuit television systems which reproduce at a high degree of magnification book pages, etc. Low vision clinics exist in some places, but a survey carried out in 1974[1] concluded that half the registered blind and partially sighted population who could benefit from low vision aids had not had an opportunity to try them. Extension of the service could reduce the need for training in the reading and writing techniques of the blind.

Conclusions and recommendations

6.61 The present national priorities set for the NHS are services for the elderly, the mentally ill and mentally handicapped, and children. The emphasis is on community care. These priorities are not the result of objective analysis but of subjective judgment. Our own view is that they are broadly correct at the present time, but they are certainly not the only possible choices. It is important to recognise that national priorities emerge from a variety of conflicting views and pressures expressed in Parliament, by the health professions and various patient or client pressure groups amongst others. So far as possible discussion which leads to the establishment of priorities should be conducted in public and illuminated by fact.

6.62 Implementing priorities gives rise to other problems. There are considerable practical problems to be overcome in shifting resources from one patient or client group to another, or in favouring one part of the NHS against others, particularly when funds are short. It remains to be seen how far the NHS planning system introduced after reorganisation will turn out to be an effective mechanism for this purpose. National priorities can in any case only be uniformly applied to a limited extent. Some of the difficulties may be seen

---

[1]Silver, J, Gould, E, Thomsitt, J, *Transactions of the Ophthalmic Societies of the UK,*1974, pages 94, . 310.

in the efforts to promote community care, and unless additional resources are made available progress will be slow.

6.63 Services for the elderly will make increasing demands on health and local authorities for the rest of this century. We are concerned that without greater shifts in resources than are yet evident neither health nor local authority service: will be able to cope with the immense burden these demands will impose. Inevitably the community as a whole will have to share the responsibility and cost of caring for the elderly at home with appropriate support from the health and personal social services. The health departments are already tackling the implications and integrated planning of services at all levels is essential. In the NHS the burden of caring for infirm old people will fall mainly on nurses, and efforts must be made to encourage them in undertaking this work.

6.64 Hospital provision for the mentally ill and mentally handicapped is discussed in Chapter 10, but most problems with a psychiatric aspect are first identified by GPs. It is clear that many GPs would benefit from more training in this part of their work. We doubt whether medical care for the elderly and mentally handicapped is best organised on the basis of separate specialties. Other doctors should be involved in the care of these patients, and we see the development of special interests by doctors in related specialties as being a promising way of achieving this.

6.65 The Court Committee has recently looked in depth at services for children and we have not considered it necessary to go over that ground again in detail, but, like others, we have doubts about the wisdom of introducing new specialist staff into this field. Finally, we welcome recent developments in services for the deaf, and would like to see improved services for the partially sighted.

6.66 We recommend that:

(a) the health departments should make public more of the professional advice on which policies and priorities are based (paragraph 6.7);

(b) all professions concerned with the care of the elderly should receive more training in understanding their needs (paragraph 6.34);

(c) further experiments in different ways of meeting the needs of elderly and other patients requiring long-term care should be undertaken urgently (paragraph 6.37).

Chapter 7 Primary Care Service

7.1   When we seek health care or medical aid we look in the first place to services available in the community, and usually that is as far as we need to go. For this reason it is impossible to over-rate the importance of the quality of and easy access to services of this kind. At the same time it should be understood that the NHS is by no means the only provider of health care in the community, its most noticeable allies being the local authorities who provide a wide range of complementary services. In this chapter we shall concentrate on some aspects of community care, namely, general medical practice, community nursing,[1] health centres and the serious problem of providing health services to those who live in declining urban areas.

7.2   Historically, general practice has been an important element in publicly provided medicine. Even before the National Insurance Act 1911, which introduced the panel system, many general medical practitioners (GPs) treated Poor Law patients. In 1948 general practitioner services became part of the NHS. In nursing and midwifery too significant developments came in the second half of the 19th century, largely as a result of the public health movement. Before 1948 nursing services in the community were principally provided by voluntary associations. These services have grown rapidly since 1948 and at NHS reorganisation in 1974 health authorities took over the employment of local authority nursing staff.

7.3   The demands made on services in the community are already large and there is every reason to think that they will continue to increase. As we noted in Chapter 6, the proportion of elderly people in the population is growing and so is employment among women who would in the past have been available to care for dependent relatives. The trend in treatment of the mentally ill and handicapped is towards enabling them to live as far as possible in the community. Increased demand may, well be generated by better health education and more screening of high risk groups, and the more interventionist approach of GPs and community nurses. Efforts towards shortening the length of stay in hospital benefit patients and stimulate the efficiency of the hospital service but necessarily throw an added burden on community services. Compared with most other countries we have an extremely well developed primary care system and we would be foolish to allow it to deteriorate.

7.4   A recent development of great significance has been the growth of teamwork in primary care. The grouping of practices and the spread of health centres have brought GPs into closer working contact with each other and with their nursing and administrative colleagues; and in some cases, too, with dentists, pharmacists, clinical psychologists and social workers. Teamwork in

---

[1]We define community nursing in paragraph 7.19.

71

primary care is at an early stage. It will have a major contribution to make to raising standards of service to patients in the community and this makes the development of joint training for the professions involved of considerable importance.

7.5   Choice of doctor by patient and of patient by doctor is an important freedom; and though its existence is largely theoretical for some people, it is highly valued. However, it makes rational planning of the delivery of primary care services more difficult. A general practice normally has no defined catchment area. The general practitioner and other members of the primary care team (unless they are employed directly by him) often do not serve the same geographical locality. The development of group practices and health centres, which provide a degree of choice for both patient and doctor, may encourage greater concentration of catchment areas and movement towards zoning or sectorisation. If that were to occur, it would provide a strong impetus towards the planning and delivery of co-ordinated patient care by hospital and community services for a given population in a given locality; and it would tend to blur the boundaries between these services. We support such developments.

7.6   In our work we have given much attention to NHS services in the community and although we have no doubt that the way in which the NHS provides health care in the community is good, and the general level of care is satisfactory, we are just as sure that there is room for improvement. The professions themselves have done much to assist changes in practice and attitudes to the benefit of patients. An example is the work of the Royal College of General Practitioners (RCGP) in raising professional standards to which we refer below. The criticisms which we make later in this chapter should be set against that background.

General medical practice

7.7   The following definition, quoted in evidence to us by the RCGP, commands general acceptance in the UK and Western Europe:

"The general practitioner is a licensed medical graduate, who gives personal, primary and continuing care to individuals, families and a practice population, irrespective of age, sex and illness. It is the synthesis of these functions which is unique. He will attend his patients in his consulting room and in their homes and sometimes in a clinic or hospital. His aim is to make early diagnoses. He will include and integrate physical, psychological and social factors in his consideration about health and illness. This will be expressed in the care of his patients. He will make an initial decision about every problem which is presented to him as a doctor. He will undertake the continuing management of his patients with chronic, recurrent or terminal illnesses. Prolonged contact means that he can use repeated opportunities to gather information at a pace appropriate to each patient and build up a relationship of trust which he can use professionally. He will practise in co-operation with other colleagues, medical and non-medical. He will know how and when to intervene through treatment, prevention and education to promote the health of his patients and their families. He will recognise that he also has a professional responsibility to the community."

Although general medical practice exists in other countries, it differs from ours in one important respect; in this country patients do not normally have direct access to the hospital consultant and the GP is usually the first point of contact. The different approaches found in other countries are more likely to reflect their different history, geography and social organisation than a systematic attempt to provide the best system of doctoring. Those who gave evidence to us both in this country and abroad valued the concept of general practice, but services often fall below the ideal standard described in the quotation. We deal with the role of the GP in Chapter 14.

7.8 GPs are not employees of the NHS but contract with Family Practitioner Committees (FPCs) in England and Wales and health authorities in Scotland and Northern Ireland to provide all necessary and appropriate services within the scope of general practice to patients registered with them. There are variations within this contract; for example, not all GPs provide maternity services but receive extra remuneration if they do. GPs have considerable freedom to choose their own premises, methods of work and the extent to which they are personally available to deal with patients. It is open to them to practise privately, or to hold part-time hospital or other appointments within the NHS, to work in industry or for an insurance company, although the evidence suggests that most GPs undertake little work outside general practice.[1] It is also open to a GP to arrange for a locum tenens or deputy to stand in for him when he is sick, on holiday or chooses not to be available, but the responsibility for his patients remains with him, except where a deputy is on the same FPC or health authority list. This is not true in Scotland and we recommend that the position there should be brought into line with the position elsewhere in the UK.

7.9 Most GPs contract to provide a 24 hour service, although it will be rare for a GP to be personally available all the time. In a well organised group practice GPs cover for each other and may be on call only one or two nights during the week. However, the use of commercially organised deputising services to undertake this responsibility has grown rapidly over the last ten years and about one third of all GPs now make some use of them. In large cities the proportion is much higher. Deputising services are seen by some as a sensible arrangement which enables GPs to get proper rest and relaxation, but by others as striking at the root of general practice. In recent years public concern about the quality and use of commercially provided deputising services by GPs has grown. Complaints most often made in evidence were that the deputy lacked personal knowledge of the patient and access to his medical records, that contacting the service could be difficult, that deputies were slow in responding to emergencies and that the standard of some deputies was unsatisfactory. But there are advantages in having a deputising service

---

[1]Work in hospitals, for local authorities and government departments gives the average GP less than two per cent of his income, and private practice probably accounts for about a further six per cent. Source: *Review Body on Doctors' and Dentists' Remuneration. Fourth Report 1974*, (Cmnd 5644), London, HMSO, 1974.

73

available, especially for GPs who work single-handed. They can provide an element of flexibility and relieve the burden of night visits and weekend duties.

7.10   In our view, it is in the patient's interest that GPs should normally ensure continuity of care by providing their own out-of-hours cover. At present FPCs and health authorities have the power to control the use of deputising services by individual GPs and to withdraw approval to use services which are unsatisfactory. They are advised on the use of these powers by representatives of local GPs. We recommend that health authorities should keep under review the operation of deputising services in their areas and, if they are unsatisfactory, improve or replace them. We look forward to the end of unsupervised deputising services.

7.11   The use of appointment systems in general practice has increased substantially during the last 15 years. One recent study suggests that the GPs of three-quarters of all patients surveyed used them, but, in spite of this, surgery waiting times have not declined substantially.[1] Our published study of access to primary care suggests that the introduction of more flexible systems, including sessions with appointments and others where appointments are not necessary, is helpful to patients.[2]

7.12   We received complaints about GPs' receptionists from patients and from a number of community health councils (CHCs). The main difficulty seems to be that some receptionists appear to patients to make it hard for them to see their doctor. These receptionists may be over-protective of the GP and inclined to take too much on themselves. A receptionist's life is not always an easy one and the pressures exerted on her by patients may sometimes be considerable. Adequate training for this demanding work is essential. We recommend that, where this does not happen already, the full costs of attendance of GPs' receptionists at training courses should be met by the FPC or health authority concerned. We hope that education and health authorities will make more courses available for training receptionists, and welcome the health departments' intention to give guidance on the content of training courses.

7.13   Continuity of care is widely regarded as one of the benefits of general practice. However, patients sometimes find it difficult to see the doctor of their choice for successive consultations and continuity is broken. Very brief consultations, particularly for patients with psycho-social problems, are unsatisfactory and may encourage over-prescribing of psychotropic drugs. Admission to and discharge from hospital without the proper exchange of information between health workers impairs continuity of care. Adequate warning of discharge is required to enable community services to be mobilised. It is not going too far to say that continuity of care may simply not exist in many large cities. The OPCS study on access to primary health care suggests that in one year 15% of people had occasion to use (or take their children to) the accident

[1]Cartwright, A & Anderson, R, *Patients and their Doctors* 1977, Institute for Social Studies in Medical Care, Royal College of General Practitioners, Occasional Paper Number 8, 1979.

[2]Simpson, Robin, *Access to Primary Care*, Royal Commission on the NHS, Research Paper No. 6, London, HMSO, 1979.

and emergency departments of large hospitals rather than consult their GP.[1] Fifty per cent of them said that their reason for using the hospital was because it was better equipped to provide the service they required.

7.14   The BMA, in their proposals for a revision of the GP contract, record that:

"In the course of his practice the family doctor recognises his ethical obligation to his patient to provide continuing care. In our view the community is fortunate that GPs' sense of ethical responsibility for the continuous care of their patients still features so strongly in their attitude to their work, despite the current pressure of demand."[1]

7.15   We share the view that continuity of care is an important objective for NHS services in the community, particularly for those groups like children and the elderly, who make most use of these services. We now examine whether there is a significant shortage of personnel which might adversely affect the prospects for continuity of care, and more generally the quality of service provided to patients.

7.16   Table 7.1 shows an increase in the number of GPs in the last ten years, and average list sizes have been falling as have the number of home visits. The BMA in its new charter proposals has suggested that average list size should be brought down from its present level – about 2,300 – to about 1,700 patients. Because GPs are free to select and reject patients they can, for the most part, adjust the size of their lists to suit themselves. There is considerable variation in list size, but little is known which would help determine an optimum range of sizes. Consultation time could be extended either by increasing the numbers of GPs, and thus reducing average list size, or by increasing the numbers of other professions who work with GPs and delegating more of the GP's work to them. We recommend that before a maximum or minimum list size is adopted, considerable research on this important question should be undertaken.

7.17   List size is affected, particularly in areas which are regarded as over- or under-doctored, by the willingness of the Medical Practices Committees (MPCs) to approve the appointment of GP principals. Some GPs restrict their lists, either because they are elderly or not in good health, or because they have other commitments, but the MPC is powerless to introduce new practitioners if an area is numerically over-doctored. Another problem is that list sizes may be inflated in areas where the population is highly mobile. These problems are particularly marked in London. We recommend a review of the present controls exercised by the MPCs to see whether they should be strengthened.

7.18   There are two other measures which we think should be considered. Many GPs over the normal retirement age provide an excellent service, but

---

[1]OPCS, *Access to Primary Care*, (to be published).

[2]British Medical Association, *Report of the New Charter Working Group*, London, BMA, 1979, paragraph 6.4.

there seems to us no reason in principle why retirement arrangements for GPs should differ from those for hospital consultants. We recommend that the health departments should consider offering an assisted voluntary retirement scheme to GPs with small lists who have reached 65 years of age. We also recommend that the health departments should discuss with the medical profession the feasibility of introducing a compulsory retirement age for GPs. We are conscious that both these measures may present practical difficulties, notably in relation to pension arrangements, but we would expect that these could be overcome.

Nursing in the community

7.19   We quote below the description of the roles of nurses in primary health care services from a recent circular from the Chief Nursing Officer at the DHSS:

> *"The Health Visitor* is a family visitor and an expert in child health care. She is trained to understand relationships within the family and the effects upon these relationships of the normal processes of growth and ageing and events such as marriages, births and deaths. She is concerned with the promotion of health and the prevention of ill health through giving education, advice and support, and by referring to the general practitioner or to other NHS or statutory or voluntary services where special help is needed. The Health Visitor is a professional in her own right, and she initiates action on behalf of her clients and refers to other agencies as she considers appropriate. She makes a very special contribution by visiting families who may have no other regular contact with health services, or who may be visited by no other voluntary or statutory worker, so that she alone may be in a position to identify physical, mental or social illness or family breakdown, and to alert others as appropriate. She is the leader of a team which may include SRNs, SENs and nursing auxiliaries working in schools or clinics. The scope for the employment of supporting staff, and the nature of the tasks which the Health Visitor delegates to them, will vary according to the needs of the population she serves.
>
> *The School Nurse* is involved in the health surveillance of school children and in the health education of school children of all ages. The present trend is away from regular medical inspections and towards a more selective system by which school doctors see children brought to their attention by parents, teachers and school nurses. Certain regular screening tests, e.g. for vision and hearing, remain important. Infestation remains a problem in some areas, and must be looked for and treated by school nurses. In some areas school nurses work direct to Health Visitors. There is much benefit to be derived from the closer integration of the school nurse into the primary health care team.
>
> *The District Nurse* is a SRN who has received post basic training in order to enable her to give skilled nursing care to all persons living in the community including in residential homes. She is the leader of the district nursing team within the primary health care services. Working with her may be SRNs, SENs and nursing auxiliaries. It is the District Nurse who

is professionally accountable for assessing and re-assessing the needs of the patient and family, and for monitoring the quality of care. It is her responsibility to ensure that help, including financial and social, is made available as appropriate. The District Nurse delegates tasks as appropriate to SENs, who can thus have their own caseload. The District Nurse is accountable for the work undertaken by nursing auxiliaries who carry out such tasks as bathing, dressing frail ambulant patients, and helping other members of the team with patient care.

Treatment room nurses are employed by some AHAs. These nurses undertake a wide variety of treatments in health centres or general practice premises. In other AHAs the district nursing team undertake these tasks as well as their domiciliary work.

Midwives are, in most areas, working within Midwifery Divisions, but there is an important role for them as a member of one or more primary health care teams in the provision of ante and post-natal care, and health education. They attend confinements of those mothers delivered in their own homes, and may deliver mothers in hospital. Those mothers discharged early from hospital come under their care until responsibility is transferred to the Health Visitor. Midwives in primary health care are professionally accountable for their own work. Midwives are becoming increasingly involved in family planning and genetic counselling.

Practice nurses. Some general practitioners employ nurses on nursing and/or reception duties, and these are known as practice nurses. They may work alongside AHA employed nurses who are attached to the practice, but seldom undertake work outside the surgery premises. They may be included in training programmes organised by the AHA."[1]

7.20   Although these roles are distinct, they can on occasions be combined. Some nurses in rural areas undertake all three. Nurses in most of these categories are employed by health authorities and form an integral part of an authority's nursing resources. A health visitor, for example, may be attached to work with a particular group practice but she remains accountable to the nursing management of the authority. Many GPs also directly employ practice nurses who work under their supervision.

7.21   As Table 7.1 shows, the numbers of health visitors and district nurses have increased in recent years but the number of community midwives has decreased with the falling numbers of home confinements. There has been a marked increase in visits and treatments carried out by district nurses although numbers of staff are well below target level. Cases attended by district nurses in Geat Britain have risen from 39.6 per 1,000 population in 1972 to 57.6 in 1976. The rate of increase in the number of health visitors has not been as great as that for hospital nursing staff and this at a time when there has been an increasing emphasis on care in the community. The Royal College of Nursing drew attention to the shortage of community nurses in their evidence to us and to the strain which this places on nurses working in the primary care

---

[1]CNO(77)8, *Nursing in Primary Health Care.*

services. It also reduces the effectiveness of other members of the primary care team.

TABLE 7.1
Numbers of General Medical Practitioners, Health Visitors, District Nurses and Community Midwives: Great Britain 1967–1977

whole time equivalents

	1967	1972	1977
General Medical Practitioners (number)	24,005	25,183	26,810
Health Visitors	6,403	7,608	10,248
District Nurses	9,369	11,359	14,929
Midwives	5,685	4,654	3,399

Source: compiled from health departments' statistics.

7.22   Community nursing services are highly important to the improvement of services in the community. They have not yet been fully developed, and we recommend that the health departments continue their current plans for their expansion. Community nursing services are an essential element in the support of patients and their families, giving care in their own homes, and we have been impressed by the satisfaction which most community nurses find in their work. But there is a need for more research into the way nursing services are provided. As the Royal College of Nursing said in its evidence to us:

"The provision of primary care has grown up in the rough and tumble of empiricism and little research has been done into the changed needs for primary care in the community. There are a number of questions that need to be asked about the traditional roles of the various members of the team and the training they receive to fit them for those roles."

7.23   There has been a growing trend towards the attachment of district nurses to general practices. Attachment can mean that a nurse works exclusively with one general practice or with a number of them. A survey in England carried out in 1974 found that 68% of practices had attached nurses.[1] Well equipped and designed health centres encourage attachment of district nurses to general medical practices, but the development of a team approach to primary care requires an understanding of and respect for the professional roles of its various members. Attached district nurses may be torn between the heavy demands of maintaining patients in their own homes and treatment work in GPs' surgeries. In addition patients on a GP's list may be widely dispersed and this may mean additional travelling for district nurses. Many see home nursing as their primary function. We welcome the introduction of a new syllabus and mandatory training for district nurses.

7.24   Increasing numbers of health visitors are attached to general practices, but here the working relationship is more complex and they retain a

[1]Reedy, B L E C et al: "Nurses and nursing in primary medical care in England", *British Medical Journal*, November 1976, Vol 2, pages 1304–6.

geographical responsibility in addition. Florence Nightingale was the first to comment on the distinctive features of nursing the sick and what she called "nursing the well". Health visitors are unique in the health team because of their contact with the "well population". They visit families on their own initiative in the absence of crisis and hence are often the first point of contact with the NHS. The health visitor is a key worker in the primary health care team and makes a major contribution to its role in prevention and health education. Her training equips her to assess the social aspects of health and disease and gives her a knowledge of epidemiology. The health visitor's work may be aided by access to the age/sex register of the GP's list, but she also needs an identifiable geographical area for case-finding. Her work relates to that of the community physician and the GP and she needs to have a working relationship with both. We welcome the advances which have been made in the education and training of health visitors which should help them to achieve their full potential.

7.25 Nurses working in the community, who are employed by health authorities and attached to work in a health centre or group practice, sometimes experience a conflict of loyalties between the team with which the nurse works and her superiors in nursing management. The problem is not unique to the community nurse – the hospital nurse has also a dual loyalty to the clinical team, of which she is a member, and to nursing management in the health authorities. The difference is that the community nurse works in relative professional isolation. Community nurses certainly need access to professional advice and support, and it is important for nursing management to ensure that community nurses keep up-to-date with professional developments and to prevent unnecessary distortions in their workload, but these matters need to be handled sensitively.

7.26 We think that there is considerable scope for expanding the role and responsibilities of health visitors and district nurses. As Dr Jillian MacGuire pointed out in a review of the current literature on nursing roles which she prepared for us:

"the involvement of nurses in screening both the very young and the elderly is already well accepted ... It is not yet routine in all practice settings for nurses to be the main contact for elderly patients ... In many cases the nurses are effectively making first contact decisions anyway though this may not always be recognised for what it is."[1]

We consider that there are increasingly important roles for community nurses, not just in the treatment room but in health surveillance for vulnerable groups and in screening procedures, health education and preventive programmes, and as a point of first contact, particularly for the young and the elderly.

7.27 We recommend that the health departments promote research into nursing in the community. Some of the issues which need investigation are:

the workload of district nursing and the respective demands of domiciliary care and treatment room work;

---

[1]MacGuire, J, *The Expanded Role of the Nurse*, (unpublished paper prepared for the Royal Commission on the National Health Service), October 1977.

the respective roles of district nurse, treatment room nurse and practice nurse vis-à-vis the GP;

their training and lines of responsibility;

the use of aides in community nursing; and

standards of care.

Quality of care

7.28   In Chapter 3 we pointed to the difficulties of measuring the performance of the NHS. We deal generally with quality control questions for the health professions in Chapter 12, and standards of nursing care in Chapter 13, but there are particular difficulties in general practice and good reason to think that standards of competence are not always as high as they might be. The RCGP told us:

"our picture of the assets of good general practice must be balanced by the frank recognition that care by some doctors is mediocre, and by a minority is of an unacceptably low standard."

7.29   We agree with this admirably candid view and we think there are three main reasons for this state of affairs. First, GP training is often inadequate. Whereas several years hospital training, and normally a further qualification, is required before a doctor can be appointed as a consultant, the would-be GP can go straight into general practice as soon as he has completed his pre-registration clinical year. The undergraduate education of doctors gives relatively little emphasis to experience in the community yet, in contrast to the hospital specialities, there is no requirement for GPs to undertake extensive post-graduate training. This will be largely remedied when the National Health Service (Vocational Training) Act 1976 makes post-registration training for GPs compulsory in 1981. The GP will then be obliged to spend three years in further training before becoming eligible for a post as an unrestricted prinicpal in general practice. This will help to raise standards; but, as in other specialities, experience in itself will not be a sufficient indication of quality of performance; it will need to be tested and competence demonstrated. As with hospital specialities, possession of the post-graduate qualification of the relevant Royal College should become the norm for appointment as a principal in general practice. There are two aspects of the post-graduate education of GPs to which we would like to see prominence given; further experience and training in the psychological aspects of general practice and in clinical pharmacology.

7.30   Second, there is no mechanism for setting national standards in the selection of principals in general practice. GP partnerships choose their own new partners, subject to the formal approval of the FPC or health authority. In the case of single-handed vacancies, FPCs and health authorities set up committees on equal numbers of lay members and representatives of local GPs to advise on new appointments. For the most part the system seems to work reasonably well, but on some occasions selection committees have to choose between poor quality applicants and it may then be in patients' interests that no appointment is made. The appointment of a poor applicant will simply tend to perpetuate a poor quality service. However, there is a statutory obligation on the MPC to make appointments to single-handed posts even if no suitable applicant is available. We recommend that consideration be given to this obligation being removed. We recommend, also that national or regional panels are set up to provide external assessors[1] for each new appointment of a principal in general practice. The constitution of such a panel or panels should be discussed between the health departments, the RCGP and the BMA.

7.31 Third, GPs are often isolated and lack the close contact with professional colleagues which is available to those who work in hospitals. There are no mechanisms for ensuring that their standard of work is high, and their earnings depend mainly on the amount, rather than the quality of care provided. GPs have in the past rejected an extension of the distinction awards system to general practice. By contrast, hospital medicine provides elaborate financial inducements. In the training grades, doctors work towards a consultant appointment, for the new consultant there is the possibility of a distinction award, and for the consultant who already holds an award there is the prospect of one at a higher level.

7.32 In some places forms of audit of GP services have already been introduced or are under consideration. Better record keeping, systematic self-criticism, and the inspection of training practices should lead to improvements in standards. In our view a more formal mechanism is required. We suggest that in each health authority area a "division" of general practice to which all GPs would belong should be set up. It might be developed out of the local organisation for post-graduate education, or it might take a form similar to that of the clinical divisions in hospitals. It would act as a forum for medical audit and other methods of raising professional standards. The health departments and health authorities have a duty to encourage good standards of practice and should check progress, but the detailed arrangements should be a matter for local professional decision and experiment. We recommend accordingly.

7.33 We had evidence which suggested that in many practices the system of record keeping was antiquated. Reliable and comprehensive records are vital to the primary health care team and to health service planning. Data are required for identification of populations at risk, and for screening and prevention. GP records need to be brought up to a high standard and to be in a form which facilitates linkage with hospital records and those kept by other health workers in the community. Better record keeping would encourage practice-based research and assist in peer review. We recommend that the introduction of the A4 records system should be given high priority.

7.34 The GP is ideally placed to study the natural history of disease, the

---

[1]The consultants' selection procedure provides assessors to ensure that standards are maintained. For hospital consultant appointments in England and Wales external assessors are found by the appointing health authority after consultation with the appropriate Royal College or Faculty and the university; in Scotland they are drawn from a panel of names selected by the Secretary of State after consultation with the Royal Colleges and Faculties and universities. In Northern Ireland they are appointed by the Central Services Agency, on behalf of the relevant health and social services board, after consultation with the Royal College concerned.

family setting of illness, and recurrent or chronic conditions. The RCGP has made notable contributions to research, particularly in studies of morbidity and multi-centre treatment trials. Individual practitioners have also made important observations, and more can be expected from the departments of general practice which have been set up in many medical schools. Until recently the lack of an established post-graduate training programme for GPs, and the fact that the GP's contract makes no financial provision for research, has meant that much less research has been carried out in general practice than in hospitals. However, the spread of health centres and group practices should provide a better base for collaborative studies, and the increasing numbers of GPs with post-graduate qualifications should lead to an expansion in research. Neither the Medical Research Council nor the health departments earmark funds for research in general practice, but there is no doubt that good quality projects will be supported. Further research is required into for example, the functions of primary care teams, the use of drugs, the relationship between hospital and community care, the size of GP lists (referred to in paragraph 7.16).

7.35 FPCs and health authorities have power to ensure that the provisions of GPs' contracts are complied with, and to inspect their premises. During our own visits to primary care services in different parts of the UK we saw some premises which were clearly unacceptable. We recommend that FPCs and health authorities should use their powers vigorously to ensure that patients are seen by their GPs in surgeries of an acceptable standard. More generally, FPCs and health authorities should monitor carefully the way in which GPs' contracts are discharged.

Prescribing

7.36 In 1977–1978 the total cost of drugs, dressings and appliances prescribed by GPs in the UK was £539.5m. The cost of all other prescriptions was about £127m, most of which was incurred in hospitals. The bulk of the £539.5m went on drugs. Although international comparisons suggest that the health departments have been fairly successful in keeping drug prices down,[1] we have been concerned at the size of the GP drug bill. Total prescriptions dispensed and the average quantity of drugs prescribed have been rising steadily; and there are indications of over-prescribing, particularly of psychotropic drugs. There is a particular problem of high levels of GP prescribing costs in Wales. Some figures are given in Table 7.2.

---

[1]Organisation for Economic Co-operation and Development, *Public Expenditure on Health,* Paris, OECD, 1977.

TABLE 7.2

Number and Cost of Prescriptions: Great Britain 1949–1977

	Unit	1949	1959	1968	1969	1970	1971	1972	1973	1974	1975	1976	1977
Number of prescriptions	Thousands	219,188	236,055	295,875	292,339	295,462	294,389	304,944	313,797	326,019	334,648	348,490	351,331
Total cost	£thousand	33,838	81,336	169,550	182,386	200,865	224,266	255,270	279,465	327,497	431,613	542,251	665,200
Net ingredient cost	£thousand	—	51,777	122,742	134,714	148,339	164,674	186,486	205,581	245,857	317,611	412,255	520,600
Persons on NHS prescribing lists	Thousands	—	47,590	52,072	52,065	52,796	52,903	53,126	53,279	53,609	53,544	53,566	53,696
Average prescriptions per person on list	Number	—	4.96	5.68	5.56	5.60	5.56	5.74	5.89	6.08	6.25	6.51	6.54

Source: health departments' statistics.

Note: these figures represent the number of NHS prescriptions for drugs, medicines and specified appliances dispensed by retail pharmacies, drug stores and suppliers of surgical appliances in contract to FPCs and health authorities; most of the items are supplied on NHS prescriptions given by family doctors (other than doctors who themselves dispense for their patients) but a small number are given by dentists and at NHS hospitals and clinics at such stations of Service Departments that have no dispensing facilities.

7.37   The GP controls what is prescribed, but patients' expectations may encourage him to prescribe even though there may not be a clear clinical need. Medicines prescribed in hospitals are set against health authorities' cash limits, but there is no such limitation on GP prescribing; in effect the NHS has an open-ended commitment to meet the cost of whatever GPs prescribe. This can encourage GPs in bad and expensive habits, such as leaving repeat prescriptions to be handed out by receptionists and prescribing drugs by brand name when cheaper therapeutic equivalents are available.

7.38   GPs are also subjected to massive pressure from the drug companies. A study in 1974–1975 showed that a typical GP may be exposed to over 1,300 advertisements for 250 drugs each month.[1] In 1977 the cost of sales promotion in the UK by drug companies was about £71m, most of it aimed at GPs. The relative isolation of many GPs from pharmacologist and clinical colleagues adds to their problems in evaluating this mountain of material.

7.39   From time to time, health ministers have exhorted the public not to ask for medicines which they feel they need and for which a prescription is unnecessary, but most of the effort in keeping down the GP drug bill is rightly directed at GPs themselves. It consists of a mixture of information, exhortation and threat.

7.40   Last year the health departments agreed with the drug industry that advertising material would have to contain specified information on the active ingredients of the drug, the circumstances in which it should and should not be used, dosage, side effects, precautions and cost. Approved fact sheets have to be given to a GP when he is visited by a drug company representative. The amount of tax deductible sales promotion expenditure allowed to drug companies is also to be reduced, a measure which we support. More positively, the health departments distribute the British National Formulary (BNF) and the Prescribers Journal free to all GPs, draw up charts which compare the costs of similar drugs, and, except in Scotland, help the Consumers Association to distribute the Drug and Therapeutics Bulletin to young doctors at no cost. We recommend the early re-issue of the BNF in portable loose-leaf form. It should be kept up-to-date and should include separate information about costs.

7.41   GPs' prescribing is monitored but subsequent comment reaches individual GPs very slowly. In England and Wales if analysis shows a GP's prescribing habits to be markedly out of line with those of other colleagues in the area, a regional medical officer of the health department may visit him and discuss his prescribing. However, in England about 7% of GPs are visited in this way each year although some 10% prescribe at a cost of 25% or more above the average per person for GPs in their FPC area. In principle, excessive prescribing may, if it persists, lead to the GP having part of his remuneration stopped but in practice this rarely happens and no GPs in England have been "fined" in this way since 1972.

---

[1]The Medical Sociology Research Centre, University College of Swansea, Wales, "Prescribing in General Practice," *Journal of the Royal College of General Practioners,* Supplement No. 1, Vol 26, 1976, page 76.

Controls and incentives

Charges

7.42 We discuss the general question of charging for NHS services in Chapter 21. At present prescription charges are made at a flat rate of 20p[1] for most items although 60% of all prescriptions are dispensed at no cost to the patient. It is often suggested that charges should be adjusted to reflect the full cost of prescriptions to bring home to patients and GPs the cost of their treatment. It seems clear that the benefits of a scheme of this kind are likely to be outweighed by the drawbacks. In any case a patient cannot get a prescription unless a GP agrees to give him one.

Limited list

7.43 Some countries have drawn up lists of essential and effective drugs. In Denmark, Australia and New Zealand listed drugs are prescribed free or at low cost, but patients are charged in full for drugs not on the list. This means that the GP is free to prescribe what he thinks is best for the patient but the cost of prescriptions is transferred from the taxpayer to the patient if a drug not on the list is prescribed. A limited list should lead to improvement in the quality of prescribing by the elimination of ineffective and unnecessarily expensive drugs. It is difficult to estimate the potential savings that would result as much would depend on the composition of the list but a reasonable estimate is of savings of the order of £10-£20m per annum.

Generic prescribing

7.44 Another approach is to require GPs to prescribe by the generic name of the medicine, as opposed to its brand or proprietary name. Some GPs do this already but in 1977 only about 14% of NHS prescriptions in the UK were non-proprietary. If there is a good deal of difference in the price of drugs whose therapeutic qualities are virtually identical, generic prescribing should yield some savings. Adoption of this measure would be likely to reduce the amount of promotional literature from the drug companies to GPs. However, it seems uncertain that savings would be considerable and it might be necessary to recast the level of payment to chemists to take account of the new prescribing patterns.

Quantity limitation

7.45 A further possibility is to require GPs to prescribe for a limited period. In New Zealand, for example, GPs are generally restricted to a week's supply per prescription. But one result might be an increase in repeat prescriptions, and unless GPs were strict in checking them the benefits would be slim.

7.46 The measures listed above are generally applicable both in hospitals

[1]Prescription charges were increased in June 1979.

and general practice. Improvement in the quality of GPs' prescribing probably depends most on their being given the training and information necessary to make sensible choices. In this the educational role of university departments of clinical pharmacology and post-graduate medical education committees is of great importance. There is no evidence that patients benefit from the flood of promotional literature which descends on GPs each week. The most promising of the methods of securing a greater economy and effectiveness in GPs' prescribing which we have considered are the limited list and generic prescribing. We recommend that the health departments should introduce a limited list as soon as possible and take further steps to encourage generic prescribing.

Health Centres

7.47   A recent DHSS circular defined health centres as:

"premises provided by an area health authority where primary health care services are provided for patients by general medical practitioners, health visitors and district nurses and possibly other professions."[1]

Although not every health centre provides all these services, ante-natal, pre-school and school health services, immunisation and vaccination are usually provided in health centres in addition to GP and community nursing services. The circular suggests that health centres may also provide facilities for:

"health education, family planning, speech therapy, chiropody, assessment of hearing, ophthalmology, physiotherapy and remedial exercises, and community dental services; general dental, pharmaceutical and general ophthalmic services, hospital out-patients services and supporting social work services may also be provided."

7.48   Health centres represent a departure from the traditional pattern of general practice. Their supporters emphasise the opportunities they offer for providing integrated services and closer links with hospitals. Their opponents see them as undermining the independence of the general practitioner. In a rapid expansion of the health centre programme in recent years in England and Wales there has been an increase from 212 in 1972 to 731 health centres in 1977 with more than 200 planned for the future. Development has been even more rapid in Scotland and Northern Ireland. However, there is evidence from a recent survey that health centres are by no means universally popular with either GPs or patients.[2]

7.49   The increase in health centres has been less rapid in the conurbations where they are most often needed and is slowing down in places where there is already a high concentration, in Northern Ireland, for example. Only 15% of GPs in the metropolitan counties in England work in health centres against a national average of 17%, and at the end of 1975 Greater London had only 54

[1]HC(79)8, *Health Centre Development*.
[2]Cartwright, A and Anderson, R, *Op cit*.

health centres, hardly more than Greater Manchester. Some health centres are being provided in inner city areas through the current inner city area partnership scheme. Under this scheme, government and local authority provide new facilities in a number of inner city areas with additional resources provided by central government.

7.50 Doctors, nurses and the other professions who together provide care in the community do not necessarily require purpose-built premises to work together efficiently. Nor does working under the same roof guarantee good communication. But it seems to us that health centres serve several purposes: they can set standards, they can make it easier to experiment with different methods of providing primary care and they can house a wide range of services – for example, consultant out-patient clinics, diagnostic and paramedical services. In our view they can significantly improve the quality and accessibility of services to patients. GPs are not obliged to work in health centres although the recent rapid expansion suggests that many find them attractive. Improvement grants are available to those practising from their own premises, but health centres require no capital from the GP and the rent (but not running costs) is fully reimbursed by the FPC or health authority. They appear to offer clear financial advantages to GPs but in some cases a rapid rise in running costs has led GPs to withdraw from participation in proposed new or existing centres. We recommend that the health departments consider whether high running costs are acting as a significant disincentive to GPs to work in health centres. We understand that in Northern Ireland a standard charge is being introduced and that a similar arrangement is under consideration in Scotland.

7.51 It would be foolish and unprofitable to try to force general practice into one particular mould. There is no reason why standards should not be as high and facilities as good in premises which are owned by GPs as they are in the best health centres. However, the development of health centres or other suitable premises to attract GPs to London and other inner city areas where sites are particularly expensive and difficult to obtain, must be given priority. We recommend that the health departments consider urgently how best this can be done. In some places local authorities can assist health authorities by releasing land for new development. An increase in the current level of improvement grants for practice premises, and better terms for loans from the General Practice Finance Corporation might also help.

Problems of Rural Areas

7.52 We received some evidence, in particular from the National Federation of Womens' Institutes, which suggested that both patients and health workers face particular problems in remote rural areas. We mention the difficulties of providing pharmaceutical services in country areas in Chapter 8. Public transport in rural areas is dwindling. Many GPs are single-handed and often cannot find locums to enable them to leave their practices for postgraduate education or holidays, or even to substitute for them when they are ill. A research project commissioned by the Scottish Consumer Council highlighted the special difficulties of providing a full range of primary care services in the Western Isles.[1] An inducement scheme to attract GPs to the remoter areas already exists and similar measures may be required to attract other health workers. We are aware of the impressive contribution made by those who work in these areas, often under difficult conditions, and we urge the health departments to improve conditions of service for them, particularly in the provision of locums.

Problems of Declining Urban Areas

7.53 There are problems, also, in providing health services in declining urban areas. Many arise in industrial towns and peripheral post-war council housing estates as well as in decaying inner city areas. Obviously, not all cities suffer from the same problems. The White Paper "Policy for the Inner Cities"[2] drew attention to a number of symptoms common to the decline of many inner city areas. These include high unemployment due to firms closing and moving out of the city centre, high concentrations of semi-skilled and unskilled workers, old and poor housing, high population density, and concentrations of the homeless and destitute and of members of ethnic minorities. Some of these symptoms are due to economic decline and the accompanying poverty and social problems, but others may arise from the high cost of accommodation or the special demands of an aged, migrant or homeless population.

7.54 These features of urban decline add considerably to the difficulty of providing health services. A study of the Birmingham inner city area in 1975[3] recorded that local doctors considered that medical problems prevalent in the area, such as respiratory disorders, poor hygiene and anxiety, were directly connected with poor housing, environmental and, to a lesser extent, cultural problems. Low take up of health services is common in inner city areas. Staff may be discouraged from working in them by poor working conditions and the effects of vandalism and crime

7.55 Many health professionals are coping courageously and effectively in these areas, but there is evidence in some places that services are inadequate. GPs, nurses, health visitors, social workers, receptionists and secretaries are no more likely than anyone else to want to live and work in unattractive urban areas. In England metropolitan AHAs have lower than average health visitor and district nurse staffing ratios in spite of their greater needs. Where health authorities can fund an agreed complement of nurses in the community it may still be difficult to fill vacancies. The GPs tend to be older and to have large lists. The accepted view today is that a GP will work most efficiently in a group practice or partnership with several other GPs and there may be some connection between the extent of single-handed practice and low quality of care although there are many excellent single-handed GPs. More single-handed practices are found in inner city areas.

7.56 In these areas, health professionals have an innovative part to play in

---

[1]Scottish Consumer Council, *Island Health Care*, Institute of Medical Sociology, Occasional Paper Number 3, Aberdeen, 1978.

[2]*Policy for the Inner Cities*, (Cmnd 6845), London, HMSO, 1977.

[3]Birmingham Inner Area Study, *Small Heath health study*, draft report, 1975.

reaching those people who do not make sufficient use of NHS services. This is particularly important in the care of children and here the health visitor's role is highly important. The development of a special interest in paediatrics and the appropriate training among inner city GPs should be strongly encouraged.

London

7.57 London's size, density of population and concentration of medical teaching facilities give rise to particular problems. We deal here with the city's primary health care difficulties, and in Chapter 17 we recommend that an enquiry into London's problems should be mounted, including the special difficulties of providing primary care services in the metropolis. Some of the problems of inner city areas are seen at their most acute in London. In 1977 31% of London GPs were single-handed compared with an average of 16% in England and their average age was 51 (1978). Many practices have small lists; 35% of London practices have fewer than 2,000 patients (against the national figure of almost 20%). Some London boroughs and health authorities are chronically short of social workers and nurses. GPs and other health workers generally live some way from where they work. This inhibits the provision of a 24 hour service by the GP and encourages the use of deputising services. In parts of London GPs' involvement in private practice may lead to a restriction of NHS list sizes.

7.58 In some declining urban areas and in parts of London in particular the NHS is failing dismally to provide an adequate primary care service to its patients. While the NHS cannot be expected to solve all the problems of these areas we consider that it has a clear responsibility to improve the quality of its services in them and we outline below ways in which this might be achieved.

7.59 The complex and disparate problems we have referred to suggest that no single solution will suffice. Good practice premises are a vital incentive to staff of high quality to work where they are most needed. The NHS has a clear responsibility to ensure that adequate premises are provided. We were pleased therefore to note that recent DHSS advice[1] urges health authorities to give priority to building health centres in "health deprived" localities and specifically allows the building of health centres, even where there is no assurance that local GPs will staff them. We recommend that health authorities, when establishing such new health centres, should experiment with offering salaried appointments and reduced list sizes to attract groups of doctors to work in them.

7.60 In some urban areas patients use out-patients departments of large district hospitals for primary care rather than local GP services. Many teaching hospitals are found in inner city areas. We think these hospitals have the responsibility, which they have not always shouldered, to foster and improve the quality of primary care services in their surrounding areas. One possibility, since they already give primary care in their accident and emergency departments, would be for them to provide teaching practices within their own perimeter to help to meet the needs of their neighbourhood. Professional

---

[1]HC(79)8, *Op cit.*

incentives for GPs working in inner city areas are often lacking and teaching hospitals could do more to fill this gap by co-operating with local practitioners in providing teaching and research opportunities and encouraging hospital practitioner appointments. Consultant sessions in health centres would also help to promote the integration of hospital and community services.

7.61 A more imaginative approach to dealing with the special needs of inner city populations is needed. Homeless people in particular may find it difficult to use the NHS. The evidence we received from the Campaign for the Homeless and Rootless quoted a survey by a Liverpool CHC in 1976 which suggested that 6 out of 10 homeless people in Liverpool were without a GP. Experiments in providing services for them have been carried out in a number of cities, including Edinburgh and Leeds, and further research and experiment is required. Inner city area partnership funds could be a useful source of finance. The special needs of patients who come from ethnic minorities require sensitive handling by the NHS. The evidence we took from their representatives suggests that many NHS workers are not aware of cultural, language, literacy and dietary problems which may affect these groups. Training in their needs and problems for personnel who work with them is needed.

7.62 New financial inducements to attract GPs and other health personnel to work in inner London and elsewhere in severely deprived urban areas may be required. At present GPs, for example, do not receive a London weighting allowance. It might be feasible to provide differential capitation fees for GPs in such areas to take account of their heavier workloads. Other possible incentives are the provision of housing, a car, clerical support and a telephone.

7.63 Improving the quality of care in inner city areas is the most urgent problem which NHS services in the community must tackle. Many of the difficulties are severe. Additional financial resources are needed and, in the case of London in particular, this will involve hard choices. We recommend that they are provided. Many London health authorities' expenditure is being squeezed as a result of the application of the RAWP formula. The London RHAs must make additional provision in distributing funds for primary care services to inner city AHAs to ensure that the improvement to services which we recommend is not impeded by lack of finance.

Conclusions and Recommendations

7.64 Changes in the structure of the population and in health care priorities mean that the demand on and for general practitioner, nursing and related services in the community will increase during the next decade. These services are generally provided to a good standard but improvements are needed in a number of directions. The development so far of the primary health care team has been encouraging, but there is a continuing need to encourage closer working relationships between the professions who provide care for the community. District nurses and health visitors have a particularly important part to play. There have been a number of promising developments which have enhanced the quality of general practice, but more should be done to improve the training and continuing education of GPs. Improvement of the standard of existing premises is required and so are more health centres. Better training is needed for receptionists, and deputising services should be brought under closer control. More research should be undertaken into a number of aspects of community services.

7.65 To a large extent GPs can control their own prescribing costs but they have little incentive to keep them down and they are subject to pressures from pharmaceutical companies and patients to prescribe expensively and often ineffectively. A more radical approach to this problem is required.

7.66 The major challenge to community services is the provision of services in declining urban areas. The health needs of patients who live in these areas are complex, and the health departments alone cannot provide all the answers. A much more flexible and innovative approach to improving services in them is needed.

7.67 We recommend that:

(a) the legal position regarding responsibility in the use of deputising services in Scotland should be brought into line with that elsewhere in the UK (paragraph 7.8);

(b) health authorities should keep under review the operation of the deputising services in their areas and, if they are unsatisfactory, improve or replace them (paragraph 7.10);

(c) where this does not happen already, the full costs of attendance of GPs' receptionists at training courses should be met by the FPC or health authority concerned (paragraph 7.12);

(d) before a maximum or minimum list size is adopted, considerable research on an optimum range of list sizes should be undertaken (paragraph 7.16);

(e) there should be a review of the controls on the appointment of GPs exercised by the Medical Practices Committees (paragraphs 7.17 and 7.30);

(f) the health departments should consider offering an assisted voluntary retirement scheme to GPs with small lists who have reached 65 years of age (paragraph 7.18);

(g) the health departments should discuss with the medical profession the feasibility of introducing a compulsory retirement age for GPs (paragraph 7.18);

(h) the health departments should continue their current plans for the expansion of community nursing (paragraph 7.22);

(i) research is required into a number of aspects of primary care (paragraphs 7.27 and 7.34);

(j) national or regional panels should be set up to provide external assessors for each new appointment of a principal in general practice (paragraph 7.30);

(k) GPs should make local arrangements specifically to facilitate audit of the services they provide and the health departments should check progress with these developments (paragraph 7.32);

(l) the introduction of the A4 records system in general practice should be given high priority (paragraph 7.33);

(m) FPCs and health authorities should use vigorously their powers to ensure that patients are seen by their GPs in surgeries of an acceptable standard (paragraph 7.35);

(n) the British National Formulary should be re-issued soon in portable, loose-leaf form with separate information on drug costs, and be kept up-to-date (paragraph 7.40);

(o) the health departments should introduce a limited list of drugs as soon as possible and take further steps to encourage generic prescribing (paragraph 7.46);

(p) the health departments should consider whether high running costs are acting as a significant disincentive to GPs to work in health centres (paragraph 7.50);

(q) the health departments should consider urgently measures to assist the development as a priority of health centres or other suitable premises to attract GPs to London and other inner city areas where sites are particularly expensive or difficult to obtain (paragraph 7.51);

(r) health authorities when establishing health centres in inner city and deprived urban areas, should experiment with offering salaried appointments and reduced list sizes to attract groups of doctors to work in them (paragraph 7.59);

(s) additional financial resources should be provided to improve the quality of primary care services in declining urban areas (paragraph 7.63).

Chapter 8   Pharmaceutical, Ophthalmic and Chiropody Services

8.1   In this chapter we deal with the general pharmaceutical and general ophthalmic services, and have a brief look at chiropody services. Although chiropody is not provided on the same basis as the "contractor" services, and most chiropodists work in private practice, we include them here because their relationship to patients is similar in many ways to the relationship between the members of the contractor professions and their clients.

8.2   Apart from the evidence we have received about these services, we have had available to us the results of a study on access to primary health services commissioned by the DHSS and undertaken by the Office of Population Censuses and Surveys (OPCS). We ourselves commissioned jointly with the National Consumer Council (NCC) a study which complemented the OPCS survey.[1] We have drawn on these studies in this chapter.

Pharmaceutical Services

8.3   The evidence we received about the general pharmaceutical services concentrated on two distinct but linked aspects – access to pharmaceutical services and the role of the pharmacist in the community.

Access

8.4   Most of those who submitted evidence about pharmacists were concerned with the reduction in the number of pharmacies which has occurred in recent years. Although numbers of trained pharmacists and those in training have been rising, the number of pharmacies in the community has fallen by more than a quarter since 1963. Most of the closures have been in urban areas but their effect has been felt particularly in rural areas, and was the subject of comment by a number of community health councils. Bath CHC told us:

"the increasing trend for small pharmacies to close is giving more and more cause for concern particularly in the small and rural communities where the alternative service may be some distance away."

8.5   However, this experience does not appear to be general and both surveys of access to primary care showed that relatively few patients

---

[1]Office of Population Censuses and Surveys, *Access to Primary Care* (to be published). Simpson, Robin, *Access to Primary Care*, Royal Commission on the National Health Service, Research Paper Number 6, London, HMSO, 1979.

experienced difficulties in getting a prescription dispensed. Nine out of ten people interviewed in the OPCS study said that they found it very or fairly easy to get to a chemist from where they lived, and about the same proportion usually went to one which was less than one mile from their home or from the doctor's surgery. Difficulties were greater in rural areas, where the OPCS survey reported that 15% of people living in these areas found it fairly or very difficult to get to a chemist, particularly the elderly disabled and those who did not own cars.

8.6   Nevertheless, numbers of pharmacies have been declining in all parts of the UK, and if the trend continues the difficulties that some people are now experiencing in getting to a pharmacist are likely to become more widespread. The main reason for the decline in numbers seems to be that many pharmacies are simply not profitable. The Pharmaceutical Services Negotiating Committee (PSNC) told us:

> "Because of the system of reimbursement, over 4,000 pharmacies in England and Wales, i.e. those dispensing up to 23,399 prescriptions per annum ... are estimated not to recover their costs. These pharmacies can be sustained if they have a substantial volume of retail trade but ... figures show that pharmacies are experiencing a 10% drop in volume sales over the counter."

8.7   An important influence on the distribution of pharmacies is the distribution of GPs. Patients find it convenient to visit a pharmacy close to GPs' premises to have their prescriptions dispensed. The OPCS survey found that 51% of the people who had taken at least one prescription to be dispensed during the previous year said that their "usual" chemist was near (i.e. within one mile) to the doctor's surgery. The concentration of GPs in group practices has led, in some places, to a process of leapfrogging in which pharmacies try to move nearer to practice premises. Pharmacists complain about the dispensing of drugs by GPs in certain rural areas, though there has been only a small increase in numbers of dispensing doctors in recent years.

8.8   The falling numbers of pharmacies may mean that patients have to travel further to get their prescriptions dispensed. In rural areas many patients will be quite happy to collect their medicine at the doctor's surgery, usually after a consultation, or to have it brought when the doctor visits, or collected by relatives or neighbours. In urban areas concentration of pharmaceutical services in fewer, larger shops may enable better and less costly services to be provided. It is not clear how far, if at all, small pharmacies should be preserved from the effects of competition. A differential system of payment for dispensing NHS prescriptions has recently been introduced in England and Wales which will benefit smaller pharmacies at the expense of larger ones. In the short term some £5m will be provided by the taxpayer to phase the scheme in. It remains to be seen what effect the new system will have.

8.9   We had available to us the report of a committee on dispensing in rural areas, which was chaired by one of our members.[1] The Clothier

---

[1]Report of the National Joint Committee of the Medical and Pharmaceutical Professions on the Dispensing of NHS Prescriptions in Rural Areas, DHSS, 1977.

Committee recommended that a new independent statutory body be set up to regulate significant changes in dispensing arrangements in rural areas. The proposals of the Committee have been accepted by the medical and pharmaceutical professions and are at present under consideration by the DHSS.

8.10   A number of suggestions were put to us to improve the distribution of pharmacies. One was that there should be a system of classification of areas, on the pattern of the control of general medical practice exercised by the Medical Practices Committees (discussed in Chapter 7) to prevent pharmacists opening businesses in areas which were already well or over-provided. In rural areas this proposal has been largely met by the recommendations of the Clothier Committee. Another suggestion was that the NHS should run the service directly in some places and pay pharmacists' salaries, in the same way as those employed in hospitals are salaried, so that they would not be dependent on making a profit from their businesses. In some isolated communities a pick-up and delivery service for prescriptions has been developed.

8.11   We are not convinced that there is sufficient difficulty in getting NHS prescriptions dispensed to warrant the introduction of a national system for controlling the location of pharmacies. This is not to deny that there are local problems in some rural areas or for some groups of patients, but we doubt whether there is one solution which will meet all circumstances. We think that, as for the salaried GP and dentist, there may well be a place for a salaried pharmacist, perhaps employed by the health authority in some places and possibly located in a health centre. We hope that the health departments will support experiments in this field. A flexible approach and a balancing of the needs of people living in rural areas, who seem to be those most likely to be inconvenienced by closures of pharmacies, with the costs of any changes should permit the development of local solutions suited to local conditions.

Role of the pharmacist

8.12   Traditionally it is the function of a pharmacist to dispense medicine to the prescription of doctors.[1] In the past the bulk of medicines had to be made up, but this skilled task has increasingly been taken over by the pharmaceutical companies and many medicines now need no preparation by the pharmacists. Perhaps for this reason much of the evidence we received from the profession was concerned with developing a new role for pharmacists to make fuller use of their extensive training. Since 1970 pharmacists have had to take a three year degree course followed by a pre-registration year in a recognised pharmacy.

8.13   It was suggested to us that pharmacists might develop their role of giving advice to the public. The PSNC said:

"The training and experience of the general practice pharmacist allows the public access to responsible advice on the actions and uses of medicines

---

[1]Although dentists may prescribe, their prescriptions do not account for a significant amount of the pharmacist's work.

wherever a pharmacy is situated. With the growing concentration of medical practitioners serving a wide area in health centres, it will be even more important in the future to ensure that members of the public have convenient and ready access to advice about matters and information about medicines."

The Pharmaceutical Society of Great Britain pointed out that "the general practice pharmacist is regarded as one of the main sources of advice in relation to minor ailments". This is substantiated by both the OPCS and NCC surveys referred to and by previous studies. In the OPCS survey 15% of the people interviewed said that they had gone to a chemist for advice instead of to their doctor during the preceding year. Over two-fifths of them had gone with various respiratory conditions and with stomach or skin complaints.

8.14   This seems to us to be an important and useful service, and one which should contribute towards keeping down demands on other parts of the NHS. If a pharmacist is able to provide his clients with remedies for their aches and pains he is likely to be saving his medical colleagues' time and possibly the cost of an NHS prescription. In the OPCS study nearly a fifth of those who had gone to the chemist instead of their doctor had been told to consult their GP by the pharmacist. In Chapter 5 we emphasised the importance of patients caring for their own health, and the pharmacist may be well placed to help them do so though it must be remembered that he is not trained in diagnosis. He can and should respond helpfully to people who ask his advice, but we do not see him as a quasi-doctor.

8.15   One way of making better use of the present under-used skills of the pharmacist is the establishment of pharmacies in health centres. This would enable the pharmacist to provide a better service to patients, foster good working relationships with his medical colleagues and might lead to collaboration to improve the accuracy of prescribing. We recommend that it should be encouraged. The possibility of pharmacists being used to advise on the safe keeping and administration of drugs in nursing homes, and establishments for the handicapped and elderly, and to monitor repeat prescriptions also deserves consideration.

8.16   There are nearly 3,000 pharmacists employed in the hospital and community health service in the UK. There are recruitment difficulties in the basic grades (one out of every six posts is currently vacant), but there appears to be no difficulty in attracting new entrants into the profession as a whole, and the shortage may have arisen as the result of a discrepancy between earnings in the public and private sectors. Hospital pharmacists can play an important part with their medical colleagues in improving prescribing and in restraining drug costs. Local drug information centres, staffed by salaried NHS pharmacists, can also help to improve the quality of prescribing in general practice by providing information perhaps in the form of a newsletter, on new drugs and on drug interactions. We welcome recent developments along these lines.

General Ophthalmic Services

8.17 Eye problems may be dealt with under the NHS by hospitals or in the general ophthalmic services (GOS). The GOS provides sight-testing and the supply, replacement and repair of spectacles. Opticians, like pharmacists, derive part of their income from NHS work, but perhaps three-quarters of their gross profit comes from other activities, including private practice, and the sale of sunglasses, etc, which are not obtainable under the NHS. There are about 6,500 opticians' establishments in the UK.

8.18 Two-thirds of the people interviewed in the OPCS survey said that they had had glasses or lenses prescribed through the GOS. Considering the high proportion of spectacle wearers in the population we received surprisingly few complaints from patients about the service. The principal complaint was that NHS spectacle frames were often not displayed and non-NHS frames did not carry prices so that patients were encouraged to buy relatively expensive private frames. We also had some complaints about the poor range of NHS frames. Both the level of NHS charges and confusion over eligibility for exemption, emerged as problems from the NCC study, though the OPCS study found no clear evidence that charges put people off going for sight tests if they did not already wear spectacles.

8.19 We had representations from the profession about insufficient rewards for NHS work, the restrictions on what could be prescribed, and the lack of a fee for a domiciliary visit to patients who were confined to their homes or who lived in local authority residential homes.

8.20 So far as patients' complaints are concerned, we understand that the health departments are discussing with the profession a requirement for NHS opticians to display the full range of NHS spectacle frames. If agreement on this can be reached, it will meet one of the frequent criticisms of existing arrangements. The gradual extinction of NHS charges, proposed in Chapter 21, would reduce confusion amongst patients about prices and charges. Until that time we recommend that charges for NHS and non-NHS items and details of eligibility should be prominently displayed and publicised. It would be difficult to show that the existing range of NHS frames was unsatisfactory so far as patients' vision was concerned, and fashions in spectacle frames may change. A larger range of frames is likely to mean greater cost and should not be given much priority.

8.21 In general the GOS is likely to provide a cheaper service than hospitals, as well as being more convenient for most patients, and we recommend that serious consideration be given to widening the range of items, such as magnifying glasses for the partially sighted, which can be prescribed and dispensed under the GOS. Our evidence does not suggest that many people require domiciliary consultations with an optician, but there will be some, particularly the elderly and the handicapped, and those in residential accommodation, and it is important that they should be provided for.

Chiropody

8.22 Chiropodists, like pharmacists and opticians, engage partly in private practice and partly in NHS work. Access to chiropody is not normally via referral from a doctor. However, while the NHS aims to provide pharmaceutical and ophthalmic services to all who need them, chiropody on the NHS is currently restricted to certain priority classes – the elderly, the handicapped, expectant mothers, school children and some hospital patients. Anyone else needing chiropody has to pay for it themselves. Health authorities have no powers to charge for chiropody treatment.

8.23   In 1977 about six and a half million NHS chiropody treatments were provided to just over one and a half million people in Great Britain. This represents an increase of 19% on the number of treatments provided three years earlier. Over 90% of patients receiving these treatments were aged 65 or over. Treatments are mainly provided in clinics, but about one-quarter take place in the patient's home, and a further one-eighth in the chiropodist's own surgery. Chiropody is an extremely important service for the eight million aged 65 and over in the UK. The Elderly Invalids Fund pointed out to us that:

"Painful feet can mean that people do not go out to shop or to lunch clubs and can easily become isolated and possibly undernourished. They become less mobile indoors, sit still for longer periods and so become cold, may take to their bed for warmth, become weaker and possibly bedfast."

Providing chiropody may well be an alternative to providing other, more costly community services.

8.24   NHS chiropody is essentially a community service provided for the elderly. The complaints made about it, mainly in evidence to us from community health councils, were for the most part that more and better distributed services were needed. Perhaps surprisingly the issue of whether a chiropody service should be provided by the NHS for the whole population was barely touched on. The main problem seems to be a shortage of chiropodists to undertake NHS work and consequent delays in getting treatment. Some of this treatment is of a very simple kind, such as cutting toe nails, which a more active person would be able to undertake for himself and which could be performed by an assistant with relatively little training; but some of it is more complicated and may, for example, involve giving injections. At present the demand for NHS chiropody outstrips the supply. The OPCS survey found that 13% of the over-65s who had had chiropody treatment during the past two years had used private chiropody services, though the numbers of treatments provided by the NHS has been rising.

8.25   Chiropodists employed in the NHS must be state registered. The normal qualification for registration involves a three year course of training to the syllabus of the Society of Chiropodists. At least five "O" levels or their equivalent are needed to start training. There are about 5,000 chiropodists on the register but only about two-thirds of those work for the NHS (figures are imprecise because much of the treatment provided by the NHS is paid for on an item of service basis). There are, therefore, a substantial number of chiropodists who would be eligible for NHS employment but who work only in private practice. In addition, there is an unknown number, possibly amounting to several thousands, of people who practise some chiropody, perhaps on a part-time basis, and are not registered.[1] The NHS is competing for registered chiropodists with the attractions of independent private practice.

8.26   About £15m per annum is spent on chiropody in the NHS at present, and the DHSS Priorities Documents[2] propose that chiropody services should be increased by more than 3% per annum. The ability of health authorities to meet this objective depends on their success in attracting staff as well as finding the money to pay them. At present numbers of registered chiropodists are increasing at under 1% per annum, and existing training schools are doing little more than keeping up with natural wastage. There are proposals to open new schools but, under the provisions of the 1960 Professions Supplementary to Medicine Act, the approval of the Chiropodists Board is required.[3] The Board is at present reluctant to approve any further schools, than one in Belfast, on the grounds that there would be difficulties in staffing new schools. This does not seem to us to be an insurmountable problem, and we recommend that more training places should be provided and that services to the elderly in the community should be increased.

8.27   We support the suggestion put to us by the Association of Chief Chiropody Officers for the introduction of more foot hygienists who undertake, under the direction of a registered chiropodist, "nail cutting and such simple foot-care and hygiene as a fit person should normally carry out for himself".

8.28   While accurate assessment of need is not available, our evidence suggests that there is plenty of work amongst the existing priority groups for all the chiropodists likely to be employed by the NHS in the foreseeable future. In the circumstances, we do not think that it would be sensible to attempt to extend the service to the rest of the population.

Conclusions and recommendations

8.29   The main problems in the pharmaceutical services appear to be falling numbers of pharmacies and the erosion of the pharmacist's traditional role with the development of modern packaging of medicines. While surveys suggest that access to a pharmacy is not yet a serious problem for many people, it may well become so in the future. Pharmacists will continue to have an important role since the use of potent drugs in medicine has increased substantially. We do not consider, however, that they should develop a quasi-medical role, and we think their expertise can most usefully be employed in advising doctors on prescribing matters and the public on self-medication.

8.30   The complaints about the general ophthalmic services were mainly

---

[1]The 1971 census showed 6,000 people in Great Britain giving chiropody as their main occupation, but did not identify those for whom chiropody was only a secondary or spare-time occupation.

[2]Department of Health and Social Security, *Priorities for Health and Personal Social Services in England 1976. A Consultative Document,* London, HMSO, 1976, page 41. Department of Health and Social Security, *Priorities in the Health and Social Services. The Way Forward,* London, HMSO, 1977, page 12.

[3]In Chapter 15 we discuss registration arrangements for the professions supplementary to medicine and recommend an independent review of the machinery.

lack of information about NHS treatment and spectacle frames. The optician has a financial interest in encouraging patients to buy non-NHS frames, but we see no reason why he should not be required also to display NHS frames and the prices of both NHS and non-NHS items.

8.31 The NHS does not attempt to provide a comprehensive chiropody service. Within the NHS chiropody is mainly provided to the elderly, and there are shortages of qualified chiropodists prepared to undertake the work. One reason for this is a shortage of training facilities for chiropodists; another is the attractions of the private sector in which most chiropodists work at present. The health departments should promote the introduction of foot hygienists.

8.32 We recommend that:

(a) the establishment of pharmacies in health centres should be encouraged (paragraph 8.15);

(b) charges for NHS and non-NHS items and details of eligibility should be prominently displayed and publicised by opticians (paragraph 8.20);

(c) serious consideration should be given to widening the range of items which can be prescribed and dispensed under the general ophthalmic services (paragraph 8.21);

(d) more chiropody training places should be provided and services to the elderly in the community increased (paragraph 8.26).

Chapter 9   Dentistry

9.1   This chapter differs in character from the other chapters in our report. In it we deal with a full range of issues relating to NHS dentistry and look at the subject in greater technical detail than is the case with most of the other topics. We felt it appropriate to treat the issues about dentistry in this way mainly because dental health and dental diseases are fairly readily measurable and because there is an obvious prospect of making significant improvements in dental health. We are conscious also that while other aspects of health services have been examined from time to time, often in considerable detail since the NHS was set up, there has been no general review of NHS dental services in the last 20 years.

9.2   In this chapter, we review the development of NHS dental services, assess ways in which NHS dental care can be improved and comment on possible future changes in the pattern of treatment. We have not dealt with education to any degree because of the work being done by the Nuffield Committee of Inquiry into Dental Education[1] which is expected to report in 1980. We welcome this inquiry because of the importance which the changes we recommend will have for dental education.

9.3   There is good evidence that dental diseases have increased considerably in the past two centuries although it is only since 1968 that national surveys have provided any reliable information about their occurrence in the UK. Until 1859 there was no formal qualification for the providers of dental treatment and it was only in 1921 that the practice of dentistry was limited to those who were professionally qualified. There are now more than twice as many registered dentists per 10,000 population in the UK than there were in 1921.

9.4   As with general medical practice, publicly funded dental services predate the NHS. However, by 1948 only two thirds of those who were entitled to sickness benefit were eligible for dental benefits, and of these only six per cent claimed them.

9.5   School dental services provided by local authorities developed slowly after the first service of this kind was set up in Cambridge in 1907. However, since 1953 local authorities have had a statutory duty to make comprehensive dental treatment available to pupils, but undermanning has prevented the school dental service from fulfilling this requirement.

---

[1]This Committee is chaired by Professor T. Thomas and has the following terms of reference:

"To review, in the light of the current and foreseeable needs of the community, education and training for the practice of dentistry in the United Kingdom, taking into account advances in dental science and technology, changes in concepts of the provision of dental care, and possibilities for the prevention of dental disease; to advise on what principles future developments should be based; and to make recommendations."

9.6 NHS dentistry is provided by the general dental service, the hospital service and the community dental service. Initially NHS dentistry was free at the time of use but charges to patients were introduced in 1951 and have remained, being increased from time to time to take account of inflation. The manpower and finance required to provide NHS dentistry was seriously underestimated in 1948. In order to improve the supply of manpower, existing dental schools were expanded and one new one established in Cardiff. Dental auxiliaries have been introduced in the hospital and community service. However, despite the visionary concept of a comprehensive national service, the sobering reality is that there has been a continuing failure to match the unmet need for dentistry with the resources required.

The nation's dental health

9.7 Dental health is part of general health and by any standards the dental health of the nation is poor. This is vividly illustrated by the statistics. Total tooth loss is a good measure of the ultimate breakdown of dental health. In 1968 37% of the population of England and Wales over the age of 16 had no natural teeth.[1] In Scotland in 1972, 44% of the population over 15 had no natural teeth.[2] The prevalence of caries (decaying teeth) and periodontal disease (diseases of the gums, bone and other supporting structures of the teeth) is also high. In 1973, in England and Wales, 31% of children by the age of five had five or more teeth affected by caries and, at the age of 14, five or more permanent teeth of 72% were affected.[3] Of all the general anaesthetics given for dental purposes in the UK in 1976, 56% were given for the extraction of teeth in the 5–14 age-group.[4] Periodontal disease was present in 73% of the 16–34 age-group and in 90% of those over 35 in 1968.

9.8 In spite of these gloomy figures there is a strong impression amongst practising dentists that there has been a continuing improvement in oral health in the last 30 years. There is now much more emphasis on the conservation of teeth. Relatively more money is being spent on periodontal care, orthodontics and more advanced conservation, and relatively less on dentures, routine conservation and surgical treatment.[5] Table 9.1 shows changes in the nature of dental treatment for both adults and children in England and Wales.

---

[1]Gray, P G, Todd, J E, Slack, G L & Bulman, J S. *Adult Dental Health in England and Wales in 1968*, London, HMSO, 1970, page 21.

[2]Todd, J E & Whitworth, A. *Adult Dental Health in Scotland, 1972*, London, HMSO, 1974.

[3]Todd, J E. *Children's Dental Health in England and Wales in 1973*, London, HMSO, 1975. Part IV, Tables 4 and 6.

[4]Dinsdale, R C W & Dixon R A. "Anaesthetic Services to Dental Patients England and Wales 1976", *British Dental Journal*, 1978, 144, 9, pages 271-9.

[5]Annual Reports of the England and Wales Dental Estimates Board.

9.9   We shall not know with any precision what effect the considerable effort by the dental profession and other factors are having on the control of dental disease until surveys comparable to those of 1968, 1972 and 1973 are repeated. There is some evidence to suggest that edentulousness (toothlessness) may now be proportionately less than it was in 1968. The initial results of the 1978 adult dental health survey[1] indicate a fall in England and Wales in edentulousness in all ages from 37% in 1968 to 29% in 1978 (28% in England: 37% in Wales). The 1978 all ages figure for Scotland was 39%. Table 9.2 shows total tooth loss by age in England and Wales in 1968 and 1978.

TABLE 9.1

Changes in the Nature of Dental Treatment: Adults and Children: England and Wales 1935–1976

Adults	Ratio permanent teeth filled to permanent teeth extracted	Ratio permanent teeth filled to full dentures provided
1935	1:6	2:1
1976	6:1	50:1

Children	Ratio permanent teeth filled to permanent teeth extracted	Ratio of first teeth filled to first teeth extracted
1938	2:1	1:22
1976[1]	7:1	1:1

Source: unpublished research by Dr J S Bulman.

Notes: [1] England only.

[1]OPCS, *Adult Dental Health for the UK: 1978* (to be published in 1980).

TABLE 9.2
Proportion of People with no Natural Teeth by
Age: England and Wales 1968 and 1978

percentage

Age	1968	1978
16–24	1	—
25–34	7	3
35—44	22	12
45–54	41	29
55–64	64	48
65–74	79	74
75 and over	88	87
All ages	37	29

Sources: Gray P G et al *Adult Dental Health in England and Wales in 1968,* London, HMSO, page 27.
OPCS, *Adult Dental Health in the UK: 1978* (to be published in 1980).

TABLE 9.3
Child Dental Health: England and Wales 1973

percentage

Children with untreated dental disease 1973	Age in years		
	5	9	14
Caries	63	76	62
Periodontal disease	47	78	74
Malocclusion (irregularities of the teeth)	17	55	28
Needing some dental attention	79	96	90

Source: Todd J E, *Children's Dental Health in England and Wales 1973*, London, HMSO, pages 23, 48, 63, 74.

9.10 The five yearly surveys of the Department of Education and Science indicate an improvement of the dental health of five year olds in England but Table 9.3, taken from the 1973 Children's Dental Survey, gives an indication of the daunting amount of untreated dental disease still present in various age groups.

The present provision of dental treatment

General dental service

9.11 Most of the dental treatment carried out in the UK is provided by general dental practitioners under contract to family practitioner committees (FPCs) in England and Wales, and directly to the health authorities in Scotland and Northern Ireland. Like general medical practitioners, they are free to carry out private as well as NHS work. Unlike general medical practitioners, however, they do not have a list of patients but enter into a contract with the patient to render him "dentally fit". Once the necessary work has been done, the dentist's responsibilities to that particular patient end and a new contract is entered into the next time the patient visits the dentist. Most dentists work on a continuing family practice basis. They may choose whether or not to accept the patient for treatment under the NHS, but having done so, must not charge him privately for any treatment necessary for dental fitness. A very small number of general dental practitioners are salaried. A few have a salary plus bonus type of remuneration but the vast majority operate independently receiving payments authorised by the Dental Estimates Boards[1] (DEBs) for their NHS patients on a fee for item of service basis or directly from the private patients.

Allegations of failure

9.12 Some of the evidence we have received alleges that in addition to its other difficulties the general dental service is seriously failing the patient. The main complaints made to us by Citizens Advice Bureaux, the Patients' Association and also by some dental practitioners were:

the difficulty of finding a dentist who takes NHS patients;

the unwillingness of some dentists to provide certain kinds of treatment which depend on laboratory support, eg. bridges, crowns, dentures;

the difficulty of obtaining out-of-hours emergency treatment;

unavailability of preventive items on the NHS;

confusion amongst patients about what is available under the NHS and about the level of charges;

high charges to patients for NHS treatment; and

decline in the quality of treatment (this complaint has come from some members of the dental profession).

Complaints about NHS dental services occurred in about a quarter of the 166 evidence submissions we received from community health councils (CHCs). Of

---

[1] Central Services Agency in Northern Ireland.

these, 26 were about the availability of dentistry under the NHS, 11 about the lack of emergency services and nine about patient confusion over charges for NHS treatment.

9.13 While we have had ample anecdotal evidence to cause us some disquiet, we have found it difficult to quantify the seriousness and extent of these complaints. Also, most of our evidence was prepared at a time when there was a dispute between the dental profession and the government over practice expenses and a consequent move away from NHS provision by some general dental practitioners.[1] Some of the complaints appear to be related to the shortage of dental manpower and its uneven distribution. Others are related to the way dentists are paid and we consider these matters in the following paragraphs. Our views on patients' charges, emergency care, patient confusion over the availability of NHS treatment and the quality of care are set out in paragraphs 9.24–9.27. We consider in 9.66 the question of the availability of preventive items in NHS dentistry.

9.14 About 14,000 general dental practitioners in the UK in 1977 were contracted to provide services under the NHS. Given the present level of disease and methods of practice, regular dental care can be given to considerably less than half the population. The fact that, in general, demand is much lower than need saves the service from breakdown. In addition to the overall gap between need and provision there are wide regional differences in the distribution of dental resurces (see Table 9.4) and even wider intra-regional differences, similar to those found generally in the NHS: for example, the dentist population ratio in 1977 in Sunderland was 1:7317 compared with 1:3522 in Newcastle-on-Tyne.

9.15 There has been some improvement in patient attitudes to dental care. Forty-six per cent of adults with some of their own teeth in England and Wales regularly attended a dentist in 1978 compared with 40% in 1968.[2] The proportion of patients seeking regular dental care varies by region and by social class and with the distribution of dentists. The variations in total tooth loss by social class and region are shown in Table 9.5. This is another illustration of poorer health among the less well-off referred to in Chapter 3. The unequal distribution of dental manpower and the difficulty of recruitment in unattractive areas are problems shared throughout the NHS. There is, however, some evidence that as the number of registered dentists increases recruitment is improving in previously neglected areas.[3]

9.16 On the basis of current estimates of need there is a considerable shortfall in dental manpower and a much smaller and locally variable shortfall on the basis of demand. There is a real prospect that a preventive approach through fluoridation of water supplies and effective dental health education could transform this position. A preventive strategy of this kind would lead to

---

[1]The number of courses of NHS treatment did in fact increase during this period, but there was a noticeable drop in items like crowns and dentures requiring laboratory services. The position now shows a more normal spread of treatment.

[2]OPCS, *Adult Dental Health in the UK*, 1978, *Op cit.*

[3]Scarrot, D M. "Changes in the regional distribution of general dental service manpower". *British Dental Journal*, 1978, Vol. 144, No. 11, pages 359–363.

TABLE 9.4
Distribution of Dentists in the General Dental Services: UK 1977

	Total number of dentists	Number of principals	Number of assistants	Number of persons per dentist
ENGLAND	11,784	11,629	155	3,914
NW Thames	1,371	1,358	13	2,494
SW Thames	1,027	1,015	12	2,773
South Western	935	918	17	3,367
SE Thames	1,034	1,016	18	3,434
NE Thames	1,024	1,007	17	3,604
Wessex	706	699	7	3,674
Oxford	555	553	2	3,992
Mersey	603	601	2	4,104
East Anglia	397	395	2	4,535
Yorkshire	777	767	10	4,582
North Western	856	851	5	4,722
West Midlands	1,079	1,064	15	4,769
Trent	848	829	19	5,333
Northern	572	556	16	5,445
SCOTLAND	1,204	1,163	41	4,293
WALES	576	567	9	4,794
N IRELAND	345	306	39	4,413

Source: health departments' statistics.

TABLE 9.5
Proportion of People with No Natural Teeth by Social Class, Region and Country: Great Britain 1978

percentage

	Social Class		
	I, II, IIIa non-manual	IIIb manual	IV, V
North	24	35	38
Midlands and East Anglia	23	30	37
South West	22	22	40
South East	15	17	33
Scotland	32	38	45
Wales	29	38	40

Source: OPCS, *Adult Dental Health in the UK: 1978*, (to be published in 1980.)

the substantial control of dental diseases and people would keep their teeth longer. The reduction of dental decay following water fluoridation could mean that eventually the same number of dentists would be able to serve more people, although this could be upset by a change in the style and content of dental practice to one providing more comprehensive care for individual patients. On the other hand, the effective use of less highly trained manpower for procedures which do not require the skills of the fully trained dentist, would release them to carry out more complex treatment for a larger number of people. In the short term the dental health education component of a preventive strategy would need careful co-ordination to prevent stimulating a demand which could not be met.

9.17   Nevertheless, in no other area of health is the way forward so clearly signposted as in the handling of the two major dental diseases. Wholehearted application of known preventive measures would bring treatment needs to manageable proportions. The control of dental caries in children could be a reality in twenty years time and the full effects felt in a generation. Although it is a more difficult area, much can also be done to control periodontal disease.

9.18   Whilst we have no doubt that this approach to the control of dental diseases is the proper way forward, it nevertheless has serious manpower and educational implications. A general strategy for preventive, curative and restorative services should be worked out as part of the review of dental policy which we recommend in paragraph 9.74. Only then can the tasks to be performed and the types of manpower necessary to undertake them be identified, their numbers assessed and educational requirements logically considered. Continuing evaluation is an essential corrective feature of any strategy of this kind. Until the implications of such a shift in policy have been identified we recommend that the dental student entry numbers are not altered but that flexibility in meeting demand is achieved through the increased use of dental ancillary workers.

Remuneration

9.19   At this point we discuss how dentists are paid. Although a secondary issue, it is nevertheless at the root of some of the problems we referred to above. The present system of remuneration for the vast majority of general dental practitioners consists of payment of a fee for each item of service. After completing a course of treatment the dentist claims reimbursement from the DEBs and is paid according to a scale of fees determined annually by representatives of the health departments and the dental profession who meet under independent chairmanship in the Dental Rates Study Group. The scale of fees is designed to provide "the average dentist" with the target net income recommended by the Doctors and Dentists Review Body, plus an amount for practice expenses based on average expenses.

9.20   We received complaints both about the method of payment and its amount. We are concerned here only with the method and, while we do not regard it as our business to offer views on levels of remuneration, it is clear to us that the willingness of dentists to provide treatment under the NHS depends largely on their NHS earnings. It is alleged that a relatively poorly funded piece-work system encourages quantity at the expense of quality. In addition, charges made for work done by the private dental laboratories for such items as the construction of crowns or dentures have been increasing faster than dentists' NHS fees. A dentist is not obliged to offer treatment under the NHS to a patient who needs an "unprofitable" course of treatment. Any substantial imbalance between the fee scale and laboratory costs will tend to result in people having difficulty in finding a dentist prepared to carry out such procedures. This can be particularly noticeable when dentists' fees are being squeezed by an incomes policy and laboratory costs are rising disproportionately.

9.21 There are other complaints about pay arrangements. These include the suggestion that the fee structure could be considerably simplified and the numbers of items in which the prior approval of the DEBs is required be further reduced; that new forms of treatment are discouraged because of the time it takes for these to appear in the scale of fees; and that the reimbursement of dentists who attend post-graduate courses is inadequate. The system has been condemned by many of those concerned and the British Dental Association's (BDA) Tattersall Committee took the view as long ago as 1964 that:

> "there is no future for the profession, or indeed for general dental practice as an art and a science, in the system of remuneration as presently operated."[1]

However, the task of finding a more acceptable system is by no means easy. The dental profession, we were told, has actively and regularly explored alternatives for many years.

9.22 There are a number of possibilities in addition to payment by item of service; grant-in-aid, capitation fees, salary, reimbursement of expenses or a combination of some of these. The Tattersall Committee recommended a part-capitation, part scale of fees system which would consist of a "payment for the maintenance of dental fitness and an additional payment by item-of-service for complex dentistry and dentures".[1] Some of those giving evidence to us recommended that all dentists should be salaried as they are in the community and hospital dental services. Another suggestion was that the salary plus bonus scheme, such as that in operation in several health centres in Scotland and England, should be introduced more widely. The Court Committee[2] in 1976 recommended experimentation with the capitation system for children using an annual fee for maintaining the dental fitness of a child.

9.23 The drawbacks of each method or combination of methods are well known to both government and profession. It seems likely that no one system could suit every type of practice in every part of the country, and it may therefore be preferable for practitioners to opt for a particular method of payment. It appears to us, however, that any systems considered should:

---

[1] *The report of an ad hoc sub-committee of the General Dental Services Committee on the Remuneration of Dentists*, British Dental Association, London, 1964, page 1.

[2] *Fit for the Future. The report of the Committee on Child Health Services*, (Cmnd 6684), London, HMSO, 1976, paragraph 13.39.

be geared to an overall strategy for dental care and encourage a preventive approach rather than one which seeks only to repair the effects of disease;

provide incentives to patients for self care and regular attendance;

enable practitioners to earn a reasonable income while at the same time providing a good quality and cost effective service;

enable practitioners to undergo post-graduate training without personal loss;

ensure a good standard of premises, equipment and ancillary help and the use of materials of high quality; and

encourage the development of new techniques and co-operative research by practitioners.

We support the recommendation of the Court Committee for an experimental capitation system for children. We recommend profession and government to experiment with other alternatives to the present system of remuneration for general dental practitioners. A method of payment must be tested and seen to work fairly in the interests of both patients and dentists before being generally implemented.

Charges

9.24 We discuss in Chapter 21 the general question of charges to patients, and note here that they are undoubtedly a disincentive to regular dental care. The OPCS Primary Care study[1] suggests that 24% of those with no natural teeth and six per cent of those with some natural teeth found the cost of NHS treatment the main reason why they did not visit the dentist or did not go as often as they thought they should.

Out-of-hours services

9.25 Although some dentists conscientiously look after their own patients requiring emergency "out-of-hours" treatment, many do not. More than half the population have no regular dentist on whom to call when they require attention urgently. The problem of obtaining treatment for acute toothache has been made worse by recent additional Monday bank holidays and the now long Christmas and New Year breaks. In a few towns, for example Glasgow, there are emergency dental services, some run on a voluntary or private basis. The British Dental Association has been negotiating with the health departments about the setting up of four experimental schemes in England, Scotland and Wales. However, these have been prevented from starting by a disagreement over the level of fees. We endorse the recommendation in paragraph 53 of the Eighth Report of the Doctors' and Dentists' Review Body that agreement on the appropriate level of remuneration should be reached without delay. There is no doubt that individual suffering can be intense. Robert Burns in his "address to the Toothache" called it "thou Hell o' a' disease!" We recommend profession and government to make rapid progress with these experimental schemes with a view to early general provision.

---

[1]Office of Population Censuses and Surveys, *Access to Primary Care*, (to be published).

Patient confusion about the availability of NHS treatment

9.26 The National Consumer Council study found that:

"there was widespread 'leakage' into the private sector and, in general, considerable confusion over the boundary between private and NHS treatment and fees".[1]

We also received complaints from a number of CHCs to the same effect. There is a clear ethical responsibility for dentists to make plain to patients the basis on which they propose to treat them and they should fulfil it.

Quality of care

9.27 Questions of quality control are dealt with generally in Chapter 12 but there are a number of specific points about dentistry to be made here. We have received no evidence from individual patients or consumer organisations to suggest that the quality of treatment provided falls below an acceptable standard. The evidence from the British Dental Association on this is illuminating:

"In 1975, for example, the Department's dental officers in England found that completed treatment was 'entirely unsatisfactory' in only 72 out of 17,932 cases examined. The number of complaints or queries of such a nature as to give rise to formal Service Committee investigations is well under 300 annually and in over 50% of these the practitioner is exculpated; viewed against a background of 28 million courses of treatment these figures hardly give cause for disquiet."

However, individual dentists have told us of their concern that the present system of payment puts the emphasis on quantity rather than quality and militates against the achievement of the highest attainable standards. They have told us that anything less than the best is false economy. High standards require accurate diagnosis and painstaking precision work, using first class materials. The present method and levels of remuneration do not help towards this ideal. Standards also depend on other factors, such as professional education, self-respect, peer judgment, type of patient demand and the inspection of work. In the belief that the NHS should strive for the highest standards we make the following suggestions:

further work should be undertaken on the difficult area of definitions of the quality of dental care;

some form of protected educational environment is required, to help the new graduate make the transition to general dental practice;

continuing education for the general dental practitioner should be improved (in this context we are pleased to note the stimulus which will be provided by the establishment of a Diploma in General Practice by the Faculty of Dental Surgery of the Royal College of Surgeons of England);

---

[1]Simpson, Robin, *Access to Primary Care*, Royal Commission on the National Health Service, Research Paper Number 6, London, HMSO, paragraph 4.29.

the development of group practices should be encouraged whether in private accommodation or in health centres: group working brings its own stimulus to improved practice and makes peer review possible; and

the Regional Dental Officer service which carries out random inspections of patient treatment should be strengthened so that on average four or five patients per dentist could be inspected by the service each year.

Health centres

9.28 Dentistry has played a part in the growth of primary care provision from health centres. As we point out in Chapter 7 there are certain advantages to patients from the increased possibilities for co-operation and team work between health professionals working under the same roof. These apply as much to dentistry as to other professions. When health centres are planned consideration needs to be given to including appropriate accommodation and facilities for dentistry. Too often dental suites in health centres have been added as an afterthought. Without adequate planning and provision health centre dentistry can appear a second class alternative to practice in privately provided accommodation. So far only a small number of dentists work in health centres. The reluctance of general dental practitioners to work in them may stem from conditions imposed by health authorities. Health authorities should also make it possible for part-time dentists to work in health centres.

9.29 We are concerned that dental services are insufficiently developed in areas of social deprivation, although demand may not be very high in these areas. We are pleased to note the announcement of an experimental scheme in four selected areas for participating dentists to work in publicly provided premises and to be paid a basic salary supplemented by payment related to output exceeding a certain level.[1] In addition there is a role for the community dental service to initiate provision on a pump-priming basis with the employment of salaried dental practitioners. Demand for dental services in these areas is likely in time to grow to a point where it becomes attractive for general dental practitioners to provide them. New initiatives are required to improve dental care in areas of social deprivation not only by attracting staff to work in them but also by experiment with different approaches to the provision of care. This field might attract the interest and support of the charitable foundations.

Community dental services

9.30 The community dental service was formed from the former local authority school dental service at the time of reorganisation in 1974. The present service provides dental inspection and treatment to school children, pre-school children and to pregnant women and mothers of infants under one year old. Recently the health departments have allowed discretion to health authorities to provide limited facilities for the dental treatment of handicapped adults who are not hospital in-patients. This extension of service is subject to authorities first meeting their primary responsibilities.

---

[1]Department of Health and Social Security, *On the State of the Public Health for the year 1977*, London, HMSO, 1978, page 86.

9.31   The community dental service employed the whole-time equivalent of approximately 1,980 dental officers in the UK in 1977. They were assisted in their work by approximately 370 dental auxiliaries, 2,900 dental surgery assistants (DSAs), 70 hygienists and 140 dental technicians. The school dental service was introduced at a time when there was no state funded alternative. Most children are now treated in the NHS general dental service. This development, together with the probability of water fluoridation and a falling child population, calls for a careful review of the future functions of the community dental service. This is an important issue which we deal with later in the chapter in the context of the reorganised dental services. The health departments should include this as part of the review of dental policy which we recommend in paragraph 9.74.

Hospital dental services

9.32   Since 1948 there has been a remarkable development of consultant dental services in the UK based mainly on the district general hospitals and plastic and jaw surgery units. The equivalent of approximately 400 consultants are now employed. Appointments are in oral surgery, in orthodontics, and much more recently in restorative dentistry. In general these services are organised and administered in a similar way to hospital medical services. We consider it to be in the patients' interest that they should remain so. Hospital dentists share with hospital doctors similar problems about their career structure and these are discussed in Chapter 14. The internationally recognised high quality of UK dental consultants has unfortunately not always been matched by NHS provision of staff and facilities.

9.33   Apart from the provision of specialist services, it is the duty of the hospital service to look after the routine dental needs of long-stay patients, such as those in geriatric wards in hospitals. In most areas there has been serious under-staffing of this work, particularly for the mentally handicapped. At the moment it is an area of considerable neglect and is a major gap in the provision of an adequate level of dental care under the NHS. This deficiency must be remedied. We recommend that dental care for long-stay patients should be as readily available as it is for men and woman in the community.

9.34   In addition to the many dental units in district general hospitals, there are 17 undergraduate dental hospitals and one post-graduate institute in the UK. Although they all have important specialist functions, their primary role is to provide clinical facilities for the teaching of students. Most of their patients would otherwise be treated by the general dental service. The dental hospitals have therefore rather a different function from that of general hospitals. It has been suggested to us by the British Dental Association and others that this difference has not been recognised in their funding. The Association, in oral evidence, told us that they thought that as dental hospitals have a national training function, they should be centrally financed, and divorced from the competing claims of district finance. More specific to the dental hospitals is their contention that the service increment for teaching

(SIFT) in England and Wales determined by the Resource Allocation Working Party (RAWP) at 25% of the medical equivalent, was wrongly conceived.[1]

9.35   In view of the very different balanced functions and the relatively small component of district services compared with medical teaching hospitals, we recommend that the dental teaching hospitals be directly funded by region or by the health departments. In Scotland dental teaching costs are already allocated directly to those health boards which have dental schools. We also agree with the criticism of SIFT for dental teaching hospitals and are pleased to notice that the DHSS is looking at how to define more accurately the additional costs of dental teaching.

Other dental staff

9.36   Dentists may be assisted by workers of several kinds. They include dental surgery assistants who work closely with dentists much as a theatre nurse works with a surgeon; dental technicians, many of whom are employed in private dental laboratories making dentures and other appliances; dental hygienists, who give advice to patients and carry out preventive procedures; and dental auxiliaries who, in addition, carry out certain operative procedures for children to the diagnosis and prescription of the dentist.

9.37   There is no doubt that increased specialisation and the appropriate delegation of functions by dentists increases the effectiveness of scarce dental manpower. However, increased delegation must be carefully monitored and evaluated to ensure that roles do not become inflexible and that patients do not suffer undue dilution of services. Evaluation must take account also of patients' preferences: the provision of a personal service like dental care by different people may not prove acceptable to some patients.

Dental surgery assistants

9.38   Dental surgery assistants form the largest group of dental ancillaries. Their numbers are hard to estimate precisely but are in the region of 20,000. If a dentist works with the close support of one or two DSAs, not only does his output increase substantially, but the stresses on him are reduced. There appear to be no problems in recruitment. Through lack of finance, however, undergraduate dental schools are unable to employ DSAs or trainees in sufficient numbers. This results in inadequate training in "close support" dentistry and a substantial waste of undergraduate time.

---

[1]Department of Health and Social Security, *Report of the Resource Allocation Working Party*, London, HMSO, 1976, paragraph 4.27.

Dental hygienists

9.39   Dental hygienists undergo a twelve month course of training and work in all branches of the dental service. The number of enrolled hygienists rose from 464 in 1972 to 1,145 in 1978. A much greater increase in their numbers must be an important element in a preventive programme. We support the expansion of training facilities recommended in the report of the Working Party on Dental Services.[1]

9.40   Dental auxiliaries, soon to be known as dental therapists, take a two year training at the New Cross School. The school was opened in 1960 and has an intake of 60 students a year. The number of enrolled dental auxiliaries has risen from 286 in 1970 to 533 in 1978. Dental auxiliaries are mainly employed in the community service and do not work in the general dental service. The functions of auxiliaries are closest to those of dentists and they carry out much routine treatment. The expansion of this category of staff has been opposed by some dentists who fear, for example, that there might be a tendency to fragmentation of care if this group developed a corporate identity, increased educational requirements and adopted inflexible roles. In our view the risk of the formation of a two-tier profession should be recognised and avoided. We endorse the recommendation of the Court Committee for an expansion of training facilities for dental auxiliaries. We trust that the dental profession will now review this matter most carefully in their own and the national interest.

9.41   The expansion of dentistry which we envisage will require more manpower and in particular an increase in the number of ancillary workers who, in support of the dentists, can improve the service provided for the public. In these professional developments, however, patients' preferences must not be ignored. To his supporting workers the dentist can delegate simpler duties and procedures; but he must supervise and monitor their work to ensure that it is carried out to a high standard of technical efficiency, and the development of the team must be coherent and balanced. A flexible curriculum is needed which would allow joint training in aspects common to all dental ancillary work and make possible movement between the careers of DSA, hygienist and auxiliary. This would facilitate the flexible development of team roles. The training of ancillaries should take place alongside that of dental students.

Dental technicians

9.42   The dental technician is important in all spheres of dental practice. Against a background of general shortage there is a particular shortage of technicians capable of advanced work in the hospital services. We agree with the BDA that their career prospects should be improved, and we recommend that the present technical college/dental hospital training schemes should be expanded to avoid a breakdown in dental services.

The Reorganised Dental Services

9.43   Before 1974 the general dental service, the community dental service

---

[1]Department of Health and Social Security, Welsh Office: *Working Party on the Dental Services Interim Report: Recruitment and Training of Dental Hygienists*, London, HMSO, 1974.

and the hospital dental service were organised separately, but at reorganisation all became the responsibility of the new integrated health authorities. The general dental service is, however, administered in England and Wales by the FPC,[1] the community dental service by the Area Dental Officer and the hospital dental service by the District Management Team, or Area Team of Officers and their equivalents in Scotland and Northern Ireland, and the consultants concerned.

9.44 The introduction of the Area Dental Officer (ADO) at reorganisation was greeted with suspicion by many members of the dental profession. The development and integration of dental services require an appointment of this kind in order to represent and interpret the interests of the profession within the NHS management structure, and the priorities of the NHS to the profession. A wide knowledge of dentistry and the dental services needs to be combined with epidemiological and management skills. At the present time, not all ADOs are equipped for this role and it is doubtful whether a full time appointment is justified in every health authority.

9.45 If our proposals for changes in management structure in Chapter 20 are adopted, there will need to be an examination of the appropriate number of administrative dental officers, taking into account the availability of suitably trained and qualified staff. Rearrangement of responsibilities should be introduced in stages as vacancies occur. Firm decisions need to be made to assist those responsible for the training programme.

9.46 In order to use scarce resources efficiently, it is essential to know the extent of disease and its distribution. It is desirable that such dental epidemiological data are available at operational level and this must be one of the most important tasks of the ADO. To facilitate comparisons of local need and progress, we recommend that data should be collected by community dentists on a nationally agreed basis.

9.47 The present Area Dental Advisory Committee represents all dental interests at area level and, together with the ADO, should shape policy for the best use of local resources. In some areas, this has already begun, but it can be achieved only when all concerned recognise the importance of the job and provide it with the support and co-operation it requires.

9.48 Authorities with different needs and resources will not find their best solutions if confined by rigid national policies. The three arms of the dental service tend, for historical reasons, to overlap. It is important at local level that they should have the flexibility and willingness to complement each other's services.

9.49 We recommended above a review of the future functions of the community dental service. Added weight is given to this by the present uncertainty over the respective roles of the general dental practitioner and the community dental services in the routine treatment of children and the

---

[1]In Scotland and Northern Ireland there is no separate FPC.

development of specialist community officers, particularly in orthodontics. The community service might develop into a high quality specialist service for children providing skills in, for example orthodontics, general anaesthetics and the management of child and adult handicapped patients; or into a comprehensive service for children removing the treatment of children from the general practitioner; or into the spearhead of a preventive dentistry programme and as a safety net for those children whose parents do not obtain regular care for them through the general dental service.

9.50   A recent collaborative study by the World Health Organisation[1] has raised the question of the appropriateness of double systems with different services for children and adults, and indicates that dental services should be available for all age groups alike in the same environment. Routine treatment for children is readily available in the general dental service and, under present methods of payment, is more economically carried out there. Although it seems that dental care for children may best be provided in the setting of a family practice, there will continue to be a need for a safety net for those children who cannot or will not go to a general dental practice. The size of this net will vary; in some parts of the country the routine treatment element of the school dental service will need to be built up and in others to be run down.

9.51   It is not our intention to go over ground so ably covered in the Court Report, but we want to emphasize that the primary functions of the community dental service should include:

> the annual inspection of all children of school age and where possible pre-school children, and the collection of epidemiological data;
>
> the encouragement of those needing treatment to attend their family dentist;
>
> the identification of those who are not getting treatment;
>
> the capacity to offer a comprehensive service to those children who are not getting treatment in the general dental service; and
>
> the organisation of dental health education and preventive measures in school and community.

The presence of a salaried service alongside the independent contractor service allows a potentially flexible method of meeting difficult needs. We recommend that manpower in the community service should be increased so that it can fulfil the primary roles mentioned above. Further development would depend on the identification of reasonable local needs by the ADO and the Area Dental Advisory Committee and local rather than national determination of the best use of resources.

9.52   As we have noted the efficient and flexible use of the community service will depend largely on the quality of the basic data which it can collect and maintain. This is particularly important in keeping track of those children who receive care from a general dental practitioner and those who do not. In Scotland a system has been developed whereby all information about the

---

[1]Cohen L K, *WHO/US. Public Health Service International Collaborative Study of Dental Manpower Systems in relation to oral health status*, a paper presented at a conference in international dental care delivery systems, Washington DC, 1977.

dental treatment of children either by the community or by the general dental service is recorded in the same way. The linking of that information makes it possible to identify those children who are getting no treatment. Steps can then be taken to offer it to them. We recommend that a similar system is adopted in England, Wales and Northern Ireland.

9.53 As we noted earlier, handicapped patients of all ages, and many elderly patients in particular, need special dental care and it is encouraging that the regulations governing the community dental services have been relaxed so that this care can be given to adults as well as children by that service. Although their treatment is inevitably more time consuming, many handicapped people can appropriately be treated by general dental practitioners. We recommend that the availability of services to the handicapped should be further improved by the payment of fees, authorised on a discretionary basis by the DEBs.

The Future

9.54 Our assessment of dental health and dental care in the UK can give no grounds for complacency. Due to a number of factors, but mainly to the highly efficient and cost-effective service provided by general dental practitioners, there has been a substantial improvement since 1948, but it is also true that the level of dental disease is still unacceptably high. Many of the complaints we have received from the public and the profession spring from the present commitment to a comprehensive service which is not matched by adequate resources. We noted above that dental manpower is not evenly distributed. In some areas, NHS dentistry is difficult to obtain whilst new graduates are beginning to find difficulty in getting employment in the areas of their choice. On the whole, demand is probably being substantially satisfied. However, as we have seen, only a minority of those who need treatment seek regular dental care.

9.55 How far the gap between aspiration and performance is closed will depend on the political will. We consider this as part of the general problem of the level of funding and public expectation of the NHS in Chapter 21.

9.56 If we regard the retention of a natural set of teeth for life as a fundamental aim for a national service, the present approach via the treatment of established diseases has little prospect of success. People living in London and the south east of England have the best access to treatment and also the best record of dental health, but no one would pretend that even here the general standards of dental health approach this aim. Even so, it appears from Table 9.4 that if the same access to care as in North West Thames RHA were to be enjoyed by the other English regions then the number of dentists would have to increase by about 60%.

9.57 The dental service is no longer a pain – extraction – denture service but has become substantially a repair service. A major shift in policy towards prevention is long overdue. This will require changes in the attitude and practice of dentists and their teachers and in the public's apparent indifference

118

to dental health. A much more positive approach to dental health must be adopted if progress is to be made. Four main measures seem to be required:

fluoridation of water supplies;

better financial recognition for preventive work by dentists;

effective dental health education supported by relevant behavioural studies; and

increased support for biomedical research directed towards prevention.

Fluoridation

9.58   We have been impressed by the weight of written evidence in favour of fluoridation. The Royal College of Physicians of London commented on the enormous body of information on the subject of fluoride and health which justified their conclusions not only on the effectiveness of fluoridated water in caries prevention but also its safety both from personal and environmental viewpoints. Fluoridation of water supplies has also been repeatedly advocated by the World Health Organisation,[1] by the DHSS[2] and by the Court Committee on Child Health Services. Eighty four of the 90 English area health authorities have agreed to the measure, as have four out of eight AHAs in Wales, all·15 health boards in Scotland and all four health and social services boards in Northern Ireland. Nevertheless, only 12% of the population in Wales, 9% in England, 0.9% in Scotland and 0.5% in Northern Ireland receive fluoridated water.

9.59   Despite the fact that fluoride occurs naturally in the water supply in a number of places in the UK with obvious benefits for dental health, and that the safety of fluoridation in recommended quantities is no longer in doubt, an effective campaign waged by a small group continues to dissuade some local authorities from agreeing to it on the grounds that it would interfere with personal freedom. However, as the Royal College of Physicians' report points out, substances such as copper sulphate and chlorine, aluminium and calcium are already regularly added to water supplies without arousing protest. The Court Report puts the matter succinctly:

"the cost (of not fluoridating water supplies) in unnecessary disease, personal pain and discomfort, misuse of professional resources and national expenditure has been immense."[3]

9.60   Caries is a disease which attacks almost every child in the UK. We have the power to reduce its incidence substantially without requiring personal effort from any child or parent by using a method which is not only effective and safe but also by far the cheapest available. We are not simply convinced of the wisdom of introducing fluoridation, if necessary compulsorily; we are

---

[1]World Health Organisation, *Twelfth Plenary Meeting. Resolutions*, WHO 22.30, WHO (1968) 28th World Health Assembly, Thirteenth Plenary Meeting WHO 28.64, 1975.

[2]Department of Health and Social Security, *Priorities for Health and Social Services in England. A Consultative Document*, London, HMSO, 1976: announced that £2 million would be set aside to help area health authorities with the capital cost of fluoridation schemes.

[3](Cmnd 6684), *Op cit*, paragraph 13.20.

certain that it is entirely wrong to deprive the most vulnerable section of the population of such an important public health measure for the sake of the views of a small minority of adults for whom its benefits come too late. We recommend that the government introduces legislation to compel water authorities to fluoridate water supplies at the request of health authorities. Otherwise children who cannot choose for themselves will continue to suffer the ravages of a disease which can be substantially reduced by a method that has been shown not to have any deleterious effect.

9.61   What this means in human terms is illustrated by treatment figures from Birmingham where the water supply was fluoridated in 1964 (Tables 9.6 and 9.7). The staffing of the community dental service and the number of practitioners in the general dental service remained remarkably constant throughout this period, as did the number of children, with the exception of a slight rise in 1974 when 23,000 children from unfluoridated Sutton Coldfield were added. In terms of demands on the service these figures provide a striking indication of the relief of misery among the young. Tables 9.6 and 9.7 are based on treatment records with no control group. However, a recent statistically controlled trial in Northumberland on smaller groups of five year olds indicated a very similar reduction in toothache and the need for extractions under general anaesthetics.[1]

TABLE 9.6

Emergency Visits to the Dentist: Birmingham Children 1965–1976

Year	"Emergency" visits for the relief of pain				
	0–4 yrs	*5–9 yrs*	*9–15 yrs*	*15+ yrs*	*Total*
1965	Not collected	5,978	3,399	891	10,268
1966	722	5,648	3,015	602	10,037
1976	43	994	878	420	2,335

Source: Data provided by Birmingham AHA(T) Community Dental Service.

TABLE 9.7

Child Dental Health: Birmingham 1964 and 1977

Year	*General anaesthetics given*	*First teeth extracted*	*Permanent teeth extracted*
1964	22,628	44,410	13,429
1977	3,851	11,487	5,290

Source: Data provided by Birmingham AHA(T) Community Dental Service.

[1]Rugg, Gunn, et al. "Fluoridation in Newcastle and Northumberland", *British Dental Journal*, 1977, Vol 142, No. 12, pages 395-402.

9.62   In fluoridated areas the first contact with the dentist is now much more rarely a frightening general anaesthetic and the extraction of aching teeth with all that this implies in the formation of negative attitudes to dental treatment. Carious teeth are few, they appear later and are much simpler to treat. Following fluoridation, a changed attitude develops towards dentistry, there is a greater uptake of treatment and more interest in the prevention of dental disease.

9.63   Fluoridation of water supplies also makes good economic sense in the short-term. There is no doubt that expenditure on repair work in a dirty mouth is often a waste of time and money. Prevention of dental caries is much less costly than the repair of its effects and fluoridation of water supplies is much cheaper and more effective than other methods of preventing such decay.[1] Because, however, the aim of maintaining teeth for life will be brought nearer, it is likely that more sophisticated care will be demanded in the longer term.

9.64   If general fluoridation were agreed, it would take about two years for production of the main fluoride compound to be expanded to the necessary level. Installation of equipment might take as little as 18 months in some areas. It is estimated that 75% of the population of Scotland could be receiving fluoridated water within five years of starting the operation, but it might take 25 years to reach as many as 90%. The time factors make it urgent that a decision be made so that work can begin.

Alternative means of using fluoride

9.65   Even if fluoridated water were reaching more areas, there would still be some small communities in the UK not sharing the public water system. We have therefore considered some of the alternative measures which are said to reduce caries. They fall into two categories:

   forms in which fluoride can be swallowed to strengthen developing teeth, eg. by fluoridation of individual school water supplies, or flour, milk or salt, or by the use of fluoride tablets. With all these methods, there are significant practical or economic disadvantages or a lack of adequate data on which to form a sound judgment. The use of fluoride tablets has been more widely researched but the results have not been consistent; and

   ways of applying fluoride to the surfaces of erupted teeth, eg in fluoride toothpaste. A recent market estimate suggested that fluoride toothpaste sales now account for 90% of all toothpaste sold in the UK. In addition, the application of various formulations of fluoride to the teeth has been investigated in short term clinical trials and found to give encouraging results.

9.66   The general dental service is a treatment service. We doubt whether an item of service system of payment can provide the structure for a fully satisfactory preventive programme. The present fees schedule could be modified to encourage dentists to give preventive advice and individual

---

[1]Gish, C W, American Dental Association Newsletter, 1968, Vol 21, Number 23. Davies G N. *Cost and benefit of fluoride in the prevention of dental caries*, WHO, 1974.

application of preventive measures. There are difficulties, however. By no means all of the preventive measures used in private practice have been tested sufficiently rigorously for use in a national system. In addition, the introduction of preventive measures generally into the present scale of fees would have major consequences for the fees structure itself. We are pleased to learn that the DHSS are to look at this difficult area.

Dental health education

9.67   Recent work in Sweden[1] has demonstrated the value of plaque control in adults by the intensive use of hygienists. This resulted in the almost total prevention of caries and periodontal disease over the three years of the experiment which covered 555 patients. Regular conventional dental care was given to the control group and proved to be much less effective. This work may well have a fundamental influence on the "best use of resources" and demands further study in the UK.

9.68   While the precise value of personal, intensive dental health education can be measured in such studies as those of Axelsson and Lindhe, public dental health education is a more difficult field. We comment generally on health education in Chapter 5. To increase the number of people cleaning their teeth efficiently, to persuade them to adopt sensible dietary habits, to increase the level of awareness and interest in dental health, to make tooth loss less acceptable and to persuade people to visit a dentist regularly must all be important objectives. However, much more evaluative effort is needed to define the best methods of approach in health education, taking into account the need for it to reach people of all social classes and backgrounds, against a variety of opposing influences. We also note from the White Paper "Prevention and Health"[2] that restriction on advertising which may lead to undesirable dietary habits, particularly in children, is under consideration. We recommend that the health departments pursue an active policy in this field.

9.69   Fluoridation of water supplies would cut the incidence of caries by half and is a true public health measure. The application of other methods of caries prevention, and indeed all the available methods of periodontal disease control, demand personal co-operation and effort. The behavioural sciences have an important part to play in innovation and evaluation of health education.

Research

9.70   We must look further ahead. The recognition of caries as a bacterial infection is relatively recent, and considering what has been achieved in the conquest of most bacterial diseases this has enormous implications. The Medical Research Council[3] (MRC) has accorded high priority to an expansion

---

[1]Axelsson, P & Lindhe, J. "Effect of controlled oral hygiene procedures on caries and periodontal disease in adults", *Journal of Clinical Periodontology* (1978) 5, pages 133-151.

[2]*Prevention and Health,* (Cmnd 7047), London, HMSO, page 47.

[3]*Review of Dental Research: a report by the Medical Research Council Dental Committee,* London, MRC, 1977.

of research directed towards counteracting disease processes initiated by bacterial aggregations on the tooth surface. It is from advances in biomedical research that methods for the antimicrobial control of dental diseases are most likely to accrue.

9.71   There appear, however, to be two problems. Research manpower is in short supply. Young researchers need a more adequate training programme and, once trained they are often discouraged from continuing in research by the lack of a career structure. Where clinical trials are involved most projects are funded over too short a period to establish the service value of the findings. Such clinical research has a long time scale and needs sustained support. We recommend that the dental profession should consider ways of overcoming these difficulties.

Conclusions and Recommendations

9.72   There is no doubt that dental health in the UK has improved since 1948, but the prevalence of dental disease remains at an unacceptably high level. The NHS should strive for the highest standard of care. We have recommended a number of detailed changes which should, if implemented, improve the quality of service offered to patients and the efficiency of the present system.

9.73   The prevention policies which we recommend for the future offer a real and attainable – perhaps unique – improvement in public health. A determined swing of policy towards a greater emphasis on prevention is needed. The most immediate requirements are for the full implementation of water fluoridation and for the funding of research on prevention and dental health education and the training and employment of more ancillary workers. Individual preventive work should be carried out by the general dental service and a way found for providing fees for treatment of this kind.

9.74   While these policies will require time to implement and will not bring changes overnight, their effect on the numbers, composition and training of the dental team will be profound. The appointment of the Nuffield inquiry to which we referred at the start of this chapter is, therefore, timely. Because NHS dentistry is likely to change significantly we recommend that a small committee representing government and other interested parties is set up to review the development of dental health policy and in particular a preventive strategy and the future functions of the community dental service. Its purpose would be to ensure that the impetus for improvement is not lost. Its starting point could be this report and that of the Nuffield Committee.

9.75   We recommend that:

(a) until the implications of a shift in policy towards prevention have been identified dental student entry numbers should not be altered but flexibility in meeting demands should be achieved through the increased use of dental ancillary workers (paragraph 9.18);

123

(b) the dental profession and government should experiment with alternative methods of paying general dental practitioners in addition to a capitation system for children (paragraph 9.23);

(c) the dental profession and government should make rapid progress to the introduction generally of an out-of-hours treatment scheme (paragraph 9.25);

(d) dental care for long-stay hospital patients should be as readily available as it is for men and women in the community (paragraph 9.33);

(e) dental teaching hospitals should be funded directly by region or health department (paragraph 9.35);

(f) the present technical college/dental hospital training schemes for dental technicians should be expanded (paragraph 9.42);

(g) a standardised national basis for the collection of dental data should be introduced (paragraph 9.46);

(h) manpower in the community dental service should be increased (paragraph 9.51);

(i) the Scottish system for recording all information about the dental treatment of children in the same way should be adopted in the rest of the UK (paragraph 9.52);

(j) the availability of services to the handicapped should be further improved by the payment of fees, authorised on a discretionary basis by DEBs (paragraph 9.53);

(k) the government should introduce legislation to compel water authorities to fluoridate water supplies at the request of health authorities (paragraph 9.60);

(l) the health departments should pursue an active policy in restricting advertising which may lead to undesirable dietary habits, particularly in children (paragraph 9.68);

(m) the dental profession should consider ways of overcoming the problems of long-term clinical research in dentistry (paragraph 9.71);

(n) a small committee representing government and the other interested parties should be set up to review the development of dental health policy (paragraphs 9.18, 9.31 and 9.74).

Chapter 10   Hospital Services

10.1   In this chapter we consider some aspects of the services provided for patients in NHS hospitals. We discuss patient attitudes to the services, government policies on providing hospitals, the problem of ageing hospital buildings and the relationship with the community health services. We deal with hospital dental services in Chapter 9, hospital staff in Part III of the report, the problems of teaching hospitals in Chapter 17, and hospital management in Chapter 20.

10.2   There are about 2,750 NHS hospitals. They range from the large psychiatric hospital with over 1,500 beds and about 800 staff, drawing its patients from a wide area, to the cottage or general practitioner hospital with under 50 beds and a handful of full-time staff providing local service to a small community. The total number of hospital beds is about 480,000, of which 80% are occupied on any one day. Out-patient and accident and emergency departments serve some 100,000 patients daily. Hospital services account for about 70% of total NHS expenditure. They aim to provide a comprehensive range of treatment and care for people who are ill and cannot be adequately looked after in the community.

Services and patients

10.3   Most people rarely have to use hospital services. When they do they are usually at their most vulnerable, removed from the security of their home, dependent on others for their daily living needs and for the treatment which will allow them to resume a normal life. In the main, hospital staff are highly regarded by their patients. This was amply confirmed by the survey of hospital patients' attitudes which we commissioned from the Office of Population Censuses and Surveys (OPCS)[1] and we draw heavily on its findings in this part of our report.

10.4   The OPCS survey found that the majority of patients were satisfied with the overall service provided in hospital, but there were many detailed complaints and we deal with the most important of these below. We commend the report to all who plan and provide services to patients.

Waiting lists

10.5   Waiting lists in general, and the size of waiting lists in particular,

---

[1]Gregory, Janet, *Patients' Attitudes to the Hospital Service,* Royal Commission on the National Health Service, Research Paper Number 5, London, HMSO, 1978.

attract a good deal of attention in Parliament and in the press. In the words of an article in The Lancet last year:

"The impression conveyed is that the problem reflects a general one affecting the NHS, due to inadequate resources, money, and beds, to administrative inefficiencies, or to lack of concern by hospital staff."[1]

Surprisingly, waiting lists attracted relatively little comment in our evidence.

10.6 Discussion of waiting lists seems often to generate more heat than light. There are some basic points to clarify. First, the number of people recorded as waiting for hospital admission is not by itself a useful figure. There are a number of reasons for thinking that it can be misleading, but more importantly it does not indicate by itself how long people have to wait for hospital treatment, especially treatment which they require urgently. The psychological effects of a long wait for admission must not be underestimated, though the OPCS survey found that 80% of all in-patients said that they were not caused inconvenience or distress by waiting for admission.

10.7 Second, interest tends to focus on in-patient admissions, though the waiting time for an out-patient appointment may be just as or more significant. This is because the majority of patients are admitted after they have been seen first as out-patients. There may be a long wait for an out-patient appointment but only a short one for admission as an in-patient. Separate waiting times for out-patient and in-patient are therefore required to give a reliable picture.

10.8 Third, waiting lists are one mechanism for controlling access to services free at time of use. Other countries use other methods, often financial. Immediate admission to hospital for non-urgent treatment implies spare capacity. Waiting lists are likely always to be with us, but that does not mean we should not try to reduce waiting times.

10.9 Generally the acute hospital services provide excellent and rapid treatment of urgent cases. Problems are greatest for non-urgent cases where the longest waiting lists and times are, in the main, for in-patient surgery; and within surgery, for orthopaedics and for some of the commonest operations, for example, hernia repair, and cataract removal. These operations relieve conditions which, although not life-threatening, cause much disability and distress. Many are prevalent in the elderly and demand for them will therefore increase in the future.

10.10 Much effort has been put into studying waiting times for admission to hospital. Guidance issued by the DHSS in 1975 referred to a survey which showed that in six major surgical specialties 37% of patients had been waiting longer than a year, nearly 20% for more than two years, and some for four years or more.[2] A number of recommendations were made for reducing waiting times, including pooling of beds and greater use of day surgery. Influences on

---

[1]Avery Jones, Francis and McCarthy, Mark, "Understanding Waiting Lists", The Lancet, 1 July 1978, page 34.

[2]HSC/IS/181, Reduction of Waiting Times for In-Patients Admission: Management Arrangements, DHSS, August 1975.

waiting times include the effect of strikes, longer holidays and shorter working hours for staff. Returns by health authorities to the DHSS in 1976 mentioned shortages of theatre staff, particularly anaesthetists and trained nurses, and theatre facilities amongst the causes of long waiting times. Only limited success was reported in meeting the suggested objective of reducing waiting times for urgent admissions to a maximum of one month and for all patients of one year. Our OPCS survey did not differentiate between urgent and non-urgent cases, but found that 45% of all in-patient admissions took place within one month of the patient being put on the waiting list, but that six per cent had to wait longer than one year.

10.11   There are startling differences in the rate per thousand population on in-patient waiting lists between health authorities, and even between neighbouring districts. The answer to a parliamentary question on 14 March 1978 showed, for example, that in South Camden there were about 73 people per thousand on the in-patient waiting list, while in North Camden there were ten. In Central Manchester health district there were 39 per thousand and in nearby Bury there were six.[1] Other surprising variations can readily be found.

10.12   In view of the importance of out-patient waiting times it is surprising that more information is not available. There has been little research and there are no data held centrally. Our OPCS survey found that 28% of patients waited seven days for their first out-patient appointment and 60% were seen within three weeks. However, 17% waited more than six weeks and of these 44% were distressed by the delay. The main reasons for distress were physical pain or discomfort, and anxiety to know what was wrong.

10.13   There are evidently many aspects to the waiting lists question. We understand that the DHSS have commissioned a large scale study of the subject from OPCS. We have no instant solutions to offer, though it seems clear that methods of improving the position will have to be worked out locally according to the particular difficulties. More day surgery linked to effective community services, better use of operating theatre time, and more cross-boundary referrals may help in some places. A substantial improvement in the position would probably require considerably increased resources of both manpower and finance. Even if the importance of waiting lists is exaggerated, it seems to us that very long waiting times must represent a significant failure in the service.

Out-patient services

10.14   We discuss here both attendance at hospital out-patient clinics and day patient admissions. In the UK the number of new out-patients has remained relatively stable in recent times at about nine million per annum, but there has been a considerable growth in the number of day patients, normally for minor surgery or investigation, who do not stay in hospital overnight. In 1976 there were about 560,000.

10.15   The OPCS survey found that patients' most common complaints

---

[1]*Hansard*, 14.3.1978, Col. 150–158.

about out-patient clinics were difficulties in obtaining satisfactory information about their progress (25% of all out-patients), and the total time spent in the out-patient clinic (19%). We deal with communication between patient and doctor later in this chapter.

10.16 The fact that only a minority of patients complain does not mean that services are as good as they should be. The OPCS survey showed that 16% of patients waited over an hour to be seen after their appointment time and another eight per cent more than 45 minutes. This is too long, and even though well over half the out-patients were seen within about 15 minutes of the time of the appointment, it seems plain that more effort should be made to arrange for patients to be seen promptly. We recognise that much of the difficulty may be due to overloaded clinics, but the staff manning them should take a realistic view of what they can hope to achieve, and block booking of a large number of appointments at one time should be avoided. Individual bookings waste staff time when patients arrive late or not at all, but this can be ameliorated by appointments for two or three patients at a time. We would like to see investigation into the greater use of evening clinics which would reduce the need for patients to be absent from work and would make more intensive use of hospital facilities.

10.17 We were told that some hospitals keep out-patients on their books too long. The most frequent causes are probably an unwillingness by over-cautious junior doctors to discharge a patient to the care of his GP, and the lack of a satisfactory review arrangement by the consultant. The consultant should check regularly what goes on in the out-patient department under his name, and the hospital medical divisions should keep in touch with GPs about the balance to be sought between out-patient and GP treatment.

10.18 The OPCS survey did not find that the time taken to get to hospital, whether by the patient's own means or by ambulance, was a major source of dissatisfaction. The great majority made their own way and of these 19% spent over half an hour on the journey. However, there were complaints about the time patients had to wait for the ambulance or hospital car to take them home: one in four usually waited an hour or longer.

10.19 As we said earlier there has been in recent years an increase in the practice of admitting day patients. This may be convenient both for the patient and the hospital and may be economical. Both the Royal College of Surgeons of England and the British Hospital Doctors Federation supported the practice and suggested that it might help to reduce waiting lists. Abortion clinics could be provided more widely on this basis. We would like to see more research both on the acceptability of day admissions to patients, and on the benefits to the NHS, and we recommend that the health departments promote this.

Accident and emergency services

10.20 The problems of accident and emergency (A and E) departments stem mainly from their different functions. Some A and E departments have four different functions – dealing with accidents, such as road accidents, involving severe injuries; handling medical emergencies, such as poisoning;

undertaking functions which might otherwise have been performed by a GP; and acting as a clearing house for admitting patients. A and E departments, particularly in large cities, may also have to deal with patients suffering from alcoholism or drug dependence who are often aggressive and difficult to manage. The main questions we consider here are whether A and E departments should perform, in effect, a GP function; and the staffing problems raised with us in evidence.

10.21 In large cities the local hospital has sometimes been used as a walk-in GP surgery by patients who find it convenient to receive their medical attention there. This may discourage patients from registering with GPs, as well as imposing an extra load on the department. The strengthening of GP services in large cities should improve the situation. Meanwhile in certain places it can be a considerable burden: a study of a London casualty department in 1977 showed that 16% of all patients were not registered with a GP, and of the new patients who did not require emergency treatment only 19% had consulted a GP before coming to the hospital.[1] Where the tradition of using the department in this way is strong it may be preferable for the hospital to accept the role and make specific arrangements for fulfilling it rather than to try and resist established local preferences.

10.22 We do not consider that it is practicable to prohibit self-referral since at least some such cases will be genuine emergencies. The OPCS primary care survey[2] suggested that people often had good reasons for going directly to A and E departments. For example, they had gone because they needed treatment for fractures, cuts and bruises; the hospital was better equipped to provide the necessary treatment; or because treatment was needed outside GP surgery hours.

10.23 There have been problems about staffing A and E departments, particularly with doctors. In the past such departments were normally in the charge of an orthopaedic surgeon. However, consultant appointments in the new specialty started towards the end of 1972, and there are now over 120 major departments run by full-time A and E consultants. At present there is a shortage of junior staff, and a high proportion of doctors from overseas. The medical staffing of A and E departments was the subject of a recent report[3] which the Joint Consultants Committee is discussing with the DHSS. We hope that the result of these discussions, and the recent training programme established by the Joint Higher Training Committees in medicine and surgery, will lead to improvements in the staffing of these departments.

10.24 A consultant appointment in the specialty may not be justified or possible. In that case the responsibility should be clearly placed with a named consultant in another specialty. We think it preferable to leave to local decision the best way of meeting the demands on A and E departments.

[1]Wilkinson, A, et al, "Attendance at a London Casualty Department", Journal of the Royal College of General Practitioners, Vol 27, December 1977, pages 727–733.

[2]Office of Population Censuses and Surveys, Access to Primary Care, (to be published).

[3]Joint Consultants Committee, Report on Medical Staffing of Accident and Emergency Services, 1978.

In-patients

10.25   In this part of the chapter we deal with communications between staff and patients, privacy and wakening times for hospital in-patients. These are not the only subjects of complaint by patients, but they were those on which patients had strong feelings.

Communications

10.26   The OPCS survey found that 31% of in-patients and 25% of out-patients considered that they had not been given sufficient information about their treatment and progress. This was also an issue often mentioned in our evidence. The Royal College of Nursing, for example, told us:

"From the complaints that have come to light through research the most important appear to centre on the failure to give patients and their relatives the right informaion in the right way at the right time."

10.27   The OPCS survey suggested that apart from the difficulties of getting information, patients often felt they were ignored. One in four adult in-patients reported that doctors had discussed their condition or treatment with other people "as if they were not there".[1] Another complaint was of difficulty in understanding what was being said, either because medical jargon was used, or for some other reason such as the doctor's insufficient command of English.

10.28   About half the in-patients in the OPCS sample said they were not really bothered by not understanding what they were told, but this is certainly not a reason for hospital staff not to make every effort to answer questions which patients have about their condition or treatment. And though it may be important for teaching purposes for a consultant, for example, to explain to students what is wrong with a patient, it is grossly inconsiderate for this to happen without the patient having been consulted. It is also essential for patients and relatives to be seen at times in private. A busy corridor or ward waiting room is not acceptable and we recommend that all hospitals should provide facilities for this purpose.

10.29   Another point about communications made in our evidence was that more general information about the hospital and its routine should be made available to patients. The OPCS survey showed that about 60% of in-patients were given an explanatory booklet or leaflet about the hospital either before they were admitted or soon after, and nearly all of them had found it useful. The main complaints about the booklets were that they did not contain enough information, or that the information they did contain was wrong. The survey showed that many patients would have liked to have information about facilities at the hospital, for examaple shops and day rooms; and the parents of children going into hospital would like to have known whether they should take their child's own clothes and toys with them. This seems to be a simple and necessary requirement, and so much more easily conveyed in a booklet than by waiting for patients to ask, and we recommend that all hospitals

---

[1]Gregory, Janet, *Op cit.*, page 112.

should provide explanatory booklets. They should also include information about the suggestions and complaints procedures. Whenever possible admissions should be planned with the patients. Once in the hospital, patients should also be told what is going to happen to them, for example when and why they are being X-rayed or having blood samples taken.

Privacy

10.30   Many patients feel strongly about the privacy they are permitted in hospital. We were told by the Western Provident Association:

> "Our experience leads us to believe that one of the principal reasons (perhaps the strongest) which leads people to subscribe to Provident Associations is to ensure the privacy of their own room when in hospital."

The OPCS survey found that 11% of in-patients would have preferred on a future occasion to have a room on their own, compared with over 60% who would favour a small ward. It may of course be that the Provident Associations are supported by people who feel particularly strongly about having their own room in hospital, and who do not make use of the NHS for that reason, or it may be that actual experience of hospital changes one's views.

10.31   The OPCS survey recorded that:

> "over half (52%) of the 74 patients who, given the choice, would opt for a room on their own said this was because it would be quieter. Preferring not to see other ill people or hear about their complaints or operations was mentioned by 18%, and one in four admitted to simply preferring their own company or not being particularly sociable. More privacy was a deciding factor for a considerable proportion of patients (20%) either when being examined or treated or when visitors were there, and a small number of informants thought there was more freedom for patients in single rooms – visiting arrangements would be more flexible, they could choose which TV programme to watch, and so on."[1]

10.32   There are probably other reasons why patients prefer their own room, and it seems to us that the NHS should aim so far as possible to meet this preference. In some modern hospitals a high proportion of beds are in single rooms or small wards, but in older hospitals larger wards may be the rule. Amenity beds in single rooms or small wards are sometimes available at a charge which has, since 1 August 1975, been £3 per day for a single room and £1.50 for a bed in a small ward, for patients who prefer privacy. There are roughly 4,000 amenity beds, but not all hospitals can offer them. Amenity beds are not bookable before a patient goes into hospital, and may have to be vacated if they are required for urgent medical reasons by another NHS patient. All the patient is buying for his £3 is privacy: his treatment and amenities are the same as those provided for other NHS patients in the hospital.

---

[1]Gregory, Janet, *Op cit.*, page 74.

10.33 Although authorisation of amenity beds is freely given by the health departments, both the number and their occupancy have been falling steadily. They represent under one per cent of hospital beds at present, and not all of those are in single rooms, though we have seen that 11% of patients would prefer their own rooms. The reason for the disparity would seem to be a combination of the rooms not being bookable in advance and few patients knowing of their existence. One argument against meeting these points is that to do so would create separate waiting lists if the demand outstripped the supply. Other possible reasons are that the physical separation of amenity beds might create additional work for nursing staff, particularly in times of staff shortages, and that patients might have unrealistic expectations. Whatever the reasons, we understand that there has been a marked reluctance on the part of hospital management to publicise the availability of amenity beds.

10.34 This attitude seems to us to be absurd. If amenity beds are to be provided under the NHS then their existence should be made known to the public in the same way as other facilities provided. If there are shortages, that should be explained also. If this results in pressure for more amenity beds to be provided, then steps should be taken to meet this demand. We see nothing wrong about waiting lists for amenity beds developing; this is a matter of patients' personal preference. There may be places where staffing or other considerations make the provision of amenity beds impracticable, but that does not mean that they should not be provided where they can be. The phasing-out of pay beds should have made amenity beds more available. We recommend that hospitals should ensure that their availability is routinely made known to patients when they are given a date for admission.

10.35 Another aspect of the question of privacy raised in evidence was mixed sex wards. Some patients find it embarrassing to share wards with members of the opposite sex. There may be occasions when the efficient provision of services requires mixed sex wards, but there cannot be very many, and patients should be given the choice.

Wakening times

10.36 The OPCS survey found that nearly half the patients surveyed complained of being woken too early. This is scarcely surprising when 44% of patients were being woken before 6 am, and 76% before 6.30 am. We have singled the problem out because so many patients evidently find this aspect of hospital life unsatisfactory.

10.37 In 1961 a sub-committee of the Minister of Health's Standing Nursing Advisory Committee produced a report on the pattern of the in-patient's day. The opening sentence of the report was "In many hospitals the patient's day begins sometimes between 5 am and 6 am".[1] It is evident that there has been all too little improvement in the last 18 years. Obviously some people are used to getting up early and to do so is no hardship, but equally obviously it is a hardship for others. There seem to be a number of reasons for early wakening – the amount of work expected of night nursing staff before

---

[1] Ministry of Health, *The Pattern of the In-Patient's Day*, London, HMSO, 1961, paragraph 1.

they go off duty and the timing of the changeover of shifts, often controlled by the availability of public transport; medical rounds; medicine rounds and the need to collect laboratory specimens; and the design of the ward (Nightingale wards tend to mean "one awake, all awake"). Tradition probably plays a part in the hospital routine also.

10.38 This seems to us a prime example of the hospital being run for the convenience of the staff rather than the patient. We do not believe that the in-patient's day cannot be so organised that the majority of patients are able to wake up at roughly their usual time. We have seen the latest report on the organisation of the in-patient's day[1] which discusses the problem. We would like to see a much tougher line being taken on this matter, and we recommend that health authorities should review forthwith the practice in the hospitals for which they are responsible.

Provision of Hospitals

10.39 In general it is no easier to define the need for hospital care than the need for other health services. It varies over time and from place to place. However, the demand – as opposed to the need – for hospital care is largely determined by GPs who are responsible for most out-patient referrals. In doing this they may be influenced by such factors as the availability of other appropriate institutional or community care, the expectations of individual patients, and waiting times for admission to hospital.

10.40 There are other problems in working out a strategy for providing hospital services. In 1948 the NHS inherited over 3,000 hospitals, mainly old, inadequately equipped and badly distributed. The process of replacing and redistributing hospital services involves heavy capital expenditure, but successive economic crises have interfered with and modified strategic planning. The effective planning of hospital services is of major importance. Health authorities must be chiefly responsible for determining their own requirements and will need good information about the state of hospital stock, morbidity, local population trends and the effectiveness of methods of treatment. They will also need to consult interested local authorities.

10.41 In this section we consider the health departments' policies on the provision of hospitals. We concentrate on England and Wales. In Scotland and Northern Ireland, policies seem to have been applied more flexibly with local solutions being preferred. There may, however, be messages in what we say about England and Wales for the other parts of the UK.

District General and Community Hospitals

10.42 In England and Wales the district general hospital (DGH) has been

---

[1]Department of Health and Social Security and Welsh Office, *The Organisation of the In-Patient's Day – Report of a Committee of the Central Health Services Council*, London, HMSO, 1976.

the basis for hospital planning since the Hospital Plan[1] was introduced in 1962. Its role is to provide a full range of specialist services, but different views have been taken of how many beds and what services. The 1962 Hospital Plan proposed 600 to 800 beds as the normal size for a DGH serving a population of 100,000 to 150,000. Subsequently the report of the Bonham-Carter Committee proposed 1,200 to 1,800 beds serving a population of 200,000 to 300,000, based on the view that DGHs should be planned around teams of not less than two consultants in each of the major in-patient specialties.

10.43   In addition the Bonham-Carter Committee envisaged a need for a number of linked small hospitals to be responsible for:

"the continued in-patient care of local patients who have already been assessed and treated by a consultant at the district general hospital, and who in the consultant's judgement no longer need specialist medical attention but still need nursing beyond what can be provided in the community".[2]

10.44   Current strategy in England and Wales is to provide a network of 250 DGHs supplying:

"a full range of specialised treatment, and including a maternity unit, a psychiatric unit, a geriatric unit containing at least half of the district geriatric beds, and a children's department, as well as specialised surgical and medical facilities. Some, but not all, DGHs would have accident and emergency units, and some would have in-patient units for ENT and ophthalmology. Some would also provide regional specialties (such as neurosurgery)."[3]

The DGH would be supported by community hospitals and ideally be on a single site to facilitate the provision of laundry, pathology and other common services. Where this is not possible the DGH is composed of linked local hospitals. In some places completely new buildings are required, and a "nucleus hospital" is being developed by the DHSS to provide a range of standard departments selected to suit local needs. The nucleus hospital would be of about 300 beds and would be capable of expansion later on up to the now preferred range of 600-900 beds. It is being designed with economy in capital and running costs as a prime objective.

10.45   The elderly are important users of hospital services but many of them, and indeed other patients, do not require the full specialist facilities of a DGH. Instead it is envisaged that community hospitals of between 50 and 150 beds serving a population of 30,000 to 50,000 would provide a limited range of services, in smaller units and nearer patients' homes, under the care of general practitioners. The Priorities Consultative Document for England said:

---

[1]Ministry of Health, *National Health Service. A Hospital Plan for England and Wales*, (Cmnd 1604), London, HMSO, 1962.

[2]Department of Health and Social Security and Welsh Office, *The Functions of the District General Hospital. Report of the Committee*, London, HMSO, 1969, paragraph 35.

[3]Department of Health and Social Security, *Priorities for Health and Personal Social Services in England: A Consultative Document*, London, HMSO, 1976, paragraph 4.2.

"up to a quarter of all in-patient beds and many day places might eventually be in community hospitals. It is intended that up to two-thirds of community hospital beds should be for geriatric patients and for elderly patients with severe dementia. The remainder would be medical or post-operative surgical patients including pre-convalescent cases transferred from the DGH."[1]

Since the issue of the Consultative Document in 1976 additional functions, such as minor and intermediate surgery, and radiology and other diagnostic techniques, have been assigned to community hospitals. There has been great difficulty in getting this approach accepted in the NHS, and very few community hospitals have been established.

Criticisms

10.46   Although it is generally agreed that DGHs should be responsible for the delivery of specialised services, they have disadvantages. The TUC, for example, in their evidence to us pointed out:

"There is a limit, however, beyond which the general hospital becomes too large and impersonal and the sheer physical distances within the hospital become too great."

The larger the DGH, the greater the population served, the more serious the problems of communication within it and of access to it are for patients and staff. The size of the hospital will also affect capital and revenue costs.

10.47   The optimum size for a DGH has yet to be determined, but a range of sizes, to take account of local conditions and needs, will probably be required. The "nucleus hospital" approach looks to offer the greatest flexibility in response to what are certain to be changing needs. We believe that increasingly the human aspects of hospital size, such as good communications, building up group loyalties and good industrial relations, will be seen to be important for both patients and staff. These are matters which need to be researched.

10.48   Most of the criticism of the present hospital policy in England and Wales centred on the community hospitals. There was support for having small local hospitals manned by GPs, but concern that such hospitals would simply turn into long-stay units for the elderly, a high proportion of whom would be severely mentally infirm. There is no dispute about the need to provide for these patients, whose numbers are increasing, but fears were expressed about the staffing implications of transferring them from the mental hospitals into community hospitals, in the care of GPs.

10.49   The development of nursing homes mainly staffed and run by nurses, might, we consider, make a useful contribution to the problem. Some small hospital might be converted to nursing homes, others might be purpose-built. They could reduce the number of dependent elderly patients who require little

---

[1]*Ibid*, paragraph 4.2.

but nursing care in local hospitals, but they would make heavy demands on the nurses who staff them and this must be recognised. Nursing homes are already widely used on the continent and, as we said in Chapter 6, there should be more experimentation in this country. The increased use of nursing homes for elderly or chronically disabled patients would leave more scope for GPs to look after their other patients who need only the limited facilities a cottage or GP hospital can offer. We understand that the DHSS is reviewing their policy on community hospitals, and we hope they will take these factors into account.

Acute hospitals

10.50 The main debate about acute hospital services has centred not on their quality but on the amount of resources devoted to them. The specialist general hospital services are well distributed over the country and their quality is high. Our evidence contained much praise and little criticism of them, and we endorse the view of their contribution that this implies. The man, woman or child who becomes acutely ill in this country is well cared for.

10.51 Not surprisingly, those who work in the acute services tend to believe that too few resources are allocated to allow them to sustain, far less enhance, the quality of treatment and care of the acutely ill. Those who work in the services which are currently given priority consider that acute services have been too favoured, that too much attention has been given to cure and too little to care, and that the less dramatic and more persistent conditions of illness and disability have been neglected. We do not propose to judge between these views, but we would be unwilling to see a redistribution of resources occuring at the cost of reducing the quality of acute services.

10.52 Elsewhere in our report we deal with the deficiencies of the hospital capital stock, unit management, medical and nursing careers, teaching and non-teaching hospitals, professional advisory structure, and other matters which immediately affect the services provided by acute hospitals. We hope we have made some contribution to solving their problems, and indeed those of peripheral hospitals which we next discuss.

Peripheral hospitals

10.53 The particular problems of teaching hospitals are discussed in Chapter 17. They have recieved a good deal of public attention and much of our evidence related to them. However, the problems of of the non-teaching or peripheral hospitals are at least as serious. Many of the buildings are very old, the facilities are poorer than those in the teaching hospitals, and they are less generously staffed. Nonetheless, they provide the bulk of care and treatment up and down the country.

10.54 The redistributional effects of the Resource Allocation Working Party approach to resource allocation will normally work in favour of peripheral hospitals, and the health departments have, with the support of the central medical manpower bodies, been endeavouring to secure a better distribution of medical training posts. The increasing use of non-teaching hospitals in undergraduate medical education is to be welcomed and encouraged, but more teaching facilities and staff will be required if this development is to be fostered. Pressures of work may mean that staff in these hospitals find it difficult to take study leave, and while the needs of the service must of course be placed first, a more generous attitude on the part of health authorities may pay long-term dividends. Measures of this kind will help to break down "us and them" attitudes of staff in hospitals which have in the past been separately managed and financed but which with recent educational developments have become less distinct from the traditional teaching hospitals.

Mental illness hospitals

10.55 In England and Wales there has been a departmental policy to run down and close mental hospitals, replacing them with other facilities. The 1962 Hospital Plan stated that "there will be no place for many of the existing mental hospitals . . . a large number will in course of time be abandoned".[1] It was expected that 13 mental hospitals with over 400 beds each would be closed by 1975. In fact only one large hospital for the mentally ill has been closed in England and Wales, and it has been converted to the care of the mentally handicapped.

10.56 The 1962 Hospital Plan was based on statistical projections of mental hospital populations rather than on a major breakthrough in the prevention or cure of mental illness. There has certainly been considerable progress in treatment, and the number of mental hospital in-patients in England and Wales has fallen from nearly 150,000 in 1955 to 80,000 in 1977. But major mental illnesses, such as schizophrenia, and the dementias of old age, still present intractable problems, and the numbers of the very old and demented are rising steadily in the population, both inside and outside the hospitals.

10.57 It was hoped that the mental hospitals could be replaced by psychiatric units placed in DGHs, supported by small local in-patient units and generally by an enhanced provision of services in the community. The feasibility of this has not yet been demonstrated. The relatively small size of the DGH units, the lack of money to create many more of them, and the nature and extent of the patient populations which the psychiatric services have had to continue to look after, have frustrated the departments' plans. Some DGH units have been selective either in their admission policies or about those for whom they would continue to care, and the mental hospitals have had to receive those patients whom the DGH units have thought were unsuitable in the first place or whom they had failed to cure. In-patient facilities in community hospitals and hostels have not materialized. As we have noted, little or no progress has been made in developing community hospitals, and we understand that only one district has a "hospital hostel" for the long-stay mentally ill.

10.58 The departments' plans have depended heavily also on increased provision for community care by local authorities. Despite a sustained drive to

---

[1] (Cmnd 1604), *Op cit*, paragraph 37.

discharge to and maintain mentally ill people in the community, the build up of the necessary social services has been slow. The provision of day centre places in particular has fallen far behind expectations. The capacity of local authorities to develop services, and in particular residential accommodation, for those who are considerably mentally disabled or disturbed may have been over-estimated. Local communities have not always welcomed such developments.

10.59   The DHSS told us that its 1975 White Paper made clear that the closure of mental illness hospitals is not now an objective of their policies:

"We welcome this opportunity to stress that our aim is not the closure or rundown of the mental illness hospitals as such; but rather to replace them with a local and better range of facilities."[1]

And again in its Priorities Consultative Document:

"The closure of mental illness hospitals is *not* in itself an objective of Government policy, and the White Paper stresses that hospitals should not encourage patients to leave unless there are satisfactory arrangements for their support. The possibility of closing a hospital depends both on the existence of the necessary range of health and local authority facilities, and on the length of time for which care must be provided for the hospital's remaining long-stay patients."[2]

We do not find these statements an unambiguous declaration of policy; and probably most of those who work in mental hospitals in England and Wales still believe that they are to be closed at least in the long run. There have been other consequences of a policy which has been unclear or has not been carried through. New hospitals have not been built and old ones have been inadequately maintained and upgraded. Critics and pressure groups have been encouraged to believe that mental hospitals must have harmful effects on patients and should be abandoned. For example MIND told us:

"Better services for the mentally ill will only be achieved if within the next 10 years we can look forward to the phased closure of the majority of islolated psychiatric hospitals."

It is not surprising that the morale of staff in these hospitals has been damaged, and recruitment to what have seemed to be condemned relics of the past has been affected.

10.60   We are certain that there is a continuing need for most of the mental illness hospitals, and we recommend that the health departments should now state categorically that they no longer expect health authorities to close them unless they are very isolated, in very bad repair or are obviously redundant due to major shifts of population. It should be made clear that they will be required

---

[1]*Better Services for the Mentally Ill.*(Cmnd 6233), London, HMSO, 1975, paragraph 11.5.

[2]*Priorities for Health and Personal Social Services in England: A Consultative Document, Op cit,* paragraph 8.3.

throughout the remainder of this century and for as long ahead as it is possible to plan.

10.61 The placing of psychiatric units in DGHs was a notable development in that it brought the psychiatric services into the main stream of medicine and made provision for the care of mentally ill people who might not otherwise have been willing to seek treatment. But the creation of these units, dealing mainly with the acute and more easily treatable problems, has led to what amounts in many places to a two-tier service a first-rate service, for the acutely ill and a second-rate service for the remainder; and to much resentment in the mental hospitals. It is evident now that both mental hospitals and DGH units are essential to a well-balanced psychiatric service. We suggest that not all acute services should be provided in the latter: there should be some specialisation of function between the two but not entirely on the basis of short or long term treatment and care. Some at least of the staff might rotate between the two institutions or work in both, and both should be used for training and share out-patient and other community facilities.

10.62 Some patients need to be restrained for their own effective treatment and safety or, less often, for the protection of the public. All large mental hospitals should provide for this, and the hospitals should feel confident enough in their purposes and integrity to be able to strike the right balance between freedom and constraint. The prison services are now having to look after a good many men and women who are suffering from an identifiable mental illness, who should be in psychiatric care and are not sufficiently disturbed to require admission to a Special Hospital such Broadmoor. It is the mental hospitals which should take such cases. Some consultants have refused to do so on the grounds that these people are not susceptible to treatment and so do not need their specialist care. Some of the nursing staffs of these hospitals also have been ambivalent towards, or antipathetic to, receiving such patients. It is often said that society has become more violent in its behaviour both outside and inside hospitals; in hospitals it is the nursing staff who receive the brunt of this violence. Despite professional codes of practice, nurses have still felt uncertain about how far they are entitled to restrain violent behaviour, in face of critical public opinion bolstered by well-publicised cases of staff assaults on patients. This is an area of practice where strong medical and nursing leadership could enhance morale and raise levels of tolerance. The provision of regional secure units will provide a valuable base for improving practice through training and research, but they should be introduced on an experimental basis before being generally introduced.

10.63 We realise the great difficulties which those working in mental hospitals have had to face in the past decade or more, with an uncertain future, shortages of staff, a greater degree of patient dependency because of the increasing numbers of old people, and often poor facilities. We believe that given the necessary encouragement and practical assistance they can fully recover their self-confidence.

Mental handicap hospitals

10.64 We have dealt with the provision of services for the mentally handicapped in Chapter 6 and will discuss in Chapter 16 the possibility of these services becoming the responsibility of the local authorities. In addition we are conscious that consultation on the recent Jay Committee report has only just commenced. Here we look briefly at the future of the mental handicap hospitals.

10.65 The position of the mental handicap hospitals is similar in many respects to that of the mental illness hospitals, but there is greater scope for contraction since they have had to care for large numbers of people who did not need hospital care or treatment but were rejected by society. In addition, although the mental handicap hospitals have a growing geriatric population they are not under the same pressure as the mental illness hospitals to admit geriatric cases from the community.

10.66 It seems clear to us that hospital provision will continue to be required for many mentally handicapped people, both children and adults. The Development Team for the Mentally Handicapped classified those in residential care into four groups. Group IV was composed of those with "severe double incontinence, multiple physical handicaps, severe epilepsy, extreme hyperkinetic [i.e. overactive] behaviour, aggression to self and others". The proportion of hospital residents in this group was 54.3% for adults (with 3.5% over 65) and 68.3% for children.[1] Severely mentally handicapped people lack basic self help and self preservative skills and have little verbal capacity. The prospect of transferring these patients to community care seems remote. There is therefore much to be done, in nearly all these hospitals, to make the environment more suitable both for long-term care and for active rehabilitation. It must not be forgotten that for many of these patients, the hospital is their home. The fact that these hospital patients are becoming more disabled, and so more demanding to care for, imposes increasing strain on the staffs looking after them. We are conscious of the recent concern about the standards of care and treatment in some of these hospitals and we comment on this in Chapter 19. It is clear that the staff should be supported in every way: by being given good working conditions and equipment, and the opportunity to keep abreast of the latest methods of treatment and care, through the provision of study leave and secondment; and they should if possible work both in the hospital and in the community parts of the service.

Hospital Buildings

10.67 We noted above that the process of replacing hospitals had been slow, and the strategy subject to variation. Professor Abel-Smith has remarked that:

"Compared to some other advanced countries, particularly those that have enjoyed higher rates of growth, the task of renewing hospitals or replacing them with more appropriate places of care was started late."[2]

---

[1]Development Team for the Mentally Handicapped, *First Report 1976-77*, London, HMSO, 1978, pages 4–5.

[2]Abel-Smith, Brian, *National Health Service: The first thirty years*, London, HMSO, 1978, page 53.

Because piecemeal upgrading and renovation has been carried out in many hospitals, it is misleading to talk in terms of "new" and "old" hospitals, but in England probably about one-third of hospital beds are provided in new or converted accommodation built since 1948. The proportion is higher in Northern Ireland, but lower in Scotland and Wales. On the other hand, a survey undertaken in England of the age of hospitals showed that over one-third of the stock, in terms of floor area, had been originally built before the turn of the century, and that the average age in 1971 was over 61 years.[1]

10.68   Although we do not have reliable information about the age of the hospital stock of other advanced countries, we were told in evidence that generally hospitals in Europe and in North America are expected to have a life of only 25 to 40 years. This was largely confirmed by our experiences abroad; for example in Schleswig-Holstein in West Germany all hospitals built before 1955 will have been replaced by 1982. If this rate of replacement had been accepted in the UK about three-quarters of existing NHS hospitals would already have been pulled down and replaced.

10.69   It should not be assumed that because a building is old it is unsatisfactory. Hospitals put up 50 or 60 years ago were built to last and the fabric may often be perfectly sound. The case for replacing a hospital building is not made when it has been established that it was erected before the introduction of the health service, or even before the turn of the century. The UK is not so wealthy that it can afford to scrap perfectly usable hospitals merely because they are getting old. We should be aiming at making the maximum use of what we have got, and this will often mean adapting, upgrading and extending rather than replacing.

10.70   On the other hand, there may be difficulties in adapting old buildings to modern technology and it may be cheaper in the long run, and better for patients, simply to replace them. Movements in population may have reduced the usefulness of a building in a particular place. For example, it was recognised before the first world war that London was over-provided with hospitals and although a number have been moved out of the centre, the problem is still with us. Elderly buildings are also often gloomy, though they have no monopoly of this, and in many cases, particularly in those for long stay patients, facilities such as kitchens may be antiquated. It hardly needs saying that despite inconvenient, depressing and difficult surroundings the vast majority of hospital staff are giving devoted service to their patients. We visited, for example, a surgical ward, overcrowded and squalid, and yet found nurses and other ward staff cheerfully efficient and surgeons doing excellent work. The replacement or upgrading of such old buildings should lift the spirits both of those who work in and those who use them.

10.71   One aspect of the present position that should be noted is the priority which has been given to acute and maternity services since 1948. For example in England, only 12% of hospital accommodation for mental illness (measured in floor space) has been provided since 1948, 23% of geriatric accommodation and 27% of mental handicap, against 35% for acute units over 200 beds and 44% for maternity.

---

[1] Department of Health and Social Security, *Hospital Maintenance Survey 1972*, (unpublished).

10.72   It is difficult to prove that a particular sum is required to replace our hospitals. A complicated balance has to be struck between the kind of factors referred to above. It should also be remembered that it takes at least ten years to design and build a large hospital by which time there may have been changes in the population served, the other facilities available and medical technology. However, many of those giving us evidence felt strongly that greater funds should be made available to rebuild our hospitals.

10.73   Launching a "crash programme" to modernise our hospitals is often suggested. The idea is that the government would set aside much larger sums of money than have so far been available, earmarked for NHS capital development, to be spent over a relatively short period. Once the programme had been completed, capital spending would return to its previous level. Unfortunately, it is not merely a question of making money available, though of course that is an important consideration. A large and rapid expansion in the hospital building programme would make heavy demands on the architects and engineers employed by health authorities and the building and engineering industries. Furthermore, if the new buildings are not to be wasted, it would be necessary to take account of the consequences for revenue expenditure and reappraise existing plans for health and community services which would have been prepared on the assumption of a lower level of capital expenditure.

10.74   Despite the uncertainties and difficulties alluded to above we recommend that the government should find extra funds to permit much more rapid replacement of hospital buildings than has so far been possible; and, more important, they should stick to their plans. The constant delays and shifts of policy so that a hospital promised is long delayed and then has to be modified or scrapped or cannot be opened because of lack of resources, inevitably leads to staff and public becoming bitter. We hestitate to call it a "crash programme", but we think a planned programme of replacement and upgrading is needed over the next 15 years. This should be a top priority which needs to be tackled jointly by the departments and health authorities, in consultation with local authorities. Initially the emphasis should be on the oldest and worst facilities, whether they are for acute or long-stay patients. We have concentrated on hospitals but what we say applies equally to other NHS buildings.

Hospitals Community Relationships

10.75   We conclude this chapter with a brief discussion of some aspects of the relationships between hospital and community health services. From the patient's point of view it is most important that these services should operate in an integrated and consistent way. The services should be provided so that the patient can move easily from being cared for in the community to hospital, and as he improves, back to the community. This requires good communications between those who work in hospitals and those who work in the community, and some overlap between what might be considered the spheres of responsibility of staff who are hospital or community based. The rehabilitation services exemplify some of the difficulties particularly well. Elsewhere in the report we deal with aspects of community and hospital care, and the relationship between health and local authority services.

10.76　The reorganisation of the NHS was, of course, intended to integrate health services in the community with those in hospitals, but at working level, with which the patient is concerned, the effects will often not have been felt. The employer may be the same but health service workers in the community and in hospitals may still go their own way. The NHS depends heavily on the personal social services – social workers, home helps, etc – provided by local authorities, and is affected by other local authority services, such as housing and education. Close links between the NHS and local authority services are therefore just as necessary as those between hospital and community services.

10.77　There is frequent criticism of communications across the hospital/community boundary: hospital staff complain of patients being referred to them without adequate documentation, and GPs complain of patients being discharged to their care without warning or information. While there are well established conventions between doctors for handing over a patient from hospital to community, or vice-versa, the development of such conventions between nursing staff has been slow. This seems to us to be a point worth following up.

10.78　There are already arrangements for certain community health workers to work in hospitals and hospital workers to work in the community. In Great Britain about 9,000 GPs work for a session or two each week in hospitals, and the introduction of the hospital practitioner grade should make hospital work more attractive in future. There has long been provision for a consultant to visit a patient at home at the request of his GP, but the value of such visits will be reduced if there is no proper consultation between GP and consultant at or after the time of the visit. There is provision, also, for consultant sessions to be held in health centres, though the consultant often cannot function to maximum efficiency without the support of his usual staff and specialist facilities.

10.79　There is little cross-boundary working by other health service workers. Some psychiatric nurses based in a mental hospital may provide a community pyschiatric nursing service for discharged patients and some successful liaison posts have been developed by district nurses and health visitors. In some local hospitals, nurses work both in the hospital and the community. Such developments need to be evaluated and the results made widely known. In addition, some hospital based occupational therapists and physiotherapists undertake domiciliary work, and speech therapists and those concerned with the deaf may be employed either in hospitals or the community, but rarely in both. The need to co-ordinate the flow of information between professionals in the interests of the patients remains all the more important.

Rehabilitation

10.80　Many patients who leave hospital not completely well are capable of looking after themselves with minimal assistance from community workers, and the help of relatives or friends. However, the division between hospital and community services will be particularly important for paients who require long-term rehabilitation. We commissioned a paper from Mildred Blaxter of the MRC Medical Sociology Unit in Aberdeen on the principles and practice of rehabilitation. Her revealing paper, which is reproduced at Appendix G, drew attention to some of the difficulties. She quoted the results of a previous study:

"The consultants observed by Forder *et al*. assumed, quite wrongly, that the GP would ask for advice if he needed it; they assumed, quite wrongly, that the patient's circumstances and family would be already known by the GP; and they assumed, quite wrongly, that the GP would see himself as having a co-ordinating function, and would ensure that rehabilitative and community services swung into action."

Often responsibility for the patient's employment, etc. after leaving hospital remains substantially in the hands of the consultant.

10.81   Mildred Blaxter drew attention also to the dilemma that while the hospital consultant whose "short-term responsibility for the patient and a limited knowledge of his life circumstances, has unlimited power to prescribe therapies, aids and appliances", the general practitioner "with long-term responsibility and potentially better knowledge is unsure of his responsibilities and limited in his access to services". She stressed the importance of the GP being given better facilities and permitted more responsibility for referral to specialist therapies, a view which we would support. This will be particularly important if day-care rehabilitation centres are to be further developed.

10.82   There are a number of other problems in providing rehabilitation services apart from those referred to above. The division between community and local authority services to which we have already drawn attention, and between local authority and voluntary services, give rise to further problems. In particular, the complexity of the various rehabilitation services, and the financial support available, hinder action and themselves generate problems. Mildred Blaxter told us:

"The ludicrous situation has now been reached . . . where the regulations for the conglomeration of benefits, compensation, pensions, special allowances, discretionary payments, and so on . . . fill a fat book."

These divisions were also given as a "major cause of the general dissatisfaction about the aids, appliances and domestic adaptations provided for disabled people." Clearly the need for effective rehabilitation services will increase in the future as provision for caring for patients in the community is further expanded. It seems to us that this must be an important factor in future NHS planning.

10.83   The problems in the relationships between hospital and community health services are not instantly resolvable. Some of them may be ameliorated by the recommendations we make elsewhere. For the rest, we stress their importance to the patient but must leave others to pursue their solutions.

Conclusions and Recommendations

10.84   Most patients are well satisfied with the treatment they receive in NHS hospitals as they are with other parts of the service, but there were two grumbles which were both frequent and long-standing. Patients are not given enough information about their treatment, and despite constant complaints over the years they may still feel they are ignored when doctors discuss them with colleagues. Hospitals persist in waking patients at the crack of dawn.

10.85　We did not hear a great deal about waiting lists in our evidence, and our OPCS survey found that most patients were not caused great distress by waiting for admission to hospital. The significance of waiting lists has certainly been exaggerated, partly for political reasons, and it is waiting *times* which should in any case attract attention. The DHSS have now commissioned a large scale study on the subject and this may throw more light on the matter.

10.86　We have no quarrel with the DGH approach to providing specialist services, though flexibility is plainly required. We think the "nucleus hospital" approach is sensible. There is still dispute over the best use of the many small hospitals which are not part of the DGH. It is clear that the community hospital approach is not acceptable and we were relieved to hear that the DHSS are rethinking the present policy. There is plenty of room for experiment in this as in so many other parts of the NHS, and we would deplore too rigid an approach. The development of nursing homes could make a major contribution to the care of the elderly.

10.87　Acute hospital services are generally excellent. Most of them are provided by peripheral non-teaching hospitals, often in old buildings ungenerously staffed. We hope that our recommendations will improve the position of both those who use them and those who work in them.

10.88　We think the mental illness hospitals need to be rescued. Despite the statement in the DHSS Consultative Document on Priorities, there is a widely held view that the specialist mental hospitals are to disappear. There is no sign of our being able to dispense with them in the foreseeable future. The development of acute psychiatric units in DGHs, itself an admirable development, has tended to leave the mental illness hospitals with the chronic and most difficult patients. They need to be clearly reassured about their future, to be integrated fully into a unified psychiatric service, and to receive a proper share of capital monies.

10.89　Finally, communications between the hospital and the community services are not all that they should be and the arrangements for community workers to work in hospitals and vice-versa need to be improved. Strong links are particularly important in the rehabilitation services.

10.90　We recommend that:

(a) the health departments should promote more research both on the acceptability of day admissions to patients, and on the benefits to the NHS (paragraph 10.19);

(b) all hospitals should provide facilities for patients and relatives to be seen in private (paragraph 10.28);

(c) all hospitals should provide explanatory booklets for patients before they come into hospital (paragraph 10.29);

(d) hospitals should ensure that the availability of amenity beds is routinely made known to patients when they are given a date for admission (paragraph 10.34);

(e) health authorities should review forthwith wakening times for patients in the hospitals for which they are responsible (paragraph 10.38);

(f) the health departments should now state categorically that they no longer expect health authorities to close mental illness hospitals unless they are very isolated, in very bad repair or are obviously redundant due to major shifts of population (paragraph 10.60);

(g) the government should find extra funds to permit much more rapid replacement of hospital buildings than has so far been possible and they should stick to their plans (paragraph 10.74).

Chapter 11 The NHS and the Public

11.1 The interest, support and influence of the public are essential to the well being of the NHS. Nearly all of us are its patients from birth, and over one million of us work in it. Many more contribute as members of health authorities, or through leagues of friends and other voluntary bodies. There has always been a strong tradition of involving the public in the NHS, but specific and separate consumer representation was introduced for the first time at reorganisation in 1974 when community health councils[1] (CHCs) were set up. They were experiments, though inheritors of a long tradition. In this chapter we consider how they are getting on. We also look at arrangements for making suggestions and complaints in the NHS, and the role of informal, but nonetheless important arrangements for voluntary effort in the NHS.

Community Health Councils

11.2 The White Paper on NHS Reorganisation in England defined CHCs as "bodies to represent the views of the consumer". The need for health authorities to know and take account of the views of local communities was emphasised and "lively and continuing interaction between management and the users of the services" identified as being of "benefit to both parties".[2] The NHS reorganisation legislation established a CHC in each health district. In England and Wales half a CHC's members are appointed by local authorities, one-third by voluntary organisations and one-sixth by regional health authorities or their equivalent. In Scotland and Northern Ireland the proportion of local authority members is smaller. Appointments are normally for four years. Finance is provided by Regional Health Authorities (RHAs) in England and areas elsewhere.

Function and role

11.3 The functions of CHCs outlined in the 1972 White Paper and the subsequent DHSS circular on NHS reorganisation[3] included representing the interests of the public in each health district to the area health authority (AHA); contributing ideas on how services should be operated and developed; providing information and advice about formal complaints procedures and monitoring the volume and type of individual complaints as a measure of public satisfaction; and commenting on health authority plans and on proposals

---

[1] Known as local health councils in Scotland and district committees in Northern Ireland.

[2] *NHS Reorganisation: England*, (Cmnd 5055), London, HMSO, 1972, paragraphs 105, 107.

[3] HRC(74)4, *Community Health Councils*: similar functions were identified for Welsh CHCs, local health councils in Scotland and district committees in N Ireland.

to vary services affecting the public (e.g. hospital closures), and on collaboration between health and related local authority services. To help CHCs carry out these functions, they were given statutory powers to secure information, visit hospitals and other institutions and access to health authorities and their senior officers. The DHSS have advised AHAs to allow a CHC representative to attend AHA meetings with the right to speak but not to vote, and to attend family practitioner committee (FPC) meetings, as observers, at the discretion of individual FPCs.

11.4　CHCs were conceived and should be seen as consumer bodies, and not as part of the management machinery of the NHS, but it is evident that in practice this simple principle is not easy to apply. Our evidence reveals much uncertainty and confusion about their role within CHCs and amongst health authorities and other bodies. Conflicting opinions were expressed about how early CHCs should be consulted and whether they should be given a formal part in the decision-making process. The Association of District Councils said:

> "Given a full democratisation of the management of the health service, it would not be necessary to have CHCs and there would be a considerable administrative saving. Short of this it has been suggested to the Association by member councils that the role of the CHCs should be strengthened by giving them some powers of decision in relation to the assessment of priorities."

Not surprisingly the Association of CHCs in England and Wales took a different view in oral evidence:

> "Consumer representation is stronger when it is not involved with management, and some confusion of the representative and management roles is evident amongst members of AHAs: even if a health authority were established at district level there would continue to be a role for CHCs."

11.5　Many CHCs submitting evidence felt that they did not have the power or the resources to fulfil their functions effectively. East Hertfordshire CHC said what many others implied:

> "At the moment there is much criticism of CHCs from some quarters as a waste of money in hard times. If CHCs can achieve nothing in gaining improvements, or even in mitigating hardships, this criticism will be justified. And yet, the system is loaded against the CHC. It has little money, few staff, and no sanctions save those of public opinion."

Indeed, some hostility towards CHCs and the way they interpreted their role was expressed in evidence to us. One district nursing officer said:

> "They watch aggressively and seem permanently to be seeking to find fault with the loyal and hard pressed National Health Service staff on whose patients they are constantly requesting surveys and for whom they offer little, if any, practical help."

However, this point of view was not widespread. Many health authorities commented on the positive part CHCs played in helping to develop health services in their districts.

CHCs at work

11.6   A survey of the activities of 180 CHCs in 1977 gives some idea of the way they went about their work.[1] Three out of four had carried out surveys of local services and most were represented to some degree on NHS planning teams. Almost a third of those in the survey attended Joint Consultative Committee meetings and 30% had been involved in helping complainants to present their cases at service committee hearings. One in four CHCs were allowed to send observers to FPC meetings.

11.7   It is almost impossible to determine from the available evidence whether or not CHCs are fulfilling their functions of representing consumers and channelling local opinions to health authorities, and five years is not long enough for any new institution to realise its full potential. However, some aspects of their role deserve review at this stage.

Informing the public

11.8   It is part of a CHC's role not only to tell people how to complain about services but to contribute ideas for the development of services. To do this they need to inform the public about the availability of local services and propose changes and developments in them. Most CHCs acknowledge that this task is difficult to perform well with limited resources. The siting of CHC offices is also important here and health authorities should encourage them to find "High Street" or easily accessible premises wherever possible.

Monitoring local services

11.9   To do this effectively, CHCs clearly need full access to relevant information. In the main they have the co-operation of health authorities with one major exception. In England and Wales family practitioner committees often appear to resist CHC attempts to assess family practitioner services. Many CHCs told us that this was their greatest stumbling block. We recommend that CHCs should have right of access to FPC meetings and their equivalent in Scotland and Northern Ireland. If FPCs are abolished as we propose in Chapter 20, CHCs should have access to the meetings of the committees which take over FPC functions.

Representing public opinion

11.10   CHCs are better able to pursue the interests of the consumer if they survey opinion about local health services from time to time. Many CHCs have done this, but effective public opinion sampling is expensive and health authorities may not find it easy to meet the costs involved. In addition, if CHCs are to make an effective contribution to the way in which health services

---

[1]"CHCs at Work", *CHC News*, December 1977, pages 6–7.

are provided in the future they need to be fully consulted by health authorities about their plans. They may need more support if they are to assess local health issues effectively. On the other hand, it is not their function to do the health authority's job. A balance has to be struck. We recommend that CHCs are given more resources to enable them to inform the public fully about local services.

Summary

11.11 In our view CHCs have been an experiment which should be supported further along the lines suggested above. They need to be involved at the formative stages of policy development. The health departments should give them more specific advice on the role they are expected to play. If the structural changes recommended in Chapter 20 are introduced it will be important that the close identification of CHCs with relatively small populations is retained.

Suggestions and Complaints Procedures

11.12 It is difficult to write about complaints without giving the impression that the NHS is constantly being criticised by the people who use it, that the normal relationship between patient and health worker is one of confrontation, and that only elaborate procedures will protect the patient from the risks of going to his GP or being admitted to hospital. This is a wholly misleading picture: there are about 200 million contacts between GPs and their patients each year and a similar order of contacts between patients and those who provide dental, pharmaceutical and ophthalmic services. In 1978 there were 1,465 complaints about these services which got as far as a hearing in the UK. Over six million in-patient treatments were provided in hospitals and nearly nine million new out-patients were seen. Written complaints were made by less than one per cent of patients. What we say in the following paragraphs should be read with these figures in mind.

11.13 However well intentioned those who provide the services are, things can go wrong. The NHS is just as liable to human error as any other large organisation. There has to be a mechanism for mistakes to be corrected. This should be seen as a positive contribution to making the NHS more efficient. We have referred in the heading to this section to "suggestions and complaints" and the emphasis should be that way round. Nonetheless, few of us actively welcome suggestions from outsiders about how to do our jobs, however kindly they are meant, and however beneficial to our ultimate welfare they may be. There needs, therefore, to be a simple and well understood mechanism through which people who use the NHS can suggest how it can be improved and complain when things go wrong.

Family practitioner services

11.14 In England and Wales complaints about GPs, dentists, opticians and pharmacists providing NHS services have to be made in writing to the FPC administrator within eight weeks of the event which gave rise to it. An informal procedure also exists which aims to explain and clarify matters and remove misunderstandings between patient and practitioner without resort to the full service committee procedure. Where this informal procedure is used, a lay member of the FPC is appointed to conduct the investigation, with medical advice if necessary, within a fortnight of the complaint being received. If the matter is not resolved there the complaint can be dealt with formally. However, there are many complaints which, not being concerned with breach of contract, fall outside this procedure.

11.15   A formal complaint is referred to the appropriate service committee, whose chairman will initially consider whether a breach of contract is involved. If a hearing is necessary, the complainant and practitioner are invited to present their cases and can call witnesses. Both are allowed to use paid or voluntary help in the preparation of their case, but at the hearing only unpaid "friends" can take part. The decision reached by the service committee can be appealed against by either party to the Secretary of State. If an appeal is made, an oral hearing can be arranged at which both parties are entitled to legal representation. Although there are no separate FPCs in Scotland and Northern Ireland the service committee procedure operates in these countries. In 1978, 1,253 service committee cases were dealt with in England, over half of which were related to general medical practice. A breach of contract was found in just under a third. In the same year 48 cases were dealt with in Wales, 134 in Scotland and 30 in N Ireland.

11.16   It was put to us that this procedure favoured the practitioner because complaints had to be made to those who are responsible for administering the service in question. However, the decision about whether a complaint should be referred to a service committee is made by a layman and the service committee itself has a majority of lay members. Other criticisms are that the service committee cannot require the production of patient records or insist that they should be made available to the complainant to help him to prepare his case and that the time limit of eight weeks for making a complaint is too short. Many feel that the procedures are generally too formal and complicated.

11.17   An approach to tackling these problems was made in a consultative document published by the DHSS in 1978.[1] The proposals provide for an extension of the informal procedure with the aim of removing misunderstandings and attempting to resolve a complaint quickly and simply. Committees for dealing with formal complaints should be independent, the Chairman being selected from a panel of three appointed by the Lord Chancellor from within each region, with voting rights. The service committee would also include two independent members, one lay and one professional. This might go some way to removing the criticism of bias. Service committees would also have the power to ask for the case notes to be released for examination by the complainant. The time limit for submission of complaints would be extended from eight weeks to six months. Finally, in an attempt to simplify the procedure, the DHSS suggested that service committees should be reduced in

---

[1]DHSS proposals for reform of FPC procedures were first circulated to interested bodies in 1976 and were ammended after consultation. Further consultation is now taking place and a White Paper is expected in 1979. The SHHD and DHSS(NI) are closely associated with these developments and the former issued a similar document in 1978.

size from seven to five members (including the chairman and the two independent members), and that oral complaints to an FPC officer should be allowed.

11.18 In general these recommendations, together with proposals to improve publicity and the public's understanding of the complaints procedure, should go a long way to meeting the criticisms of the existing system. However, we have reached no conclusion on the recommendation that case notes should be released to complainants. It can be argued that the release of case notes will often be important when there is dispute about a practitioner's actions, and that in the long run it might lead to greater frankness between doctor and patient. On the other hand, the present confidentiality of case notes allows a practitioner to record fully his impressions and judgments in detail which is of considerable value to himself and others caring for the patient later. The potential release of case notes might in some cases result in the keeping of a brief defensive set of notes with perhaps another set in some other form. We are not convinced that extending the time limit for complaints is necessary. If oral complaints are allowed then eight weeks seems to be an adequate time for formal complaints to be lodged.

Hospital services

11.19 No statutory procedure is laid down for patients to complain about hospital services[1] or make suggestions for improving them. Each health authority has the right to deal with complaints in its own way, subject to guidance from the health departments.[2] If a patient wishes to complain formally about some aspect of the hospital service, he must do so in writing to the district administrator responsible for a particular hospital. Informal complaints or suggestions may be dealt with on the spot by the head of a department. If investigations follow from either kind of complaint, the complainant has to be told of the outcome of the investigation and that he can pursue his complaint with higher authorities if he remains dissatisfied.

11.20 In 1976 there were about 15,600 written complaints resulting from hospital treatments in England and Wales and 1,570 in Scotland in 1975.[3] The Health Service Commissioner received 712 complaints in 1978 although he was able to accept only 138 of these as falling within his terms of reference. There is no record nationally of the number of complaints about hospital services which come into CHC offices, but one estimate suggests that in England and Wales this figure might have been more than 9,000 in 1976.[4] Nor is there any record of complaints made orally.

---

[1]A clearly defined informal procedure has existed in Scotland since 1969 following the report of a working party: Scottish Home and Health Department, *Suggestions and Complaints in Hospitals*, Edinburgh, HMSO, 1969.

[2]HM(66)15 England and Wales 1966. GEN(58) Scotland 1976. HMCs 23/72, 72/71, 26/69 N Ireland.

[3]First Report from the Select Committee on the Parliamentary Commissioner for Administration: *Independent Review of Hospital Complaints in the National Health Service*, London, HMSO, 1977, paragraph 8.

[4]Johnson, M, "Have you heard the one about the fly in the soup?" *Health and Social Services Journal* 8.4.77, page 625.

11.21   The Davies Committee on hospital complaints procedure in England and Wales published its report in 1973.[1] The committee identified gaps in the procedures which they felt were inevitable because existing guidance did not provide properly for handling suggestions and complaints. The main recommendation of the Committee, that health authorities should have a uniform written code of practice for handling complaints in the hospital service, was accepted by the DHSS and the Welsh Office in 1976. After consultation, a code of practice was drawn up which applies to all complaints about health services, except those which relate to family practitioner services. This code is currently being re-drafted by the DHSS in the light of comments made during consultation and is likely to be published later this year.

11.22   A major recommendation of the Davies Committee was that an investigating panel outside the jurisdiction of the Health Service Commissioner should be established in each health service region to investigate complaints, including complaints involving clinical matters. The then Secretary of State asked for a review of the present jurisdiction of the Health Service Commissioner for England, Wales and Scotland, by the Select Committee on the Parliamentary Commissioner. The main reason for this was concern that there might be an overlap of functions between the suggested regional panels and the Health Service Commissioner which would lead to confusion.

11.23   The Select Committee's report, "An Independent Review of Hospital Complaints in the NHS", was published in 1977 and criticised existing procedures and mechanisms on the grounds that they were complicated, fragmented and slow. The Committee also felt that when difficult cases occurred (almost always cases with a clinical element) the enquiry procedures used had sometimes been disquieting. A further criticism was that even after using existing procedures many complainants were left dissatisfied. The Committee concluded that "a more radical approach is needed, scrapping much of the existing structure and replacing it with something better".[2] The report included the recommendation that there should be a simple, straightforward system for handling complaints in every hospital with the emphasis on listening carefully to the patient's or relative's concern and dealing with it promptly. All other cases not resolved in this way, including clinical matters, should be referrable by the complainant or the health authority to the Health Service Commissioner.

11.24   The main criticisms of existing arrangements made to us were similar; that there was no single established procedure; that procedures were complicated and slow; and that there was no recognised or simple procedure for an external review. We find ourselves here in the position of having to repeat much of what the two other enquiries (the Davies Committee and the Select Committee on the Parliamentary Commissioner for Administration) have already said. There is an undoubted need for a single straightforward complaints procedure. This will be facilitated by the abolition of FPCs in England and Wales which we recommend in Chapter 20.

---

[1]Department of Health and Social Security, and Welsh Office, *Report of the Committee on Hospital Complaints Procedures*, London, HMSO, 1973.

[2]First Report from the Select Committee on the Parliamentary Commissioner for Administration, *Op cit*, paragraph 40.

11.25   Since no procedure is likely to be known or immediately understandable to all who might have cause to use it, there is a good case for making the CHCs' role in complaints procedures a more active one. We suggest that in the literature supplied by hospitals informing patients of suggestions and complaints procedures the name and telephone number of local CHC offices is given prominence, together with a statement that patients can seek advice about procedures from them. CHCs should make it their business to ensure that this kind of information is readily available in all their local hospitals. However, it may be possible for CHCs to undertake a more active role as adviser and "friend" in complaints procedures only at the expense of other important aspects of their work. The full burden of the extra work should not fall on CHC secretaries; members or other volunteers might act as the patient's friend if they are adequately briefed. More resources may be necessary in some areas if these changes are to be introduced and we so recommend.

11.26   If CHCs are to develop their role as patients' friends, we suggest experiments with "patient advocates", on the lines of those in the USA. The advocate's function would be to take up problems as they arose with the person or department responsible quickly and informally. He or she would be based at a hospital or health centre, and would be a paid employee, part-time or full-time, of the CHC.

11.27   In all this we emphasise that CHCs should not seek to encourage and advance irresponsible or trivial complaints. Although it seems clear that the great majority of complainants are not acting maliciously, every care should be taken not to encourage those who do not have genuine grievances.

11.28   All complaints procedures should include adequate informal arrangements for settling small problems and resolving trivial disputes. The Davies Committee made suggestions for procedures at hospital ward and departmental level which would encourage patients to make suggestions and which we hope to see included in the code of practice. FPC arrangements already include informal procedures which will be strengthened by the implementation of the recommendation (made in the DHSS consultative document) to allow oral complaints.

11.29   We agree with the Select Committee's recommendation that the Health Service Commissioner should be allowed to accept cases involving clinical matters. We recognise the difficulties involved and it is important to ensure that patients do not use the Health Service Commissioner procedure as a trial run to collect evidence for taking legal action. Both the Davies Committee and the Select Committee acknowledged this risk, and the latter said:

"We are deeply concerned about this problem of double jeopardy and see no complete solution to it ... The only more definite means of alleviating the danger of double jeopardy is to insert a statutory bar to the courts when a complainant elects to ask the Commissioner to investigate his case. There are some relevant precedents but we ourselves doubt whether this is feasible or desirable. Therefore some danger of double jeopardy must remain. It will continue to be one of the many difficulties of the Health Service Commissioner's task to minimise this danger."[1]

In his evidence to the Select Committee the then Commissioner said that he did not know of a case having been taken to court after he had dealt with it. He subsequently notified the Committee of one such case. We share the concern of the Select Committee on this issue but feel, as they did, that an independent mechanism for the review of such complaints is necessary.

11.30   Complaints procedures may operate against the best interests of patients. Whatever procedures are devised most patients will remain hesitant about using them, and this is why informal arrangements and sympathetic staff attitudes are so important. Equally important is the need to develop an effective role for CHCs, not simply as an aid to complainants, but on the much wider front of influencing health service provision to meet the needs of patients. We think that if their role is clarified and strengthened along the lines suggested earlier in this chapter, they will be able more easily to represent the views of the consumer and fulfil the functions envisaged for them at reorganisation more effectively.

The Voluntary Contribution

11.31   We have received a great deal of evidence from voluntary organisations and others pointing to the unique and varied contribution made by volunteers to the NHS. The Volunteer Centre identified in its evidence nine types of activities through which voluntary organisations and individual volunteers help the NHS. They were: befriending patients; providing skilled help in occupational therapy; providing specific services like canteens, libraries and trolley shops; entertaining patients; fund raising; setting up special interest groups, for example for mentally handicapped patients; running self or mutual help groups; engaging in pressure group activities; and pioneering new forms of care. The health departments recognise this contribution and encourage it by making grants to national organisations to enable them to extend the range of their activities or simply to continue their work when other sources of income are inadequate.[2] Local organisations and effort probably make an even larger contribution to services in their area.

11.32   There can sometimes be difficulties in using volunteers. Permanent staff may, for example, resent them, seeing them as a potential threat in the market for labour and occasionally volunteers can make their work more difficult. The haphazard use of volunteers is obviously unwise and their activities need to be co-ordinated carefully. Many health authorities have appointed voluntary service organisers to ensure that this is done. Some training of volunteers may be useful. One of the most valuable contributions made by voluntary organisations is to initiate new methods of local service provision and they should be left to get on with this without undue interference

---

[1]First report from the Select Committee on the Parliamentary Commissioner for Administration, *Op cit*, paragraphs 38–39.

[2]In 1978/79 the health departments' grants to voluntary organisations totalled about £1.5m.

and without well-meaning attempts to professionalise their activities. In some areas, for example, volunteers arrange medicine deliveries for people who cannot get to the chemist, and voluntary organisations have long been pioneers in the provision of hostels. We recommend that health departments and health authorities continue to give financial support and to encourage voluntary effort in the NHS.

11.33 A variation in voluntary work in the NHS is self-help groups and organisations. There are many such groups in the UK at the present time. The contribution they make to patients suffering from particular diseases and to the development of services for them, is considerable.

11.34 Another recent development has been the establishment of patient committees in individual health centres and group practices. Their development seems to have been spontaneous resulting from the desire of one or two GPs to improve their service in line with patients' suggestions. There are now about 20 patient committees in England and Wales with a National Association. There are local variations in function and composition, but their general aim is to encourage health professionals and patients to meet informally and work together to improve services. Patients can make suggestions and voice complaints in an accessible and relaxed forum. Patient committees are an interesting development and may offer opportunities for the advancement of health education and community care in the local setting but they need initiative from both doctors and patients. Most of them, up to now, have been set up by highly motivated doctors and seldom in practices where there is a real need for developing a dialogue between doctors and patients. We would like to see positive steps taken to encourage the setting up of such committees and recommend that financial support should be given to enable them to get off the ground.

Conclusions and Recommendations

11.35 Since their introduction at reorganisation CHCs have made an important contribution towards ensuring that local public opinion is represented to health service management. They need additional resources to fulfil this task more effectively, and further guidance from the health departments on their role.

11.36 It is very important that patients should be able to make suggestions for improving health services. Those who have complaints about the way the NHS has treated them or their relatives must also be able to make them through a simple, fair and effective mechanism. The changes in procedures which we have discussed are likely to improve matters considerably.

11.37 The contribution made by the public, voluntary bodies and volunteers is of major benefit to the service. It should be encouraged. The development of informal patient committees is a constructive way of bringing patient views to bear on the provision of neighbourhood primary care services.

11.38 We recommend that:

(a) CHCs should have right of access to FPC meetings and their equivalent in Scotland and Northern Ireland. If FPCs are abolished as we propose in Chapter 20, CHCs should have access to the committees which take over their functions (paragraph 11.9);

(b) CHCs should be given more resources to enable them to inform the public fully about local services (paragraph 11.10);

(c) more resources should be made available where necessary to allow CHCs to act as the "patients' friend" in complaints procedures (paragraphs 11.25 and 11.26);

(d) health departments and health authorities should continue to give financial support and to encourage voluntary effort in the NHS (paragraph 11.32);

(e) financial support should be given to encourage the setting up of patient committees in general practice (paragraph 11.34).

Part III The NHS and its Workers

The chapters which follow deal for the most part with matters which concern directly those who work in the NHS, and concern patients somewhat less directly. Those who have read our earlier chapters will know that we see this to a large degree as a somewhat artificial distinction, but it is a convenient one. There are issues where the interests of patients and of those who work in the NHS conflict, and we deal with one such – industrial strife – in Chapter 12. But it is in everyone's interest that patients should be cared for to the best of the ability of those whose high responsibility this is.

Chapter 12   General Manpower Questions

12.1   This chapter deals with some important general matters affecting NHS workers. We begin with a discussion of the difficult issue of morale, a matter on which we have received much evidence. This leads on to the related issue of industrial relations. We then consider the way NHS workers see their roles and the way they relate to one another. Next we deal with methods of measuring and controlling the quality of the work done by NHS staff and the problems of manpower planning. We finish with a discussion about occupational health services for NHS staff.

Morale

12.2   We said in Chapter 4 that we did not think that the NHS was about to collapse because of the low morale of people who work in it, though some have tried to persuade us of this and many have told us that it is dangerously low. Professor Kogan's study unequivocally supports the view that morale is low. But morale is difficult to assess, and our view is that while it is lower than we should like to see it, low morale is curiously patchy in its distribution, geographically and among different groups of workers. We set out below what we see as some of the main general causes of low morale amongst NHS workers.

12.3   The following factors affect all sorts and grades of NHS workers to a greater or lesser extent:

> *the short-term effects of reorganisation* – whatever the long-term merits of reorganisation, it is certain that in the short-term the changes in the organisation of the NHS, and of key administrators in it, led to extensive dislocation of work. Although relatively few staff were directly affected by reorganisation in the sense of having to change jobs, the effects were widely felt. Traditional loyalties were broken. Another aspect of this is the disappointment of many NHS workers that the long heralded reorganisation has achieved so little of what it set out to do. It could well be that in the short-term Professor Kogan was correct in saying:
>
>> "The disappointments expressed about reorganisation may say as much about unrealistic expectations as they do about what is happening";[1]
>
> *the country's economic difficulties* – NHS workers have been affected by

---

[1] Kogan, Maurice, *et al, The Working of the National Health Service,* The Royal Commission on the National Health Service, Research Paper Number 1, London, HMSO, 1978, paragraph 1.18.

inflation like everyone else and they have also seen the effects on staffing levels and buildings of continuing public expenditure restraint;

changing roles and relationships – quite apart from the stresses and strains of reorganisation, the NHS has been subject to pressures arising from changes in attitudes of those who work in the service. Obvious examples are the increasing use of industrial action at all levels, and the growth in influence of nurses and other groups in decisions about the management of services and the treatment of patients;

criticism of the NHS – unfortunately bad news about the NHS is more likely to be prominently featured in newspapers and elsewhere than good news. However well intentioned criticism of this kind may be, its cumulative effect is to undermine the confidence staff feel in what they are doing. An example of this, which we mentioned in Chapter 4 and refer to again below, is the constant criticism of administrators and administration which has certainly had a most damaging effect.

12.4   Nearly half the evidence submissions which mentioned low morale in the NHS were from doctors. Doctors are important in any discussion of morale because of their influence on other groups of staff. Some consultants felt that their position had been adversely affected by the increasing influence of other hospital staff and the development of an explicitly multi-disciplinary approach to patient care. As one of the best paid groups of health workers, consultants had been considerably affected by pay restraint (though no more than others in the public service at their pay levels), and this had been made no easier to bear by the introduction of the junior doctors' new contract which resulted in some junior doctors' earnings exceeding those of some consultants. Again, many doctors had been deeply disturbed by government decisions about the NHS, which they regarded as often having been taken for political reasons. These include the phasing out of pay beds which we deal with in Chapter 18, and the health departments' priorities for the NHS. Many doctors were critical of these decisions and felt that they were arrived at without adequate consultation. Some also felt that the development of a stronger consumer influence, for example through CHCs, and the more critical attitude towards doctors and other health service workers it encourages, had undermined their position.

12.5   NHS reorganisation was an administrative measure, and administrators have had more than their fair share of difficulties since it took place. They have carried much of the burden of making the new system work, and have been the main recipients of criticism when it does not. The increase in their numbers, dealt with in Chapter 4, has been the subject of criticism both within and without the service. The more senior among them suffered the stresses of applying for jobs in the reorganised service, which clinical staff did not, and one of the consequences was that many found themselves in new places dealing with unfamiliar problems, with no established administrative machine to help them. Finally, uncertainty about the future structure of the service remains. As the Institute of Health Service Administrators said to us:

"Despite government assurances that no further major reorganisation is contemplated in the short term, many AHAs are actively discussing radical change at local level and the spectre of change resulting from devolution and the Royal Commission itself has appeared on the scene. In such a climate of uncertainty it is little wonder that morale is low."

12.6   Other groups of staff have their own particular problems, and we have referred to doctors and administrators as illustrations of the importance of the particular circumstances of individual groups in any general discussion of morale. We attempt to deal in later chapters with some of the problems raised, but it is obvious that there is no panacea: each grievance needs to be considered separately. We hope that the recommendations we make elsewhere in this report will, if they are implemented, make some contribution towards a more contented workforce in the NHS.

Industrial Relations

12.7   There is no doubt about the importance of good industrial relations to patient and health service worker alike. This is a difficult and complicated area, and we are conscious that we shall not contribute much to the discussion simply by striking moral postures. In many respects the NHS is quite unlike industry, but some of its industrial relations problems are reflections of national problems which require national solutions. It is apparent, too, that health workers have felt that the NHS has not dealt fairly with them, and this can be seen in their attitude to the service. We hope that the suggestions we make below will help to dissipate this feeling. The importance of enlisting the support and harnessing the idealism of NHS staff cannot be over-emphasised.

12.8   The success or failure of industrial relations is often measured by the frequency of industrial action. This is not a particularly good criterion and is in any case imprecise. There are many kinds of industrial action other than complete withdrawal of labour which can seriously dislocate the service – working to rule, going slow, and selective refusal to co-operate with management are common enough examples. The failure to stimulate the enthusiasm of health workers, or to make the best use of their talents cannot be measured in these terms.

12.9   Table 12.1 gives some figures about strike action in the NHS and compares the average number of days lost per 1,000 workers in the NHS and in Great Britain as a whole. These are the only figures of industrial action available, a fact which reflects the difficulties of definition in this field. The table is to be studied with the reservations referred to above prominently in mind. In terms of days lost it suggests that the NHS has a much better record than the country as a whole. It also suggests that numbers of stoppages and days lost have increased markedly in the last decade.

12.10   As the largest employer in the country, the NHS will be affected by the same developments which affect other workers in the UK. The most obvious of these in recent years has been the government's strict control of wages at a time of high inflation. Second, there has been an expansion of trade union membership amongst professional and white collar workers, including those in the NHS.

162

TABLE 12.1

Comparison of Days lost through Strike Action in the NHS with the Workforce as a Whole: Great Britain 1966–1977

Year	Number of NHS staff	Number of stoppages	Number of staff involved	Number of days lost	Average number of days lost per 1,000 NHS staff	Average no. of days lost per 1,000 employees in Great Britain
1966	728,838	2	500	500	0.69	100.0
1967	753,486	1	78	200	0.27	124.7
1968	761,747	1	80	80	0.11	211.4
1969	778,998	8	2,500	7,000	8.99	309.1
1970	792,307	5	1,300	6,700	8.46	499.2
1971	799,673	6	2,900	4,700	5.88	625.9
1972	831,753	4	97,000	98,000	117.8	1,104.3
1973	843,119	18	59,000	298,000	353.5	324.4
1974	859,468	18	4,070	23,000	26.84	661.5
1975	914,068	19	6,000	20,000	21.88	270.6
1976	945,877	15	4,440	15,000	15.86	149.3
1977	970,900	21	2,970	8,200	8.44	448.0

Source: compiled from statistics provided by health departments and the Department of Employment.

Third, the attitudes of professionals to their work has been changing. In the NHS this may be seen in the departure from an open commitment form of contract for junior hospital doctors and dentists, which may be followed by consultants and GPs; and their willingness to take industrial action. Finally, health workers and others in the public service have seen workers in other industries apparently benefiting from strike action. Some of the factors peculiar to the NHS were referred to in paragraph 12.3 above.

12.11   Unfortunately the NHS has so far lacked a systematic approach to dealing with industrial relations problems which arise at local level. This was borne out by a memorandum prepared for us by the Advisory, Conciliation and Arbitration Service (ACAS), with which the health departments were broadly in agreement, and which is reproduced in full at Appendix H. It identified a number of weaknesses in existing arrangements. Clarification of management relationships and responsibilities – not only for industrial relations – would itself be an important step forward. Personnel officers often lacked experience, some districts were without a district personnel officer, and where one had been appointed he might not get adequate support from the district management team. There were defects on the trade union side also. There were inter-union rivalries over recruitment and areas of influence, and in a few places there were problems with participation in local machinery. Machinery for settling disputes at district level was often lacking, but the Whitley Councils were too remote to deal with local problems. The ACAS memorandum emphasised the need for better industrial relations training for both staff representatives and management, including health authority members who are increasingly involved in industrial relations matters, and we recommend that the health departments and staff organisations and unions give this urgent attention.

12.12 Other evidence and Professor Kogan's report confirmed many of ACAS's conclusions. ACAS summed up their evidence as follows:

"In our view the NHS has reached the stage where it should review its IR policies and practices. Unless effective remedies are introduced urgently, we can see little prospect of avoiding continued deterioration in IR with associated frustration of management and staff, increased labour turnover, and noticeably poorer quality patient care."

A number of detailed recommendations are made in the ACAS memorandum and we commend them to the health departments. A recent and welcome development in Northern Ireland is the employment of the Labour Relations Agency, the Northern Ireland equivalent of ACAS, to carry out a review of industrial relations in the health and personal social services.

12.13 The weaknesses in arrangements in the NHS for dealing with local disputes were the subject of a series of meetings held last year by the then Secretary of State for Social Services with representatives of health authorities, the professions and health service unions. The outcome was a draft procedure for dealing with disputes at local level. It was proposed that so far as possible disputes should be dealt with where they occurred. Those that could not be resolved at that level would be referred to area, and if necessary to regional disputes panels. If all else failed it would be open to either party to refer the dispute to ACAS. The proposals are currently being considered by the General Whitley Council and we hope that an agreed procedure can be reached very soon.

Whitley Councils

12.14 At national level, pay and conditions of service are negotiated for most staff by the Whitley Councils. They were established early in the life of the NHS, and there are at present eight functional councils in operation, each dealing with a particular group of staff, and the General Whitley Council which deals with matters common to all. Each council is composed of representatives of staff and management, including the health departments who also provide the secretariat to the management side. They cover England, Scotland and Wales; in Northern Ireland there is comparable machinery which ensures that agreements reached for Great Britain are followed closely. Between them the Whitley Councils cover all NHS staff, except doctors and dentists and a comparatively small number of other NHS workers who negotiate directly with the health departments. Doctors' and dentists' remuneration is subject to the recommendations of the Doctors' and Dentists' Review Body. Regulations require health authorities to apply the terms of agreements reached when they have been approved by the health ministers, who, in effect, have power of veto over arrangements, though this is rarely directly used.

12.15   A number of criticisms of the Whitley Councils were made to us in evidence. The Association of Scientific and Technical and Managerial Staffs told us that:

"The present Whitley Council system should be replaced by proper collective bargaining structures, including agreed procedures for settling problems at the workplace."

but this was not the generally held view, and most complaints were about the lack of flexibility in the agreements to meet local needs, the complexity of the agreements themselves, and delays in reaching them. The Association of Chief Administrators commented:

"there must be an improvement in the 'quality' of the agreements reached by the Whitley Councils. Many of the agreements reached in the past have proved to be complicated to apply, with resultant confusion and discontent, thus aggravating the industrial relations situation. The greatest step towards improving the quality of the agreements would be a more informed and co-ordinated Management Side of the Whitley Councils. Second in importance to the quality of the agreements, is the need for speed and clarity in the communication from the Whitley Council to local management of agreements reached."

12.16   There are some general comments we should like to make. First, it seems to us that a Whitley Council system of some kind is needed in the NHS for the great majority of staff. Standardised, centrally negotiated terms and conditions promote the unity of a national service and relieve staff and management of the complexities of local bargaining on basic matters such as pay and hours of work. However, some questions need to be settled locally, and it may not be easy to decide where the line between central and local negotiations should be drawn. There is also the perennial difficulty of leaving sufficient flexibility in national agreements to enable local problems to be overcome. This is why the involvement of representatives of NHS management in negotiation is particularly important.

12.17   Second, we see no escape from government involvement in negotiations. The Society of Radiographers said to us:

"It has been a constant source of irritation to the Society that the majority of members of the Management Side appear to have little or no control over the total amount of money available. The Society believes that this has often prevented serious negotiation from taking place ... We believe that if negotiation is to have any real meaning then all the Management Side members must be able to take a full part in negotiations and not be over-ruled by a few powerful DHSS members."

However, in a public service the size of the NHS, almost wholly Exchequer financed, and in which 70% of expenditure is on staffing, the government has a duty to the taxpayer to keep a close watch on negotiations. This would be true even if there were not a defined government incomes policy which often requires interpretation in individual cases.

165

12.18   Third, a weakness of the existing arrangements is that the government apparently acts as both judge and prosecuting counsel in disputes about NHS pay and conditions: the health departments are represented on the Whitley Councils and the final arbiters on matters not settled there are the central departments.[1] This has made the idea of an independent commission or review body to deal with pay seem more attractive. The Doctors' and Dentists' Review body is one example, and the Standing Commission on Pay Comparability in the public sector proposed by the last government is another. Other approaches of this kind in the past were represented by the Industrial Court and National Board for Prices and Incomes.

12.19   The Whitley Council system was reviewed in detail by Lord McCarthy in 1976,[2] and his recommendations were subsequently widely discussed. The main points about Whitley Councils made to us in evidence were dealt with in his review. We consider that changes are needed to streamline the system generally, and, in particular, reduce the lengthy periods sometimes taken to reach agreements. Such delays may be resented by the staff concerned and may themselves lead to disputes.

Avoidance of industrial action

12.20   Those who work in the NHS have special responsibilities towards patients, and it is clear that the great majority are conscious of this. It is essential that they should be, but it is equally important that the government should not take advantage, or seem to take advantage, of the obligation health workers feel towards patients. We have already noted that some health workers feel that the NHS has not dealt fairly with them. When disputes occur the fault is unlikely to be wholly on one side or the other. It is too soon to forget the sad events of last winter, but the object should be not to apportion blame but to prevent them occurring again.

12.21   A suggestion made is that NHS workers should forego the right to strike, for example in exchange for compulsory arbitration. While this looks attractive at first sight, we do not think it goes to the root of the problem, or could provide a guarantee of industrial peace. Health workers, like other workers, will not find it necessary to take industrial action if they are satisfied with the arrangements for settling disputes over pay and conditions of service and if disputes which have arisen are seen to be fairly dealt with. If they are not so satisfied, it seems unlikely that the outlawing of industrial action could be made to stick. In the future, workers would not necessarily consider themselves bound by an agreement reached by their predecessors, possibly in different circumstances. There might be difficulties in defining what counted as industrial action. But although it is easy to write down these arguments against agreements of this kind, the benefits which would result both for patients and those who serve them are so great we would not want to dismiss the possibility out of hand, and would encourage those who might have the essential will and tenacity to see such agreements made.

---

[1]These are the Civil Service Department, the Department of Employment and the Treasury.

[2]McCarthy, Lord, *Making Whitley Work. A review of the operation of the National Health Service Whitley Council System,* London, HMSO, 1976.

12.22 We have referred to some of the weaknesses in arrangements for settling disputes at local level, and welcomed the procedures proposed for dealing with them. Procedures need also to be worked out for dealing with national disputes. They need to be rapid and generally understood if they are to be effective. Such procedures cannot be worked out when industrial action is taking place: they have to be discussed coolly and agreed when a broad view is possible. Because pay is such an important factor in national industrial disputes, the arrangements for settling disputes need to be linked to those for negotiating or determining pay.

12.23 We consider that a review is needed of the arrangements for negotiating pay and settling disputes at national level. We do not think this can be undertaken by the General Whitley Council, both because the review should cover the role of Whitley Councils themselves, and because it should include all groups of NHS workers some of whom are not represented in the Whitley Council machinery. It would be possible to establish a committee for this purpose, or to remit the responsibility to the Secretary of State for Social Services, but the talking has to start somewhere. We would ourselves suggest that the Secretary of State should reserve his position initially because in the end it is he who has to speak for the patient. On the other hand we were impressed by the progress last winter of the discussions mounted by the TUC with its affiliated unions and other bodies to work towards a national disputes procedure.

12.24 We therefore recommend that the TUC should take the necessary steps in initiating discussions which must involve not only those bodies affiliated to the TUC but bodies representing the interests of other NHS workers as well. Once a basis for wider discussion had been established, it might be helpful for a wider range of opinion to be brought to bear, perhaps at a series of conferences involving NHS management as well as staff interests. The object would be to recommend agreed procedures to the Secretaries of State. The method of reaching that objective would depend on progress made.

12.25 We do not attempt to predict the outcome of the discussions we propose should be launched, but two matters seem to us certain. First, the process we have sketched will take a considerable time, certainly months and quite possibly more than a year. It should be started as soon as possible, but it cannot be rushed. It requires patience and goodwill from those concerned, and above all a determination to succeed. Second, the eventual outcome will not seem startling or even novel in its basic approach. There are no magic wands to be waved in this field. It will be important that those most closely involved in the exercise should not start with preconceptions of its outcome. An approach which has been unsuccessful in the past may turn out to be acceptable today.

Roles and Relationships

Flexibility

12.26 The role of health workers is subject to many kinds of change but particularly those brought about by developments in techniques in health care. As the Regional Medical Officers told us:

"The character of health care is constantly changing, sometimes rapidly and extensively, more often quietly and imperceptibly, and this condition in turn gives rise to a continuous although unstructured process in which tasks and functions are redistributed between professions."

To meet these changes staffing structures need to be flexible and so must be the attitude NHS workers adopt to their roles. Staff should be prepared to take on new work, if necessary with additional training or retraining, and be given the incentives to do so. Duties need to be defined, but not over zealously provided responsibilities are clear. In a service in which resources are in short supply it is also important that aides and unqualified staff should be used where possible, releasing skilled workers for jobs which require their expertise. The attitude of both staff and management should be one of encouragement towards innovation and experiment in the use of staff.

12.27 It is easier to advocate flexibility than to achieve it. The heavy investment in existing personnel, training syllabuses and institutions, Whitley Council agreements and professional codes of practice ensures that even the most marginal changes in activity are often extremely difficult to achieve. Staff may feel that their jobs are at risk, particularly in times of high unemployment, and that their status may be eroded if their traditional functions are not jealously guarded. In a few cases there may be legal problems.

12.28 One illustration of the difficulties can be seen in the efforts to amalgamate the professions of remedial gymnastics and physiotherapy. There are about the equivalent of 350 remedial gymnasts employed in the NHS in the UK. They have only one training school. The differences between the training, qualifications and activities of a remedial gymnast and physiotherapist are marginal. The Report of the McMillan Committee, on which both physiotherapists and remedial gymnasts were represented, said "Although each has a particular contribution to make, we recognise that there are great similarities between them",[1] and went on to recommend that the two professions should amalgamate. Despite this recommendatioin and the encouragement of the health departments, amalgamation has still not occurred.

12.29 The Institute of Health Service Administrators drew our attention to the growth of professionalism in the NHS:

"The high degree of professionalism in the NHS, which is fundamentally good, does, however, generate problems of using staff flexibly as skills become increasingly narrow. The pathology service provides a good example of this. The various branches of pathology are now largely separated and the professional and technical staff are no longer interchangeable."

They went on to suggest that:

---

[1] Department of Health and Social Security, *The Remedial Professions,* London, HMSO, 1973, paragraph 8.

"The professional ethic is dominant in the NHS and leads quite naturally to the desire of non-professional staff to achieve this status. Specialist training has developed in a wide range of fields – theatre attendants, mortuary attendants, porters and many groups in the scientific fields. Whilst there is little doubt that the NHS has benefited from these increased skills, it has meant that the total manpower available is increasingly more difficult to re-deploy without re-training."

The Institute saw the development of common-core training schemes[1] as a way of encouraging flexibility between staff groups.

12.30   We think that it is certainly "in the interests both of the patients and of those who work in the NHS" that health workers, be they doctors, nurses or ambulancemen, serving the patient should feel pride in their work, should feel their jobs to be worthwhile and well-regarded, and should practise them to the best of their ability. But it will be the exception rather than the rule that patients will be looked after by only one kind of health worker, and if those caring for them are more concerned with their own status than the patients' health and well being then the patients will be the losers.

12.31   At the same time staff will want to know what their broad responsibilities and duties are. In a team working closely together, for example, the surgeons, anaesthetists, nurses and orderlies working in an operating theatre, this should not be a problem, but in a less defined and constrained environment uncertainty about role can lead to trouble.

12.32   The solution does not lie in attempts to define precisely the roles of those caring for the patient. An interesting illustration of the difficulties of such an approach is provided by the Dentists Act 1957. This Act defines dentistry with the intention of confining the practice of dentistry to those on the Dental Register. It provides the following definition:

"For the purposes of this Act, the practice of dentistry shall be deemed to include the performance of any such operation and the giving of any such treatment, advice or attendance as is usually performed or given by dentists."[2]

In other words, dentistry is what dentists do. The Medical Acts wisely do not attempt to define medicine or to confine its practice to those on the Medical Register. If they did then the mother who diagnosed measles in her child and the wife who offered her husband aspirin for a headache would soon be in trouble. More seriously, the present-day nurse or physiotherapist now undertakes procedures which the doctor of yesterday would certainly have held to himself.

12.33   We consider it to be extremely important to the interests of the patient that flexibility of roles be exploited and built upon. Of course there will

---

[1]These are schemes where two or more staff groups share those basic parts of their training which are common to all.

[2]*Dentists Act 1957*, Section 33(1).

be procedures which can be undertaken safely only by a nurse trained in a particular way or a doctor with particular skills, and it will be the responsibility of all those caring for the patient to see that nothing but the best standards of care and treatment are offered to him.

12.34 Flexibility in training arrangements is particularly important. The Todd Royal Commission's[1] concept of an initial "general professional training" for doctors, with the emphasis on a common ground of experience and training before specialisation, has not prospered. The opportunities for switching over from one path of specialist education to another, for those uncertain about their career choice or wishing to change it, has not been facilitated. But many doctors still change their decisions about which specialty to pursue, and we think that there should be a further effort to create a wider and more flexible base for their post-graduate education. There is likely also to be an increasing demand for re-training; not only because changes in the need for particular services may require it, but because it may be stimulating for a specialist after a number of years of practice to enlarge or re-direct his interests. Where re-training is not incompatible with the needs of the service, it should be done without financial loss to the individual.

12.35 Another aspect of flexibility is the importance of the NHS making arrangements to employ those with domestic commitments who can only work part-time. Women constitute about 70% of the total NHS workforce, but the proportions vary between different categories of workers. About 90% of nurses, 75% of administrative and clerical staff and about 67% of hospital ancillary workers are women, but only 18% of doctors. Part-time workers account for about half the workforce of hospital ancillary workers and one third of nurses, and the great majority of part-time workers are women. It is obviously extremely important that, relying as heavily as it does on part-time women workers, the NHS should make every effort to ensure that the best use is made of them, and maximum opportunity given to them to work in the health services. This will involve flexible working times, the provision of crêches, and opportunities for part-time training and re-training.

Aides and unqualified staff

12.36 Roughly one-quarter of all nursing staff in the UK are nursing auxiliaries and assistants who at best will have received only a brief in-service training. Substantial numbers of helpers are employed also in occupational therapy (where they outnumber registered staff) and physiotherapy. A few are employed in chiropody, radiography and speech therapy departments and in medical laboratories. The Briggs Committee,[2] the McMillan Working Party[3] and the Quirk Committee on Speech Therapy[4] all supported the use of aides. The Briggs Committee saw them as an indispensable part of nursing teams.

---

[1] *Royal Commission on Medical Education 1965–1968*, (Cmnd 3569), London, HMSO, 1968.

[2] *Report of the Committee on Nursing*, (Cmnd 5115), London, HMSO, 1972.

[3] *The Remedial Professions, Op cit.*

[4] Department of Education and Science, *Speech Therapy Services*, London, HMSO, 1972.

They also noted that the borderline between the role of the qualified and the unqualified nurse was indistinct and liable to change.

12.37　Aides require proper supervision, and there are limits to what unqualified people can be expected to do. In some cases they have been employed in response to shortages of trained staff in particular categories, and while the demand for qualified nursing and para-medical staff remains strong, they are likely to be welcomed by the professions. If there is over-production of trained staff, however, they may be seen as a threat – a cheap way of manning the service. There is already resistance to employing·aides, particularly from dentists, radiographers and the medical laboratory scientific officers. Nonetheless, where there are simple unskilled tasks which cannot be automated, as there are in laboratories, it is wasteful to use skilled staff to perform them. We understand that the introduction of a grade of aides for laboratories has been opposed by the Staff Side of the Whitley Council, and we regret this. The NHS should make the best use it can of the skilled manpower available and we think that more should be done to assess the scope for employing aides for the simpler tasks.

Inter-professional relationships

12.38　Uncertainties over role, the drive for professionalism, developments in the approach to treating patients, and the difficulty of giving guidance on how health professionals should work together in the treatment of patients may all be observed in the evidence we have received about what is referred to as the "multi-disciplinary clinical team" (MDCT). By this is meant a group of colleagues acknowledging a common involvement in the care and treatment of a particular patient. The staff in question may be doctor, nurse, social worker, and members of other disciplines, depending on what is wrong with the patient. The relations between members of the MDCT are unlikely to be formalised. The same questions arise whether one is talking of care in hospital or the community. Some of the problems put to us about the MDCT were questions of leadership, corporate responsibility, legal responsibility and confidentiality of records.

12.39　Most heat is generated over which member of the MDCT is to be regarded as its leader. The BMA told us:

> "No doctor fails to recognise the necessity of co-operation with the nursing profession and with other medical workers and the benefit which he can derive from their experience. But this does not mean that the doctor should in any way hand over his control of the clinical decisions concerning the treatment of his patients to anyone else or to a group or team."

12.40　The question then arises of what are to be regarded as "clinical decisions". In practical terms the decision to operate on a severely injured patient is unlikely to be one to which the social worker, for example, will normally be expected to contribute. At the other end of the spectrum, the decision to discharge an elderly person into the community may depend crucially on the social worker's view of the home circumstances. The Royal College of Nursing told us in oral evidence that:

"In the MDCTs the leadership role should be determined by the situation; in some circumstances, e.g. geriatrics, the nurse may reasonably assume the leadership role in continuing care situations, this currently happens and should be formally recognised."

These examples will probably not be seriously disputed by any of those involved in patient care: it is those in between which seem to cause the difficulty.

12.41   In the past the doctor's long and broad training, and his higher pay and status, made him pre-eminent amongst his non-medical colleagues. Many factors have come together to change this, among them changes in social attitudes and the increasingly sophisticated nature of the training undertaken by other professions. Whereas formerly the doctor probably took most decisions affecting patients on his own, he may now look to the nurse, speech therapist or dietitian for advice on particular aspects of treatment or care. Non-medical members of the MDCT will be experts in their own right, and as we have seen, there will be aspects of care where the doctor is not necessarily the best person to judge the patient's interests. But if he is not, who should be "in charge" of the patient?

12.42   It would be impracticable to answer this question by specifying how an MDCT should work in all circumstances. The possible combinations of staff involvement and patient needs are infinite. In any case, we doubt whether in practice the problem is as difficult as it appears to be in principle. It is sufficiently clear that each health professional is likely to have the last word on matters which are clearly within his professional competence. It is pointless for us to rule on who should be "leader", or indeed whether there should be a team leader in the ordinary sense. We are in no doubt that it is in the patient's interests for multi-disciplinary working to be encouraged, provided that it is clear to the patient or his relatives, and to those professionals involved in his care, where responsibilities lie.

12.43   At national level the health departments do not regard it as their business to determine professional matters, or to settle demarcation disputes that may arise. This function is performed by a number of bodies, including for the medical and dental professions the General Medical and General Dental Councils and the Royal Colleges; for nursing and midwifery, the General Nursing Councils, Royal College of Nursing and Royal College of Midwives; and the Council for Professions Supplementary to Medicine. There are other bodies, statutory and otherwise, that govern other health service professions, and some Whitley Council agreements specify the functions of the staff they cover. What appears to be lacking is a mechanism for considering the functions of the different groups of health service workers looked at together and arbitrating between them. It seems clear to us that management of the NHS involves consideration of the roles of those who work in it, and that this is something to be undertaken by the health departments in consultation with the national bodies responsible for staff matters. We recognise that the handling of differences between the professions as to what their roles should be is, to put it mildly, a delicate matter, but it is one that the departments cannot duck. We recommend that they should intervene on those occasions when the health professions cannot reach agreement.

Measuring and Controlling Quality

12.44 The importance of ensuring high quality of treatment and care offered by those working in the NHS is certainly not something that need be argued. We have referred to the difficulties of measuring the performance of the NHS, and some of the same problems arise over deciding whether the right treatment is being used and the right sort of care given. Medicine is still an inexact science, and many of the procedures used by doctors, nurses and the remedial professions have never been tested for effectiveness. They are used because they have always been used and patients seem to get better. But patients get better anyway in most cases and a particular procedure or treatment hallowed by time and use may have little to do with it: certainly, the fact that one procedure helps does not mean that another procedure may not help more.[1]

12.45 In attempting to measure quality of care the first thing is to establish standards. This is by no means easy. The obvious approach is to assess the outcome of treatment or care – is the patient better as a result of whatever treatment he has received? But the difficulties we refer to in Chapter 3 of defining and measuring health arise here also. The end product of health care must be the benefit to the patient. Uncertainties about whether and how far a patient has improved and what his improvement has been due to, or whether he has been well cared for, will be reflected in difficulties of establishing standards or norms for staffing or procedures.

12.46 It is usually accepted that data about quality of health care may be of three types:

input – the resources used, mainly staff and institutions, but including such factors as the type and qualifications of staff and the accessibility and equipment of institutions;

process – what is done to the patient under treatment, which includes diagnosis and care, and the after-care given;

outcome – the effects of treatment and care, or the lack of it, on the patient.

These three approaches to the measurement of quality are linked. A favourable outcome to treatment depends on sufficient input of resources and the right processes being used. The old joke that "the operation was a success but the patient died" illustrates the risk of concentrating on process at the expense of outcome. An increasingly important consideration is the cost effectiveness of treatment. The development of sophisticated procedures, often extremely

---

[1]See, for example, Cochrane, A L, *Effectiveness and Efficiency. Random Reflections on Health Services,* London, Nuffield Provincial Hospitals Trust, 1972.

expensive in terms of staff and equipment, poses special problems. This is an aspect which cannot be ignored.

12.47 It is not easy to set national standards for any of these aspects of quality of care, even for input. It is easy to count hospital beds and numbers of staff, but attempts to set norms have usually met with failure or at best a good deal of resistance. Part of the problem is the difficulty of determining the need for services. The demand for services may not accurately reflect need, and may be internal, deriving from the health professions and reflecting in part perhaps a wish for extended career opportunities. Another aspect of the problem is the way health services have developed locally: hospital beds may be plentiful in some areas and the pattern of treatment and manning may reflect this. Some types of staff may be in short supply in particular areas. Trends in treatment change.

12.48 A number of techniques have been developed to assist evaluation of quality of care. One method of measuring the outcome of treatment is the randomised controlled trial (RCT) which is a method of obtaining a bias free result in comparing two treatments, or a treatment with no treatment. Professor Cochrane told us:

"there are large areas very much neglected, e.g. GP prescribing, length of hospital stay, and place of treatment, or looking at it from another angle Psychotherapy, Physiotherapy, Rehabilitation, Dermatology, Geriatrics and Obstetrics (although the situation in Obstetrics seems likely to be remedied in the near future)."

Large scale studies of this kind raise many practical problems. Large numbers of patients may be involved. Studies may take several years to set up and carry through, and reliable measures of outcome will be required. Studies of this kind may also raise ethical problems: a doctor's obligation is primarily to his individual patient, but if a doctor taking part in an RCT comes to consider that his "control" patient would benefit from the treatment under examination, he has either to withdraw the patient from the RCT or suppress his own views. Nor can an RCT show how acceptable to patients the treatment may be. Nonetheless, there seems little doubt that the more widespread use of RCTs could eliminate procedures whose benefits are at present accepted simply because they have never been systematically challenged.

12.49 RCTs can also be used to evaluate services; and it would be a major advance if the health departments would as a matter of routine promote the testing of new and expensive services before their general introduction. The difficulties are formidable, the gains would be great.

12.50 Reliable case records are an invaluable vehicle for studying outcomes of treatment and quality of care. Far too often clinical records are illegible, incomplete and badly kept. The problem-oriented medical record is a form of structured record keeping which facilitates the retrieval of information and evaluation of outcomes; and we hope that current experimentation in its use will be continued and expanded. In Chapter 7 we discussed the need for upgrading generally the quality of record keeping in general practice. In hospitals standard extracts from in-patient records are processed by computer

174

for the Hospital Activity Analysis (HAA); and a 10% sample of the HAA cases is analysed by the Office of Population Censuses and Surveys and the results published as the Hospital In-Patient Enquiry (HIPE). The data thus produced are required for examining the use of resources; for example, the throughput per hospital bed. They can be used also to some extent for studies of outcome: but relatively little use of them for this purpose has been made by clinicians and the reports of the HIPE have had less attention than they deserve. There is room here for progress, as there is in the development of record linkage (ie the linking of medical records which relate to the same individual) which allows outcomes of treatment to be evaluated more clearly.

12.51 We have referred to techniques for evaluating the outcome of treatment. We now turn to methods of improving the performance of individual health workers. Most NHS professions are hierarchically organised, and the junior will normally look to his superior for praise, blame and correction. However, medical and dental consultants and general practitioners, for example, are their own masters. There is no one to tell a consultant that he may not prescribe a particular drug or undertake a particular procedure, and in practice there are limits to the extent to which such staff as senior nurses and physiotherapists can supervise juniors. This independence is highly prized by the professions. A number of methods have been developed to ensure that staff who are exercising their own judgment should be aware of how their performance compares with that of their colleagues elsewhere. One form of checking is "professional audit" which involves, like financial audit, an examination of the books, in this case to see what treatment a patient has received. The idea is that clinical decisions should be checked, errors pointed out, and future improvements in performance achieved. While there is the difficulty of establishing standards already referred to, there are plenty of occasions when it would be agreed that a treatment was "bad" or "good" in particular circumstances. A successful application of this approach is the Confidential Enquiry into Maternal Deaths, launched in England and Wales in 1952 under which doctors review with a representative of the Royal College of Obstetricians and Gynaecologists the avoidable risks in each case of maternal death.

12.52 An informal variation on professional audit is peer review under which practising clinicians evaluate the quality and efficiency of the services provided by themselves and their colleagues. This may be no more than an informal discussion between two or three colleagues on the best way of dealing with particular problems, but in many hospitals it has become more formalised in regular clinical reviews of the treatment and progress of individual patients, or "death and complications" conferences. Peer review has the advantage that it is not imposed by some external body, and it avoids the difficulty of appearing to apply some ill-defined national standard, but unless it is undertaken systematically it will lack public credibility. We welcome the trend towards the introduction of regular peer review sessions and consider that it should be given every encouragement.

12.53 At an institutional level, the NHS has its own form of quality checking body in the Health Advisory Service in England and Wales and the

Hospital Advisory Service in Scotland.[1] These are teams of doctors, nurses and other staff who are seconded to work with the advisory service and who visit and evaluate mental illness, geriatric and, until recently, mental handicap services. On the whole their activities have been welcomed by the great majority of staff working in the field. We consider in Chapter 19 whether the functions and powers of the advisory services should be extended.

12.54　There are other approaches to encouraging higher standards: for example, NHS laboratories which do not take part in the UK National Quality Control Scheme may be refused approval as training institutions. Such an approach could be extended and we recommend that the Joint Higher Training Committees for post-graduate medical education should approve only those units and departments where an accepted method of evaluating care has been instituted. There may also be a place for "demonstration centres" of good practice and innovation in hospitals and elsewhere.

12.55　Systems of monitoring, whether run by a profession itself, or imposed by health departments or some other organisation, have their disadvantages. The feeling that someone may come round and blame you for your mistakes is not necessarily a healthy one. In the USA where a great deal of litigation is undertaken against doctors and where the courts have been willing to award high damages, "defensive medicine" has developed, characterised by doctors insisting on many expensive tests and procedures more designed to ward off blame than to establish a diagnosis. There is also a danger of establishing and perpetuating a rigid orthodoxy of approach and so discouraging innovation and experiment. We understand that there is also a legal difficulty here. Communications between doctors are not "privileged" for legal purposes, and, as the law stands, a doctor who had "audited" another doctor's treatment of a patient could be obliged to reveal what the audit had shown. If it suggested that a mistake had been made it could form the basis for legal action against the doctor who had made the mistake. This consideration would need to be borne in mind if the introduction of any system of compulsory audit were under discussion.

12.56　While we are well aware of the difficulties of establishing standards it does not seem to us that they need discourage experiment in procedures for raising the quality of care. One issue is whether some form of audit should be imposed on the professions from outside. The Royal Colleges have for long given leadership in maintaining and raising standards of practice, and they have promoted much discussion of and some experimentation with clinical audit. Evaluation of patient care and post-graduate education are also closely linked and this is widely recognised. Audit is a responsibility of the clinical divisions in hospitals, but its progress in this setting has been slow. We are in no doubt that initiatives in this field can best come from the professions

---

[1]There is no comparable body in Northern Ireland, but the position is currently being reviewed.

themselves, but despite recent developments we are not convinced that the professions generally regard the introduction of audit or peer review of standards of care and treatment with a proper sense of urgency. We recommend that a planned programme for the introduction of such procedures should be set up for the health professions by their professional bodies and progress monitored by the health departments.

Manpower Planning

12.57 Over one million people are employed in the NHS in the UK. The major staff groups are shown in Table 12.2. It is impossible with our present knowledge to say how many workers the NHS needs and of what type: roles are not always clearly defined, the level of training required may not be clear, and the difficulty of establishing standards of quality, referred to in the last section, is reflected in the absence of generally accepted staffing standards.

This lack also makes it difficult to monitor effectively over- and under-manning even locally. Nor do international comparisons of staffing levels offer much guidance. Finally, calculations about numbers of staff needed must take account of their relative cost and the availability of cash to pay them. The aim should be to provide as much good quality care as possible from a given budget.

TABLE 12.2
NHS Staff: UK 1977

Category of staff	Unit	Numbers/wtes of staff (rounded)	Percentage of the total
Total	number/ wte	1,003,000	
Doctors[1]			
Hospital, community and school health medical staff and locums[2]	wte	39,500	3.9
General medical practitioners	number	27,700	2.8
Dentists[1]			
Hospital, community and school health dental staff and locums[3]	wte	3,200	0.3
General dental practitioners	number	13,900	1.4
Other Practitioners[1]			
Hospital pharmacists and opticians	wte	3,000	0.3
Ophthalmic and dispensing opticians in the GOS, ophthalmic medical practitioners and pharmacists in the GPS	number	24,800	2.5
Nursing and Midwifery Staff			
Hospital, community, school health, blood transfusion service and agency staff	wte	430,500	43.0
Professional and Technical (excluding works) Staff			
Scientific, technical, dental ancillary and remedial staff	wte	64,700	6.5
Ancillary Staff and Others			
Catering, laundry, domestic, portering etc staff	wte	219,700	21.9
Ambulance Service Staff			
Ambulance officers, control assistants and ambulancemen[4]	wte	20,900	2.1
Administrative and Clerical Staff			
Administrators, clerical staff, support services managers etc	wte	123,200	12.3
Works and Maintenance Staff			
Regional, area and district works staff and hospital maintenance staff	wte	31,600	3.2

Source: compiled from health departments' statistics.

Notes: [1] The addition of numbers and whole-time equivalents involves an element of duplication as some practitioners are included in both categories.

[2] GPs holding hospital appointments are excluded.

[3] Dentists holding hospital appointments are excluded.

[4] Other ambulance service staff are included under the respective staff category.

12.58 Several of those giving evidence drew attention to a lack of national manpower planning for the NHS. The Institute of Health Service Administrators suggested that consideration should be given to establishing a national manpower committee comprising representatives of employing authorities and professional associations. National planning of medical manpower was regarded as particularly important, and the Regional Administrators suggested to us that:

"The key to the redeployment of manpower resources in the NHS is the redeployment of medical staff, for the necessary support in terms of other professional staff will follow providing the financial resources are likewise redeployed."

12.59 There are two broad aspects to manpower planning: estimating the total numbers needed, for example how many physiotherapists overall are required; and getting them to the right places, for example ensuring that doctors are correctly distributed both geographically and by specialty. It is important to bear this distinction in mind when it comes to considering what the arrangements for manpower planning might be.

Existing arrangements

12.60 While strenuous efforts have been made to assess the numbers of doctors needed and to arrange for their proper distribution, comparatively little attention has been paid to other health service workers. The reasons for this neglect are partly historical: since 1948 the object has been to recruit more nurses, physiotherapists, technicians, without much regard to how many were needed. Attempts to establish norms have been made in the past, but have not commanded general acceptance. Furthermore, the majority of NHS staff, including ancillary and clerical workers, and many nurses and other professional and technical staff are recruited and trained locally, and there has been advantage in leaving local employers to recruit them in the numbers and mixtures they could afford and attract. This arrangement leaves the management function of manpower planning largely to health authorities and the function of estimating numbers largely in abeyance. It has the advantage of flexibility.

12.61 On the other hand, numbers of doctors required have been the subject of a succession of studies[1] and there is elaborate central machinery to

---

[1] The main ones were the 1944 Report of the Interdepartmental Committee on Medical Schools (Goodenough Committee), the 1957 Report of the Committee to Consider the Future Numbers of Medical Practitioners and the Appropriate Intake of Medical Students (Willink Committee) and the 1968 Royal Commission on Medical Education (Todd Commission).

direct them to specialties and areas where they are most needed.[1] There is obvious sense in this: doctors' training takes a long time and is expensive. It also involves the universities. The expansion of medical training facilities is therefore a complicated and long-term business. However, attempts in the past to determine the numbers of doctors required have not been altogether successful for several reasons; role flexibility and the resource implications of alternative forecasts were not considered, and the data base was inadequate. The health departments are aware of the deficiencies of the statistical information, and their discussion paper, Medical Manpower – The Next Twenty Years,[2] is a welcome development in this field.

Central planning machinery

12.62 Some of those who sent us evidence proposed a central planning body which would be independent of and advisory to the government and have the function of assessing the numbers and types of staff required for the NHS and the implications for the educational system. We are doubtful about establishing such an advisory body, and particularly one which would attempt to deal with all types of NHS staff, because we think it would have little to contribute to what we see as the main difficulty for the NHS in this field, that of ensuring the proper distribution of its workers. In our view this must remain the business of health departments and the health authorities. Furthermore, it would be a force for centralisation, whereas we consider that in general it should be left to the health authorities to recruit and train the staff they need within an overall policy. It is essential that those concerned with manpower planning at all levels should consult fully the representatives of the staff concerned and the health departments should ensure that they do so. There are already a number of bodies for the main groups of NHS staff with responsibilities for their recruitment, training and development. For example, in England and Wales there are the National Staff Committees which cover administrative and clerical, nurses and midwives, and some other groups of staff (though not doctors or dentists). These bodies are comparatively recent creations and should be left to get on with their jobs.

12.63 Nor do we see a lot of point in replacing the Central Manpower Committee for doctors and its equivalents in Scotland and Northern Ireland. However, the existing machinery is concerned with the distribution rather than the overall numbers of doctors, and we do not regard the present system of collecting views on numbers of doctors needed ad hoc every decade or so as satisfactory. It seems clear to us that there should be regular and more frequent reviews (approximately every two years) of the medical manpower position, following open and public discussion, and supported by better data than have so far been available. The responsibility for conducting these reviews should rest with the health departments. We recommend accordingly.

---

[1] See Chapter 14 for an account of this machinery.

[2] Department of Health and Social Security, Scottish Home and Health Department and Welsh Office, *Medical Manpower – The Next Twenty Years,* London, HMSO, 1978.

12.64   The manpower planning for one staff group needs to take account of changing roles, etc, of other related staff and while we do not advocate new central manpower planning bodies, we do consider that a more positive approach to manpower planning generally is required. The need for adequate data, which should be available locally, is urgent. It is important that local managers should keep records of staff turnover, their reasons for leaving, etc, and pay proper attention to planning career development of those who work for them.

12.65   In addition to improved statistical information more work is needed on numbers and roles. Experiments with different mixes of staff in different contexts, and the development of inter-professional training should be encouraged and we so recommend. Unless matters of this kind are studied deliberately changes in function to meet changing circumstances may occur haphazardly and become established before they can be evaluated. The health departments should ensure that the results are evaluated and make the information available to those involved in manpower planning. There is a role here for the independent Health Services Research Institute which we recommend in Chapter 17.

Occupational Health Services For NHS Workers

12.66   Occupational health was discussed in Chapter 5. Here we comment on the need for an occupational health service for NHS staff. There was considerable support in our evidence for the proposal that the NHS should develop an occupational health service for its own employees. As the TUC said:

> "We firmly hold the view that an occupational health service is essential for staff employed within the NHS and that this should be established as a matter or urgency."

Most of the evidence urged that the proposals of the Tunbridge Committee should be implemented without delay. This Committee, which reported in 1968, recommended that hospital authorities "should aim at setting up an occupational health service for all their employees",[1] and added that while their recommendations were too wide-ranging to be quickly implemented throughout the hospital service, the NHS had a particular responsibility in occupational health which had in their view been neglected, and that a start needed to be made on a broad front.

12.67   The Tunbridge recommendations were accepted in principle by the government, but progress towards their implementation has been slow and uneven largely because of limitations on financial and manpower resources for which there are many competing demands. The health departments are consulting the NHS professions and trade unions on guidance to be issued on occupational health services for NHS staff. We hope that these discussions can be brought to an early conclusion. The NHS should assume the same

---

[1] Ministry of Health, Scottish Home and Health Department, *The Care of the Health of Hospital Staff, Report of the Joint Committee,* London, HMSO, 1968, page 36.

responsibility as any other employer for the health and safety of its staff and set up an occupational health service. We recommend accordingly.

Conclusions and Recommendations

12.68   In this chapter we began by considering the morale of workers in the NHS. We were told by many people that morale was low, but we see this as a symptom rather than an underlying or constitutional disorder. We make no recommendatons about morale itself, but we hope that the recommendations we make here and elsewhere in the report will lead to improvement.

12.69   We are in no doubt that industrial relations in the NHS are in need of improvement. At local level adequate machinery and staff are often lacking and it is clear that urgent action is needed. We welcome the proposals for procedures to deal speedily with local disputes which have been put to the General Whitley Council and hope they can soon be introduced. We also welcome the survey into industrial relations in the health and personal social services which is being undertaken in Northern Ireland. There is no single solution to the problem of industrial action in the NHS, but better local procedures should help to eliminate local disputes of the kind which have plagued the service in recent years.

12.70   The pay of NHS workers is a major cause of dispute at national level. The Whitley Council system has a number of faults: in particular, its sometimes cumbersome procedures may lead to excessive delays in reaching new agreements. We hope that Lord McCarthy's review will lead to improvements. As pay negotiating bodies, the Whitley Councils are weakened by being insufficiently independent of government. This means that pay disputes may have to be resolved in some other forum.

12.71   We think it essential that a procedure should be worked out for resolving national disputes about pay. This will involve a review of existing pay arrangements, including the role of the Whitley Councils. It will take time and patience. We think the initiative can best come from the TUC. In due course proposals should be put to the Secretaries of State and the NHS management interests.

12.72   The changing character of health care requires flexibility in the roles of those working in the NHS. On the other hand responsibilities and duties should be clear. In certain circumstances the two may pull in opposite directions. Multi-disciplinary working brings out some of the difficulties. Another aspect is the need to assess the quality of the treatment and care provided by NHS workers. This can best be undertaken by the professions themselves, but the health departments should ensure that adequate progress is made. We considered whether it would be possible to lay down staff norms, to forecast needs and deficiencies, and eliminate shortages. We concluded that the needs and resources of different parts of the UK varied so greatly that centralised planning for all NHS staff would be wholly impracticable. Recruitment decisions should, for the most part, be made locally in the light of local needs within an overall policy. An exception to this is medical and dental manpower, both because it takes ten years or more to expand facilities for training doctors and dentists, and because of the extent of the involvement of the universities. In all cases staff interests need to be consulted and health departments should ensure that the machinery for this is adequate.

12.73 We consider that the NHS should assume the same responsibility as any other employer for the health and safety of its staff.

12.74 We recommend that:

(a) the health departments and staff organisations and unions should give urgent attention to industrial relations training for staff representatives and management (paragraph 12.11);

(b) the TUC should take the necessary steps in initiating discussions on a procedure for dealing with national disputes in the NHS which must involve not only those bodies affiliated to the TUC but bodies representing the interests of other NHS workers as well (paragraph 12.24);

(c) the health departments should intervene on those occasions when the health professions cannot reach agreement on staff roles (paragraph 12.43);

(d) the Joint Higher Training Committees for post-graduate medical education should approve only those units and departments where an accepted method of evaluating care has been instituted (paragraph 12.54);

(e) a planned programme for the introduction of audit or peer review of standards of care and treatment should be set up for the health professions by their professional bodies and progress monitored by the health departments (paragraph 12.56);

(f) the health departments should undertake, approximately every two years, a review of the medical manpower position, following open and public discussion, and supported by better data than have so far been available (paragraph 12.63);

(g) experiments with different mixes of staff in different contexts, and the development of inter-professional training should be encouraged (paragraph 12.65);

(h) the NHS should assume the same responsibility as any other employer for the health and safety of its staff and set up an occupational health service (paragraph 12.67).

Chapter 13   Nurses, Midwives and Health Visitors

13.1   Nurses, midwives and health visitors play a vital part in the care of patients in hospitals, nursing homes and the community. They have constant and direct contact with patients, in most cases the service is provided throughout 24 hours, and they give more personal care than many other groups of staff. They are the largest staff group in the NHS and command the largest salary bill, accounting for over one-quarter of the total current expenditure in the NHS. For all these reasons the part that they play in the NHS is profoundly important.

13.2   In this chapter we discuss some of the main problems of nurses, midwives and health visitors put to us in evidence. We dealt with the allegation of increased numbers of administrators following the Salmon Committee Report[1] in Chapter 4, and with community nursing in Chapter 7, and we touched on aides and manpower planning in Chapter 12. We concentrate here on roles, manpower requirements, an improved career structure for clinical work, and some aspects of education and research, but we start by commenting on the standards of care provided to patients. Much of what we say here applies equally to nurses, midwives and health visitors and our use of "nurse" and "nursing service" should be interpreted accordingly.[2]

The Briggs Committee

13.3   In preparing this chapter we have been conscious of the major review of the nursing service undertaken by the Briggs Committee which reported in 1972.[3] The Committee's terms of reference were:

> "to review the role of the nurse and the midwife in the hospital and the community and the education and training required for that role, so that the best use is made of available manpower to meet present needs and the needs of an integrated health service".

The Committee made a detailed study of the role of the nurse and important proposals for the statutory framework of nurse education and training, manpower, conditions of work, reorganisation of nursing and midwifery functions, career structure, and research. We have drawn heavily on their work.

---

[1]Ministry of Health and Scottish Home and Health Department, *Report of the Committee on Senior Nursing Staff Structure*, London, HMSO, 1966.

[2]For simplicity and because most nurses are women they are referred to as such.

[3]*Report of the Committee on Nursing*, (Cmnd 5115), London, HMSO, 1972.

13.4   We are concerned that relatively little progress has been made on the major recommendations scheduled by the Committee for "immediate action" and not needing legislation, for example an effective manpower policy, increased recognition of clinical skills and a major drive to produce more nursing and midwifery teachers. Although some progress has been made, the "period of intense activity" envisaged by the Committee as occurring after their report did not take place. Indeed, it took seven years before legislation to set up the statutory framework recommended by the Briggs Committee was enacted.

Standards of care

13.5   We received much evidence expressing concern about declining standards of nursing care. It was often attributed to the structural changes arising from the Salmon and Mayston[1] Committees' recommendations and their alleged tendency to withdraw good clinical nurses into administration. We dealt with these points in Chapter 4. Further, in a submission to the Secretary of State for Social Services in October 1978 the RCN claimed that standards had been put at risk because of financial constraints, increased work loads and manpower shortages. They submitted that the main areas of risk were:

"*in hospitals*
untrained staff left in charge of wards
inadequate supervision of learners
neglect of basic nursing routines
employment of agency staff

in the community
increased workloads which cause severe pressure on nursing staff with the consequent curtailment of time allocated to patients and learners
abandonment of patient care programmes because of the need to cope with emergency cases and high dependency patients."[2]

13.6   These are serious matters. There is no doubt that nurses are under pressure in many places, and services to patients suffer. We refer later to increased workloads inherent in NHS policies and developments, training arrangements, and the balance of trained to untrained staff. Nurses expect to provide a high standard of care; their morale may be seriously affected if the standard of care they are able to offer their patients falls, and this may lead to some of them leaving the service.

13.7   In earlier chapters we have pointed out some of the difficulties in measuring quality in health care. Progress has been made by the profession in

---

[1] Department of Health and Social Security, Scottish Home and Health Department and Welsh Office, *Report of the Working Party on Management Structure in the Local Authority Nursing Service*, London, HMSO, 1969.

[2] Royal College of Nursing of the United Kingdom, *An Assessment of the State of Nursing in the National Health Service, 1978*, London, RCN, 1978, page 35.

the evaluation of care through the use of nursing audit, research into clinical nursing methods, and staff appraisal schemes. Although some of these are in their infancy, the profession has shown it is well aware of the need for quality control. We were pleased to hear that the RCN has set up a working party to study standards of nursing care. We welcome this and other research initiatives and we hope that what we say in this chapter will contribute to improving both the quality of the nursing service provided to the patient and the nurse's own role.

Role and numbers

13.8 At present the NHS employs the equivalent of over 430,000 whole-time nurses, midwives and health visitors, approaching half of all NHS workers (see Table 13.1). The availability of nurses depends on such factors as the finance available for nursing budgets, the state of the local labour markets, recruitment and training policies and wastage. Demand for nursing care is related to morbidity and mortality trends, the organisation of care in institutions or community, and trends in medical treatment. These are constantly changing and the nurse's role also changes. It has developed to take account of the increased nursing involvement in administration as well as changes in nursing practice. It overlaps with that of other health workers; for example, the nurse may carry out duties normally undertaken by a domestic worker, physiotherapist or doctor. All these factors make for difficulty in establishing the number of nurses the NHS needs.

TABLE 13.1
Numbers of Nurses: UK 1977[1]

Whole-time equivalents

	ENGLAND	WALES	SCOTLAND	N. IRELAND	UK
Hospital Nursing Staff					
Registered Nurses	87,966	5,385	12,217	4,766	110,334
Enrolled Nurses	50,527	3,221	7,186	2,274	63,208
Student Nurses	53,765	2,353	7,006	2,923	66,047
Pupil Nurses	20,288	1,378	3,206	697	25,569
Other Nurses	73,494	5,322	15,859	2,689	97,364
TOTAL	286,040	17,659	45,474	13,349	362,522
Primary Health Care Service Staff					
Health Visitors	8,477	522	1,249	375[2]	10,623
District Nurses	12,649[3]	1,088[3]	1,192	351[2]	15,280
School Nurses	2,330	114	373	78[2]	2,895
Other Nurses	7,482	498	1,193	67[2]	9,240
TOTAL	30,938	2,222	4,007	871[2]	38,038
Midwives					
Certified Midwives					
—Hospital	12,142	775	1,997	783	15,697
—Primary Health Care	3,041	100	92	351[2]	3,584
Pupil Midwives					
–Hospital	4,572	218	1,106	203	6,099
—Primary Health Care	166	—	—	—	166
Other Midwifery Staff	—	705	—	—	705
TOTAL	19,921	1,798	3,195	1,337	26,251
Administrative Nursing and Midwifery Staff	1,863	107	400[1]	396[2]	2,766
Blood Transfusion Service Nurses	896	40[5]	—	33[2]	969[1]
GRAND TOTAL	339,658	21,786	53,076	15,986	430,506

Source: compiled from health departments' statistics.

Notes: [1] Figures for N. Ireland are for 1978.
[2] Numbers, not WTE.
[3] Includes district nurse trainees.
[4] Includes staff of Common Services Agency.
[5] Included under appropriate grade of hospital nursing staff.

Role

13.9　Within nursing there are many levels of skill and different roles. Nursing in the NHS may involve providing unskilled but devoted care which might otherwise be given by relatives and friends. It is carried out by nursing assistants and auxiliaries with the minimum of in-service training, under the supervision of trained nurses, and it forms a substantial part of the care given to patients. Skilled professional nursing care is provided by trained nurses or those in training for enrolment or registration. The Briggs Committee remarked:

"Although enrolment and registration are distinct qualifications, leading to very different career prospects within the profession, the actual level of work assigned to some enrolled nurses is often very similar to that assigned to some registered nurses in the staff nurse grade. We believe this can only lead to confusion and bitterness."[1]

13.10　At present nurse training aims to produce different levels of skill. There are courses of up to two years leading to State Enrolment (SEN), and of three years leading to State Registration (SRN), with one of the General Nursing Councils or with the Northern Ireland Nurses and Midwives Council. The SRN course has the greater theoretical content. There are also a small number of courses which combine SRN training with an undergraduate degree programme. The registers are divided into general, sick children, mental and mental sub-normality parts, and in England and Wales the roll is similarly divided except that there is no sick children category. Early specialisation is encouraged by this arrangement, and flexibility in deploying nursing staff is reduced. The Briggs Committee put forward proposals for a system of nursing education with a single portal of entry and a common certificate in nursing practice. This should help to resolve the problem of lack of flexibility but still allow some nurses to progress to registration and higher certificates which would replace the present post-basic nursing qualifications. It will be the task of the new United Kingdom Central Council for Nursing, Midwifery and Health Visiting to review these proposals and plan accordingly.

13.11　Nursing is an immensely varied profession. In hospitals, nurses work in acute, long-stay, children's, psychiatric, maternity and other specialised units. Outside hospital there are health visitors, home nurses, midwives, and nurses working in clinics and in general practice as part of the primary health care team (dealt with in Chapter 7). Nurses work in administration in the NHS and health departments, in education and research, the armed forces, voluntary organisations such as the Red Cross, occupational health and international agencies. There is a great deal of overlap in the knowledge required in many branches of nursing.

13.12　Midwifery has long been recognised as a separate profession, although the majority of midwives are also trained nurses. The midwife makes her own judgments about the supervision, care and advice to women before and after childbirth. She is responsible for deliveries, and cares for the new-

---

[1](Cmnd 5115), *Op. cit*, paragraph 188.

born and infants. It is part of her duty to detect abnormal conditions in mother and child, to decide when to summon the doctor, and to deal with emergencies in his absence. The Royal College of Midwives told us that in 75% of deliveries the midwife is the senior person present. Health education and counselling are an important part of her work. The role of the midwife may serve as a model of the extended role and clinical responsibility which nurses could carry.

13.13   The nature of nursing has been debated for years. Florence Nightingale remarked:

"the very elements of nursing are all but unknown."
and
"I use the word nursing for want of a better."[1]

In her view nursing had been limited to a restricted range of tasks. She outlined an expanded role in which the nurse was responsible for the control of the patient's environment, and this remains an essential part of the nurse's function. The Briggs Committee saw nursing and midwifery as "the major caring profession",[2] at least in the mind of the public. They referred to "the unique caring role"[3] of the nurse which involves skills of observation and assessment, planning and taking responsibility for a comprehensive and continuous oversight of patient care. This view was supported in our evidence, for example by the General Nursing Council for Scotland who told us that:

"it is of the utmost importance that the comprehensive role of the nurse to give care and support to meet all patients' needs, should be maintained".

We endorse the view that the caring role, the functions of which the nurse initiates and controls, is central to nursing.

13.14   Nurses do not work in isolation. The care of patients requires the skills of many different staff, working together as a team. The nurse's functions overlap particularly with the doctor's. The Briggs Committee said that "it is essential from the start to dispel the notion ... that nursing and midwifery constitute a substitute profession for medicine",[4] but accepted that the roles of doctor and nurse are complementary and may be on occasions interchangeable. The overlap between the roles of nurses and doctors, and indeed other professionals such as physiotherapists, is an essential element in the continuity of care of patients.

13.15   Because of their availability and continuity of service to the patient, nurses may be misused. The Briggs Committee remarked:

"where treatment or care cannot be adequately maintained by other professional members of the health team because of insufficient staff or

---

[1]Nightingale, F, *Notes on Nursing – What it is and what it is not*, (First published in 1860), Dover Publications Inc, 1969 edition, page 8.

[2](Cmd 5115), *Op cit*, paragraph 38.

[3]*Ibid*, paragraphs 39–41.

[4]*Ibid*, paragraphs 141–142.

workload inadequate to justify the employment of specialist staff in small hospitals or units, nurses and midwives, on account of their availability and continuity of service, are usually the staff expected to attempt to take over the functions of other specialists".[1]

Nursing time may be eroded by nurses accepting other duties. The tasks of other groups should not as a matter of course be handed over to nurses simply because they are always there, and staff shortages whether of domestic or other professional staff should not be made an excuse for persistent misuse of nurses.

13.16   We were told of many different ways in which nursing roles are being extended and expanded. There is increasing recognition that the major health need of groups such as the chronic and long term sick, and the elderly, is for nursing care. The Regional Nursing Officers in England suggested to us that:

"Examination should be given to the possibility of extending the role of the nurse and enabling them to undertake tasks traditionally the province of the medical staff. . . . There is a need in some long stay care areas for nurses to take the lead. Nurses should be enabled and encouraged to prescribe nursing care programmes, including the mobilisation of other services such as physiotherapy and occupational therapy."

This seems to us a logical extension of the nurse's caring role. Adequate preparation for an extended role will be needed.

13.17   Extended roles for nurses are developing as a result of specialisation, for example in renal dialysis, care of spinal injuries, and special care baby units. Advances in medical science often require parallel advances in nursing care, and nurses working closely with doctors are pioneering new roles. During our visit to North America we found a growing interest in the role of the clinical nurse specialist. The health departments told us of similar appointments in the UK, usually at nursing officer or ward sister level. Specialist nurses may also have an advisory or an executive function in a health district. The RCN submitted a list of posts showing the range of specialties which have developed. While we recognise the danger that specialisation may lead to inflexibility, there is clearly a growing demand for specialist nursing skills in the care of certain groups of patients. We comment later on the need to reward special expertise, and on the preparation needed for advanced roles in nursing.

13.18   Nurses working in the community have long had a considerable degree of independence. For example, as we saw in Chapter 7, health visitors initiate their own visits, assess the development of children, undertake screening of the normal population, assess and care for the elderly, and advise on family planning. It is possible that district nurses could undertake more first visits to patients in their home. An experiment carried out at the Woodside Health

[1]*Ibid*, paragraphs 141–142.

Centre in Glasgow suggested that decisions made independently by nurses and doctors about what to do for patients in the community were very similar.[1]

13.19   In considering an extension of nursing roles in the community we were referred to the development of nurse practitioners in North America. We commissioned a study of the literature on nurse practitioners from Dr Jillian MacGuire. This showed that in North America a number of problems had stimulated the wider use of nurses in the community, including the shortage of doctors in general practice, maldistribution of health facilities, cost of health care, and pressure from the nursing profession itself. Nurse practitioners work mainly, but not exclusively, in primary care, and may be involved in hospital out-patient clinics. They work closely with doctors, but in some rural areas the nearest doctor can be many miles away and they have considerable independence. They take health histories from patients, act as first point of contact, provide teaching and counselling, and deal with a case load of patients with self-limiting diseases. Nurse practitioners have proved to be perfectly acceptable to patients, and indeed are often felt to be more accessible than the doctor, particularly as in the main they operate in under-doctored areas. We do not see nurse practitioners as providing a second class medical service, but there is scope for further development in the roles of community nurses this side of the Atlantic.

13.20   In 1974 a joint working party of representatives of the nursing and medical professions and the DHSS identified a range of activities being undertaken by nurses both in the general and psychiatric fields which were clearly an extension of their normal functions.[2] We consider that decisions about the respective responsibilities of the professions for different aspects of patient care should be made by the health departments after consulting the professions concerned, and with due regard to the interests of the patient and the level of knowledge and skill required. Where a function is identified as part of the nurse's role it should be incorporated into basic or post-basic nursing education and be professionally supervised.

13.21   A main concern in our evidence was that any extension in the nurse's role should not be at the expense of her caring functions. The GNC for Scotland warned us that "some technical procedures may distract from true patient care, and the nurse's involvement in those which have this effect should not be encouraged". The RCN told us that comments of community nurses in 1974 (which are still valid today) had shown that there was concern also in the community services at:

> "the extended duties of both health visitors and home nurses, the running of immunisation and vaccination clinics, taking blood, performing venepuncture, making 'first assessment' visits in place of the doctor and the using of new and more sophisticated equipment and drugs in patients' homes where, in the case of an untoward event, there was no medical aid nearby".

[1]Moore, M F, *et al*, "First contact decisions in general practice", *The Lancet*, 14 April 1973, pages 817–819.

[2]HC(77)22, *Health Services Management. The Extending Role of the Clinical Nurse – Legal Implications and Training Requirements.*

13.22 There are other risks in nurses taking on new tasks. The Briggs Committee pointed out:

"A nurse or midwife, whether working in the community or in a hospital, has a legal duty of care towards her patient. In giving this care she is required to exercise the degree of knowledge and skill which could reasonably be expected of one trained in her particular profession. If she falls below this standard and the patient is thereby harmed she will be regarded as negligent in common law and will be legally liable for the damage resulting from her negligence."[1]

Concern about their legal position may make nurses cautious about taking on new functions for which they have not been adequately trained. Extension of the nursing role needs to be planned and to take account of both training and staffing implications.

13.23 There will be able nurses who prefer to widen the scope of their work and make their careers in the clinical field rather than to move into administration or education. We believe that they should be encouraged to do so, and it seems to us to be a mistake to define or to confine the nursing role rigidly. Its development should be encouraged and experiment pursued, and we recommend that the profession and health departments take the necessary steps. It is clear that both the health departments and the professional organisations concerned are keeping a close watch on the position. They will need to ensure that new developments do not take place at the expense of the nurse's caring role which is so important to patients and which itself is a prime candidate for expansion.

Numbers

13.24 Attempts have been made to calculate the numbers of nurses the NHS needs. Bed or population ratios, staffing norms, and workload indices based on patient dependency studies have been used, but none has proved wholly satisfactory. Minimum staffing standards have been set, for example in mental illness, mental handicap and geriatric nursing, but these do not purport to measure need. The Jay Committee[2] found difficulty in making even a rough estimate of staffing needs for mental handicap. The DHSS commented to us that:

---

[1](Cmnd 5115), *Op cit*, paragraph 152.

[2]Department of Health and Social Security, Scottish Home and Health Department and Welsh Office, *Report of the Committee of Enquiry into Mental Handicap Nursing and Care*, London, HMSO, 1979.

"Each health authority sets its own nursing establishments and to some extent engenders its own demand. Except for health visitors and home nurses where staff/population ratios have been recommended, the Department has not issued guidance to health authorities about assessing staffing needs."

13.25   Recruitment of student and pupil nurses has fluctuated considerably in recent years. For example in England in 1976/77 there was an overall fall of 7.6% in numbers of nurses entering training, and in 1977/78 a further fall of over 21%. These fluctuations may reflect the financial difficulties of health authorities rather than an unwillingness of young people to enter nursing, and the 1978/79 figures showed a considerable improvement. Wide fluctuations of this kind make for difficulties in years to come and cannot be in the best interests of the service. There will be a decline in the number of 18 year olds in the population in the 1980s. Recruitment policy in the NHS will need to take account of this and the needs of mature students, male nurses and those from overseas. Also there should be better arrangements for training nurses who want to return to the service, for example after their children have grown up.

13.26   There are frequent complaints both in the press and in our evidence of shortages of nurses despite considerable increases in the numbers of nurses nationally over the years: between 1971 and 1977, for example, total numbers of nurses in England increased by about 23%. However, increases in numbers may be partly offset by a reduction in availability of staff: Table 13.2 shows that the increase between 1971 and 1977 fell to about 12% when this is taken into account. Further, the rate of increase has been tailing off: in 1976–1977 it was less than one-half per cent. Although the minimum staffing requirements for mental illness, mental handicap and geriatric nursing have been met (though these may need to be reviewed), and the number of health visitors has increased, the growth in district nursing is below the target set by the DHSS in 1976.[1]

13.27   Factors which have contributed to a reduction in nurses' availability include a shorter working week, longer holidays, additional bank holidays and revised training schemes which have been widened to include community and psychiatric aspects. The benefits of a broader based training and ultimately greater flexibility are gained by some sacrifice of the service contribution during training. A sense of shortage of nurses may be produced by the greater

[1]Department of Health and Social Security, *Priorities for Health and Personal Social Services in England. A Consultative Document*, London, HMSO, 1976.

TABLE 13.2

Numbers of Nurses, Midwives and Health Visitors Adjusted for Availability: Hospital and Primary Health Care Services[1]: England 1971–1977

	1971	1972	1973	1974	1975	1976	1977
Total Staff (numbers)	272,630	290,233	295,302	301,295	324,115	332,598	335,081
Total Staff (adjusted[2])	272,630	276,412	280,050	276,752	297,843	305,505	306,300
Total Staff (indexed[3])	100	106.5	108.3	110.5	118.9	122.0	122.9
Total Staff (adjusted and indexed)	100	101.4	102.7	101.5	109.2	112.1	112.4
Changes in nurses' conditions		40 hour week 1st January 1972		Revised leave 1st April 1974			Additional Public Holiday

Source: compiled from published and unpublished statistics provided by the DHSS.

Notes: [1] Excluding tutorial staff, RHA headquarters staff, blood transfusion staff, nursing cadets and agency staff.

[2] Adjusted figure = Total staff × (Annual Hours per WTE Staff Member for year) ÷ (Annual Hours per WTE Staff Member for 1971).

[3] Index 1971=100.

194

throughput of patients in hospital, more people being cared for in the community, and nurses' increasingly specialised and technical roles. Finally, the increase in the number of doctors which has taken place has resulted in greater demand for other services, including nursing.

13.28   Growth in total numbers may conceal local shortages, high wastage rates of learners, and difficulties in manning the relatively unpopular psychiatric and geriatric units. As with other NHS workers, the geographical distribution of nurses is uneven. Table 13.3 shows that in 1977 Scotland had over 68% more nurses and about 57% more midwives (though fewer health visitors) per 1,000 population than Oxford RHA. There are also variations within regions. A further factor is the number of overseas nurses particularly in the training grades. For example, in England in 1976 over 16% of all nurse learners were born overseas. The problems experienced by this group are similar to those of overseas doctors and some of what we say in Chapter 14 is relevant here.

13.29   The NHS has long been dependent on unqualified staff. About 50% of the nursing workforce is unqualified, fairly equally divided between nurse learners, nursing auxiliaries and assistants, some of whom receive only a short basic in-service training. The Briggs Committee welcomed "the increasing contribution" of these workers "in view of the differing levels of work to be done".[1] However, the high proportion of unqualified staff may produce problems; for example, the development of specialised units requires extra qualified staff and this may result in other units becoming more dependent upon auxiliaries and assistants. We were told of instances where unqualified staff were left in sole charge of wards, particularly in geriatric and psychiatric units, in which the patient/staff ratios were already low and demands on staff high. There has been little research into the effect of this on patient care, or into the best composition of the ward team in different settings for both service and educational purposes. We recommend that this should be rectified.

13.30   There is little or no nurse manpower planning to meet national requirements, though the mental and geriatric "leads" negotiated by the Whitley Council recognise the difficulties of recruitment in those areas. There are normally sufficient applicants for training and in practice the factors which most influence recruitment are probably the availability of funds and the local employment situation. The RCN pointed out:

"In spite of research the balance of the nursing team has been based on empirical considerations, the two most important being: which groups are easily available and how many can be paid for out of the current budget. In good times the service recruits, in bad it cuts back and replaces trained staff with untrained."

[1](Cmnd 5115), *Op cit*, paragraph 411.

The Briggs Committee considered that the absence of a manpower planning strategy was a serious deficiency, a view which we support.

TABLE 13.3

Nurses, Midwives and Health Visitors[1] per 1,000 Population: UK 1977

Whole-time equivalents

	Nurses	Midwives	Health Visitors
ENGLAND	6.64	0.43	0.20
Northern	6.45	0.40	0.20
Yorkshire	6.67	0.40	0.19
Trent	5.90	0.38	0.19
East Anglia	5.90	0.43	0.17
NW Thames	6.82	0.43	0.22
NE Thames	6.93	0.49	0.17
SE Thames	7.33	0.46	0.21
SW Thames	6.98	0.34	0.23
Wessex	6.16	0.43	0.20
Oxford	5.50	0.40	0.25
South Western	6.82	0.42	0.19
West Midlands	6.10	0.43	0.19
Mersey	7.34	0.47	0.19
North Western	6.67	0.49	0.22
WALES	6.99	0.65	0.20
SCOTLAND	9.28	0.61	0.24
N IRELAND[2]	9.00	0.87	0.27

Source: compiled from health departments' statistics.

Notes: [1] Excludes administrative staff, blood transfusion staff, agency staff and community student nurses.
　　　　[2] Figures for N. Ireland are 1978.

13.31   The major planning problem is to get the right number of nurses into the right places, particularly unpopular areas and specialties. The health departments are aware of this and have been working with the profession and the NHS to develop manpower planning expertise. Better methods of quantifying need might be a proper subject for study by the Health Services Research Institute we recommend in Chapter 17, but the most immediate requirement is that nurse managers at every level should have adequate manpower information on which to base their future plans. The development of computerised personnel records would be a great help here. We do not advocate the establishment of new and centralised planning machinery, still less that the health departments should control nursing establishments. We recommend that the health departments should undertake such central planning as is necessary, that is develop a national recruitment policy, assist the setting of standards and objectives, propagate good practice and ensure an adequate data base which will be of considerable importance to the new statutory educational bodies.

Clinical career structure

13.32   We recorded in Chapter 4 that the Salmon Committee's recommendations on the senior nursing staff structure were often alleged to have resulted

196

in a marked increase in the number of nurses employed on administrative duties. We concluded that the figures did not support this view. The structure was also unfairly blamed for the loss of experienced ward sisters, whereas it was demographic factors, such as changing patterns of marriage and child-bearing and the changed expectations of women in society, which were the main influences on the availability of ward sisters and the length of their working lives.

13.33 A workforce as large as nursing's must be efficiently managed and this requires the involvement of many nurses in planning and decision making processes. A nurse should continue to be a member of management teams at all levels, and we agree with the RCN that the "concept of the team of equals must not be lost". Nurse administrators will often need supporting staff to do their jobs properly, and we hope that health authorities will bear this in mind when considering their needs for clerical staff.

13.34 A major concern in the evidence from both medical and nursing organisations was that career prospects for nurses in clinical work should be improved. The British Association of Oral Surgeons, commenting on the Salmon structure, said that:

"This system, which requires experienced ward sisters to abandon clinical nursing and enter the administrative field in order to obtain promotion, aggravates the serious skilled nursing shortage ... a career structure which offers high levels of promotion in clinical nursing should be reintroduced."

We have referred to the way in which clinical nursing roles are developing, and the support for this of the regional nursing officers in England. The RCN told us that:

"there is a need to identify new roles for nurses as specialists and consultants, in different spheres of practice ... This proposed extension of the role of the nurse is seen primarily as a means of promoting high standards of care; it would also provide an avenue of advancement for nurses who wish to continue in clinical work. The RCN believes that this development should proceed in two stages. The role of the nurse specialist is already capable of identification ... The role of the nurse consultant should be the subject of research".

At present the nurse who wishes to continue with and specialise in clinical work will suffer financially, as can be seen from Table 13.4. We discuss below ways in which career prospects in clinical nursing could be improved.

13.35 A satisfactory career structure in clinical nursing should be linked to the establishment of criteria for the evaluation of clinical expertise by a systematic analysis of clinical nursing functions. It seems to us that rewards in clinical nursing should depend more on a developing expertise and growing responsibility for clinical decision making than on a line responsibility for the

197

TABLE 13.4
Nursing Salary Levels[1], Relationship Between Main Groups: England 1978

Administration	Education	Clinical[2]
Regional Nursing Officer (£10,866)		
Area Nursing Officer (£10,266)		
District Nursing Officer (£9,930)		
Regional Nurse (£8,430)		
Area Nurse (£8,073)	Director of Nursing Education (£7,656)	
Divisional Nursing Officer (£7,209)		
Principal Nursing Officer (£6,516)		
Senior Nursing Officer (£5,277)	Senior Tutor (£5,403) Tutor (£5,028)	
Nursing Officer[2] (£4,848)		
	Clinical Teacher (£4,695)	Nursing Sister/ Charge Nurse (£4,695)
		Staff Nurse (£3255)

Source: compiled from published and unpublished statistics provided by the DHSS.

Notes: [1] Maximum salary for the highest grade in each category at April 1978.

[2] There are a comparatively small number of clinical nurse specialists who are, in the main, graded as nursing officers.

management of other workers. In the process of developing satisfactory clinical career prospects, existing relativities may need to be disturbed.

13.36 A clinical career structure must be based on the staff nurse and ward sister grades and it is essential that their roles are reviewed and modified in the light of advances in nursing care. The importance of the team approach to nursing care giving co-ordinated physical and psychological care was stressed by the Briggs Committee, and we referred above to the need for research into the composition of the ward team. We welcome the research which is being undertaken into methods of organising patient centred nursing care and the roles of the ward sister and nursing officer.

13.37 There seem to be the following approaches to improving career prospects for nurses specialising in clinical work:

revision of the ward sister's salary scale to provide incentives for distinction or excellence in clinical practice;

development of the existing nursing officer role to approach more closely the model originally envisaged;

developing specialist and expanded roles for nurses on the lines referred to in paragraphs 13.16–13.23;

linking teaching and research with clinical work.

The first approach is a matter for the Whitley Council, but the comparatively unfavourable position of nurses employed on clinical work is clear. One possibility would be the introduction of an open system of distinction awards on the lines of the one that applies to hospital consultants. This would involve developing criteria for clinical excellence which could include factors such as innovation in clinical methods, research and teaching.

13.38   The Salmon Committee envisaged that the nursing officer in the hospital would be in charge of a unit, and would be responsible "for seeing that patient care is of a high order, that the requirements for nurse education are met and that the unit is efficiently managed."[1] Her functions would include keeping abreast of clinical developments, advising unit nursing staff on nursing practice and helping to solve problems of patient care, as well as dealing with managerial matters such as deployment of staff and arrangements for nurse education.

13.39   It seems to us that the nursing officer should have a satisfying role with combined professional, administrative and personnel functions. However, her professional functions of acting as consultant in nursing practice, developing new ideas and methods, and teaching have emerged only in a few places. There are a number of reasons for this. First, the management content of the role is often so demanding that little time is left for clinical involvement, and training for nursing officers has often emphasised the management role to the exclusion of preparation for an advanced clinical role. Second, the medical profession have traditionally consulted the ward sister, and the Regional Nursing Officers told us that "the Nursing Officer has in most cases been 'relegated' by medical staff to administrative duties only". Third, there is a real difficulty for grades above ward sister acting as consultants and advisers on clinical care if they do not take responsibility for the care of individual patients. Expertise and special knowledge are quickly outdated. In the present system the ward sister has effective control of the clinical nursing care of patients in her ward, while the nursing officer has limited access to patients and her role as consultant has no base. She rarely has training in research methods and the clinical teacher may effectively exclude her from a teaching role.

13.40   We consider that the original concept of the nursing officer has much to commend it and we recommend that her clinical role should be developed along the lines envisaged by the Salmon Committee. There is scope for experiment, for example in the nursing officer specialising in *either* the clinical *or* the management aspect of her role. It seems to us that a clinical nursing officer should assume responsibility for a group of selected patients and combine clinical, research and teaching functions.

---

[1]Department of Health and Social Security and Welsh Office, *Progress on Salmon*, London, DHSS and WO, 1972, page 52.

13.41 We have already referred to the development of nurse specialist/ consultant posts in the hospital service. There was some criticism of this development in our evidence. As COHSE said:

"Who is going to consult the nurse consultant? We don't think that the ward sister will. It would undermine the role of the sister. In fact it would change her role beyond recognition – the key role in the nursing structure. Perhaps the doctor will consult the nurse consultant then? We don't think so. The doctor will also want to consult the ward sister – and rightly so when he or she wants information about the patient."

While we think this overstates the case, healthy scepticism about the creation of new jobs is certainly desirable. On the other hand nurses may well acquire considerable expertise in a special area, for example in the control of infection, which can and should be put to good use elsewhere in the service. The nature of this role and the specialist's relationship with her colleagues will need to be worked out. This is a matter for the profession itself and research will assist it in dealing with these issues. The grading of nurses who develop specialist or consultant roles is of course for the Whitley Councils to determine, but we would expect that nursing officer or above would often be appropriate.

13.42 Hard and fast rules will prevent the best use being made of highly skilled manpower. The 30 years of the NHS have seen the emergence of many professional groups in response to service need, and there is no reason why this should not occur in nursing also. The nurse is to some extent in the same position as the newly qualified doctor: she has had her general training but her usefulness will be further improved by experience and the development of specialist knowledge and skills. We recommend that the development of such specialisation, both in the community and hospital, should be encouraged. The continued expansion and improvement of post-basic education will be essential and we refer to this later.

13.43 The fourth approach to improving the career prospects of nurses engaged in clinical work is to combine clinical work with teaching and research. We see this combination at different levels in both the ward sister's and clinical nursing officer's roles, and we suggest that joint appointments between the schools of nursing and the nursing service could be developed with benefit to both nursing education and patient care. We deal with education and research in the next section.

13.44 The approaches to improving the nurse clinical career structure considered above are not exclusive. They complement each other and all four should be encouraged. This should do much to ensure that the nurse who wants to remain in the clinical field will have a worthwhile and rewarding job.

Education and Research

13.45 The Nurses, Midwives and Health Vistors Act 1979 is a notable, if long-awaited, contribution to nursing education. It provides for a single United Kingdom Central Council supported by powerful national boards in each of the four parts of the UK which replace the existing separate bodies responsible for the education and regulation of the professions. The Central Council has a duty to prepare and maintain a central register of qualified nurses, midwives and health visitors, and to determine the education, training and other requirements for admission to the register. Such a structure is consistent with the Briggs Committee view that:

> "what the branches of a united profession have to give to each other is more significant and more fundamental than the respects in which they differ. We believe that a structure can be created in which essential differences are safeguarded within the overall unity".[1]

We endorse this view and welcome the Act.

13.46   The Briggs Committee proposed a broad training for all entrants leading to a certificate of nursing practice fitting "a nurse to work in any field at the basic level of membership in a nursing team".[2] Experience in different fields of nursing during training would help to break down the barriers that exist at present, provide a greater flexibility in deployment, and promote a better understanding of the diverse professional roles in an integrated service. The Committee went on to recommend courses at registration and higher certificate level for more specialised roles. It will be part of the task of the new Central Council to review these recommendations in the light of more recent educational and professional developments. Reports from the Court, Jay and Warnock Committees[3] have implications for paediatric and mental handicap nursing and midwifery and health visiting. In addition the EEC requirements will affect the range of experience required.

Nurse learners

13.47   Student and pupil nurses are employees of the NHS and form some 25% of the total nursing staff employed in the hospital service. Not surprisingly there are occasions when patient and educational needs conflict. Training arrangements should be designed to minimise pressures on students and pupils, and provide adequate support and supervision by qualified staff. There has long been an argument about whether nurse learners should be bona fide students rather than employees, and it appeared also in our evidence. The General Nursing Council (GNC) for England and Wales told us that their concern for the nurse learner could be expressed in two related questions:

> "(A) is the trainee nurse being recruited/employed for her immediate availability as a worker in hospital or for her future potential as a trained nurse?
>
> (B) is the trainee nurse being trained/educated for her own benefit or for the overall needs of the NHS?"

---

[1](Cmnd 5115), *Op cit*, paragraph 621.

[2]*Ibid*, paragraph 271.

[3]*Fit for the Future. The Report of the Committee on Child Health Services*, (Cmnd 6684), London, HMSO, 1976; *Report of the Committee of Enquiry into Mental Handicap Nursing and Care, Op cit*; *Special Educational Needs. Report of the Committee of Enquiry into the Education of Handicapped Children and Young People*, (Cmnd 7212), London, HMSO, 1978.

The truth is that the nurse learner is being recruited for both her availability as a worker and her future potential as a qualified nurse; and for both her own benefit and the overall needs of the health service. However, there is inherent conflict in these aims.

13.48 The GNC for England and Wales drew to our attention the proportion of time which learners can contribute to service needs after educational requirements have been met and the problems this creates for nurse managers, teachers, ward sisters and the learners themselves. The GNC recommended that the trainee should remain an employee. The RCN did not agree:

> "recent legislation, relating to the employment situation has made untenable the student/employee status of the nurse learner ... In urging that nurse learners should be accorded student status the RCN is not departing from its strongly held view that nursing can only be taught and learnt in the context of giving care. In the course of training students will contribute to the service; this does not require that they be employees of the service authority ... There is need to review the status of nurse learners as a matter or urgency".

13.49 A Working Group was set up by the DHSS following the Briggs Committee report to consider the status of the nurse learner and it supported the view of the Committee that:

> "students should not consider themselves as nor be considered as part of the ordinary labour force of the National Health Service".[1]

The Working Group concluded that although there should be no immediate change in the present "employee" status, the question should be pursued by the new educational bodies. We support this conclusion. We consider it essential to the quality of the service that patients should not be nursed by untrained staff unless they are adequately supervised, and that the nurse's basic education should prepare her for an exacting future role. We also set out some broad principles:

> clinical practice is the "core" of nursing education;
>
> clinical practice is best taught by practising nurses in real situations;
>
> in learning practical skills the nurse learner will inevitably give service to the NHS whatever her status;
>
> adequate demonstration of skills and supervision of practice must be given by trained staff and standards of supervision need to be established;
>
> whatever the nurse learner's status her educational needs must be safeguarded.

Post-basic training

13.50 Nursing, midwifery and health visiting have a long and honourable history of post-basic preparation for advanced roles in the profession. These

---

[1](Cmnd 5115), *Op cit*, paragraph 361.

include preparation for management, nurse teaching and clinical roles in hospital and the community. At present a number of different bodies have responsibility and courses are organised in higher and further education establishments, within the NHS and by the Royal Colleges. The United Kingdom Central Council for Nursing, Midwifery and Health Visiting will be able to take a broad view of both basic and post-basic education and a great deal of rationalisation should be possible.

13.51 Basic nursing education can only be a foundation. It needs to be followed by systematic updating and more advanced preparation for specialised roles through post-basic educational programmes. We approve the diversity of provision that is available. In particular we welcome the work of the Council for the Education and Training of Health Visitors since its inauguration, the introduction of mandatory training for district nurses by the Panel of Assessors for District Nursing, and the progress made by the Joint Board of Clinical Nursing Studies (JBCNS) since it was established in 1972. By the end of 1978 the JBCNS had approved 375 education centres, and outline curricula had been prepared for 64 courses leading to a certificate and a further 16 leading to a statement of attendance. Although this represents considerable progress there is room for further development.

13.52 We were told that financial support for post-basic nursing education was not always available. We believe that nurses, midwives and health visitors should be adequately prepared for advanced roles in clinical specialties, education, management and research. Post-basic education is essential, and we recommend that health authorities should establish budgets and develop programmes for their nurses.

Nurse teachers

13.53 We referred earlier to the Briggs Committee recommendation that pending the establishment of the new educational bodies:

"As a matter of utmost urgency, a major programme to increase the nurse and midwife teaching strength should be launched."[1]

This has not happened. The number of qualified teachers has been slow to expand despite their relatively favourable financial position compared with the clinical grades (see Table 13.4). The DHSS told us that although attempts have been made to increase the numbers, a high wastage rate has kept the ratio of qualified teachers to learners constant at about 1 to 25 since 1972. While the ratio has improved in Scotland from 1 to 36 in 1972 to 1 to 21 in 1977, it still falls substantially short of the 1 to 15 aimed at for Scotland. The ratio in Northern Ireland was 1 to 17 in 1977, and in Wales 1 to 23 in 1978.

13.54 The delay in implementing this specific recommendation of the Briggs Committee may in part have caused the uncertainty about the future which has affected the supply of nurse teachers. The GNC for England and Wales highlighted three problems; inadequate support for the development of

---

[1]*Ibid*, paragraph 710.

new curricula, shortages of trained staff in clinical practice, and shortages of qualified teachers carrying clinical responsibilities. The GNC recommended a number of measures to solve these problems, but they are still under discussion with the DHSS. This lack of progress underlines our concern at the apparent failure of the parties involved to recognise the need for urgent action in developing nursing education and increasing the number of nurse teachers.

13.55 Part of the difficulty in recruiting sufficient nurse teachers has undoubtedly been that once a nurse goes into education she may effectively lose touch with clinical work. One solution to this problem would be to ensure that tutorial staff also carry a clinical load in the same way as university medical teaching staff have clinical responsibilities for NHS patients. It seems to us that joint appointments between service and education have several advantages: they enable the teacher to keep in touch with clinical work and to avoid a too theoretical "classroom" approach to teaching; the nurse who is interested in teaching but does not want to give up her clinical work need not do so; and the more attractive salary scales at present available to the tutorial grades might be open to the nurse interested in clinical work who wished to improve her career prospects. We have not gone into this in depth, but although apprehensions have been expressed about such appointments we recommend that developments in joint appointments between schools of nursing and the service should be vigorously pursued. We envisage that this role could combine clinical research and teaching, and it could be seen as an expansion of the clinical teacher's role or as specialisation within the nursing officer role. In addition we consider it important that full-time clinical nurses should receive adequate training for their teaching role, and should be encouraged, say by honorary appointments or attachments to nursing schools, to pursue it. The increase in nurse teachers recommended by the Briggs Committee seven years ago, a recommendation which we endorse, is now urgent, and unless it takes place the other reforms of nurse education proposed by the Committee will not be possible.

Nursing research

13.56 Although nurses are the largest staff group in the NHS, few nursing methods have been examined for their effectiveness. A much more critical approach towards nursing is required, and nurses themselves should obviously be involved in researching it. We were pleased to learn of recent improved arrangements for enabling nurses to undertake research. In particular the RCN Research Society are encouraging research-minded nurses. There is a useful dissemination of research findings in the RCN research series, and in the Index of Nursing Research and Nursing Research Abstracts published by the DHSS. The Nursing Research Unit at the University of Edinburgh has an outstanding reputation and there is a growing amount of research associated with departments of nursing in the universities and polytechnics. We welcome the establishment of the Nursing Education Research Unit at Chelsea College, the Nursing Practice Research Unit at Northwick Park Hospital, and the World Health Organisation collaborative units for research on the nursing process at Edinburgh and Manchester Universities. There is heartening evidence in the literature and in practice that nurses are beginning to apply research findings in their work, in for example, the prevention of pressure sores, feeding the unconscious patient, the management of pain, and promotion of continence.

13.57 Despite this it seems to us that there is considerable scope for developing nursing research further. However, competent researchers cannot be created overnight. Nursing fellowships are available from the health departments and though numbers awarded have risen slightly, demand from well-qualified applicants has been small. We hope that the education arrangements recommended by the Briggs Committee will, in due course, provide a basis which will enable nurses with an interest in research to develop their potential. We should also like to see health authorities do more to encourage their nurses to assist in, or undertake themselves, perhaps on a part-time basis, approved research projects. This is, after all, the way that much of the clinical research undertaken by doctors is arranged. We consider that our earlier suggestion of incorporating a research function into clinical and teaching roles will assist development in this field. We say more about research in Chapter 17.

Conclusions and Recommendations

13.58 It is difficult to overestimate the importance of nursing services in the NHS. Nurses are the most numerous and the most costly group of health workers, but more important is the close relationship they have with patients. We were therefore disturbed by criticisms of standards of care made by the Royal College of Nursing and referred to in our evidence.

13.59 Our whole approach to the questions discussed in this chapter has been coloured by the report of the Briggs Committee. The Committee dealt with matters which we would otherwise have had to discuss. We were disappointed that more progress had not been made with implementing their recommendations. There was disagreement in the profession over some aspects of the Committee's recommendations, and, like many other desirable reforms, the follow-up work on the report was held up by NHS reorganisation. In particular little progress has been made on the clear recommendation, which we endorse, for more nurse teachers. However, the Nurses, Midwives and Health Visitors Act 1979, which sets up the new statutory educational bodies is a welcome, if long-awaited, development.

13.60 The profession is going through a difficult period. It has suffered major structural changes following the Salmon and Mayston Reports and was considerably influenced by the management changes introduced at reorganisation. Nurse administrators fulfil a necessary function, but to do their jobs properly need adequate supporting staff. The role of the nurse is varied and it is being further extended and expanded by, for example, research into the caring function of the nurse, and development of specialisation. There is a need to improve the clinical career structure, and to encourage flexibility in the way nurses work.

13.61 Developments in nurse education have been delayed pending the new statutory bodies. The Central Council for Nursing, Midwifery and Health

Visiting will need to review both basic and post-basic education. Linked to this we see a need to develop the research capacity of the profession.

13.62   We recommend that:

(a) the profession and the health departments should encourage and pursue experiments in the development of the nursing role (paragraph 13.23);

(b) research is required into the effect of the use of unqualified staff on patient care and into the best composition of the ward team in different settings (paragraph 13.29);

(c) the health departments should undertake such central manpower planning as is necessary, that is develop a national recruitment policy, assist the setting of standards and objectives, propagate good practice and ensure an adequate data base which will be of considerable importance to the new statutory educational bodies (paragraph 13.31);

(d) the clinical role of the nursing officer should be developed along the lines envisaged by the Salmon Committee (paragraph 13.40);

(e) the development of specialist knowledge and skills, both in the community and hospital should be encouraged (paragraph 13.42);

(f) health authorities should establish budgets and develop programmes of post-basic nursing education for their staff (paragraph 13.52);

(g) developments of joint appointments between schools of nursing and the service should be vigorously pursued (paragraph 13.55).

Chapter 14   Doctors

14.1   The vast majority of people will when they are ill expect the doctor to diagnose what is wrong and prescribe treatment. Although doctors account for only seven per cent of NHS workers they are responsible in the end for initiating most of the expenditure in the NHS. They also play an important part in the management of the financial resources, and of the service.

14.2   In this chapter we discuss the main problems presented to us in evidence which are specific to the medical profession, particularly those members of it who work in hospitals. In other chapters we deal with aspects of general medical practice, private practice, and other matters which affect doctors. Here we concentrate on the role and number of doctors needed and their distribution in the specialities; problems of particular groups of doctors (those from overseas, women doctors, community physicians, and community health service doctors); and contractual matters, including the hospital doctors' career structure, distinction awards, the proposed new consultant contract and the GP's contactor status.

Role, Numbers, Distribution

14.3   The number of doctors needed depends both upon the nature of their activity and upon its effectiveness. Their role has changed in response to developments in medicine, and as a consequence of changes in attitude and aspiration. It is not defined and it varies according to individual inclinations and circumstances. Few detailed studies have been made of medical work in the UK, and this is an important area for future health services research.

14.4   Hospital medicine is likely to become increasingly specialised as advances are made in scientific knowledge and technology. Numbers of general physicians and general surgeons have been declining as specialities develop within these two broad fields. Increasing specialisation and the rigidity in staff roles which accompany it are likely to lead to higher staffing levels. So are patient expectations and influences, which increasingly demand more personal medical attention, though it is not yet clear how hospital-based doctors will respond to this. Doctors in the acute specialities may see their role as being predominantly physically oriented and dependent on the findings of biomedical research and on developments in technology. In other hospital specialities, such as those dealing with the behaviourally disturbed, the emphasis more certainly will be on development of the relationship between doctor and patient.

14.5   Other factors may affect the nature of hospital doctors' work. The junior hospital doctor's contract, and the proposed new consultant contract, link pay to periods of time and particular activities. The present policy of increasing numbers of consultants relative to numbers in the training grades will lead to them taking on work at present done by their juniors. An increase in GP involvement in hospital care, for example through development of the hospital practitioner grade, desirable in itself, may affect hospital doctors' work. What doctors do will also be influenced by developments in the roles of other professions.

14.6   We discussed developments in general practice in Chapter 7. The GP deals with about 90% of all illness, both physical and mental, but it is only recently that the Royal College of General Practitioners has proposed explicitly a comprehensive approach to the physical, psychological and social aspects of patients' illnesses. Many people expect such a role from their GP, but it is not always reflected in his attitude, nor in the way in which general practice is run. Sympathetic personal attention is time consuming, and patients complain that their GPs do not give them enough time.

14.7   It is not certain that the smaller lists that will come with the increased output of the medical schools and the increased popularity of general practice will necessarily lead GPs to devote more time to their patients. Studying 22 doctors in general practice, Buchan and Richardson found "little evidence that list size is a major factor governing the length of time spent with patients".[1] Cartwright and Anderson in evidence to us reported:

"92% of the general practitioners in our sample in 1977 thought there was a growing tendency for people to seek help from doctors for problems in their family lives. At the same time the proportion of doctors who felt it was appropriate for people to seek help from their general practitioners for problems in their family lives had fallen from 87% in 1964 to 67% in 1977 ... Doctors in their fifties were more likely than their younger colleagues to feel that consultations for family problems were appropriate: 75% of them did so, 62% of younger doctors."[2]

14.8   The primary care team may influence the GP's role. Nurses are already undertaking dressings, injections, and other procedures traditionally performed by GPs. It is not clear how the counselling role can best be undertaken and distributed between members of the team. Nor is it known what implications a greater emphasis on the psychological aspects of care would have for training and staffing levels. Accepted policy is to reduce list sizes, but again it is not known if this influences the effectiveness or humane quality of patient care. Systematic study of these questions may lead to some answers, but it is just as likely that the role of doctors will be affected by the numbers available as the reverse. The fundamental problem that we have drawn attention to in earlier chapters remains: no limits have yet been set to the potential demand for health care.

---

[1]Buchan, I C and Richardson, I M, "Time study of consultations in general practice", *Scottish Health Service Studies,* Number 27, 1973, page 16.

[2]Cartwright, A and Anderson, R, "Patients and their Doctors 1977", Institute for Social Studies in Medical Care, *Royal College of General Practitioners Occasional Paper,* Number 8, March 1979.

Numbers

14.9   The number of doctors the UK should train is clearly of great concern
to the profession, especially those of its members in the hospital training
grades. The BMA's written evidence to us recommended "a major review of
the manpower situation" forthwith, and considered "that this problem is of
sufficient urgency to justify the Royal Commission reporting on this in advance
of its main report". We have not felt able to do so both because it would have
meant stopping other work and devoting several months to the study of a
narrow, if important, problem, and because we thought that others more expert
than us in this field could do the job better. However, in view of the concern
expressed in the evidence to us we commissioned and published a study on
doctor manpower up to the year 2000.[1] The health departments have also been
active: a fact-finding group of representatives of the departments, the BMA
and the NHS has been established, and a valuable discussion paper[2] which
considered how many doctors will be employed in Great Britain up to the end
of the century was published last year.

14.10   Table 14.1 shows the growth in numbers of doctors in GB since
1949.

TABLE 14.1

Growth in Numbers of Doctors: Great Britain 1949–1978

Whole-time equivalents

	1949	*1974*	*1975*	*1976*	*1977*	*1978*
Hospital Doctors[1]						
England	11,735	25,618	26,922	27,686	28,397	29,293
Wales		1,472	1,528	1,578	1,648	1,705
Scotland	1,900[2]	4,417	4,509	4,591	4,737	—[5]
General Medical						
Practitioners[3]						
England	18,000[4]	21,531	21,752	22,015	22,327	22,651
Wales		1,354	1,370	1,362	1,394	1,418
Scotland	2,000[4]	2,959	3,006	3,041	3,089	3,148
Community and School						
Health Services						
England	—[5]	2,347	2,565	2,681	2,745	2,782
Wales	—[5]	176	193	205	209	204
Scotland	—[5]	307	417	436	452	—[5]

Source: compiled from health departments' statistics

Notes: [1] Excludes locum staff, (except in 1949), and GPs holding hospital appointments.

   [2] 1948. Excludes honorary staff.

   [3] Numbers rather than whole-time equivalents.

   [4] Estimated.

   [5] Figures not available.

While the number of hospital doctors has more than doubled during the period
at an average growth rate of over three per cent per annum, number of GPs
have increased by only about 36% at an average rate of something under two
per cent per annum. Table 14.2 shows the numbers of doctors per 10,000

[1]Maynard, Alan and Walker, Arthur, *Doctor Manpower 1975-2000* Royal Commission on the
National Health Service, Research Paper Number 4, London, HMSO, 1978.

[2]Department of Health and Social Security, Scottish Home and Health Department and Welsh
Office, *Medical Manpower – The next Twenty Years. A Discussion Paper,* London, HMSO, 1978.

population for selected "developed" countries. Scotland comes in about the middle of the table, Northern Ireland further down, and England and Wales are nearly at the bottom. On these comparisons there is no reason to think that the UK has, or is likely this century to have too many doctors.

TABLE 14.2
Number of Doctors per 10,000 Population;
International Comparisons: 1974

Country	Doctors per 10,000 population
Italy	19.9[1,2]
W Germany	19.4
Canada	16.6
USA	16.5
Norway	16.5
Sweden	16.2
Scotland	16.1
N Ireland	15.3
Netherlands	14.9
France	13.9[2]
Australia	13.9[3]
Finland	13.3[1]
England and Wales	13.1
Japan	11.6

Source: McKinsey & Co, *International Comparisons of Health Needs and Health Services*, April 1978

Notes: [1] Registered personnel.
         [2] 1973.
         [3] 1972.

14.11   We referred in Chapter 12 to the studies of medical manpower needs which have taken place at roughly ten year intervals. The Royal Commission on Medical Education (the Todd Commission)[1] which reported in 1968 recommended an expansion in the entry to medical schools to 4,300 by 1979. While the build up has been slower than originally intended, about 4,000 students entered medical schools in the UK in 1978. The stock of doctors is likely to increase substanially in the next few years. Just what the increase will be depends on factors such as the balance between immigration and emigration, the present overproduction of doctors in some EEC countries, and the number of women in the workforce. These and other factors influencing the supply of medical manpower are considered in the health departments' discussion paper and in our research paper.

14.12   Some of the factors influencing demand for doctors are the birth rate; the performance of the national economy (because employment prospects for doctors depend, like those for the rest of us, on money being available to pay for them); the role of doctors and their relationship with other health workers who may undertake work which would otherwise be done by doctors;

---

[1]*Report of the Royal Commission on Medical Education 1965-68*, (Cmnd 3569), London, HMSO, 1968.

developments in medicine; and changes in hours worked by doctors. Health department policies may influence demand: for example, the DHSS told us that the White Paper "Better Services for the Mentally Ill"[1] required 290 more consultants than at present and something like ten per cent more GPs would be required to bring the average list size in England down to 2,000 patients. Changes such as these would depend on the funds being available to pay for the doctors as much as on there being doctors available to employ.

14.13   The evidence of the Hospital Junior Staffs Committee of the BMA analysed the position and concluded:

"That the annual output of medical graduates should be reduced to 2820 by an immediate reduction in medical school intake."

They estimated that the "total economically-active British graduated doctors" would be about 91,000 by the year 2013, which is not out of line with other projections. The Committee's essential argument was that "the economic circumstances of this Kingdom will preclude any great increase of expenditure on the Health Services", and that unless student numbers are cut there will be medical unemployment. They calculated that reducing the intake of medical students would save about £94m in training costs over the next five years, plus another £9.4m annual salary saving. This kind of calculation can be criticised, and the health departments' paper showed that if the medical school intake remained at 4000 per annum to the end of the century, resources should be available to support the additional doctors. We have suggested in Chapter 12 that there should be regular and more frequent reviews of the medical manpower position, and we consider it to be most important that discussion of a matter which affects the profession so closely should be conducted publicly.

14.14   The health departments have much more information available, and more time to digest it than we did. However, the difficulties of forecasting the birth rate, and the uncertainties of the performance of the economy, make long-term prediction of medical needs a particularly hazardous business. Both the Willink Committee[2] and the Todd Royal Commission misjudged the trend in the birth rate, and the Todd Commission's expectation of steady economic growth of three per cent per annum has not been realised. The Royal College of Surgeons of England commented:

"Previous attempts to forecast the staffing needs of the NHS have not met with conspicuous success and the most important lesson to be learnt from the past is that the future is unpredictable."

14.15   Nonetheless we chance our arm here. We think that the planned output of medical graduates is about right at present, and that there is unlikely to be medical unemployment this century. It may be that doctors will not have the choice of specialty and place of practice they have at present, but this is not peculiar to the medical profession. We noted that the BMA's GP Charter

[1]*Better Services for the Mentally Ill*, (Cmnd 6233), London, HMSO, 1975.

[2]*Report of the Committee to Consider the Future Numbers of Medical Practitioners and the Appropriate Intake of Medical Students*, London, HMSO, 1957.

Working Group[1] provided for a reduction in list size from 2000 to 1700 patients. The trend nationally and internationally has been towards employing more doctors rather than fewer, and we have no reason to think that this will be reversed.

Distribution

14.16 The distribution of doctors is uneven geographically and there are shortages in particular specialties. We have already commented on some aspects of medical manpower distribution: in Chapter 3 we drew attention to geographical inequalities in the distribution of doctors and other health service workers in the UK; and in Chapter 7 we commented on the special difficulties of persuading GPs to work in inner city areas. In Chapter 12 we made some suggestions for changes in manpower planning arrangements in the NHS. There are some other general points to be made before we go on to consider the problems of improving the distribution of doctors within the UK and between specialties.

14.17 First, geographical and specialty shortages may be linked. Places which find it difficult to recruit doctors generally will find it particularly difficult to recruit in the shortages specialties. Another aspect of this is that a shortage of, say, surgeons may mask a shortage of anaesthetists because fewer anaesthetists are needed if fewer operations are being carried out. There is also the possibility that a shortage in one specialty will lead to the under-use of another.

14.18 Second, there are few generally accepted staffing standards. Table 14.2 shows that numbers of doctors per 10,000 population in 1974 ranged from 11.6 in Japan to nearly 20 in Italy. Within the UK the range in 1977 was from 9.68 in Trent RHA to 15.17 in Scotland, but Trent RHA has a much better health record than Scotland on most of the accepted indices. How then are shortages to be measured?

14.19 Third, quantity may not be a satisfactory substitute for quality. In recent years there have been larger than average increases in several of the shortage specialties, but these may be made up in part by recruits who have taken the jobs because career prospects are good, and such recruits may bring little enthusiasm to their work. In 1977 consultant geriatricians on first appointment had spent only four years in the specialty against an average for all specialties in England and Wales of seven years.

Geographical Distribution

14.20 It is not difficult to show that the geographical spread of doctors in the UK is very uneven. Table 14.3 shows the distribution of GPs and hospital doctors by population. Population by itself is an unsatisfactory measure: it takes no account of factors such as the movement of patients across administrative boundaries, the incidence of disease, or the distribution of non-

---

[1]British Medical Association, *Report of the New Charter Working Group,* London, BMA, 1979.

212

medical staff. Furthermore, different populations will have different needs: an elderly population will generate more work than a relatively young one.

14.21 A great many factors affect health – itself an elusive concept, as we pointed out in Chapter 2 – and the availability of doctors is only one of them, but it is usually assumed that a more even distribution is desirable, and this has been one of the objectives of those concerned with medical manpower planning. Although considerable progress has been made since 1948, Table 14.3 shows that wide variations remain. There are also intra-regional differences, for example we were told that the medical staffing in peripheral hospitals was often a problem.

14.22 In England and Wales the establishment of the Central Manpower Committee, the Manpower Advisory Committee on Community Medicine and the Medical Practices Committee, and equivalent machinery for Scotland and Northern Ireland,[1] has led to a more systematic attempt to improve the geographical distribution of medical manpower. Progress has necessarily been slow. The constraints on resources over recent years have had an effect, but

TABLE 14.3

Distribution of GPs and Hospital Doctors; Numbers per Head of Population: UK 1977

	General Medical Practitioners per 10,000 Population	Hospital Doctors[1] per 10,000 Population
ENGLAND	4.84	6.13
Northern	4.55	6.22
Yorkshire	4.70	5.62
Trent	4.54	5.14
East Anglia	4.85	5.71
NW Thames	5.48	7.84
NE Thames	5.10	7.40
SE Thames	5.01	6.85
SW Thames	5.17	6.25
Wessex	4.98	5.45
Oxford	4.73	6.04
South Western	5.17	5.32
West Midlands	4.56	5.45
Mersey	4.60	6.13
North Western	4.55	6.59
WALES	5.05	5.96
SCOTLAND	5.98	9.19
N IRELAND	5.56	7.84
UNITED KINGDOM	4.98	6.45

Source: health departments' statistics.

Note: [1] whole-time equivalents.

---

[1]For Scotland the equivalents are the Advisory Committee on Hospital Medical Establishments, the Advisory Committee on Community Medicine Establisments and the Scottish Medical Practices Committee, and for Northern Ireland the Northern Ireland Medical Manpower Advisory Committee. All these bodies are advisory, their recommendations being subject to decision by the health ministers. We refer to them collectively as "central manpower machinery".

perhaps the main reason is the length of time doctors in the career grades, consultants and GPs,[1] spend in post. On average a hospital doctor gets his first consultant appointment when he is about 37, and may go on working past the normal retiring age of 65. Nationally applied terms and conditions of service mean that there is likely to be little incentive for a consultant to move once appointed and he may stay in his first post for 30 or more years. GPs are often appointed in their 20s and may spend even longer in the same place. Contraction in the number of career posts in a region therefore depends primarily on vacancies occurring and not being filled — which carries implications for the work of other doctors in the area. Expansion depends on the creation and funding of new posts.

14.23   There are different reasons for shortages. Some shortage specialties, like radiology and anaesthetics, have been created by a rapid increase in demand combined with attractive opportunities abroad; others, like the laboratory specialties, lack opportunities for private practice; and others, perhaps like the psychiatric specialties, may only appeal to relatively few doctors. Teaching hospital traditions, conditions of work, and opportunities for research may also play their part. By definition career prospects are good in the shortage specialties. The average doctor will make the consultant grade sooner and will have a larger choice of post. The health departments and medical schools make information on career available to medical students.

14.24   The creation of new consultant and senior registrar posts in England and Wales is controlled by the Central Manpower Committee. Since 1974 the Scottish Advisory Committee on Hospital Medical Establishments has also controlled other medical training grades, but outside Scotland grades below senior registrar are not at present centrally controlled, and it is up the employing authority to decide how many junior doctors it should employ. A number of factors, such as availability and recognition of posts for training purposes will influence this decision, but probably the most important will be the number of vacancies there are in the existing establishment and the funds available. Recent pressures on health authorities' funds, and the redistributive effects of the Resource Allocation Working Party (RAWP) formula and equivalents outside England, will no doubt encourage authorities to look more closely at their medical staffing needs. The best staffed regions are also those which have in the past been proportionately well off for revenue funds and would stand to suffer most under the strict application of the RAWP formula.

14.25   Scotland is relatively well provided with doctors with over 15 per 10,000 population compared to 11.43 for the UK as a whole. The reasons are mainly historical: the Scottish Home and Health Department estimate that "approximately 300 – 350 doctors per annum are required for Scotland's permanent needs" whereas the intake of medical students to the Scottish medical schools has averaged 650 students in recent years. In 1976/77 per capita expenditure on health services in Scotland was 21.2% higher than that in England and 18.4% higher than in Wales (Northern Ireland was higher still but had a lower doctor/population ratio than Scotland).

---

[1]We are primarily concerned here with hospital medicine and general practice, but some of the same difficulties arise in respect of doctors working in community medicine.

14.26   While it is difficult to show that difference in medical staffing ratios are reflected in the health of the population, the unevenness of distribution gives rise to resentment in the less fortunate parts of the country. The process of correction is necessarily slow: authorities do not find it easy to close down posts themselves. In the absence of generally accepted yardsticks it is not possible to say with certainty that a particular area must have a certain number of doctors, and for the same reason it is not possible to identify those places which are overstaffed. There is much to be said for allowing health authorities, so far as possible, to provide services in their own way and to determine the level and balance of staffing in the light of their own circumstances. The combined pressures of controls exercised by the central manpower machinery referred to above, and the redistributive effects of RAWP and equivalents, will probably eventually lead to greater equality in medical manning levels. Some local shortages are inevitable, and the difficulties of predicting shifts in population 10 or 15 years ahead – the kind of time scale which is involved in the production of new consultants or GPs – suggests that too rigid an approach is not justified.

Specialisation and shortage specialties

14.27   We are concerned here with hospital specialties. The problems of community medicine are dealt with below, and general practice is discussed in Chapter 7. We start by making some general points about specialisation in medicine.

14.28   A clinical specialty is one recognised as such by the Royal College and Faculties concerned. There are currently 47 hospital clinical specialties, 11 of them introduced in the last ten years, and some of them having only tiny numbers of consultant posts so far. The process of recognition of a new specialty need not involve anyone but the members of the specialty and the Royal College and Faculties. However, since the establishment of new consultant and senior registrar posts is regulated by the central manpower machinery, new appointments cannot be made in an emergent specialty without the agreement of the health departments.

14.29   Clinical specialties have developed for various reasons. Some have been closely linked with major developments in technology, such as radiology; some have focussed on particular organs of the body, such as cardiology, nephrology, and ophthalmology; some are linked with age groups, such as paediatrics and geriatrics; and others have developed according to the locus of the work, such as general practice, forensic psychiatry, or blood transfusion. These developments have not necessarily had anything to do with the NHS, in the sense that they probably would have occurred whether or not the NHS existed.

14.30   The advantages of greater specialisation are that standards of care and training are raised and research is promoted. But there may be disadvantages also. When a specialty is created those in the specialty become reluctant to perform non-specialised activities, while those who had previously cared for the kind of patients which the specialty has been promoted to serve, may no longer see it as their responsibility to do so. A specialty often cannot cope on its own with all those patients who might be thought to fall within its remit. Thus the development of geriatrics as a specialty was encouraged as a means of enhancing the quality of care of elderly people, and it has in many places succeeded in this; but it has also influenced some physicians to take less interest in the old and to look to geriatricians excessively for the care of the elderly who now form a great part of those needing hospital treatment.[1] The division and sub-division of specialties encourages expertise, but it involves loss of flexibility in the manning of the service and tends to result in a fragmentation of patient care.

14.31 We have commented on the difficulty of knowing whether and to what extent there are shortages of doctors. The DHSS told us that they considered that a shortage specialty was one in which the demand for new consultants at any time exceeded the supply of suitable candidates. The demand for new consultants is shown by requests received from health authorities to establish new posts; while the supply of candidates can be estimated from the number of doctors in that specialty known to be in training. On this basis, and making allowance for impending retirements, etc, the main shortage specialties are regarded by the health departments as being mental illness and mental handicap, geriatrics, radiology, anaesthetics, and the pathological specialties. There are differences between the four parts of the UK. For example, anaesthetics is not considered a shortage specialty in Northern Ireland, and the SHHD told us that:

"apart from local and usually temporary problems there are no real shortages especially in the consultant grades in Scotland. Difficulties do occur from time to time in specialties such as anaesthesia, radiology, psychiatry and laboratory medicine, especially in less attractive areas."

As Table 14.4 shows, there have been large increases in all the shortage specialties in recent years, and most of them have increased faster than the average of all specialties.

TABLE 14.4
Increase in Number of Consultants in Post in Selected Specialities: Great Britain 1966–77

Specialty	Number of Consultants in post			% Increase	
	1966	1971	1977	1966–77	1971–77
Anaesthetics	1,209	1,438	1,730	43.1	20.3
Geriatric Medicine	190	265	401	111.1	51.3
Mental Illness	842	979	1,197	42.2	22.3
Mental Handicap	103	135	148	43.7	9.6
Radiology	639	718	863	35.1	20.2
All Specialties	10,075	11,542	13,530	34.3	17.2

Source: compiled from health departments' statistics.

[1]We say more about this in Chapter 6.

14.32   The increasing numbers of doctors resulting from the expansion in university medical school places may improve the position of shortage specialties though it has not solved the problem in England and Wales so far. The present strategy of the health departments is to control, through the central manpower machinery, appointments of consultants and senior registrars, and to favour the shortage specialties. At best the building up of shortage specialties will be a slow business because of the relatively small number of posts that are created each year. It will also be important to maintain the quality of recruitment. We recommend that the health departments should show more determination in enforcing their priorities in the shortage specialties, if necessary by blocking expansion of other specialties; and should be more critically involved in the development of new specialties. At present the creation of new specialties is too often seen by the health departments as a way of correcting neglect in particular fields, and the medical profession appears sometimes to be too ready to accept the claims of small sectional interests.

14.33   It is plainly important that students should be encouraged to work in the specialties which the NHS needs to man. In addition to career prospects, we think it likely that the quality of teaching in the subject, the facilities that can be offered for clinical practice and for research, and above all the attitude of the teachers themselves towards the specialties are important factors in attracting students into specialties the NHS needs. In Chapter 6 we have suggested the greater use of doctors with joint appointments to work in geriatrics and mental handicap. We recommend that the development of special interests in other shortage specialties amongst doctors who are working in related fields should be encouraged and appropriate training programmes provided.

Problems of Particular Groups

Overseas doctors

14.34   There are probably about 18,000 registered doctors in the UK who were born outside the UK and the Republic of Ireland.[1] About half of them were born in India or Pakistan, a quarter in other commonwealth countries (including Australia, Canada and New Zealand), and the rest elsewhere in the world. Most of them are employed in NHS hospitals. Table 14.5 shows the proportion of overseas born doctors by grade in the four parts of the UK. Roughly one-third of doctors employed in the NHS in the UK were born overseas. The turnover of these doctors is high: about 3,500 to 4,000 of them enter the NHS annually and about 3,000 leave. There is no doubt that they have made, and are making, a valuable contribution to the NHS: the BMA told us that "the importance of their contribution to the NHS cannot be over emphasised", a view which we endorse.

14.35   The proportion of overseas doctors in hospitals varies greatly between

---

[1]"Overseas qualified" is more useful than "overseas born" since there have been large numbers of immigrants to the UK in the last 20 years or so, some of whom will have gone through our educational system but will nonetheless be shown as "overseas born" in the statistics. Unfortunately figures for "overseas qualified" are not available for England and Wales (they are available for Scotland and Northern Ireland) and we have made do with overseas born, therefore. Using place of birth exaggerates the extent to which the UK is dependent on doctors who are likely to leave the NHS. We use the term "overseas doctors" to mean doctors born overseas.

TABLE 14.5

Proportion of Overseas Born[1] Doctors by Grade: UK 1978

Grade	England		Wales		Scotland[2]		N Ireland	
	Total in grade wte	% overseas born	Total in grade wte	% overseas born	Total in grade wte	% overseas born	Total in grade wte	% overseas born
Hospital Staff[3]								
Consultant	10,382	16	614	13	1,781	8	429	7
Medical Assistant	760	43	65	32	236	17	63	13
Senior Registrar	2,227	27	95	24	414	13	91	21
Registrar	5,087	57	319	60	1,133	44	181	35
Senior House Officer	8,159	53	476	54	841	26	382	34
House Officer	2,617	14	133	8	603	5	146	14
Other[4]	61	22	3	—	32	—	—	—
All grades	29,293	35	1,705	34	5,040	19	1,292	21
GPs with hospital appointments (para 94)	1,604	26	107	20	187[5]	—	55[6]	—
Hospital Practitioner	117	15	—	—	—	—	—	—
General Practitioner[7]	22,327	20	1,394	17	2,820[6,8]	6	780	2
Community & School Health	2,782	21	204	11	555[6]	10	80[6]	5

Source: compiled from health departments' statistics.

Notes: [1] Overseas born means born outside the UK and Eire.
[2] Scotland figures are for 1977.
[3] Locums are excluded.
[4] Mainly Senior Hospital Medical Officers.
[5] Whole time equivalent.
[6] 1976.
[7] Numbers (not WTE) of restricted and unrestricted principals, trainees and assistants in 1977.
[8] Unrestricted principals only.

specialties and regions. Table 14.6 shows the percentages of posts in hospital specialties they fill in England and Wales (the proportions in Scotland and Northern Ireland are generally much smaller, as Table 14.5 demonstrates). Table E2 in Appendix E shows their distribution by regions. Posts in the NHS are normally competed for, and on the whole overseas born graduates compete less successfully than UK trained doctors. As a result, they tend to get pushed into the "unpopular" specialties such as geriatrics, and to get left with the less attractive posts.

TABLE 14.6

Percentage of Posts in Hospital Specialties Filled by Overseas Born Doctors: England and Wales 1978

Percentages

Specialty	Consultants[1]	Senior Registrars	Registrars	Senior House Officers
ALL SPECIALTIES	15.9	26.5	57.0	52.8
General Medicine	8.0	8.7	34.5	30.6
General Surgery	8.3	11.3	53.8	66.3
Paediatrics	14.4	9.9	41.6	31.1
Anaesthetics	15.8	25.2	61.5	57.1
Radiology	17.8	37.8	39.6	55.6
Mental Illness	23.4	34.0	66.8	53.7
Geriatric Medicine	40.9	53.8	84.6	75.4

Source: health departments' statistics.

Note: [1] Includes SHMOs with allowance.

14.36   It is expected that the expansion of entry to UK medical schools to over 4,000 students per annum in the early 1980s will eventually result in a reduction in the number of overseas doctors employed in the NHS. It is clear that the growth of the NHS will not sustain both net immigration on the scale of recent years and a greatly increased output from UK medical schools. It is assumed that competition for posts will make it progressively harder for overseas doctors to find jobs in the NHS and will result in a reduction in the numbers employed in the UK. The rate of reduction will depend on factors such as the output from the UK medical schools, the proportion of women doctors (since they tend to have shorter careers), the expansion of the NHS, the extent to which overseas doctors compete successfully for UK posts, the effect of the Professional and Linguistic Assessments Board (until January 1979 the Temporary Registration Assessment Board) tests,[1] the new registration arrangements, and the rate of emigration of UK trained doctors. Calculating the various permutations has become something of an industry, and the uncertainties of the situation are a source of considerable anxiety both to UK trained and overseas trained doctors.

---

[1]The TRAB tests were introduced by the General Medical Council in 1975. They test both the candidate's professional knowledge and his knowledge of English, and unless he reaches a satisfactory standard he cannot work as a doctor in the NHS. Broadly, all overseas doctors joining the NHS after July 1975 have had to sit the tests. Failures have been running at between 65% and 68%.

219

14.37 The influx of overseas doctors, especially in the last decade, has enabled numbers in the hospital service to expand much faster than would otherwise have been possible, but there are fears that the NHS has become excessively dependent on overseas doctors holding short-term contracts (training posts below senior registrar are normally held for only one or two years), and therefore vulnerable to a sudden drying up of supply, for example as a result of a decision by a foreign government to control emigration.[1] It is also argued that the concentration of overseas doctors in particular specialties and places conceals real weaknesses in the medical career structure and the distribution of doctors between specialties and geographically. We are primarily concerned with the interests of the NHS, but from a less parochial viewpoint it cannot be desirable that the UK should be attracting doctors from countries who are much less well supplied than we are, and offering in exchange a training which is geared to the needs of an industrialised, predominantly urban society which may well be inappropriate for them.

14.38 There are broadly two groups of overseas doctors working in the UK; those who have come to gain experience and a higher qualification with a view to returning home after a few years; and those who have settled in this country, who have families and homes, and who are making a career in the NHS. The dividing line is not clear but it is important to remember that overseas doctors represent substantial proportions of doctors in the career grades: 15% of consultants and 20% of general practitioners in England in 1977 were overseas born. It cannot be assumed that overseas born doctors can easily return whence they came once they can no longer find work in the NHS, though the Overseas Doctors' Association take the view that "most of the overseas doctors do come here for a limited period, mainly to obtain higher degrees and experience".

14.39 The Overseas Doctors' Association put a number of criticisms to us of the present arrangements. Some of these have been referred to already. They are well summarised in an extract from the Association's evidence:

"Most of these doctors come with high hopes of gaining expert knowledge in the field of medicine to obtain degrees and diplomas in the respective specialties. But, in cold reality, they end up in the most unpopular branches of medicine in the peripheral hospitals where the service demands are high, teaching facilities are very little or inadequate. Most of these doctors are obliged to work in casualty, orthopaedic, geriatric, psychiatric departments in district hospitals totally outside the influence of the teaching hospitals. These overseas doctors do not get the opportunity of training in the teaching hopitals and in the popular branches of medical discipline. Hence, it is not surprising that their performance is not as good as it should be in the professional examinations."

These criticisms were largely confirmed by a study of overseas doctors in the NHS undertaken by the Policy Studies Institute,[2] which showed, for example, that only 19% of overseas graduates work in teaching districts and that overseas doctors generally are under-represented in the medical specialties (apart from geriatrics), in general surgery, radiology, radiotherapy, and in pathology.

---

[1] In 1977 Pakistan introduced stricter emigration control which could affect the flow of doctors to this country.

[2] Policy Studies Institute, *Overseas Doctors in the National Health Service*, (to be published).

14.40   Some of the training deficiencies to which the Overseas Doctors' Association drew attention are not peculiar to overseas doctors, though they may be more apparent in their case. UK graduates may suffer from poor training arrangements at peripheral hospitals as much as doctors from overseas. The less popular specialties have to be manned, and someone has to work in the unattractive areas. The answer is not to make special arrangements for overseas doctors, but to improve conditions for all. There is a need for closer links between peripheral and teaching hospitals and we comment on this in Chapter 10, and the balance between career and training grades needs to be improved.

14.41   We were impressed by the moderate and helpful way the Overseas Doctors' Association put their case to us. Overseas doctors who come to the UK for a career in the NHS ask to be treated neither better nor worse than UK graduates. It is right that they should have to compete for NHS posts and it is in the interests of patients that the registration arrangements should ensure that they have an acceptable knowledge of medicine and of the English language. But they should not arrive here with false hopes. The Policy Studies Institute study found that most had no reliable information about training and career prospects in the NHS, despite the efforts of the London based National Advice Centre which was set up for that purpose. There is an obligation on both the UK and other interested governments to make clear to doctors who want to come here what their prospects are. We recommend that the UK government takes the necessary steps.

14.42   Finally, the health departments and the universities should consider developing post-graduate education and training specifically geared to the needs of overseas countries, concentrated in a small number of special centres, outside the NHS training structure, and financed either by the countries using them or through the Overseas Development Administration or some similar agency. We recommend that a few such centres should be started on an experimental basis. We do not think it either feasible or desirable to establish posts within the NHS reserved for overseas doctors.

Women doctors[1]

14.43   About one in five doctors in the UK is a woman but not all women doctors are active in medicine. Some are retired, some are bringing up children, and some have other reasons for not working. About 70% of all women doctors are thought to be active in medicine, compared with nearly 90% of men. Although women at present constitute a small proportion of medical manpower in the UK, they formed nearly 38% of the entry to medical schools in 1978 and this proportion could increase to about 50% by 1985. In the 1990s, therefore, half the new doctors in the UK may be women.

14.44   Women doctors suffer the same difficulties of combining a career with raising children as women in other occupations. These include conflict between their own and their husbands' careers, and the costs, emotional and material, which this generates. Moreover, women doctors have a problem not met in most other careers of having to undertake several years' training which cannot easily be part-time. Women with families are often immobile and find

---

[1] We refer to "women doctors" as a convenient shorthand, but what is said in this section applies to all doctors who because of domestic or similar commitments are unable to work full-time in the NHS.

it all but impossible to take jobs, whether in the training or career grades, far from home.

14.45 Doctors in the training grades traditionally spend long hours on duty. Consultants will normally have spent eight to ten years in the training grades, and implementation of the National Health Service (Vocational Training) Act 1976 will require a GP to spend three years in training after full registration before becoming eligible for a post as an unrestricted principal in general practice. Hospital doctor training requires trainees to take a succession of jobs which may be in different parts of the country and which may last only a year or two. Furthermore, part-time training is discouraged by some of the Royal Colleges, especially in the surgical specialties; and where it is permitted, it may have to amount in total to the equivalent of the full-time period specified, which greatly extends the period spent in training. In the circumstances, it is not surprising that in England in 1978 only about 10% of consultants were women, against 16% of GPs and 54% of doctors working in the community health service. Over 40% of medical assistants in hospitals are women, in a grade for which a fellowship or equivalent is not normally required, and which contains many doctors specialising in paediatrics, obstetrics and gynaecology.

14.46 There is obviously a limit to the extent to which the NHS can and should provide employment for women doctors on demand. The health departments have for many years encouraged hospitals to enable women doctors to return to work on a part-time basis. An instruction issued by the DHSS in 1969 said that the Secretary of State was prepared:

"to consider sympathetically proposals for increases in medical establishments at all levels for part-time posts specifically for women doctors and for other doctors who are unable to work more than part-time in the health service."[1]

The circular also invited hospital authorities to consider splitting existing posts into two or more part-time appointments and provide retraining and refresher courses. In England and Wales between 70 and 80 registrars and senior registrars have been appointed under HM(69)6 each year, many of them in the shortage specialties, particularly mental illness and anaesthetics. The Women Doctors' Retainer Scheme, introduced in 1972, enabled doctors who could not work more than the occasional session to keep in touch with professional activities.[2] Similar arrangements were introduced in other parts of the UK.

14.47 Progress has been made, but someone who can work only part-time still faces real difficulties in completing the training necessary for appointment as consultant. We should like to see the Joint Higher Training Committees (JHTCs) taking a more flexible attitude towards the requirements for part-time training. We wonder whether, for example, it is always necessary for part-time training to be at least a half-time commitment; or if its total duration

---

[1] HM(69)6, *Re-employment of Women Doctors*, DHSS, 1969.
[2] HM(72)42, *Women Doctors' Retainer Scheme*, DHSS, 1972.

need, in the case of a part-timer, always add up to the normal period. We wonder also if part-time training cannot be further developed in most of the surgical specialties. These are matters for the JHTCs and they must put patients' interests first, but there seems to us to be a risk that over-strict application of the rules may prevent able women from following their choice of specialty, and in the long run this may not be to the advantage of patients. On the other hand, realism is necessary: the Royal College of Physicians of Edinburgh put it to us that:

"The implications of practising in each of the medical specialties should be impressed on all medical students during their training, and girls should not be led to believe that it is possible to stop work, or to undertake prolonged part-time employment, without detriment to their eventual careers and professional satisfaction."

This should be made clear in the career advice which is now available to all students, and to all girls who propose to take up medicine as a career.

Community physicians

14.48 The Faculty of Community Medicine told us that community physicians are:

"those doctors who try to measure and predict the health care needs of the population, who plan and administer services to meet those needs, and those who teach and research in this field."

This definition excludes doctors working in the community health services who are employed on clinical work, for example in the school health service, and with whom we deal later in this chapter. We are talking here of regional medical officers, specialists in community medicine, district community physicians, and equivalents in Scotland and Northern Ireland. There are currently in post in the UK over 800 staff in these grades and about 130 trainees. In addition there are about 160 doctors who were transferred to the NHS from local health authorities at the time of reorganisation and who are engaged in administrative functions of one kind or another but have not been appointed to one of the substantive posts referred to. Numbers of these "latched on" doctors are declining as they retire or are appointed to substantive posts. Table 14.7 shows the number of community physicians in post in the four parts of the UK. As with many of the medical professional problems we have encountered, the position in Scotland is more favourable than that in the rest of the UK. What we say, therefore, applies mainly to England, Wales and Northern Ireland.

14.49 Community physicians in the NHS are drawn from services which, before reorganisation, had different traditions and roles. The great majority were employed by local authorities before reorganisation. They included medical officers of health, their deputies and others working with them. The report of the Hunter Working Party[1] estimated that in 1971 there were 1,147

---

[1]Department of Health and Social Security, *Report of the Working Party on Medical Administrators*, London, HMSO, 1972.

TABLE 14.7

Number of Community Physicians in Post and Number of Vacancies: UK
1978

	Region	Area	District	Trainees	Total	Vacancies
England	14	90	506	108	718	180
Wales	—	8	30	9	47	5
Scotland[1]	—	15	135	7	157	13
N Ireland[1]	—	11	17	5	33	10

Source: compiled from health departments' statistics.
Note: [1] 1977.

such doctors. The remainder of those transferred to the NHS in 1974 had been employed by regional hospital boards: there were 128 in England and Wales in 1971. Whereas the medical officers of health and their departments were concerned for the most part with aspects of preventive medicine (such as health education, food hygiene, environmental control, screening of children, immunisation and tackling epidemics), the ex-RHB doctors had been concerned with the administration of the hospital service. Study of the incidence of disease (epidemiology) was also undertaken by university-based community physicians.

14.50 Community medicine is a new specialty. Although the Todd Commission referred to it in its 1968 report, it was not until 1972 that a Faculty of Community Medicine was established by the Royal Colleges of Physicians. Outside the health service community physicians are employed in universities, the armed forces and government administration. Their main functions which are medical administration, environmental health and preventive medicine in the community, and epidemiology, combine to give the community physician a unique role in the planning of comprehensive health care for the community as a whole. The community physician should be responsible for:

> "highlighting the health problems in his particular population, for stimulating different health professionals to plan their services to meet these problems, and for evaluating and monitoring the success of these services".[1]

In addition he should keep in contact with and advise the related local authority services.

14.51 The problems of the specialty derive mainly from a combination of teething troubles to be expected where roles have to be established and acknowledged, the different origins of community physicians, and the disruptive effects of NHS reorganisation. It is difficult to separate these elements, and together they contribute to the specialty's serious shortage of recruits.

14.52 Whatever the deficiencies of the pre-reorganisation arrangements, at least the role of medical officers of health and their departments on the one

---

[1] Evidence from community physicians in the Oxford region.

hand, and administrative medical officers in the hospital service on the other, were reasonably clear and accepted. Reorganisation broke traditions which had been built up over many years, and launched the holders of the new posts in the reorganised NHS on largely uncharted waters. While the role of the regional medical officer and his department in the reorganised NHS was not unlike that of the senior administrative medical officer before reorganisation – and indeed most RMO posts were filled by ex-SAMOs – all other community medicine posts were new creations. In the case of area medical officers and their teams of specialists in community medicine, not only were the jobs new, but the authorities themselves were new. Furthermore, the filling of community physician posts was by competition and this created a good deal of bitterness amongst the unsuccessful. The BMA put it to us:

> "The appointment process by which every member of the specialty had to apply for what was in effect his own job has left many bitter and disillusioned, and has given rise to some real personal tragedies."

14.53   Community physicians have also had to contend with the marked unpopularity of administration, well illustrated in a comment made to us by the British Hospital Doctors Federation:

> "Furthermore, new posts have been created in some specialties – e.g. Area Pharmacist, Area Chiropodist, Area Nursing Officer – whose function is difficult to determine, let alone understand. Such people perform a purely administrative function which we regard as a waste of their special training and skills which were acquired for the treatment of patients. The same applies to the large number of doctors in purely administrative posts and as Community Physicians."

In the face of these difficulties, it is not surprising that community physicians have found it difficult to find their feet in the reorganised NHS.

14.54   Table 14.7 showed that there are substantial numbers of vacancies in the specialty. Some health authorities found the calibre of applicants too low, or their experience inadequate, to permit all the new post to be filled at the time of reorganisation. We understand that the age structure of the specialty will mean that many community physicians will be retiring in the next few years. There is a risk that numbers in post will decline, and the possibility of the specialty collapsing altogether has been raised. The failure to fill posts will mean that the work is undertaken by other staff, or not done at all, and this may lead to a contraction of opportunities, discourage recruits futher, and in turn cause further contraction.

14.55   We received evidence that, while community physicians should be able to develop a role in planning, health education, epidemiology and environmental control, if they failed to do so the specialty should disappear. We ourselves believe that the specialty has a future and that the present decline should not be allowed to continue. We understand that good quality recruits are now coming forward, though more are needed, and we agree with the Faculty of Community Medicine that it is bad policy to lower standards at this stage. We welcome moves to encourage mature entrants from clinical disciplines by offering them shorter training and no loss of rank.

14.56   The Regional Medical Officers told us that:

"Many community physicians are appointed without management support, ie they lack administrative and secretarial help and management structures preclude the employment of essential research and information assistants in their medical departments. They are in the position of attempting professional practice with no tools of their trade."

This was confirmed by a recent report[1] and although the cut-back in administrative staff will plainly have made it difficult for health authorities, we recommend that community physicians should be given such support. Data processors, statisticians and field workers would help them carry out their epidemiological functions. The specialty clearly needs all the help it can get in the next few years.

14.57   We also support the view put forward in the report referred to that there should be a closer relationship between the university departments of community medicine and the NHS. An honorary NHS attachment, with for some a specific local service commitment, would assist university staff in undertaking operational research and benefit the community.

Community health service doctors

14.58   In 1978 there were about 8,000 community health service doctors in the UK employed primarily on child health, but also on family planning, environmental health and other work. Before NHS reorganisation they worked for local authorities. Only about 1,500 were working on a full-time salaried basis, the rest working part-time or on a sessional basis, so that the whole time equivalent of the 8,000 doctors was about 2,500. About two-thirds of them are women. Salaried staff may be graded clinical medical officer or senior clinical medical officer. The maximum of the senior clinical medical officers' salary scale is close to the third point of the consultants' scale.

14.59   The work of community health service doctors with pre-school and school age children overlaps that of both GP and paediatrician, but perhaps because of their local authority origins, they have been somewhat isolated from their GP and hospital colleagues. Nonetheless, they represent a valuable fund of knowledge and experience which must clearly be properly integrated into the NHS. Generally action on this has awaited publication of the Court Committee Report[2] and discussion of its recommendations. In Scotland the Brotherston Committee Report[3] had recommended for doctors working in child health clinics and the school health service in Scotland a status within a wider specialty of paediatrics, and this remains the basis for action in that part of the UK.

---

[1] British Medical Association and Faculty of Community Medicine, *Report of a Working Party on the State of Community Medicine,* London, BMA Publications, 1979.

[2] *Fit for the Future. The Report of the Committee on the Child Health Services,* (Cmnd 6684), London, HMSO, 1976.

[3] Scottish Home and Health Department, *Towards an Integrated Child Health Service,* Edinburgh, HMSO, 1973.

14.60　The Court Committee envisaged that these doctors would be absorbed into the staffing structure the Committee proposed for the child health services, but not all of the Committee's proposals were accepted by the government. We understand that discussions have been taking place between representatives of the profession and the health departments on the future of community health service doctors. A working party set up by the BMA Central Committee for Community Medicine under the Chairmanship of Dr Preston reported in December last year, and its findings[1] are under discussion in the profession. We make no recommendation in respect of this group, but it seems clear to us that they should not become an independent specialty and should be properly integrated into whatever pattern of child health services ultimately emerges. They are too valuable a group to waste.

Contractual Matters

14.61　In this section we comment on the contracts of NHS doctors and make some suggestions for a revised hospital career structure. We also look at the distinction awards system.

Hospital doctors' contracts

14.62　There is a widely held belief in the profession that doctors have been exploited by the governments of the day. Some of the evidence we received from individual doctors reflected this point of view, and it may be seen in the columns of the medical journals every week. We have already commented in Chapter 12 on doctors' morale, but we mention the point here because one expression of their dissatisfaction has been the search by the profession for a more satisfactory form of contract which would reward hard work and long hours, and yield more remuneration. The profession have made no secret of this last point: the junior doctors' contract introduced in 1976 had that effect and the BMA told us in oral evidence that the main purpose of the proposed new consultant contract "was to restore financial reality to consultant remuneration . . . the contract would be put to the profession when it had been priced and rejected if it were not found to benefit consultants". The question was raised with us whether the changes involved in the new contracts might not be more damaging than any benefits which could result from them. We concentrate on the proposed consultant contract but most of what we say applies equally to the present junior doctors' contract.

14.63　The old consultant contract has stood, with minor alterations, since the early days of the NHS. It provides for a consultant to be an employee of the health authority (unlike the GP), and to be assessed in his workload and remuneration on the basis of broadly defined "notional half days" (NHDs). In the past it has been assumed that the consultant has a continuing responsibility for his patients after he has worked his NHDs. While a number of modifications and additions to the contract have been made over the years,

---

[1]British Medical Association, "Community Health Doctors", *British Medical Journal*, 1979, Vol. 1, pages 503-504.

they have not altered the open-ended commitment that it implies. Many consultants have unquestionably spent very long hours working for the NHS.[1]

14.64 The other feature of the old contract relevant here was that if a consultant wished to undertake private practice, it was open to him to do so but he then sacrificed in NHS salary the equivalent of two notional half days, ie two-elevenths of the full-time rate.

14.65 Proposals for changes in the contract were put forward by the professions (hospital dentists were involved) in the early 1970s. Negotiations with the health departments continued in the Consultant Contract Working Party under the Chairmanship of the then Minister of State, Dr David Owen, but discussions broke down in December 1974. The subsequent dispute was settled in April 1975, and the proposed new consultant contract built on commitments given at the time of the settlement. It differs from the old, open-ended contract mainly in the extent to which aspects of the consultant's work, previously covered by his salary, are separately contracted and paid for. Thus, the basic commitment is reduced to ten notional half days, but fees would be paid for emergency recall, for being on call, and for certain other forms of duty. The distinction between NHS whole-timers and consultants undertaking private practice would be retained, though in a different form.

14.66 The professions' negotiators hoped that the introduction of the new contract would lead to an increase in earnings. The other main advantage seen was that, being more "workload sensitive" than the old contract, it would reward those who have to work long hours, for example because they are in a shortage specialty or lack adequate supporting staff; and would encourage consultants to undertake work which might otherwise have been left to their juniors. It is seen by its supporters as being a fairer way of paying consultants.

14.67 The view of those who criticised the proposed new consultant contract were clearly influenced by experience of the junior hospital doctors' and dentists' contract introduced in 1976. They argued that it was unprofessional, that it would adversely affect recruitment to certain specialties, including some shortage specialties, and that it would have a serious effect on university employed doctors and dentists. On the first point, some think it wrong that a consultant's commitment to the service and his patients should be limited by a contract which specifies hours of work and payment much more closely than in the past. This is felt to be close to an industrial type of contract in which workers are checked in an out of their place of work and paid for overtime.

14.68 More specifically it was argued to us that the new contract would make recruitment to certain shortage specialties more difficult. The Royal College of Physicians of Edinburgh told us:

"We consider that a Consultant contract based on the present junior

---

[1]The Doctors' and Dentists' Review Body carried out a survey of consultants' pattern of work, the results of which were published in their Eighth Report (Cmnd 7176), London, HMSO, 1978. The mean hours of duty, other than on-call commitments or emergency recall, reported by consultants were just under 49 a week for whole-time and about 43 a week for maximum part-time consultants.

hospital contract with extra duty payments might well lead to further reduction in those training in the less popular specialties and further problems in staffing these specialties especially in district general hospitals."

The argument is that it would be easier to undertake private practice, and that NHS earnings would be higher in those specialties which have a lot of out-of-hours work and duty. The surgical specialties would be expected to benefit most; geriatrics, psychiatry and the laboratory specialties have fewer opportunities for extra earnings. Anaesthetics, on the other hand, is a shortage specialty which might benefit from the new contract. There are fewer opportunities for private practice and other additional earnings for consultants in most of the shortage specialties under the old contract, but the fear is that the new contract will make the discrepancies worse and affect recruitment. Community medicine is another shortage specialty which would be put at a disadvantage, and at a time when it is having great difficulties in attracting recruits.

14.69 A number of university faculties of medicine and clinical teachers expressed great concern at the effects of the juniors', and the likely effects of the consultants', contracts on recruitment of clinical academic staff. Universities employ doctors and dentists as teachers in medical and dental schools, and on research. Most, but not all, also have honorary contracts to provide clinical services to the NHS. Those that have honorary consultant appointments are paid by the university on the higher NHS consultant rates. Junior staff are paid on university rates which are kept broadly in line with those payable to junior hospital doctors and dentists in the NHS. However, university staff do not have the same opportunities to undertake extra remunerated work as their colleagues in the NHS, and the new contract would widen the gap in earnings between the two groups. Universities already report difficulties in recruiting clinical staff, and the new contracts are expected to make things worse. The Committee of Vice-Chancellors and Principals of the Universities of the UK told us:

"The system of extra duty allowances [for junior hospital doctors and dentists] has also had a damaging effect on the universities' ability to recruit staff for research posts since NHS posts are now much more financially attractive. Proposals at present under discussion for changes to the consultants' contract could pose similar difficulties for the universities. If the terms and conditions of service in the NHS continue to be more favourable than those for clinical academic staff, there is a serious threat in the long term to the very existence of medical education in the universities."

14.70 University interests also argued to us that the notion that working hours should be closely accounted for and remunerated accordingly was alien to university traditions and practice. They considered that the closed contracts would import a new and undesirable element into academic life.

14.71 Unless the new contract is introduced, and its effects judged, it is impossible to say with certainty what its results will be. In theory a contract which rewards long hours of duty might benefit consultants in difficult areas and shortage specialties, and encourage them to take part in administration

229

and teaching. In practice, we suspect that it is likely to be of most benefit to the surgical specialties and to be injurious to those shortage specialties and clinical areas which the health departments have identified as priorities. We believe also that whole-time commitment to the service should continue to be recognised in NHS remuneration. Over large areas of the UK there is little or no opportunity for private practice, and doctors working in these areas should not be disadvantaged. The effects on the recruitment of university clinical staff depend on what efforts are made to keep their remuneration in line with NHS earnings.

14.72   The professions and the health departments should be fully aware that both the juniors' contract already introduced, and the new consultant contract, are steps away from the traditional, flexible way that doctors and dentists have been employed in hospitals. Separate payment for work outside office hours is one step towards regarding such work as an option – a favour to the patient – rather than being part of the normal business of providing care. It undermines what has been described in our evidence as "the traditional role of a doctor in assuming the total care of his patients regardless of times of duty or other commitments".[1] This point is difficult to make without sounding unctuous, but remains of great importance.

GPs' contracts

14.73   We discussed in Chapter 7 some of the criticisms of the general practitioner services, and in Chapter 11 we dealt with the mechanism for making complaints against GPs. We turn here to the advantages or otherwise of the GP's present contract, and particularly whether a salary should replace existing arrangements.

14.74   We noted in Chapter 7 that GPs are not employees of the NHS but contract with FPCs or health authorities to provide services to people registered with them. This arrangement is considered by most GPs to give them the freedom to organise their work which a salaried hospital doctor, for example, lacks. Indeed, independent contractor status remains an article of faith of many GPs. The BMA said in their evidence to us:

"The independent contractor status of family practitioners enjoys overwhelming support in the profession and must continue, whether they practise from health centres or from their own premises. It offers advantages to patients, doctors and the Service which would not be found if family doctors were employees."

What are these advantages?

14.75   The Royal College of General Practitioners put it to us that there were advantages to the patient in the GP's existing form of contract:

"the preservation of this status is not only consistent with the responsibilities of the primary health care service we envisage in the future but

---

[1]Evidence received from the Faculty of Medicine and Dentistry, University of Birmingham.

essential if patients are to have an independent medical advocate and adviser in a State dominated health service."

The BMA suggested that the GP's independent status "with personal control and responsibility for his staff and premises, is an added safeguard for this principle of confidentiality and encourages patients to trust their doctor personally with their particular problems". The flexibility in the way a GP can organise his work was, they suggested, "a source of confidence in him, which in itself is of therapeutic value".

14.76   The BMA saw advantages to the doctor also. "His independent status is a guarantee against excessive interference in his practice from the administrative structure of the NHS", it "reduces the danger of interference by the State in matters of clinical judgement", and he can organise his work as he pleases so long as he fulfils his NHS duties to his patients. The BMA suggested that "a heavy administrative and financial burden would be placed upon the NHS" if medical care were not based on a system of independent contractors.

14.77   We do not find these arguments altogether compelling and it may be that others, such as the advantages of tax assessment under Schedule D rather than Schedule E, also weigh with GPs. However, it would be pointless to depart from existing arrangements to which many GPs are plainly much attached unless there were strong reasons to do so. The main criticisms put to us in evidence about the GP's contract were that it did not give the NHS sufficient control over the development of the service and the distribution of GPs, patients were at a disadvantage if they wanted to complain, arrangements for paying GPs were unsatisfactory, out-of-hours cover was inadequate, and GPs had too many commitments outside their practices. We have already dealt with the complaints point in Chapter 11 and with the last two points in Chapter 7.

14.78   The most important of the remaining criticisms is that the development of the service and the better distribution of GPs is hindered by the existing contract. So far as distribution is concerned, the Medical Practices Committee for England and Wales told us that "some chronically grossly under-doctored areas continue to be a problem", but this does not prove that the fault lies in the contract. GPs cannot be forced – though they can be encouraged – to work in unpopular areas, and this would be true whether they held the existing form of contract or were, for example, salaried. The distribution of hospital doctors and other NHS employees is also unsatisfactory despite their different form of contract. Unless the NHS is to resort to direction of labour – which we certainly do not recommend – distribution of manpower can be improved only by financial and other inducements, and any negative controls, such as those exercised by the Medical Practices Committees, that may be available.

14.79   As matters stand, the GP is, in many respects, a small businessman. He provides his own premises and offers a service which patients are free to take up or not. If he is an efficient doctor and businessman he prospers: if he is inefficient, he loses patients. This, it is argued, provides an incentive to good medicine and efficient practice, but the picture is somewhat misleading. A patient may have little choice but to go to the GP who will take him. Numbers on GP lists have been falling, but there are not many places where there is competition between doctors for patients. The GP who provides a barely passable service, and never bothers to improve his premises is still unlikely to starve.

14.80   It was suggested to us that GPs should be paid a salary. Those who advocate this assume that the GP would be more closely controlled (for example in not having the choice of accepting or rejecting patients), and that the NHS would provide premises and supporting staff. As a salaried employee he would be taxed in the same way as NHS hospital doctors, and it is argued that he would be more closely integrated into the NHS.

14.81   It tends to be assumed that with a salary would go loss of present independence – regarded as a good or bad thing according to one's point of view. It is difficult to visualise how a salaried service for all GPs would be implemented. No doubt if introduced it would develop over time, but if the general practitioner service were to provide the same kind of cover as it does at present, then it seems to us likely that GPs would continue to be very much their own masters. Furthermore, there look to be great difficulties in transferring all GPs to salaried status even if, which we do not think is the case, the majority favoured this. The introduction of a salary would be costly: either it would have to be set high enough for no GP to be worse off, or the existing high earners amongst GPs would have to have their position protected – which might mean that the introduction of a salary for all would take 30 or 40 years to implement. There would be complications and wrangles over the transfer of GPs' staff and premises, new terms and conditions of service would have to be negotiated, and legislation would be required.

14.82   All this might be worthwhile if it were certain that patients would benefit, but the case seems to us to be unproven. We have identified a number of weaknesses in general practice, but these can be remedied by means other than a salaried service. Most GPs oppose the introduction of a salary for all, and while, as we have said, we think that some of their arguments are thin, their views are strongly held. This is not to say that some GPs would not benefit from, or indeed favour, being paid a salary: for example those with small lists in remote parts of the UK tend to support the introduction of at least a salary option, though even this is opposed by some members of the profession, and the salary option which is already provided for in legislation has not been activated. We recommend that such an option should be introduced and be open to any GP who prefers it. Such an option should include provision of premises by health authorities, and might be particularly helpful in facilitating the staffing of health centres in deprived inner-city areas. Details would need to be worked out and the financial consequences considered by the Doctors' and Dentists' Review Body.

14.83   A BMA Working Group has proposed wide-ranging changes to the GP contract. While recognising his "ethical obligation to his patient to provide continuing care"[1] the Report recommends the introduction of a contract

---

[1] BMA, Op cit, paragraph 6.4

relating pay to particular activities, and extending item of service payments. Discussion of this new contract has just begun, but we wish to say now that we are strongly of the view that item of service payments, except possibly for preventive measures, should not be extended in general practice. They distort patterns of services and may be expensive. The kind of contract proposed would also have the disadvantages we have seen in the hospital doctors' contracts, and we hope the profession will think very carefully before pursuing it.

Hospital career structure

14.84 One of the few subjects on which our evidence seemed to be unanimous was the need for improvement in the hospital career structure for doctors. Unfortunately there was no such unanimity on methods of putting right what was wrong. This is a long-standing problem and we hope that our suggestions may contribute to its solution.

14.85 Almost all doctors spend at least a few years in hospital grades. Typically, the UK trained graduate will take his first post, as house officer, when he is about 24. Those who intend to make a career in the hospital service will work for about five years in the house officer, senior house officer and registrar grades, and another three or more years in the senior registrar grade before being appointed consultant. However, for a number of reasons the median age of first consultant appointment is about 37.[1] Doctors who go into general practice, community medicine, or the community health services may only spend two or three years in the hospital grades. Table 14.5 showed the distribution of NHS medical manpower by grade in the UK.

14.86 The existing structure is criticised on a number of grounds. In the first place, there are said to be too many doctors in the training grades below senior registrar for the number of consultant posts available. The central manpower machinery controls numbers of senior registrar posts so that doctors appointed to that grade can be reasonably sure of being appointed as a consultant in due course. But below senior registrar there is no such certainty.[2] Since a consultant may spend over 30 years in the grade there should be many more consultants than juniors if equilibrium is to be achieved. In fact, Table 14.5 showed that registrars and SHOs together outnumber consultants.

14.87 The calculations are complicated by the existence of overseas doctors, who in England and Wales comprise over half SHOs and registrars, and who, as we have noted above, are often not intending to make careers in the UK. However, these doctors are helping to meet the service needs of the NHS at present, and while a sudden decision by them to leave the UK might bring the career structure abruptly into something like equilibrium, the hospital service would be considerably endangered. It is not sufficient, therefore, to rely

---

[1]Some of the reasons are that doctors may spend time overseas, or may prefer to wait for an appointment of their choice (there may be considerable competition for posts in some specialties); and overseas doctors are usually older than UK graduates of equivalent seniority.

[2]The position in Scotland is better controlled and the Advisory Committee on Hospital Medical Establishments hope to be able to bring the career structure into equilibrium.

on the gradual replacement of doctors from overseas with the home grown product: the disequilibrium of the career structure will remain unless steps are taken to correct it.

14.88   The second major criticism of the structure is that it makes no provision for trained and competent hospital doctors to carry clinical responsibility for their patients except in the consultant grade. Training to consultant level in the UK normally lasts eight or more years. Although it is not necessarily relevant here, we understand that in the rest of the EEC specialist status and clinical responsibility is achieved after between three and five years' training, and of course in general practice a doctor may carry independent clinical responsibility in his twenties.

14.89   There are other consequences. Junior doctors' training is unsatisfactory in some places because there are too few consultants to supervise their work properly, and they are used simply as pairs of medical hands. Professor Sir John Walton, Dean of Medicine at the University of Newcastle, told us:

> "the next single factor [after pay] which has been in large part responsible for medical emigration and unrest is the present unsatisfactory career structure in the hospital service. Registrars and senior registrars whose appointments were specifically designed for training purposes, are nevertheless used as 'pairs of hands' and if they were not the Health Service would collapse."

Often senior registrars and medical assistants, though ostensibly working under supervision, carry clinical responsibility in all but name. Many competent doctors who have not had the opportunity to acquire the training and higher qualifications necessary for consultant appointment, or who are perhaps unable to find a consultant appointment within reach of their homes, are obliged to take posts as medical assistants, a grade which was formally closed ten years ago.

14.90   The present policy of the health departments, which is supported by most of the professions' representatives, is to expand the numbers of consultant posts faster than numbers of training grade posts so that, in due course, the two will be brought into equilibrium. At the time the policy was introduced, following the reports of the Royal Commission on Medical Education in 1968 and of the Working Party on the Consultant Grade[1] it was estimated that if numbers of consultant posts expanded by four per cent per annum and training grade posts by two and a half per cent per annum a state of equilibrium would be produced by 1978. This has manifestly not occurred. It was agreed between the departments and the professions that the length of post-graduate training should be determined by educational and not service requirements; that there should be no permanent "sub-consultant" career grade; that training and career posts in each specialty should be balanced; and that a new grade, the hospital practitioner grade, should be introduced mainly filled by GPs but not restricted to them.

---

[1]Department of Health and Social Security, *Report of the Working Party on the Responsibilities of the Consultant Grade,* London, HMSO, 1969.

14.91 The present strategy has the advantages of being accepted by the professions and of being reasonably straightforward: it does not seek to introduce new hospital grades or ones which are difficult to define, the hospital practitioner being a development of existing arrangements under which GPs work in hospitals. Its main and very damaging disadvantage is that it has not delivered the goods: the career structure is further out of equilibrium than when the policy was introduced. The numbers of overseas doctors have increased, more women doctors are entering medical school, and there are difficulties over the hospital practitioner grade. Currently many junior doctors are pressing for urgent action to bring the career structure into equilibrium by reducing numbers of training places.

14.92 We set out a possible alternative to the present career structure in Appendix I. We do not make a recommendation in this difficult and contentious area, but we hope our suggestions will make at least a useful contribution to the debate. It is clear that a solution must be found.

Distinction awards

14.93 Many consultants are appointed in their 30s. They have then no higher grading to look forward to, and their only financial incentive to excellence is the possibility of a distinction award.

14.94 All consultants and their community medicine equivalents are eligible for distinction awards. In England, Scotland and Wales they are made by the health ministers on the advice of the Advisory Committee on Distinction Awards. This is a predominantly professional body traditionally headed by a distinguished and respected doctor.[1] Members and Chairman are appointed by the health ministers. A similar scheme operates in Northern Ireland. Details of awards are set out in Table 14.8. The total value of awards is currently about £20m per annum, or about ten per cent of total consultant remuneration. Once allocated, awards are held until the consultant leaves the NHS. University teachers holding honorary NHS contracts are eligible. Consultants with part-time contracts receive the appropriate proportion of the full award.

14.95 Distinction awards were introduced on the recommendation of the Spens Committee,[2] and endorsed by the Royal Commission on Doctors' and Dentists' Remuneration in 1960.[3] The system was introduced because consultants in the NHS would otherwise have no prospects of promotion, nor higher earnings, to look forward to. As the Pilkington Royal Commission put it:

"we consider the awards system is a practical and imaginative way of securing a reasonable differentiation of income and providing relatively

---

[1] The current Chairman is Sir Stanley Clayton, past-President of the Royal College of Obstetricians and Gynaecologists.

[2] *Report of the Interdepartmental Committee on the Remuneration of Consultants and Specialists,* (Cmd 7420), London, HMSO, 1948.

[3] *Report of the Royal Commission on Doctors' and Dentists' Remuneration 1957–60,* (Cmnd 939), London, HMSO, 1960.

TABLE 14.8
Distribution and Value of Distinction Awards: UK 1979

Type of Award	Number		Value in Payment[1]
	Great Britain	Northern Ireland	
A+	135	5	£11,880
A	505	17	£8,916
B	1,444	50	£5,409
C	3,308	113	£2,664
Totals	5,392	185	

Source: health departments' statistics.

Notes: [1] The "fully up-to-date" 1 April 1979 values recommended by the Doctors' and Dentists' Review Body are: A+ £14,982, A £11,508, B £6,873, and C £3,060.

high earnings for the 'significant minority' to which the Spens Committee referred."[1]

About half of all consultants receive an award during their careers (at any one time, just over one-third are award holders), and there is promotion through the various levels.

14.96   The main criticisms made to us of the system were that the awards did not always reflect hard, but perhaps unpublicised, work which benefited the NHS, and that the policy of not publishing the names of those with awards introduced an undesirable element of secrecy into the system. On the first point, the critics argue that awards tend to go to consultants in teaching hospitals and in the "glamorous" specialties: thus, in England and Wales in 1977 73% of consultants in thoracic surgery held an award, 64% of those in cardiology and 67% of those in neuro-surgery; while only 23% of those in geriatrics, 25% of those in mental health and 26% in rheumatology and rehabilitation held awards. On the same lines, one consultant who had been involved in the system argued to us that "these awards, especially the A awards, have in the past been allocated to too great an extent to distinguished academics with a small NHS commitment at the expense of NHS consultants".

14.97   There are also those who would like to abolish the whole system and use the money for something else. A consultant surgeon told us:

"The merit award system was justified in 1948 by the need to induce distinguished consultants to join the NHS. It has outlived its usefulness. It is quite impossible to assess merit fairly throughout the service, nor is it possible to equate one kind of merit with another. The system should be abandoned without prejudice to existing holders."

The money might be used, for example, to introduce seniority awards, paid automatically after certain periods of service or at certain ages; or for

[1]*Ibid,* paragraph 224.

responsibility awards; or in inducement payments for posts that are hard to fill; or simply added to consultant remuneration generally.

14.98 Distinction awards were discussed between the professions and the health departments when the consultant contract was under review, and we understand that some modifications to the existing system have now been agreed. Their effect is to relax the secrecy provisions by allowing a limited number of outsiders access to the lists. Health authorities should also in future have a much stronger influence over the distribution of awards so that the consultant who has been carrying the heat and burden of the day should more readily receive recognition.

14.99 We are pleased to hear that some relaxation of the secrecy provision is proposed. We appreciate the argument that the possession or otherwise of a distinction award might mislead the public about the relative merits of consultants, but this danger does not seem to us a very serious one compared with the suspicions engendered by wrapping the whole process in secrecy. We also welcome the modifications to the system that will give health authorities more say. We hope that whether or not the new consultant contract is adopted these reforms will be implemented.

14.100 More generally, it seems to us desirable that there should be opportunities in the NHS for earnings which go some way to match salaries paid to distinguished medical men elsewhere in the world. The gradations of award provide a useful career ladder and incentive. It is not clear to us that these benefits would be obtainable through any of the other systems offered.

Conclusions and Recommendations

14.101 We started this chapter with a brief look at the role of doctors. What doctors do underlies many of the other problems referred to, particularly the question of how many doctors we should be training. This is an extremely complex matter, but it seems to us that it would be a mistake to cut back the planned output of medical graduates from UK universities at a time when there are shortages in some specialties and many places and more doctors are likely to be needed in future.

14.102 We gave special attention to certain groups of doctors with special problems. We are concerned that the interests of overseas doctors who have made a valuable contribution to the NHS should not be overlooked. Many of them are established residents in the UK. It is particularly important that doctors coming here from overseas should be made aware of the career prospects and standards required. Proper provision must also be made for the post-graduate education of women doctors who are coming out of the medical schools in increasing numbers. The Joint Higher Training Committees should look carefully at their policies. Community physicians are another group with problems. The specialty must be supported in the next few years if it is to survive. This will mean both imaginative recruitment policies and the willingness of health authorities to provide the supporting staff necessary. Those working in universities could be encouraged to have a service commitment in the NHS.

14.103   We do not like the new contracts negotiated for hospital doctors. They seem to us to be inappropriate to a leading profession and ultimately contrary to the interests of patients. We do not regard the proposed new contract for GPs with any more enthusiasm. On the other hand, we think the importance of the relationship between GPs and NHS, the contractor status, is exaggerated. A salary option should be introduced for those GPs whose circumstances require it, but we do not propose that all GPs should be salaried. For hospital doctors, the present career structure has obvious defects. We fear that the current strategy will yield results too slowly and we set out one possible alternative in Appendix I. One aspect of the hospital career structure is the distinction awards system where we welcome a relaxation of secrecy and a shift of emphasis towards rewarding those consultants who deserve most of the NHS.

14.104   We recommend that:

(a) the health departments should show more determination in enforcing their priorities in the shortage specialties, if necessary by blocking expansion of other specialties, and should be more critically involved in the development of new specialties (paragraph 14.32);

(b) the development of special interests in shortage specialties amongst doctors working in related fields should be encouraged and appropriate training programmes provided (paragraph 14.33);

(c) the UK government should take the necessary steps to make clear to doctors who want to come to the UK what their prospects here are (paragraph 14.41);

(d) a few post-graduate centres to provide medical education and training specifically geared to the needs of overseas countries should be started on an experimental basis (paragraph 14.42);

(e) community physicians should be given adequate supporting staff (paragraph 14.56);

(f) a salary option should be introduced and open to any GP who prefers it (paragraph 14.82).

Chapter 15   Ambulance, Ancillary, Professional, Scientific and Technical, Works and Maintenance Staff

15.1   In this chapter we deal with the professions supplementary to medicine, and scientific and technical staff. We also look at ambulance, ancillary, and works and maintenance staff about whom we heard in evidence relatively little. We dealt with matters common to health workers in Chapter 12.

Professions Supplementary to Medicine[1]

15.2   The eight professions covered by the Professions Supplementary to Medicine Act, 1960 (the PSM Act) are chiropodists, dietitians, medical laboratory technicians (now designated in Whitley Council agreements as medical laboratory scientific officers), occupational therapists, orthoptists, physiotherapists, radiographers and remedial gymnasts. Speech therapists are usually included in this group though they are not covered by the Act. Table 15.1 shows how many staff have been employed in the NHS during the period 1974–1977. Chiropodists, most of whom work in private practice, were discussed in Chapter 8 and we do not deal with them in detail here. The other professions fall into two broad groups – the remedial group consisting of occupational therapists, orthoptists, physiotherapists, remedial gymnasts and speech therapists; and the scientific group consisting of dietitians, medical laboratory scientific officers and radiographers.

15.3   Our evidence concentrated on two linked problems common to these professions, arrangements for regulating them, and shortages.

Regulating the professions

15.4   The PSM Act established for each of the eight professions supplementary to medicine registration boards with the general function of promoting high standards of professional education and conduct. The boards cover the UK and are responsible for maintaining registers, and for approving courses of training, qualifications and training institutions. Each registration board has a majority of elected members of the profession concerned. In practice one professional body dominates each of the boards and can normally secure the election of all its professional members. The boards operate under the general supervision of the Council for Professions Supplementary to Medicine (CPSM)

---

[1]The term "professions supplementary to medicine" is used in the Act, but we think these professions might better be referred to as professions *complementary* to medicine.

TABLE 15.1
Members of Professions Supplementary to Medicine,[1] Speech Therapists, and Helpers Employed in the NHS: UK 1974–1977[2]

Whole-time equivalents

Profession	1974	1975	1976	1977
Chiropodists	1,511	1,660	2,121	2,484
Dietitians	572	627	707	755
Occupational Therapists	1,988	2,340	2,561	2,774
Orthoptists	385	403	441	457
Physiotherapists	5,737	6,222	6,866	7,073
Radiographers	6,204	6,890	7,154	7,754
Remedial Gymnasts and Trainees	252	277	295	351
Speech Therapists	1,180	1,156	1,481	1,539
Helpers[3] in:				
chiropody	—	36	23	21
industrial therapy and occupational therapy	2,400	2,638	2,885	2,979
physiotherapy	1,217	1,411	1,530	1,659
radiography	94	88	96	91
remedial gymnastics	—	31	34	48
speech therapy	3	18	24	28

Source: health departments' statistics

Notes: [1] Medical Laboratory Scientific Officers are covered in Table 15.2.

[2] Figures for Northern Ireland are estimates.

[3] Figures for Scotland not available.

whose membership is composed of representatives of the eight professions, plus eight medical and seven lay members. On major matters the boards require the approval of the CPSM and the CPSM requires the approval of the Privy Council.

15.5   The Act itself does not prevent unregistered members of the professions practising, though it does limit the use of the titles "state registered", "registered", and "state". However, when the Act became fully operative in 1964 regulations were made which prevent the employment of unregistered members of the professions in the NHS, though not outside it. Comparable regulations apply to speech therapists. The effect of the registration machinery was to give control of standards and qualifications to the professions themselves.

15.6   These arrangements have been criticised on the grounds that they place too much power in the hands of the professional bodies who have an interest in limiting entry to the professions. Developing longer and more thorough training may be perfectly consistent with the duties of the registration boards but may not be necessary to meet the needs of the NHS. However, with the possible exception of chiropodists, which we comment on in Chapter 8, there has been little sign that the professions have tried to limit entry to their ranks, and numbers in the NHS have been increasing in most groups, as can be seen from Table 15.1.

15.7   Another criticism of the registration arrangements is that while they confer status and recognition on the professions they could induce rigidity rather than flexibility in staffing. In discussing the need for flexibility in Chapter 12 we noted the difficulties of integrating the two professions of remedial gymnastics and physiotherapy, and we comment below on the limited progress made in developing a common core training for some of the PSMs. Changes in training arrangements are the key to greater flexibility in the role of these professions, but the relationship between registration boards and CPSM could mean that desirable reforms are blocked. We consider that it is now time for an independent review of the operation of the machinery set up under the PSM Act and we recommend accordingly. The review should include manpower and training needs of the professions.

Shortages

15.8   As with other professional staff groups the potential demand for the services provided by the PSMs is very large. We have already noted that there have been increases in most of the professions in recent years, but despite this COHSE told us in evidence that there "are tremendous shortages of the various grades of staff who constitute the PSMs". The 1975 Halsbury Committee of Enquiry into the pay of PSMs and speech therapists, while accepting that there "are no nationally recognised standards of staffing" and that "the figures must be treated with caution, as staffing standards vary and the scale of need is bound to some extent to be impressionistic",[1] recorded NHS shortages in some of the professions in Great Britain, for example 25% in the case of radiographers and 55% in the case of occupational therapists. While the Halsbury figures are clearly not to be regarded as accurate assessments of shortages, they suggest that the demand for staff in these groups markedly outstripped supply. With the exception of radiographers, where one recent study[2] suggests a surplus, the position has probably not altered since 1975. The shortages occur mainly, but not exclusively, in hospitals where the great bulk of these professions are employed, speech therapists excepted.[3]

15.9   Our evidence indicated widespread concern about shortages in these professions, although to some extent the shortfall has been taken up by the

---

[1]Department of Health and Social Security, *Report of the Committee of Enquiry into the Pay and Related Conditions of Service of the Professions Supplementary to Medicine and Speech Therapists*, London, HMSO, 1975, paragraph 63.

[2]Nuffield Provincial Hospitals Trust, *Patterns for Uncertainty – Planning for the Greater Medical Profession*, London, Oxford University Press, 1979, pages 100-101.

[3]Roughly twice as many speech therapists are employed in the community health services as work in hospitals. The speech therapy services were considered by the Quirk Committee: Department of Education and Science, *Speech Therapy Services,* London, HMSO, 1972.

appointment of helpers, particularly in occupational therapy and physiotherapy departments, where, as Table 15.1 shows, numbers have increased considerably since 1974. The growing number of the elderly and pressure on the rehabilitation services will increase demand for most of the PSMs.

15.10   There are evidently difficulties in increasing markedly the number of trainees in the PSMs. Training arrangements vary: most orthoptists, physiotherapists, radiographers and remedial gymnasts are trained at NHS based schools; but most occupational therapy (and speech therapy) schools are outside the NHS, though making use of the NHS for practical work; while dietitians take a polytechnic or university course. There are three NHS chiropody schools, the rest of those training to registration standard being in colleges of further education. The main difficulty in increasing training places is a shortage of teachers, which has been long-standing in the case of the chiropody and physiotherapy schools, and was commented on by the Halsbury Committee. It is clearly essential to have an adequate supply of teachers if the numbers in these professions are to be increased.

15.11   Several of those giving evidence commented on the extent to which the training of the PSMs overlaps, and suggested that more could be done to integrate training. Dietitians apart, standards at entry are broadly similar; a minimum of five "O" levels is required, though most of the professions now seek an additional one or two "A" levels. Most training courses last for three years. Attempts have been made to establish integrated training schools, for example in Cardiff and London, but although those taking part were enthusiastic, problems arose between the professions and the courses ran into difficulties. A small step in the right direction is the recent decision to set up joint courses for remedial helpers. It seems to us that if there is to be an expansion in training facilities, it should take place at schools which provide for several of the PSMs. Prime candidates for integrated training are occupational therapists, physiotherapists and remedial gymnasts.

15.12   Our evidence about speech therapists, occupational therapists, physiotherapists and remedial gymnasts stressed the importance of evaluating techniques and the effects of treatment. This is recognised by the health departments, and indeed by the Chartered Society of Physiotherapy who emphasised to us the need for research. Proper evaluation of the work of these professions should influence decisions on the content of training courses and the number of staff required. This seems to us to be as urgent as increasing training places. We recommend that the health departments should continue their efforts to generate more research into the work of these four professions.

15.13   The Council for Professions Supplementary to Medicine put to us the desirability of the Council taking on a manpower planning role in addition to its existing functions. It is true that at present the registration boards and CPSM operate without firm guidance on the numbers needed in the professions for which they are responsible, but our view is that manpower planning at national level is a matter for the health departments and we do not support the Council's proposal. Since the NHS employs the great majority of members of the professions, its needs should be made clearly known to the CPSM and the boards. There is an obvious lack of an agreed and coherent manpower policy for the PSMs and we hope this will be developed. The remarks we made in Chapter 12 about manpower planning are relevant here.

Scientific and Technical Staff

15.14   There are over 20 separate staff groups in the scientific and technical services of the NHS. They range in size from the whole-time equivalent of 11 medical artists to nearly 16,000 medical laboratory scientific officers. They include university trained biochemists, physicists and psychologists and grades for which there are no specific educational requirements above "O" level. Numbers have grown rapidly (see Table 15.2) and new groups have emerged.

15.15   In the last ten years the dominant influence over the organisational development of this group of workers has been the Report of the Zuckerman Committee.[1] Most of our evidence has revolved around the implementation or otherwise of the recommendations of this Committee. The other main problem put to us is the responsibility for management of laboratories.

TABLE 15.2

Growth in Certain Scientific and Technical Staff Groups[1] in the NHS: Great Britain 1957–1977

Whole-time equivalents

Grade	1957[2]	1967[2]	1977	% increase 1957–77
Biochemists and Physicists	337	753	1,627	383
Psychologists	153	336	965	531
Dark Room Technicians	877	1,204	1,428	63
Medical Laboratory Scientific Officers	2,942	9,657	15,878	440
Medical Physics Technicians	125	410	1,767	1,314
Physiological Measurement Technicians	579	1,172	2,149	271

Source: compiled from health departments' statistics.

Notes: [1] Dietitians, orthoptists and radiographers are covered in Table 15.1 and dental auxiliaries in Chapter 9.

[2] Hospital service only but numbers employed in the community were negligible.

Implementation of the Zuckerman proposals

15.16   The Zuckerman Committee Report was published at the end of

---

[1]Department of Health and Social Security, Scottish Home and Health Department, *Report of the Committee on Hospital Scientific and Technical Services*, London, HMSO, 1968.

1968. Its principal recommendations were the setting up of a scientific service to ensure the orderly development of scientific and technical services in support of medicine, and the creation of a new staffing structure which would provide a broader training and better career opportunities for the specialised groups involved in the service. The government accepted the report in principle in 1970 and a certain amount of progress has been made in implementing its recommendations, but it has proved impossible to implement the important staffing structure recommendations, or to introduce the organisation proposed for the hospital scientific service. There seem to have been two main difficulties: some groups of staff did not favour integration into a scientific service (and the negotiations were made much more difficult by pay policy); while the broader structural proposals were overtaken by NHS reorganisation which undermined the centralised, regional hospital board based pattern proposed by the Committee. Responsibility for providing scientific services at present rests with the area medical officers and equivalents.

15.17   In view of these difficulties the Secretary of State for Social Services set up a departmental team in 1977 to review the position. Their report and a draft circular were widely distributed last year. Their main conclusion was:

"a single scientific service – in terms of organisation, management and staff structure and grading – is not practicable nor acceptable; rather we should recognise the present development of three main scientific services – medical laboratory services, radiological services, and clinical engineering and physical sciences services".[1]

The team excluded from the three main services a number of specialties which had been mentioned in the Zuckerman Report, amongst them pharmacy, psychology, dietetics, orthoptics, and medical illustration and photography. They also recommended that dental and maxillo-facial technology should be excluded.

15.18   The Zuckerman Committee had envisaged that unification of scientific services would enhance the career prospects of the non-medical staff involved. The DHSS team acknowledged that their own proposals did not advance this strategy, but pointed out that while career prospects were extremely important the linking of grading to numbers of staff supervised was not necessarily appropriate to workers in the scientific services. In other words, it was not necessary to bring the scientific and technical classes together into one grading structure to improve their prospects. However, they recognised the "attractions of a single non-medical grade system",[2] for the scientific services if this could be introduced in the future.

15.19   The report of the DHSS team and subsequent actions were directed specifically at the scientific and technical services in England, and future development of the services in the rest of the UK will be considered in light of developments in England. At the time of writing, the team's proposals are still

---

[1]Department of Health and Social Security, *Scientific and Technical Services in the NHS – Report following a Review by a Departmental Team*, 1977/78, page 2.

[2]*Report of the Committee on Hospital Scientific and Technical Services, Op. cit*, page 6.

being considered. Subject to what we say in paragraph 15.29 below, we think that the DHSS approach is on the right lines and hope it will be developed.

15.20   Our evidence does not suggest that present staffing arrangements are giving rise to serious problems generally: we discuss the particular question of managing laboratories below. The introduction of a common grading "spine" which has been supported, particularly by medical laboratory scientific officers, should probably be postponed until the future pattern of the services is clearer. It is important that high standards for appointment to senior posts in the scientific services are maintained, and it is our emphatic opinion that staff in these posts should normally be graduates in a scientific discipline and we recommend accordingly. We consider that the effective development of these services which underpin the delivery of patient care requires honours graduates who hold a PhD and have had a rigorous scientific training.

15.21   In the main, the laboratory services have developed in an ad hoc manner, based on individual hospitals, in close support of physicians and in response to local demands. However, technological developments, particularly in rapid means of communication, may make it unnecessary for them to be so closely linked to the delivery of patient care. Our own view is that the long term planning of these services should be considered on a regional basis if there is not to be overlapping and even duplication of provision, and if the rationalisation of services is to be promoted. It has been put to us that there has been a loss of impetus in planning since reorganisation and this needs to be recovered. We recommend that pilot experiments should be carried out to see whether a regional service for one or more specialties (for example, clinical chemistry and microbiology) might not be both more economical and more efficient, and give a better basis for training. In any event the Public Health Laboratory Service and the Supra-regional Assay Services should continue to fulfil their present, very valuable role in the provision of the scientific services.

15.22   At the national level there is no body similar to those for dentistry, medicine, nursing and the professions supplementary to medicine, to look after education and professional standards. Some of those who gave evidence to us considered that the Zuckerman proposal for a National Scientific Council should be implemented. It seems logical that there should be such a body and moves to establish one should be encouraged.

Laboratory management

15.23   NHS laboratories are usually based on hospitals. A laboratory may provide a number of pathology services depending on the local organisation of services, and may cover chemical pathology or clinical chemistry, haematology, histopathology, microbiology and immunology. Some, but not all, microbiology laboratories are linked to the Public Health Laboratory Service which deals with the control of communicable disease in England and Wales. The specialist services are provided by medical, scientific, and technical staffs. The head of a laboratory is usually a consultant pathologist or occasionally a non-medical graduate scientist. There was dispute in our evidence about how responsibility for the management of laboratories should be allocated.

245

15.24 In the past the policy on this matter has been quite clear. For example, the guidance issued by the DHSS following NHS reorganisation said:

"The fundamental unit is the *department*, comprising a body of people associated in a single discipline (eg chemical pathology or clinical chemistry, microbiology, radiodiagnosis), managed by a medical consultant or a non-medical scientist of equivalent standing who is the *head of the department*."

It was envisaged that in some places disciplines might be linked in a combined department. Management arrangements were defined as follows:

"The head of department will be responsible for the proper functioning of the department. This does not mean that he must undertake all the management duties himself. There are some aspects of management which are commonly undertaken by a suitable member of his department (eg chief technician, superintendent radiographer). Particular examples of such delegated management functions are the organisation of technical training, the maintenance of proper technical standards, the deployment of technical staff and quality control procedures."[1]

15.25 In their evidence to us the Institute of Medical Laboratory Sciences,[2] disputed these arrangements. Commenting on the DHSS guidance, they said it:

"failed to confirm and consolidate the changes in laboratory management that had taken place over the previous 30 years. Indeed it appeared to be trying to remove management responsibilities from technicians who were in charge of laboratories and to resurrect an obsolete laboratory management structure in which they exercise only those functions delegated to them".

They said that "medical laboratory scientists do not seek medical responsibility, which properly belongs to pathologists", but argued that they "have a responsibility to pathologists and the district management team . . . for the technical competence of the laboratory". They proposed that "separate departments of the laboratory should be organised under one medical laboratory scientist who would be managerial head of the whole laboratory" and "managerially responsible for all medical laboratory work carried out within a district".

15.26 The Institute went on to propose a staff structure which would integrate medical laboratory scientific officers and NHS scientists (biochemists and physicists). Pointing to increasing numbers of graduate entrants to the technician grades they said:

"Frequently it is a matter of chance or opportunity whether a graduate

---

[1]HSC(IS)16, *Organisation of Scientific and Technical Services,* DHSS, 1974, page 2.

[2]The Institute is the professional body for medical laboratory scientific officers. Before 1975 it was known as the Institute of Medical Laboratory Technology.

enters the career structure for medical laboratory technicians or that for biochemists and other scientific officers. Thereafter the graduate is likely to remain within the same career structure regardless of his abilities, interests or job performance."

15.27 The evidence we received on behalf of the scientists recognised that it should be possible for the technical grades to achieve promotion, though the Association of Clinical Biochemists argued that transfer from technical officer to clinical biochemist grade would require an honours science degree or equivalent qualification at least. The Institute of Biology said that "the merging of the classes of technician and graduate scientist would lower standards of professional competence to the detriment of patient care within the NHS".

15.28 Evidence from the pathologists emphasised the medical aspects of laboratory management and the importance of a pathologist being in charge. The Royal College of Pathologists said that:

"all laboratories should have a senior medical pathologist on the staff to be responsible for the medical aspects of their work. The heads of the departments in hospital diagnostic laboratories should ordinarily be medically qualified pathologists, but there are laboratories where the head could be a non-medical graduate scientist with appropriate training and experience."

Other points made on behalf of the pathologists were that it was essential that "the pathologist should be the budget holder of his department", and that the head of the department would "usually delegate some of his managerial duties and decisions to technicians".[1]

15.29 The management of laboratories was considered by the DHSS team referred to in paragraph 15.17. They proposed as a compromise that there should be both a head (or director) and a manager. We cannot support this proposal. It seems to us that a responsible head of department must manage, and that the proposal would lead to conflict.

15.30 It is unlikely that there is a solution to this problem which will be acceptable to all parties at present. The NHS needs now, and will increasingly need in future, the most able scientists it can get. On the one hand NHS scientists have recently felt threatened by the ambitions of the medical laboratory scientific officers; on the other, they feel that their scientific ability has not been adequately recognised by their medically qualified colleagues. There is a risk that unless the position of the scientists is secured by, for example, facilities for further training and research, and good prospects of getting to the top of their specialty, the NHS will not be able to recruit high quality staff.

15.31 It was put to us that the head of the laboratory should always be medically qualified because a doctor would be better able to collaborate with

---

[1] Evidence received from the BMA Consulting Pathologists' Group and the Association of Clinical Pathologists.

247

clinicians, judge the relevance of the laboratory's work to clinical practice, and persuade clinicians not to make excess demands on laboratory services. We are not convinced. The weight of argument concerning the desirability of a medical qualification varies with the clinical responsibility of the department; it is stronger, for example, in the case of pathology than in medical physics or clinical chemistry. In our view possession of a medical qualification should not outweigh an individual's capacity as a scientist, though where there are two candidates of equal scientific ability it is reasonable, given that there is nothing to choose between them on other grounds, that preference should be given to the one who is medically qualified. Accordingly we recommend that the head of a laboratory should be the most able scientist available.

15.32 The head of the laboratory, whether medically or non-medically qualified, should of course be concerned about possible excessive demands on its services. Examples were brought to our attention of what appeared to be unnecessary investigations being carried out on patients, particularly the elderly. Hospital clinicians have a clear personal responsibility here towards their patients, and so have the clinical divisions, which should be monitoring the quality and effectiveness of services. Laboratory heads have a responsibility to inform clinicians not only about advances in laboratory techniques but also about the costs of procedures. Automation should be encouraged, as should the use of aides for simple tasks. Greater cost consciousness is required.

Ambulance Staff

15.33 In England and Wales the ambulance service was transferred from the control of local authorities to the NHS at the time of NHS reorganisation. The Regional Ambulance Officers' Committee told us that before reorganisation:

> "there was considerable local variation in the quality of the service provided, particularly in relation to vehicles, staff and equipment. Most Services were administered by Local Authorities through their Medical Officer of Health and his Ambulance Officer, a few were under the aegis of the Fire Service, whilst others relied upon agency methods for the provision of part or all of their services."

15.34 An effect of reorganisation was a reduction from 142 separate services to 53 in England and Wales. Outside the metropolitan counties and London the ambulance service is the responsibility of area health authorities. In the metropolitan counties it is run by the appropriate RHA, while the South West Thames RHA runs the ambulance service for London. One of the disputes in the evidence was whether all services would be better run on a regional or an area basis.

15.35 In Scotland the service was operated before reorganisation by the St Andrews' Ambulance Association under contract to the Secretary of State. In 1974 it was transferred to the NHS and the service is one of the functions of the Common Services Agency. The Director of the service is at the head-quarters in Glasgow and there are eight local operational centres. In Northern Ireland the service was the responsibility of the Northern Ireland Hospitals

Authority before reorganisation, and is now run by the four health and social services boards.

15.36 The work of the ambulance service, which in the UK in 1977/78 cost about £138m, falls into two distinct parts. First, it provides transport for emergency and urgent cases, which requires sophisticated equipment, trained staff, and vehicles able to take stretchers. Second, there is a non-emergency service which the health departments told us accounts for about 90% of the work: it takes to and from hospitals, out-patients and day patients who are not able to get there by other means. In Great Britain the ambulance service includes the hospital car service which is usually manned by volunteers and deals with some 14% of the non-emergency work. We have been told that the trend towards shorter in-patient stay, day surgery, and the concentration of resources on large hospitals are placing demands on the ambulance service which will be difficult to meet from existing resources.

15.37 Including workshop staff, there are the equivalent of over 20,000 ambulance staff in the UK. They divide into ambulance officers who are responsible for managing and controlling the service, for example directing ambulances to emergencies and drawing-up "runs" for out-patient clinics; and ambulancemen who man the vehicles. Ambulance officers are generally recruited from the qualified ambulancemen. Ambulancemen are locally recruited and trained. Training consists of a six weeks' course in ambulance aid at a regional centre followed by 12 months' practical experience, and refresher courses thereafter. About 80% of staff are qualified. One of the issues raised in evidence was whether, bearing in mind that the great majority of patients transported make little demand on the skill of the ambulancemen beyond the ability to drive the vehicle, less training was required. Staff interests argued that there should be more rather than less training of ambulance staff.

15.38 In Great Britain the pay of ambulancemen has since 1973 been negotiated on the Ambulancemen's Whitley Council. The pay of ambulance officers, on the other hand, is dealt with by the Administrative and Clerical Staffs Whitley Council. It was put to us that this separation was based on a "false military analogy",[1] and made for divisions in the ambulance service. A similar division exists in Northern Ireland.

15.39 We received evidence from the Director of the Scottish Ambulance Service, the Regional Ambulance Officers' Committee, and from four ambulance organisations about the management of the service. The regional officers argued that the opportunity to create an integrated and standardised service provided by NHS reorganisation had not been realised. They complained that:

"Regional Ambulance Officers, except in Metropolitan Services, have no line management, their monitoring and co-ordinating role over Areas being restricted because no executive power exists at Region."

They disliked the "corporate management system which is incapable of making rapid decisions" required by the ambulance service and proposed that in England the service should be run by regions.

---

[1] Evidence received from the London Ambulance Service (Trade Union Side).

15.40 The four ambulance organisations[1] argued for the "tiering" of the service. They suggested to us that the "role of the Ambulance Service of the future should be divided into two distinct functions, ie Accident and Emergency Service and Community Transport Service". They pointed out that it was uneconomical to use skilled staff and expensive ambulances for what was little more than a taxi service. The use of "tiering" is not new but there are different views on its value. The advantages are evidently greatest in large conurbations, and we understand that this arrangement is being tried out in some places. The DHSS told us, however, that experience had shown that in rural areas a more efficient cover for emergency and non-emergency work could be provided by a unified service.

15.41 It seems to us that the way ahead is to encourage experiment in ways of providing an ambulance service, for example by linking it with local authority transport services. In particular we recommend that in one or two instances the accident and emergency service should be organised experimentally on a regional basis with "community transport services" being provided by the lower tier NHS authorities; and the results closely monitored. When the structure is right then related manpower and training problems will need to be tackled.

Ancillary Staff

15.42 In the UK the NHS employs the equivalent of over 200,000 ancillary staff; only nurses form a larger group. Nearly half of them work as domestics or ward orderlies, but there are many catering staff and porters. Other ancillary workers include laundry workers, telephonists, vehicle drivers, stokers, storekeepers and workers in central sterile supply departments and gardens. Over 70% of ancillary workers are women, and over half work part-time. This is an important group of staff providing important services for patients such as cooking and laundry, and assisting in wards and theatres. They work closely with other staff groups and what we say in Chapter 12 on roles and relationships is relevant here.

15.43 The DHSS told us that "there is no evidence of stortage of ancillary workers" in England, and this is also true for other parts of the UK. Local shortages of particular groups of staff occur from time to time, as might be expected with locally recruited staff paid on national rates which have to compete with local industry. This is a particular problem in the London area. There seem to be two main reasons for the generally satisfactory recruitment position. The first is the UK's high rate of unemployment, and the second is that the rates paid to women, which have been the same as those paid to men since 1974, are seen to be competitive for the kind of work undertaken. The DHSS told us:

"While the basic rate does not compare so favourably for men, there are incentive bonus schemes of "lead-in" payments applying to some 40% of staff and overtime is a significant feature in the pay packets of many".

---

[1]Association of Chief Ambulance Officers, Institute of Ambulance Officers, Institute of Certified Ambulance Personnel and National Institute of Ambulance Instructors.

15.44 There has been little investigation of roles and expectations of ancillary staff in the NHS. One study undertaken of catering, domestic and portering staff in a number of London hospitals in 1975 by the City University Business School, supported by the DHSS, showed that most of the staff interviewed liked the hospital at which they were working and the job they did. Most of them, too, were satisfied with their pay, hours of work and working relationships. However, four major problem areas were identified:

"(a) *Induction and training* Frequently when staff began work they were not made familiar with the hospital, the people with whom they would be working, or the correct way to do their job. This often led to initial difficulties and may have encouraged the less confident newcomers to leave their job . . . Lack of induction and training was a particular problem for staff who were not fluent in English.

(b) *Conditions of work* It has been commonly reported that working conditions for ancillary staff lag behind those provided for other hospital staff. Conditions of work described by some respondents were undoubtedly poor and contributed to low morale. Particular criticisms were made of changing, washing and rest room facilities, and of uniforms.

(c) *Status* Many ancillary staff considered that their status in the hospital was low and that they were treated with thoughtlessness and a lack of consideration, in particular by some members of the nursing staff.

(d) *Promotion* Most ancillary staff felt that chances for promotion were poor, although almost half of those interviewed said they would not accept a more responsible job if they were offered one. Predictably, people who would have liked promotion but who felt that they did not have any opportunities for advancement, had lower levels of job satisfaction than others."[1]

The study concluded that the "most fundamental needs are for systematic induction and training schemes and an improvement in working conditions."

15.45 Our evidence showed that some of the problems identified in the study referred to above are still with us. For example, the Community Relations Commission told us that it is particularly important for staff who were born overseas[2] that language courses and induction training should be provided. A radiologist in London referred to one of the consequences of the low status of this staff group as "the increasingly aggressive attitude on the part of the "forgotten" members of the Health Service – porters, cleaners, etc." He went on: "Having for a long time been taken for granted they have realised that their contribution is an essential one and have 'flexed their muscles' on many occasions of late."

15.46 The development of policies for the recruitment, training and role development of most ancillary staff in England and Wales has been undertaken by the National Staff Committee for Accommodation, Catering and Other

[1]Williams, Allan et al, "Ancillary Staff in the Hospital Service", *The Hospital and Health Services Review*, March 1978, pages 83-86.

[2]In 1974 in one RHA 34% of domestic staff and 31% of catering staff were in this category.

Support Services since 1975. Training is considered to be a function of local management and is mainly on-the-job. The National Staff Committee has produced training kits for stores staff and is currently studying the training needs of other staff such as porters and telephonists.

15.47   The Confederation of Health Service Employees described ancillary staff as:

"A forgotten army where training and role development is concerned. There is a large reservoir of talent to be tapped here."

They are a critically important group and the NHS has an obligation to see that they are given at least as much consideration as other NHS staff. We welcome the efforts of the National Staff Committee, but recommend that health authorities should ensure that adequate induction training (including access to language courses where appropriate) is available.

Works and Maintenance Staff

15.48   This group of staff includes architects, surveyors and engineers employed mainly at regional, area and district level; and craftsmen employed on building and engineering maintenance mainly at unit level. There are about 6,000 in the first group and about 25,000 in the second in the UK. Between them these staff plan and maintain the stock of NHS property. As we said in Chapter 10, a considerable part of the hospital stock which comprises the bulk of this poroperty is old and its maintenance problems are considerable.

15.49   Most of the evidence we received from or about this group of staff was submitted by works officers. This is not surprising because one of the effects of NHS reorganisation was to create the works officer. His responsibilities, at various management levels, comprise:

"the organisation and execution of (a) capital building and engineering works and (b) estate management ie the economic use of assets, maintenance of buildings, engineering plant, equipment and services and grounds and gardens . . . and operation of engineering plant and services; it also includes the professional (surveying) and technical aspects of property management – advice on land and property transactions."[1]

15.50   The works officers were concerned about their position. Whereas in England the regional works officer is a member of the regional team of officers, this is not the case at area or district levels. We were told that some area works officers had difficulties in gaining access to their health authority. Several of those giving evidence emphasised the importance of protecting the maintenance budget from the depredations of other functional departments. The National Association of District Works Officers told us:

"It is apparent that any budget which can be readily diverted as problems

---

[1]HRC(74)37, *Works Staff Organisation and Preparation of Substantive Schemes*, DHSS, 1974, page 1.

arise will always be at risk but in a Service, where the average age of buildings is 70 years, it is clear that such actions can only have a long term and cumulative detrimental effect on the Service."

They went on to say:

"In our view these reductions in allocations for work, which is essential for the safe operation of the Health Service, is entirely due to inadequate representation of Works Departments at the management levels where revenue allocations are determined."

15.51 Another cause of complaint was of staff shortages. The South Western Region Works Officers said:

"It should not be overlooked that generally speaking, there are no more managers in the Works field than pre-Reorganisation in the hospital service, but responsibilities taken over in April 1974 from Local Authorities have increased the workload by about 10%."

We were also told of shortages of craftsmen at unit level which may have given rise to many complaints in our evidence about delays in carrying out minor repairs and other maintenance work.

15.52 There were several criticisms of the lack of a career structure for craftsmen. It was put to us that the change in the type of work since the introduction of the NHS has meant a change "from labour intensive tasks to those requiring less manual but more intellectual input".[1] This means that in future a younger, more highly qualified workforce may be needed. If it is, it will need to be matched by improvements in career prospects and training. The basic training of most craftsmen has been carried out before they join the NHS. This has been satisfactory in the past, but we are given to understand that there may now be a need to develop apprenticeship schemes within the NHS.

15.53 The Merseyside Branch of the NHS Works Officers Association concluded their evidence with the cheering words:

"it should not be thought that Works Officers are critical of the reorganisation [of the NHS]. This is not the case, for from it have derived many improvements ... the concept of 'Works Officer' ... has brought together what were two largely separate disciplines – building and engineering into one team with very much improved credibility. This has in turn created good working relationships with medical and administrative officers both at District and Area levels."

This was not the universal view, however. The Royal Institute of British Architects considered that reorganisation had substituted for previous arrangements "a cumbersome and expensive works structure which has little chance of allowing sensible design and estate management policies to evolve". It is

---

[1]Evidence received from the National Association of District Works Officers.

perhaps too early to gauge the success of the new category of works officer and we recommend that the works staffing structure should be kept under review by the health departments, as should the numbers and training of craftsmen. As has been said, many of our buildings are exceptionally old and a programme for their replacement and upgrading is required. It will be essential to ensure that the works and maintenance staff group has the necessary expertise for such a programme.

Conclusions and Recommendations

15.54 The Professions Supplementary to Medicine Act 1960 established elaborate registration machinery for eight professions, the vast majority of whose members are employed in the NHS. It has been criticised as leaving too much power in the hands of professional bodies so that desirable developments, such as integrated training for some of the professions, have been blocked. It is time that the machinery set up by the Act was reviewed.

15.55 Scientific and technical staff were considered by the Zuckerman Committee who published their report in 1968. Its main recommendations, though accepted in principle by the government, have not been implemented, partly because NHS reorganisation interfered with the structural proposals and partly because of the difficulties in negotiating the necessary staffing arrangements. The health departments are considering the best way forward and we support their general strategy. Much of our evidence on these services was about who should head and manage laboratories. We do not think that the solution suggested by the DHSS of dividing the managerial responsibilities is realistic. The best available scientist should be appointed as head; the possession of a medical qualification will be an advantage when there are two candidates of equal ability. Moves towards the establishment of a National Scientific Council proposed by the Zuckerman Committee, should be encouraged.

15.56 We received comparatively little evidence about the other groups of staff considered here and we do not feel justified in proposing major changes. We suggest experimenting with ways of providing an ambulance service and we think it important that more effort should be put into providing induction training for ancillary staff. Works officers are a new group, formed at reorganisation, and it will be important to keep the framework within which they operate under review. They are essential to the success of the accelerated building programme we proposed in Chapter 10.

15.57 We recommend that:

(a) there should be an independent review of the machinery set up by the Professions Supplementary to Medicine Act 1960. It should include manpower and training needs of the professions (paragraph 15.7);

(b) the health departments should continue their efforts to generate more research into the work of speech therapists, occupational therapists, physiotherapists and remedial gymnasts (paragraph 15.12);

(c) staff in senior posts in the scientific and technical services should normally be science graduates (paragraph 15.20);

254

(d) pilot experiments should be carried out in providing a regional scientific service for one or more laboratory specialties (paragraph 15.21);

(e) the head of a laboratory should be the most able scientist available (paragraph 15.31);

(f) in one or two instances the accident and emergency ambulance service should be organised experimentally on a regional basis with "community transport services" being provided by the lower tier NHS authorities; and the results closely monitored (paragraph 15.41);

(g) health authorities should ensure that adequate induction training (including access to language courses where appropriate) is available for ancillary staff (paragraph 15.47);

(h) the works staffing structure should be kept under review by the health departments, as should the numbers and training of craftsmen (paragraph 15.53).

Part IV   The NHS and Other Institutions

In this part of the report we look at the important links which the NHS has with services and institutions outside it. Perhaps the most important of these is the relationship between the NHS and local government. Many health services and programmes of care will be fully effective only if there are close relationships with the complementary services provided by local authorities. We consider, too, the important relationships, particularly so far as education and research are concerned, which the NHS has with universities. Finally, we consider the relationship between the NHS and private practice, a subject which was generating much heat when the Royal Commission was set up.

Chapter 16   The NHS and Local Authorities

16.1   In this chapter we consider the relationship between the services the NHS provides and those provided by local authorities. There are important relationships between the NHS and housing, environmental health, education and other services provided by local authorities, but the most direct is with the personal social services.[1] The importance of effective collaboration between the NHS and the personal social services, and indeed their interdependence, was a recurring theme in much of the evidence we received. Caring for people in the community is of increasing importance, and it is essential to have the easiest and most efficient collaboration between the NHS and local authorities.

Collaboration

16.2   Good co-operation between the NHS and local authorities is important because their responsibilities overlap. The most common example of joint responsibility is the care of infirm elderly people. Many of them can be looked after at home without overburdening the family if the local authority is able to provide a home help and meals on wheels, or day care and social work support, or sheltered housing; and the NHS provides family practitioner, health visiting and home nursing services. If these services are not available and properly co-ordinated where they are needed, an elderly person may need to go into an old people's home, or hospital. Effective co-operation is similarly important to the other main patient and client groups who require help from both NHS and local authority services – the mentally ill, the physically disabled and the mentally handicapped – and for the individual person at risk. Cost considerations apart, most of us would prefer to live at home rather than in an institution or hospital, however congenial. It is obviously desirable that services should be provided in a way which makes the life of the patient as independent and satisfying as possible.

16.3   The importance of collaboration between health and personal social services was fully recognised at the time when the NHS and local government were being reorganised. Government white papers[2] published in 1971 and 1972 emphasised the point, and NHS reorganisation legislation laid a duty on health and local authorities to co-operate with one another in order to "secure and

---

[1]The term "personal social services" is used to cover services (including residential and day care facilities) provided by social workers and related staff in social service departments in local authorities in England and Wales, social work departments in local authorities in Scotland and the health and social services boards in Northern Ireland.

[2]*National Health Service Reorganisation: England*, (Cmnd 5055), London, HMSO, 1972; *Reorganisation of the Scottish Health Services*, (Cmnd 4734), Edinburgh, HMSO, 1971 and *National Health Service Reorganisation in Wales*, (Cmnd 5057), London, HMSO, 1972.

advance the health and welfare of the people of England and Wales".[1] There was a similar provision in the Scottish legislation. In Northern Ireland health and personal social services are administered jointly, and we deal with them below (paragraphs 16.26-28). A special working party on collaboration between the NHS and local government in England and Wales was set up and produced three reports between 1972 and 1974.[2] A similar Scottish working party reported in 1977.[3] Post-reorganisation experience shows that effective collaboration requires that those involved should have appropriate training and sufficient authority within their own organisations to carry out the task which is to be performed jointly. Continuity in post of the personnel involved is particularly necessary. Before any collaboration begins, its purpose, form and resource implications should be identified with the different agencies and professions involved, and we so recommend.

16.4   Before dealing with the problems of collaboration we comment briefly on the arrangements for the provision of social work support to the NHS. Since NHS and local government reorganisation this has been the responsibility of local authorities. Before that the qualifications of hospital social workers were prescribed. The indications are that since reorganisation social work support to the health service has been maintained and is developing, particularly in attachments to general practice and in liaison schemes where the stimulus of joint financing has encouraged progress. The provision of social work services is essential to good patient care. However, by 1976 fewer than half of all social workers in the UK were professionally qualified and fewer than 5% of those in residential social work had a recognised social work qualification.[4] The Central Council for Education and Training in Social Work stressed in its evidence to us the need to sustain a 5% growth in training in the short term and we fully accept the importance of this to the NHS.

16.5   There are a number of formal arrangements for facilitating effective collaboration:

coterminosity— at NHS reorganisation health authority boundaries were drawn so as to conform to those of the reorganised local authorities responsible for providing education and personal social services, ie the non-metropolitan counties and metropolitan districts in England and Wales, and the regional councils in Scotland;[5]

common membership of local goverment and NHS authorities— one-

---

[1]*The National Health Service Act 1977*, Section 22(1).

[2]Department of Health and Social Security, Welsh Office, *Reports from the Working Party on Collaboration between the NHS and Local Government on its activities to the end of 1972; from January to July 1973; from July 1973 to April 1974, London, HMSO, 1973 and 1974.*

[3]Social Work Services Groups of the Scottish Education Department, Scottish Home and Health Department, *Social Work Services in the Scottish Health Service; report of the Working Party*, Edinburgh, HMSO, 1977.

[4]Department of Health and Social Security, *Manpower and Training for the Social Services*, London, HMSO, 1976.

[5]This could not be achieved in London which had not been covered by the local government reorganisation of 1974, or in Strathclyde which covers four health boards, and there were one or two other minor exceptions.

third of AHA members in England and Wales are selected directly by the local authorities in their area. Ministerial appointments to RHAs are made in consultation with local authorities as well as other organisations. In Scotland a proportion of health board members are appointed by the Secretary of State after consultation with local authorities;

interchange of staff— health and local authorities have power to provide each other with goods and services. Health authorities make staff available to local authorities to help them to discharge their environmental health, education and personal social services functions; and local authorities make available social workers to health authorities;

joint consultation— in England and Wales a statutory joint consultative committee for each health and associated local authority is appointed to advise the authorities on the performance of their duties. Joint liaison committees with similar functions are being established administratively in Scotland;

joint financing— since 1976 joint financing of projects of benefit both to health and local authorities has been possible in England and similar arrangements have more recently been introduced in Wales and are under consideration in Scotland.

Criticisms of Present Arrangements

16.6   Despite the considerable efforts made at the time of reorganisation to ensure the close co-operation of health and local authorities, we have heard a great deal of criticism of the existing arrangements. The main complaint has been that responsibility for the individual patient or client is unclear, and that as a result he or she may fall between two parts of what should be an integrated service.

16.7   There are more specific complaints. For example, we were told that a patient may have to be sent to hospital or kept in hospital, because of a lack of suitable accommodation or support in the community. On the other hand, some local authorities considered that because of shortages of hospital beds the community services had to deal with people who should really have been in hospital. The Association of District Councils told us:

"In some instances there has been a tendency to regard the warden service provided by a housing authority as a reason for leading an elderly or disabled person in his or her home long after institutional care has become necessary".

16.8   Another complaint is that patients may be discharged from hospital without proper arrangements being made to support them in their homes because of lack of communication and understanding between professionals in the two services. Despite the obvious need for close co-operation between health and personal social services in such cases, doctors and social workers were often critical of each other's roles and capacity to fulfil them. We were told that in some social services departments, collaboration arrangements did not run smoothly because the liaison officers at senior level, recommended by the collaboration working parties, had not been appointed. Better mutual understanding and planning of services is needed to co-ordinate social work support to the NHS and to contribute to joint planning.

16.9 The disappearance of the medical officer of health, with his dual responsibility for preventive and many environmental services, has been mourned in some places since reorganisation. There were also complaints that in Scotland the relative responsibilities of health boards and local authorities for the control of communicable diseases was unclear. We deal in Chapter 5 with the role of environmental health services in preventing ill-health and in Chapter 14 with the important role of the community physician.

16.10 These and other deficiencies occur despite the elaborate arrangements described in paragraph 16.5. A number of causes were suggested, the most important of which is that NHS and local authority priorities are different when it comes to providing complementary services. There are at least two reasons for this. One is financial: since the NHS is funded centrally there is a built-in incentive for the local authority to push as much expenditure as possible onto the NHS. Equally, of course, a health authority's expenditure will be reduced for every potential hospital patient who is looked after in his own home or in local authority accommodation. Second, health and local authorities have different functions: while health is the sole preoccupation of health authorities, it is only one of several competing responsibilities of local authorities. The provision of hostels by local authorities to enable patients to be supported in the community instead of in hospital has to compete with new schools or housing, both of which may be more attractive to the local politician and voter.

16.11 The lack of progress made by some joint consultative committees may be a symptom of health and local authorities' differing priorities. The Institute of Health Service Administrators told us:

"The way in which the joint consultative committees and their officer groups have developed clearly differs enormously. Some health service administrators find it very difficult to see how far they have had any beneficial effects on what they have achieved, whereas others are able to report upon them as vehicles of close collaboration and worthwhile development."

The Institute also commented:

"It is perhaps significant that local government officer participation in joint consultative committees has tended to be at a lower level of seniority than that of the health service".

16.12 Effective co-operation is clearly in the interests of both services. A fresh impetus is needed. There was a strong feeling in the evidence that many of the problems of collaboration could be overcome, or at least eased, if money were not so tight. Local authorities have been under the same kinds of financial pressures as other public authorities in recent years, and it is hardly surprising that they should have found it difficult to develop their services as fully as they and the interested health authorities wished. Joint financing seems to have helped, but as the report of a working party, set up jointly by the Personal Social Services Council (PSSC) and the Central Health Services Council put it:

> "Inadequate resources are clearly a great obstacle to adequate service of any sort ... Joint financing ... is clearly insufficient to overcome the overall shortage of resources."[1]

16.13   Finally, there is the question of coterminous boundaries. Opinion on the value of coterminosity was sharply divided. There was support for it particularly from those concerned to see the development of a more integrated service and closer links between hospital and community services. On the other hand Professor Kogan found in his study that:

> "A surprisingly large number of respondents, and in all disciplines, positively expressed the view that the principle of coterminosity was irrelevant, or worse, to the running of the health service and the relationship with the cognate local authority services."[2]

We deal in Chapter 20 with co-terminosity in the context of our discussion of the structure of the NHS at local level.

Suggested Solutions

16.14   The three health departments in Great Britain told us in their introductory evidence that they were keeping a close watch on the progress being made towards the aims of collaboration but added:

> "there is a general impression that [joint consultative committees] have not yet been able to reach their full potential".

A more positive step is the growing amount of money health authorities can make available for joint financing of health and local authority projects. This was expected to rise in England from £34.5m in 1978/9 to £44m in 1980–81 and we hope that it will enable more rapid progress to be made in developing complementary services. Although the take-up of the funds available under the scheme has improved considerably, we understand that some local authorities are reluctant to commit resources to projects which they would have to take over in the long term, We hope the current discussions between the DHSS and the local authority associations will resolve these outstanding difficulties.

16.15   Several more radical solutions have been suggested to help overcome complaints and criticisms. We discuss here suggestions that responsibility for the NHS should be transferred to local government; that the personal social services should become the responsibility of the NHS; and that responsibility

---

[1] Personal Social Services Council, Central Health Services Council, *Collaboration in Community Care – a Discussion Document*, London, HMSO, 1978 page 49.

[2] Kogan M. et al, *The Working of the National Health Service*, Royal Commission on the National Health Service, Research Paper Number 1, London, HMSO, 1978, paragraph 7.4.

for certain "client groups" should be transferred from the NHS to local government or vice versa.

Transfer of NHS to local government

16.16 The proposal that the MHS should be wholly run by local government is not new. Before the introduction of the NHS in 1948 most hospitals and a number of other health services were provided by local authorities. The 1944 White Paper "A National Health Service", pointed out that:

"in a long series of Public Health Acts and similar measures Parliament has placed the prime responsibility for providing the health services – hospitals, institutions, clinics, domiciliary visiting, and others – on local, rather than central, authority"[1]

The possibility of transferring the hospital service to local authorities was considered and rejected by the Guillebaud Committee in 1956,[2] although Sir John Maude, a member of that Committee, looked forward to the day when a reorganised local government would assume responsibility for a unified NHS. Thirteen years later, the Royal Commission on Local Government in England[3] envisaged the transfer of the NHS to a reorganised local government. The government of the day rejected this recommendation. Mr R H S Crossman's Green Paper published in 1970 which preceded NHS reorganisation, concluded:

"that the unified National Health Service cannot be directly or indirectly controlled by local authorities, and that special area health authorities must be established to administer it".[4]

Despite the fact that local authority control of the NHS has been rejected more than once in the past, some of the organisations sending us evidence continue to support it.

16.17 Transferring responsibility for the NHS to local authorities would certainly be a logical way of dealing with problems that arise at present from divided responsibility for the complementary health and local authority services. Local government has made in the past, and continues to make, a very important contribution to health, in particular through housing, environmental health and personal social services. If responsibility for health were transferred to local government all these services would be concentrated in the hands of one organisation and this would facilitate comprehensive planning. The local administration of health services could no doubt be carried out in

---

[1] Ministry of Health, Department of Health for Scotland, *A National Health Service,* (Cmd 6502), London, HMSO,1944, page 12.

[2] *Report of the Committee of Enquiry into the Cost of the National Health Service,* (Cmnd 9663), London, HMSO, 1956.

[3] *Royal Commission on Local Government in England 1966–1969,* (Cmnd 4040), London, HMSO, 1969.

[4] Department of Health and Social Security, *The Future Structure of the National Health Service,* London, HMSO, 1970, paragraph 21.

much the same way as the administration of education services, supervised by a committee of the authority. Finance could be provided through the existing rate support grant mechanism or by direct grant from government. National priorities could be set and their achievement encouraged by a combination of exhortation and earmarked funds. Central negotiation of terms and conditions of service, and the control, for example of medical manpower, could continue. Those who, like the local authority associations in England and Wales, argue for local government control of the NHS point out that health is no more expensive to run than education, and suggest that special arrangements could be made to safeguard the interests of the health service professions.

16.18   A further substantial argument for putting the NHS in the hands of local government is that the health services would be controlled by people directly elected and accountable to local users of the services. Local priorities – the closure of a hospital, the provision of a health centre – would be settled at local level. It can be argued that local government control of the NHS would bring greater local accountability. The chairman of a health authority is appointed by a health minister; the chairman of a local authority health committee would be elected by his fellow councillors. Officials of local authorities might be more accountable than health authority officers who are responsible to appointed rather than elected members. In the course of making a strong case to us for transferring the NHS to local government control, the Association of County Councils said:

"The Association believe that the most crucial decision before the Commission is whether the service will be returned to the public. Such a step, with the agreement of the professions, would go a long way to ensure a Health Service which belongs locally and to which people feel committed".

The Association also argued that community health councils would not be needed if the NHS were democratically controlled at local level. A further advantage would be that additional funds could be levied from the rates to help meet local priorities and express local commitment.

16.19   The 1970 Green Paper[1] which we quoted earlier gave two main reasons for rejecting the transfer of the NHS to local government control:

"First, the professions believe that only a service administered by special bodies on which the professions are represented can provide a proper assurance of clinical freedom. Secondly, the independent financial resources available to local authorities are not sufficient to enable them to take over responsibility for the whole health service".

16.20   Our evidence suggests that there would be great resistance in the NHS to a local government "take over". The Confederation of Health Service Employees, for example, were emphatic that "the NHS has no place in local politics". The Regional Administrators in England declared themselves "totally opposed" to a transfer. Part of this opposition no doubt comes from those who

---

[1]*The Future Structure of the National Health Service, Op cit*, paragraph 19.

have an interest in the management of the service at present, plus fears that the special needs of the NHS could not be properly appreciated by those outside it. Moreover it is inevitable that the service would be run by those committed to the policies of one political party or another, and committed to many interests other than those of the NHS.

16.21 A number of other objections to the transfer of the NHS to local government have been advanced. First, there is no equivalent in the present pattern of local government to the regional tier which has been considered necessary for the effective administration of the NHS in England. Second, although collaboration between the present local government services and the present NHS services might be improved, there is no strong reason to think that health services would be better run by local government as presently constituted. Third, while it is true that local authorities are responsible at present for public education, the addition of another public service as large again would inevitably impose great pressures on local authority administration. Finally, it is arguable that the gain in local responsiveness would be matched by a loss in momentum towards achieving national standards.

16.22 Proper consideration of the question of transferring the NHS to local government requires thorough inquiry into local government itself as well as the NHS. This would have been clearly outside our terms of reference, and would in any event have taken far more time than we could afford. After much debate, we decided that, although a transfer has many attractions and is in some ways a logical development from the present structure, we could not recommend it at the present time. We think that a further reorganisation of the NHS of such major dimensions should be avoided at least in the short term, and we note that at present there is no regional level of local government. Joint administration of health and local authority services might become feasible if regional government reached the political agenda; and we consider that any small scale changes which may take place in the structure of the NHS or of local government in the next few years should not make more difficult an eventual joint administration of these services at regional level.

A transfer of personal social services to the NHS

16.23 There was also support in the evidence for transferring responsibility for the personal social services to the NHS. The British Medical Association told us:

"The administration of the health and personal social services should be functionally reintegrated. This is particularly important in those areas – care of the elderly, of the mentally ill, handicapped (mentally and physically), and those requiring after care – where health and social workers are dealing with the same patients."

This would be a less radical solution to the collaboration problem and would avoid some of the objections to shifting responsibility for the NHS to local government. A number of professional bodies and trade unions, the Royal College of Nursing and the National Union of Public Employees, for example, supported it. It would integrate the NHS with that part of local authority

265

responsibilities with which it has most contact. There is a precedent for it in Northern Ireland. For those social workers who were previously employed by the NHS it would mean reverting to a position similar to that before 1974.

16.24 On the other hand, the potential benefit from this less radical solution looks to be smaller than that from transferring the NHS to local government, and for the majority of social workers it would mean a major and unwelcome change. It would not by itself produce the integrated planning of the full range of health and local authority services which many people consider necessary. It would shift the dividing line between the NHS and local government but the dividing line would still remain: housing and education with which the NHS is also closely involved would remain on the local authority side of the line. In any case, while the NHS depends heavily on personal social services, it probably generates well under half the caseload of social workers, the rest coming from their other responsibilities. Transferring the personal social services into the NHS would disrupt these other functions and import into the NHS responsibilities for matters outside its scope. It would certainly be strongly resisted by local authority interests.

Transfer of client groups

16.25 Another suggestion is that the primary responsibility for the care in the community of particular patient or client groups might be wholly assigned to one service or the other with the object of achieving greater continuity of care for the groups in question. For example, the NHS might assume responsibility for all services for the elderly, while local authorities might take over those for the mentally handicapped. This would have the advantage of making quite clear where responsibility for particular groups lay and of avoiding the criticisms of divided responsibilities to which we referred in paragraph 16.6. However, it would also mean that local authorities would have to employ nurses and doctors, and the NHS social workers and home helps. This would cut across the grouping of the professions following reorganisation. Difficult problems of definition such as when a patient is to be considered "geriatric" rather than "acute" would still need to be resolved, and financial arrangements would need to be worked out. We think the possibilities of transferring the main responsibilities of services for particular patient or client groups might be the subject of local examination and experiment. The effectiveness of such arrangements in practice cannot be assumed.

Northern Ireland Experience

16.26 Experience in Northern Ireland is particularly interesting because of the integration, since October 1973, of the health and personal social services. There were special factors which led to the transfer of major local government functions to the four health and social services boards. The structure of local government in the Province had been reviewed and the pattern adopted was one of 26 single-tier local authorities which, with one exception, covered small populations ranging from 13,000 to 90,000. They were not considered an adequate base for the provision of personal social services. In addition these authorities did not carry the other related local government functions of housing and education.

16.27 The integration of health and personal social services has been criticised. There was a fear that the personal social services would be dominated by the health services and absorption into the new boards would lead to a de-personalisation of social work. On the other hand there have been advantages. The director of social services is a member of the management team at area and district levels. This has made the job of planning health and social services simpler and more effective. The Department of Health and Social Services in Northern Ireland told us that the total resources can be more easily allocated through the PARR formula,[1] not only at departmental level but throughout the services. Services can be planned without recourse to the more difficult exercises of joint funding and joint planning which are required in Great Britain where the services are administered separately.

16.28 It seems clear that the full potential of this experiment has not yet been realised. The planning systems are still in an embryo stage and as we saw on our visits to Northern Ireland, there are practical difficulties in the field which need to be ironed out. However, Professor Rea and Dr O'Kane found that:

"While some respondents considered that the system was not working as well as it should, nevertheless the impression gained was that integration was inherently beneficial with, at its best, an improved continuity of care between hospital and community for all patients and special care groups."[2]

Although special political factors present in 1973 may have encouraged integration there should be no turning back. We recommend that in Northern Ireland the present integration of the health and personal social services should be encouraged and further developed.

Conclusions and Recommendations

16.29 There is no doubting the importance of effective collaboration between health and local authority services. While eventually the integration of these services may become possible, there is little in the present administrative arrangements to prevent or even hamper such collaboration, though its success depends on the attitude of the parties to it. If there is determination on both sides to work together, many of the problems referred to above could be solved. If, however, authorities or professions are at loggerheads, coterminous boundaries, overlapping membership and joint committees will be ineffective. Post-reorganisation experience shows that effective collaboration requires that those involved should have appropriate training and sufficient authority within

[1]Department of Health and Social Services (Northern Ireland), *Proposals for the Allocation of Revenue Resources for the Health and Personal Social Services*, Belfast, DHSS (NI), 1978.

[2]Perrin John et al, *Management of Financial Resources in the National Health Service*, Royal Commission on the National Health Service, Research Paper Number 2, London, HMSO, 1978, page 232. Professor Rea and Dr O'Kane provided the Northern Ireland Appendix to Professor Perrin's report.

their own organisations to carry out the task which is to be performed jointly. Continuity in post of the personnel involved is particularly important.

16.30   It is clear from our evidence that relations between health and local authorities range from indifferent to excellent. It is hardly surprising that this variation exists, given the differing circumstances in which the new authorities found themselves when the new services were introduced. Changes which we recommend in Chapter 20 to the local management of the NHS will, we believe, greatly improve working relationships.

16.31   The improvement will be assisted if there is more emphasis in the education and continuing training of health and social work professionals on the importance of inter-professional collaboration and we recommend accordingly. The PSSC/CHSC document[1] on collaboration identifies such training carried out jointly, and better communication, the development of multi-disciplinary working and the development of agreed procedures as ways in which better collaboration can be achieved at field level. Good working relationships are clearly of the essence. We endorse the PSSC/CHSC Committee's approach and in paragraph 16.3 we identified a number of requirements for effective collaboration and planning at all levels.

16.32   We recommend no radical changes in the responsibility for either the health or the personal social services. The evidence we received tended to divide according to the interest of the organisation concerned: local authorities often argued for local government control of the NHS, and health authorities advocated the absorption by the NHS of the social work services. We are also doubtful of the benefits which might arise from an allocation of responsibility for patient and client groups. It is obvious that no radical structural solution would command general support, but in any case we do not think changes of this kind are necessary at present simply to achieve better collaboration between the NHS and local authorities. Joint administration of health and local authority services might become feasible if regional government were introduced in England. If such a change reached the political agenda in the next 20 years, joint administration of health and local authority services would merit serious consideration.

16.33   We recommend that:

(a) before any collaboration begins, its purpose, form and resource implications should be identified with the different agencies and professions involved (paragraph 16.3);

(b) in Northern Ireland the present integration of the health and personal social services should be encouraged and further developed (paragraph 16.28);

(c) there should be more emphasis in the education and continuing training of health and social work professionals on the importance of inter-professional collaboration (paragraph 16.31);

---

[1] Personal Social Services Council, Central Health Services Council, *Op cit.*

(d) there should be no radical change in the responsibilities for either the health or the personal social services (paragraph 16.32).

Chapter 17   The NHS, the Universities and Research

17.1   Education and training for NHS staff is carried out in a wide range of educational institutions; these include universities, polytechnics, colleges of technology, colleges of further education, NHS training schools and private institutions. We have not attempted to review these educational and training arrangements comprehensively but have concentrated on examining the links between the NHS and the universities because our evidence suggested that this relationship presented particular problems and because of the wide range of NHS workers who receive undergraduate and further education in the universities. They include all or some doctors, dentists, nurses, midwives, health visitors, psychologists, ophthalmic opticians, pharmacists, biochemists, physicists, administrators, dietitians, speech therapists and the remedial professions. This does not mean that we in any sense devalue the considerable contribution which other educational institutions make to the education and training of NHS staff. We received little or no evidence about these institutions and we discovered nothing in our work to suggest that the NHS received other than excellent service from them.

17.2   In addition to training many NHS staff, the universities make a major contribution to medical and health services research, some of which the health departments fund, either directly or by commissioning work from them. Some staff appointments in university departments are funded by the health departments.

17.3   The close relationship between the NHS and universities has advantages for both sides, but it has been under strain since 1974 for several reasons. NHS reorganisation broke established working arrangements especially in England and Wales; the financial aspects of this relationship were given undue prominence by the pressure on resources in the public sector; and the introduction of the new junior hospital doctors' contracts in the NHS had serious implications for the universities. We discuss these problems in this chapter. We also consider the criticisms of medical education put to us in evidence, and the arrangements for research in the NHS.

Consultation Arrangements

17.4   Before NHS reorganisation most teaching hospitals in England and Wales were administered by boards of governors and funded directly by the Secretary of State. The universities were represented on the boards and the medical schools had an influential voice in the management of teaching hospitals. However, the administrative separation of the teaching hospitals from those hospitals administered by the regional hospital boards was thought

270

to be a barrier to comprehensive planning of health services in the regions. The White Paper on NHS Reorganisation in England stated:

"Administrative unification is essential if there is to be a properly balanced development of community and hospital facilities to meet the needs of teaching, of research and of services to the public. Teaching hospitals have in recent years gone a long way in providing district hospital services. Unification will help them to take this further, and in so doing, will bring great benefit to the districts concerned."[1]

The NHS Reorganisation Act abolished the separate boards of governors of teaching hospitals except for the 12 boards of the London specialist post-graduate teaching hospitals, and the administration of these hospitals became the responsibility of the Area Health Authorities (Teaching) (AHA(T)s).

17.5   Arrangements for the administration of the 12 specialist post-graduate teaching hospital boards were left unchanged at reorganisation pending consideration of their future. The advantages of integrating them into the regional structure of the NHS were not thought to be great because they concentrate exclusively on particular specialties and provide a national service. They are all in London and employ a high proportion of national specialist staff resources. The government has recently extended the life of the boards until 1982 and has proposed that a new authority is set up to administer them to pave the way for their full integration in the NHS structure. We are not certain that this is the right solution. Later in this chapter we recommend that a special inquiry is mounted to look at a number of the problems of health services in London and the future administrative arrangements for the post-graduate teaching hospitals.

17.6   In Scotland and Northern Ireland the teaching hospitals have been administered in the same way as other NHS hospitals since 1948. The Committee of Vice Chancellors and Principals (CVCP) told us, however, that many of the problems of the Scottish universities with medical schools are similar to those in England.

17.7   Under arrangements introduced in 1974 each regional health authority (RHA) has a representative from each university with a medical school in the region. Each AHA(T) in England with a medical school has up to three such members with experience in the administration of teaching hospitals.[2] For each RHA and AHA(T) there is also a university liaison committee consisting of representatives of the health authority and the university or universities involved in medical and dental education. Its purpose is to advise on the university's needs for NHS facilities and the resource implications of those needs. At district level the university is not formally represented on the district management team, although in most districts a university teacher has been nominated to work with it. In most cases university interests are also

---

[1]*National Health Service Reorganisation: England* (Cmnd 5055), London, HMSO, 1972, paragraph 115.

[2]AHAs which do not have teaching hospitals have one university representative. Health authorities in Scotland, Wales and Northern Ireland have representatives of universities where appropriate.

represented in the medical advisory committee structure, but there are no formal arrangements for this.

17.8   The main complaint made in evidence about these arrangements was that the university's interests tend to be submerged in the struggle to deal with the daily problems of the NHS. This conflict is seen at its sharpest when financial matters are under discussion. If there were less pressure on resources, the difficulties would doubtless seem less serious. Moreover, in England and Wales the one-to-one relationship of medical school to board of governors has been replaced by the more complex structure of the reorganised NHS. The CVCP commented:

"The three level structure inevitably imposes a strain in relation to the distribution of resources for medical education and adds to the delay and complexity in obtaining decisions."

17.9   It was suggested to us that the university representation on RHAs and AHA(T)s should be strengthened. In Chapter 20 we propose some development of the role of RHAs and it is likely that increased university representation will be needed. More spokesmen do not necessarily mean more influence, however, and we think that the main requirements are to strengthen links at operational level and to make sure that university representation on health authorities is at a sufficiently senior level. It may be appropriate for the Vice Chancellor or Principal, or Dean of the Medical Faculty to sit on the health authority, but that would be a matter for the university to decide.

17.10   We were told that generally the joint NHS/university liaison committees have not been working as well as they should. It is the responsibility of the health authorities to see that they work well, in particular that the medical schools and their teachers are involved in all planning which affects their interests and to which they can usefully contribute. For their part the universities could do more to help health authority members to understand the functions and contribution of the medical schools within the NHS.

17.11   At national level there should be regular discussion between the universities' representatives and the health departments about the development of NHS policies and their implications for medical education. They will cover such subjects as the need for expansion or contraction of medical schools, the provision of specialist clinical laboratory services by universities, the impact of formulae for resource allocation, facilities for clinical research, the provision for teaching in non-teaching hospitals, the functioning of NHS/university liaison committees, the contribution of universities to the education of paramedical personnel and the implications for universities of new NHS terms and conditions of service. The University Grants Committee (UGC) told us that liaison between the health departments and the appropriate sub-committee of the UGC was satisfactory. However, it has not always been apparent to those in the field that central policies have been adequately balanced and co-ordinated between the interests concerned; and too great reliance may have been placed on personal relationships and informal contacts. These were perhaps adequate in a less stressful era but may no longer be so.

17.12   The CVCP drew our attention to a particular anomaly which has arisen in the arrangements for liaison between the universities and the health departments. Arrangements exist in London, Scotland, Wales and Northern Ireland, but in England are lacking for the medical schools outside London. We think this gap should be filled in view of the growth of medical schools outside London and the importance which they are likely to have in the future. A more formal central structure to co-ordinate the policies of the health departments, the UGC and the universities may be required. We recommend that this should be considered by the parties concerned.

Teaching Hospitals Finance

17.13   Before 1974 the teaching hospitals in England and Wales were directly funded by the health departments. With the disappearance of the boards of governors of the undergraduate teaching hospitals responsibility for their funding passed to the AHA(T)s. This need not have presented serious problems; seven university hospital management committees in England and the teaching hospitals in Scotland had been funded through the regional hospital boards and there were no indications that this arrangement was unsatisfactory. But the change roughly coincided with two other developments, a significant reduction in the rate at which spending on the NHS was increasing, and the introduction of formulae for the allocation of resources within the NHS. The effect has been that at a time when much of the NHS has suffered from financial restraint the teaching hospitals have felt themselves to be particularly hard pressed.

17.14   Teaching hospitals are generally more expensive to run than comparable non-teaching hospitals. The extra cost is only partly due to their teaching activities, but it is difficult to separate the costs of teaching from those associated with the provision of specialist services and their traditional role as hospitals where higher standards of treatment and care than are normally possible are achieved. The Resource Allocation Working Party[1] (RAWP) estimated that in England 75% of the excess costs of teaching hospitals could be attributed to their teaching functions, and the formula the Working Party proposed gave them an increase for this known as Service Increment for Teaching (SIFT).[2] The SIFT is based on the median hospital excess cost per student: hospitals above the median lose in the redistribution of funds, those below it gain. One effect is that most of the London teaching hospitals lose. It has to be said that the basis for the allocation of funds in this way has been much criticised.

Centres of excellence

17.15   Teaching hospital costs contain an element which is impossible to quantify, attributable to "excellence". There is no doubt that in teaching hospitals clinical standards are high and that most medical research is

---

[1]Department of Health and Social Security, *Sharing Resources for Health in England, Report of the Resource Allocation Working Party,* London, HMSO, 1976, page 76.

[2]A broadly similar approach has been adopted in the resource allocation formulae in Scotland, Wales and Northern Ireland.

concentrated in them. In these hospitals the leaders of the professions and teachers are trained, many specialist services provided, specialisms advanced, new techniques developed and new equipment evaluated. They embody a tradition of high standards, contain a high concentration of professional and scientific expertise and have an influence in attracting and fostering talent which does not exist elsewhere in the NHS. They are an invaluable asset and are rightly called "centres of excellence". The teaching hospitals have served the nation well in advancing medical knowledge and in pioneering high standards of care. This is not to say that centres of excellence of research and development are not to be found outside the teaching hospitals. They are, but they tend to be the creation of one man or of a small group, possibly within a relatively narrow field. Standards of clinical care are often as high outside the teaching hospitals as within them, but less uniformly so.

17.16 Part of the quality of care provided by the teaching hospitals is due to their higher staffing levels, particularly of medical and nursing staff. There is a difficult decision to be made about how far the non-teaching costs of "excellence" should be protected from the redistributive effects of RAWP and efforts to promote the more even distribution of doctors. Not surprisingly those who work in the less well provided hospitals and areas are not always sympathetic to arguments for more resources based on the need to maintain very high standards.

London

17.17 Particular problems arise in the case of the London teaching hospitals. It has been a major achievement of the NHS to spread the specialist services including some supra-regional specialties more evenly across the country. This, and the creation of new medical schools in other parts of England has resulted in the birth of many new "centres of excellence". There is no doubt that RHAs have looked, and will look, less to London for specialist expertise. However, despite the recommendations of the Royal Commission on Medical Education[1] in 1968 that the number of medical schools in London should be reduced little progress has been made. There is still an excessive concentration of teaching and research facilities in London and more hospitals than its population needs. They include the famous and long-established teaching hospitals which between them train about one third of all the doctors of the UK as well as many nurses and other health professionals. They have been hard hit by RAWP. The University of London recently set up a working party under the chairmanship of Lord Flowers to examine the future of the London medical and dental schools. One of the options of the working party is to consider the closing of one or more medical schools in London.

17.18 We welcome this action by the University. We are conscious, however, that London has a number of specific problems which in our view require independent detailed examination. We have already referred to the need to examine the administration of the post-graduate teaching hospitals in London. Other matters which an inquiry should consider are whether London

---

[1]*Report of the Royal Commission on Medical Education, 1965–68,* (Cmnd 3569), London, HMSO, 1968.

needs four RHAs, whether some special adjustment to the RAWP formula is required to take account of the high concentration of teaching hospitals in London, and what additional measures can be devised to deal with the special difficulties of providing primary care services and joint planning discussed in Chapters 7 and 16. We recommend that such an inquiry is set up as a matter of urgency.

Alternatives

17.19   We are in no doubt that the well-being of the teaching hospitals is as essential to the NHS as it is to the universities with medical schools. The Welsh National School of Medicine argued that:

"Some way must be found to insulate the teaching hospital from the conflict between short-term patient care and the longer-term needs of medical education",

and suggested that teaching hospitals should be financed and run by the Department of Education and Science. Another suggestion was that they should revert to being directly financed by the health departments in England and Wales (or that their funds should be earmarked in the regional allocations). We do not believe that such a degree of insulation is desirable or in their long-term interests. At whatever level the needs of teaching hospitals are considered they will have to be balanced against other demands on available resources. However, their important national and regional functions must not be allowed to suffer. This places an important responsibility on the health authorities concerned.

Cost sharing

17.20   The close relationship between universities, especially those with medical schools, and the NHS means that there are grey areas where financial responsibility between the university and the NHS is unclear. These include the balance of time spent on clinical work by university staff and time spent on teaching by NHS staff; responsibility for buildings and equipment; and for post-graduate education. Neither side has operated a strict system of accounting for shared costs. They have followed "the principle of uncosted mutual assistance", to quote the UGC. This "knock-for-knock" arrangement is a gentlemen's agreement based on goodwill and the knowledge that anything much more refined would be infinitely laborious and in many respects entirely arbitrary. The arrangement has derived strength from its flexibility: its weakness is that responsibilities are not clearly defined, and in recent years financial restrictions and different conditions of service in the universities and the NHS have put a serious strain on their relationship.

17.21   The cost-sharing relationship between the universities and the NHS is complex as far as medical education is concerned. The undergraduate medical course normally lasts for five years. The typical arrangement is for a two year pre-clinical period of study in the basic sciences followed by three years clinical training. The pre-clinical period is entirely the responsibility of the university, but the education in the clinical years is shared with the NHS. As a result, clinical NHS staff are involved in teaching and academic university staff participate in patient care. The exact balance depends on local circumstances and could not readily be ascertained, even if this were desirable. Hospital doctors' contracts carry no defined teaching commitment, but consultants usually welcome the opportunity to take part in clinical teaching.

17.22   The interdependence of the NHS and the medical schools extends to the joint use of buildings and equipment. Responsibility for the capital cost of teaching hospital building schemes is apportioned between the NHS and the university concerned according to the Pater Formula of 1957[1], and this seems to have worked reasonably well. There has been no such agreement about paying for the running costs of buildings shared by NHS and university departments, or in the new integrated teaching hospitals and medical schools; and local negotiations about running costs have often been protracted and difficult. There seems to be a need for a formula for the shared payment of running costs which corresponds to that for capital costs.

17.23   The escalating costs and demands of post-graduate medical education have added to the strain on NHS/university relationships. The costs are unknown in total, those that can be identified are large, and the NHS meets the bulk of them. It is right that the NHS should do so, since post-graduate medical education is vocational and its main purpose the improvement of the quality of care provided to patients. Trouble stems from the fact that the UCG does not specifically fund the universities' share of post-graduate medical education. If a university runs post-graduate courses it can recover their costs from fees, but these fees are normally not sufficient to meet the cost of recruiting extra staff. Thus university departments, serving the NHS in this way, meeting rising demands, have sometimes felt hard done by. The concordat which has determined the financial responsibilities of NHS and university authorities for post-graduate medical and dental education, agreed by the UGC and the health departments in 1973, has been under strain.

17.24   Clearly in times of economic stringency there will be pressure to minimise obligations and scrutinise expenditure very carefully. We believe that this should not be carried too far. General formulae can be helpful providing they are not too specific, but it is sensible to accept the existence of a "grey area" of obligation and accounting between the NHS, the UGC and the

---

[1]The formula was set out in HM(57)74:

"(a) Teaching. The Board of Governors should provide facilities for teaching done in connection with the medical school staff's duties under their hospital contracts and arising out of their hospital work, e.g. ward rounds, operations, out-patients, laboratory work. These facilities might well include accommodation for clinical demonstrations, seminars, etc, and enough laboratory space for pathology students. The university should provide facilities for professional and academic duties and teaching, and for formal lecture theatres.

(b) Research. The Board of Governors should provide facilities for research on patients actually under treatment or investigation. The university should provide for all other research, including work with normal subjects and academic work, though the Board of Governors would give access to necessary hospital material. Thus, clinical laboratory space would be proper to the Board of Governors but the extensive animal houses and laboratory accommodation required for physiological, pharmacological and biochemical research would be provided by the university."

In this formula the words "to provide" mean "to finance" and not merely "to put up a building".

universities. Rigid definitions of responsibility might lead to neater accounting but would impair good relationships and efficiency.

Hospital Doctors' Contracts

17.25 We remarked in Chapter 14 that we had received representations from university interests that the new NHS contract for junior medical staff with its introduction of units of medical time, defined duties and payments for overtime, had from the point of view of university recruitment, teaching and research been wholly injurious. The proposed new contract for consultants, if introduced, is likely to do far greater damage and further impair relationships between the NHS and the universities. It goes directly against the ethos of academic life and commitment. We recommend that NHS staff, if expected to teach students, should have that requirement written into their contracts. To go further than this, to prescribe individually the amount of teaching to be done, would be to replace flexibility and goodwill with rigid obligations; while to pay for it as an item of service would lead to endless wrangling.

Medical Education

17.26 The main areas of criticism of undergraduate medical education in our evidence were that the medical curriculum was inappropriate to the needs of the NHS, and that some medical schools' selection procedures were biased in favour of certain kinds of applicant.

17.27 The aims of university education are of course wider than those of the NHS which are more concerned with the vocational aspects of medical or dental education. The tension between these interests is wholly understandable and should be constructive in its effects. While post-graduate medical education is explicitly vocational, the under graduate curriculum has also always had a vocational bias. The majority of the teachers are clinicians, not scientists; and if the curriculum did not have this bias it would not be acceptable to the majority of students, and would seem to them inappropriate to their future professional needs.

17.28 Critics of the undergraduate medical curriculum argued to us that medical education was not well adjusted to the working world, that it was too concentrated on acute general hospital medicine, and that it produced a doctor whose skills, attitudes and expectations were sometimes poorly related to the health problems and needs of the community.

17.29 The need for preparation for multi-disciplinary team working was also remarked on. The British Association of Social Workers said:

"Opportunities should be provided for all health professionals to have multi-disciplinary training ... This is especially relevant to the medical training courses, where doctors have a crucial contribution if effective teamwork is to take place between different staff groups."

We agree that the medical student should be far better prepared than he is at present for team working with other disciplines. There are few things more important for the NHS than that its health professionals should work well together.

17.30 Medical education should be relevant to the major health problems of the day, and amongst these are now geriatric illness, mental illness, disability and handicap and the potentially preventable diseases and injuries which result from an unhealthy life-style. There should be more emphasis on community care and the importance of continuity of care. There has been some change in these directions in the curricula of the medical schools since the Royal Commission on Medical Education reported in 1968 but not enough. These are matters for which the General Medical Council (GMC), now reconstituted under the Medical Act 1978 with much broader powers, is responsible. We believe that we can rely on the newly constituted GMC to use its new powers wisely, and give this important matter its continuing attention.

17.31 The universities have been criticised for being slow to develop academic departments in fields which have been chosen by the health departments as deserving priority. Geriatrics, mental handicap, and rehabilitation are examples. A wholesale invasion of educational territory by the NHS would be quite inappropriate; but it should continue to help the universities by funding academic developments in specialties where it is important to raise standards or pioneer change. We recommend that the health departments should, as a matter of national policy, fund chairs or senior lectureships, or promote joint university/NHS appointments as in Northern Ireland, in the priority specialties. There are already a number of appointments of this kind; for example, the Welsh Office supported the chair of geriatric medicine at the Welsh National School of Medicine in 1978 and the government endowed the Europe chair of rehabilitation at Southampton University in 1973.

17.32 Another aspect of medical education criticised in our evidence was the selection of medical students, although some of the criticisms would apply equally to the arrangements for selecting students in other faculties. Most medical students are selected from the science forms of the secondary schools and from the middle classes. There is some evidence of a slight increase in the already high proportion of final year medical students with fathers from social classes I and II between 1966 and 1975.[1] Most medical students enter university straight from school. In their selection increasingly high academic school qualifications have been required; they are now at least as high as those for entry into any other university faculty; but no reliable techniques have been developed to test motivation. We recommend that universities should encourage and monitor experiments in medical student selection which take account of factors other than the traditional academic criteria. We suggest that they should retain some pre-medical courses which will allow the student who has not made his choice of career early in his teens, or who has not studied the requisite science subjects at school, or not to a sufficient degree, to switch to science and medicine. A more positive policy towards the admission of mature students to medical schools is needed, including some entrants from the other health and social services professions.

---

[1]Donnan, S P B, "British Medical Undergraduates in 1975. A student survey in 1975 compared with 1966", *Medical Education,* 1976, 10, pages 341–347.

17.33   The development of post-graduate specialist education has had less influence that it should have had on the undergraduate medical curriculum in reducing some of its specialist vocational content. Similarly the existence and planned expansion of continuing education seems to have taken place apart from the development of specialist training. The duration of training in most of the medical specialties has been very similar, despite apparent differences in the complexity and sophistication of their subject matter and techniques of investigation and treatment. No doubt these are matters which the new GMC will view critically.

Research

17.34   Research is vital to improve standards of patient care. It increases knowledge and fosters a critical attitude to existing patterns of care and treatment. The government currently spends about £80m a year in the UK on medical and health services research. The money is allocated through the Medical Research Council (MRC)[1], the health departments and health authorities. In England in 1978 the Department of Health and Social Security (DHSS) devolved responsibility for the administration and funding of health authority sponsored research to RHAs. Immediately before this more than £2m a year was made available for locally organised health services research. This new arrangement should be monitored to make sure that RHAs do not neglect research. In addition a valuable contribution is made by charitable foundations and by the pharmaceutical companies.

17.35   It is convenient to classify research into biological and biomedical, clinical and health services research, although the boundaries are somewhat blurred. A wide range of disciplines make a contribution to research. We deal in Chapter 7 with primary care research and in Chapter 13 with nursing research. Biomedical research is concerned with the biological mechanisms which operate both in normal functioning and in disease. It is not clinically oriented but may result in advances important for clinical medicine. In the UK it is funded mainly by the MRC and its record has probably not been bettered in any other country with comparable resources.

17.36   Clinical research starts with the detection and delineation of the phenomena of disease or illness. Trials of new regimes of treatment and of new drugs are some of the most common examples. It is the kind of research most obviously relevant to the treatment of individual patients. Clinical research is undertaken mainly, but by no means exclusively, in the clinical academic departments of the universities and is funded by the MRC, by the NHS and by the universities themselves. We commented above that the changing contractual arrangements for NHS staff pose a threat to the recruitment of suitable staff to clinical research. Another problem is that the post-gradute education of doctors, and some specialist training programmes in particular, are too inflexible. While some allowance is generally made for research, it is

---

[1]Estimated expenditure on the MRC will be £54.9m in 1979/80. Spending on the other research councils ranges from £17.8m for the Social Science Research Council to £176.7m for the Science Research Council.

commonly insufficient to foster clinical research which should be accepted as an integral part of post-graduate education.

17.37   Health services research has only been undertaken on any scale within the last decade. It embraces many disciplines, including epidemiology, statistics, sociology, psychology and economics. It is concerned with topics such as the demand for health care, the needs of client groups, the organisation of services and their cost-effectiveness, the ordering of priorities, manpower and industrial relations and more generally with the efficient and effective use of resources. Although the health departments, the universities, the Social Science Research Council (SSRC) and charitable trusts have promoted health services research, its development has been slow in comparison to clinical research.

17.38   There is an acute shortage of trained researchers in the relevant disciplines. Health services research is a complex process in which continuity is essential. The present arrangements for funding and commissioning research do not meet this requirement. The London School of Hygiene and Tropical Medicine told us that they:

"make it very unlikely that a cadre of able and experienced workers can be built up in health services research".

The DHSS has tried to overcome this problem to some extent by channelling a significant part of its research budget to a number of multi-disciplinary units which are guaranteed support for a few years ahead. This improves security of tenure for a few essential staff, but still does not provide researchers with the secure career structure enjoyed by academic staff in universities. It is recognised that recruitment, especially of senior or experienced staff, is hampered. An alternative approach might be for the health departments themselves to employ a cadre of scientists to undertake research in the same way as government departments like the Ministry of Agriculture, Fisheries and Food and the Ministry of Defence, but this is open to other objections. The Institute of Health Service Administrators told us:

"To be of real value such research would have to be sponsored at a high level and undertaken by bodies of sufficient standing and independence to command general support and acceptance."

We accept this view.

17.39   A solution to this critical problem of encouraging systematic research into health care issues would be the establishment of an Institute of Health Services Research. Such an institute should be sufficiently large to provide secure employment, and even a career structure, to at least some research workers from a wide range of disciplines, and would provide opportunities for full-time and part-time research activity by those pursuing academic and scientific careers. The institute would need substantial independent sources of funds, and this might be provided by linking it to the SSRC, and perhaps also the MRC. Such funding would enable coherent research programmes to be developed. The institute could undertake specific research projects within the customer-contractor relationship on behalf of the health departments, health authorities, community health councils and other bodies, and supplement its funds in this way. It would encourage the development of a corpus of knowledge and experience in the sphere of health services research, and could help to co-ordinate the research undertaken by universities and other agencies. It could also provide training in research methodology for health service professionals, and participate in post-graduate training programmes. We believe that such an institute could contribute greatly to the development of health services research and we recommend that an Institute of Health Services Research should be established in England and Wales and its activities and output carefully evaluated. The health departments in Scotland and Northern Ireland should consider their position as separate institutes may not be appropriate there.

17.40   Although public spending on medical and health services research is the equivalent of only about one per cent of total expenditure on the NHS, it represents a large sum and it is important that research expenditure is properly evaluated and co-ordinated. The annual research budget of the DHSS totals about £26 m, of which the largest proportion goes on commissioning research from the MRC which also informally co-ordinates much clinical research, whether funded publicly or privately. More than £8m is spent by the DHSS itself on research in the health and personal social services, in fields determined by its own administrative divisions. Following the Rothschild Report,[1] a Chief Scientist organisation was set up at the DHSS. It has attracted criticism; the scientific community thought that the department had not yet made effective arrangements to represent its interests as a customer for research. We have been pleased therefore to note that recently the office of the Chief Scientist has been reorganised and that new arrangements have been introduced for the control of the department's total expenditure with the aim of underpinning the Chief Scientist's role in providing a single focus for research in the department and in advising ministers on research and development matters. A Chief Scientist was appointed also in Scotland and the developments there have been more harmonious and fruitful. A review of the arrangements between the MRC and health departments will be made later this year.

Conclusions and Recommendations

17.41   The arrangements that existed for consultation between the NHS and universities were disturbed by NHS reorganisation. The transfer of responsibility from boards of govenors with direct access to the health ministers to area health authorities would have given rise to difficulty at any time until the new arrangements had settled down, but was made much more difficult by the financial pressures on the NHS. Both parties have to work at getting the new relationship going properly: on the NHS side this means making sure that universities are properly consulted on matters which affect them, and on the university side it may mean that the Vice Chancellor or Dean of the Medical School has to be personally involved. We are doubtful whether consultation arrangements at national level between educational and health interests are adequate.

17.42   It is likely that teaching hospitals would have found themselves

---

[1] *A Framework for Government Research and Development*, (Cmnd 4184), London, HMSO, 1971.

under financial pressure even if NHS reorganisation had not occurred because of the general pressures on NHS resources since 1974. There is a conflict between the short-term needs of the NHS and the importance of providing for the future. The teaching hospitals feel themselves exposed to the pressures of keeping the NHS going, but this would have to be faced whatever the financing arrangements. We are strong supporters of centres of excellence, but we think the teaching hospitals will in the long run gain through their closer integration into the NHS. It is a difficult time for the teaching hospitals, but the example of Scotland should offer some encouragement. Another aspect of the financial pressures is the tendency for both university and NHS to start counting the cost of services provided to the other. This is a profitless occupation since the funds being argued over come from the Exchequer and the loss of flexibility, not to mention the complexities of computation, would merely make for future difficulties.

17.43 There have been criticisms of undergraduate medical education, but this is not an area into which we have gone in detail. The curriculum has been criticised on the grounds that it is not as relevant as it should be to the work of doctors in the NHS, and the selection of medical students has been criticised on the grounds that universities rely too much on academic performance and too little on other evidence of suitability. We think there is room for development in both these areas.

17.44 Biomedical and clinical research are adequately catered for by the existing agencies, particularly the MRC. Health services research needs to be developed.

17.45 We recommend that:

(a) a formal structure at national level to co-ordinate the policies of the health departments, the UGC and the universities should be considered by the parties concerned (paragraph 17.12);

(b) an independent enquiry should be set up to consider the special health service problems of London including the administration of the post-graduate teaching hospitals, whether London needs four RHAs, whether some special adjustment to the RAWP formula is required to take account of the high concentration of teaching hospitals in London, and what additional measures can be devised to deal with the special difficulties of providing primary care services and joint planning in London (paragraph 17.18);

(c) NHS staff who are required to teach students should have this requirement written into their contracts (paragraph 17.25);

(d) the health departments should as a matter of national policy fund chairs or senior lectureships, or promote joint NHS/university appointments as in Northern Ireland, in the priority specialties (paragraph 17.31);

(e) universities should encourage and monitor experiments in different approaches to student selection which take account of factors other than the traditional academic criteria (paragraph 17.32);

(f) an Institute of Health Services Research should be established for England and Wales to encourage systematic research into health care issues and its activities and output should be carefully evaluated. The health departments in Scotland and Northern Ireland should consider their position as separate institutions may not be appropriate there (paragraph 17.39).

Chapter 18   The NHS and Private Practice

18.1   Our terms of reference cover private practice only so far as it affects NHS resources. But the connections between the NHS and private practice are such that, although we have no wish to enter into the "pay beds" dispute, we felt that out contribution might best be made by putting in summary form some of the more important facts about private medicine. We first survey the extent of private practice as far as it is known, then consider the arguments for its benefiting or harming the NHS, and finally we look more closely at pay beds in NHS hospitals.

18.2   Private practice is often discussed in terms of broad principles such as individual freedom of choice and equality of opportunity. We have deliberately tried to avoid such emotive issues by concentrating on the facts. Nevertheless, we have no doubt that this matter will continue to be debated. We hope that in the light of our discussion some of the more extreme attitudes which have been struck in the past might be avoided.

The Extent of Private Practice

18.3   Private practice is an imprecise term. It may include:

registered private hospitals, nursing homes and clinics, some of which also treat NHS patients on a contractual basis;

private practice in NHS hospitals, including treatment of private in-patients (in pay beds), out-patients and day-patients;

private practice by general medical practioners, general dental practitioners, and other NHS contractors, including opticians and pharmacists, who provide NHS services but usually also undertake retail or other private work;

private practice outside the NHS undertaken by medical and dental practioners, and other staff such as nurses, chiropodists and physiotherapists, who are qualified for employment in the NHS but choose to work wholly or partly outside it;

treatment undertaken by other practitioners not normally employed in the NHS, such as osteopaths and chiropractors.

Private hospitals and nursing homes

18.4   Private hospitals and nursing homes are required to register with health authorities under the Nursing Homes Act 1975 (in Scotland the Nursing Homes Registration (Scotland) Act 1938 and in Northern Ireland the Nursing Homes and Nursing Agencies Act (Northern Ireland) 1971). The total number of private hospitals and nursing homes registered, and the number of beds they contain, is shown in Table 18.1.

TABLE 18.1

Registered Private Hospitals and Nursing Homes:
UK 1977

	Institutions	*Beds*
England	1,110	30,457
Wales	45	986
Scotland[1]	84	2,847
Northern Ireland	10	256
UK TOTAL:	1,249	34,546

Source: health departments.
Note: [1] 1979

18.5   There is no formal distinction between private hospitals and nursing homes. Their beds are approved by health authorities for use by four broad categories of patient – medical, surgical, mental health and maternity – but these classifications are not exclusive and some beds are approved for more than one purpose. About 73% of the beds shown in Table 18.1 were for medical patients, 15% for surgical, 11% for mental health, and 2% for maternity.

18.6   Of the institutions referred to in Table 18.1, 117 were private hospitals with facilities for surgery, 31 of these being run by religous orders and 44 by other charitable or non-profit making organisations. They concentrate on "cold" surgery.[1] Although no comprehensive figures are available, 88% of the patients treated in the largest group of private hospitals (the Nuffield Nursing Homes Trust) in 1977 received surgical treatment. The distribution of acute beds in private hospitals and nursing homes is shown in Table E3 in Appendix E.

18.7   Beds approved for medical patients are used mainly for the convalescence, rehabilitation and care of the chronically sick and elderly. The great majority of these patients are elderly. They receive nursing care and any necessary medical attention is often provided under the NHS by local GPs in the same way as it is for people living in their own homes. Such nursing homes are distributed throughout the country, but there are concentrations in coastal areas, such as Kent, Sussex, Devon and North Wales. There is no doubt that many patients in private nursing homes would otherwise need care in NHS hospitals or local authority accommodation,[2] or would make heavy demands on community services.

18.8   Private hospitals and nursing homes may treat NHS patients on a contractual basis and there are currently about 4,000 beds in the private sector

---

[1]"Cold" surgery refers to non-emergency surgical procedures which can be arranged well in advance. Examples are operations on varicose veins or hernias, or hip replacements.

[2]In 1977 there were 116,564 people aged 65 or over in residential accommodation provided by or on behalf of local authorities, compared with 51,800 patients in hospital departments of geriatric medicine.

occupied by NHS patients under the care of NHS doctors, about 0.8% of the total beds available to the NHS.

18.9   We visited a number of private hospitals with acute beds, including ones run commercially and by charitable organisations. We found that the disparities between one hospital and another in premises and facilities and in general atmosphere were at least as great as the variations to be found within the NHS. We were not able to judge the quality of medical and nursing care provided, but in some the standard of accommodation was higher than that normally provided by the NHS. Others seemed to offer no advantages over the NHS except a room to oneself, and in some cases not even that. There are of course substantial variations in the cost of private hospitals, but we did not always find that the most expensive hospitals offered the best facilities.

18.10   People turn to the private sector for a number of reasons. One is for the privacy of a single room. Illness is usually distressing and some patients prefer to be alone in their discomfort. Others may wish as far as possible to continue to conduct their day-to-day business and may require privacy and access to a telephone. The convenience of being able to book a date for admission to suit business or personal commitments is obviously important to many people. In our view it should not be necessary to seek private treatment to obtain these advantages (we discussed the availability of NHS amenity beds in Chapter 10). Others may seek private treatment to reduce the time they have to wait for an out-patient appointment or in-patient treatment, particularly where cold surgery is involved. Another reason is to guarantee seeing a particular consultant.

Abortion facilities

18.11   Since the passing of the Abortion Act 1967 (which does not apply in Northern Ireland) most abortions have been performed in private clinics and nursing homes. In 1978 121,754 abortions were performed on women resident in the UK, and 28,015 on non-resident women. Table E4 in Appendix E shows the number of abortions perfomed in the NHS and in approved nursing homes on resident and non-resident women since 1968. About half the abortions on resident women, and nearly all those on non-resident women, were performed privately. Sixty registered private nursing homes were approved under the Abortion Act, of which 19 were regarded as specialising in abortions.

18.12   Abortion cannot be delayed and if an NHS operation is not readily available a patient must resort to the private sector. There is considerable geographical variation in the proportion of women obtaining an abortion in the NHS, ranging from nearly 90% in the Northern Region to about 22% in the West Midlands Region and 31% in the Mersey Region. This suggests that lack of availability of NHS facilities, rather than real desire for private treatment, is the major factor in most cases where the full cost of treatment has to be met by the patient. Some health authorities have been able to meet most of the local demand but others have not. Equality of access to health services was one of the objectives we set out in Chapter 2 and abortion is a conspicuous example of lack of such equality.

18.13   We doubt whether the NHS could meet the demand for abortion in the immediate future without reducing other services, and this will not normally be justified. Nevertheless, there are ways in which health authorities could increase the number of abortions provided. There is evidence that many abortions can be safely carried out on a day-care basis, with considerable savings in resources compared with in-patient treatment; and it may also be possible in some areas for abortions to be undertaken, with suitable supervision, by outside agencies on behalf of the NHS. We recommend as a broad objective that health authorities in Great Britain should aim to increase to about 75% of all abortions on resident women the proportion performed within the NHS over the next few years. The additional cost might eventually be about £2.5m per annum (less if day-care abortions were widely introduced).

Private practice in NHS hospitals

18.14   Consultants who undertake private practice may, if facilities are available, admit their private patients to designated private beds (pay beds) in NHS hospitals or as day patients, or see them as out-patients. Not all NHS hospitals have pay beds and the number of pay beds and the proportion of consultants undertaking private practice has been falling for many years. Table 18.2 gives figures.

TABLE 18.2

Number of Pay Beds and Proportion of NHS Consultants with Part Time Contracts: UK 1965 and 1976

	1965	1976
Number of pay beds	6,239[1]	4,859
Part-time consultants as a percentage of all NHS consultants[2]	56.9%	42.8%

Source: compiled from health departments' statistics.

Note: [1] Excluding Northern Ireland.
      [2] Excludes academic staff and consultants with honorary contracts.

18.15   Under half of all NHS consultants work part-time.[1] While there may be a few who work part-time for other reasons, the great majority do so because they want to undertake private practice. However, the opportunities for private practice vary according to specialty and locality and this is reflected in the proportion of consultants with whole-time contracts shown in Table E5 in Appendix E. In England and Wales in 1978 only about 15% of consultants in the major surgical specialties had whole-time contracts, while about 90% of those in pathology, geriatrics and mental handicap worked whole-time in the NHS. Over 69% of consultants in the Northern region had whole-time contracts, compared with under 40% of those in the Thames regions.

18.16   Up-to-date information on consultants' earnings from private practice is not available, but figures for 1971/72 published by the Doctors' and Dentists' Review Body showed that part-time consultants on average derived

---

[1]The figures exclude medical staff employed by academic and other authorities who have honorary contracts with the NHS. Some of these may undertake private work.

about one third of their income from private practice.[1] In current terms, this would represent about £6,000 per annum.

18.17   We referred in Chapter 14 to the proposed new consultant contract. It is impossible to predict with confidence its effect on consultants' private practice, though it is intended to offer more encouragement than present arrangements. However, this will not be the only influence, and the volume of private practice will probably depend as much on the adequacy of NHS services, the demand for private treatment and the availability of facilities as it will on the consultants' form of contract.

18.18   A certain amount of non-NHS work, mainly for public authorities may be undertaken by consultants who hold whole-time NHS contracts and are not eligible to undertake private practice as defined in their terms and conditions of service. This includes examinations and reports for industrial injuries or court purposes. For most consultants, earnings from this source are probably very small.

General medical and dental practitioners

18.19   General medical and dental practitioners are free to accept as much private work as they wish, subject to it not interfering with their NHS obligations. Probably almost all general medical practitioners undertake work, such as examinations and certificates for insurance or employment purposes, for which they charge a fee. For the majority, income from this and from private treatment of patients will represent a very small part of their total earnings. In 1971/72 about two per cent of general practioners' income was derived from hospital, local authority and non-NHS public sector work, and about six per cent from private practice.[2]

18.20   Private practice by general dental practioners is more substantial. In 1977 some 11% of their time was spent on work other than in the general dental service, probably mainly on private practice.[3] The evidence we have received has expressed concern at the tendency for general dental practitioners to restrict their NHS practices to concentrate on private practice or provide only some forms of treatment on the NHS.

Patients

18.21   About 50% of private patients treated in NHS pay beds or receiving acute treatment in private hospitals are covered by provident associations. Altogether there were some 1.12 million subscribers to provident schemes in 1978, of whom 869,000 were members of group schemes. Subscriptions often cover more than one person and in 1978 a total of 2.39m people were covered.

---

[1] *Review Body on Doctors' and Dentist' Remuneration, Fourth Report,* (Cmnd 5644), London, HMSO, 1974, page 42.

[2] DDRB 1974, *Op cit,* page 41.

[3] *Review Body on Doctors' and Dentists' Remuneration, Ninth Report,* (Cmnd 7574), London, HMSO, 1979, paragraph 76.

The total number of subscribers rose in 1978 after remaining fairly steady in recent years, but within the total, group subscriptions have tended to increase and individual subscriptions to fall. As might be expected, such evidence as there is suggests that most individual subscriptions are taken out by older members of the community and people with relatively high incomes. The proportion of private patients from overseas is not known, but except in some of the larger private hospitals in London is probably small.

Size of the private sector

18.22   The overall scale of private practice in relation to the NHS is small. In England about two per cent of all acute hospital beds and six per cent of all hospital beds are in private hospitals and nursing homes. The proportions in the rest of the United Kingdom are lower. In 1976 about four per cent of "acute" patients, and about seven per cent of surgical patients, were treated in private hospitals. However, about 50% of abortions on women normally resident in the UK were performed in the private sector, and private nursing homes make a significant contribution to the long-term care of the elderly.

18.23   A recent estimate put expenditure on private health care in the UK in 1976 at £134 million.[1] This figure excluded most expenditure on abortions and on long-term care in nursing homes (neither of which is normally covered by private health insurance), and on private general medical and dental care. Information from the Family Expenditure Survey for 1976 suggested that total expenditure on private health care was of the order of £200 million.[2] This compares with the total NHS expenditure in 1976 of £6,249 million, and on this basis the private sector accounted for about three percent of total expenditure on health care in the UK in that year.

Private Practice and the NHS

18.24   The difference in scale of the private and public health care sectors suggests that private practice could have at most a marginal and local effect on the NHS. Nonetheless, it was put to us that the private sector subsidises the NHS in some ways, and that the NHS subsidises the private sector in others. We consider these arguments briefly below.

18.25   A point frequently made by supporters of private practice is that patients who opt for private treatment in effect pay twice for their health care: they contribute to the NHS through taxation and NHS National Insurance contributions, but they also pay for the private care that they receive. Much the same argument is made in relation to private education.

18.26   Second, most consultants who undertake private practice are on "maximum part-time" contracts. Under such a contract a consultant may undertake private practice but is required to devote "substantially the whole of his time" to NHS work. He is paid nine-elevenths of the full-time salary.

[1]Lee, Michael, *Private and National Health Services*, London, Policy Studies Institute, 1978.
[2]Unpublished table.

Some consultants argue that this arrangement constitutes a subsidy for the NHS since the consultant is paid only a proportion of the full-time rate but is required to carry the same case load as a full-time consultant. The situation is further complicated because the present consultant contract is open-ended and there are no stipulated hours of duty. In a survey undertaken by the Doctors' and Dentists' Review Body in 1977 whole-time consultants reported averaging 48.7 hours per week and maximum part-time consultants 43.2 hours per week on NHS work.[1] There is room for argument both about the interpretation of the survey and the nature of the consultant contract, but the 5½ hours difference is less than the two-elevenths difference in salary. If the proposed new consultant contract were to be introduced this particular grievance would disappear.

18.27   Third, we were told that private practice contributed towards the funds available for medical research. Academic staff holding honorary NHS contracts may not normally benefit personally from any private practice they undertake. The arrangement is that such fees are paid over to the university department and used for research purposes. The amounts involved are likely to be a small proportion of the total funds available for medical research, although they may be significant for some medical schools.

18.28   Others argued to us that the taxpayer subsidises the private sector by financing staff training and the provision of radiology and pathology services. It was also said that skilled manpower was attracted away from the NHS. The argument about training is that the private sector does not have to incur the expense of training its own doctors, nurses, and other staff but relies on those trained in the NHS. Few private hospitals are approved by the General Nursing Council for nurse training, and post-graduate medical training takes place exclusively in the NHS. Pathology and radiology carried out in the NHS for private patients is normally paid for, but the availability of such facilities may relieve the private sector of providing what might in some places be an uneconomic service.

18.29   There is no doubt that the NHS has from time to time suffered from shortages of particular groups of staff both locally and nationally. However, bearing in mind the modest size of the private sector it is difficult to believe that such shortages were often due to NHS workers leaving for the private sector. A number of the private hospitals we visited employed a high proportion of married women. They argued that the NHS was unable to provide sufficient opportunity for part-time employment. We did not find this argument wholly convincing – in 1977, 38% of hospital nursing and midwifery staff in the UK were employed part-time – but the private sector may be able to offer more flexible working hours and better conditions of service for some staff. Hard information on the effect of the private sector on NHS staffing is difficult to come by. Our view is that the impact of private health facilities on NHS staffing will depend mainly on the local employment position and could only be determined by detailed local enquiries. We have no information that would enable us to assess the effect nationally of the private sector on NHS staffing but it cannot be large.

---

[1]*Review Body on Doctors' and Dentists' Remuneration, Eighth Report,* (Cmnd 7176), London, HMSO, 1978, paragraphs 7,8.

18.30 Some less specific points were put to us. It was suggested that the existence of a private sector provides a yardstick against which the performance of the NHS can be measured and shows where the NHS is failing to meet consumer demand. We accept that demands on the private sector may well show where the NHS is deficient, but we think that there is ample scope within the NHS for comparing standards of performance and identifying strengths and weaknesses. A related point made was that the strict financial discipline imposed on the private sector enables resources to be used more efficiently than in the NHS. This kind of point is virtually impossible to test.

18.31 Most of the considerations referred to above are unquantifiable. There is no doubt that the private sector contributes to the health care of the nation, albeit on a small scale. In two particular areas, provisions for the elderly and abortions, the contribution is significant. It would be virtually impossible to establish how far health workers are diverted from employment in the NHS. We have reached no conclusions about the overall balance of advantage or disadvantage to the NHS of the existence of a private sector, therefore, but it is clear that whichever way it lies it is small as matters now stand.

Pay Beds and the Health Services Board

18.32 Under the NHS Acts, health ministers may designate beds in NHS hospitals for use by private patients. The patients are required to pay the full cost of accommodation and services provided by the hospital. Fees for medical treatment are paid directly to the consultant concerned. Pay beds have always constituted a small proportion of total NHS beds, and their number was declining before the Health Services Board started work in 1976. Tables 18.3 and 18.4 show this trend.

TABLE 18.3
Pay Beds in NHS Hospitals: UK 1956–1979

Number of pay beds

	1956	1965	1970	1976	1979[1]
England	5,723	5,534	4,353	4,150	2,666
Wales	106	91	68	60	39
Scotland	929[2]	614	328	234	1,14
Northern Ireland	430[3]	—[4]	376	415	149
UNITED KINGDOM	7,188	6,239	5,125	4,859	2,968

Sources: compiled from statistics provided by the health departments' and the Health Services Board.

Notes: [1] 1979.
  [2] 1951 only available.
  [3] Estimated.
  [4] Figure not available.

18.33 The number of patients treated in pay beds has also declined from a peak in 1972, as Table 18.5 shows. Average daily occupancy by private patients of paybeds in the UK was 1,762 (45.6%) in 1977.

18.34 The Health Services Act 1976 established an independent Health

TABLE 18.4

Pay Beds as a percentage of total beds in NHS hospitals:
Great Britain 1965 – 1976

	1965	*1970*	*1976*
England	1.25	1.02	1.07
Wales	0.30	0.26	0.25
Scotland	1.00	0.52	0.39

Source: compiled from health departments' statistics

TABLE 18.5

Patients Treated in Pay Beds: England and Wales 1950 – 1977

1950	1966	1971	1972	1973	1974	1975	1976	1977
78,274	101,696	114,856	120,274	116,272	113,221	97,641	94,323	93,877

Source: Lee, Michael, *Private and National Health Services,* London, Policy Studies Institute, 1978.

Services Board to be responsible for the progressive withdrawal from NHS hospitals of authorised accommodation for the treatment of private patients, and for the regulation of the development of private hospitals and nursing homes. The Board's powers of regulation apply only to hospitals and nursing homes which have, or would have, more than 100 beds in Greater London or 75 elsewhere. Smaller developments have to be notified to the Health Services Board but are not regulated. The Act also provided for the revocation within 6 months of Royal Assent of 1,000 pay bed authorisations and the submission of recommendations by the Board for the introduction of common waiting lists for private and other patients in NHS hospitals. Although the Act does not extend to Northern Ireland, the government of the day indicated its intention to pursue a similar policy on private medical practice there when the Act was passed.

18.35   The first 1,000 revocations of pay bed authorisations required by the Act were made in 1977, and the Health Services Board has since made four further sets of proposals for revocations. At 1 January 1979 there were 2,819 pay beds in Great Britain, compared with 4,444 in 1976. The initial revocations were based on the non-use or under-use of authorised pay beds for which average daily occupancy was taken as evidence, but the Board has now begun to take into account also the the availability of suitable alternative accommodation and whether "reasonable steps" have been taken to provide private sector alternatives.

18.36   The strongest argument put to us in favour of the retention of pay beds was that as far as possible a consultant should be able to undertake private practice while remaining "geographically full-time", in other words that he should be able to treat both his private and NHS patients in the same place. "In this way the waste of time and effort involved in travelling to and from private consulting rooms and clinics elsewhere, and the need to maintain a separate office staff and to arrange for independent laboratory investigations can be avoided."[1] The presence of pay beds in NHS hospitals makes it more likely that consultants will be on hand to attend to their NHS patients, and has the additional advantage that the full facilities of the NHS are available to private patients in an emergency.

18.37   One argument against pay beds is that the charges made do not meet the full cost of treating private patients, and that the NHS is therefore subsidising private practice. Charges for private patients are determined by health ministers on the basis of the average costs incurred in the appropriate class of hospital. They are intended to include a reasonable contribution towards capital expenditure but do not take account of variations in facilities provided in individual hospitals. In general, the charges appear to cover the revenue costs of treating private patients in NHS hospitals, but we are not convinced that they cover the capital element adequately. The calculation of the capital element is based on average capital expenditure on all hospital beds in recent years, expressed as a cost per occupied bed per week. This bears little relationship to the full capital cost of providing a hospital bed in the private sector. The Employment and Social Services Sub-committee of the Expenditure Committee of the House of Commons pointed out in 1971 that the weekly charge to meet the full capital cost of a hospital bed would be very much higher.[2] A new private hospital, unless supported by charitable funds, would need to cover in its charges both the interest and depreciation costs of its capital, and we recommend that the NHS should determine the capital element of pay bed charges in the same way.

18.38   We were told that the existence of private practice within the NHS facilitates and encourages abuse. It was suggested that hospital staff, including junior doctors, nurses and domestic staff, were expected to provide services for private patients outside their normal range of duties without additional pay, and that payment was not always made when hospital equipment and facilities were used for private work. The most frequent and serious allegations, however, concerned the speedier admission of private patients, either to pay beds or after a private consultation to NHS beds. We have no firm evidence that such abuses are extensive, and we consider that it should be possible to deal with them administratively. Nevertheless, we regard it as important not only that the NHS should be fair to all its patients, but also that it should make every effort to be seen to be fair, and we deplore such "queue jumping". Agreement has now been reached between the health departments (Northern Ireland excepted) and the medical profession on the introduction of common waiting lists for urgent and seriously ill NHS and private patients. We welcome this and hope that these arrangements can soon be extended to all hospital patients.

18.39   There has been speculation that the phasing out of pay beds will lead to an increase in the number of private hospitals. The Health Services Board recognise that there is likely to be a "significant expansion of the private sector from late 1979 onwards".[3] This will probably provide more facilities for

[1]*Report of the Royal Commission on Medical Education 1965 – 68,* (Cmnd 3569), London, HMSO, 1968, paragraph 515.

[2]*Fourth Report from the Expenditure Committee,* London, HMSO, 1972, pages. xii and 14-15.

[3]Health Services Board, *Developments in the basis of revocation proposals to be made by the Health Services Board in 1979 and beyond,* 1978.

surgery. We see no objection to such expansion, which at least initially may amount to little more than the replacement of the pay beds removed from the NHS, providing that the interests of the NHS are adequately safeguarded. This is one of the responsibilities of the Health Services Board. However, although the Board has powers to control larger developments (over 100 beds in London and 75 elsewhere) they cannot regulate developments below these limits; nor, more importantly, can the Board consider how the aggregate of several such developments within a locality may affect the NHS.[1] We think that if the interests of the NHS are to be adequately safeguarded the Board should have the power to consider the aggregate of several developments within a locality, perhaps on the basis that authorisation should be required for any proposal which increases the total number of private beds within a locality above a specified level. We recommend that the powers of the Health Services Board should be extended in this way.

18.40   Pay beds arouse strong emotions. Many doctors regard them as an essential element of their professional independence as well as a source of additional income. Other health service workers, including some junior doctors, resent both the additional work they claim is imposed by private patients and what they see as the purchase of privilege by a small minority within a public service. When the controversy is raging, patients suffer. We do not consider the presence or absence of pay beds in NHS hospitals to be significant at present from the point of view of the efficient functioning of the NHS.

Conclusions and Recommendations

18.41   We are concerned with private practice only insofar as it affects the NHS. We have concentrated on the facts so far as they are known. Information is lacking that would enable us to reach precise conclusions about the relationship between the NHS and private practice, but it is clear that the private sector is too small to make a significant impact on the NHS, except locally and temporarily. On the other hand, the private sector probably responds much more directly to patients' demands for services than the NHS, and provides a useful pointer to areas where the NHS is defective. One such is clearly the provision of abortion services: half the abortions performed on residents of the UK are undertaken privately. Another is in the provision of nursing homes for the elderly; and patients waiting for cold surgery in the NHS may opt to pay rather than suffer discomfort and inconvenience for months or even years. Other important reasons for choosing the private sector are the convenience of being able to time your entry to hospital to suit yourself, being assured of reasonable privacy and choosing your own doctor. The NHS should make more effort to meet reasonable requirements of this kind.

18.42   From the point of view of the NHS the main importance of pay beds lies in the passions aroused and the consequential dislocation of work which then occurs. The establishment of the Health Services Board led to a welcome respite from discussion of this emotional subject. However, for the Board to carry out its function of safeguarding the interests of the NHS, it seems to us

---

[1]The Health Services Board told us that they had received notification of two proposed developments in one part of London, one of which would provide 99 beds.

that it should be able to control the aggregate of private beds in a locality: this appears to be a loophole at present.

18.43   We recommend that:

(a) health authorities in Great Britain should have the broad objective of providing for about 75% of all abortions on resident women to be performed in the NHS over the next few years (paragraph 18.13);

(b) the capital element of pay bed charges should cover both the interest and depreciation costs of the capital investment in pay beds (paragraph 18.37);

(c) the Health Services Board should be given power to control, and a responsibility to consider, the aggregate of beds in private hospitals and nursing homes when any new private development is considered in a locality (paragraph 18.39).

Part V   Management and Finance

In Chapter 4 we reviewed some of the matters most often put to us in evidence. Most of them concerned the way in which the NHS was administered, its structural organisation and its financing. In this section of the report we look in detail at how the present system operates and at what can be done to improve it. For many who work in the NHS this may be the part of our report of greatest interest. We think that while these matters are of great importance, not least because those who work in the NHS have given us so much evidence about management and finance questions, they are essentially secondary to those subjects which bear directly on patient care.

Chapter 19   Parliament, Health Ministers and their Departments

19.1   In each of the four parts of the UK the NHS is the direct statutory responsibility of a Minister of the Crown and to help him in his task each has a health department staffed by civil servants. Health ministers devolve the day to day management of the NHS to health authorities. These authorities employ staff, provide buildings and equipment and ensure that patients receive care. Their members are appointed, as opposed to elected, for the most part by the responsible minister or, in the case of Area Health Authority (AHA) members in England, by the appropriate Regional Health Authority (RHA). They look to central government for their funds. Formal overall responsibility to Parliament for their actions rests with the appropriate minister.

19.2   There are financial reasons for this form of organisation. More than 95% of NHS funds are drawn from general taxation and NHS National Insurance contributions, most of the balance coming from charges for certain NHS goods and services. These funds are voted annually by Parliament and it is a major function of a health minister to negotiate with his Cabinet colleagues an appropriate share of public expenditure for the NHS. He must then account to Parliament, and through Parliament to the people of the UK, for the proper use of these funds. In each health department a senior civil servant is the accounting officer and is subject to examination by the Public Accounts Committee (PAC) of the House of Commons for all the expenditure by his department on the NHS. Health ministers are accountable to Parliament, not only for the determination of national policy but also for actions carried out by or on behalf of individual health authorities. In principle health ministers and their departments are expected to have detailed knowledge of and influence over the NHS. In practice, however, this is neither possible nor desirable and detailed ministerial accountability for the NHS is largely a constitutional fiction. That is not to say that it is without virtues.

19.3   The NHS differs from local authorities in that it has no significant independent source of income and no direct accountability to a local electorate.

19.4   Nor is the NHS like a nationalised industry where central government delegates detailed control over the management of a particular service or industry to a public corporation. Those corporations are expected to operate like businesses and have to find a large part of their own capital and resources. The NHS is thus not subject to the financial discipline of having to meet a target rate of return on capital.

19.5   The formal ministerial and central control by civil servants means that the NHS differs from those parts of the public services whose administrative independence from the state is accepted but which are nevertheless dependent on central funds. For example, the universities derive over 90% of their income from central government, but they are independent corporations and although subject to the usual rules of financial accountability under the scrutiny of the Comptroller and Auditor General, the control and guidance exercised over them by the University Grants Committee is light.

19.6   On the other hand, the size of the NHS, the power of the health authorities and the influence of the health professions mean that central government cannot in practice administer the NHS in the detailed way that it can the social security system or the armed forces. Nor would it be sensible to try to do so. The Department of Health and Social Security put the position like this:

> "Because of the size and complexity of the NHS budget, it would not be practicable for DHSS to control expenditure in great detail. In any case to attempt to do so would seriously undermine one of the major concepts on which the present structure of the NHS is based, namely, the maximum delegation to Regional and Area Health Authorities of responsibility for providing services in accordance with national policies, objectives and priorities. Broad financial control is exercised by giving RHAs fixed allocations, which they must not exceed but within which they have considerable freedom to manage as they judge best. The essential counterpart of this degree of delegation is a clear line of accountability and an efficient system of monitoring."[1]

It is clear that there is a gap between the formal, detailed accountability that a minister and his chief official carry for all that goes on in the NHS and every penny spent on it, and the realities of the situation described above. It is not surprising that difficulties occur.

19.7   In the remainder of this chapter, we examine in turn the parts played by Parliament, the health minister, his permanent secretary and his department. Our analysis is primarily concerned with the Secretary of State for Social Services and the DHSS. Nevertheless, much of what we say will apply to Scotland, Wales and Northern Ireland.

Parliamentary Control

19.8   Parliament supervises the NHS in a number of ways. Individual MPs can raise matters of constituency or more general interest with the minister concerned by letter, or by parliamentary question, or by initiating adjournment debates and so on. MPs will take part in debates on health policy in the NHS initiated by the government or opposition, and in the process of scrutinising legislation on the NHS. There is no select committee on the NHS but the Social Services and Employment Sub-committee of the Expenditure Committee periodically considers aspects of health services. The PAC, served by the Comptroller and Auditor General and his staff, examines the way NHS funds are spent.

---

[1]*Eleventh Report from the Expenditure Committee*, Volume II (Part I), London, HMSO, 1977, page 381.

19.9　Ministers have encouraged MPs to raise points about the local operation of the NHS with the appropriate health authority in the first instance, and they do so. However, the health departments told us that over 3,000 parliamentary questions were asked by MPs on health topics in session 1976/77. Our discussions with former ministers and members of the Expenditure Committee confirmed that MPs value the direct access to health ministers which the present system allows them, but we think that on occasion they raise matters which can and should be dealt with by the NHS and dealt with at its lowest level. They expect health ministers to be in a position to provide accurate and detailed information quickly over the whole NHS field for Parliament. This requires a large and staffed intelligence gathering capacity which in practice involves both the health authorities and the health departments.

19.10　Some critics of present arrangements suggest that the creation of a public corporation or health commission would "take the NHS out of politics" in general, and in particular relieve ministers of much of their present obligation to provide information to MPs. We discuss the merits of this proposal later, but whatever else it might do it certainly would not take the NHS out of politics. We do not believe that this is in any wider sense desirable. Obviously there are aspects of the nation's health which would be better left out of *party* politics, but we believe it is both inevitable and right that the affairs of the NHS should be kept firmly at the centre of public debate.

19.11　It was suggested to us that the establishment of a select committee on the NHS would assist parliamentary control of the health service. We noted that a select committee to examine the work of the DHSS was proposed by the House of Commons Select Committee on Procedure in their 1977/78 report.[1] We recommend that a select committee be set up. We consider that it would make a valuable contribution to public debate on the NHS, and, provided it were properly served, with the power to examine health ministers, civil servants and expert witnesses, would enable Parliament to influence health policy and keep in touch with the work of the NHS in a more systematic way. We think its establishment should be accompanied by a reduction in the volume of routine work imposed by MPs on health departments. There should be a clear understanding that matters of local significance should be raised and dealt with by the appropriate health authority. We recognise that MPs must retain their important right to raise matters affecting their constituents with the minister responsible if such matters cannot be dealt with satisfactorily locally, but we hope that they would use that right sparingly.

The Minister

19.12　The lot of a Secretary of State and his junior ministers cannot be an easy one. He is accountable to Parliament for the NHS and carries management responsibilities for it. The Secretary of State for Social Services is a cabinet minister with the heavy responsibility which any office of cabinet rank carries. He will be an MP and may hold office in his political party. The

---

[1]*First Report from the Select Committee on Procedure*, Volume 1, London, HMSO, 1978, paragraphs 5.22–5.24.

functions of the DHSS include not only the NHS but wider health matters, local authority social services in England and the administration of the social security system in Great Britain. In other parts of the UK the NHS is the responsibility of the Secretaries of State for Scotland, Wales and Northern Ireland. They carry portfolios for many other functions in addition to the NHS and the pressure of responsibilities on them means that, if anything, they are even more remote from the NHS.

19.13   We took the advice of former prime ministers and health ministers about the role of the ministers responsible for the NHS. One view was that ministers' powers were limited and that all that could be reasonably expected of them and their departments was an inspectorial function. Another was that under present financial arrangements a large bureaucracy was required to ensure accountability to Parliament. The importance of the NHS having a voice in the Cabinet was also stressed. Our informants united in discounting the possibility of the NHS being taken out of politics.

19.14   Nonetheless, the Secretary of State for Social Services, and his colleagues with health responsibilities in other parts of the UK, are clearly overburdened at the present. We hope our recommendations in this and other chapters will relieve them to some extent.

The Permanent Secretary

19.15   It is difficult to separate the role of the permanent secretary[1] from that of his department, but there is one feature of that role which demands separate consideration. As the permanent head of the department, he is its accounting officer. This means that he is personally accountable for the proper and efficient use of funds allocated by Parliament. His accountability is increasingly interpreted by Parliament as including the policies which give rise to expenditure as well as financial propriety. We were told by the Comptroller and Auditor General that while the DHSS permanent secretary would not be blamed for everything that went wrong in the NHS, he would be expected to make sure that faults in management that might be exposed were corrected. We think it would be possible to divide up the present accountability of the DHSS permanent secretary and devolve defined areas of it to the health authorities themselves. We recognise that this would not be achieved without a re-definition of the roles of the minister and the department responsible for the NHS.

19.16   Ours is not the accepted view of Whitehall. Evidence presented to the PAC in 1977 by senior officials from the health departments, the Treasury and the Civil Service Department reviewed alternatives to the permanent secretary's present accountability for the NHS. The departments concluded that the accounting officer responsibility of the permanent secretary must

---

[1]The DHSS has two permanent secretaries. The second permanent secretary carries responsibility, including accounting officer responsibility, for social security matters. We are speaking here of the first permanent secretary who carries overall responsibility for the department and leads its work in relation to the NHS. In the other health departments the chief official responsible for the NHS is also the accounting officer.

remain personal to him. In their view the alternative of separate financial accountability for each health authority would require the creation of suitable accounting officer posts in health authorities and would, in any case, not relieve the health departments significantly of the burden of responsibility. Any change in the position of the accounting officer implies significant structural change in the top management relationships of the NHS. We return to this below.

The Department of Health and Social Security

19.17   In considering the role of the department we found the Expenditure Committee's report referred to above most helpful, particularly the memoranda submitted to it by the DHSS on its own organisation. We have also carefully studied the report of an enquiry into the department's work carried out by three RHA chairmen and the very considerable documentation of the management review carried out by the department itself.[1] In all this, as with all other matters, we have received the fullest and friendliest co-operation of officials in the DHSS and the other health departments.

19.18   In the memorandum to the Expenditure Committee the DHSS described its functions as follows:

"Across the Health, Social Security and Personal Social Services the Department has a major policy development role. The Department is also directly responsible for administering the various Social Security schemes, for promoting the establishment of a comprehensive Health Service, for public and preventive health measures and for ensuring the provision of personal social services by local authorities. The total expenditure for which the Department is responsible is of the order of £17,000m a year. Its staff numbers about 93,000."[2]

The memorandum went on to distinguish the department's role in relation to social security and to health:

"The nature of policy formation and of the administrative tasks for Social Security differ in many important ways from those for Health and Personal Social Services. Through its own network of central, regional and local offices, the Department deals direct with claimants for social security benefits in accordance with rules affecting benefits and contributions laid down under statute. In its health and personal social services roles, however, the Department does not directly treat patients – except at the Special Hospitals and Artificial Limb and Appliance Centres – or advise individual members of the public. It is responsible for seeing that there is adequate organisation, with a full range of services to ensure that patients are treated and individuals helped. It is a centre for developing

---

[1]The primary purpose of the review which was carried out by a team of civil servants from the DHSS and the Civil Service Department was to help the top management of the DHSS improve the efficiency and effectiveness of its organisation and management and in particular the planning and control of its resources.

[2]*Eleventh Report from the Expenditure Committee, Op cit*, page 375.

general advice and guidance to the authorities concerned. It has important co-ordinating and research roles to help it discharge these responsibilities. It decides the allocation of finance among authorities and monitors expenditure. Its oversight of and assistance to authorities is generally more by administrative guidance than by legislation."

The vast majority of staff employed by the DHSS work on the social security side of the department, but about 5,000 work on health and personal social services. About another 1,000 staff work in the other UK health departments.

19.19 The most frequent criticism of the DHSS is that it is too large and complicated. The Rt Hon Dr D Owen MP, Minister of State at DHSS 1974–76, has written:

"The department has become bogged down in detailed administration covering day to day management that has been sucked in by the parliamentary process. The answerability of Ministers to Parliament may have given the semblance of control, but on some major aspects of health care there has been little central direction or control."[1]

The three chairmen's report made the following points about DHSS:

"(a) There must be a clear statement of the precise function of the department.

(b) The structure of the DHSS has become complicated, partly because of the centralising tendencies of successive governments, and partly because of the confusion over the years between its executive and its advisory responsibilities.

(c) The complication of functions, both advisory and executive unconnected with the NHS has made the lines of responsibility even more diffuse.

(d) The Department has in consequence grown steadily in size in recent years, to the detriment of its effectiveness, ability to take decisions, and capacity to manage the Service as it should.

(e) This has resulted also in considerable duplication of effort between the Department and Regions with consequent duplications of staff and hence, of cost."[2]

In oral evidence to us the three chairmen expressed their disappointment that, although some progress on peripheral changes in the organisation of the DHSS had taken place as the result of their report, and of the management review in the department, in general their comments and criticisms had not been accepted.

---

[1]Owen, David, *In Sickness and in Health,* London, Quartet Books, 1976, page 7.

[2]*Regional Chairmen's Enquiry into the working of the DHSS in relation to Regional Health Authorities,* London, DHSS, 1976, ["The Three Chairmen's Report"], paragraph 245.

19.20   It is never easy for the outsider to obtain a balanced and accurate view of how large organisations operate. This is perhaps particularly true of government departments whose organisation is affected by political factors and which have many traditional and advisory functions. Simple management models are rarely relevant. Organisational change in very large institutions always takes a long time to come fully into effect and usually longer than others estimate. These considerations caution us against recommending hasty structural change in the top management of the NHS. We were also impressed by Professor Kogan's finding that at working level in the NHS there was little sign of widespread dissatisfaction with the DHSS or the other health departments. Nevertheless, we have been left with a sense of unease about the present size and structure of the DHSS and with the way it controls the NHS.

19.21   The two main functions of the Secretary of State for Social Services are to give general directions and policy guidance to the NHS. We consider that wherever he gives guidance to the NHS which has financial consequences, he must provide the resources necessary to follow his guidance. Again, if he feels that savings can be made the Secretary of State should indicate what he expects these savings to be. To do less than this is to raise expectations on the part of the public which the NHS is unable to fulfil.

19.22   We think we detect some lack of co-ordination between policy formation within the department which leads to the development of priorities in health spending and the reflection of this policy through the RAWP formula which mainly determines the financial allocations made by the DHSS to the regions. In our view the DHSS has tended to give too much guidance to the NHS both on strategic issues and matters of detail. Too often national policies have been advocated without critically evaluated local experiment. As we noted in Chapter 6 close co-operation with other government departments responsible for social policy is also important.

19.23   It seems to us that the fact that the Secretary of State and his chief official are answerable for the NHS in detail distorts the relationship between the DHSS and health authorities. It encourages central involvement in matters which would be better left to the authorities. In consequence no clear line is drawn where the department's involvement ends. In our view the essential functions of the DHSS in the health field are to:

obtain, allocate and distribute funds for the NHS;

set objectives, formulate policies and identify priorities;

monitor the performance of health authorities so as to enable the Secretary of State to discharge his responsibilities;

undertake national manpower planning;

deal at national level with pay and conditions for NHS staff;

advise on legislation;

liaise with other government departments on matters related to the NHS and health policy;

take a lead in promoting policies designed to improve the health of the nation and prevent ill-health;

promote experiment, evaluation and the exchange of ideas on health questions.

In addition there will inevitably be a departmental involvement in such matters as capital building, supplies and international health.

The other health departments

19.24 Although some of the comments we have made about the DHSS apply to the health departments in Scotland, Wales and Northern Ireland they operate in a very different context. In general relations between them and the health authorities, professions and trade unions are more direct and informal. This is probably because their scale of operation is smaller, their populations being analogous to that of an RHA in England, and because many contentious issues, such as the settlement of pay and conditions for health service workers, are handled nationally. At reorganisation central agencies were set up in Scotland, Wales and Northern Ireland to deal with functions, such as supplies, which it made sense to administer centrally. Our impression is that for the most part these organisations work well and have proved useful innovations.

19.25 We received some evidence that a regional tier in Wales was required. The Association of Welsh CHCs and the Society of Secretaries of Welsh CHCs told us in oral evidence:

"with the passing of the Welsh Hospital Board, there was no longer an all Wales body with widespread geographical representation which could debate health topics in public. Administration by Welsh Office civil servants did not fill the gap."

These remarks about the structure of the NHS in Wales are consistent with our general view that greater power should be devolved from the health departments.

Alternative Models

19.26 The problems we have identified in the top management of the NHS have led us to consider a number of alternative forms of top management which have been proposed to us. We have looked at four broad approaches to the problem:

transferring the NHS to local government;
the establishment of a health commission;
devolving power to health authorities; and
strengthening the arrangements for monitoring the quality of services which are the responsibility of health authorities.

The local government option

19.27 We concluded in Chapter 16 that transferring the NHS to local government would not be desirable. Further consideration of the joint administration of the NHS and local authority services might be appropriate if regional government became a serious possibility in England.

A health commission

19.28   A health commission is usually seen as having management functions in relation to the NHS, but a central monitoring body or super-inspectorate is sometimes advocated.

19.29   The establishment of an independent health commission or board to manage the NHS was one of the solutions most frequently advocated in evidence. There are a number of possible models including the British Broadcasting Corporation, the Post Office, the University Grants Committee and the Manpower Services Commission. Although most of those who favoured the proposal were not specific about the role of a commission, some of the functions suggested were the co-ordination of planning by health authorities, pay and conditions for NHS staff, manpower planning and training, research and guidance in areas such as hospital building and equipment, and perhaps the allocation of funds to health authorities within guidelines laid down by Parliament.

19.30   Setting up a commission would radically affect the relationship of the health departments, and indeed of Parliament itself, with the NHS. The departments would lose their direct involvement in the management of the NHS, and MPs would have to raise local issues with the commission or the health authorities. The very large sums of public money required by the NHS would, however, make some continued parliamentary supervision inevitable. Parliament would, as now, be involved in legislation, the provision of funds and securing financial accountability. The Secretaries of State and the health departments would continue to have major functions, for example in appointing the commission's chairman and members, negotiating the appropriate level of funding and setting priorities and objectives. A commission might act as a buffer between the NHS and Parliament but the NHS would remain dependent on the willingness of Parliament to vote funds. The effect, therefore, might be to duplicate functions that at present are carried out, however unsatisfactorily, by the health departments and the top tier of health authorities. The latter's role would be little changed.

19.31   On the other hand, a health commission might have the important advantage of providing the permanent and easily identifiable leadership which the service at present lacks. An NHS view would be presented publicly by a body representing the whole of the NHS and only the NHS. Planning and decisions on use of resources would be seen to be carried out by an independent body.

19.32   Although many of the arguments presented to us in favour of setting up a health commission are attractive, we have not been persuaded that the management of the NHS would benefit from a major structural innovation of this kind. Improvements are possible within the existing structure. A commission would be necessary only if it became clear that the health departments and authorities could not discharge their responsibilities satisfactorily and that no improvement could be achieved within the existing framework. We consider that this is an important matter about which it is not possible to be categorical at this time, and that it is one that ministers should keep under review.

Devolving responsibility to health authorities

19.33   We have ruled out the two most radical approaches to resolving the inconsistency between the theoretical responsibilities for the NHS carried by health ministers, permanent secretaries and health departments, and the practical realities. There is a third approach, and we think it is one which the government should pursue, though the temptation not to will be strong. In our view the direct and detailed accountability for the NHS which Parliament requires can best be provided by health authorities themselves. In England, RHAs should become accountable to Parliament for matters within their competence. This would include most of the activities of the NHS, but not those, such as apportioning revenue and capital funds between RHAs, which clearly have to be undertaken centrally. A more precise division of responsibility would have to be worked out.

19.34   The main reason for transferring to regional health authorities the accountability at present held by the DHSS is that it would transfer formal responsibility to the authorities responsible in fact for running the service. The RHA chairman, or some nominated officer, or both, would appear before the PAC. Enquiries from MPs about local matters would be routed to and dealt with by health authorities. The representatives of RHA chairmen told us in oral evidence that they would welcome an arrangement of this kind. As we noted above, the main problems appear to be the practical difficulty of finding a suitable accounting officer, and the need to define the responsibilities respectively of health authorities and the DHSS. We think these problems could be overcome and recommend that accountability at present held by the DHSS should be transferred to RHAs.

19.35   The formal transfer of responsibility from the DHSS to health authorities should result in a smaller range of functions for the DHSS. Time-consuming parliamentary business should be reduced, and it should no longer be necessary for the department to intervene to the same extent in the way health authorities discharge their responsibilitites. A contraction in the present DHSS regional liaison and service development functions could be achieved. This should have two importants benefits: a closer integration within the DHSS of policy making and resource allocation; and for the NHS a clearer view of where particular responsibilities lie within the department. The responsibilities of health authorities under the new arrangement would need to be spelled out.

Monitoring quality of service

19.36   Mechanisms for reviewing services in NHS hospitals were set up in 1969 in England and Wales and in 1970 in Scotland following public disquiet about conditions in a number of long-stay hospitals. Originally the remit of the Hospital Advisory Services (HAS) in England and Wales and in Scotland was confined to long-stay hospitals, but in 1976 the HAS in England and Wales was renamed the Health Advisory Service and its remit extended to cover community services, including those provided in collaboration with local authorities. The needs of the mentally handicapped are dealt with separately in England by the Development Team for the Mentally Handicapped.[1]

19.37   These institutions are doing useful work, but it is clear that in some places the quality of NHS services still falls seriously below an acceptable standard. An extreme example may be seen in the report of the inquiry at Normansfield Hospital.[2] We were aware that Normansfield was not an isolated case of a disastrous decline in standards of patient care, and that the HAS had visited this hospital in 1970 and 1972.

19.38   The HAS and Development Team perform an advisory service and function by persuasion rather than coercion. Because they deal with matters that impinge on the clinical responsibilities of staff the limitation of their powers may be inevitable if they are to be acceptable to those who are looking after patients, However, we received evidence from Mr Frank Pethybridge, the Administrator of the North Western RHA, supported by his regional administrator colleagues, that the function of these services should be considerably extended and centralised. He pointed to the existence of inspectorates in other fields, for example the police, the probation service and education. We do not think that developing these existing services in this way would be appropriate. An inspectorate would be costly and unlikely to be effective outside the management system of the NHS.

19.39   We have referred in other chapters to the importance for safeguarding high standards of patient care, of the high quality and integrity among all of the health professions, expressed in their own self-scrutiny, peer reviews and clinical audits. The health departments have a responsibility to promote and facilitate this professional activity. But there is also a case for separate administrative monitoring services. This is the responsibility of the health departments and the health authorities. Standards of care are very closely linked with the facilities provided for care. One of the main ways in which health ministers and their departments can raise standards is to ensure that more resources are devoted to underdeveloped services. Services where standards of care have been so poor that there have been public outcries and enquiries have almost without exception been the under-funded and administratively neglected areas of the NHS. Ministers must face the need to make their priorities stick. It is neither just nor efficient to allow one scandal after another to erupt, to institute an enquiry and then to pillory those who have drifted into these often neglected services.

19.40   The necessary priorities will not be established at any level of the NHS unless there is strong continued public concern and pressure. In the next

---

[1] In Scotland and Wales the HASs have retained responsibility for the mentally handicapped.

[2] *Report of the Committee of Inquiry into Normansfield Hospital,* (Cmnd 7357), London, HMSO, 1978.

chapter we propose that the public contribution to management of the NHS should be at the lowest administrative level, and in Chapter 11 that community health councils should be assisted to carry out their functions more effectively. These changes would help public concern to be expressed more effectively. However, at all levels health authority authority members should play an active part in visiting the institutions and services for which they are responsible. If health ministers and health authorities are unable to monitor services effectively within the structure then we suggest that stronger measures may be called for. One possibility would be to set up an independent special health authority for the purpose. We do not think that this is required at the present time provided that the other changes that we recommend are adopted.

Conclusions and Recommendations

19.41   The roles of health ministers, permanent secretaries and the health departments, and their relations with the NHS, seem to us to stem from the way that the NHS is financed. Arrangements for accounting for NHS finance follow the classic Whitehall model under which the minister is answerable to Parliament, and the permanent secretary personally accountable, for every penny spent and every action taken in the NHS. This arrangement seems to us to be quite inappropriate to an organisation the size of the NHS whose staff are not civil servants and some of whom – for example, doctors – may not be answerable to anyone else for the expenditure they incur. The system has been made to work by those immediately concerned, to their credit, but there is nonetheless a gap between the theoretical and the actual position. The effect of this may be seen in the uncertainties over the respective roles of the health departments and the NHS.

19.42   After a good deal of reflection, and having considered a number of alternatives, we concluded that the best solution to this fundamental difficulty was to place responsibility for the detailed working of the NHS in England with the regional health authorities themselves. We mention the position outside England in paragraphs 19.24 and 19.25. This would end the anomalous position of the Secretary of State for Social Services and his permanent secretary being held responsible for actions over which in practice they can have little control. The division of responsibility between the regional health authorities and the DHSS would need to be worked out, but in broad terms we see the former as accountable for the delivery of the service and the latter for national policies and functions.

19.43   It is clear that neither the DHSS and the Welsh Office nor some of the health authorities in England and Wales, are carrying out their monitoring functions adequately, and this responsibility should have their urgent attention.

19.44   We recommend that:

(a) a select committee on the NHS should be set up (paragraph 19.11);

(b) formal responsibility, including accountability to Parliament, for the delivery of services should be transferred to RHAs (paragraph 19.34).

Chapter 20 Health Authorities and Their Organisation

20.1 In the last chapter we discussed the responsibilities carried by Parliament, health ministers and their departments for the NHS. In this chapter we discuss the organisation and administrative structure of the NHS itself. The recurring theme of our report is that the NHS is a service to patients. It follows that the structure and management of the NHS must be judged by how well they serve patients and the efficiency and humanity with which the resources put at the command of the NHS are used. These resources, paid for in the end by the patient, are on a huge scale. Good, clear administration is therefore essential.

20.2 We deal with three broad topics in this chapter. We discuss first a number of aspects of management; the "consensus" style of management by representatives of different disciplines, the involvement of health professions in the planning and management of health care and administration below district level. Second, we consider the structure of the administration of the NHS, including the role of each of the tiers in the structure, and we include in this the important matter of the separate existence in England and Wales of family practitioner committees (FPCs). Last, we discuss the arrangements for making health authorities accountable to the communities they serve.

Present Arrangements

20.3 The reorganisation of the NHS took effect on 1 October 1973 in Northern Ireland and in Great Britain on 1 April 1974. It was the result of a lengthy process of discussion and consultation.[1] The generally held view before reorganisation was that unification of the health services which were the responsibility of separate hospital, family practitioner and local health authorities would bring undoubted benefit. Unification of the tripartite structure was the starting point for NHS reorganisation. Speaking in a debate on his Green Paper, Mr R H S Crossman, then Secretary of State for Social Services, said:

"most of the faults and failings of the system derive from its tripartite structure",[2]

---

[1] The first Green Paper proposing the unification of administration of health services was published in 1968 by Mr Kenneth Robinson, Minister of Health, and further discussion documents were published in 1970 (the Crossman Green Paper) and May 1971 (the Consultative Document). There were parallel discussion documents in Wales. A separate Scottish Green Paper was issued in 1968 and a consultative document on restructuring the health and personal social services in Northern Ireland in 1971.

[2] *Hansard*, 23.3.1970,.Column 998.

and the 1972 White Paper for England said:

"unification offers solid advantages to the individual and the family, because their needs for health and social services are not divided into separate compartments. A single family, or an individual, may in a short space of time, or even at one and the same time, need many types of health and social care, and these needs should be met in a co-ordinated way. Otherwise they will get an unsatisfactory service or even no service at all."[1]

20.4   We were told in evidence from the DHSS that in addition to unification the main principles underlying reorganisation were:

"the integral involvement of the health care professions in planning and management at all levels of the service;

decentralisation and delegation of decision making but within policies established at a higher level;

a territorial structure and organisational mechanisms which allowed closer collaboration with local authorities and facilitated joint planning and working on matters of common concern;

provision for effective central control over the money spent in the service to enable the Secretary of State to discharge responsibilities laid upon him by Parliament."

20.5   These principles were followed in the four parts of the UK. Although the arrangements introduced to implement them differed slightly, there were several common features. Below each health department there were a number of tiers. *Regional health authorities* (RHAs) in England only[2], *area health authorities* (AHAs) or *boards,* and *health districts.* The health district was seen as the basic unit for planning, management and operation of health care services. Each tier had a team of officers drawn from various disciplines and working, as equals, by consensus. Collaboration between health and local authorities was facilitated in most places by coterminus boundaries. Management of the service was separated from representation of the views of consumers as expressed by district based *community health councils* (CHCs) and their equivalents. There have been minor modifications of these arrangements since 1974, the most important of which has been the conversion of some multi-district AHAs into single district areas in England. Below district level are *sectors* covering hospital and community services. *Units* relate to individual hospitals.

Criticisms of the present arrangements

20.6   In Chapter 4 we noted a number of factors affecting the NHS at the time of reorganisation. They included the grave economic difficulties which the country has faced since 1974; the consequent effect on remuneration and the

---

[1]*National Health Service Reorganisation: England,* (Cmnd 5055), London, HMSO, 1972, paragraph 7.

[2]In Scotland, Wales and Northern Ireland central agencies carrying out some 'regional' functions were set up at reorganisation.

development of the NHS generally; changes in the organisation of nursing following the 1966 Salmon Committee Report; the increased unionisation of staff and the development of more "industrial" attitudes; the shortage of personnel officers in the NHS, and the emergence of new professional groups, for example in the laboratories. To quote Professor Kogan:

> "We emphasise that many of the sources of low morale have nothing to do with reorganisation. It is a bad time to be a public servant. Management faces virtually incessant bombardment from employees wanting changes of status as well as of conditions and salaries, from clients who want a voice in the management of the system, from members who are under far more political pressure than used to be the case within the former hospital service."[1]

The NHS is, of course, by no means unique among public services in attracting criticism about the way it functions.

20.7   Many of the complaints heard today were being made about the NHS before 1974. For example, Mr Crossman speaking in a Parliamentary debate in 1971 referred to:

> "the insensitivity of the health service to local feeling and patient criticism, the remoteness of the service, its bureaucratic nature, its refusal to understand local needs, the setting up of hospitals with no transport to them, the creation of great marble palaces and the closing down of well-loved small hospitals."[2]

20.8   Much the most common criticism of the reorganised NHS is that the machinery for decision making is expensive, cumbersome and slow. "Matters which should be corrected in minutes or hours now take weeks or months with the obvious effect of slowing down the whole service", as one doctor told us. The reasons given for this vary. The King's College Hospital Group Medical Executive Committees said:

> "The proliferation of committees and introduction of democracy has meant unlimited opportunities for extremists to manipulate the system for their own ends, and for postponement of decisions to faceless committees at higher levels."

Another favourite cause of delay offered in evidence was the number of tiers. Another doctor commented:

> "The present reorganisation. . . has proved too cumbersome and involves too many tiers at which decision-making is expected to take place. All too frequently it has meant that decision-making has been deferred for fear of what the next tier up may say."

---

[1]Kogan, Maurice, et al, *The Working of the National Health Service,* Royal Commission on the National Health Service, Research Paper Number 1, London, HMSO, 1978, paragraph. 31.

[2]*Hansard,* 1.7.1971, Col 612.

It would be possible to multiply these quotations many times. The research we commissioned from Professors Kogan and Perrin has helped us to assess these criticisms more thoroughly and Professor Kogan's report confirmed that there was:

> "a great deal of anger and frustration at what many regard as a seriously over-elaborate system of government, administration and decision making. The multiplicity of levels, the over-elaboration of consultative machinery, the inability to get decision making completed nearer the point of delivery of services, and what some describe as unacceptably wasteful use of manpower resources were recurrent themes in most of the areas where we worked."[1]

Much the same conclusions were reached by Pofessor Perrin in his report.

Our approach

20.9   We have seen our task throughout as helping the NHS to help itself. We do not intend, therefore, to lay down a detailed blue-print for the organisation and management of the service although we indicate later where the main responsibilities for reform should lie and what these reforms should be. Some discipline needs to be imposed on the structure, for example to enable monitoring and review to be carried out at the appropriate levels, but we feel strongly that there is plenty of room for variation in local arrangements and local initiatives and experiments should be encouraged. It seems to us obvious enough that the way health care should be brought to the people of Wester Ross and to the people of Tower Hamlets will be entirely different; and that there is no reason, other than the false god of administrative tidiness, why the service management arrangements should be the same or, indeed, why they should even resemble each other to any great degree. This theme of introducing flexibility into the administration of the NHS is behind much of our thinking in this chapter.

20.10   Our impression is that management arrangements have tended to be inflexible and to follow too closely the guidance issued by the health departments. This may not be suprising given the pressures under which the reorganised service started work. For most of the UK there were only nine months between the passing of the enabling legislation and its implementation, during which several thousand appointments had to be made, authorities established, and so forth. But it is not to be expected that all health authorities can be organised and managed in the same way. With flexibility should go more experiment to test how the NHS can be better run locally.

20.11   In the "Task of the Commission" we said:

> "we think that large organisations are most efficient when problems are solved and decisions taken at the lowest effective point."[2]

---

[1]Kogan, Maurice, et al, *Op cit*, page 231.

[2]Royal Commission on the National Health Service, *The Task of the Commission*, London, HMSO, 1976, paragraph 8.

Nothing we have learned since has led us to change our minds. The advantages hardly need to be laboured, but the main benefits are likely to be speed in decision taking and responsiveness to local needs. NHS workers have complained without cease that management decisions are removed from the people best suited to make them. Despite the emphasis in the 1971 Consultative Document and the 1972 White Paper on "maximum delegation downwards matched by accountability upwards", it is all too clear that so far the emphasis has been on the latter. We discuss the reasons for this later in this chapter, but a major cause is that many of those in all the disciplines responsible for administering the reorganised service found themselves in jobs in unfamiliar places performing unfamiliar roles and working with colleagues who were in much the same position. In the circumstances it is not surprising that decision makers looked for help higher up the ladder and felt anxious about the rungs below them.

Consensus Management

20.12   Consensus management predates the reorganisation of the NHS. It is one aspect of the general complaint about excessive consultation. It was explained in guidance from DHSS at reorganisation in terms of the district management team (DMT) as follows:

> "the DMT will take decisions jointly on matters which are not exclusively the responsibility of any one of them and which are not provided for in approved plans nor regulated by established policies of the AHA."[1]

The decision to involve different professions as equals was a reflection of the growth in influence of the non-medical professions, nurses in particular, in the NHS. The alternative was some form of chief executive.

20.13   Professor Kogan and his team found that "support for consensus management was wide-ranging, and only a small minority of respondents thought that it could never be successful". The main advantages seen were that it "gave a wider dimension to decision making, bringing in different points of view, allowing these different views to confront each other, and portraying the impact of one set of factors upon others"; and that it brought "a stronger commitment to decisions and [resulted] in better implementation".[2]

20.14   Problems with consensus management were reported to us. Clashes of personality, domination by an individual and the need to reach compromises could make its operation difficult. Consensus management might encourage team members to ignore a difficult problem or to present a united view to their authority where their proper role was to present health authorities with options for decision. Difficulties occurred in extreme form at Solihull where in 1977 unresolvable differences between members of the area team of officers led to their replacement. Consensus management may mean that decisions take longer to reach, but when they are reached they may be better ones and more

---

[1]HRC(73)3, *Management Arrangements for the Reorganised National Health Service.*

[2]Kogan, Maurice, et al, *Op cit,* pages 44-45.

rapidly implemented. This is debatable, but Professor Kogan's findings suggest that the chief executive alternative would not be popular in most places.

20.15 It is important not to exaggerate the extent to which consensus management has changed the way workers in the NHS go about their jobs. It must always have been necessary in the NHS, as in other large organisations, for those responsible for particular services to be at least in broad ageement with their colleagues in different disciplines about decisions which directly affected their own responsibilities. Before reorganisation, no sensible hospital or group secretary would have tried to tell the matron how to do her job. There was consultation and discussion then as now. Perhaps the main difference is the extent to which this has been formalised. Consensus management need not itself be a cause of inefficiency, provided that there is a clearly identified responsibility to implement team decisions. The co-ordinating role of the administrator is highly important here. There is a risk that consensus management may sap individual responsibility by allowing it to be shared: it is important that managers should not be prevented from managing the services for which they are responsible. Clearly consensus management works best where individual team members have a firm grasp of the distinction between their personal responsibility and those of the team. We recommend further guidance from the health departments to clarify this question. Greater involvement by health authority members in monitoring services as we recommended in Chapter 19, and the changes in the structure of the NHS, which we recommend later in this chapter, will affect the operation but should not detract from the principle of consensus management. But like all "principles" of management, it is good only so far as it is useful and leads to greater efficiency.

Advisory Committees

20.16 The 1972 White Paper said that:

> "Strong professional advisory machinery will be built into the new structure ... It will function at each level of management, and will ensure that the RHA and AHA and their staffs make decisions in the full knowledge of expert opinion. It will ensure, too, that at all levels the health professions exercise an effective voice in the planning and operation of the NHS."[1]

Legislation lays a duty on health ministers to "recognise" representative committees of doctors, dentists, nurses and midwives, pharmacists and ophthalmic and dispensing opticians at health authority level.[2] In multi-district areas there are district medical committees representing both hospital doctors and general practitioners. At hospital level medical advice is given through the divisional system. The divisions consist of clinicians from one or more hospitals, grouped in specialties. Their main functions are advice giving and clinical audit, plus an element of management.

---

[1]*National Health Service Reorganisation: England, Op cit*, paragraph 100.

[2]National Health Service Act 1977, Section 19(1), National Health Service (Scotland) Act 1978, Section 9(1).

20.17 It is important to distinguish principle from present practice in this field. Professional advice, arising out of the practical needs of daily patient care, is essential to the NHS and professional advisory committees are an integral part of the multi-disciplinary approach to running the NHS. The number of disciplines represented reflects the growth in influence of the non-medical professions. Their introduction was generally supported by the professions concerned at the time of reorganisation and their involvement in decision taking should improve the quality of decisions and increase professional commitment to them. The principle that the professionals should be involved in the running of the NHS through advisory committees is right.

20.18 In practice, however, the process of consultation has proliferated unduly, particularly in the medical profession. Medical committees of one kind and another are particularly numerous. In a multi-district area, for example, there may be local medical committees of GPs, divisional and medical staff or executive committees of hospital doctors, district medical committees, and area medical committees. Although the arrangements differ in Scotland and Northern Ireland, the machinery is similarly elaborate. This is vividly illustrated in Appendix J prepared for us by staff of the Regional Medical Officer's Department at Trent Regional Health Authority. A survey carried out for the Doctors' and Dentists' Review Body found that:

"Some 95% of consultants were members of one or more professional committees and about one in six consultants of five or more."[1]

20.19 Commenting on the arrangements in general, the Regional Medical Officers in England said:

"Professional advisory machinery is extravagant of professional time in the way it relates to over-complicated management structures. Representatives find themselves debating the same issues with very nearly the same people on different occasions. In practice one 'tier' of professional advisory machinery tends to lapse."

Furthermore, some of the committees may not be particularly good at their jobs. Professor Kogan's report noted that "nurses themselves commented strongly on their inexperience of committee work".[2] In our view the amount of discussion of and consultation about forward planning is often disproportionate to the amount of change which is possible in the NHS in the short term. It is this that leads to much of the frustration with the consultative process. The task of monitoring and improving the quality of services which are actually being delivered to patients should not be hindered by time spent on excessive consultation.

20.20 No doubt some of the problems in the professional advisory structure are to do with making unfamiliar machinery run smoothly. The changes to the structure of the NHS which we recommend later in this chapter should lead to

---

[1]*Review Body on Doctors' and Dentists' Remuneration, Eighth Report 1978*, (Cmnd 7176), London, HMSO, 1978, page 75.

[2]Kogan, Maurice, et al, *Op cit*, page 65.

some reductions in the number of committees; others may simply fall into disuse as their limited usefulness emerges. However, in our view stronger measures are called for and we recommend that the health departments should urgently consider with the professions concerned the best way of simplifying the present structure.

Hospital Management

20.21 There were many complaints in the evidence about the quality of hospital administration in the form of allegations that the local administration could or would not take decisions, and that as a result of the development of different functional hierarchies getting quite minor problems dealt with was unnecessarily difficult and delayed. Professor Kogan reported a widespread feeling that arrangements were working significantly less well than they had before reorganisation. It is clear to us that the three main professions involved in the efficient management of a hospital, administrators, nurses and doctors, need to devise mechanisms to ensure that decisions can be made quickly and implemented effectively. This will best be achieved by the creation of an executive team representing these three disciplines, advised as appropriate by the other professions involved. It would have responsibility for the day to day management of the hospital.

Administrators

20.22 Although the paragraphs that follow deal with the problems of hospital managers, much of what is said, particularly about status and pay, applies equally to those who administer community services below district level. In Chapter 4 we referred to the often repeated allegation that there are too many administrators in the NHS. We recorded that they were often blamed for what has gone wrong in the NHS since reorganisation. For the most part we think this blame unfair. Administrators have perhaps been seen as the personification of new and unpopular management arrangements. The passing of the hospital secretary, the group secretary and board of governors' administrator is mourned by many doctors. The Royal College of Surgeons, England, said:

"before reorganisation, there were at the hospital level many experienced and capable administrators who performed this task well and some who performed it with great distinction."

It is impossible to assess the quality of NHS administration with precision, but we have been impressed by the many able administrators we have met, the products either of in-service training or the national graduate trainee schemes, who are performing highly responsible tasks with distinction.

20.23 While some administrators in their fifties opted to retire at the time of reorganisation, the cadre of administrators must have been much the same on 1 April 1974 as it was on 31 March 1974. Many of the secretaries to hospital management committees or boards of governors were appointed administrators to the new districts and areas. At this level, the administrator is

317

involved in the management and planning of all NHS services and inevitably he does not have the close relationship with hospital administration that the group secretary had before 1974. This is as it should be; the decisions taken at district should reflect not just the interests of the hospital service but those of all parts of the NHS at that level.

20.24   Because important decisions about hospital matters affect patients and will have repercussions for other parts of the NHS, they cannot be taken by administrators alone without consultation with other colleagues in different disciplines, nor can they be taken by administrators whose responsibilities are solely for hospitals. A consequence is that the unit (hospital level) administrators often find themselves fourth or fifth in line in the administrative structure whereas before reorganisation the secretary of a large hospital would have been the second most senior administrator in a substantially autonomous authority. Their grading and pay in the reorganised service reflects the change. Before reorganisation the secretary of one of the large hospital groups could receive the same salary as a secretary to a regional hospital board. While the hospital secretary was paid less he had reasonable prospects of promotion to a group secretary job. Although there are good promotion prospects in the NHS administrative structure, the hospital administrator, may have to move into a wider field of administration rather than, as in the past, being able to make his career exclusively in hospital administration.

20.25   One of the results of NHS reorganisation has therefore been to down-grade the importance of administrators who deal solely with hospital matters. This has been compounded by the fact that membership of health authorities – previously at hospital group level, with house committees taking an interest in individual units – was concentrated at area level. We have more to say about this later in the chapter.

Functional management

20.26   Some supporting services are organised on a district, area or even regional basis. A hospital engineer, for example, is answerable for his professional work to his immediate superior, though his day-to-day responsibilities, and the workload that he carries, arise at the hospital where he works. There are potentially more than 20 such "functional" disciplines, including works, catering, supply, personnel and engineering, which may be represented at various management levels.[1] Professor Kogan's report points out that functional management is not new in the NHS and was fairly well developed before reorganisation although the new structure considerably increased its importance and scope. Functional management was said to conflict with the collective decision-making of district teams. One effect of strengthened functional management has been to reduce the discretion of officers at sector and unit levels. Professor Kogan noted that:

"The boundaries of roles of different functional managers were said to be unclear, and there were misunderstandings about the extent of authority

---

[1]The term "functional management" does not apply to medical, nursing etc. services provided in a hospital.

of functional managers, and about how much ought to be delegated to lower levels. Functional managers were in a service-giving relationship to other staff, yet it was not clear that the meaning of this was understood."[1]

20.27   It is clear that the quality of management of institutions has suffered substantially since reorganisation for the reasons we have indicated. The administrator in charge of the hospital (graded as a sector or unit administrator depending on the size of the hospital) is a key figure. His grading must reflect the substantial responsibilities he carries. Perhaps new titles are needed for hospital administrative posts. We consider that the chief administrator in a hospital should be clearly responsible for co-ordinating all services in the institution. This means that staff who are part of a functional hierarchy in hospital, while remaining professionally answerable for their services, should be responsible to the administrator in charge for their day-to-day work. The administrator should co-ordinate the budget for all the functional services in hospitals, although decisions on the use and allocation of the budget should be taken jointly with the unit and functional managers concerned. Functional management at levels above the institutional level may well be required in certain of the more specialised disciplines like engineering, but the role in most cases is likely to be advisory rather than supervisory. We would expect that some of the posts above institutional level would be unnecessary. We recommend that the role of the hospital administrator at unit or sector level should be expanded. This may lead to the regrading of many posts and will need to be discussed by the Whitley Council concerned. We recommend also that there should be a review of the number of functional managers above unit level.

Nursing

20.28   The implementation of the Salmon Committee's recommendations for senior nursing staff preceded reorganisation. The structure has proved adaptable and in some cases has resulted in fewer levels of nursing management. The grade of the chief nurse in a hospital may vary, but in all cases there is a clearly identifiable nurse in charge. The management of community nursing and hospital nursing services has been integrated in a number of different ways under one nurse at district or area level. We deal with the nursing career structure in Chapter 13.

Doctors

20.29   A doctor should be a member of the executive team to which we referred in paragraph 20.21. The health departments expected that a representative of the doctors in a hospital would be found from the membership of the specialist clinical divisions, elected by his colleagues. The concept of clinical divisions is sound but its implementation has been very patchy. In many places the divisional system has not been developed effectively; and problems have been particularly acute in the large multi-specialty district general hospitals. Here it was envisaged that the chairmen of the various clinical divisions would

[1]Kogan, Maurice, et al, *Op cit*, page 39.

meet together to co-ordinate their policies, that they would elect a chairman and that he would make the medical contribution to administration on behalf of them all. This has rarely taken place and the lay administrator has had in many hospitals to negotiate with each specialty separately. Various types of ad hoc and usually more or less unsatisfactory mechanisms have been set up to bridge the gap; for example, deriving a medical advisory committee from the divisions. In many places community physicians have been brought in from district on a sessional basis, to act in effect as part-time medical superintendents, although this is clearly a misuse of their role. The situation has been further confused by the existence in hospitals of groups of doctors in more or less informal staff and house associations and committees outside the advisory structure.

20.30   There are important problems here which should have the serious attention of the health departments and the medical profession. Decisions made by clinical divisions can have implications for other services and good links with nursing management in particular are important. An effective medical contribution to administration at unit level is essential. We do not ourselves see any practical alternative to making the divisional system work, short of returning to the appointment of medical superintendents to hospitals which we believe would be a retrograde step. We realise the difficulties: many clinicians do not have the time, the desire or the skills to engage in administration and get little or no education about their role in management. However, the chairmanship of a division, and more so the chairmanship of a committee of divisional chairmen, is a position of considerable responsibility and must be recognised. Election to such positions should be for long enough to give stability and continuity and for the individual to make his mark (probably for three to five years). There should be adequate secretarial support and information services. This essential part of the advisory and administrative structure is unlikely to function properly unless these appointments are given status, facilities and reward.

Psychiatric hospitals

20.31   The problems of hospital administration which we have dealt with in the preceding paragraphs apply to all hospitals, but psychiatric hospitals have had special difficulties. We see no reason in principle why they should be administered differently from other kinds of hospitals; but their administration may be particularly difficult because they are often large, isolated and have complex catchment areas. Instead of the strong administration they need there has been sometimes almost an administrative vacuum. Psychiatric hospitals particularly need administrative staff of good quality.

20.32   The quality of psychiatric hospital administration in recent years has been affected by several factors. Medical or physician superintendents, the heads of the old hierarchical and patriarchal structure, have been abolished, and the chairmen of clinical divisions have often not provided the drive and leadership which was given by the best of the medical superintendents, not least because they have not had the time to do so. Here, as elsewhere, hospital or group secretaries have been replaced by junior and less experienced sector or unit administrators. The functions of the old hospital management committee have been assumed at least in part by the district management team, but often there has been no member of the DMT with experience of psychiatric hospital administration. A multi-disciplinary approach to management and to the delivery of clinical services may have gone further in these hospitals than elsewhere and run into more difficulties. Trade union activities have led to unit concerns being referred to higher levels. The clinical functions of the hospitals have often been undertaken by sub-divisions or independent teams, serving different populations. The DHSS has now realised how serious their administrative problems are and has set up a working group which is likely to report shortly.[1]

Structure

20.33   There was general agreement in our evidence that the structure of the NHS needed slimming. Evidence from England was the most emphatic on this point, perhaps because of the existence of the regional tier, but criticism was by no means confined to England. In Scotland, Wales and Northern Ireland the district was sometimes seen as the redundant tier. Abolition of a tier seemed to have assumed symbolic importance and was seen as the universal solution to the problems of managing the NHS. We do not ourselves regard abolition of a management tier as a panacea. There are many reasons for the present difficulties in the NHS and structure is only one of them.

20.34   Indeed, talking simply of abolishing a tier is not necessarily helpful. We have preferred to think in terms of the levels at which functions can best be performed. There are two broad groups of functions discharged by health authorities, the planning of services and their delivery to the patient. Although these activities are related, and it may not always be possible to distinguish them clearly, we have found it helpful to bear the distinction in mind.

Regions versus areas

20.35   In England, the discussion about structure has tended to focus on whether regions or areas should be abolished. Not surprisingly, most of the evidence we received from those working in, or associated with, areas put forward the view that the area was more useful than the region; those working in regions and districts saw the area as the redundant level. In terms of weight of criticism, there was no doubt that the areas were the most often attacked. Some of the issues were referred to in Chapter 4. We consider below the arguments for and against abolishing region or area, but there are two prior points to be considered.

20.36   The first consideration is what might be achieved by abolition of a tier. Regions are responsible for strategic planning, major building and specialised clinical services. If regions were abolished, these services would either have to be performed by the area or the health department; and if the area disappeared its responsibilities would similarly have to be redistributed. We agree with Professor Kogan that:

---

[1]Working Group on the Organisational and Management Problems of Mental Illness Hospitals.

"Any reduction in [the] number of levels must simplify decision making if only by a reduction in the communication and co-ordination inevitably required where authority is located in many centres."[1]

However, the results may not be as startling as many of those giving us evidence seem to expect.

20.37   Second, it is clear that the abolition of a tier would have significant implications for the staff involved and their interests must be kept firmly in mind when major upheavals are considered.

20.38   The health departments told us that AHAs were introduced as:

"the main operational health authorities [with] boundaries which match those of the non-metropolitan counties, metropolitan districts and the London boroughs or groups of London boroughs since these were to be the local authorities responsible for providing personal social services."

The AHA's broad functions were described in the England 1972 White Paper as:

"operational NHS authority, responsible for assessing needs in its area and for planning, organising and administering area health services to meet them."[2]

The area is also the level where lay membership is involved which is closest to the consumer. AHAs come in different sizes ranging from Essex, Kent, Lancashire and Surrey with populations of well over one million to others below the 200,000 mark. There are much smaller areas in Scotland, Wales and Northern Ireland. The largest AHA in population terms, Kent, is only slightly smaller than the smallest RHA, East Anglia, both of them with populations of about 1.5 million. The largest AHAs contain five or even six health districts.

20.39   The main arguments advanced to us for abolishing the area tier were that its collaborative functions with local government had not turned out to be very successful and that there was a duplication of planning between area and district. Area was too remote from the delivery of services to be effective in organising and administering them, or to be responsive to local needs; and the separate area team of officers confused the relationship between the AHA and the district management team. We dealt in Chapter 16 with criticisms of the effectiveness of collaboration between the NHS and local authorities. At reorganisation hospital management committee roughly translated into district, and regional hospital board into regional health authority, and for workers from the hospital service AHAs seemed an unnecessary addition.

20.40   The main objections to the RHA were that it duplicated the planning and personnel function of AHAs and was altogether remote from local

---

[1]Kogan, Maurice, et al, *Op cit*, page 231.

[2]*National Health Service Reorganisation: England, Op cit*, paragraph 53.

requirements; and the role of the RHA member was sometimes in practice confined unsatisfactorily to a narrow range of functions, for example regional services and consultant appointments.

20.41   One effect of abolishing AHAs would be that in the larger regions RHAs would have to deal with 15 to 20 districts. Another effect would be to remove the involvement of health authority members even further from the point of delivery of service, a matter to which we return below. The abolition of RHAs would leave the DHSS dealing with AHAs, and the view taken by the government at the time of reorganisation was that:

> "a central Department operating from London could not hope to exercise effective and prompt general supervision over area authorities."[1]

Arrangements would have to be made also for the regional planning and centralised services to be performed if RHAs disappeared.

Districts

20.42   The health district was described in paragraph 45 of the 1972 White Paper for England as forming "the natural community for the planning and delivery of comprehensive health care". We consider that it is also the natural management unit. Whereas the area and regional levels are primarily concerned with planning, the emphasis at district level is on the delivery of services. District boundaries do not conform, except in the case of single-district areas, to those of local authorities. For the most part they are determined by the catchment area of the district general hospital or equivalent. In England there are about 200 districts each with an average population of about 230,000. In 1977 the typical district in England had about ten hospitals and working within it about 145 hospital doctors, 1,400 hospital nurses, 110 GPs, 60 general dental practitioners and 150 community nurses. It employed directly almost 4,000 workers. It thus forms a very large management unit.

20.43   In England the DMT is responsible to the AHA; outside England there is a line relationship between officers at area and district. In multi-district areas, therefore, the districts compete with each other for area resources. Professor Kogan found that single-district areas function more harmoniously than multi-district areas and this is supported in the evidence we have received. For example, the Confederation of Health Service Employees said:

> "If there has been any success stories in the management structures of the reorganised NHS we must say that these have been the single district areas."

Single-district areas also have the advantages that their management costs appear to be significantly lower than multi-district areas and member involvement is closer to operational level. On the other hand, the general feeling about multi-district areas was that the relationship between district and area was difficult and led to duplication of work, frustration and delay. The

---

[1]*National Health Service Reorganisation: England, Op cit*, paragraph 31.

solution for these problems was often felt to be the development of more single-district areas. This can be done by merging existing districts or by splitting existing areas.

20.44   As we remarked earlier, the health district is mainly concerned with delivery and the area and region mainly with planning services. The current structure of the NHS, therefore, effectively separates authority members from involvement in detailed arrangements for health care delivery. This results in these members being remote from the patients they serve and the health workers they employ, a very unsatisfactory situation. The substantial majority of members should be laymen and it is essential that the authority they serve should not be so big that its size stifles the influence and participation of members at all levels.

Proposals for change

20.45   In the NHS we consider that there is one tier too many in most places. We recommend that in England RHAs should continue to be principally responsible for planning and for the major functions they carry out at present, for example in relation to regional specialties. In addition, they will have greater responsibilities devolved from the DHSS as we recommend in Chapter 19. The relationship between regions and lower tier health authorities should remain on the same basis as that which exists between RHAs and AHAs at present, backed by the powers which regions have to direct AHAs to perform certain functions. The DHSS should ensure that this is clearly spelled out.

20.46   Below region in England, and elsewhere in the UK below health department, we recommend that, except in a minority of cases, one management level only should carry operational responsibility for services and for effective collaboration with local government. These authorities would be formed from existing single-district areas, by merging existing districts, or by dividing areas. They need not be self-sufficient in all facilities, nor would their boundaries always conform to existing health authority boundaries. However, in some places it will not be appropriate for reasons of geography, history and population to depart from existing area boundaries. In these circumstances health services may be more easily organised on a wider basis than can be provided by existing districts.

20.47   Very large authorities would be difficult to manage, and here the answer may be to retain a managerial structure below authority level. In these cases there should be a line relationship between teams of officers. It is not essential uniformly to have both sector and unit management below authority level.

20.48   The NHS is not a tidy construction and it still bears the marks of the haphazard growth of health services before 1948. Arrangements which will suit one part of the UK well will be wholly unsuited to another. We referred earlier in this chapter to the need for flexibility of structure.

20.49   A strong argument for making all health districts into health authorities is that one tier could be abolished in multi-district areas, but there are other considerations. Most important of these is the relationship between health and local authorities. In single-district areas there would normally be no change from the present position, but where new health authorities were based on the existing health districts, coterminosity with the matching local authority would be lost. One place where coterminosity does not apply, but where in the view of those concerned good relationships have been developed between health and local authorities, is Strathclyde where the regional council and the four health boards within its boundaries have established one liaison committee. In London, however, problems arise through the lack of coterminosity which affects 12 out of the 16 London AHAs. The London Boroughs Association commented in evidence to us:

"the arrangements subsequently made in some, but not all, Area Health Authorities for the Health Districts to overlap AHA boundaries, with complicated and somewhat theoretical 'agency' provisions, damaged and in some cases virtually destroyed the principle coterminosity."

A good deal of doubt was expressed in our evidence about the usefulness of coterminous health and local authority boundaries. As we noted in Chapter 16, effective collaboration does not depend on coterminous boundaries, although it may be assisted by them. The benefits of coterminous boundaries have, therefore, to be balanced in each locality against other considerations.

20.50 If our approach is adopted, the position of the FPC will need consideration in England and Wales. We discuss later the relationship of the FPC to the NHS and we will simply note here that this is a highly sensitve matter for the contractor professions. Changes in the structure below region would also have implications for community health councils. At present they represent the users of the NHS at district level. We dealt in Chapter 11 with the important part which CHCs have to play. Where districts are amalgamated it may be appropriate to retain more than one local CHC.

20.51 We recommend that each RHA in England and the health departments in Scotland, Wales and Northern Ireland should institute a review of the structure for which it is responsible. The DHSS should monitor this review in England. The review would be carried out with full consultation of all those concerned, including health and local authorities, staff and CHCs. Its aim should be to set up a structure which is the most appropriate to the area concerned.

20.52 Since we are recommending no simple, universal panacea for the cure of the administrative ills of the NHS – indeed, we are against uniform solutions – it perhaps behoves us to recapitulate the broad ideas behind the recommendations we have made in the preceding paragraphs. They are:

it is convenient, and will lead to better administration, to think of the management of the NHS as made up of a planning level and a service level;

each of these levels will have authorities composed largely of laymen; that is to say, not employed by the NHS and so able to represent patients easily;

only rarely will it be administratively useful and in the interest of the patient to interpose a layer between the two levels we describe;

the authorities at the service level should be of a size to encourage natural and easy discourse between authority members, patients and health service workers; and to link effectively with other services;

we would encourage a flexible and imaginative approach to management arrangements at both the planning and service levels and to interaction between them.

Family practitioner committees

20.53 We consider elsewhere questions arising from the independent contractor status of the four contractor professions (general medical practitioners, general dental practitioners, pharmacists and opticians). We are concerned here only with the family practitioner committees (FPCs) in England and Wales. In Scotland FPCs do not exist, the functions of the former executive councils having been taken over at reorganisation by the health boards.[1] Our evidence suggested that this arrangement was satisfactory, and had brought some advantages.

20.54 FPCs in England and Wales were established at reorganisation. They administer the contracts and terms of service of individual practitioners and the statutory disciplinary arrangements. They deal directly with the health departments on these matters and are centrally financed. However, the 1972 White Paper indicated that the AHA would have significant responsibilities for:

"the planning and development of health centres; the approval where necessary of practitioners' own proposals for providing premises; plans for contractor services in new towns and redevelopment areas; and general arrangements for the nursing and other skilled staff employed by the AHA or by the local authority to work with family doctors in their own practices, whether in health centres or elsewhere."[2]

20.55 The main criticism of the arrangements in England and Wales made in evidence was that complete integration of the three parts of the NHS was prevented so long as FPCs retained their independent status and membership. It was also argued that they were poor at dealing with service problems such as inadequate waiting room accommodation, waiting times, appointment arrangements and so forth; and they did not always help GPs, for example to improve their premises; and that FPC administrators had divided responsibilities between the AHA and FPC. Some of the difficulties turn on the contractual status of the practitioners with whom they deal, but we propose no considerable change here.

---

[1] In Northern Ireland before reorganisation, administration of family practitioner services was carried out by the Northern Ireland General Health Services Board. Since 1973 GPs in Ulster contract to the four Health and Social Services Boards with the Central Services Agency arranging payments to GPs centrally on behalf of the boards.

[2] *National Health Service Reorganisation: England, Op cit,* paragraph 70.

20.56 By and large health authorities supported some form of close intergration between FPCs and AHAs, while the evidence from the representatives of the medical profession and bodies representing family practitioner committees supported the status quo. The latter argued that it was convenient to have specialist staff to administer contracts; that integration of the FPC with the AHA would reduce the independence of professional contractors which was provided by the direct relationship between the FPC and the health departments; and that an AHA could not conveniently and satisfactorily run services provided both by contractors and salaried workers. It was also argued that since the family practitioner services represented an open-ended financial commitment, whereas the rest of the NHS was run on cash limits, the AHA would have a difficult problem in managing the FPC's finance.

20.57 Experience in Scotland and Northern Ireland suggests these objections are not conclusive. In these parts of the UK it appears that the absence of separate machinery for administering family practitioner services assists the integrated planning of health services. We recommend the abolition of FPCs in England and Wales and the assumption of their functions by health authorities as a step towards integration. It must allow them to influence more positively than they can at the present the distribution and quality of surgeries and other practice premises, the balance and relationship between hospital and community care, the movement of staff across institutional boundaries and deputising services. AHAs or their replacement authorities should take over existing FPC responsibilities and we recommend accordingly. The position of existing FPC staff would need to be safeguarded and handled sensitively.

Accountability

20.58 We discussed in Chapter 19 the implications of the relationship between Parliament, the health departments and the NHS for central financing of the service, and in Chapter 11 we considered the role of community health councils. We comment here on the membership of health authorities, some of the considerations which affect them and some of the proposals for change.

20.59 The membership of health authorities is important because members make the broad strategic decisions about what goes on in the NHS. They are answerable for the expenditure of exchequer funds to Parliament through the health departments and secretaries of state, but they have responsibilities also towards the communities they serve and the workers they employ. They have to be responsive to, or at least be aware of, pressure groups in the community and the NHS. They may be pulled in several different directions: local interests versus national pressures, contradictory staff pressures and local authority interests which may be incompatible with those of the NHS.

20.60 The 1972 White Paper said:

"The Government believes that, as in the past, the NHS should be administered by trained staff, under the general direction of authorities composed of part-time members who give their services voluntarily. Members of the area and regional health authorities will serve in an unpaid capacity though they will be entitled to travelling and other allowances. The chairman will however have a specially heavy and time-consuming job and it is desirable that there should be no financial barrier that would prevent those with other commitments from giving adequate time to the health service."[1]

We think this general principle and approach are correct. We are reassured by Professor Kogan's research which confirmed that those working the NHS were satisfied with the calibre of health authority members.

20.61   We concluded in Chapter 16 that the NHS should not be transferred to local government at the present time but that the question should be looked at again if regional government became a possibility in England. One of the main arguments advanced by those who advocate that the NHS should transfer is that the NHS is "undemocratic" because health authority members are for the most part nominees. At present the chairmen and members of RHAs and the chairmen of AHAs are appointed by health ministers after consultations. AHA members in England are appointed by RHAs after consultation. Outside England members of health authorities are appointed by the health ministers. They reflect a cross-section of local interests and include professional members and representatives of trade unions, voluntary organisations and local authorities. The detailed composition of authorities varies with the authority's teaching responsibilities, but outside Scotland roughly one third of members are local authority nominees, one third are drawn from the professions and the universities and the rest from other sources. In Scotland the proportion of local authority members is lower.

20.62   A number of trade unions giving evidence to us, and the TUC itself, suggested that health authorities would be more "democratic" if the membership were equally divided between the nominees of local authorities and the trade unionists working in the NHS. In a consultative document published in 1974, the DHSS canvassed the possibility that each health authority might include among its members two elected representatives of the staff who worked for the authority, in addition to workers already appointed under existing arrangements. The publication of the Bullock Committee Report[2] gave some stimulation to this question, although the committee itself did not deal directly with the NHS. We hope that all health authorities could be constituted in a way which reflects the fact that their prime task, over-riding all other considerations, is to serve the patient and that those members who are NHS workers would keep this constantly in mind. Since we believe firmly that the NHS must work easily with local authorities, we see no reason for departing from the principle that there should be representation of local authority members, as well as health workers and the public at large. A health authority should not normally exceed 20 members, though multi-district authorities might require a slightly larger membership. Authorities should work through properly constituted sub-committees which could, of course, contain members who were not also members of the authority.

20.63   For the most part, members of authorities are nominees of some

---

[1] *National Health Service Reorganisation: England, Op cit,* paragraph 91.

[2] *A Report of the Committee of Enquiry on Industrial Democracy,* (Cmnd 6706), London, HMSO, 1976.

kind. It was put to us that they should instead be elected, on the grounds that if health authorities are to run the service for the benefit of local communities they should be responsible to them in the same kind of way as local authority councillors are responsible to their electorate. There are one or two countries, notably New Zealand, where health authorities are elected. There are, however, a variety of difficulties and objections to elections of this kind. Some of the more obvious ones are obtaining the right mix of professional experience and lay membership, the costs and complications of running a new set of elections, the inevitable involvement of party politics in the arrangements and the possible lack of public interest (judging by turn-outs in local authority elections) in the procedure. The present appointment arrangements are similar to those which existed before 1974, and we think it preferable to retain them in something like their existing form. If our proposals for structural change are adopted, the involvement of health authority members will be brought closer to the services they provide. We stressed in Chapter 19 the importance of effective monitoring of services by members, including visiting hospitals and other facilities.

20.64   Although health authority chairman receive an honorarium, health authority members at present may only receive out of pocket expenses and financial loss allowances. We understand that a scheme to introduce payment of elected members of local authorities is being discussed. If local authority appointed members of health authorities receive some form of payment matching provision should be made for other health authority members.

Implementation

20.65   We hope that the proposals we make here and elsewhere in this report will improve the working of the NHS but there are two important questions of timing. The first is whether any significant change should be made in the structure of the NHS for the moment, and second is whether the changes to be introduced should be carried out rapidly or gradually. In Chapter 4 we mention problems not caused by reorganisation which became more apparent after it was introduced. Further structural change would not help those problems, and we do not in any case propose any alterations on the scale of 1973/1974. However, there was, and probably still is, a strong body of opinion that, with all its faults, the present structure should be left untouched until the scars of reorganisation have healed completely, people have got used to working the new system and a better appreciation can be made of what changes are required.

20.66   It is easy to write down proposals for change as we have done in this chapter. To put them into effect requires consultation, thought and time, all of which will properly inhibit precipitate and ill-considered action. That seems to us entirely right when the working habits of so many people will have to change. Nevertheless, we would urge that those who will be responsible for acting upon this chapter of our report should do so with the greatest speed consistent with making changes with humanity. "Planning blight" is not something which settles only upon buildings; it can settle upon human organisations too. We acknowledge that our approach calls for different solutions for different communities and that it will take some time for the best

329

solutions to be identified. We recommend that the process of introducing these changes should be completed within two years from the end of the period of consultation.

Conclusions and Recommendations

20.67 Although the reorganisation of the NHS came under attack in the evidence, the pre-1974 system was criticised on many of the same grounds. Other factors over which the NHS has little control adversely affected the morale of those who worked in the service at the time reorganisation was being implemented. We have tried, therefore, to see the changes in perspective.

20.68 The introduction of consensus management and the proliferation of advisory committees have been criticised and we suggest ways in which practical difficulties in their operation may be overcome. A more serious problem is the decline in the quality of hospital administration. The status of the institutional manager must be improved and a satisfactory medical contribution to hospital administration achieved.

20.69 Although the importance of structure in the efficient operation of the NHS can be exaggerated, we received an impressive weight of evidence which suggested that in most places there was one tier too many. We have already recommended that in England RHAs should assume additional powers from the DHSS. In our view RHAs should be the main planning authorities and the structure below region should be simplified. We consider that, except in a minority of cases, there should be one tier below RHA or health department. In most cases this would mean the creation of more single-district areas. In some it would mean merging existing districts or creating new authorities by dividing existing areas. However, a flexible approach to structural change will be very important. The other main change we should like to see in the structure is the abolition of separate FPCs in England and Wales and the adoption there of the Scottish pattern of administration of family practitioner services.

20.70 We recommend that:

(a) the health departments should give further guidance about the role of members of consensus management teams (paragraph 20.15);

(b) the health departments should urgently consider with the professions concerned the best way of simplifying the present professional advisory committee structure (paragraph 20.20);

(c) the role of the hospital administrator at unit or sector level should be expanded (paragraph 20.27);

(d) there should be a review of the number of functional managers above unit level (paragraph 20.27);

(e) RHAs in England should continue to be principally responsible for planning and for the major functions they carry out at present (paragraph 20.45);

(f) below region in England, and elswhere in the UK below health department, except in a minority of cases, one management level only should carry operational responsibility for services and for effective collaboration with local government (paragraph 20.46);

(g) each RHA in England and the health departments in Scotland, Wales and Northern Ireland should institute a review of the structure for which it is responsible. The DHSS should monitor this review in England (paragraph 20.51);

(h) FPCs in England and Wales should be abolished and their functions assumed by health authorities as a step towards integration (paragraph 20.57);

(i) the process of introducing the changes recommended in this chapter should be completed within two years of the end of the period of consultation (paragraph 20.66).

Chapter 21   Finance

21.1   Our terms of reference require us to consider "the best use and management of the financial and manpower resources of the National Health Service". In practice these resources are linked and about three quarters of the expenditure of the NHS goes on salaries and wages. It is important to remember that discussions of NHS finance must take account of its implications for NHS workers who account for about 1 in 20 of the total working population of the UK.

21.2   In this chapter we consider what should be spent on the NHS, how it should be raised, its distribution and its management. To help our work we commissioned studies on the management of financial resources[1] and a critique of the health departments' arrangements for allocating finance to health authorities.[2] These studies have provoked some public discussion and we hope have been useful to those working in the NHS. They have certainly been most useful to us.

What Should be Spent on the NHS?

21.3   Expenditure on the NHS in the financial year 1978/9 was about £8,100m, or over £140 for every person in the UK. Over 94% of this was revenue expenditure: only about £460m was spent on hospital building and other capital development. Since 1949 total expenditure on the NHS in real terms has more than doubled and the volume of resources devoted to the NHS has increased in every year except 1952. Total NHS expenditure has grown faster than the rest of the economy in almost every year since 1954, rising from 3.4% of the gross domestic product (GDP) in 1954 to 5.6% in 1977.

---

[1]Perrin, John et al; *Management of Financial Resources in the National Health Service,* Royal Commission on the National Health Service, Research Paper Number 2, London, HMSO, 1978.

[2]Buxton, M and Klein, R E, *Allocating Health Resources: A Commentary on the Report of the Resource Allocation Working Party,* Royal Commission on the National Health Service, Research Paper Number 3, London, HMSO, 1978.

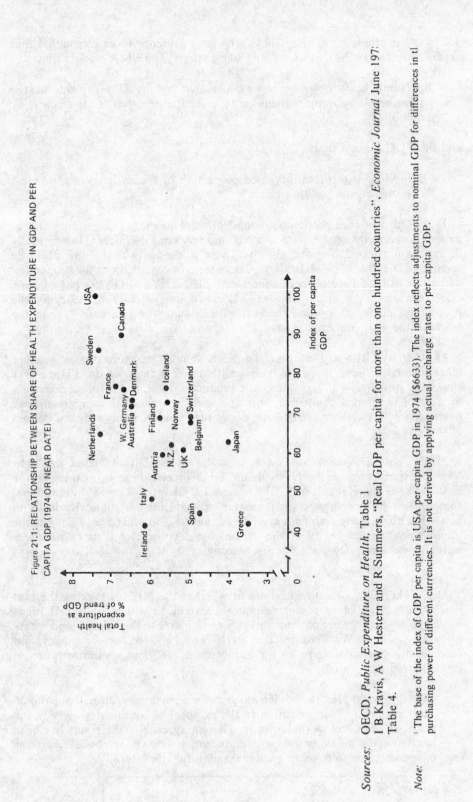

Figure 21.1: RELATIONSHIP BETWEEN SHARE OF HEALTH EXPENDITURE IN GDP AND PER CAPITA GDP (1974 OR NEAR DATE)

Sources: OECD, *Public Expenditure on Health*, Table 1

I B Kravis, A W Hestern and R Summers, "Real GDP per capita for more than one hundred countries", *Economic Journal* June 197: Table 4.

Note: [1] The base of the index of GDP per capita is USA per capita GDP in 1974 ($6633). The index reflects adjustments to nominal GDP for differences in tl purchasing power of different currencies. It is not derived by applying actual exchange rates to per capita GDP.

21.4　Nonetheless, many of those who gave evidence to us considered that expenditure on the NHS was nothing like enough. The BMA told us that:

"for some years now the money allocated by the Government for the service has been quite inadequate to meet the demands made upon it by the public"

and the TUC argued that:

"In the longer term an increased proportion of the national income must be devoted to the health service."

21.5　Our evidence proposed amongst other things that more money should be spent on improving the hospital stock and services for children, the mentally ill and handicapped, and the elderly. There is no doubt that more could be spent, and spent well, on all of these. There were few suggestions for economies. The effect of lack of resources on morale in the NHS, and the low pay of some NHS workers were also mentioned. We had no difficulty in believing the proposition put to us by one medical witness that "we can easily spend the whole of the gross national product."

21.6　It was also argued that the NHS should get more money because other countries spend more on their health services than we do. Figure 21.1 shows the proportion of gross domestic product devoted to health services by a number of developed countries. Although such international comparisons are not wholly reliable there seems little doubt that the UK is towards the bottom of the league.[1]

21.7　These arguments do not take us far in establishing what the right level of expenditure on the NHS should be, if indeed there is meaning in the concept of "the right level". We noted in Chapter 3 that international comparisons do not suggest that greater expenditure automatically leads to better health in those countries considered, and it is at least arguable that the improvement in the health of the nation would be greater if extra resources were, for example, devoted to better housing.

21.8　There are also the questions of whether the NHS is making the best possible use of existing resources and the extent to which additional funds would be used to benefit patients directly or to increase the salaries and wages of NHS workers. We consider that NHS gives good value for money, but there is still considerable room for improvement. Regional Administrators in England told us:

"The National Health Service has become accustomed throughout the 25 years preceding reorganisation to the prospect of continual growth in the financial resources available to it. Though agreeable, the result has been to allow slack management, with no incentive to examine obsolete patterns of spending, or to develop a coherent plan for the future."

---

[1]See also Table 3.6.

This view was supported by other evidence that we received, by the research studies we commissioned and by much unofficial and official published material. The government's priorities document, "The Way Forward",[1] for example, contains an interesting appendix listing ways in which resources could be more efficiently used. It is essential that a service which spends three quarters of its budget on manpower should make efficient use of its labour force.

21.9　Figure 21.1 indicates that many of those countries which devoted a greater share of their resources to health services in 1974 were richer than the UK. They could better afford to spend more on health care both absolutely and relative to their gross domestic product. The relatively slower rate of growth of the UK economy since 1974 compared with many developed countries will tend to widen the gap in health spending.

21.10　We naturally accept that the resources the nation devotes directly to health care must stand in competition with other claimants on the public and private purse, particularly when those claimants may well contribute themselves to the good health of the nation. Nor have we any evidence to suggest that the NHS has fared badly in this competition. But this does not mean that we are satisfied with the nation's present level of expenditure – no thoughtful person could be – and indeed our recommendations would, if adopted, add significantly to NHS expenditure. The national income is growing, if relatively slowly, and it is right that as it does, more resources should be devoted to the care of the nation's health.

21.11　But we should sound two notes of caution. The first is that spending more on the NHS will not make us proportionately healthier or live proportionately longer, though it may improve the comfort and quality of life of patients or the pay and conditions of staff. The other is that whatever the expenditure on health care, demand is likely to rise to meet and exceed it. To believe that one can satisfy the demand for health care is illusory, and that is something that all of us, patients and providers alike, must accept in our thinking about the NHS.

Methods of Financing the NHS

21.12　The NHS is funded almost entirely by the Exchequer. In 1978/9, 88% of NHS finance was raised through general taxation, 9.5% from NHS national insurance contributions, 2% from prescriptions and other charges, and the balance from other sources such as sale of land and port health charges. The proportion of finance from general taxation has risen since the early 1960s, while the importance of both the NHS insurance contribution and revenue from charges has declined. At no stage has less than 94% of NHS expenditure been raised from general taxation and NHS insurance contributions.

21.13　We received several proposals for changing the arrangements for financing the NHS. Their purpose was either to supplement the Exchequer contributions, or to replace it with a system which might encourage more

---

[1]Department of Health and Social Security, *The Way Forward: Priorities in the Health and Social Services,* London, HMSO, 1977, Appendix III, pages 35-42.

efficient use of resources or which might have greater public appeal. We discuss the main proposals below, but there is one general point to be made first. It must be understood that there is no escaping government supervision of health service expenditure whatever system of raising funds is adopted. Some advocates of an insurance system evidently see it as a mechanism for automatically increasing expenditure on the NHS as costs rise. They delude themselves if they do. The rising cost of health care is a major concern in most developed countries, and measures to control it may be, and are, introduced whatever the method of financing health services.

Insurance financing

21.14   We noted in Chapter 4 that in Western Europe and North America health care is commonly financed by insurance schemes. A number of those who sent us evidence thought that this should be the arrangement in the UK. We consider the advantages and disadvantages of insurance based schemes below, but it is important to understand that their existence elsewhere is not usually the result of some careful weighing of the advantages or disadvantages of different methods of financing health care. Health insurance schemes come in a great variety of shapes and sizes, they have in most cases grown up over many years, and they reflect the peculiarities of the countries they serve. The UK in unusual in that a deliberate decision was taken in 1946 to introduce an Exchequer financed national health service.

21.15   There is no standard system of health insurance, and when considering the theoretical virtues of such a system we made assumptions about what its main characteristics might be, based on the private health insurance schemes in the UK at present. There are perhaps four essential differences between the NHS and the kind of health insurance scheme that might be introduced:

   charges to patients – each patient would be charged accordingly to the service used and wholly or partly reimbursed by an insurance agency;

   insurance could be undertaken by private agencies on a commercial basis or by some form of public undertaking;

   all those covered by insurance would have some choice of the extent of the cover they purchased;

   the individual or his employer would pay for insurance cover.

People would buy health insurance much as they buy house or motor insurance. There would be competition between companies, and there might be a compulsory minimum level of health insurance in much the same way as owners of motor cars are obliged to take out third party cover. There would be good risks and bad risks among users, and premiums might vary accordingly.

21.16   We have assumed that the system would be voluntary, perhaps with compulsory elements, because arrangements under which everyone had to pay for the same cover for themselves and their families would not in practice be significantly different from those we have at present. Instead of paying for the health service through taxation, individuals would be compelled to do so through insurance institutions. Indeed, many foreign insurance based systems contain such a large compulsory element that they could be described as "tax financed". The introduction of choice, and the competition that goes with it, would be essential if an insurance system were not to be indistinguishable from an Exchequer Financed system.

21.17   The introduction of an insurance system would not itself lead to more resources being devoted to the NHS, but there might be other advantages. It might be that patients, becoming more directly aware of what health care costs, would become more responsible in their demands on the service. However, fully insured patients would have little direct incentive to economic use of the service, because the extra costs imposed by their demands on it would be spread over the premiums of all those insured. By the same token, there would be little inducement for providers of the service to keep their costs down.

21.18   Some doctors and other health professionals favour a system of remuneration based on item of service payments. They argue that the detailed itemisation necessary would provide rapid and useful information which could be used for the monitoring of services, and that while health professionals are often paid more under such systems they work harder and more effectively so that labour costs are lower than under a salaried system. But insurance financing does not require that professionals should be paid on an item of service system, though it is often associated with it. Nor does item of service remuneration require insurance financing.

2.19   There are two important disadvantages which arise in most insurance based schemes. First, there are groups in the community who are both bad health risks and too poor to pay high premiums. They include elderly people, children, and the mentally and physically handicapped. Over 60% of NHS expenditure is currently accounted for by these groups, and nearly half of the community are exempted for one good reason or another from prescription charges, for example. We noted in Chapter 3 that poorer people tend to have worse health, but they are of course also least able to pay insurance and are most likely to be deterred by charges at time of use. The imbalance between ability to pay for health care and the need for it is met in most countries by government support. However, an insurance scheme which offered a range of benefits according to ability to pay would inevitably favour the wealthier members of society. It is true that there are inequalities now in the availability of health care: private medical care may be purchased, and, as we have seen in earlier chapters, there are geographical and social differences in access to health services under the NHS. But private medicine is provided outside the NHS, and the differences of availability of health services within it are recognised as faults to be eradicated so far as possible. The introduction of an insurance system would incorporate into the NHS a new principle, namely that a different standard of health care under the NHS was available to those who chose to pay for it. Some may feel such a change to be desirable, but at least it should be clearly recognised for what it is.

21.20   The second disadvantage is the cost of administration. The bulk of NHS funds are collected through general taxation. No special mechanism is required. An insurance system would require insurance companies to determine premiums, collect them and distribute them in the form of payment for services

337

either to the claimant or to the hospital or practitioner who had provided the treatment. A mechanism for helping those too poor to pay premiums would be needed. It seems to us that this would inevitably lead to more forms to fill in and more people to handle them. An OECD study in 1977 indicated that the expense of collecting contributions and making payments to suppliers of medical services were probably higher in most countries than in the UK.[1]

21.21   We do not think that the NHS should be funded by health insurance. The advantages of the market place could well be real but there would certainly be significant disadvantages. In addition the introduction of such a system in the UK would mean a great deal of upheaval – everyone would have to get used to making the new system work. The advantages of change would have to be much more clearly demonstrable than they are at present to make this worthwhile. No doubt there are grounds for criticising the equity and efficiency of the current system, but we do not think that an insurance based system is the best means of effecting improvements.

21.22   We have ruled out a complete change to insurance finance but what of less radical alternatives? It was suggested to us that the existing private insurance arrangements in the UK might be encouraged and extended in a variety of ways. For example, free use of the NHS might be restricted to those below certain income levels and the richer and healthier members of the community expected to finance their consumption of health care through private insurance. Insurance premiums could be made allowable against income tax. The effect might be to inject extra resources into health care with benefits to both NHS users and those who opted for the private sector.

21.23   Partial insurance financing implies expansion of the existing private health care sector. It would have many of the advantages and disadvantages of a system based primarily on insurance funding but would not involve the same major upheaval and its associated costs. However, there would be the danger of producing the two tier system of health care we have referred to. We would have serious reservations about actively encouraging a system in which the richer members of our society received better care than the less well off.

Supplementary finance

21.24   We have said that the government was likely to control NHS expenditure whatever the method used to finance it. Unless Parliament concludes that more money is indeed needed, a new scheme for raising substantial extra funds for the NHS is likely to be adopted only if it either represents a more politically acceptable approach than the equivalent Exchequer financing, or if it is seen as a means of changing the way that those who use and work in the NHS behave. Trivial additions to NHS resources might be disregarded by those who control NHS expenditure, but would not assist an under-financed service; while a substantial addition would probably lead to a reduction in funds made available from the Exchequer.

---

[1] Organisation for Economic Co-operation and Development, *Public Expenditure on Health*, Studies in Resource Allocation No. 4, Paris, 1977, pages 22-23.

21.25   Charges to NHS patients[1] yield about £125m per year or about 1.6% of the cost of the NHS.[2] About half of this arises from dental charges and about a quarter each from charges for prescriptions and ophthalmic services. As Table 21.2 shows, their revenue yield in recent years has fallen in proportion to the cost of the services. It was suggested to us that there should be both a considerable increase in existing charges and that new ones should be introduced. The new charges proposed included "hotel" charges for non-medical services in hospital, for visits to hospital accident and emergency departments, and for consultations with general practitioners.

21.26   *Purely as an illustration* we show in Tables 21.3 and 21.4 what might have been the effect in the 1975/6 financial year of increasing the prescriptions charge to 50p, and introducing a hotel charge for inpatients of £20 per week, an accident and emergency visit fee of £5, and GP consultation charge of £2. On these figures Table 21.3 shows that after adjustments for reductions in use of the service due to the charges and for increases in social security payments, public expenditure would have been cut by approximately £440m. This saving would have been reduced by the administrative costs of collecting revenue from new charges. An estimate of what would have been the revenue in 1975/6 from unchanged dental and ophthalmic service charges, a higher prescription charge and possible new hospital and GP consultation charges is given in Table 21.4. On the assumptions made, but without allowing for higher administrative costs, the total revenue from charges to NHS patients would have amounted to about £423m or 8.0% of NHS expenditure in 1975/6.

21.27   Though a small proportion of total NHS expenditure, this is too large a sum to be ignored when the Exchequer contribution to the NHS is calculated. The only reasons for introducing the charges referred to would therefore be to discourage patients from using the services in question or to transfer part of the financial burden of the service from the taxpayer to the patient. But the patient does not become a major user of NHS resources until he becomes a hospital patient, and he becomes a particularly large user if he is admitted as an in-patient. In general, to be admitted as an in-patient requires not only the willingness of the patient himself but also the clinical judgement of at least two doctors. It follows that there can be little abuse of hospital resources by patients, and that if incentives and disincentives are to have a major effect on the use of hospital resources then they must be offered to doctors and not to patients. This does not apply to visits to GPs, but would the extra administrative costs and inconveniences of charges be compensated for by keeping away from GPs those who demand his service frivolously? We doubt it, and we would be uneasy that it could well discourage patients from seeking help when they really needed it.

21.28   We have put forward only the practical arguments against NHS charges though we acknowledge that there is a sizeable body of opinion that

---

[1]Excluding charges to private patients.

[2]The paragraphs that follow were written, and the calculations made, before increased NHS charges were announced by the Government on 12 June 1979.

TABLE 21.1
Revenue from Principal NHS Charges[1]: Great Britain 1972/3–1978/9

Financial years

Service	Charge revenue, £m							Revenue as % of cost of service						
	1972/3	1973/4	1974/5	1975/6	1976/7	1977/8	1978/9	1972/3	1973/4	1974/5	1975/6	1976/7	1977/8	1978/9
General pharmaceutical	27	28	28	27	28	28	29	9.9	9.4	7.8	5.8	4.8	3.9	3.4
General dental	30	33	34	37	45	58	63	23.4	23.2	19.4	16.0	17.7	22.5	19.1
General ophthalmic	16	17	19	20	26	27	31	51.6	50.0	45.2	27.8	34.2	35.2	34.4

Source: compiled from health departments' statistics.

Note: [1] Charges to private patients are excluded. Charges to NHS patients are also made for amenity beds, for certain items, such as wigs, dispensed in hospital out-patient departments and under the Road Traffic Act which permits the recovery through motor insurers of a contribution towards the hospital cost of treating road accident casualties.

TABLE 21.2

Estimated Effects of Illustrative New and Increased Charges: Great Britain 1975/6

£ million

	50p prescription charge	£2 GP consultation fee	£5 accident and emergency department visit fee	£20 per week "hotel" charges for inpatients	Total
Increase in revenue[1]	35	134	27	143	339
Reduction in NHS costs[2]	14	13	6	84	117
Reduction in NHS expenditure	49	147	33	227	456
Increase in social security payments[3]					16
Reduction in public expenditure					440

Sources: health departments' statistics;

CSO, Social Trends 9, 1979 HMSO;

J W Hurst, Saving Hospital Expenditure by Reducing In-patient Stay, HMSO 1977;

R J Lavers, "A demand model for prescriptions", 1977, Institute of Social and Economic Research, University of York.

Notes:

[1] It has been assumed that (a) 60% of prescriptions, g.p. consultations, visits to A and E departments and inpatient days would have been exempted from these charges; (b) the new charges would have caused a 10% reduction in the non-exempted g.p. consultations, A and E department visits and inpatient days; (c) the higher prescription charge would have reduced the number of non-exempt prescriptions by the 7.9% suggested by Lavers' study.

[2] The cost reductions have been estimated by taking the average NHS cost of a prescription, a g.p. consultation and a visit to an A and E department in 1975/6. The reduction in hospital inpatient costs arising from a hotel charge is based on the assumption that the charge reduces the length of stay in hospital, not the number of stays, so that the cost saved is that of days at the end of stays which is about half the average cost of all days in hospital.

[3] It is assumed that those inpatients who received reduced social security payments in 1975/6 while in hospital would have had their benefits increased to cover the hotel charge. If such patients had instead not had to bear the charge the increase in NHS revenue would have been reduced by £16 m.

[4] No allowance has been made for the additional administrative costs of the new charges.

TABLE 21.3
**Estimated Yield of Illustrative New and Increased Charges to NHS Patients[1]:
Great Britain 1975/6**

Charges	Revenue	
	£m (1975/6 prices)	% of service cost
New charges:		
Hospital (£5 accident and emergency visit fee, £20 weekly 'hotel' charge)	170	4.2
GP consultation fee (£2)	134	41.9
Higher prescription charge (50p)	62	13.7
Unchanged charges:		
Dental	37	16.0
Ophthalmic	20	27.8
TOTAL:	423	8.0

Source: compiled from health departments' statistics.

Notes: [1] Excludes charges to private patients and hospital outpatients, amenity bed and Road Traffic Act charges.

[2] The effect of the possible new and increased charges on use, and hence the cost, of the services has been allowed for in calculation of the proportion of the cost of the services recovered in charges.

[3] No allowance has been made for the additional administration costs of the possible new charges.

sees them as wrong in principle. But it will be apparent that we are not enthusiastic about charges. Indeed, we feel that, particularly with the irrational structure of charges we now have, there is a good case for their gradual but complete extinction, and we so recommend. The cost to the taxpayer of complete abolition might be about £200m of which £80m would represent the costs of meeting the resulting increase in demand.

21.29   We should not want to be misunderstood on this important issue. The way the public pays for the NHS is a matter which lies within our terms of reference only insofar as it affects the way the NHS uses its revenue or the way the public uses the NHS. The external issues of how tax or charges affect the public and public policy are certainly not our concern and must lie in the hands of the government. If we could see that the charges, which exist now made for better doctoring or discouraged frivolous use of the NHS by the public, then we should applaud them. But we do not see them in that light.

Other sources of finance

21.30   Other suggestions for supplementing sources of finance included a state lottery and some form of local voluntary funding. The main drawbacks to relying on a lottery to fund a signficant part of the cost of the NHS, are its unreliability and the expense of collecting funds in this way. It should also be remembered that the yield from a national lottery would, in comparison with the £8,100m spent on the NHS at present, be very small. The Royal Commission on Gambling[1] advocated a "National Lottery for Good Causes". They calculated that this would yield in the first year about £37.5 million. Even if the whole of this were spent on the NHS it would still amount to under 0.4% of its cost. While we would certainly not wish to suggest that such an additional sum be rejected if it were offered to the NHS, its effect, though

---

[1] Royal Commission on Gambling, *Final Report*, (Cmnd 7200), London, HMSO, 1978.

important at the local operational level, would be at very best marginal in a national context. The experiences of local authorities with fund raising from lotteries has not always been very encouraging.

21.31 We were told that the public would, with suitable encouragement, be prepared to make a significant extra financial contribution to the NHS. There is already much public involvement in the NHS through organisations such as Hospital Friends and the various societies for helping particular groups of patient. At one remove from the NHS, there are fund raising and research organisations like Age Concern, MIND and the Imperial Cancer Research Fund, which give valuable help but have a national rather than local impact. Local fund raising by voluntary workers is normally directed to a specific purpose, and can be a most welcome contribution. On the other hand, the more glamorous causes – new buildings or expensive equipment – are not always those for which the need is greatest, and may themselves commit NHS funds which are urgently needed for other purposes. We would like to see a continuation and expansion of the present voluntary effort, but we do not see it contributing significantly to NHS funds.

21.32 We can see advantages in local authorities being able to contribute to NHS funds if they so wish. There may be circumstances in which it would be in the rate payers' interests to do so, and a local authority contribution to the NHS – the reverse of the present joint financing – would be a tangible expression of local government's involvement, as well as giving its representatives more influence on the health authority.

Hypothecation

21.33 Some of our witnesses favoured greater hypothecation of tax revenue to cover NHS expenditure, i.e. setting aside from general tax revenue some or all of the proceeds of a particular tax or taxes to be spent exclusively on the health service. The arguments for this suggestion varied depending on the precise arrangements proposed, but two common themes were, first that the health service should have a source of revenue outside the control of politicians and insulated from the fluctuations in government economic policy; and, second, that hypothecation would increase the funds available to the NHS. It was also suggested that hypothecated taxes on health harming goods such as tobacco and alcohol would both appropriately penalise their users, and reduce their consumption and therefore the need for health service expenditure. Others felt that a hypothecated "health tax" levied directly on individuals on the lines of the NHS National Insurance contribution would be a useful reminder of the cost of health services.

21.34 We have noted above that no government is likely to relinquish control over NHS expenditure however it is financed. Hypothecation by itself would therefore neither increase spending on the health service nor remove it from political control. There are also objections to the particular arguments for a health tax or hypothecated taxes on health harming goods. A health tax levied at a flat rate would bear most heavily on the poorest tax payers; but if such a tax varied with income it would not provide the same signal to all individuals about the cost of the NHS. In any case since payment of a health tax would be unrelated to demands on the service made by the individual it would provide little incentive to its more economical use. Increasing the price of health harming goods by taxation might make consumers more aware of their dangers, but this could be achieved whatever the revenue of such taxes was spent on.

Distribution of Resources

21.35 In the discussion of the objectives of the NHS in Chapter 2 we stated our belief that the NHS ought to aim to provide equal access to health services for those equally in need irrespective of where they lived. We concluded in Chapter 3 that while there had been some improvement since 1948 in meeting this objective much remained to be done. We commissioned a critique of the health departments' arrangements for allocating financial resources in the NHS from Martin Buxton and Rudolf Klein (referred to in paragraph 21.2 above), published in August 1978. We limit ourselves here to describing briefly some of the main issues. As usual, the problems in England seem to be greater than those in the other parts of the UK, and for that reason our discussion concentrates on England.

21.36 The big spenders in the NHS are hospitals and they account for over 70% of all NHS spending. In 1950/51 the best provided regional hospital board had received more than twice the allocation per head of the worst provided. By 1971/72 the best provided RHB received only about one-third per head more than the region with the lowest allocation. There had been no systematic attempt to assess overall need, though various mechanisms, including in particular the 1962 Hospital Plan, had attempted to direct resources to where they seemed to be most required.

21.37 In 1970, in an attempt to reduce geographical inequality further, the DHSS introduced the "Crossman" formula as the basis for distributing funds to RHBs. Under it, half the money allocated was based on the population served, and a quarter each on the number of beds and the number of cases treated.

21.38 The Crossman formula was succeeded by the arrangements recommended by the Resource Allocation Working Party (RAWP) which reported in September 1976. RAWP recommended that revenue funds should be allocated according to relative need for health care, and that no account should be taken of previous allocations. The formula used population, adjusted for age and sex and marital status as well as standardised fertility ratios and standardised mortality rates as the basic measures of need. Adjustments were made for cross-boundary flows of patients and the high cost of providing services in London. Separate allowance was made for teaching activities through the service increment for teaching (SIFT). The Working Party recommended that its principles should be applied within regions, and that a population based formula should be used for calculating capital funding.

21.39 In Scotland, Wales and Northern Ireland similar exercises took place and broadly similar recommendations were made.[1] Teaching hospital costs were more fully protected than in England, and there were other differences related to the size and particular needs of those parts of the UK.

21.40 The introduction of the RAWP formula was an important step towards determining a rational and equitable system of allocating resources to health authorities. It represents a clear commitment to reduce inequalities in health care provision, which have existed since 1948. The ingredients of the formula itself are partly a matter of subjective judgement and political decision, and we consider it essential that they should be open to public inspection and debate. The publication of the RAWP report provides for this. We hope that developments of the formula will similarly be laid open to public inspection.

21.41 While the RAWP approach is sound in principle, it has been subject to a good deal of criticism. The use of mortality rates as measure of morbidity, the valuation of the capital stock and the failure to include, or allow for, family practitioner services have aroused much concern. Nor does the formula take account of factors which may be important locally in determining the need for resources, such as the occupational status of the population, social deprivation and the availability of other public services. Its application *within* regions has been widely criticised. It is clear that judgement must be used to temper any rigid application of the formula below the regional level. These and other issues are discussed in the commentary prepared for us by Buxton and Klein referred to above and we do not propose to go into them in detail here. We understand that the DHSS have established an advisory group on resource allocation to consider how the formula may best be modified. A formula is only as good as the data on which it is based, and if this is unsatisfactory confidence in it will be undermined. The RAWP report listed a number of aspects of their study on which research was required, and we do not doubt that the DHSS and the other health departments will encourage this.

21.42 We discussed in Chapter 17 the particular problems faced by the teaching hospitals, especially in London, as a result of the introduction of the RAWP formula. While a part of the additional cost of teaching hospitals is covered by the SIFT element of the RAWP formula, this still leaves a substantial part of the additional cost to be met from the normal RAWP allocation. In particular the additional costs arising from research activity and from the role of the teaching hospitals as "centres of excellence" are not explicitly recognised. RAWP recommended that research should be set in hand on these matters, and we endorse the recommendation.

21.43 RAWP and the equivalent exercises outside England relate only to distribution of NHS funds within these parts of the UK. There is no explicit formula for the distribution of funds to the four parts of the UK, though there are marked differences in the resources provided, as the Buxton and Klein

[1]Scottish Home and Health Department, *Scottish Health Authorities Revenue Equalisation,* Edinburgh, HMSO, 1977; Welsh Office, *Report of the Steering Committee on Resource Allocation,* 1977; Department of Health and Social Services in Northern Ireland, *Proposals for the Allocation of Revenue Resources for the Health and Personal Social Services,* 1978.

study shows.[1] There may be adequate justification for these differences, but if so it should be explained and made public in the context of an explicit formula for the distribution of funds to the health service in the four parts of the UK. We recommend accordingly.

Financial Management

21.44   We asked Professor Perrin and his team to investigate the financial management of the NHS. The report which they produced concluded that NHS funds were being "'properly spent' in the sense of the technical probity of the spending, and on purposes broadly consistant with [health] departmental policy".[2] However, they identified a number of weaknesses, some of them serious, in the system of financial management of the NHS. The financial control systems were "little used for planning and decision-making in any positive sense of resource allocation or conscious testing of alternatives"[3] and the system of financial management was not conducive to the efficient and economical use of the service's resources. We commend the report to the health departments and health authorities. We examine briefly below some issues to which we would like to draw particular attention or which were outside the scope of the Perrin study.

Equipment and supplies

21.45   The NHS spends over £900 million a year on a wide variety of equipment and supplies. These include food, fuel, bed-linen, surgical dressings, surgical equipment and drugs as well as major items of scientific and medical equipment. The suppliers of the NHS range from very large multi-national companies to small local firms. The regional supplies officers described the supplies organisation of the NHS in evidence as:

"the logistic arm of the NHS; its task is to ascertain and to provide whatever supplies are legitimately required by the operational arm of the service for those who treat patients or are in 'close support' of them."

Purchasing occurs at all levels in the NHS, from the hospital to the health department. Most of these contracts are "call-off" arrangements, ie not based on fixed quantities. About 25% of the NHS revenue expenditure on goods and services is arranged under central contracts placed by health departments or by using contracts arranged by other government departments. Many other items are bought on bulk contracts arranged by the supplies organisations of health authorities. The value of these latter contracts now exceeds 30% of total NHS expenditure on supplies.

21.46   The health departments involvement in equipment and supplies differs in the four parts of the UK, although the DHSS takes the leading role

---

[1]Buxton, M J and Klein, R E *Op cit,* page 21, Table 1.

[2]Perrin, John et al *Op cit.*, paragraph E1.1.

[3]*Ibid,* paragraph E2.1.

346

on general purchasing policies. In Scotland the SHHD has no executive responsibility for contracts and its role is confined to ensuring that government policy is followed, that resources are used efficiently and economically and in determining policy on equipment, research, development and evaluation. The Welsh Office monitors purchasing. Central executive functions are undertaken by the supplies divisions of the Common Services Agency in Scotland and the Welsh Health Technical Services Organisation in Wales. The arrangements for central purchasing in Northern Ireland are very similar to those in Scotland with the Central Services Agency having executive functions.

21.47 Supplies organisation and policies in the NHS have been extensively studied. Most recently a working party chaired by Mr A J Collier reported in 1976 on "Buying for the National Health Service".[1] Its main recommendation was that a "limited list" approach to medical equipment should be developed, "subject to the institution of adequate facilities for evaluation and acceptability to the users". We understand that this proposal has met with opposition from some health authorities and the industries supplying the NHS. A supply board working group under the chairmanship of Mr B Salmon reported in 1978 on the arrangements for procuring NHS supplies (but not those related to the family practitioner service). The Salmon working group recommended that supplies policy should be determined at AHA level and that a supply council should be established as a special health authority whose policy decisions should be binding on DHSS and on health authorities. Its main functions would be to formulate policy at health department, region and area level; to arrange for the production and introduction of a comprehensive and universal computer based supplies information system; and to establish policy for the evaluation of the equipment and supplies used in the NHS.

21.48 Professor Perrin's report recommended that:

"health departments should further encourage health authorities towards an early change-over to the use of central stores, where this has not yet been done, and also that NHS authorities should give urgent attention to improving stores management and control systems ... additional staffing and training, and improved systems should be provided for central purchasing functions just as quickly as resources permit."[2]

21.49 Our interest in these questions is principally to ensure that resources in the NHS are used in an efficient and effective way. The NHS is a major purchaser of supplies and equipment and the problems of supplies policy appear to have been thoroughly researched in recent years. There is obviously a need for better specification of equipment required, improved arrangements for research, development and evaluation of new equipment, and more effective ways of ensuring that users are aware of the results of evaluation. At regional level there should be provision for an equipment information and advisory service. Some pieces of machinery are now enormously expensive and the cost of housing and using them may also be very large. It is essential therefore that

---

[1]Department of Health and Social Security, *Buying for the National Health Service*, 1976: (an unpublished consultative paper).

[2]Perrin, John et, al *Op cit*, paragraph D 26.3.

they be evaluated before they are brought into general use. This should be a health department responsibility, and accepted by the health authorities as such; but at present the health authorities can buy any item of equipment, however expensive, which they can afford. We were disturbed to hear that whole body scanners, which can cost £0.5m to buy and £40,000 per annum or more to run, had been purchased by health authorities before they had been properly clinically tested and their uses and running costs ascertained. The Collier suggestions for a "limited list" would obviously be useful in this context and we recommend that the main proposals of the Collier report be implemented as quickly as possible.

Budgets and incentives

21.50 There are formidable obstacles to the efficient use of resources in the health service. The individual patient will gain little if he uses the service more economically. The information necessary to monitor and evaluate decisions taken may not be available. Responsibility for expenditure may not fall on those who actually control the use of resources and there are few incentives for efficiency. If budget holders manage to achieve economies they are likely to find that their budget next year has suffered a corresponding cut and the savings used to cover expenditure elsewhere in the health service. A selfless concern for the generality of tax payers and patients is an insubstantial basis for efficient resource allocation. It is too easily turned into apathy, even cynicism by seeing others acting wastefully.

21.51 The weakness of financial management cannot be remedied without a clear agreement on what tasks should be carried out, some ranking of priorities and enforcement of budgetary discipline. In this respect it is interesting that we heard NHS administrators and treasurers welcome the introduction of cash limits because these made authorities decide on priorities and enforce economies.

21.52 W attach great importance to improving incentives to NHS service providers to use resources effectively. We would like to see budget holders permitted to keep and spend as they think best within the service a proportion of any savings they may achieve and possibly be allowed to carry over a greater proportion of funds from one budget period to the next. We recognise that there are difficulties in arranging this: the efficient unit may be penalised because there is little scope for economy while the inefficient unit benefits, and measures of service output have to be developed to ensure that savings do not arise merely from a reduction in service provision or quality. However, schemes of this kind have been tried in the NHS, and we recommend that they should be encouraged.

Clinicians and resource management

21.53 The clinical decisions that doctors make heavily influence NHS expenditure. GPs prescribe great quantities of drugs and decide whether to refer patients to hospital. Hospital doctors decide whether to admit patients or treat them as outpatients, whether to order diagnostic tests, to prescribe or recommend surgical, pharmaceutical or nursing treatment, and when to discharge their patients. A doctor has clinical responsibility but is not usually accountable for the resource and financial implications of his decisions. No doubt many doctors are cost-conscious and careful, but the individual doctor normally has no direct incentive to economy. Doctors also need information about costs if they are to be cost-conscious. Apart from the expense of new equipment which they may request, they are often in the dark about the financial aspects of their work. They are told neither their unit costs nor the cost of the investigations and tests which they use. Some information about drug costs is made available to them but in no systematic or emphatic way. Much more could and should be done to inform them. The Perrin Report recorded that:

"Amongst health service finance staff, it is generally considered that the best way to encourage redeployment of resources . . . and also the best way to encourage cost consciousness more generally amongst medical staff, is to involve clinicians more positively in the managerial dimension of financial control . . . the key to the feasibility of this development is the willingness of clinicians to become involved, firstly in the resource allocation process, and secondly in the responsibility for, and 'control' of, resource spending/consumption for/by their specialties"[1]

21.54   One way of involving doctors in the resource allocation process is to make them budget holders and thus accountable for the expenditure generated by their decisions. This approach was supported by the King's College Hospital Group Medical and Medical Executive Committees who told us:

"More autonomy needs to be granted to each hospital or hospital group in order to redevelop local pride and encourage economy and good house-keeping. Financial autonomy for Divisions or Departments with allocation of Unit Budgets could, by freeing doctors to decide and finance their own priorities, bring a greater sense of responsibility in the individual use of taxpayers' money with saving to the country at large, and benefit to patients in hospital served communities."

21.55   There are considerable practical difficulties in clinician budgeting to be overcome and some doctors may see it as restricting their clinical freedom. It is worth stating, therefore, that there can be no such thing as absolute clinical freedom. A doctor must exercise his judgement as to which of the best available courses should be taken, but there will continue to be, as there is now, a limit on the courses available. As medicine becomes more technically advanced and expensive, the limitations on its practice are likely to increase. By becoming explicit resource managers doctors would gain a greater measure of control over their work within clearly defined resource constraints. We recommend that experiments with clinician budgeting should be encouraged.

Information

21.56   The best use of the resources of the NHS requires that its decision-

---

[1]*Ibid,* paragraph C8.11.

makers be provided promptly with relevant information on needs and on the volume and cost of resources used in meeting those needs. Unfortunately the information available to assist decision-makers in the NHS leaves much to be desired. Relevant information may not be available at all, or in the wrong form. Information that is produced is often too late to assist decisions and may be of dubious accuracy.

21.57 Without explicit measures of the need of groups of patients for health care rational decisions on priorities and geographical distribution of resources are impossible. The lack of outcome measures means that judgements of the efficiency of service delivery rest on insecure foundations. Professor Perrin concluded that health authorities are:

"not well served by their information systems in monitoring their own progress; in particular, the data on patients are poor . . . and the financial control system does not show care groups used in planning, nor report output."[1]

21.58 If an organisation cannot keep track of its resources it is unlikely to be using them effectively and decisions on how those resources ought to be developed are made much more difficult. We were dismayed by the lack of information on the physical capital of the NHS. Professor Perrin's report noted that:

"Another criticism levelled at the information system was the almost total lack of reliable data concerning the type, cost, age and location of equipment in everyday use. Without such data it was difficult to implement a planned replacement programme or to ensure the maximum utilisation of resources."[2]

21.59 Sensible decisions at all levels in the service require information on the costs of resources used in providing services to patients, but Professor Perrin's team found that:

"The existing system of annual financial accounts (and linked functional 'cost accounts') do not appear to provide significantly-valuable information for improved resource allocation or other decision making . . . Cost data necessary for planning, decision making and resource allocation are difficult to derive. Important decisions have to be taken with only approximate knowledge of their cost . . . "[3]

21.60 We have urged the importance of improving the information available to decision makers in the NHS in a number of places in our report. We also support the sensible recommendations contained in Professor Perrin's report. In particular we feel that it is essential that information on costs must be improved and costed options considered if the best use is to be made of the service's resources. Improvements in information will initially require addi-

---

[1]*Ibid*, paragraph D20.2.

[2]*Ibid*, paragraph C2.25 (b).

[3]*Ibid*, paragraphs D28.3, E.2.2.

tional expenditure on administration but we would expect that the quality of decision making would thereby be much improved.

Family practitioner services

21.61　The family practitioner services (FPS) account for about £1,800m, or over one-fifth of all NHS expenditure. About half of this is spent on pharmaceutical services, mainly on drugs and dressings. Unlike the rest of the NHS the FPS are not subject to cash limits, except for the small expenditure on administration. The bulk of expenditure incurred in the services is automatically reimbursed by the health departments. The open-ended budget of the FPS was defended by the BMA on the grounds that:

> "there is no way of controlling absolutely the amount of illness or disease and while it is possible, for example, to defer many surgical operations for 6 months or a year because of limited resources, similar action cannot be taken in the field of general medical care."

21.62　Although the FPS are "demand determined" this does not mean that their expenditure cannot be forecast and influenced and hence budgeted for. The level of remuneration of doctors, dentists, pharmacists and opticians is subject to the ultimate control of the government; prices of drugs and optical appliances are subject to price control and negotiation; and there are arrangements for vetting the prescribing habits of doctors and the treatment given by dentists in the FPS. Prescribing, dental and optical charges have been used to control demand. In the past FPS expenditure has tended to rise more slowly than that of the NHS as a whole, though this trend has been reversed in the last few years.

21.63　The open-ended nature of FPS expenditure has disadvantages. First, the FPS is shielded from the effects of financial stringency, and the burden of any cut-back in NHS expenditure falls on the hospital and community services. This may accord with spending priorities, but it would be preferable it it were the result of an explicit decision rather than the accidental effect of a particular method of budgeting. It may encourage the misallocation of resources. Second, finance cannot be readily used to remedy geographical inequalities in the FPS. Third, and perhaps most important, the separate FPS budget does nothing to encourage joint planning of FPS and hospital and community services.

21.64　In Chapter 20 we recommended that family practitioner committees should be abolished and family practitioners contracted to health authorities in England and Wales as they are in Scotland and Northern Ireland. The closer involvement of the FPS in health service planning and decision making that this will imply might be further assisted by the FPS being coverd by the same budget as the hospital and community services. However, there are some obvious practical problems to be overcome and we recommend that a study of the desirability and feasibility of a common budget for the family practitioner and hospital and community services should be undertaken.

Capital

21.65 Our recommendations in Chapter 10, if adopted, will lead to a significant increase in capital expenditure in the NHS. In 1978/79 this was running at the rate of about £460m per year or some 5.7% of total NHS expenditure. This is a considerable sum in itself but capital expenditure also has a profound influence on the pattern of revenue expenditure. It is therefore doubly important that capital projects are examined within a framework which is conducive to sensible decisions. This will require that alternative means of satisfying service objectives are systematically identified and all the significant costs and benefits of alternatives are considered explicitly. Many of the factors in investment decisions, particularly the benefits, are difficult or impossible to quantify or evaluate so that such decisions will continue to depend heavily on professional judgements. However, as Professor Perrin's team noted, it is important that a procedure should be adopted which:

"focuses attention on the desirability of making implicit policy judgments explicit, and ensuring that all can see clearly just what decision has been made and why."[1]

We understand that DHSS is considering how best to issue guidance, in consultation with health authorities, on the planning and appraisal of investment decisions. We welcome this approach and hope guidance can be issued swiftly to encourage rational appraisal of capital expenditure.

21.66 Capital expenditure in the NHS is controlled by the earmarking of capital funds in health authorities' allocations. Greater flexibility between capital and revenue funds has been introduced in recent years. Professor Perrin's team reported that:

"The consensus view within the authorities studied was that the separation between revenue and capital monies (limited virement notwithstanding) was not conducive to the proper (ie economic) evaluation of the choice between consumption and investment."[2]

The Regional Treasurers considered that RHAs were better able than DHSS to make the decision on the optimum mix of capital and revenue expenditure necessary to meet the service needs of the population they serve.

21.67 The Treasurers also considered that health authorities should be able to raise loans and service them from their annual allocations. The interest on such loans would bring home to users of capital funds the costs of their investment decisions and encourage a better balance between capital and other resources in the NHS. Access to the capital market would also enable health authorities to postpone or bring forward expenditure from one period to another.

21.68 These two questions are linked. One of the arguments against abolishing the distinction between capital and revenue is that in a centrally financed health service authorities might be tempted to spend on capital

---

[1]*Ibid*, paragraph D22.2.

[2]*Ibid*, paragraph C2.7.

projects without taking full account of the revenue consequences. Exposure to the financial discipline of the capital market might solve this difficulty. A problem with giving health authorities access to the capital market is that they are not elected and publicly accountable bodies with independent revenue resources. Some authorities might be rated as worse risks than others and be faced with higher interest charges. This particular problem might not arise if health authorities were given access to an internal NHS capital market administered by the health departments perhaps along the lines of the borrowing and lending arrangements for temporarily surplus SHARE funds recently introduced in Scotland.[1]

21.69 There are clearly potential disadvantages which may outweigh the theoretical attractions of charging interest on NHS capital funds, and Professor Perrin considered, and we agree, that detailed research would be needed before it could be considered a workable alternative to current methods of capital allocation. In the meantime health authorities can take advantage of the considerable degree of flexibility that has recently been introduced.

Conclusions and Recommendations

21.70 There is no objective or universally acceptable method of establishing what the "right" level of expenditure on the NHS should be. Some of our recommendations would increase NHS expenditure, but others should lead to savings. On balance our recommendations will increase the cost of the NHS, but our judgement is that these additional resources will be justified by the benefits which will flow from them. We also consider it right that the nation should spend more on the NHS as it gets wealthier.

21.71 We made our own broad assessment of the financial implications of our recommendations, but in most cases we have not included them in our report. The accurate costing of any recommendation that affects the NHS in the four parts of the UK would be difficult enough if undertaken by the health departments themselves. For obvious reasons we could not ask them to do this exercise for us, and we had neither the time nor resources to make other than the most rudimentary estimates.

21.72 No method of financing a part of national expenditure as large and as politically sensitive as the health service is likely to remove it from government influence. Discussion of the merits of alternative methods of finance must therefore focus on their implications for the way the health service is organised and performs, rather than on the total amount of finance they will generate. We are not convinced that the claimed advantages of insurance finance or substantial increases in charge revenue would outweigh their undoubted disadvantages in terms of equity and administrative costs. The same disadvantages arise from the existing NHS charges.

21.73 The geographical distribution of the provision of health care has become fairer since the NHS was founded but there is still some way to go. It

[1]*Hansard*, 18 January 1978, written answers, columns 250-1.

is essential that the resource allocation procedure adopted should be the subject of informed and public scrutiny and we welcome the recent change to explicit formulae based on estimates of need.

21.74 The system of financial management in the NHS does not sufficiently encourage efficient resource use. Much of the information required for effective management is not produced, or is inaccurate, or too late to be of value. Those held responsible for expenditure are often not in a position to control it. We commend Professor Perrin's Report to the health departments.

21.75 We recommend that:

(a) it is for government to decide how the NHS should be funded, but there is a firm case for the gradual but complete extinction of charges (paragraphs 21.28 and 21.29);

(b) the health departments should prosecute the research necessary for improvement of the resource allocation formulae (paragraphs 21.41 and 21.42);

(c) there should be an explicit formula for the distribution of funds to the health service in the four parts of the UK (paragraph 21.43);

(d) the main proposals of the Collier report on equipment and supplies should be implemented as quickly as possible (paragraph 21.49);

(e) health departments should encourage experiments with budgeting (paragraphs 21.52 and 21.55);

(f) a study of the desirability and feasibility of common budgets for FPS and hospital and community services expenditure should be undertaken (paragraph 21.64).

Chapter 22   Conclusions and Recommendations

22.1   In this Chapter we bring together our conclusions and recommendations, but we thought it would be helpful to put them in the context of a brief account of our main lines of work and thinking.

22.2   We should wish to emphasise first that we have tried always to relate our discussion, no matter what the topic, to the patient, his family and those serving them. Will our recommendations help the patient, and help those who serve him to do so more effectively?

22.3   We have tried to take the widest possible view of the NHS and to see it whole. We have also tried to view it not in isolation but in the context of the many links it has with other services and institutions. At no time have we thought that any other approach to our task would be useful, if indeed any other were possible, but this has the disadvantage that we have dealt only cursorily, and sometimes perhaps even superficially, with important topics. Our work can therefore be regarded only as a beginning. It is not for us to say whether it is good or bad, and it must now be put to the refining fire of public discussion. But we hope that even in those areas where we have necessarily had to work sketchily those who will be discussing this report will at least have no trouble in seeing which way we are pointing.

22.4   We are all too conscious that our report will be disappointing to those who have been looking to us for some blinding revelation which would transform the NHS. Leaving to one side our own capacity for revelation of this kind, we must say as clearly as we can that the NHS is not suffering from a mortal disease susceptible only to heroic surgery. Already the NHS has achieved a great deal and embodies aspirations and ideals of great value. The advances to be made – and which undoubtedly will be made – will be brought about by constant application and vigilance.

22.5   In this connection we should like to quote the wise words of the late Sir Richard Clarke who was Second Secretary at the Treasury when he spoke in 1964 about the management of public expenditure in the following terms:

"In the dispersed services such as education and hospitals ... units of administration are small, and their performance must be uneven. It is difficult to form a judgement about how efficient those relatively small independent units are, and how much scope there may be for saving, and by what management techniques and services this potential saving can be realised – without of course endangering the quality of local responsibility and flexibility to local circumstances which is fundamental to these services."

355

22.6   Sir Richard continued:

"Altogether, there is clearly no room for complacency. But it would seem difficult to argue that there is widespread inadequacy; or to point to substantial improvements which could be made readily. To improve performance is a long slogging job."[1]

The NHS has come a long way since 1964 but if we had to sum up our general view of the present-day NHS we could think of no better words to use than those we have just quoted.

22.7   The NHS reflects the society around it – both society's aspirations towards good health and its careless attitudes towards bad health. Then again, the NHS mirrors, and always will, not only the imperfect nature of medical science but the diffuse and ill-defined understanding we have of our own health, whether good or bad. It would be comforting to think that one day we shall be able to mend broken minds as effectively as we can broken limbs, but we know that that must be a very distant prospect.

22.8   It follows therefore that, within its large and complex framework, the NHS must be sensitive always to the individual voice and its cry for help. It must never lapse into insularity or complacency. It should always strive for improvement and be open to new ideas and influences, rewarding initiative and leadership wherever they may be found.

22.9   We now summarise our conclusions and recommendations. We should warn the reader that what follows is a very brief summary of often detailed and complex material which is dealt with in the earlier chapters of the report.

Part I A Perspective of the Nation's Health and Health Care

22.10   We started this part of our report with a statement of what we felt should be the objectives of the NHS. We believed the NHS should:

encourage and assist individuals to remain healthy;

provide equality of entitlement to health services;

provide a broad range of services of a high standard;

provide equality of access to these services;

provide a service free at the time of use;

satisfy the reasonable expectations of its users;

remain a national service responsive to local needs.

22.11   We then looked at how good the service is now. We concluded that we need not be ashamed of our health service and that there were many aspects of it of which we can be justly proud. However, social and geographical inequalities and variations in the provision of resources persist. Although the

[1]Sir Richard, Clarke, "The Management of the Public Sector of the National Economy," *Public Expenditure Management and Control: the Development of the Public Expenditure Survey Committee (PESC),* (editor Sir Alec Cairncross), London, Macmillan, 1978.

NHS by itself cannot overcome these problems, they must remain a cause for concern and areas in which the performance of the service can be improved. In spite of the problems of measuring efficiency in health care we were convinced that, apart from improvements which may be achieved through the use of more resources, the NHS can provide a better service by making better use of the resources now available to it.

22.12 We went on to summarise some of the major failures of the NHS and remedies to correct them which had been put to us in evidence. For the most part we discuss these in detail in the main body of our report, and we shall not summarise them all here. We did, however, discuss in some detail in Chapter 4 allegations about the swollen numbers of administrators in the service, including administrative nurses. We found that the figures for nurses administrators did not support the allegation that the Salmon Committee's recommendations had increased the proportion of nurses in the grades above ward sister. In England there had been an increase of about 28% in numbers of administrative and clerical staff between 1973 and 1977, but the causes of this were not clear, and there was in any case no way of establishing the "right" number of administrators. Some of the expansion in numbers would have occurred whether or not NHS reorganisation had taken place. We formed an encouraging view of how well many administrators had coped with the real difficulties caused by reorganisation, and we rejected criticism of them as a group. We considered, nonetheless, that there was much that could be done to make their work more effective, including improving standards of recruitment.

Part II Services to Patients

22.13 We began this part of our report with an identification of the four categories or gradations of care which an individual may need. They were:

the care which a healthy person will exercise for himself so that he remains healthy;

the self-care which the slightly ill person will exercise which may involve medication and treatment;

the care provided by the person's family and by the health and personal social services outside hospital;

the care which can only be provided in hospital or other residential institution.

These categories merge into each other and the administration of health services must not create barriers between them. The chapters which form this part of our report follow the path of these gradations of care, and end with a discussion of the influence of the consumer on health services.

Good health

22.14 We concluded in Chapter 5 that preventive measures were by no means the exclusive responsibility of the NHS, but that a significant improvement in the health of the people of the UK could come through prevention. We considered that there were major areas where government

357

action could produce rapid and certain results: a much tougher attitude towards smoking, towards preventing road accidents and mitigating their results, a clear commitment to fluoridation and a programme to combat alcoholism, were among the more obvious examples. But such action had to be matched by other measures. We saw a need for more emphasis on health education and the development and monitoring of its techniques, for greater involvement of GPs and other health professionals, and for better in-service training for teachers in health education. The imaginative use of radio and television would be important. We felt that much more could be done to emphasise the positive virtues of health and the risks of an unhealthy life style, and that this should include environmental and occupational hazards as well as personal behaviour. We were concerned that local authorities should not let standards of environmental health slip. We considered that the NHS needed to face its responsibilities in prevention.

22.15   Occupational health and safety is not a responsibility of the NHS at present, though some evidence we received suggested it should become so. This is a complicated field and one which in many respects has little to do with the central functions of the NHS.

Priorities

22.16   In Chapter 6 we considered how priorities in the NHS were set and implemented. The present national priorities were services for the elderly, the mentally ill and mentally handicapped, and children, and the emphasis was on community care. These priorities were not the result of objective analysis but of subjective judgment. Our own view was that they were broadly correct at the present time, but that they were certainly not the only choices. We thought it important to recognise that national priorities emerge from a variety of conflicting views and pressures expressed in Parliament, by the health professions and various patient or client pressure groups amongst others; and that so far as possible discussion which led to the establishment of priorities should be conducted in public and illuminated by fact.

22.17   We found other problems in implementing priorities. There were considerable practical difficulties to be overcome in shifting resources from one patient or client group to another, or in favouring one part of the NHS against others, particularly when funds were short. We could not yet tell how far the NHS planning system introduced after NHS reorganisation would turn out to be an effective mechanism for this purpose, but we were sure that national priorities could be uniformly applied only to a limited extent. Some of the difficulties were to be seen in the efforts to promote community care, and unless additional resources were made available progress would be slow.

22.18   Services for the elderly would make increasing demands on health and local authorities for the rest of this century. We were concerned that without greater shifts in resources than were yet evident neither health nor local authority services would be able to cope with the immense burden these demands would impose. Inevitably the community as a whole would have to share the responsibility and costs of caring for the elderly at home with appropriate support from the health and personal social services. We noted that the health departments were already tackling the implications and integrated planning was essential in our view. It was clear to us that in the NHS the burden of caring for infirm old people would fall mainly on nurses, and that efforts must be made to encourage them in undertaking this work.

22.19 We dealt with hospital provision for the mentally ill and mentally handicapped in Chapter 10, but in the context of priorities we noted that most problems with a psychiatric aspect were first identified by GPs. It was clear to us that many GPs would benefit from more training in this part of their work. We doubted whether medical care for the elderly and mentally handicapped was best organised on the basis of separate specialties. Other doctors should be involved in the care of these patients, and we saw the development of special interests by doctors in related specialties as being a promising way of achieving this.

22.20 We noted that the Court Committee had recently looked in depth at services for children, and we did not consider it necessary to go over that ground again in detail, but, like others, we had doubts about the wisdom of introducing new specialist staff into this field. Finally, we welcomed recent developments in services for the deaf, and would like to see improved services for the partially sighted.

Primary care services

22.21 In Chapter 7 we noted that changes in the structure of the population and in health care priorities would mean that the demand on and for general practitioner, nursing and related services in the community would increase during the next decade. We found that those services were generally provided to a good standard at present but improvements were needed in a number of directions. The development of the primary health care team was encouraging, but there was a continuing need to encourage closer working relationships and teamwork between the professions who provided care for the community. District nurses and health visitors would have a particularly important part to play. We heard of a number of promising developments in improving the quality of general practice, but we thought that more needed to be done to improve the training and continuing education of GPs. Improvement of the standard of existing premises was required and so were more health centres. In our view better training was needed for receptionists, deputising services should be brought under closer control, and more research was needed into a number of aspects of community services.

22.22 We understood that to a large extent GPs could control their own prescribing costs but had little incentive to keep them down and they were subject to pressures from pharmaceutical companies and patients to prescribe expensively and often ineffectively. We thought that a more radical approach to this problem was required.

22.23 We concluded that the major challenge to community services was the provision of services in declining urban areas. The health needs of patients who live in these areas were complex, and the health departments alone could not provide all the answers. A much more flexible and innovative approach to improving the services in them seemed to us to be needed.

Pharmaceutical, ophthalmic and chiropody services

22.24   In Chapter 8 we identified the main problems in the pharmaceutical services as a falling number of pharmacies and the erosion of the pharmacist's traditional role with the development of modern packaging of medicines. While surveys had suggested that access to a pharmacy was not yet a serious problem for many people, we thought it might well become so in the future. Pharmacists would continue to have an important role since the use of potent drugs in medicine had increased substantially. We did not consider that they should develop a quasi-medical role, and we thought that their expertise could most usefully be employed in advising doctors on prescribing matters, and the public on self-medication.

22.25   The compaints about the general ophthalmic service were mainly lack of information about NHS treatment and spectacle frames. We noted that the optician had a financial interest in encouraging patients to buy non-NHS frames, but we saw no reason why he should not be required also to display NHS frames and the prices of both NHS and non-NHS items.

22.26   The NHS does not attempt to provide a comprehensive chiropody service. We found that within the NHS, chiropody was mainly provided to the elderly, but there were shortages of qualified chiropodists prepared to undertake the work. One reason for this was a shortage of training facilities for chiropodists: another was the attractions of the private sector in which most chiropodists work at present. We considered that the health departments should promote the introduction of foot hygienists.

Dentistry

22.27   We were in no doubt that dental health in the UK had improved since 1948, but the prevalence of dental disease remains at an unacceptably high level. The NHS should strive for the highest standard of care. We recommended a number of detailed changes which should, if implemented, improve the quality of service offered to patients and the efficiency of the present system.

22.28   The prevention policies which we recommended for the future offer a real and attainable improvement – perhaps unique – in public health. It was clear that a determined swing of policy towards a greater emphasis on prevention was needed. The most immediate requirements were for the full implementation of water fluoridation and for the funding of research on prevention and dental health education and the training and employment of more ancillary workers. Individual preventive work should be carried out by the general dental service and a way found for providing fees for treatment of this kind.

22.29   We thought that while these policies would require time to implement and would not bring changes overnight, their effect on the numbers, composition and training of the dental team would be profound. The appointment of the Nuffield enquiry into dental education, referred to at the start of Chapter 9, was, therefore, timely. Because NHS dentistry was likely to change significantly we recommended that a small committee representing government and other interested parties should be set up to review the development of dental health policy and in particular a preventive strategy and the future functions of the community dental service. Its purpose would be to ensure that the impetus for improvement was not lost. Its starting point could be this report and that of the Nuffield Committee.

Hospital services

22.30 We remarked in Chapter 10 that most patients were well satisfied with the treatment they received in NHS hospitals, as they were with other parts of the service, but that there were two grumbles which were both frequent and long-standing. Patients were not given enough information about their treatment, and despite constant complaints over the years they might still feel that they were ignored when doctors discussed them with colleagues. We were also sorry to learn that hospitals persisted in waking patients at the crack of dawn.

22.31 We did not hear a great deal about waiting lists in our evidence, and our OPCS survey found that most patients were not caused great distress by waiting for admission to hospital. The significance of waiting lists had certainly been exaggerated, partly for political reasons, and it was waiting *times* which should in any case attract attention. The DHSS had commissioned a large scale study on the subject and this might throw more light on the matter.

22.32 We had no quarrel with the district general hospital (DGH) approach to providing specialist services, though flexibility was plainly required. We thought that the "nucleus hospital" approach was sensible. There was still dispute over the best use of the many small hospitals which were not part of the DGH. It was clear that the community hospital approach was not acceptable and we were relieved to hear that the DHSS were rethinking the present policy. We thought there was plenty of room for experiment in this as in so many other parts of the NHS, and we would deplore too rigid an approach. The development of nursing homes could make a major contribution to the care of the elderly.

22.33 We found that acute hospital services were generally excellent. Most of them were provided by peripheral non-teaching hospitals, often in old buildings and ungenerously staffed. We hoped that our recommendations would improve the position of both those who used them and those who worked in them.

22.34 We thought the mental illness hospitals needed to be rescued. Despite the statement in the DHSS Consultative Document on Priorities, there was a widely held view that the specialist mental hospitals were to disappear. We could find no sign of the nation being able to dispense with them in the foreseeable future. The development of acute psychiatric units in DGHs, itself admirable, had tended to leave the mental illness hospitals with the chronic and most difficult patients. They needed to be clearly reassured about their future, to be integrated fully into a unified psychiatric service, and to receive a proper share of capital monies.

22.35 Finally, we concluded that communications between the hospital and the community services were not all that they should be, and that the arrangements for community workers to work in hospitals, and hospital workers in the community needed to be improved. Strong links were particularly important in the rehabilitation services.

The NHS and the public

22.36 We noted in Chapter 11 that since their introduction at reorganisation, community health councils (CHCs) had made an important contribution towards ensuring that local public opinion was represented to health service management. We felt they needed additional resources to fulfil this task more effectively, and further guidance from the health departments on their role.

22.37 We thought it very important that patients should be able to make suggestions for improving health services. Those who have complaints about the way the NHS has treated them or their relatives should also be able to make them through a simple, fair and effective mechanism. The changes in procedures which we discussed were likely to improve matters considerably.

22.38 We found that the contribution made by the public, voluntary bodies and volunteers was of major benefit to the service. It should be encouraged. The development of informal patient committees was a constructive way of bringing patient views to bear on the provision of neighbourhood primary care services.

Recommendations on services to patients

(1) *Proven* screening programmes should be expanded (paragraph 5.7);

(2) the wearing of seat belts should be made compulsory for drivers and front seat passengers in motor vehicles (paragraph 5.12);

(3) health education should be expanded, but some of the increased resources must be spent on developing more effective methods and on monitoring and validating existing and new techniques (paragraph 5.14);

(4) education authorities should examine seriously existing arrangements for health education in schools (paragraph 5.15);

(5) health education should be emphasised in the forward planning of health authorities (paragraph 5.17);

(6) funds for the Health Education Council and the corresponding bodies in Scotland should be increased to allow them to make more use of television (paragraph 5.21);

(7) the health departments should make public more of the professional advice on which policies and priorities are based (paragraph 6.7);

(8) all professions concerned with the care of the elderly should receive more training in understanding their needs (paragraph 6.34);

(9) further experiments in different ways of meeting the needs of elderly and other patients requiring long-term care should be undertaken urgently (paragraph 6.37);

(10) the legal position regarding responsibility in the use of deputising services in Scotland should be brought into line with that elsewhere in the UK (paragraph 7.8);

(11) health authorities should keep under review the operation of the deputising services in their areas and, if they are unsatisfactory, improve or replace them (paragraph 7.10);

(12) where this does not happen already, the full costs of attendance of GPs receptionists at training courses should be met by the family practitioner committee or health authority concerned (paragraph 7.12);

(13) before a maximum or minimum list size is adopted, considerable research on an optimum range of list sizes should be undertaken (paragraph 7.16);

(14) there should be a review of the controls on the appointment of GPs exercised by the Medical Practices Committees (paragraphs 7.17 and 7.30);

(15) the health departments should consider offering an assisted voluntary retirement scheme to GPs with small lists who have reached 65 years of age (paragraph 7.18);

(16) the health departments should discuss with the medical profession the feasibility of introducing a compulsory retirement age for GPs (paragraph 7.18)

(17) the health departments should continue their current plans for the expansion of community nursing (paragraph 7.22);

(18) research is required into a number of aspects of primary care (paragraphs 7.27 and 7.34);

(19) national or regional panels should be set up to provide external assessors for each new appointment of a principal in general practice (paragraph 7.30);

(20) GPs should make local arrangements specifically to facilitate audit of the services they provide and the health departments should check progress with these developments (paragraph 7.32);

(21) the introduction of the A4 records system in general practice should be given high priority (paragraph 7.33);

(22) FPCs and health authorities should use vigorously their powers to ensure that patients are seen by their GPs in surgeries of an acceptable standard (paragraph 7.35);

(23) the British National Formulary should be re-issued soon in portable, loose-leaf form with separate information on drug costs, and be kept up-to-date (paragraph 7.40);

(24) the health departments should introduce a limited list of drugs as soon as possible and take further steps to encourage generic prescribing (paragraph 7.46);

(25) the health departments should consider whether high running costs are acting as a significant disincentive to GPs to work in health centres (paragraph 7.50);

(26) the health departments should consider urgently measures to assist the development as a priority of health centres or other suitable premises to attract GPs to London and other inner city areas where sites are particularly expensive or difficult to obtain (paragraph 7.51);

(27) health authorities when establishing health centres in inner city and deprived urban areas, should experiment with offering salaried appointments and reduced list sizes to attract groups of doctors to work in them (paragraph 7.59);

(28) additional financial resources should be provided to improve the quality of primary care services in declining urban areas (paragraph 7.63);

(29) the establishment of pharmacies in health centres should be encouraged (paragraph 8.15);

(30) charges for NHS and non-NHS items and details of eligibility should be prominently displayed and publicised by opticians (paragraph 8.20);

(31) serious consideration should be given to widening the range of items which can be prescribed and dispensed under the general ophthalmic services (paragraph 8.21);

(32) more chiropody training places should be provided and services to the elderly in the community increased (paragraph 8.26);

(33) until the implications of a shift in policy towards prevention have been identified dental student entry numbers should not be altered but flexibility in meeting demands should be achieved through the increased use of dental ancillary workers (paragraph 9.18);

(34) the dental profession and government should experiment with alternative methods of paying general dental practitioners in addition to a capitation system for children (paragraph 9.23);

(35) the dental profession and government should make rapid progress to the introduction generally of an out-of-hours treatment scheme (paragraph 9.25);

(36) dental care for long-stay hospital patients should be as readily available as it is for men and women in the community (paragraph 9.33);

(37) dental teaching hospitals should be funded directly by region or health department (paragraph 9.35);

(38) the present technical college/dental hospital training schemes for dental technicians should be expanded (paragraph 9.42);

(39) a standardised national basis for the collection of dental data should be introduced (paragraph 9.46);

(40) manpower in the community dental service should be increased (paragraph 9.51);

(41) the Scottish system for recording all information about the dental treatment of children in the same way should be adopted in the rest of the UK (paragraph 9.52);

(42) the availability of dental services to the handicapped should be further improved by the payment of fees authorised on a discretionary basis by the dental estimates boards (paragraph 9.53);

(43) the government should introduce legislation to compel water authorities to fluoridate water supplies at the request of health authorities (paragraph 9.60);

(44) the health departments should pursue an active policy in restricting advertising which may lead to undesirable dietary habits, particularly in children (paragraph 9.68);

(45) the dental profession should consider ways of overcoming the problems of long term clinical research in dentistry (paragraph 9.71);

(46) a small committee representing government and the other interested parties should be set up to review the development of dental health policy (paragraphs 9.18, 9.31 and 9.74);

(47) the health departments should promote more research both on the acceptability of day admissions to patients, and on the benefits to the NHS (paragraph 10.19);

(48) all hospitals should provide facilities for patients and relatives to be seen in private (paragraph 10.28);

(49) all hospitals should provide explanatory booklets for patients before they come into hospital (paragraph 10.29);

(50) hospitals should ensure that the availability of amenity beds is routinely made known to patients when they are given a date for admission (paragraph 10.34);

(51) health authorities should review forthwith wakening times for patients in the hospitals for which they are responsible (paragraph 10.38);

(52) the health departments should now state categorically that they no longer expect health authorities to close mental illness hospitals unless they are very isolated, in very bad repair or are obviously redundant due to major shifts of population (paragraph 10.60);

(53) the government should find extra funds to permit much more rapid replacement of hospital buildings than has so far been possible and they should stick to their plans (paragraph 10.74);

(54) community health councils should have right of access to family practitioner committee meetings and their equivalent in Scotland and Northern Ireland. If FPCs are abolished as we propose in Chapter 20, CHCs should have access to the committees which take over their functions (paragraph 11.9);

(55) CHCs should be given more resources to enable them to inform the public fully about local services (paragraph 11.10);

(56) more resources should be made available where necessary to allow CHCs to act as the "patient's friend" in complaints procedures (paragraphs 11.25 and 11.26);

(57) health departments and health authorities should continue to give financial support and to encourage voluntary effort in the NHS (paragraph 11.32);

(58) financial support should be given to encourage the setting up of patient committees in general practice (paragraph 11.34).

Part III The NHS and its workers

22.39 In this part of the report we dealt in the main with matters which concern directly those who work in the NHS. We dealt successively with general manpower matters; nurses, midwives and health visitors; doctors; and ambulance, ancillary, professional, scientific and technical, works and maintenance staff.

General manpower matters

22.40 We began Chapter 12 by considering the morale of workers in the NHS. We were told by many people that morale was low, but we saw this as a symptom rather than an underlying or constitutional disorder. We made no recommendations about morale itself, but we hoped that the recommendations we made in this chapter and elsewhere in the report would lead to improvement.

22.41 We were in no doubt that industrial relations in the NHS were in need of improvement. At local level adequate machinery and staff were often lacking and it was clear that urgent action was needed. We welcomed the proposals for procedures to deal speedily with local disputes which had been put to the General Whitley Council, and we hoped that they could soon be introduced. We also welcomed the survey into industrial relations in the health and personal social services which was being undertaken in Northern Ireland. We found no single solution to the problem of industrial action in the NHS, but we hoped that better local procedures would help to eliminate local disputes of the kind which had plagued the service in recent years.

22.42 We were aware that the pay of NHS workers was a major cause of dispute at national level. The Whitley Council system had a number of faults: in particular, its sometimes cumbersome procedures might lead to excessive delays in reaching new agreements. We hoped that Lord McCarthy's review would lead to improvements. It seemed to us that as pay negotiating bodies, the Whitley Councils were weakened by being insufficiently independent of government. This meant that pay disputes might have to be resolved in some other forum.

22.43 We thought it essential that a procedure should be worked out for resolving national disputes about pay. This would involve a review of existing pay arrangements, including the role of the Whitley Councils. It would take time and patience. We thought the initiative could best come from the TUC, and that in due course proposals should be put to the Secretaries of State and the NHS management interests.

22.44 We observed that the changing character of health care required flexibility in the roles of those working in the NHS, but that responsibilities and duties should be clear. We noted that in certain circumstances the two might pull in opposite directions, and that multi-disciplinary working brought out some of the difficulties. Another aspect was the need to assess the quality of the treatment and care provided by NHS workers: this could best be undertaken by the professions themselves, but the health departments should ensure that adequate progress was made. We considered whether it would be possible to lay down staff norms to forecase needs and deficiencies, and eliminate shortages. We concluded that the needs and resources of different parts of the UK varied so greatly that centralised planning for all NHS staff would be wholly impracticable. Recruitment decisions should, for the most part, be made locally in the light of local needs within an overall policy, but an exception to this was medical and dental manpower both because it took ten years or more to expand facilities for training doctors and dentists, and because of the extent of the involvement of the universities. We considered that in all cases staff interests needed to be consulted and that the health departments should ensure that the machinery for this was adequate.

22.45 Finally, we considered that the NHS should assume the same responsibility as any other employer for the health and safety of its staff.

Nurses, midwives and health visitors

22.46 We remarked that it would be difficult to over-estimate the importance of nursing services in the NHS. We were conscious that nurses were the most numerous and the most costly group of health workers, but more important was the close relationship they had with patients. We were therefore disturbed by criticisms of standards of care made by the Royal College of Nursing and referred to in our evidence.

22.47 Our whole approach to the questions discussed in Chapter 13 was coloured by the report of the Briggs Committee. The Committee dealt with matters which we would otherwise have had to discuss. We were disappointed that more progress had not been made with implementing their recommendations. We understood that there had been disagreement in the profession over some aspects of the Committee's Report, and, like many other desirable reforms, that the follow-up work on the report had been held up by NHS reorganisation. In particular, we noted that little progress had been made on the clear recommendation, which we endorsed, for more nurse teachers. However, we greeted the Nurses, Midwives and Health Visitors Act 1979, which set up the new statutory educational bodies as a welcome, if long-awaited, development.

22.48 We were aware that the profession was going through a difficult period. It had suffered major structural changes following the Salmon and

Mayston Reports and was considerably influenced by the management changes introduced at reorganisation. Nurse administrators fulfil a necessary function but to do their jobs properly needed adequate supporting staff. It was evident that the role of the nurse was varied and was being further extended and expanded by, for example, research into the caring function of the nurse, and development of specialisation. We found a need to improve the clinical career structure, and to encourage flexibility in the way nurses worked.

22.49   Developments in nurse education had been delayed pending the new statutory bodies. We concluded that the Central Council for Nursing, Midwifery and Health Visiting would need to review both basic and post-basic education. Linked to this we saw a need to develop the research capacity of the profession.

Doctors

22.50   We started Chapter 14 with a brief look at the role of doctors. It was clear that what doctors did underlay many of the other problems referred to, particularly the question of how many doctors the community should be training. We found this was an extremely complex matter, but it seemed to us that it would be a mistake to cut back the planned output of medical graduates from UK universities at a time when there were shortages in some specialties and many places and more doctors were likely to be needed in future.

22.51   We gave special attention to certain groups of doctors with special problems. We were concerned that the interests of overseas doctors who had made a valuable contribution to the NHS should not be overlooked. Many of them were established residents in the UK. We thought it particularly important that doctors coming here from overseas should be made aware of the career prospects and standards required. Proper provision needed also to be made for the post-graduate education of women doctors who were coming out of the medical schools in increasing numbers. We thought that Joint Higher Training Committees should look carefully at their policies. Community physicians were another group with problems. It was evident that the specialty needed to be supported in the next few years if it were to survive. This would mean both imaginative recruitment policies and the willingness of health authorities to provide the supporting staff necessary. Those working in universities could be encouraged to have a service commitment in the NHS.

22.52   We did not like the new contracts negotiated for hospital doctors. They seemed to us to be inappropriate to a leading profession and ultimately contrary to the interests of the patients. We did not regard the proposed new contract for GPs with any more enthusiasm. On the other hand we thought that the importance of the relationship between GPs and NHS, the contractor status was exaggerated. We considered that a salary option should be introduced for those GPs whose circumstances required it, but we did not propose that all GPs should be salaried. It seemed to us that the present career structure for hospital doctors had obvious defects. We feared that the current strategy would yield results too slowly and we set out an alternative approach in Appendix I. One aspect of the hospital career structure was the distinction awards system where we welcomed relaxation of secrecy and a shift of emphasis towards rewarding those consultants who deserved most of the NHS.

Ambulance, ancillary, professional, scientific and technical, works and maintenance staff

22.53   We noted that the Professions Supplementary to Medicine Act 1960 had established elaborate registration machinery for eight professions, the vast majority of whose members were employed in the NHS. It had been criticised as leaving too much power in the hands of professional bodies so that desirable developments, such as integrated training for some of the professions, had been blocked. We thought it time that the machinery set up by the Act was reviewed.

22.54   Scientific and technical staff had been considered by the Zuckerman Committee who published their report in 1968. We understood that its main recommendations, though accepted in principle by the government, had not been implemented, partly because NHS reorganisation had interfered with the structural proposals, and partly because of the difficulties in negotiating the necessary staffing arrangements. We were told that the health departments were considering the best way forward and we supported their general strategy. However, much of our evidence on these services had been about who should head and manage laboratories, and we did not think that the solution suggested by the DHSS of dividing the managerial responsibilities was realistic. We considered that the best available scientist should be appointed as head; the possession of a medical qualification would be an advantage when there were two candidates of equal ability. We considered that moves towards the establishment of a National Scientific Council, proposed by the Zuckerman Committee, should be encouraged.

22.55   We had received comparatively little evidence about the other groups of staff considered in Chapter 15 and we did not feel justified in proposing major changes. We suggested experimenting with ways of providing an ambulance service and we thought it important that more effort should be put into providing induction training for ancillary staff. Works officers were a new group, formed at reorganisation, and we concluded that it would be important to keep the framework within which they operated under review. They were essential to the success of the accelerated building programme which we proposed in Chapter 10.

Recommendations on the NHS and its workers

(59)   the health departments and staff organisations and unions should give urgent attention to industrial relations training for both staff representatives and management (paragraph 12.11);

(60)   the TUC should take the necessary steps in initiating discussions on a procedure for dealing with national disputes in the NHS which must involve not only those bodies affiliated to the TUC but bodies representing the interests of other NHS workers as well (paragraph 12.24);

(61) the health departments should intervene on those occasions when the health professions cannot reach agreement on staff roles (paragraph 12.43);

(62) the Joint Higher Training Committees for post-graduate medical education should approve only those units and departments where an accepted method of evaluating care has been instituted (paragraph 12.54);

(63) a planned programme for the introduction of audit or peer review of standards of care and treatment should be set up for the health professions by their professional bodies and progress monitored by the health departments (paragraph 12.56);

(64) the health departments should undertake, approximately every two years, a review of the medical manpower position, following open and public discussion and supported by better data than has so far been available (paragraph 12.63);

(65) experiments with different mixes of staff in different contexts, and the development of inter-professional training should be encouraged (paragraph 12.65);

(66) the NHS should assume the same responsibility as any other employer for the health and safety of its staff and set up an occupational health service (paragraph 12.67);

(67) the profession and the health departments should encourage and pursue experiments in the development of the nursing role (paragraph 13.23);

(68) research is required into the effect of the use of unqualified nursing staff on patient care and into the best composition of the ward team in different settings (paragraph 13.29);

(69) the health departments should undertake such central manpower planning as is necessary, that is develop a national recruitment policy, assist the setting of standards and objectives, propagate good practice and ensure an adequate data base which will be of considerable importance to the new statutory educational bodies (paragraph 13.31);

(70) the clinical role of the nursing officer should be developed along the lines envisaged by the Salmon Committee (paragraph 13.40);

(71) the development of specialist knowledge and nursing skills both in the community and hospital should be encouraged (paragraph 13.42);

(72) health authorities should establish budgets and develop programmes of post-basic nursing education for their staff (paragraph 13.52);

(73) developments of joint appointments between schools of nursing and the service should be vigorously pursued (paragraph 13.55);

(74) the health departments should show more determination in enforcing their priorities in the medical staff shortage specialities, if necessary by blocking expansion of other specialities, and should be more critically involved in the development of new specialities (paragraph 14.32);

(75) the development of special interests in shortage specialities amongst doctors working in related fields should be encouraged and appropriate training programmes provided (paragraph 14.33);

(76) the UK government should take the necessry steps to make clear to doctors who want to come to the UK what their prospects here are (paragraph 14.41);

(77) a few post-graduate centres to provide medical education and training specifically geared to the needs of overseas countries should be started on an experimental basis (paragraph 14.42);

(78) community physicians should be given adequate supporting staff (paragraph 14.56);

(79) a salary option should be introduced and open to any GP who prefers it (paragraph 14.82);

(80) there should be an independent review of the machinery set up by the Professions Supplementary to Medicine Act 1960. It should include manpower and training needs of the professions (paragraph 15.7);

(81) the health departments should continue their efforts to generate more research into the work of speech therapists, occupational therapists, physiotherapists and remedial gymnasts (paragraph 15.12);

(82) staff in senior posts in the scientific and technical services should normally be science graduates (paragraph 15.20);

(83) pilot experiments should be carried out in providing a regional scientific service for one or more laboratory specialities (paragraph 15.21);

(84) the head of a laboratory should be the most able scientist available (paragraph 15.31);

(85) in one or two instances the accident and emergency ambulance service should be organised experimentally on a regional basis with "community transport services" being provided by the lower tier NHS authorities; and the results closely monitored (paragraph 15.41);

(86) health authorities should ensure that adequate induction training (including access to language courses where appropriate) is available for ancillary staff (paragraph 15.47);

(87) the works staffing structure should be kept under review by the health departments, as should the numbers and training of craftsmen (paragraph 15.53).

Part IV The NHS and other institutions

22.56 In this part of the report we looked at the important links which the NHS has with services and institutions outside it. We dealt successively with the NHS and local authorities; the relationship between the NHS and universities, particularly so far as education and research are concerned; and finally with the relationship between the NHS and private practice.

The NHS and local authorities

22.57 In our view there was no doubting the importance of effective collaboration between health and local authority services. We found that while eventually the integration of these services might become possible, there was little in the present administrative arrangements to prevent or even hamper such collaboration, though its success depended on the attitude of the parties to it. If there was determination on both sides to work together many of the problems could be solved. If, however, authorities or professions were at loggerheads, coterminous boundaries, overlapping membership and joint committees would be ineffective. Post-reorganisation experience had showed that effective collaboration required that those involved should have appropriate training and sufficient authority within their own organisations to carry out the task which was to be performed jointly. Continuity in post of the personnel involved was particularly important.

22.58 It was clear from our evidence that the relationships between health and local authorities ranged from indifferent to excellent. It was hardly surprising to find this variation, given the different circumstances in which the new authorities found themselves when the new services were introduced. We considered, however, that the changes which we recommended in Chapter 20 to the local management of the NHS would greatly improve working relationships. This improvement would be assisted if there were more emphasis on the education and continuing training of health and social work professionals on the importance of inter-professional collaboration. The joint report of the Personal Social Services Council and the Central Health Services Council on collaboration had identified such training carried out jointly, and better communication, the development of multi-disciplinary working and the development of agreed procedures as ways in which better collaboration could be achieved at field level. Good working relationships were clearly of the essence. We endorsed this approach and we identified a number of requirements for effective collaboration and planning at all levels.

22.59 We did not recommend radical changes in the responsibility for either the health or the personal social services in Chapter 16. The evidence we had received tended to divide according to the interest of the organisation concerned: local authorities often argued for local government control of the NHS, and health authorities advocated the absorption by the NHS of the social work services. We were also doubtful of the benefits which might arise from an allocation of responsibility for patient and client groups. It was obvious that no radical solution would command general support, but in any case we did not think changes of this kind were necessary at present simply to achieve better collaboration between the NHS and local authorities. Joint administration of health and local authority services might become feasible if regional government were introduced in England. We considered that if such a change reached the political agenda in the next 20 years, joint administration of health and local authority services would merit serious consideration.

The NHS, the universities and research

22.60 We noted in Chapter 17 that the arrangements that existed for consultation between the NHS and the universities had been disturbed by NHS reorganisation. The transfer of responsibility from boards of governors with direct access to the health ministers to area health authorities would have given rise to difficulty at any time until the new arrangements had settled down, but had been made much more difficult by the financial pressures on the NHS. We considered that both parties would have to work at getting the new relationship going properly: on the NHS side this would mean making sure that universities were properly consulted on matters which affected them, and on the university side it might mean that the Vice-Chancellor (or Principal) or Dean of the Medical School had to be personally involved. We were doubtful whether consultation arrangements at national level between educational and health interests were adequate.

22.61 We thought it likely that teaching hospitals would have found themselves under financial pressure even if NHS reorganisation had not occurred because of the general pressure on NHS resources since 1974. We observed a conflict between the short-term needs of the NHS and the importance of providing for the future. The teaching hospitals felt themselves exposed to the pressures of keeping the NHS going, but this would have had to be faced whatever the financing arrangements. We strongly supported centres of excellence, but we thought that the teaching hospitals would in the long run gain through their closer integration into the NHS. We observed that it was a difficult time for the teaching hospitals, but the example of Scotland should offer some encouragement. Another aspect of the financial pressures was the tendency for both university and NHS to start counting the cost of services provided to the other. We considered that this was a profitless occupation since the funds being argued over came from the Exchequer in any case, and the loss of flexibility, not to mention the complexities of computation, would merely make for future difficulties.

22.62 Although there had been criticisms of undergraduate medical education this was not an area into which we went in detail. The curriculum had been criticised on the grounds that it was not as relevant as it should have been to the work of doctors in the NHS, and the selection of medical students had been criticised on the grounds that universities relied too much on academic performance and too little on other evidence of suitability. We thought there was room for development in both these areas.

22.63 Biomedical and clinical research were, we found, adequately catered for by the existing agencies, particularly the Medical Research Council. We considered, however, that health services research needed to be developed.

The NHS and private practice

22.64 We were concerned in Chapter 18 with private practice only in so far as it affected the NHS. We concentrated on the facts so far as they were known. Information to enable us to reach precise conclusions about the relationship between the NHS and private practice was lacking, but it was clear to us that the private sector was too small to make a significant impact on the NHS, except locally and temporarily. On the other hand, we felt that the private sector probably responded much more directly to patients' demands for services than the NHS, and provided a useful pointer to areas where the NHS was defective. One such was clearly the provision of abortion services: half the abortions performed on residents of the UK were undertaken privately. Another was the provision of nursing homes for the elderly; and patients waiting for cold surgery in the NHS might opt to pay rather than suffer discomfort and inconvenience for months or even years. Other important reasons for choosing the private sector were the convenience of being able to time your entry into hospital to suit yourself, being assured of reasonable privacy and choosing your own doctor. We thought that the NHS should make more effort to meet reasonable requirements of this kind.

22.65   We found that from the NHS point of view that main importance of pay beds was in the passions aroused and the consequential dislocation of work which then occurred. The establishment of the Health Services Board had led to a welcome respite from discussion of this emotional subject. However, we felt that if the Board were to carry out its functions of safeguarding the interests of the NHS it should be able to control the aggregate of private beds in a locality: this appeared to be a loophole at present.

Recommendations on the NHS and other institutions

(88) before any collaboration begins, its purpose, form and resource impli-cations should be identified with the different agencies and professions involved (paragraph 16.3);

(89) in Northern Ireland the present integration of the health and personal social services should be encouraged and further developed (paragraph 16.28);

(90) there should be more emphasis in the education and continuing training of health and social work professionals on the importance of inter-professional collaboration (paragraph 16.31);

(91) there should be no radical change in the responsibilities for either the health or the personal social services (paragraph 16.32);

(92) a formal structure at national level to co-ordinate the policies of the health departments, the University Grants Committee and the universi-ties shold be considered by the parties concerned (paragraph 17.12);

(93) an independent enquiry should be set up to consider the special health service problems of London, including the administration of the post-graduate teaching hospitals, whether London needs four RHAs, whether some special adjustment to the RAWP formula is required to take account of the high concentration of teaching hospitals in London, and what additional measures can be devised to deal with difficulties of providing primary care services and joint planning in London (paragraph 17.18);

(94) NHS staff who are required to teach students should have this requirement written into their contracts (paragraph 17.25);

(95) the health departments should as a matter of national policy fund chairs or senior lectureships, or promote joint NHS/university appointments as in Northern Ireland, in the priority specialties (paragraph 17.31);

(96) universities should encourage and monitor experiments in different approaches to student selection which take account of factors other than traditional academic criteria (paragraph 17.32);

(97) an Institute of Health Services Research should be established for England and Wales to encourage systematic research into health care issues and its activities and output should be carefully evaluated. The health departments in Scotland and Northern Ireland should consider their position as separate institutions may not be appropriate there (paragraph 17.39);

(98) health authorities in Great Britain should have the broad objective of providing for about 75% of all abortions on resident women to be performed in the NHS over the next few years (paragraph 18.13);

(99) the capital element of pay bed charges should cover both the interest and depreciation costs of the capital investment in pay beds (paragraph 18.37);

(100) the Health Services Board should be given power to control, and a responsibility to consider, the aggregates of beds in private hospitals and nursing homes when any new private development is considered in a locality (paragraph 18.39).

Part V Management and Finance

22.66 In this section of the report we looked in detail at how the present system operated and what could be done to improve matters. We thought that while this part of our report might be of greatest interest to many who work in the NHS, management and finance questions were essentially secondary to those subjects which bore directly on patient care.

Parliament, health ministers and their departments

22.67 The roles of health ministers, permanent secretaries and the health departments, and their relations with the NHS, seemed to us to stem from the way that the NHS was financed. Arrangements for accounting for NHS finance followed the classic Whitehall model under which the minister was answerable to Parliament and the permanent secretary personally accountable, for every penny spent and every action taken in the NHS. This arrangement seemed to us to be quite inappropriate to an organisation the size of the NHS whose staff were not civil servants and some of whom – for example, doctors – might not be answerable to anyone else for the expenditure they incurred. It appeared to us that the system had been made to work by those immediately concerned, to their credit, but that there was nevertheless a gap between the theoretical and the actual position. The effect of this could be seen in the uncertainties over the respective roles of the health departments and the NHS.

22.68 After a good deal of reflection, and having considered a number of alternatives, we concluded in Chapter 19 that the best solution to this fundamental difficulty was to place responsibility for the detailed working of the NHS in England with the regional health authorities themselves. We also mentioned the position outside England. This would end the anomalous position of the Secretary of State for Social Services and his permanent secretary being held responsible for actions over which in practice they could have little control. The division of responsibility between the regional health authorities and the Department of Health and Social Security would need to be worked out, but in broad terms we saw the former as accountable for the delivery of the service and the latter for national policies and functions. It was clear to us that neither the DHSS and Welsh Office, nor some of the health authorities in England and Wales, were carrying out adequately their monitoring functions and this responsibility should have their urgent attention.

Health authorities and their organisation

22.69 Although the reorganisation of the NHS had come under attack in the evidence we received, the pre-1974 system had been criticised on many of the same grounds. Other factors over which the NHS had little control adversely affected the morale of those who worked in the service while the organisation was being implemented. We tried, therefore, to see the changes in perspective.

22.70 The introduction of consensus management and the proliferation of advisory committees had been criticised and in Chapter 20 we suggested ways in which practical difficulties in their operation might be overcome. A more serious problem was the decline in the quality of hospital administration. We concluded that the status of the institutional manager had to be improved and a satisfactory medical contribution to hospital administration achieved.

22.71 Although the importance of structure in the efficient operation of the NHS could be exaggerated, we had received an impressive weight of evidence to suggest that in most places there was one tier too many. We took the view that in England regions should be the main planning authorities and the structure below regions should be simplified. We considered that, except in a minority of cases, there should be one tier below region or health department. In most cases this would mean the creation of more single district areas. In some it would mean merging existing districts or creating new authorities by dividing existing areas. We felt a flexible approach to structural change would be very important. The other main change we wanted to see in the structure was the abolition of separate family practitioner committees in England and Wales and the adoption there of the Scottish pattern of administration of family practitioner services.

Finance

22.72 We found no objective or universally acceptable method of establishing what the "right" level of expenditure on the NHS should be. Some of our recommendations would increase NHS expenditure, but others should lead to savings. On balance our recommendations would increase the cost of the NHS, but our judgement was that these additional resources would be justified by the benefits which would flow from them. We also considered it right that the nation should spend more on the NHS as it got wealthier.

22.73 We made our own broad assessment of the financial implications of our recommendations, but in most cases we have not included them in our report. The accurate costing of any recommendation that affects the NHS in the four parts of the UK would be difficult enough if undertaken by the health departments themselves. For obvious reasons we could not ask them to do this exercise for us, and we had neither the time nor resources to make other than the most rudimentary estimates.

22.74   In our view no method of financing a part of national expenditure as large and as politically sensitive as the health service was likely to remove it from government influence. Discussion of the merits of alternative methods of finance ought therefore to focus on their implications for the way the health service was organised and performed, rather than on the total amount of finance they would generate. We were not convinced that the claimed advantages of insurance finance or substantial increases in revenue from charges would outweigh their undoubted disadvantages in terms of equity and administrative costs. The same disadvantages arose from the existing NHS charges.

22.75   We found that the geographical distribution of the provision of health care had become fairer since the NHS was founded but there was still some way to go. It was essential that the resource allocation procedure adopted should be the subject of informed and public scrutiny and we welcomed the recent change to explicit formulae based on estimates of need.

22.76   The system of financial management in the NHS did not sufficiently encourage efficient resource use. Much of the information required for effective management was not produced, or was inaccurate, or too late to be of value. Those held responsible for expenditure were often not in a position to control it. We commended Professor Perrin's report to the health departments.

Recommendations on management and finance

(101) a select committee on the NHS should be set up (paragraph 19.11);

(102) formal responsibility, including accountability to Parliament, for the delivery of services should be transferred to regional health authorities (paragraph 19.34);

(103) the health departments should give further guidance about the role of members of consensus management teams (paragraph 20.15);

(104) the health departments should urgently consider with the professions concerned the best way of simplifying the present professional advisory committee structure (paragraph 20.20);

(105) the role of the hospital administrator at unit or sector level should be expanded (paragraph 20.27);

(106) there should be a review of the number of functional managers above unit level (paragraph 20.27);

(107) regional health authorities in England should continue to be responsible principally for planning and for the major functions they carry out at present (paragraph 20.45);

377

(108) below region in England, and elsewhere in the UK below health department, except in a minority of cases, one management level only should carry operational responsibility for services and for effective collaboration with local government (paragraph 20.46);

(109) each regional health authority in England and the health departments in Scotland, Wales and Northern Ireland should institute a review of the structure for which it is responsible. The Department of Health and Social Security should monitor this review in England (paragraph 20.51);

(110) Family Practitioner Committees in England and Wales should be abolished and their functions assumed by health authorities as a step towards integration (paragraph 20.57);

(111) the process of introducing the changes recommended in Chapter 20 should be completed within two years of the end of the period of consultation (paragraph 20.66);

(112) it is for government to decide how the NHS should be funded, but there is a firm case for the gradual but complete extinction of charges (paragraphs 21.28 and 21.29);

(113) the health departments should prosecute the research necessary for improvement of the resource allocation formulae (paragraphs 21.41 and 21.42);

(114) there should be an explicit formula for the distribution of funds to the health service in the four parts of the United Kingdom (paragraph 21.43);

(115) the main proposals of the Collier report on equipment and supplies should be implemented as quickly as possible (paragraph 21.49);

(116) health departments should encourage experiments with budgeting (paragraphs 21.52 and 21.55);

(117) a study of the desirability and feasibility of common budgets for family practitioner services and hospital and community services expenditure should be undertaken (paragraph 21.64).

The Future

22.77 We believe that the recommendations we have made will, if accepted, make the NHS more suited to caring for the health of the nation now and in the future. But there are numerous influences on the need for health services not all of which are predictable. This is a highly speculative area, but we felt that we should sketch out some of the more obvious possibilities.

22.78 The demographic change which will be the greatest single influence on the shape of the NHS for the rest of this century, is the growing number of old people and particularly those over 75. This will increase the need for long term care. In addition, demand for services for the mentally ill and the mentally handicapped are likely to grow.

22.79 Changes in social attitudes and life-styles could be of great significance, but their direction and extent are unpredictable. We do not know for example, what percentage of women with families will wish to go out to work and over what period or periods in their lives. What they do will affect the care of old people, sick people and of children, and may influence significantly the emotional stability of children. Life styles of young people in this country have changed dramatically since the NHS was established and further change is certain. Habits of eating, taking alcohol and sexual behaviour could alter with profound effects on health. Groups of the population, now uncaring for their health, might become more self-conscious and take a pride in it, reducing the burden on health services.

22.80 Advances in the sciences basic to medicine will increase knowledge of the causation of disease and thus assist towards its control. Advances in molecular and cell biology, for example, will lead to a better understanding of genetic susceptibility and of some inherited diseases. Immunology is at present a thriving science within medicine. New drugs have in the past decade greatly assisted the treatment of peptic ulcers, asthma, hypertension, Parkinson's Disease and some blood cancers; and there is every reason to think that progress in pharmacology will continue. Psychology is contributing significantly to the treatment of disturbed behaviour in the neurotically ill and the mentally handicapped. Sociological insights are illuminating the interaction between the providers of services and the patients who seek their help.

22.81 The impressive contribution which acute medicine has made in relieving illness and suffering seems likely to continue. Diagnosis is continually being improved and refined by technological developments. Techniques such as tomography, ultra-sound and radio-isotope scanning have been major advances. Analytical tools of great importance such as mass spectrometry, radio-immunology and radioenzymatic techniques have been added to the battery of 100 or more tests and investigations which a clinical laboratory in a district general hospital now provides. Advanced technology has contributed to the development of incubators for premature babies, renal transplantation, cardiac pacemakers and hip replacement. It is likely that bioengineering will increasingly assist orthopaedics. At the same time the emphasis on acute and high technology medicine is being challenged and more thought is being given to the care of the chronically sick and elderly. These developments are likely to continue.

22.82   Computers will more and more be used in most areas of medical research and practice, in the laboratories, in patient information services, in hospital wards in monitoring patients as well as in recording data about them and the drugs which they receive. Diagnosis in some fields is already being considerably assisted by computers. The micro-electronics revolution is certain to have a major impact in medicine, to a degree which it is likely very few of those working in the NHS at present envisage. Improved data collection would assist better planning of services.

22.83   Technological and service developments in the NHS have implications for its cost. The NHS has already to spend about one per cent more each year merely to provide its existing standard of service on account of the increasing numbers of elderly. While some scientific advances reduce costs, most tend to increase them, so the future state of the national economy will have an important influence on the NHS and its capacity to provide new or better services.

22.84   One aspect of the NHS which is unlikely to change is the importance of its staff. By its nature the NHS is labour-intensive and this places a special responsibility on it to enable its workers to contribute in an effective way.

22.85   Predictions can be made by extrapolation from the state and the trend of things now. It is possible, however, that the greatest changes will come unexpectedly. Certainly changes in society which could potentially have the widest effects are also the least predictable. The NHS should therefore be geared for the maximum flexibility in response.

22.86   In our review of the NHS as it exists we found much about which we can all be proud. Our examination of foreign health systems for the most part reinforced that view. If in considering some aspects in detail we have made specific criticisms, we have done this in the hope that in the future the NHS can provide a better service, not because we think it is in danger of collapse. The developments which we have suggested the future might bring will produce considerable change for the service and those who work in it. We are confident that they will meet the challenge.

ALL OF WHICH WE HUMBLY SUBMIT FOR YOUR MAJESTY'S GRACIOUS CONSIDERATION

Alec Merrison (*Chairman*)
Ivor Batchelor
Paul Bramley
Thomas Brown
Ann Clwyd
Peter Jacques
Jean McFarlane
Audrey Prime
Kathleen Richards
Sally Sherman
Simpson Stevenson
Cyril Taylor
Christopher Wells
Frank Welsh

David de Peyer (*Secretary*)
Roy Cunningham (*Assistant Secretary*)
Alan Gilbert (*Assistant Secretary*)

21 June 1979

Appendix A 1 Evidence Submitted to the Royal Commission

We list below the organisations and individuals who submitted evidence to the Royal Commission. Most of those listed gave written evidence. Those marked * also gave oral evidence, and those marked ** gave oral evidence only. In addition to those listed we received evidence from two organisations and 20 individuals who asked that their names should not be revealed, and a number of anonymous submissions. Except in those cases where we were asked to regard the evidence as confidential, copies of all the evidence submitted to us have been deposited with the Public Record Offices in London and Belfast, the Scottish Record Office and the National Library of Wales.

Organisations

Aberconwy CHC

Aberdare Health Patients Committee and Primary Care Team

Aberdeen Local Health Council

Action on Smoking and Health

Action on Smoking and Health (West Midlands)

** Advisory Committee on Distinction Awards

Advisory Conciliation and Arbitration Service

Advisory Council on Social Work (in Scotland)

Age Concern (England)

Age Concern (Scotland)

Age Concern (Sunbury and Shepperton Branch)

** A Group of Chairmen and Chief Officers of the Health and Social Services Boards in Northern Ireland

** A Group of Scottish Health Board Chairmen and Chief Officers

Airedale District CHC

Allied Medical Group Ltd

Anatomical Society of Great Britain and Ireland

Area and District Works Officers (Wessex)

Area Chairmen (North Western Region)

Area Dental Officers (Mersey Region)

Area Dental Officers (Thames Regions)

Area Dental Officers (Trent Region)

Area Dental Officers of Coventry Shropshire Warwickshire Hereford Worcestershire and Staffordshire

Area Dental Officers of Dudley Sandwell Walsall and Wolverhampton

Area JCC for Ealing Hammersmith and Hounslow

Area Medical Advisory Chairmen

Area Medical Committee of Merton Sutton and Wandsworth

Area Nurses/Child Health (Inner London)

Area Nurses/Child Health (North Western Region)

Area Nursing Officers (Inner London)

Area Pharmaceutical Advisory Committee Eastern Health and Social Services Board Northern Ireland

Area Scientific Advisory Committee of West Sussex Area

Area Works Officers Association (Wales)

Argyll and Bute LHC

Argyll and Clyde Health Board

Association of Anaesthetists of Great Britain and Ireland

Association of Area Medical Officers

Association of Assistant Mistresses

Association of British Clinical Neurophysiologists

Association of British Paediatric Nurses

Association of British Pharmaceutical Industry

Association of Chief Administrators (North Western Branch)

Association of Chief Administrators of Health Authorities

Association of Chief Administrators of Health Authorities (Welsh Regional Branch)

Association of Chief Chiropody Officers ·

Association of Child Psychotherapists

Association of Clinical Biochemists Ltd

Association of Clinical Pathologists

Association of Clinical Professors and Heads of Departments of Paediatrics

Association of Clinical Professors of Medicine

* Association of Community Health Councils for England and Wales

Association of Community Orthodontists

* Association of County Councils

Association of County Councils Labour Group

Association of Dental Hospitals of the UK

Association for Dental Prostheses

Association of Directors of Education in Scotland

* Association of Directors of Social Services

* Association of Directors of Social Services (Northern Ireland)

Association of Directors of Social Services North West Regional Branch

Association of Dispensing Opticians

* Association of District Committees for the Health and Personal Social Services (Northern Ireland)

Association of District Community Physicians

* Association of District Councils

Association of District Secretaries

Association of Domestic Management

Association of Education Committees

Association of General Practitioner Hospitals

Association of Headmistresses

Association of Health Careers Advisors

Association of Health Service Personnel Officers

Association of Health Service Treasurers

Association of Hospital and Residential Care Officers

Association of Hospital Secretaries

Association for Improvements in the Maternity Services

Association of Industrial Dental Surgeons

Association of Medical Advisors in the Pharmaceutical Industry

Association of Medical Records Officers

Association of Medical Secretaries

* Association of Metropolitan Authorities

* Association of National Health Service Supplies Officers

Association of Nurse Administrators

Association of Nurse Administrators (Midland Branch)

Association of Nurse Administrators (Northern Ireland Group)

Association of Optical Practitioners

Association of Pharmacy Technicians

Association of Professors of Medical Microbiology

Association of Professions for the Mentally Handicapped

Association of Professors of Obstetrics and Gynaecology

Association of Professors of Pathology

Association of Professors of Surgery

Association of Psychiatric Nurse Tutors (Scotland)

Association of Psychiatrists in Training

Association of Radical Midwives

Association of Regional Works Officers

Association of Researchers in Medical Sciences

* Association of Scientific Technical and Managerial Staffs

ASTMS (Northern Ireland Branch)

ASTMS (Sheffield Branch)

Association of Spina Bifida and Hydrocephalus

Association of Sterile Supply Administrators

Association of Supervisors of Midwives

Association of Therapeutic Communities

Association of University Teachers of General Practice

Association of University Teachers of Psychiatry

* Association of Welsh CHCs

Association of Welsh FPCs

* Association of Welsh Health Authorities

Automobile Association

Avon AHA (T)

Avon Association of Trades Councils

Avon FPC

Aylesbury District CHC

Ayrshire and Arran Committee for Hospital Medical Services

Ayrshire and Arran Health Board

Ayrshire and Arran Health Board Nursing and Midwifery Committee

Back Pain Association Ltd

Barking and Havering AHA

Barking District CHC

Barnet/Finchley District CHC

Basingstoke and North Hampshire District CHC

Basildon and Thurrock District Consultant Staff

Basildon and Thurrock District Medical Committee

Bath CHC

Bedworth (Warwickshire) Rotary Club

Berkshire AHA

Bethlem Royal and the Maudsley Hospital

Beverley Health District CHC

Biological Engineering Society

Birmingham AHA (T)

Birmingham Society for Mentally Handicapped Children

Birth Control Trust

Bishop's Council for Social Responsibility/Diocese of Coventry

Blackpool CHC

Bolsover District Council

Bolton AHA

Bolton Hospitals Medical Staff Committee

Borders Health Board

Borders LHC

Borough of South Tyneside Council

Borrow Dental Milk Foundation

Bradford CHC

Brecknock and Radnor CHC

Brent and Harrow Area Nursing and Midwifery Professional Advisory Committee

Brent and Harrow FPC

Brent CHC

Brentwood South Ward Labour Party

Brighton CHC

Brighton Society for the Welfare of Handicapped Persons

Bristol CHC

Bristol DMT

British Acupuncture Association

British Anaesthetic and Respiratory Equipment Manufacturers' Association

British Association for Behaviourial Psychotherapy

British Association for Paediatric Nephrology

British Association for Psychopharmacology

384

British Association for the Study of Community Dentistry
British Association of Art Therapists
British Association of Dental Auxiliaries
British Association of Dermatologists
British Association of Diagnostic and Therapeutic Radiologists
British Association of Occupational Therapists
British Association of Oral Surgeons
British Association of Paediatric Surgeons
British Association of Periodontology
British Association of Plastic Surgeons
British Association of Settlements and Social Action Centres
* British Association of Social Workers
* British Association of Social Workers (Northern Ireland Branch)
British Association of Social Workers Scotland Mental Health Working Groups and Health Care
British Association of Teachers of the Deaf
British Chiropractors' Association
British Council for Rehabilitation of the Disabled
* British Dental Association
British Dental Health Foundation
British Dental Students' Association
British Dietetic Association
British Endodontic Society
British Geriatric Society
British Homoeopathic Association
British Hospitals Contributory Schemes Association (1948)
* British Hospitals Doctors Federation
British Institute of Radiology
British League against Rheumatism
* British Medical Association
BMA (Blackburn Branch)
BMA (Chesterfield Branch)
* BMA (Northern Ireland Branch)
* BMA (Scotland Branch)
British Nuclear Medicine Society
British Neuropathological Society
British Optical Society
British Orthopaedic Association
British Orthoptic Society
British Paediatric Association
British Paedodontic Society
British Postgraduate Medical Federation
British Pro-Chiropractic Association
British Psychological Society
British Red Cross Society
British Society for Digestive Endoscopy
British Society for Restorative Dentistry
British Society for the Study of Orthodontics
British Society of Periodontology
British Sociological Association
British Student Health Association
British United Provident Association
British Universities Committee on Ophthalmic Optics

Bromley AHA
Bromley CHC
Bromley FPC
Bromsgrove and Redditch CHC
Broomhill Ward Labour Party (Sheffield)
Brunel Health Services Organisation Research Unit
Buckinghamshire Area Medical Advisory Committee
Buckinghamshire Health Education Officers
Burnley Pendle and Rossendale CHC
Burpham Good Companions over 60 Club
Bury AHA
Bury CHC
Bury St. Edmunds Health District Management Team
Business Graduates' Association Ltd.

Caithness LHC
Calderdale CHC
Cambridge CHC
Cambridgeshire Area Dental Advisory Committee
Cambridgeshire AHA (T) and Professional Advisory Committees
Cambridgeshire Area Pharmaceutical Advisory Committee
Cambridgeshire County Council
Camden and Islington AHA (T)
Camden and Islington FPC
Camden North CHC
Campaign for a Democratic Health Service
Campaign for the Homeless and Rootless
Campaign for the Mentally Handicapped
Campaign for Single Homeless People
Canterbury and Thanet Health District CHC
Cardiff CHC
Camarthen/Dinefwr CHC
Casualty Surgeons' Association
Catholic Union of Great Britain and Guild of Catholic Doctors of England and Wales
Central Birmingham CHC
Central Council for Education and Training in Social Work
Central Hertfordshire Consumer Group
Central Midwives Board
Central Midwives Board for Scotland
Central Nottinghamshire CHC
Central Nottinghamshire District Hospital Medical Executive Committee
Central Nottinghamshire Health District Nurses
Central Sheffield CHC
Centre for Institutional studies North East London Polytechnic
Ceredigion CHC
Chairmen of English RHAs
Charing Cross Hospital Contact Group
Charing Cross Hospital Medical Committee
Charing Cross Hospital Medical School
Charlotte Street Association

Chartered Institute of Public Finance and Accountancy

Chartered Society of Physiotherapy

Chartered Society of Physiotherapy (Birmingham Branch)

Chelmsford CHC

Cheltenham CHC

Chest Heart and Stroke Association

Chichester CHC

Chichester District Joint Medical Staff Committee

Chief Adminstrative Medical Officers of Health Boards in Scotland

Chief Administrators South Western Region

* Chief Dental Officers of the Health Departments

Chief Laboratory Scientists (Argyll and Clyde Health Board)

Child Health Services Workers (Stafford)

Child Poverty Action Group

Child Psychiatry Section of the Scottish Division of the Royal College of Psychiatrists

Christian Medical Fellowship

Church of Scotland Church and Nation Committee

City of Aberdeen LHC

City and East London AHA (T)

City and Hackney CHC

Cleveland AHA

Cleveland County Council

Cleveland Local Dental Committee

Clinical Genetics Society

Clinical Section of the British Pharmacological Society

Clwyd Health Authority

Coleraine Ballymoney and Moyle District Committee

College of Radiographers

College of Speech Therapists

* Commission for Racial Equality and Representatives of Ethnic Minority Groups

Committee for Clinical Nursing Studies (Edinburgh)

Committee of Professors of Clinical Pharmacology and Therapeutics

* Committee of Regional Health Authority Treasurers

* Committee of Vice-Chancellors and Principals of Universities of the UK

* Common Services Agency for the Scottish Health Service

Communist Party of Great Britain

Communist Party of Ireland

Community Council of Shropshire

Community Physicians (Oxford Region)

Community Psychiatric Nurses Association

Community Relations Commission

Company Chemists Association Ltd.

Confederation of British Industry (Scotland)

* Confederation of Health Service Employees

COHSE (Yeovil Branch)

COHSE (Westwood, Halifax Branch)

COHSE (Forest Hospital Branch)

Conference of Medical Royal Colleges and their faculties in the UK

Conference of Postgraduate Dental Deans/Advisors of Universities of the UK

Conference of Postgraduate Medical Deans and Directors of Universities of the UK

Congleton War Memorial Hospital Action Committee

Conservative Medical Society

Conservation Society

Consultant Medical Staff Committee Princess Margaret Hospital Swindon

Consultant Orthodontists Group

Consultants in the Avon Health Area

Consumers' Association

Convention of Scottish Local Authorities

Co-operative Party

Co-operative Union Ltd Education Department

Cornwall CHC

Cornwall and Isles of Scilly AHA

Cornwall and Isles of Scilly FPC

Cornwall and Isles of Scilly Local Dental Committee

Council for Educational Technology for the UK

Council for Postgraduate Medical Education in England and Wales

* Council for Professions Supplementary to Medicine

Council for the Education and Training of Health Visitors

Council of Governors of Guy's Hospital Medical and Dental Schools

Council of Science and Technology Institutes

Counsel and Care for the Elderly

Coventry CHC

Coventry Evening Telegraph

Coventry Voluntary Service Council

Craigavon and Banbridge District Committee

Crewe CHC

Croydon AHA

Croydon Area Hospital Medical Committee

Croydon Area Nursing and Midwifery Committee

Croydon North East Constituency Labour Party

Cuckfield and Crawley CHC

Cuckfield and Crawley District Medical Committee

Cumbria AHA

Cumbria County Council

Cumbria FPC

Dacorum Hospital Action Group

Darlington CHC

Dartford and Gravesham CHC

Dartford and Gravesham Health District Senior Hospital Staff Committee

Dental Education Advisory Council

Dental Group Socialist Medical Association

Dental Laboratories Association Ltd.

Department of Business Studies Queens University Belfast

Department of Community Medicine St. Thomas' Hospital Medical School

Department of Community Medicine University of Sheffield

** Department of Education and Science

* Department of Health and Social Security

Department of Health and Social Security Departmental Whitley Council (Staff Side)

* Department of Health and Social Services (Northern Ireland)

Department of Neurological Surgery Radcliffe Infirmary Oxford

Department of Nursing Studies University of Edinburgh

Derbyshire AHA

Derbyshire FPC

Derbyshire Local Dental Committee

Dermatology Division (Salford AHA)

Devon AHA

Dewsbury CHC

Dewsbury Health District Management Team

Directors of the Supraregional Assay Service

Disabled Living Foundation

Disabled Motorists Federation

Disablement Income Group

District Nursing Officers (Northern Region)

Division of Neurosurgery at the Institute of Neurological Sciences Glasgow

Doctors and Over-Population Group

Doncaster Area Chemists Contractors Committee

Doncaster Area Medical Committee

Doncaster CHC

Dorset AHA

Dorset Area Medical Advisory Committee

Dorset Area Nursing and Midwifery Advisory Committee

Dorset Area Pharmaceutical Committee

Dorset Area Pharmaceutical Contractors Committee

Dudley AHA

Dumfries and Galloway Health Board

Dumfries and Galloway LHCs

Dundee LHC

Durham AHA

Durham CHC

Dwyfor CHC

Dyfed Health Authority

Dyfed Health Authority Senior Nursing Management Team

Dyfed Local Pharmaceutical Committee

ENT Surgeons of Northern Ireland

East Anglia Medical Laboratory Technicians

East Anglia RHA

East Anglia RHA Regional Manpower Committee

East Anglia Regional Medical Advisory Committee

East Berkshire CHC

East Birmingham CHC

East Birmingham Hospital Social Work Department

Eastbourne CHC

East Cumbria CHC

East Cumbria District Medical Committee

East Dorset CHC

East Glamorgan CHC

East Hertfordshire CHC

East Leicestershire CHC

East Lothian LHC

East Roding CHC

East Ross and Black Isle Council of Social Service

East Somerset CHC

East Surrey CHC

East Surrey District Medical Committee

East Surrey and Crawley and Horsham Hospitals Cogwheel Committee

East Sussex AHA

Eastern Health and Social Services Board

Eastern Regional Council of the Labour Party

Eastman Dental Hospital Board of Governors and Committee of Management of the Institute of Dental Surgery

Edgware/Hendon CHC

Edinburgh Council of Social Service

Edinburgh District LHC

Edinburgh Medical Group Research Project Working Group on Ethics and the allocation of Scarce Resources in Health Care

Elizabeth Garrett Anderson Hospital Medical Council

Enfield and Haringey AHA

Enfield CHC

Environmental Health Officers' Association

Equal Opportunities Commission

Essex AHA

European Dialysis and Transplant Association

Exeter and District CHC

Fabian Society

Faculty of Anaesthetists of the Royal College of Surgeons of England

Faculty of Community Medicine of the Royal Colleges of Physicians of the United Kingdom

Faculty of Dental Surgery Royal College of Surgeons of England

Faculty of Homeopathy

* Faculty of Medicine Queens University Belfast

Faculty of Ophthalmologists

Family Planning Association

Federated Associations of Medical Technology

Federation of Associations of Clinical Professors

Federation of Bangladesh Associations

Federation of District Hospitals of Northern Ireland

Federation of Optical Corporate Bodies

Federation of Personnel Services of Great Britain Ltd.

Fellowship for Freedom in Medicine Ltd.

Fife Health Board

Fluoridation Society

Frenchay District CHC

Frenchay District Hospital Medical Advisory Committee

Frimley Park Hospital Consultants' Staff Committee

Fund for the Replacement of Animals in Medical Experiments

General and Municipal Workers' Union

General Dental Council

General Dental Practitioners' Association

General Medical Council

General Medical Services Committee of the British Medical Association

General Nursing Council for England and Wales

General Nursing Council for Scotland

General Optical Council

General Synod of the Church of England Board for Social Responsibility

Glasgow Dental Hospital and School

Gloucester Association of Leagues of Hospital Friends

Gloucester District CHC

Gloucestershire AHA

Grampian Association of Health Service Unions

Great Yarmouth and Waveney CHC

Greater Glasgow Area Committee for Hospital Medical Services

Greater Glasgow Eastern District LHC

Greater Glasgow Eastern District Medical Committee

Greater Glasgow Health Board

Greater Glasgow Health Board Consultative Committee on Psychological Services

Greater Glasgow Northern District LHC

Greater Glasgow South Eastern District LHC

Greater Glasgow Western District LHC

Greater London Council

Grimsby CHC

Guild of British Dispensing Opticians

Guild of British Newspaper Editors

Guild of Health Education Officers Ltd

Guy's Hospital Medical and Dental Schools

Gwent Area Pharmaceutical Committee

Gwent FPC

Gwent Health Authority

Gwynedd Health Authority

** HM Treasury

Hackney Trades Council

Halton CHC

Hamilton and East Kilbride LHC

Hampshire AHA

Hampshire CHCs

Hampshire Local Dental Committee

Haringey CHC

Harlow District Management Team

Harrogate CHC

Harrow CHC

Harry Edwards Spiritual Healing Sanctuary Trust

Hastings District CHC

Havering CHC

Heads of Departments of Prosthetic Dentistry of the University Dental Hospitals in the United Kingdom and Eire

Healing Research Trust

* Health Advisory Service

* Health and Safety Commission

* Health Education Council

Health Education Officers Group (North East Thames Region)

Health Service Press and Public Relations Officers Group·

Health Service Social Workers' Group

Health Services Planning Research Project Nuffield Centre for Health Services Studies University of Leeds

Health Visitors' Association

Helping Hand Organisation

Help the Aged

Hereford CHC

Hereford and Worcester AHA

Hereford and Worcester Local Medical Committee

Hereford and Worcester Social Services Department

Hertfordshire AHA

Hertfordshire Area Pharmaceutical Advisory Committee

Hertfordshire Association for the Disabled

Hertfordshire Family Practitioner Committee

Hertfordshire Local Pharmaceutical Committee

Highland Health Board

High Wycombe CHC

Hillingdon AHA

Horton General Hospital Consultants

Hospital Caterers' Association

Hospital Chaplaincies Council

Hospital Consultants' and Specialists' Association

Hospital Contributory Schemes Association (1948)

Hospital for Sick Children Board of Governors

Hospital for Sick Children Social Services Department

Hospital Scientists' Association (Northern Ireland)

Hounslow CHC

Hull District CHC

Humberside AHA

Hummingbird Housing Association Ltd.

Ida Darwin Hospital Clinical Services Advisory Committee

Independent Hospital Group

Inner London Education Authority

Institute of Biology

Institute of Child Health University of London

Institute of Group Analysis

Institute of Health Service Administrators

Institute of Hospital Engineering

Institute of Housing

388

Institute of Internal Auditors
Institute of Medical Laboratory Sciences
Institute of Medical and Biological Illustration
Institute of Medical Sociology University of Aberdeen
Institute of Neurology National Hospital Queens Square London
Institute of Operating Theatre Technicians
Institute of Personnel Management
Institute of Practitioners in Work Study Organisation and Methods
Institute of Psychoanalysis Students' Committee
Institute of Science Technology
Institute for Social Studies in Medical Care
Institute of Welfare Officers
Institution of Chemical Engineers
Institution of Mechanical Engineers
International Hospital Federation
Inverclyde LHC
Ipswich Health District CHC
Ipswich Health District Clinical Medical Officers
Irish Association for Dental Prosthesis
Isle of Anglesey CHC
Isle of Wight Area Dental Committee
Isle of Wight Area Advisory Committee
Isle of Wight AHA Health Care Planning Team for the Elderly
Isle of Wight Area Nursing and Midwifery Committee
Isle of Wight CHC
Islington Community Midwives
Islington CHC

Joint Board of Clinical Nursing Studies
Joint Boots Pharmacists Association
Joint Committee of Professional Nursing and Midwifery Associations
Joint Consultants Committee
* Joint Standing Committee of the Scottish Royal Colleges
Junior Hospital Doctors Association

Kensington and Chelsea and Westminster AHA
Kensington and Chelsea and Westminster AHA, North West District Medical Committee and St Mary's Hospital Medical School
Kensington and Chelsea and Westminster FPC
Kensington Chelsea and Westminster (South) CHC
Kensington Labour Party
Kent AHA
Kettering and District CHC
Kettering District Hospital Medical Advisory Committee
Kidderminister CHC
Kincardine and Deeside LHC
King Edward's Hospital Fund for London
King's College Hospital Group Medical Executive Committee

King's College Hospital Medical School
King's College Hospital Registrars Executive Committee
King's CHC
King's Fund Working Party – Patients and Staff
King's Health District (District Management Team)
King's Lynn CHC
Kingston and Richmond AHA
Kingston Richmond and Esher CHC
Kingston Women's Liberation Study Group
Kirkcaldy District LHC
Kirkcaldy District Council
Kirklees AHA
Kirklees Area Medical Committee

Labour Campaign for Mental Health
Labour Party
Labour Party (North West Regional Council)
Labour Party (Redditch Branch)
Labour Party (Scottish Council)
Lambeth Southwark and Lewisham AHA (T)
Lambeth Southwark and Lewisham LDC
Lanarkshire Health Board Area Dental Advisory Committee
Lanarkshire Health Board Nursing and Midwifery Advisory Committee
Lancashire Area Consultants' Committee
Lancashire AHA Advisory Panel on Mental Handicap Nursing Sub-Group
Lancashire AHA Members and Officers
Lancashire AHA Senior Works Officers
Lancashire County Local Medical Committee
Lancaster District CHC
League of Friends of Hortham and Brentry Hospitals
League of Friends of the Guildford Hospitals
League of Friends of the Mid-Wales Hospital
League of Friends of the Nuffield Orthopaedic Centre Oxford
Lee Donaldson Associates
Leeds AHA (T) Eastern District Management Team
Leeds Joint Committee of Physicians
Leicester Council for Voluntary Service
Leicester Polytechnic Health Services Management Unit
Lewisham CHC
Lewisham Health District
Liberal Party
Library Association
Lincolnshire AHA
Lincolnshire County Council
Lincolnshire FPC
Lincolnshire LMC
Liverpool Central and Southern District CHC
Liverpool Eastern District CHC
Liverpool Personal Service Society

Llanelli/Dinefwr CHC
Lochaber LHC
London Ambulance Service (Trade Union Side)
London Boroughs Association
London CHCs
Londonderry Limavady and Strabane District
Medical Advisory Committee
Londonderry Limavady and Strabane District
Medical Staff Committee
London Hospital Medical Council
London Hospital Medical College
London Hospital Medical College Dental School
London Postgraduate Committee
London Postgraduate Teaching Hospitals' Matrons
London School of Hygiene and Tropical Medicine
Lothian Area Medical Committee
Lothian Health Board

Macclesfield CHC
Maidstone CHC
Manchester AHA (T)
Manchester Principal Hospital Social Workers
Mastectomy Association
Maudsley Hospital Junior Common Room
Mebyon Kernow
Medical Commission on Accident Prevention
Medical Defence Union
Medical Directors Association
Medical Practices Committee
* Medical Practitioners Union
Medical Protection Society Ltd
Medical Research Council
Medical Social Work Department North Middlesex
Hospital
Medical Society for the Study of Venereal Diseases
* Medical Staff Committee of the Royal Victoria
Hospital Belfast
Medical Womens Federation
Medicines Commission
Medway CHC
Medway Health Campaign
Medway Health District Management Team
Mental Welfare Commission for Scotland
Mersey RHA
Merseyside Council for Voluntary Service
Merthyr and Cynon Valley CHC
Merthyr Tydfil Borough Council
Merton Sutton and Wandsworth Area Medical
Committee
Merton Sutton and Wandsworth Area Nursing and
Midwifery Committee
Middlesex Hospital Medical School
Mid Devon District Council
Mid Glamorgan FPC
Mid Glamorgan Health Authority
Mid Lothian District LHC
Mid Staffordshire CHC

Mid Surrey CHC
* MIND
Monmouth Constituency Labour Party
Moorfields Eye Hospital
Monklands and Cumbernauld LHC
Moray LHC
Moyle Hospital Action Committee

* National and Local Government Officers
Association
National Association for Maternal and Child
Welfare
National Association for the Welfare of Children in
Hospital
National Association of Ambulance Officers
National Association of Area Dental Officers of
England and Wales
National Association of Area Works Officers
National Association of Citizens Advice Bureaux
National Association of Clinical Tutors
* National Association of Health Authorities
National Association of Industrial Therapy
Managers
National Association of Family Planning Doctors
National Association of Health Authorities in
England and Wales
National Association of Hospital Head Porters
National Association of Leagues of Hospital Friends
National Association of Specialists in Community
Medicine, Child Health
National Association of Theatre Nurses
National Association of Voluntary Help Organisers
National Association of Whole-time Hospital
Chaplains
National Association of District Works Officers
National Blood Transfusion Service
National Board of Catholic Women
National Childbirth Trust
National Corporation for the Care of Old People
National Council of Social Service
National Council of Women of Great Britain
National Deaf Children's Society
National Development Group for the Mentally
Handicapped
National Federation of Consumer Groups
National Federation of St Raphael Clubs
National Federation of Spiritual Healers
National Federation of Women's Institutes
National Federation of Women's Institutes
(Sparkford Branch)
National Hospitals for Nervous Diseases and the
Institute of Neurology
National Joint Committee of Working Women's
Organisations
National Labour Women's Advisory Committee
National Pharmaceutical Association
National Schizophrenia Fellowship
National Society for Mentally Handicapped
Children

National Society of Non-Smokers

National Staff Committee for Accommodation Catering and other Support Services Staff

National Staff Committee for Administrative and Clerical Staff

National Staff Committee for Ambulance Staff

National Staff Committee for Nurses and Midwives

National Training Council for the National Health Service

* National Union of Public Employees

National Union of Students Health Student Sector

National Union of Teachers

Nature Cure Clinic

Neath and Afan CHC

Netherne Hospital Professional Executive Committee

Newcastle AHA (T)

Newcastle AHA (T) Division of Medicine

Newcastle City Council

Newcastle Upon-Tyne Social Services Department

Newham CHC

Newport Constituency Labour Party

Newtownabbey District Committee

NHS Consultants Association

NHS Works Officers

NHS Works Officers' Association

NHS Works Officers' Association (Merseyside Branch)

1942 Club of Clinical Professors

Norfolk AHA

Northallerton District CHC

Northampton CHC

Northamptonshire Area Dental Committee

Northamptonshire AHA

Northamptonshire Area Nursing and Midwifery Committee

Northamptonshire FPC

Northamptonshire County Council and AHA

North Ayrshire and Arran District LHC

North Bedfordshire CHC

North Birmingham CHC

North Cornwall District Council

North Derbyshire CHC

North Devon District Joint Staff Consultative Committee

North East District (Kensington and Chelsea) CHC

North East Essex CHC

North East Thames RHA

Northern Ireland Association for Mental Health

Northern Ireland Association of Senior Administrators in the Health Services

* Northern Ireland Central Services Agency

* Northern Ireland Committee of the Irish Congress of Trade Unions

* Northern Ireland Council for Nurses and Midwives

* Northern Ireland Council for Postgraduate Medical Education

Northern Ireland Council of Social Service

* Northern Ireland Staffs Council for the Health and Social Services

Northern Joint Ophthalmic Committee

Northern Regional Area Pharmaceutical Officers

Northern Sheffield CHC

North Camden District Senior Nursing Staff

North Gwent CHC

North Hammersmith and Acton CHC

North Nottingham District Hospitals Medical Committee

North Nottingham Teaching District Personnel Department

North Staffordshire CHC

North Surrey CHC

North Tees CHC

North Tyneside AHA

North Tyneside Area Medical Advisory Committee

North Tyneside AHA Area Pharmaceutical Committee

North Tyneside CHC

Northumberland AHA

Northumberland CHC

Northumberland LMC

North Western RHA

North West Durham Health District Senior Nurse Managers

North West Health Liaison Officers Group

North West Herts CHC

North West Surrey CHC

North West Surrey District Senior Nursing Staff

North West Thames RHA

North Yorkshire AHA Hospital Pharmaceutical Advisory Committee

Norwich CHC

Nottinghamshire AHA (T)

Nottinghamshire FPC

Nuffield Orthopaedic Centre Oxford Medical Staff

Nurses' Christian Fellowship

Nurses and Midwives Whitley Council (Staff Side)

Office of Health Economics

Office of Population Censuses and Surveys

Ogwr CHC

Oldham AHA

Oldham Area Medical Advisory Committee

Oldham CHC

Open Medicine Trust

Operational Research Society

Outer Circle Policy Unit

* Overseas Doctors' Association in the UK

Oxfordshire AHA (T)

Oxfordshire Area Medical Committee

Oxfordshire Area Nursing and Midwifery Committee

Oxfordshire CHC
Oxford Regional Nursing and Midwifery Committee
Oxford Regional Review Committee
Oxford RHA
Oxford University

Paignton Co-operative Women's Guild
PA Management Consultants Ltd
Parkinsons Disease Society (Oxfordshire Branch)
Peat Marwick Mitchell & Co
Pembrokeshire Constituency Labour Party
Personal Social Services Council
Perth and Kinross LHC
Peterborough CHC
Peterborough Child Poverty Action Group
Peterborough District Medical Committee
Pharmaceutical General Council (Scotland)
Pharmaceutical Services Negotiating Committee and Welsh Central Pharmaceutical Committee
Pharmaceutical Society of Great Britain
Pharmaceutical Society of Northern Ireland
Plaid Cymru
Plymouth CHC
Portsmouth and East Hampshire Health District Professional Advisory Committee
Portsmouth Consultants and Specialists Association
Powys Area Medical Committee
Powys FPC
Powys Health Authority
Powys Health Authority Pharmaceutical Committee
Pregnancy Advisory Service
Preseli and South Pembrokeshire District Medical Committee and Pembrokeshire County War Memorial Hospital Staff Committee
Preston Business and Professional Women's Club
Preston Muslim Society
Princess Margaret Hospital Swindon Physiotherapy Department
Princess Margaret Hospital Consultant Medical Staff Committee
Principal Group Social Workers of the London Teaching Hospitals
Private Patients Plan
Professors of Psychiatry Club
Proprietary Association of Great Britain
Psychiatric Division District 3 Wandsworth Merton and Sutton AHA (T)
Psychiatric Rehabilitation Association
Public Health Nursing and Midwifery Liaison Committee
Public Records Office

Queen's University Belfast Faculty of Medicine

Radical Statistics Health Group
Radio Chemical Centre Ltd
Radiologists Group Committee of the BMA

Reading University Operational Research (Health and Social Services) Unit
Redbridge and Waltham Forest AHA
Redbridge and Waltham Forest FPC
Redditch District Labour Party
Regional Administrators of Regional Health Authorities (England)
Regional Ambulance Officers Committee
Regional and Area Medical Officers (West Midlands Region)
Regional Medical Committee (South East Thames RHA)
Regional Medical and Dental Postgraduate Education Committee (Trent Region)
Regional Medical Officers Group
Regional Nursing Officers Group
Regional Pharmaceutical Officers of the NHS
Regional Scientific Officers
Regional Specialists in Community Medicine/Information and Research
Regional Supplies Officers Committee
Registered Nursing Home Association
* Registration Boards of the Remedial Professions
Renal Association
Renfrew District LHC
Responsible Society
RHA Chairmen
Rhondda Borough Constituency Labour Party
Rhymney Valley CHC
Rochdale Area Dental Committee
Rochdale and District Community Relations Council
Rochdale Group of Hospitals Senior Medical Staff Committee
Ross and Cromarty LHC
Rotherham CHC
Royal Association in Aid of the Deaf and Dumb
* Royal College of General Practitioners
* Royal College of Midwives
* Royal College of Midwives (Northern Ireland Board)
* Royal College of Midwives (Scottish Board)
Royal College of Midwives (Welsh Board)
* Royal College of Nursing
Royal College of Nursing (Kettering Centre)
* Royal College of Nursing (Northern Ireland Board)
* Royal College of Nursing (Scottish Board)
Royal College of Obstetricians and Gynaecologists
Royal College of Pathologists
* Royal College of Physicians
* Royal College of Physicians of Edinburgh
* Royal College of Physicians and Surgeons of Glasgow
Royal College of Psychiatrists
Royal College of Psychiatrists (Scottish Division)
Royal College of Radiologists
* Royal College of Surgeons of Edinburgh

* Royal College of Surgeons of England

Royal Dental Hospital of London School of Dental Surgery

Royal Earlswood Hospital Professional Executive Committee

Royal Free Hospital and School of Medicine

Royal Institute of British Architects

Royal Institute of Chemistry

Royal Marsden Hospital

Royal National Orthopaedic Hospital

Royal National Throat Nose and Ear Hospital

Royal Society of Health

Royal Victoria Hospital Belfast Medical Staff Committee

Salford AHA (T) Medical Executive Committee

Salford AHA (T)

Salford AHA Dermatology Division

Salford CHC

Salop AHA

Salop CHC

Salisbury District CHC

Salvation Army

Sandwell CHC

Sandwell Staff Side Representatives Committee

Scarborough Health District CHC

** Schools Council

Scottish Ambulance Service

Scottish Association of Community Medicine Specialists

* Scottish Association of Nurse Administrators

Scottish Association of Sector and Unit Administrators

* Scottish Council for Postgraduate Medical Education

Scottish Council for Single Homeless

Scottish Council of Social Service

Scottish District Dental Officers' Association

* Scottish District Nursing Association

Scottish Health Board Secretaries

Scottish Health Board Treasurers

Scottish Health Service Planning Council

* Scottish Health Visitors Association

* Scottish Home and Health Department

Scottish Joint Consultants' Committee

Scottish Liberal Party

Scottish Medical Practices Committee

Scottish National Blood Transfusion Service

Scottish National Party (Health Policy Committee)

Scottish Record Office

Scottish Trades Union Congress

Scunthorpe Health District CHC

Scunthorpe District Medical Committee

Sefton AHA

Sefton AHA Nurse Managers in Northern District

Sefton Local Medical Committee

Sehffield Area Chemist Contractors' Committee

Sheffield AHA (T)

Sheffield AHA (T) Central District Nursing Staff

Sheffield City Council

Sheffield FPC

Sheffield Health Students

Sheffield Local Dental Committee

Shetland Health Board

Sir Robert Jones Workshops Liverpool

Socialist Medical Association

Socialist Medical Association in Wales

** Social Services and Employment Sub-Committee of the Expenditure Committee of the House of Commons

* Society of Administrators of Family Practitioner Services

Society of British Neurological Surgeons

Society of Chiropodists

Society of Civil and Public Servants

Society of Clinical Psychiatrists

Society of Community Medicine

Society of Family Practitioner Committees

Society of Occupational Medicine

Society of Radiographers

Society of Secretaries of Welsh CHCs

Society for Social Medicine

Society of St Vincent De Paul

Society of Thoracic and Cardiovascular Surgeons

Solihull Area Dental Advisory Committee

Solihull Area Medical Committee

Solihull CHC

Somerset AHA

Somerset Local Pharmaceutical Committee

Soroptomist International of Leeds

Southampton and South West Hampshire District CHC

South Ayrshire LHC

South Bedfordshire CHC

South Birmingham CHC

South Birmingham Health District Nurses

South Camden CHC

South Camden Health District Management Team

South Derbyshire Health District Management Team

South East Cumbria CHC

South East England Consumer Associates

South East Kent CHC

South East Regional Association for the Deaf

South East Staffordshire CHC

South East Thames Regional Medical Committee

South East Thames Regional Nursing and Midwifery Committee

South East Thames Regional Scientific Committee

South East Thames RHA

Southend District CHC

Southern and Central Derbyshire Health District Medical Advisory Committee

Southern Sheffield CHC

South Glamorgan FPC
South Glamorgan Health Authority
South Glamorgan Social Services Department
South Gwent CHC
South Gwent Health District
South Hammersmith CHC
South Lincolnshire CHC
Southmead CHC
Southmead District Hospitals Medical Staff Advisory Committee
South Nottingham CHC
South Tees CHC
South Tyneside AHA
South Tyneside CHC
South Warwickshire CHC
South West Cumbria CHC
South West Cumbria District Hospital Consultants
South West Durham Health District CHC
South Western District (Greater Glasgow) LHC
South Western Regional Medical Committee Sub Committee on Obstetrics and Gynaecology
South West Regional Medical Committee Regional Psychiatric Sub-Committee
South Western Region Works Officers
South Western RHA
South West Thames Regional Chemical Pathology Advisory Sub-Committee
South West Thames Regional Heads of Psychology Departments Committee
South West Thames Regional Pharmaceutical Committee
South West Thames Region Clinical Pathology Advisory Group
South West Thames RHA
South West Thames RHA District Domestic Services Managers and Regional Domestic Services Officer
South Yorkshire County Council
Sparkford Women's Institute
Spastics Society
Special Hospitals Research Unit
Spinal Injuries Association
Staffordshire AHA
Staffordshire AHA Dental Officers
Staffordshire Area Medical Advisory Committee
Staffordshire Area Nursing and Midwifery Advisory Committee
Standing Conference of Representatives of Health Visitor Training Centres
St Bernard's Hospital (Middlesex) Senior Nursing Staff
St Christopher's Hospice
Stewartry LHC
St Helen's and Knowsley AHA
St Helen's and Knowsley CHC
St John Ambulance Service
St John's Hospital for Diseases of the Skin
St Mark's Hospital for Diseases of the Rectum and Colon
St Mary's Hospital Medical School Student Union

St Michael's Organisation
Stockport CHC
St Peter's Hospitals Board of Governors
St Thomas' Health District (Teaching) Medical Committee
St Thomas' Hospital Medical School
St Thomas' Hospital Medical Staff
Suffolk AHA
Sunderland CHC
Sunderland Local Medical Committee
Surrey Area Dental Committee
Surrey AHA
Surrey Area Medical Committee
Surrey Area Multi-Disciplinary Committee – Mental Illness
Surrey Area Multi-Disciplinary Committee – Mentally Handicapped
Surrey Area Multi-Disciplinary Committee - Mentally Handicapped (Working Party)
Surrey Daily Advertiser
Surrey Local Dental Committee
Sutton and West Merton CHC
Sutton and West Merton District Community Health Services Joint Consultative Staff Committee (Staff Side)
Swale Liberal Association
Swansea/Lliw Valley CHC
Swindon and District CHC
Swindon District Management Team
Swindon Whole-Time Consultants' Group

Talking Books for the Handicapped
Tameside AHA
Tameside CHC
Tameside Local Medical Committee
Tavistock Clinic
Tayside Area Medical Committee
Tayside Area Pharmaceutical Committee
Tayside Health Board
Tewkesbury Town Council
Thamesdown and District Community Relations Council
Thames Regional Postgraduate Medical Deans
The Ophthalmic Nursing Board
The Panel of Assessors for District Nurses Training
The Partially Sighted Society
The Patients' Association
The Psoriasis Association
The Psychotherapy Centre
Tower Hamlets CHC
* Trade Union Congress
Trafford AHA
Trafford CHC
Trafford Local Medical Committee
Transport and General Workers Union
Trent Faculty of the Royal College of General Practitioners
Trent Regional Action Committee

394

Trent Region Committee for Community Medicine and the Trust Region Branch of the Society of Community Medicine

Trent RHA

Trowbridge Town Council

Tunbridge Wells CHC

Tunbridge Wells Division of the BMA

UK Council for Overseas Student Affairs

Ulster Society of Pathologists

United Reformed Church

United Ulster Unionist Coalition

Unit for the Study of Health Policy Guy's Hospital Medical School

University College Hospital Medical School (University of London)

* University Grants Committee

University Hospitals Association (England and Wales)

University of Aberdeen Faculty of Medicine

University of Birmingham Faculty of Medicine and Dentistry

University of Bristol Dental School

University of Bristol Faculty of Medicine

University of Bristol Medical School

University of Cambridge Faculty Board of Clinical Medicine and Faculty Board of Biology

University of Dundee Faculty of Medicine

University of Edinburgh Faculty of Medicine

University of Glasgow Faculty of Medicine

University of Glasgow Professors of Geriatric Medicine

University of Hull

University of Liverpool Faculty of Medicine

University of Liverpool Faculty of Medicine – Group of Trainee GPs

University of London

University of London Royal Postgraduate Medical School

University of London Senior Councils

University of London Union Medical Group

University of Manchester Senior Management Development Course

University of Newcastle-upon-Tyne Faculty of Medicine

University of Nottingham Board of the Faculty of Medicine

University of Oxford

University of Sheffield Faculty of Medicine

University of Sheffield Medical School – 1st and 2nd year pre-clinical medical students

University of Southampton Faculty of Medicine

University of Strathclyde School of Pharmaceutical Sciences

Uxbridge Constituency Labour Party

Victoria Hospital Blackpool Medical Staff Committee

Voluntary Euthanasia Society

Volunteer Centre

Wakefield AHA

Wakefield District Hospital Consultants Committee

Wakefield (Eastern) CHC

Wakefield Metropolitan District Council

Wakefield (Western) CHC

Wakefield Western District Medical Committee

Wales Council for the Disabled

Walthamstow Medical Society

Wandsworth and East Merton CHC

Wandsworth Merton and Sutton AHA Health Visitors and School Nurses

Warwickshire AHA

Warwickshire AHA Northern District Mental Handicap Sector Departmental Team

Warwickshire FPC

Warwickshire Local Medical Committee

Well Wales Group

Welsh Consumer Council

Welsh Council

Welsh Counties Committee

** Welsh Health Technical Services Organisation

Welsh Information and Library Services for Health

Welsh Liberal Party

* Welsh National School of Medicine

Welsh Nursing and Midwifery Committee

* Welsh Office

Welsh Pharmaceutical Committee

Wessex Area Dental Officers

Wessex RHA

West Berkshire Health District Hospital Medical Services Committee

West Birmingham CHC

West Cumbria CHC

West Cumbria Health District Senior Nursing Staff

West Dorset CHC

West Dorset Health Care District Hospital Medical Staff Committee

Western Health and Social Services Board

Western Health and Social Services Board (Omagh District)

Western Provident Association

West Essex and District CHC

West Fife LHC

West Glamorgan Committee Against Cuts in the NHS

West Glamorgan Health Authority

West Lancashire CHC

West Midlands Administrators

West Midlands Region a group of personnel officers

West Midlands Region Public Relations Officers' Group

West Midlands RHA

Westminster Medical School

Weston CHC

West Scotland Division of Radiotherapy and Oncology

West Somerset CHC

West Surrey and North East Hants CHC

West Sussex AHA

West Yorkshire Metropolitan County Council
Whiteladies Health Centre Practice Association
Wigan AHA
Wigan FPC
William Temple Foundation
Wimbledon (Raynes Fark Sector) Health Visitors and School Nurses
Wirral AHA
Wirral AHA Consultants
Wirral Local Pharmaceutical Committee
Wirral Northern CHC
Wirral Southern CHC
Women's Rights Committee for Wales
Women's National Commission
Worcester CHC
Worcester Health District Nurse Managers
World Federation of Doctors Who Respect Human Life
Worksop and Retford CHC
Worthing CHC
Worthing District Consultants and Specialists
Wycombe District Nursing Staff

Y Gymdeithas Feddygal
York CHC
Yorkshire and Humberside Joint Library Services Committee
Yorkshire Regional Council of the Association of Community Health Councils
Yorkshire RHA

Individuals

Mr J R Adamson
Mr R Ainsworth
Dr W D Alexander
Mr Michael Alison MP
Mr F Allan
Dr R K Allday
Mr D G Alton
Mr E S Amos
Rev J E Anderson
Mrs M C Anderson
Dr G S Andrews
Mr J C Angell
Mr R Anson-Owen
Mr S Argvrou
Professor T H D Arie
Mr S Armoogum
Dr Aemash
Ms E Ashworth
Ms L Ashworth
Dr S M Asif-Akhtar

Dr C P Atkin
Mr D R Atkins
Dr J G Avery

Mrs G Backwell
Mr J Baines
Miss L E A Baker
Mr R M Bale
Dr S Balfour-Lynn
Dr D S Ball
Mr C S Bangay
Mr John Banham
Dr P J Barclay
Dr D M Barnard
Dr K Barnard-Jones
Dr B Barnett
Dr R H Barrett OBE
Dr C N Barry
Mrs E M D Bartholomew
Professor J A Bates
Mr R Bath
Mrs B H Baybrer
Dr W H Beasley
Miss G Beattie
Mrs A P Bell
Mr J R A Bell
Mrs H M Benbow
Dr R Benjamin
Mr R Bennett
Dr Linda Benson
Mrs D I Bentley
Ms S A Beresford
Mr N R Berish
Mr E R Bessell
Mrs E M P Best
Dr B Bevan
Drs T H Bewley and R B Bewley
Mr A Biczo
Mr E M Blackley
Mr J B Blades
Dr J N Blau
Mr C H Blenkiron
Mr G Bluckert
Mrs E Bold
Mrs P Bolding
Mr A Bond
Sir Desmond Bonham-Carter
Mr R Booklan
Professor C C Booth
Dr D Kumar Bose
Miss M T Bose
Mrs P M Botting
Mr P V Botto
Mr J B Bourke
Dr A R Bracey
Mr A W Brackenbury
Mr P L Bradley

Dr H M Bramley
Mrs P E M Braund
Dr A Brewerton
Mr G E Brooks
Mr A Brown
Mr D Brown
Mrs G M Brown
Miss I C S Brown
Dr J D Brown
Miss N Brown
Dr R G S Brown
Dr W A B Brown
Mr W D Brown
Dr P Bruggen
Mr F A R Brusby
Mr A Bryan Wade
Dr H M Buckland
Mrs A Bullivant
Mr J H Bulmer
Miss N Bunce
Mrs A P Burford-Mason
Mr J R Burgess
Mrs M E Burke
Dr E A Burkitt
Miss J Burnett
Mr J B Burns
Mr H Buse
Mr R Bushell
Mrs L Buxton
Miss J Byatt

Mr J A Cairns
Mr A Caldwell
Mrs A Callaghan
Mr M Calman
Mr A D C S Cameron
Mr W A Campbell
Miss M E Carey
Dr D Cargill
Mr J M Carlisle
Mr D Caro
Mrs J Carpenter
Ms C M Carr Stevens
Mr H E A Carson
Mr M Carty
Dr J E Cates
Miss V G Chadwell
Mrs C M Chalmers
Mrs G R Chapman
Miss I Chapman
Mr J Charles
Mrs M M Checksfield
Mr R Chetwood
Mr John Clare
Dr J Clark
Mr C Clarke
Dr G R Clarke

Mr J D Clarke
Mr L Clarke
Mr P J Clarke
Ms S Clarke
Dr E E Claxton
Ms B Clegg
Mr A M Clitheroe
Mr P Cobb
The Rt Hon Michael Cocks MP
Dr N F Coghill
Mr R N Cole
Dr D E Collins
Dr R M Collister
Mrs E Connett
Dr J Connolly and others
Miss R Conti
Mr D R Cook
Mr P Cook
Mrs Jane Cooper
Professor M H Cooper
Dr C W Cordin
Dr J Corkery
Dr P Counsell
Ms S G Cox
Ms H Crawford
Mr S Creed
Mrs J Cripps
Mrs G R Criscell
Dr B W Crombie
Mr J C Crowe
Dr J Cumming
Mrs G L Curbishley
Ms H Currie

Lady Dainton
Mr M C Dainty
Mr V D Dalal
Mr H L Daniels
Miss Q R A Daniels
Mr W E Daniels
Dr C M Davenport
Miss G J Davies
Dr H G Davies
Dr I J T Davies
Mr R Davies
Ms T I H Davies
Mr J A Davis
Dr S Davis
Mrs A M Dawar
Mrs M Dawson-Bowling
Mr A Dearden
Ms F C Denning
Mrs Dewar
Mrs R Dickins
Professor C J Dickinson
Dr R Dingwall
Dr F Dirmeik

397

Mr A Ditchfield
Mr S G Dixon
Mrs H Dolling
Mr F S A Doran
Ms C Douglas
Mr C F A Downie
Mr A J Doyle
Mr M F Drummond
Mr A Drummond-Rees
Sir John S Dudding
Mr A Dudley
Rev P Duncan
Dr J M Dunlop
Dr T Dunn
Rev D J Drye

Mr W H Earle
Mr B L Edwards
Dr H A Edwards
Dr H G Egdell
Mr H G Eisner
Dr P McA Elder
Mr A H Ellam
Miss R Elliot Lord
Mrs M H Eltringham
Mr D R England
Dr S R Engleman
Dr J M English
Mr A Epps
Mr and Mrs J Epsom
Dr N L Essex
Mrs M Evans
Mr V C W Evans

Dr L Feinmann
Mr C J Fell
Miss W F Fenton
Mr R C Fereday
Mr H P Ferrer
Mr C Fewtrell
Mr E P Finch
Dr I W Fingland
Dr R A Fisher
Mrs E Fitzsimmons
Miss P J Fleming
Miss E Fletcher
Mr H L Fletcher
Mr J H Fogg
Mr P J Folca
Dr B H Fookes
Mr R M Ford
Mr A S Foster
Mrs A R Fowler
Mr F T Foyle
Lady Franks
Ms B Freeman

Mr K Freudenthal
Dr J Fry
Dr G J J Fuzzey
Mr W S Fyfe

Miss A Gabell
Mr H W Gallagher
Dr M Gammon
Dr A D H Gardner
Dr A W Gardner
Dr C J Garratt
Mr J Garrett MP
Mr R Gartside
Ms M Gates
Miss M Gibson
Sir Ronald Gibson
Mr S Gibson
Mrs M T Gilbert and others
Dr A A Gildersleve
Mr C R W Gill
Mr D R Gladwell
Dr B Glaister
Professor H J Glanville
Mr M C Godin
Miss T M Goldrick
Miss C Gomme
Mrs E Goodall
Mr A Goodman
Dr M J Gordon
Mr V Gorman
Mr W R Gowers
Ms Hilary Graham
Mr David Grant
Mrs E A Grant
Mr E Grattan
Mrs M Gray
Mrs M P Gray
Professor P Gray
Mr R Gray
Mr D Green
Dr W R Greig
Mrs P M Grenfell
Mr N Griffin
Miss K Griffiths
Dr R Griffiths
Mrs V F Griffiths
Dr R N Gruneberg
Dr D L Gullick
Mr H J Gummer
Professor A Guz

Dr J Hall
Dr M S Hall
Mrs E M Halliwell
Dr T J Hamblin
Mr D N Hamilton

Mrs E Hammond
Mrs G Hann
Mr A Harding
Mr P Harding
Dr R J Hare
Dr AJM Hargreaves
Mrs E Harland
Dr J B Harman
Mr R Harris
Mr G A Harris
Mrs E Harrison
Mr H Harrop-Griffiths
Dr C R Hart
Dr D R W Hartley
Mr W Harvey
Dr W J Hay
Dr G A H Heaney
Mrs B Healey
Dr P J Heath
Mrs M K Hebblethwaite
Rev Dr Walter Hedgcock
Mr T M A Heesom
Mr C R Helsey
Mr R D Henderson
Dr S Henderson-Smith
Dr R Henryk-Gutt
Miss E M Henslow
Dr A Herxheimer
Mrs C R Hickinbotham
Mr P Hickinbotham
Dr A Hill
Dr S G Hill
Mrs M C Hillier
Dr R L Himsworth
Proffessor J R Hobbs
Mr P M Hoffman
Dr J A Hofmeyr
Mr A J Holbert
Miss K Holden
Mr R H T Holland
Professor W Holland
Ms Catherine Hollingworth
Mr D L Holmes
Professor K S Holt
Mr A Hopkins
Mr A G Hopkins
Miss L Horne
Dr C A Houlder
Mr D M R Howard
Mr & Mrs R H Howard
Dr E Howarth
Dr D D C Howat
Dr D P M Howells
Dr J Howells
Miss M M Hubrer
Dr D Hubert-Jones
Professor G Hudson

Dr P Hugh-Jones
Mr R Hughes MP
Mrs E M Hull
Mrs M Hulme and others
Dr E A Humphrey
Mr F T Hunt
Mr N R Hunter
Dr Peter Hunter
Dr Hunter Smith
Mr Tom Hurst
Dr A G Hutchinson
Mr E M Huthnance
Mr W J Hyde

Professor D Jackson
Dr H Jacobs
Mrs E J James
Mr D Jardine
Mr E W Jenkins
Miss M C Jenkins
Mr J R Jenkins
Mr T Jenkins
Mr A E Jemmott
Ms Dorthy Jobling
Dr B Johnson
Mr H H John
Mr J Johnson
Mr M Johnson
Ms P Johnson
Dr R Johnson
Mrs B P W Johnston
Mrs Myfanwy Jones
Sir Francis Avery Jones
Mr R Jones
Dr R D Jones
Miss T P Jones
Dr W T Jones
Mr M Jopling MP
Dr D H Judson

Mr B Kat
Mr R Kaye
Dr A Keable-Elliot
Mr Brian Kelly
Mr F Kelly
Mr G D Kelly
Dr K Kelly
Dr M J Kendall
Mr J Kendall
Mr R A Kennedy
Dr J Kenyon
Professor Neil Kessel
Mrs L G Killon
Mr C N King
Dr D J King
Mr J Kinnaird

Professor Rudolf Klein
Mr N J Knott
Mr T E Korzon
Mrs L A Kruger
Dr D Kumar-Bose

Mrs B Lake
Mrs P Langham
Mr C H Langley
Mrs B Lansdale
Mr J A Lane
Mr B Lapping
Miss M Laurence
Mr M R J Lavers
Dr R Law
Mrs M B Lawrie
Mrs M Lawrie
Mr A H Leaney
Professor R Leaper
Mrs O Leapman
Professor W R Lee
Dr R Lefever
Mr J Leek
Dr J Le Grand
Mr J Lendrum FRCS
Dr A F Lever
Mr A D Lewis
Mrs E M Lewis
Mr K Lewis and others
Dr I M Librach
Mrs M L Liddell
Dr J Linden
Dr W Lindsay Lamb
Dr J C Little
Dr K Little
Dr K Little
Dr J Lister
Mrs B P Llewellyn
Miss D B Lloyd
Dr Lloyd
Dr F A Lodge
Mrs C Loughrey
Mr D J Lovelock
Dr G S Lowe
Mr H G Lowe
Ms A R Lund
Ms Grace Lunn
Dr J N Lunn
Dr Brandon Lush
Mr B J Lyme
Dr J Lynn
J P Lythgoe

Councillor J T McCarthy
Dr R L McCorry
Miss M R McCulloch

Mrs H McGinis
Rev T S McGregor
Dr Ian H McKee
Mr D L MacKenzie
Dr M McKerrow
Mr D M McKinven
Dr D McLellan
Dr R D M MacLeod
Mr I C McManus
Dr H McOmie
Dr J Morag MacArthur
Miss J M Macbey
Dr R MacGillivray
Dr J B McLaren
Dr M H MacLean
Mr J Macre-Snowie
Dr C Maddox
Mr G R Maddox
Mrs I Magrath
Miss E Major
Mr K A Mallinson
Mr J Mansell
Dr Manton
Lady Marre
Miss A Marks
Dr J Marks
Professor V Marks
Mr A R A Marshall
Mrs R E Marshall
Mr A K Matthews
Mr M T Matthews
Dr L G C Martin
Mr B Maunder
Mr Alan Maynard
Dr D Maxwell
Mr R Maxwell
Dr R Meyrick
Dr J A Mead
Dr A J Mearns
Mr G Mercer
Mrs P D Merrell
Miss M Metcalfe
Mr M Miller
Mrs M A Milston
Mr C Mitchell
Mrs P Moffat
Miss S Mollo
Mr P Monahan
Dr E P Morley
Mr M Morgan
Dr G Morris
Dr J E Morris
Mr M C T Morrison
Dr B Morson
Mr R E Morton
Mr J G Mosley
Mr R S Murley

Mr H Mungur
Mr K Munro
Mr J L Munro
Mr N Munro
Mr C G Munton
Dr G Murray-Jones
Ms Anne Muscott and others

Mrs N Naish
Mr T G Nash
Dr N E Nathanson
Mr R T Needham
Mr D Neill
Mr P J Newton
Mr T Newton MP
Mr B Nicholas and others
Mr I G Nicholls
Mr G Nichols
Dr P J R Nichols
Mr R Nicholson
Dr D Norminton
Mr A Norton
Mr H S Norwich

Dr P O'Brien
Dr J M O'Brien
Dr P O'Farrell
Mr John G Oliver
Mr M O'Reilly
Mr K Osborne
Mrs P M Osborne
Mr G T Owen
Mr J W Owen
Mr K V Owen
Mr S K Owusu

Dr A Padfield
Mr J R Paine
Mrs E Palmer
Professor J Parkhouse
Mr C J Parker
Mr F W Parrott
Mr R B Patch
Mr E D Patel
Dr J W Paulley
Mr L Pavitt MP
Dr J D Paw
Mr John H Peel
Dr C S L Peiris
Dr H G Penman
Mr W G Penn
Dr P J Pereira Gray
Mr F Pethybridge
Mr A J N Phair
Mr P O D Pharoah
Dr F and Mrs A D Pheby

Professor C I Phillips
Dr T L Pilkington
Mr H J Pilling
Mr G Pinnell
Lord Platt
Mrs P R M Popat
Dr A M Porter
Mr John Porter
Mr R Porter
Dr D Pottinger
Dr D A Primrose
Mr A D Pritchard and others
Mr J S Pullin
Mrs M Purdie

Dr B Raeburn
Professor A J Harding Rains
Mr R Ramirez
Mrs C Randall
Dr A Randle
Mr H W Rawlings
Dr T A Reilly and others
Professor R W Revans
Dr H M Rhoden
Mrs D Richardson
Sir John Richardson
Mr J R Richardson
Mr P B Richardson
Mrs E G Rickards
Mr W Ridley
Mr G M Rigler
Dr J W Rippin
Mr J L Roberts
Ms B Robertson
Dr D H Robertson
Mr Ian Robertson
Mr N R E Robertson
Mr C W Robinson
Mr S E Robinson
Sir Kenneth Robson
Dr K S Rodan
Mr S Rogers
Mr Q Rowe
Mr R Rowlandson
Professor Douglas Roy
Mr T P Roy
Mrs F Russell
Dr H D L Russell
Dr T M Ryan

Mr A Sabberton
Ms M J C Sainsbury
Dr W H St John-Brookes
Mr C Sanderson
Mr G A Sanderson
Dr R A Sandison

Mr H M Saxton
Dr K E Schmidt
Mrs J Score
Mr J B Score
Mrs E M Scott
Sir Ian Scott
Mr G V Seanor
Dr J J Segall
Mr Derek Seel
Mr A Seldon
Mrs R Sell
Sir Thomas Holmes Sellors
Mr I Semple
Dr H Sergeant
Mr P E Sharp
Dr David Shaw
Ms Jane Shaw
Miss C Sheaner
Dr A Sheiham
Mr A Shener
Mrs D M Shepherd
Dr M M A Shipsey
Mr W T Sholl
Mr R J Simkin
Mrs D Simpkins
Dr M J Simpkiss
Ms B Simpson
Mrs A Sinclair
Dr F C Smales
Mr C J Smart
Dr D M Smith
Mrs E Smith
Mrs G Smith
Mr H Smith
Dr J M Smith and others
Mr J P Smith
Mr R S Smith
Professor R W Smithells
Mr M C Snell
Miss K M Solly
Professor J F Soothill
Dr Kenneth Southgate
Mr N Spearing MP
Reverend P Speck
Mr C H Spoukes
Professor M Stacey
Mrs Ruth Staines
Professor Sir John Stallworthy
Mrs M Standen-Batt
Dr D Stark Murray
Mr P Staunton
Dr R Steele
Mr R C Steele
Mr E M Steffens
Professor G T Stewart
Dr J S Stewart
Mrs J E Stirland

Mr B Stone
Dr R B Stott
Dr J Stuart Brown
Dr J Sugden
Miss M P Sullivan
Mr J C Sunderland
Dr S Surtees
Mr A Swan
Sir Michael Swann
Mr A G D Swift
Mrs Margaret Symes

Mr R V Tait
Mr R Talbot
Mr and Mrs W E Tatton-Brown
Lord Taylor of Harlow
Dr C E D Taylor
Mr E Taylor
Mr L H Taylor
Mr S Taylor
Mr S Taylor
Mr W J Taylor
Mr P Telling
Dr E R H Tennant
Miss A M Testro
Mr P R Thatcher
Mr D P Thom
Mrs Alice Thomas
Mr B Thomas
Mr B D Thomas
Dr D Thomas
Mr D E Thomas MP
Mr R J Thomas
Mr F P Thompson
Mr Stan Thorne MP
Dr A K Thould
Dr A L Thrower
Mr B Todd
Dr J W Todd
Mr R P Tong
Miss F M Tonge
Mr D J Towersey
Dr M Trimble
Dr J Tudor Hart
Miss J Turnbull
Mr G Turner
Mrs J Turner
Professor P Turner
Dr A Tuxford
Mr R S Twaddell
Mr A Twist

Dr P I Vardy
Mr D Vellacott
Mrs E Vettewinkel
Dr H R Vickers

Mr P R Vickers

Mr I Waddington
Professor O L Wade
Mr E Wadsworth
Mr Aurthur Walker
Dr E R C Walker
Miss W Wallace
Dr G Walsh
Lieutenant Colonel H C M Walton
Professor J M Walton
Mrs S N Wansbrough
Mr J R Waters
Mr A Watson
Prof. M D Warren
Dr J R G Watters
Mrs B Webster
Mr A F Weedon and others
Mrs D Wharf
Miss N Whatley and others
Dr J Wilks
Mr C E White
Mr D L White
Dr D M D White
Mrs E White
Mr K J C White
Dr R H R White
Mrs J H Whitehouse
Miss D Whittaker
Dr J A Wickens

Mr C Wicks
Mrs B Widrig
Mr C E Wilde
Dr J R Wilkie
Mrs N Wilkinson
Dr S Wilkinson
Dr P H Willcox
Mr A T Williams
Mr K Williams
Miss M Williams
Mrs A Williamson
Mrs J Williamson
Dr J D Williamson
Dr J Wilson
Mr J W Wilson
Mrs M T Wilson
Mrs S Wilson
Dr W S Wilson
Dr S Wiseberg
Mr J Wishart
Dr A Withnell and others
Dr J B Wood
Dr G E Wood
Miss J Woods
Mr R A Worsfold
Sir Robert B Wright
Professor O Wrong
Mr & Mrs Arthur Wynn

Mrs G M Young

Appendix A 2 Those who assisted the Commission in other ways

We should like to thank the following individuals, and the organisations they represent, for their help and advice in discussions, seminars and in many other ways. We also acknowledge the contributions of the countless others who have been helpful to the Commission, whom we have been unable to record individually.

Professor B Abel-Smith
Professor R C B Aitken
Professor H Allred
Mr D J Anderson
Professor T Arie
Mr W Armour
Professor J Ashford
Dr D Badenoch
Mr B H Bailey
Mr J Banham
Mr J Barker
Mr K Barnard
Miss J Baraclough
Mr G C Battye
Professor Dr F Beske
Mr G Bevan
Sir Douglas Black
Professor J Blanpain
Dr S Barley
Professor I Breckenridge
Dr S Brenner
Mr J Bridge
Dr R F Bridgman
Mr G Bromley
Professor Sir John Brotherston
Dr J Brothwood
Dr J Bulman
Mr F Burdett
Professor W J H Butterfield

The Rt Hon Barbara Castle
Dr I Chalmers
Professor J Child
Mr C E Clark
Sir Stanley Clayton
Professor A Cochrane
Professor B Cohen
Dr E Colin-Russ
Dr D Cook
Professor M Cooper
Mr H Copeman
Dr A Crichton

Mr P Dalton
Mr B Devlin
Dr D H Dick

Miss P Dixon
Professor C T Dollery
Dr M Downham
Dr P Draper
Mr T Dowell
Professor A S Duncan
Dr D Duncan
Professor R Dyson

Professor G Forsyth
Sir Arnold France

Dr A Gatherer
Mr W H George
Dr U Gerhardt
Mr M Gerrard
Mr P Gibson
Professor H J Glanville
Dr C Godber
Sir George Godber
Mr M Godin
Professor Dr L M J Groot
Mr D Guest
Dr D Gullick
Dr J Gurdon
Miss J Guy

Professor C Handy
Mr W Harvey
The Rt Hon Edward Heath MP
Dr T Heller
Sir Douglas Henley
Mr D Hobman
Dr and Mrs F Honigsbaum
Mr D J Hucklesby
Mrs M Hughes
Lord Hunter
Professor P Huntingford

Professor R Illsley and members of his Department
Dr D Irvine

Professor D Jackson
Professor E Jaques
Professor M Jeffreys

Mr J Emlyn Jones
The Rt Hon Sir Keith Joseph MP

Sir Andrew Kay
Mr D Kaye
Dr A Keable-Elliott
Professor R Klein
Professor R Kohn
Mr W H Laming
Dr A J Lane
Mr G A Lee
Mr K Lee
Dr R Lefever
Ms R Levitt
Professor K Liddelow
Miss M Lindars
Dr M Linnett
Dr D Longson

Dr J MacGuire
Dr A Maiden
Dr R Mair
Dr J Marks
The Rt Hon Sir Richard Marsh
Mr G V Marsh
Mr R Maxwell
Professor I McColl
Professor T McKeown
Mr G McLachlan
Dr T Meade
Mr P Mellor
Mr M Midda
Ms A Mills
Sir Harry Moore

Mrs B Newstead

The Rt Hon Dr David Owen MP

Mrs B Piggott
Mr G Prys-Davies

Miss E Raybould
Sir Derek Rayner
Professor R W Revans
Professor B Rexed
Ms J Reynolds
Mrs J Robinson
Mr O Roith
Dr Rosemary Rue
Professor J A Scott
Mr R Shegog
Mr A Sheiham
Dr F Seymour
Mr P Simpson
Professor G Slack
Mr M J Smith
Mr T Smythe
Dr M Spencer
Mr H Spiegelhalter
Professor J D Stewart
Miss M Storey
Sir Charles Stuart-Harris

Professor O Wade
Mrs L Wainwright
Dr M Walsh
Mr V Watts
Mr P West
Dr I Wickings
Professor A J Willcocks
Mr Kingsley Williams
Sir Robert Williams
The Rt Hon Sir Harold Wilson MP
Dr E Woodford-Williams
Mr G F Woodhead

Mr J Yates
Miss P H F Young

Dr J Zilva

Appendix B Visits by the Commission

In addition to holding formal oral evidence sessions in Edinburgh, Cardiff and Belfast, the Commission and their staff made visits in the United Kingdom and overseas and these are listed below. We wish to acknowledge the generous help and advice given to us by the many people we met in the course of these visits. We are particularly grateful to the Parliamentary Commissioner and the Committees Unit of the Foreign and Commonwealth Office in arranging the overseas visits.

United Kingdom

a) **England**

Birley Moor Health Centre Sheffield
Birmingham Area Health Authority (Teaching)
Birmingham Family Practitioner Committee
Broad Green Hospital Liverpool
Chesterfield Royal Infirmary
City General Hospital Carlisle
Dental Estimates Board Eastbourne
Dental Practice of Mr Stern East London
Dental Practice of Mr Woolf East London
Denton Health Centre Newcastle
Department of Family and Community Medicine Newcastle University
Department of Therapeutic and Clinical Pharmacology Birmingham University
Doncaster Royal Infirmary
Elswick Health Centre Newcastle
Exeter District Management Team
Fountayne Road Health Centre London
Garston Manor Rehabilitation Centre Watford
Hallamshire Hospital Sheffield
Harefield Hospital Middlesex
Hatfield Health Centre Doncaster
Highroyds Hospital Ilkley Yorkshire
Hillsborough Health Centre Sheffield
Holt House Aged Persons Hostel Liverpool
Isle of Wight Area Health Authority
King Edward VII's Hospital for Officers London
Lakeside Health Centre Thamesmead
Lathbury House Aged Persons Hostel Liverpool
Leicester Frith Hospital
Leicester Royal Infirmary
Lincoln County Hospital
Manor House Hospital Golders Green
Medical Practice of Dr Ashcroft and Partners Newcastle
Medical Practice of Dr Burton and Partners Wolverhampton
Medical Practice of Dr Freedman and Partners Newcastle
Medical Practice of Dr Goffman and Partners Liverpool
Medical Practice of Dr Grey Newcastle

Medical Practice of Dr Griffiths and Partners Birmingham
Medical Practice of Dr Jayson Liverpool
Medical Practice of Dr Julka Wolverhampton
Medical Practice of Dr MacKellar and Partners Morpeth Northumberland
Medical Practice of Dr Mahmood East London
Medical Practice of Dr Marshall and Partners Rossington South Yorkshire
Medical Practice of Dr Olusanya East London
Medical Practice of Dr Schopflin East London
Medical Practice of Dr Sherwood East London
Medical Practice of Dr Silver and Partners Newcastle
Medical Practice of Dr Taylor East London
Medical Practice of Dr Teebay Liverpool
Medical Practice of Dr Venugopal Birmingham
Newsham General Hospital Liverpool
Northern General Hospital Sheffield
North London Nuffield Hospital Enfield Middx
Princess Grave Hospital London
Prospect Road Group Medical Practice Newcastle
Ridley Medical Centre Blyth Northumberland
Royal Dental Hospital London
Royal Free Hospital London
Royal Infirmary Sheffield
Royal Liverpool Children's Hospital
Royal Victoria Infirmary Newcastle
St Andrew's Hospital Northampton
St Mary's Hospital Newport Isle of Wight
Sefton General Hospital Liverpool
Sir Alfred Jones Memorial Hospital Garston Liverpool
South Park Ambulance Station Lincoln
Southport Promenade Hospital
The London Hospital
Thorpe Road Group Medical Practice Doncaster
Wellington Hospital London NW8
Whiteladies Health Centre Bristol
Wolverhampton Area Health Authority
Wolverhampton Family Practitioner Committee
Yorkshire Regional Health Authority

b) Wales

Aberdare Health Centre
Bron-y-Garth Hospital
Clwyd Health Authority
Corris Health Centre
Denbighshire Infirmary
Dolgellau Hospital
Glyncorrwg Health Centre Near Port Talbort
Maelor General Hospital Wrexham
Mold Cottage Hospital
North Wales Hospital Denbigh
Pharmacy of Mr D P Williams Wrexham
Royal Alexandra Hospital Rhyl
St Asaph Health Centre
Trawsfynnydd Health Centre
Tywyn Hospital
War Memorial Hospital Wrexham

c) Scotland

Greater Glasgow Health Board
Institute of Medical Sociology, Aberdeen
Lewis Hospital Stornoway
Woodside Health Centre, Glasgow
Western Isles Health Board Stornoway

d) Northern Ireland

Belfast City Hospital
Dental Practice of Mr Curry Ballymena
Dental Practice of Mr Rottger Newtownabbey
Dental Practice of Mr Alexander and Mr Chesney Ballymena
Finaghy Health Centre Belfast
Northern Ireland Central Services Agency
North-West Belfast Social Work Office
Randalstown Health Centre
Royal Victoria Hospital Belfast
Ulster Hospital Dundonald
Waveney Hospital Ballymena

OVERSEAS

a) Canada

Department of Community Medicine University of Toronto
Department of Health Ontario
Department of Health and Welfare Ottawa
Faculty of Nursing University of Victoria British Columbia
Flemingdon Health Centre Toronto
Health Sciences Centre University of British Columbia
Ministry of Health British Columbia
Ottawa Civic Hospital
Preventive Medicine Centre Vancouver
St Paul's Hospital Vancouver
Vancouver General Hospital

b) Denmark

Danish Medical Association
Friheden Health Centre Copenhagen
Institute for Social Research Copenhagen
National Board of Health Copenhagen
Pedder Lykke Centre for the Elderly Copenhagen
World Health Organisation Regional Office for Europe Copenhagen

c) Eire

Department of Health Dublin

d) France

Hospices Civiles Lyon
Edouard-Herriot Hospital Lyon

French Society of Dentists
International School of Nursing Lyon
Ministry of Health Paris
Prefecture of Lyon
Salpêtrière Hospital Paris

e) Holland

Department of Oral Surgery Brunovo Hospital The Hague
Leyenburg Hospital The Hague
Ministry of Public Health and Environmental Hygiene The Hague
Ormoord Health Centre Rotterdam
Rotterdam Municipal Health Department
Sickness Fund Council Amstelveen

f) Sweden

Dalby Community Health Centre Malmo County
Department of Economics University of Lund
Federation of Swedish County Councils
Jakobsberg Health Centre Jarfalla Stockholm
Malmo General Hospital
Ministry of Health and Social Affairs Stockholm
National Board of Health and Welfare Stockholm
Sundbyberg Long-term Hospital Stockholm County
Swedish Federation of Salaried Employees in the Hospital and Public Health Services
Swedish Medical Association
Swedish Planning and Rationalisation Institute for Health and Social Services
University Hospital Lund

g) USA

American Acadamy of Physicians' Assistants Washington
American Dental Association Washington
AFL/CIO Washington
American Medical Association Chicago
American Nurses Association Washington
Chicago Health Systems Agency
Columbia Dental School New York
Columbia Presbyterian Medical Centre New York
Department of Health Education and Welfare Washington
Dr Martin Luther King Jnr Health Centre New York
Faculty of Nursing Cornell University New York
Health Maintenance Organisations Chicago
Loeb Centre for Nursing and Rehabilitation New York
Mary Manning Walsh Home New York
Multiple Sclerosis Centre Chicago
National League for Nursing New York
New York State Dental Society
Precinct 37 Dental Centre New York
Prospect Hill Health Clinic North Carolina
Rehabilitation Institute Chicago
Staff of House of Representatives Washington
Staff of Senate Health Sub-committee Washington
United Auto Workers New York
University of North Carolina

h) USSR

Central Committee of Trades Unions of Medical Workers Moscow
Department of Health Leningrad
Hospital No 142 Moscow
Institute of Advanced Medical Training Moscow
Institute of Experimental and Clinical Surgery Moscow
Institute of Stomatology Moscow
Medical Department of Leningrad Optico-Mechanical Plant Kirov
Ministry of Health Moscow
Ministry of Medical Industry Moscow
Nurse Training School Moscow
Paediatric Poly-clinic No 53 Leningrand
Poly-clinic No 60 Moscow
Rehabilitation Centre of the City of Sestroretsk Children's Sanitorium Leningrad

i) West Germany

Friederich Ebert Hospital Neumunster
General Practitioners Association of Schleswig-Holstein
Holsten Apotheke Kiel
Ministry of Labour Bonn
Ministry of Youth Family Affairs and Health Bonn
Nurse Training Institute Kiel
Old People's Home Wandendorf
Practice of Dr Blumel Vogelsang-Grunholz
Specialist Group Practice Quickborn

j) Yugoslavia

Primary Health Care Facilities Zagreb

411

Appendix C   The Commission and Its Staff

I COMMISSIONERS

Sir Alec Merrison DL FRS (Chairman)
Vice-Chancellor University of Bristol

Sir Thomas Brown (Vice-Chairman)
Chairman of the Eastern Health and Social Services Board
Northern Ireland

Professor Ivor Batchelor CBE
Professor of Psychiatry Dundee University

Professor Paul Bramley
Professor of Dental Surgery Sheffield University

C M Clothier Esq QC*
Recorder and Judge of Appeal in the Isle of Man

Ann Clwyd
Journalist, broadcaster and member of the Cardiff Community Health
Council: newly elected member of the European Parliament

Peter Jacques Esq
Secretary of the Social Insurance and Industrial Welfare Department of the
Trades Union Congress

Professor Jean McFarlane
Professor of Nursing Manchester University

Miss Audrey Prime OBE
Chairman Enfield and Haringey AHA: until 1976
Staff Side Secretary of the NHS General Whitley Council

Miss Kay Richards
Assistant Director of Social Services Hertfordshire County Council: until
1.5.77.Senior Lecturer in Social Planning National Institute for Social
Work

Lady Sherman
Member of NE Thames RHA

Sir Simpson Stevenson
Chairman of the Greater Glasgow Health Board

Councillor Dr Cyril Taylor
General Medical Practitioner Liverpool

Dr Christopher Wells OBE TD
General Medical Practitioner Sheffield (retired)

Frank Welsh Esq
Director Grindlay's Bank Limited

413

Professor Alan Williams**
Professor of Economics York University

II THE COMMISSION STAFF

The full-time staff were:

David de Peyer	Secretary
Roy Cunningham	Assistant Secretary
Alan Gilbert	Assistant Secretary
Christine Farrell	Principal Research Officer
Hugh Gravelle	Economic Advisor

Rukhsana Acharya
Janet Ball
Maxine Budd (left February 1978)
Catherine Campbell
Nora Crilly (left November 1977)
Rosemary Davies
Brian Egan
Valerie Fanning (left March 1978)

Maureen Flynn (left December 1978)
Jim Furniss
Penny Kocher (left September 1976)
Paul Matthews
Mary Meehan (left September 1978)
Angela Oslar
Susan Wilson

 *Until 3 January 1979
**Until 31 August 1978

Appendix D   Structure of the NHS in the Four Parts of the UK

The structure of the NHS differs in the different parts of the United Kingdom. The schedule which follows sets out the main differences between the four countries. These differences are also shown in diagrammatic form in charts D1 to D4.

The abbreviations used in the schedule are:–

KEY TO INITIALS

AEG	Area Executive Group (Scotland)	equivalent to Area Team of Officers in England and Wales
AET	Area Executive Team (Northern Ireland)	
AHA	Area Health Authority	
ATO	Area Team of Officers	
CHSC	Central Health Services Council (England and Wales)	
CSA (NI)	Central Services Agency (Northern Ireland)	
CSA (S)	Common Services Agency (Scotland)	
DEG	District Executive Group (Scotland)	equivalent to District Management Team in England and Wales
DET	District Executive Team (Northern Ireland)	
DHSS	Department of Health and Social Security	
DHSS (NI)	Department of Health and Social Services (Northern Ireland)	
DMC	District Medical Committee	
DMT	District Management Team	
FPC	Family Practitioner Committee	
HB	Health Board (Scotland)	
HSSB	Health and Social Services Board (Northern Ireland)	
HSSC	Health and Social Services Council (Northern Ireland)	
LA	Local Authority	
NCC	National Consultative Committee (Scotland)	
RHA	Regional Health Authority	
RTO	Regional Team of Officers	
SAC	Standing Advisory Committee (England and Wales)	
SHHD	Scottish Home and Health Department	
SHSPC	Scottish Health Service Planning Council	
S of S (SS)	Secretary of State for Social Services	
S of S (NI)	Secretary of State for Northern Ireland	
S of S (S)	Secretary of State for Scotland	
S of S (W)	Secretary of State for Wales	
WHTSO	Welsh Health Technical Services Organisation	
WO	Welsh Office	

STRUCTURE	ENGLAND	WALES	SCOTLAND	NORTHERN IRELAND
SCOPE	Health	Health	Health	Health and Personal Social Services
REORGANISED	1974	1974	1974	1973
MINISTERIAL ACCOUNTABILITY	Secretary of State for Social Services to Parliament	Secretary of State for Wales to Parliament	Secretary of State for Scotland to Parliament	Secretary of State for Northern Ireland to Parliament
STATUTORY MANAGEMENT BODIES	S of S (SS) – Boards of Governors (Postgraduate Teaching Hospitals) – 14 RHAs– 90 AHAs – 90 FPCs	S of S (W) – 8 AHAs (including one AHA (T)) – WHTSO – 8 FPCS	S of S (S) – 15 HBs – CSA (S)	DHSS (NI) – 4 HSSBs – CSA (NI) – Staffs Council
ADVISORY STRUCTURE NATIONAL LEVEL	S of S (SS) Advised by Central Health Services Council. Standing Advisory Committees (representing major health professions) advise both S of S and CHSC	S of S (W) Advised by CHSC and SACs as in England.In addition Advisory Committees for Wales representing health professions provide professional advice to S of S (W).	S of S (S) Advised by Scottish Healh Services Planning Council. National Consultative Committees (representing major health professions) advise SHSPC.	DHSS (NI) Advised by Health and Social Services Council. Central Advisory Committees (representing Personal Social Services and major health professions) advise DHSS (NI) and HSSC.

STRUCTURE	ENGLAND	WALES	SCOTLAND	NORTHERN IRELAND
ADVISORY STRUCTURE – AUTHORITY/BOARD LEVEL AND BELOW	Advisory Committees representing major health professions provide professional advice at regional and area levels. Medical Committee only at district level. In some districts, hospital members of DMC elected by local hospital medical committees (Cogwheel).	Advisory Committees representing health professions provide professional advice at area level. Medical Committee only at district level (in single district areas the recognised Area Medical Committee includes the functions of the DMC as well as its advisory role).	Local Consultative Committees representing health professions provide professional advice at board level.	Advisory Committees representing health professions provide professional advice at board level. District Medical Committee advises District Executive Team (and DMC Chairman is one of DET).
FAMILY PRACTITIONER ARRANGEMENTS	Each AHA sets up a FPC – GPs, dentists, ophthalmic medical practitioners, opticians and pharmacists contract to it to provide services.	As England.	GPs, dentists and pharmacists contract directly with HBs to provide services. Ophthalmic medical practitioners and opticians contract to Joint Ophthalmic Committees	GPs, dentists, ophthalmic medical practitioners, opticians and pharmacists contract directly with HSSBs.
COMMUNITY REPRESENTATION	Community Health Councils.	Community Health Councils.	Local Health Councils.	District Committees (also represent public interest with regard to personal social services).

417

STRUCTURE	ENGLAND	WALES	SCOTLAND	NORTHERN IRELAND
BOARD/AUTHORITY MEMBERSHIP	RHA Chairman and members appointed by S of S (SS) after consultations. 18 to 24 members including 1 hospital consultant, 1 GP, 1 nurse or midwife, 1 university nominee, 1 trade unionist, 2 other health service employees and at least ⅓ LA members.	No RHAs.	No RHAs.	No RHAs.
	AHA Chairmen appointed by S of S (SS) 18 to 33 members. At least ⅓ LA appointees, remainder RHA appointees (including 2 health service employees) after consultations.	AHA Chairmen and members other than County Council appointees appointed by S of S (W) after consultations. At least ⅓ LA representation, including 1 consultant, 1 GP, 1 nurse or midwife, 1 university nominee and 2 other health service employees (not yet appointed).	Health Board Chairmen and members appointed by S of S (S) taking into account nominations by many bodies. Membership includes 2 doctors, 1 member of nursing profession, 2 members employed by or in contract with HBs, 1 or 2 university nominees (except island boards), 2 or 3 trade unionists, at least 3 LA nominees and the balance from business and voluntary organisations.	Chairmen and members of HSSBs appointed by DHSS (NI) after consultation. Membership includes about 30% District Council nominees, about 30% health and personal social services professionals and remainder include university nominees and nominees of such interests as voluntary and community bodies, trade unions, industry and commerce.

STRUCTURE	ENGLAND	WALES	SCOTLAND	NORTHERN IRELAND
MANAGEMENT STRUCTURE	Regional Team of Officers appointed by and accountable to RHAs. Area Team of Officers and District Management Teams similarly appointed and accountable to AHAs. No line management from district to region. DMT not accountable to ATO. Individual officers also directly accountable to appointing authority for management of staff and performance of specific functions in their own professional field.	No regional authorities. ATOs and DMTs set up by AHAs but (unlike England) DMTs are subordinate and accountable to ATOs.	No regional board. AEGs and DEGs set up by HBs but AEGs are accountable to HBs and DEGs are subordinate and accountable to AEGs, both corporately and individually. No practising GPs or consultants on DEGs.	No Regional Board. AETs and DETs set up by HSSBs but only AETs directly accountable to Boards, while DETs are subordinate and accountable to AETs, both corporately and individually (except clinicians).

419

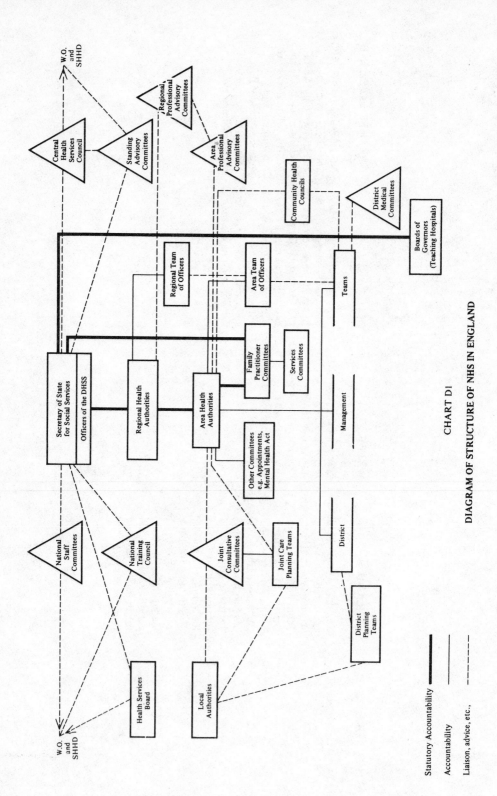

CHART D1

DIAGRAM OF STRUCTURE OF NHS IN ENGLAND

Statutory Accountability

Accountability

Liaison, advice, etc.,

420

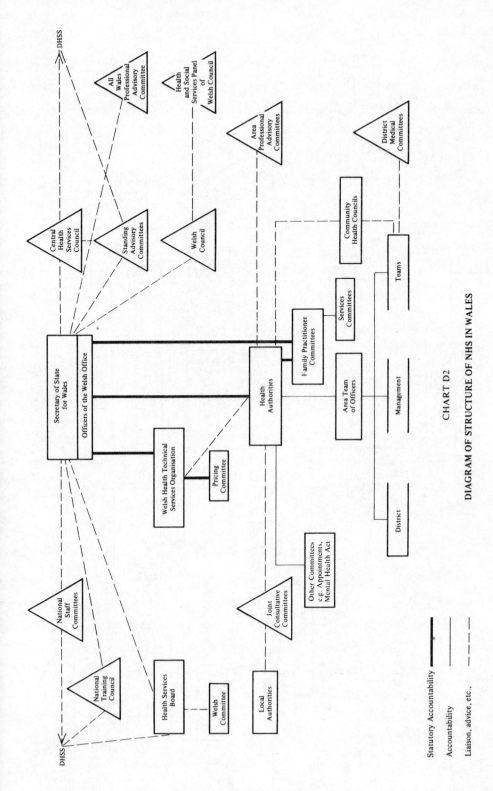

CHART D2

DIAGRAM OF STRUCTURE OF NHS IN WALES

Statutory Accountability ▬▬▬

Accountability ————

Liaison, advice, etc., — — — —

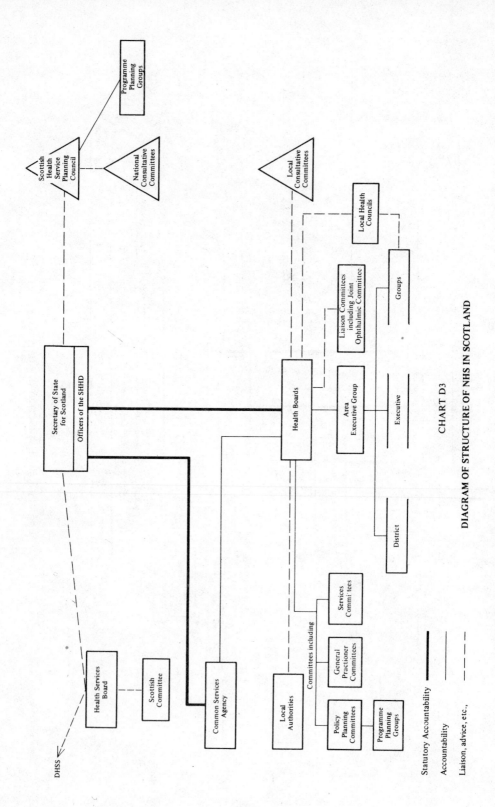

CHART D3

DIAGRAM OF STRUCTURE OF NHS IN SCOTLAND

Statutory Accountability

Accountability

Liaison, advice, etc.,

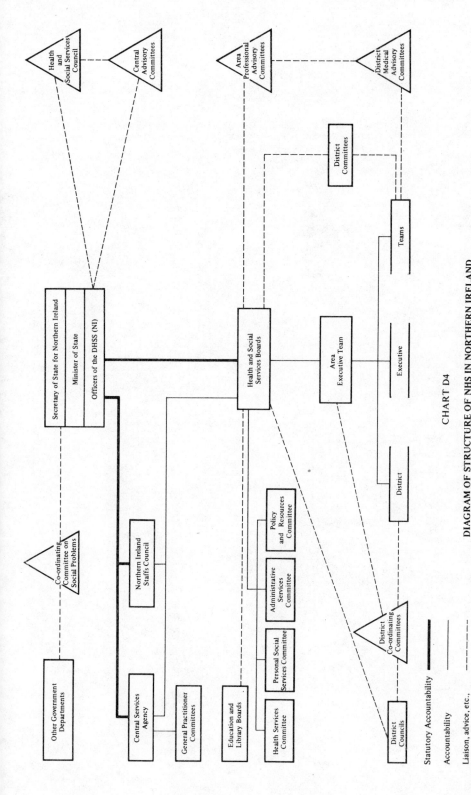

Statutory Accountability ▬▬▬▬

Accountability ───────

Liaison, advice, etc., ─ ─ ─ ─ ─

CHART D4

DIAGRAM OF STRUCTURE OF NHS IN NORTHERN IRELAND

Appendix E   Additional Tables

Table E1   NHS and PSS current expenditure by programme: England 1975/76–1977/78.

Table E2   Percentage of overseas born hospital medical staff by region and grade: UK 1978.

Table E3   Distribution of hospital beds in NHS and private hospitals for acute treatment of private patients: Great Britain 1977/78.

Table E4   Abortions performed in Great Britain: 1968–1978.

Table E5   Percentage of hospital medical consultants holding whole-time NHS appointments by region and specialty: Great Britain 1978.

Table E6   NHS expenditure and Gross Domestic Product: UK 1949–1977.

Table E7   NHS expenditure in volume terms: UK 1949–1977.

Table E8   NHS expenditure and cost terms: UK 1949–1977.

Table E9   NHS and PSS expenditure: total cost of services from all sources of finance: Great Britain 1949/50–1978/79.

Table E10   NHS and PSS expenditure; percentage of total cost on different services: Great Britain 1949/50–1978/79.

Table E11   NHS sources of finance; percentage of total by year: Great Britain 1949/50–1978/79.

Notes: [1] Where "health departments' statistics" appears as the source for tables in the text and in this Appendix, figures have been compiled from published sources and unpublished figures provided by the health departments. To avoid listing all the published sources beneath each table they are listed here for reference.

Department of Health and Social Security, *Health and Personal Social Services Statistics for England* for 1974, 1975, 1976 and 1977.

Health and Personal Social Services Statistics for Wales for 1974, 1975, 1976, 1977, 1978.

Information Services Division, Common Services Agency for the Scottish Health Service, *Scottish Health Statistics,* for 1972, 1974, 1975, 1976.

[2] UK Statistics. Our terms of reference covered the four parts of the UK and wherever possible we have provided UK statistics. There are however some problems of comparability. For example in Northern Ireland where health and personal social services operate as a unified service it has been necessary in many instances to *estimate* the proportions of expenditure, manpower etc. appropriate to health care rather than the personal social services. Where serious discrepancies occur, they are noted in the relevant table.

TABLE E1

NHS and PSS Current Expenditure by Programme: England 1975/76–1977/78

£million 1978 Public expenditure survey prices

		1975/76	1976/77	Provisional 1977/78
GRAND TOTAL		5989.2	6074.2	6213.1
PRIMARY CARE	Total	1202.9	1252.0	1259.8
Family Practitioner Services		1116.0	1169.1	1175.0
Prevention		13.9	15.6	15.1
Family Planning		13.0	12.9	12.7
Other Community Health		·60.0	54.4	57.0
GENERAL & ACUTE HOSPITAL AND MATERNITY SERVICES	Total	2319.5	2334.0	2399.1
Acute IP and OP		1810.5	1800.2	1853.0
Ambulances		112.0	111.5	115.2
Other Hospital		164.8	190.5	197.1
Obstetric IP and OP		203.9	204.4	206.0
Midwives		28.3	27.4	27.8
SERVICES MAINLY FOR ELDERLY AND PHYSICALLY HANDICAPPED	Total	789.3	801.3	820.3
Geriatric IP and OP[1]		282.9	286.0	292.8
Non-Psychiatric DP		13.3	17.1	18.6
District Nursing		84.9	91.7	92.9
Chiropody		13.6	12.2	12.7
Residential Care		180.6	182.3	183.4
Home Help		112.1	113.2	115.8
Meals		16.2	16.3	16.4
Day Care		21.4	23.5	26.2
Aids, Adaptations, Phones etc.		13.6	12.6	12.7
Services for the Disabled		50.7	46.4	44.1
SERVICES FOR MENTALLY HANDICAPPED	Total	250.6	251.9	263.0
Mental Handicap IP and OP		199.5	195.8	202.2
Residental Care		20.3	23.4	26.5
Day Care		30.8	32.7	34.3
SERVICES FOR MENTALLY ILL	Total	455.7	446.4	464.7
Mental Illness IP and OP		417.8	406.3	420.6
Psychiatric DP		16.5	17.7	20.4
Residental Care		4.6	5.1	5.8
Day Care		3.6	4.0	4.3
Special Hospital		13.2	13.3	13.6
SERVICES MAINLY FOR CHILDREN	Total	329.7	340.5	351.0
Health Visiting		49.1	49.0	52.0
School Health		57.0	54.9	57.8
Welfare Food		18.3	20.1	20.4
Residental Care		148.7	153.8	153.7
Boarding Out		17.7	20.6	23.4
Day Nurseries		33.4	36.4	36.7
Intermediate Treatment		1.0	1.1	2.0
Central Grants and YTCs		4.5	4.6	5.0
OTHER SERVICES	Total	641.5	648.1	655.2
Social Work		111.6	114.8	119.1
Other Local Authority Services		29.1	26.9	29.1
Hospital and Community Health Admin.		214.5	221.2	219.8
Local Authority Administration		140.5	141.4	143.4
Centrally Financed Services		145.8	143.8	143.8

Source: health departments' statistics.

Notes: [1] Includes units for younger disabled.

[2] Abbreviations: DP, IP, OP, YTCs – Day patients, In-patients, Out-patients, Youth Treatment Centres.

[3] A fuller explanation of the methodology of the Programme Budget from which these figures are devised can be found in Annex 2 of the DHSS Consultative Document "Priorities for Health and Personal Social Services in England", published by HMSO in 1976, and also in Appendix VI of the follow-up document, "The Way Forward", published in September 1977.

TABLE E2

Percentage of Overseas Born Hospital Medical Staff by Region and Grade: UK 1978[1]

	All Grades	Consultant	Senior Registrar	Registrar	Senior House Officer	House Officer
ENGLAND	34.6	16.0	26.5	56.8	52.8	13.5
Northern	39.0	17.5	31.2	63.2	61.1	12.3
Yorkshire	38.9	15.8	29.1	66.4	60.7	11.7
Trent	35.6	15.4	27.0	57.9	52.1	8.9
East Anglia	28.9	9.8	22.9	51.1	48.0	17.5
NW Thames	34.3	19.0	29.7	54.1	48.2	14.0
NE Thames	39.5	21.5	33.5	61.3	60.5	17.6
SE Thames	35.0	17.3	21.2	54.5	56.5	15.7
SW Thames	34.4	15.4	25.6	59.1	51.7	11.0
Wessex	25.6	13.9	26.3	44.4	39.0	10.3
Oxford	28.3	12.2	15.6	50.1	43.0	9.1
South Western	20.5	8.6	15.6	41.9	30.2	5.7
West Midlands	40.0	17.5	32.7	64.8	60.9	14.9
Mersey	34.5	11.4	33.1	55.1	53.7	16.3
North Western	39.3	18.4	21.5	63.8	58.4	16.7
London Boards of Governors	25.0	16.0	25.5	37.8	24.3	—
WALES	34.2	12.6	24.4	60.1	54.3	8.3
SCOTLAND[1]	19.3	7.8	13.3	43.5	25.7	5.0
NORTHERN IRELAND	21.0	7.3	20.5	34.8	34.0	13.7

Source: compiled from health departments' statistics.

Note: [1] Whole time equivalents except for Scotland where percentage refers to numbers. Scotland figures are for 1977.

TABLE E3

Distribution of Hospital Beds in NHS and Private Hospitals for Acute Treatment of Private Patients: Great Britain 1977–78

	Paybeds in NHS Hospitals (1.1.78)	"Acute" beds in Private Hospitals[1] (1.6.77)	Total beds for Private Acute Treatment per 100,000 population
ENGLAND	2896	3698	14.3
NW Thames	349	1049	40.9
SW Thames	165	555	25.3
SE Thames	310	240	15.5
NE Thames	290	215	13.7
London & the South East	1308[2]	2059	[3]
Oxford	173	187	16.3
East Anglia	117	117	13.0
Wessex	129	200	12.7
South Western	116	261	12.0
Yorkshire	206	186	11.0
North Western	234	160	9.7
Mersey	89	133	9.0
Trent	170	237	9.0
West Midlands	269	128	7.7
Northern	85	30	3.7
WALES	43	106	5.4
SCOTLAND	149	223	7.2
GREAT BRITAIN	3088	4027	13.2

Source: compiled from *Health Services Board Annual Report* 1978, London, HMSO, 1979; British United Provident Association unpublished statistics and Office of Population Censuses and Surveys mid-1977 civilian population estimates.

Notes: [1] Beds for the treatment of short-stay patients in private hospitals equipped with an operating theatre, excluding specialist abortion clinics.

[2] Including 194 paybeds in the London post-graduate teaching hospitals not allocated to a region.

[3] Figure not available.

428

TABLE E4

Abortions Performed in Great Britain: 1968-1978

Year	Total abortions performed in calender year	Abortions performed on women usually resident in UK	Abortions performed on women not usually resident in UK	% of all abortions performed on women not usually resident in UK	All abortions performed in NHS	% of total abortions performed in NHS	% of all abortions performed on UK residents in NHS
1968 (from 27 April)	25195	23986	1209	4.8	16064	63.8	67.0
1969	58375	53644	4731	8.1	37217	63.8	69.4
1970	91819	81721	10098	11.0	52855	57.6	64.7
1971	133110	102071	31039	23.3	59955	45.0	58.7
1972	167493	117781	49712	29.7	64596	38.6	54.8
1973	174691	120181	54510	31.2	63091	36.1	52.5
1974	170508	119130	51378	30.1	63756	37.4	53.5
1975	147029	115717	31312	21.3	58997	40.1	51.0
1976	136892	111220	25672	18.8	57087	41.7	51.3
1977[1]	140282	111624	28658	20.4	59337	42.3	53.2
1978[1]	149769	121754	28015	18.7	62793	41.9	51.6

Source: compiled from statistics provided by Scottish Health Service Common Services Agency and Office of Population Censuses and Surveys.

Note: [1] 1977 and 1978 figures are provisional.

429

TABLE E5

Percentage of Hospital Medical Consultants holding Whole-time NHS Appointments by Region and Specialty: Great Britain 1978

(a) by specialty, England and Wales

	%
All specialties	47.6
Ophthalmology	7.8
General surgery	14.4
Ear, Nose and Throat	15.5
Traumatic and Orthopaedic Surgery	15.9
Obstetrics and Gynaecology	17.6
Mental Illness	74.1
Paediatrics	80.9
Diseases of the Chest	81.3
Pathology	85.3
Accident and Emergency	85.8
Mental Handicap	91.7
Geriatric Medicine	94.0

(b) all specialties by region, Great Britain

ENGLAND	46.7
NW Thames	29.0
NE Thames	31.5
SE Thames	36.3
SW Thames	37.3
Oxford	42.1
North Western	47.5
Wessex	48.2
Yorkshire	49.8
Mersey	51.9
South Western	52.5
West Midlands	55.5
Trent	55.8
East Anglia	55.9
Northern	68.9
WALES	62.7
SCOTLAND[1]	82.2
GREAT BRITAIN	51.8

Source: compiled from health departments' statistics.

Note: [1] Scotland figures are for 1977.

430

TABLE E6
NHS Expenditure and Gross Domestic Product: UK 1949-1977

£million

Calendar year	NHS current	NHS capital	NHS other[2]	NHS total	GDP at factor cost	NHS total as percentage of GDP at factor cost
1949	414	15	4	433	10969	3.95
1950	458	16	4	478	11346	4.21
1951	476	17	6	499	12617	3.95
1952	476	15	6	497	13889	3.58
1953	500	16	5	521	14881	3.50
1954	515	18	4	537	15730	3.41
1955	555	20	4	579	16873	3.43
1956	609	20	4	633	18270	3.46
1957	655	26	4	685	19377	3.54
1958	694	29	5	728	20206	3.60
1959	750	34	4	788	21260	3.71
1960	819	37	5	861	22642	3.80
1961	879	44	5	928	24233	3.83
1962	909	55	7	971	25294	3.84
1963	968	60	7	1035	26894	3.85
1964	1047	76	7	1130	29255	3.86
1965	1176	91	8	1275	31237	4.08
1966	1290	102	9	1401	33139	4.23
1967[1]	1423	125	10	1558	34925	4.46
1968	1540	143	10	1693	37411	4.53
1969	1626	137	10	1773	39450	4.49
1970	1860	151	13	2024	43445	4.66
1971	2104	181	14	2299	49264	4.67
1972	2413	223	14	2650	54963	4.82
1973	2706	277	30	3013	63946	4.71
1974	3622	296	16	3934	73722	5.34
1975	4903	366	30	5299	92507	5.73
1976	5788	425	23	6236	109499	5.70
1977	6477	393	27	6897	123353	5.59

Source: health departments' statistics.

Notes: [1] Up to 1966 NHS current expenditure includes an imputed rent element; from 1967 this is replaced by a charge for non-trading capital consumption.
[2] Includes current grants to the personal sector and abroad and capital grants to the personal sector and to companies.

431

TABLE E7
NHS Expenditure in Volume Terms:[1] UK 1949-1977

Calendar year	NHS expenditure at 1970 prices			Indices of expenditure at constant prices 1950=100		
	Current	Capital	Total	Current	Capital	Total
1949	1065	24	1089	90.7	96.0	90.8
1950	1174	25	1199	100.0	100.0	100.0
1951	1183	23	1206	100.8	92.0	100.6
1952	1157	24	1181	98.6	96.0	98.5
1953	1177	25	1202	100.3	100.0	100.3
1954	1200	27	1227	102.2	108.0	102.3
1955	1235	28	1263	105.2	112.0	105.3
1956	1264	28	1292	107.7	112.0	107.8
1957	1293	33	1326	110.1	132.0	110.6
1958	1324	35	1359	112.8	140.0	113.3
1959	1371	41	1412	116.8	164.0	117.8
1960	1416	44	1460	120.6	176.0	121.8
1961	1424	56	1480	121.3	224.0	123.4
1962	1451	66	1517	123.6	264.0	126.5
1963	1485	76	1561	126.5	304.0	130.2
1964	1533	98	1631	130.6	392.0	136.0
1965	1602	104	1706	136.5	416.0	142.3
1966	1672	113	1785	142.4	452.0	148.9
1967	1748	119	1867	148.9	476.0	155.7
1968	1800	153	1953	153.3	612.0	162.9
1969	1781	140	1921	151.7	560.0	160.2
1970	1860	151	2011	158.4	604.0	167.7
1971	1900	165	2065	161.8	660.0	172.2
1972	1960	185	2145	167.0	740.0	178.9
1973	2041	190	2231	173.9	760.0	186.1
1974	2114	162	2276	180.1	648.0	189.8
1975	2267	175	2442	193.1	700.0	203.7
1976	2310	173	2483	196.8	692.0	207.1
1977	2360	144	2504	201.0	576.0	208.8

Source: health departments' statistics.

Notes: [1] Actual NHS expenditure deflated by an NHS price index and hence excludes the relative price effect. NHS expenditure excludes "NHS other" expenditure of Table E6.

TABLE E8
NHS Expenditure in Cost Terms[1]: UK 1949–1977

Calendar Year	NHS expenditure at 1970 prices £ million			Indices of expenditure at constant prices 1950=100		
	Current	Capital	Total	Current	Capital	Total
1949	916	33	949	91.0	94.3	91.1
1950	1007	35	1042	100.0	100.0	100.0
1951	975	35	1010	96.8	100.0	96.9
1952	895	28	921	88.7	80.0	88.4
1953	911	29	940	90.5	82.9	90.2
1954	920	32	952	91.4	91.4	91.4
1955	957	34	991	95.0	97.1	95.1
1956	989	32	1021	98.2	91.4	98.0
1957	1022	40	1062	101.5	114.3	101.9
1958	1036	43	1079	102.9	122.9	103.6
1959	1101	50	1151	109.3	142.9	110.5
1960	1182	53	1235	117.4	151.4	118.5
1961	1228	61	1289	121.9	174.3	123.7
1962	1228	74	1302	121.9	211.4	125.0
1963	1279	79	1358	127.0	225.7	130.3
1964	1349	98	1447	134.0	280.0	138.9
1965	1454	112	1566	144.4	320.0	150.3
1966	1534	121	1655	152.3	345.7	158.8
1967	1645	145	1790	163.4	414.3	171.8
1968	1721	160	1881	170.9	457.1	180.5
1969	1752	147	1899	174.0	420.0	182.2
1970	1860	151	2011	184.7	431.4	193.0
1971	1907	164	2071	189.4	468.6	198.8
1972	1984	183	2167	197.0	522.9	208.0
1973	2054	210	2264	204.0	600.0	217.3
1974	2357	193	2550	234.1	551.4	244.7
1975	2481	185	2666	246.4	528.6	255.9
1976	2568	189	2757	255.0	540.0	264.6
1977	2584	157	2741	256.6	448.6	263.1

Source: health departments' statistics.

Notes: [1] Actual NHS expenditure deflated by a general price index and hence includes the relative price effect. NHS expenditure exlcudes "NHS other" expenditure of Table E6.

TABLE E9

NHS and PSS Expenditure; Total Cost[1] of Services from All Sources of Finance: Great Britain 1949/50–1978/9

£ million current prices

Financial Year	Central Admin.	Hospital Current[4]	Hospital Capital	Executive Council Admin.[5]	General Medical[2]	Drugs	General Dental	General Ophthalmic	Welfare Foods	School Health[3]	Other Central Govt.	Local Authority Health[3 5]	Local Authority Welfare/ Personal Social Services[6]	Grand Total
1949-50	4	222	10	3	47	35	48	24	—	6	16	32	14	461
1950-51	2	247	15	3	47	39	46	22	—	6	13	38	17	495
1951-52	2	264	14	4	48	51	37	12	—	7	13	40	16	508
1952-53	3	278	13	4	85	53	31	11	—	7	23	45	18	571
1953-54	3	291	13	3	58	52	31	13	—	8	16	45	20	553
1954-55	3	309	15	4	59	55	34	13	19	8	12	48	21	581
1955-56	4	337	16	4	62	57	40	15	40	9	12	52	23	649
1956-57	4	368	17	4	66	67	44	15	30	10	11	57	27	730
1957-58	4	389	22	4	71	71	47	16	28	11	11	61	29	766
1958-59	4	416	24	5	74	77	51	15	29	11	14	66	30	814
1959-60	4	450	26	6	75	84	55	17	29	12	14	72	33	876
1960-61	5	492	30	6	101	93	59	17	29	13	16	77	37	974
1961-62	5	525	38	6	86	96	62	17	30	14	15	86	41	1020
1962-63	6	556	43	7	91	99	63	18	32	15	14	93	46	1075
1963-64	6	590	61	7	92	109	64	19	34	16	15	101	51	1163
1964-65	7	639	73	8	102	128	67	21	39	17	17	111	55	1271
1965-66	8	704	81	9	109	149	68	22	42	19	17	125	63	1408
1966-67	8	773	92	10	127	157	77	23	45	20	20	136	71	1540
1967-68	9	835	111	10	134	172	80	25	48	21	20	150	84	1690
1968-69	10	913	121	12	143	178	82	27	39	23	23	162	94	1816
1969-70	11	1013	129	13	159	196	89	30	40	25	31	105	227	2049
1970-71	14	1196	139	14	177	212	107	30	44	29	35	125	276	2398
1971-72	17	1376	173	16	191	238	118	28	18	33	42	146	335	2731
1972-73	19	1569	217	18	207	273	128	31	12	39	52	168	415	3148
1973-74	25	1778	260	19	222	299	142	34	11	44	69	196	548	3647
1974-75	29	2703	299	—	250	360	175	42	9	—	144	—	752	4763
1975-76	40	3682	395	—	333	467	231	72	15	—	185	—	1022	6442
1976-77	42	4201	415	—	373	581	254	76	18	—	209	—	1192	7361
1977-78	43	4736	378	—	395	718	265	78	22	—	233	—	1331	8199
1978-79	46	5309	448	—	450	863	329	90	27	—	303	—	1487	9352

Source: health departments' statistics.

Notes:
1 The total cost includes charges to persons using the service.
2 Because expenditure in certain years includes retrospective payments of increases in fees, strict comparisons cannot be drawn on a year to year basis.
3 Up to 1969-70 the figures include expenditure on certain local authority services which were then transferred to personal social services (including day nurseries, home helps and residential accommodation for the mentally ill and handicapped).
4 Hospitals and community health services from 1.4.74.
5 Transferred to hospitals and community health services from 1.4.74.
6 Includes expenditure on child care from 1969-70; see also Note 3.

TABLE E10

NHS and PSS Expenditure; Percentage of Total Cost on Different Services: Great Britain 1949/50–1978/79

Percentages

Financial Year	Central Admin.	Hospital Current	Hospital Capital	Executive Councils Admin.	General Medical	Drugs	General Dental	General Ophthalmic	Welfare Foods	School Health	Other Central Govt.	Local Authority Health	Local Authority Welfare/PSS	Grand Total
1949–50	0.9	48.2	2.2	0.6	10.2	7.6	10.4	5.2	—	1.3	3.5	6.9	3.0	100.0
1950–51	0.4	49.9	3.0	0.6	9.5	7.9	9.3	4.5	—	1.2	2.6	7.7	3.4	100.0
1951–52	0.4	52.0	2.7	0.8	9.4	10.0	7.3	2.4	—	1.4	2.6	7.9	3.1	100.0
1952–53	0.5	48.7	2.3	0.7	14.9	9.3	5.4	1.9	—	1.2	4.0	7.9	3.2	100.0
1953–54	0.5	52.6	2.4	0.5	10.6	9.4	5.6	2.4	—	1.4	2.9	8.1	3.6	100.0
1954–55	0.5	53.2	2.6	0.7	10.2	9.4	5.8	2.2	—	1.4	2.1	8.3	3.6	100.0
1955–56	0.5	51.9	2.5	0.6	9.6	8.8	6.2	2.3	2.9	1.4	1.8	8.0	3.5	100.0
1956–57	0.5	50.4	2.3	0.6	9.0	9.2	6.0	2.1	5.5	1.4	1.5	7.8	3.7	100.0
1957–58	0.5	50.8	2.9	0.5	9.3	9.3	6.1	2.1	3.9	1.4	1.4	8.0	3.8	100.0
1958–59	0.5	51.1	2.9	0.5	9.1	9.5	6.3	1.8	3.4	1.4	1.7	8.1	3.7	100.0
1959–60	0.5	51.4	3.0	0.6	8.5	9.6	6.3	1.9	3.3	1.4	1.6	8.2	3.7	100.0
1960–61	0.4	50.5	3.1	0.6	10.4	9.5	6.1	1.8	3.0	1.3	1.6	7.9	3.8	100.0
1961–62	0.5	51.5	3.7	0.6	8.3	9.4	6.1	1.7	2.9	1.4	1.5	8.4	4.0	100.0
1962–63	0.5	51.7	4.0	0.5	8.0	9.2	5.9	1.6	3.0	1.4	1.3	8.6	4.3	100.0
1963–64	0.5	50.7	5.2	0.6	7.8	9.4	5.5	1.6	2.9	1.4	1.3	8.7	4.4	100.0
1964–65	0.6	50.3	5.7	0.6	7.2	10.1	5.3	1.5	3.1	1.3	1.3	8.7	4.3	100.0
1965–66	0.6	50.0	5.8	0.6	7.2	10.6	4.8	1.5	3.0	1.3	1.3	8.9	4.5	100.0
1966–67	0.5	50.2	6.0	0.7	7.1	10.2	5.0	1.4	2.9	1.3	1.2	8.8	4.6	100.0
1967–68	0.5	49.4	6.6	0.6	7.5	10.2	4.7	1.4	2.8	1.2	1.3	8.9	5.0	100.0
1968–69	0.5	50.3	6.6	0.7	7.4	9.8	4.5	1.4	2.1	1.3	1.2	8.9	5.2	100.0
1969–70	0.5	49.4	6.3	0.6	7.0	9.6	4.4	1.3	2.0	1.2	1.3	5.1	11.1	100.0
1970–71	0.6	49.9	5.8	0.6	7.4	8.8	4.5	1.2	1.8	1.2	1.5	5.2	11.5	100.0
1971–72	0.6	50.4	6.3	0.6	7.0	8.7	4.3	1.0	0.7	1.2	1.5	5.4	12.3	100.0
1972–73	0.6	49.8	6.9	0.6	6.6	8.7	4.0	1.0	0.4	1.2	1.5	5.3	13.2	100.0
1973–74	0.7	48.8	7.1	0.5	6.1	8.2	3.9	0.9	0.3	1.2	1.7	5.4	15.0	100.0
1974–75	0.6	56.7	6.3	—	5.2	7.6	3.7	0.9	0.2	—	1.9	—	15.8	100.0
1975–76	0.6	57.2	6.1	—	5.2	7.2	3.6	1.1	0.2	—	3.0	—	15.9	100.0
1976–77	0.6	57.1	5.6	—	5.1	7.9	3.5	1.0	0.2	—	2.9	—	16.2	100.0
1977–78	0.5	57.8	4.6	—	4.8	8.8	3.2	1.0	0.3	—	2.8	—	16.2	100.0
1978–79	0.5	56.8	4.8	—	4.8	9.2	3.5	1.0	0.3	—	3.2	—	15.9	100.0

Source: health departments' statistics.

Notes: See Table E9.

TABLE E11

NHS[1] Sources of Finance; Percentage of Total by Year: Great Britain 1949/50–1978/79

Percentages

Financial Year	Consolidated Fund	NHS Contributions	Charges	Miscellaneous[2]
1949–50	87.8	9.8	0.7	1.7
1950–51	87.6	9.4	0.7	2.3
1951–52	88.3	9.2	1.8	0.7
1952–53	87.6	8.0	4.0	0.4
1953–54	86.5	8.3	5.0	0.2
1954–55	86.9	7.9	5.0	0.2
1955–56	87.6	7.1	5.0	0.4
1956–57	88.7	6.4	4.7	0.2
1957–58	85.0	9.5	5.3	0.3
1958–59	80.3	14.4	5.0	0.3
1959–60	80.4	14.5	4.9	0.3
1960–61	81.9	13.3	4.5	0.2
1961–62	77.7	16.5	5.6	0.2
1962–63	77.1	17.2	5.5	0.2
1963–64	77.9	16.4	5.4	0.3
1964–65	79.6	15.0	5.1	0.4
1965–66	83.8	13.3	2.6	0.2
1966–67	84.8	12.4	2.4	0.3
1967–68	86.5	10.9	2.3	0.3
1968–69	84.8	11.8	3.1	0.3
1969–70	85.9	10.3	3.5	0.3
1970–71	85.8	10.8	3.2	0.3
1971–72	85.7	10.3	3.6	0.5
1972–73	87.0	9.0	3.6	0.4
1973–74	88.1	7.9	3.5	0.5
1974–75	91.3	5.7	2.6	0.4
1975–76	89.2	8.5	2.0	0.3
1976–77	88.0	9.7	2.1	0.2
1977–78	88.0	9.6	2.1	0.3
1978–79	88.2	9.5	2.0	0.3

Source: health departments' statistics.

Notes: [1]Excludes local authority health expenditure before 1974.

[2]Includes sales of land and buildings, charges to practitioners for use of health centres, port health charges.

Appendix F   A Note on Occupational Health and Safety by Mr Peter Jacques

1   Arrangements for health and safety at work were last examined by the 1970–1972 Robens Committee on Health and Safety at Work.[1] The Committee's major conclusions were that improvements in workplace health and safety must involve employers and workers, and that the prevention of accidents and diseases involved more than traditional measures. It recommended that a more comprehensive approach was required which involved whole systems of work, including an employers' organisation, attitudes and behaviour, training and joint consultation.

2   The 1974 Health and Safety at Work Act is based on this wider approach. It imposes wide ranging general duties on employers, and others, which require a more comprehensive response to improving their workplace health and safety performance. The principle of involving employers and workers is also included in the 1974 Act and their representatives now serve on the Health and Safety Commission, and that Commission's hazard and industry advisory committees.

3   The principle of involving employers and workpeoples' organisations at national and industry level was extended to the workplace by the 1978 Safety Representatives and Safety Committees Regulations. The Regulations enable recognised and independent trade unions to appoint safety representatives at the workplace, and allow them day to day involvement in health and safety at their workplace. Every safety representative has the right to participate in a TUC or trade union's training course and over 50,000 have attended such courses.

4   The various health and safety Inspectorates, and the Employment Medical Advisory Service (EMAS) were brought together into the Health and Safety Executive (HSE) by the 1974 Act, and in addition to its enforcement role, the HSE provides information and advice to employers (including the NHS), trade unions, and others, including general practitioners, on all aspects of health and safety at work. It services the Health and Safety Commission (HSC) and its advisory committees, advises government departments, including the Department of Health and Social Security and finances and carries out research. The local authority environmental officer and other agencies also provide health and safety enforcement and advisory services under the general direction of the Health and Safety Commission and Health and Safety Executive. The HSC and the HSE have responsibility for over a million workplaces, and 25 million workpeople. In addition, they also have responsibility for the protection of the public for workplace hazards and pollution.

5   The more comprehensive approach envisaged by the Robens Committee set out in the 1974 Act is clearly necessary if a major impact is to be made on the large number of workpeople who are killed or injured at work, or die or suffer from diseases contracted at work. Each year over 1,000 workpeople are killed or die of work related diseases, and nearly 800,000 are injured and require time off from work. The construction, mining and quarrying and engineering industries continue to be the source of most fatalities and accidents:

---

[1] *Safety and Health at Work,* Report of the Committee 1970–72, (Cmnd 5034), London, HMSO, 1972.

TABLE F1
Fatalities and accidents in construction, mining and quarrying and engineering industries: Great Britain 1978

	Fatal	Total
Construction	157	34,493
Mining and Quarrying	88	47,287
Engineering	88	77,943

Source: Report of the Chief Inspector of Factories, Health and Safety Commission, London, HMSO, 1979.

6   Employers have the major responsibility for complying with the general duties under the 1974 Act but the 1976 EMAS survey of occupational health services in some industries indicated that employers lack resources to meet the legal duties.

7   The survey showed that the size of the firm is the dominant factor in determining occupational health services. For example, about eight per cent of firms employing over 60% of workers have some medical and/or nursing staff. Whereas 85% of firms with about 35% of workers have no such staff. In surveying the range of activities for which occupational health personnel employed for firms were responsibile the report revealed that the most common activity appeared to be "treatment of acute emergencies and of minor illnesses and injuries". The next most frequent activity was "pre-employment of pre-placement medical examinations/screening procedures". Only about 20% of firms said they regularly undertake activities such as rehabilitation, environmental surveillance, biological monitoring and educational work. These firms tended to be large employers with well staffed services.

8   The HSC is still considering comments on the document but the TUC evidence to the Royal Commission emphasised that since employers have legal health and safety and welfare duties, they should be required to satisfy enforcing authorities that they employ or have under some form of contract the necessary skilled personnel to carry out those duties. The range of skills required by employers would vary between industries, but at its widest point should include: occupational medicine specialists, mechanical and electrical engineers, chemists, occupational hygienists, safety advisors, and lawyers. For example, the control of lead in the working environment requires medical supervision of the workpeople, and hygienists and engineers to monitor and develop mechanical and technical control of the environment to reduce human lead absorption by employees.

9   The EMAS survey reported in the HSE's discussion document "Occupational Health Services: The Way Ahead" recognised that a range of disciplines and skills are required in the health and safety field but concentrated on the number, distribution and work of medical practitioners and nurses involved in this field.

10   There are widely differing views about who should provide these wide ranging skills, and where the administrative responsibility should lie. One of the most widely held views is that the NHS should develop or establish a comprehensive occupational health service. Employers, and others, would receive the service free of charge or be required to pay the full cost for any work carried out on their behalf.

11   It is not always clear what is meant by a comprehensive occupational health service. The Robens Committee noted that "occupational health" is subject to a number of interpretations but concluded that it is concerned with "the reactions of workpeople to their working environment and the prevention of ill health arising from working

conditions"[1]. Other definitions of "occupational health" are not only concerned with the effect of work on health, but also the effect of health on work; for example, problems such as disability, and alcoholism. Clearly, either of these approaches involves workers' safety, health and welfare and the whole range of skills are necessary to secure that end. In that respect, a comprehensive occupational health service provides an essential means for dealing with all workplace health and safety problems. It also deals with the sterile view that occupational health is the province of doctors and nurses and safety and welfare that of other disciplines. The health and safety of workpeople is too important and complex for such compartmentalisation, and each discipline has a contribution to make in all areas of the field. The major problem of occupational health is resources, and not demarcation.

12   The major Government responsibility in health and safety lies with the HSC and HSE which come within the scope of the Department of Employment. A number of bodies have suggested that the responsibility should be moved to the NHS.

13   It is not entirely clear what this may mean but there are a number of possibilities. These include the NHS becoming responsible for the occupational medicine aspects of occupational health, or that all responsibility for health and safety and welfare should be transferred from the Department of Employment to the Department of Health and Social Security/National Health Service.

14   The proposal that the NHS should provide the occupational medicine aspect to occupational health and safety would seem to imply that the HSC/HSE's medical and nursing staff in the EMAS and related laboratory services and research should be transferred. It might be that these professions employed directly in industry would also be transferred. The NHS would then presumably contribute to the work of the HSC, its advisory committees, the HSE and other enforcement bodies, employers, trade unions, general practitioners, and individuals on the same basis as it presently provides. This approach would, apart from ensuring enormous administrative complexity, undermine the co-ordinated approach proposed under a comprehensive service. Of course, unless the HSC and the HSE could be assured of full and continuing access to its former medical and nursing research staff, they could be expected to recruit medical and nursing advice themselves. While transferring the medical and nursing professions into the NHS would promote closer contact with their professional colleagues it would not necessarily contribute to total health care. Another suggestion would be to transfer responsibility for the Act and the HSC and HSE from the Department of Employment to the NHS. However, the NHS is broadly organised in geographical areas, whereas the HSE is more industrially organised; the HSC is a national organisation and there is no counterpart in the NHS. Another alternative is to transfer the responsibilty from the DE to the DHSS. This would not in itself lead to closer relations between those dealing with health and safety in the NHS and other NHS staffed departments, and indeed there are strong views that the DHSS's health and safety responsibility, particularly for dangerous pathogens, should be transferred to the HSC.

15   The 1974 Act provides the legislative framework for a comprehensive and systematic approach to health and safety, but the major problem is how this can be translated into sufficient skilled manpower and resources at the workplace. The concept of a "national" comprehensive occupation health service, along the same lines as the NHS, would be relevant if employers did not have the legal responsibility of ensuring the health and safety of their own employees (and others in relevant circumstances). It could be that such a service could advise employers, but this function is already carried out by the HSE, of which the EMAS is an integral part.

---

[1]*Safety and Health at Work: Op cit,* paragraph 356.

16   The HSC and HSE (or any other body) have a responsibility to advise, encourage and indeed enforce those duties on employers, but not to limit, divert or reduce them. The HSC has not completed its examination of what resources employers will need to carry out their legal responsibilities but it will need to progress this matter urgently. Clearly, employers will need to employ or contract more skilled manpower to meet their duties, and the HSC will need to plan and and co-ordinate this development with relevant bodies, including the NHS.

17   There are overlapping areas between the HSC, HSE and the NHS, particularly the treatment of workpeople injured or ill from work activity. The NHS, in order to treat and rehabilitate effectively, will need to have a clear view of the work undertaken by its patients. The EMAS has a responsibility for advising general practitioners and others about health and safety matters, and this should be encouraged. However, closer relations must be established with NHS authorities so that occupational health and safety can be fully taken into account in planning NHS services, treatment and training.

Appendix G   Principles and Practice in Rehabilitation.
A Paper by Mildred Blaxter

Introduction

The inadequacies of our present services in the field of rehabilitation are increasingly coming under strong criticism. This concern is not new, as a long series of reports bears witness; the Tomlinson (1943), Piercy (1956), McCorquodale (1965), Tunbridge (1972), Mair (1973), Sharp (1974) and Snowden (1976) Reports are all evidence that this is an area conspicuous for expert and concerned recommendations but not for action.

It has become apparent that greater attention needs to be given to rehabilitation, in part because of the changing pattern of disease in advanced societies and the increasing technical sophistication of rehabilitative procedures, and in part because of changing concepts of the role of medicine and health services. The current dissatisfaction has been fuelled by a considerable body of recent research findings, all showing very clearly the extent of hardship, the waste of potential, and the dysfunctional nature of many of our present structures. The Social Survey Division national study (Harris 1971), in particular, has been influential in demonstrating how large the proportion of disabled people in the population may be, and how few of them are reached by rehabilitative services.

This paper discusses primarily the short- and medium-term solutions, with speculation about long-term changes reserved for a final section.

1. Principles

1.1   Before selecting specific areas of the subject for discussion of practical remedies, some general principles ought briefly to be considered. It must be acknowledged that some of the dilemmas and problems are very fundamental. The term "rehabilitation" has been the subject of a variety of interpretations, and this has had practical consequences concerned with administrative structures and the drawing of demarcation lines. The concept has, in the past, suffered from being too narrowly defined as the application of specific therapies within a limited range of specialities (rheumatology, orthopaedics) or as training programmes aimed only at return to employment. In the reaction against this, the concept has suffered at the other extreme by being too widely applied to almost the whole of medicine and social welfare. These discussions ought by now to be resolved, since general agreement has probably been reached that the most useful definition is along the lines of "restoration of patients to their fullest physical, mental and social capabilities, within the limits of a disability" (Mair Report). Nevertheless, on the one hand the narrower concept is difficult to dislodge from the consciousness of the medical profession, or indeed of the general public, and on the other, the widest interpretation is unhelpfully vague as a prescription for action.

1.2   Who the "disabled" or "handicapped" are, to whom the concept of rehabilitation should apply, has equally raised problems. There are particular public stereotypes of "the disabled", including the blind, the crippled, the paralysed, the congenitally handicapped, and so on; the groups for whom services were first instituted. The disease-

441

oriented or physical systems-oriented structure of medicine also favours categories described by the names of disabling diseases. The current movement, however, is towards a much looser definition of disability, to include progressive and fluctuating conditions and the diseases of deterioration as well as the more stable handicaps emphasised in the past. The Harris survey has been important for its demonstration that these "stereotypical" disabilities make up only relatively small groups among those who are functionally disabled. By the definitions of handicap used, major groups living outside institutional care were shown to include those suffering from arthritis (28.4% of all the "handicapped and impaired"), diseases of the circulatory system (16.0%), diseases of the respiratory system (9.1%), senility (3.5%) and mental disorders (3.3%, probably an under-estimate). Harris also pointed out that only about 15% of the handicapped living in the community were under 50, and 58% were aged 65 and over. This loosening of the definition of the client for rehabilitative service raises obvious problems, including the dilemma (for administrative purposes) of distinguishing between "disability" and "old age".

1.3   Other fundamental dilemmas relate to the current movements towards a redistribution of resources between "cure" and "care", and towards community rather than institutional care. These newer ideologies have to be superimposed upon an extremely complex structure of statutory and voluntary services which has grown up over a long period. Categorisations and systems of assessment, in particular, may be ill-matched to newer concepts of need.

1.4   These fundamental problems must be acknowledged. However, it could be suggested that the strongest criticism which could be levelled at our society's provisions for the rehabilitation and welfare of disabled people is that they are highly hypocritical. There is considerable agreement about the general principles which ought to be applied, but action in every area of health and welfare is confined to cosmetic tinkering with the system, adding new details here and exhortations there but avoiding at all costs any fundamental change which will upset the balance of existing systems. It is, for instance, hypocrisy to congratulate ourselves on new legislation for the disabled in the community (the Chronically Sick and Disabled Persons Act) without ensuring that it can be implemented. Research on the consequences of this Act suggests that, though it has certainly had the positive effect of raising expectations and improving public awareness, it has also resulted in a great deal of conflict, cynicism, and disappointment.

1.5   In the field of work, it is agreed in principle that as many disabled people as possible should be "integrated in the community", but no real attempt is made to bring old-fashioned provisions up-to-date, or to tackle the really difficult problems involving trade unions, wage structures and employers. The equity of standardised income maintenance irrespective of the nature or cause of a disability (though probably including provision for special needs) is generally accepted, and the rational concept of "partial incapacity", replacing the more common "all or nothing" provisions, is established in peripheral areas of the social security system. The ludicrous situation has now been reached, however, where the regulations for the conglomeration of benefits, compensation, pensions, special allowances, discretionary payments, and so on, which may be applicable, fill a fat book.

1.6   The result is that Britain, once in the forefront, is generally acknowledged to have been left behind by many other nations whose provisions for the rehabilitation of disabled people are simpler, bolder, and less clogged up with the residues of a long history.

2.   Rehabilitation Services in the Hospital Sector

2.1   Although not all the people to whom rehabilitation services are relevant have received hospital treatment, the hospital is an obvious starting-point for the examination of specific services. Follow-up studies of various sorts have offered clear evidence that the rehabilitative needs of the majority of patients have not been considered while they were in hospital (e.g. McKenzie et al. 1962; Butler and Pearson 1970; Hewett 1970; Sainsbury 1970; Skeet 1970; Goble and Nichols 1971; Johnson and Johnson 1973; Blaxter 1976) and criticism has been levelled at hospital medicine for its "succeed or fail" attitude to patient care, based upon the traditional diagnostic-therapeutic model.

2.2   In an attempt to raise the status of rehabilitative medicine, the suggestion has frequently been made that a full-time speciality of rehabnilitation medicine should be developed (Piercy Report, Tunbridge Report, Mair Report) and departments of rehabilitation established. In recent years a training programme for the speciality has been instituted and some consultants appointed, and a notable focus has been provided by the foundation of the Europe Chair of Rehabilitation at Southampton with its expressed aim of "promoting further integration between hospital and community services". Despite a few successful examples, however, the idea has not been received with enthusiasm by the medical profession as a whole. There has been some dispute about whether rehabilitation specialists ought to be independent consultants with their own units, to whom patients could be referred as to any other speciality, or a resource to be used by other specialists. There is an uneasy, and unclarified, relationship between rheumatology (a speciality which has been designated as "rheumatology and rehabilitation") and the newer and more widely conceived speciality of rehabilitation medicine, which has tended to obscure the particular needs and problems of both. Some geriatricians, orthopaedic surgeons and psychiatrists have seen a speciality in rehabilitation as overlapping with their own and administrative control over rehabilitative therapies may be resented. Other doctors may resist the proposals as a challenge to their professional competence, and suggest that they already undertake comprehensive rehabilitation. Because of these conflicts, change from within the profession is likely to be slow.
2.3   The proposal has repeatedly been made, however, that regional rehabilitation services should be set up, based on district general hospitals (e.g. BMA 1968; Agerholm 1972) to provide a basic assessment service, specialised therapies, teaching, research and development programmes, and an information service. Limb-fitting and appliance services should also be centred here. Nineteen "Medical Rehabilitation Demonstration Centres" have so far been established and some of these (e.g. Garston Manor Rehabilitation Centre) provide model examples. These centres are, however, variable in scope and structure, as yet too few, and notably absent in geographical areas where need is probably greatest. Fourteen out of nineteen are south of a line from the Wash to the Bristol Channel, with none in Wales or Scotland.

2.4   The contribution of the remedial professions of physiotherapy, occupational therapy, orthotics, remedial gymnastics, speech therapy, bioengineering and vocational rehabilitation, which should all be represented at such centres, is generally appreciated. Some inefficient use of these therapies arises, however, from the frequently-expressed feeling of clinicians that scientific evaluation of their effects is not well developed. The contribution which clinical psychology may be able to make, not only to the better understanding of patient problems, but also in the fields of behaviour modification and training in biofeedback, probably remains to be evaluated and exploited (Meyerson and Kerr 1975). This is likely to be an important area of development.

3.   Hospital and Community

3.1   In 1972 the Tunbridge Report asserted:

"A major complaint in all the evidence was the general failure of co-ordination and communication between the hospital, the general practitioner, the community services, and the services of the Department of Employment, and the unnecessary delays in starting rehabilitative treatment which result from this."

There is little evidence from the follow-up studies which have been mentioned that this situation has changed. Exhortations to the medical profession seem unlikely, however, to effect change, since the causes of poor communication appear to lie very deeply within professional practices.

3.2 The division of labour between specialist and community doctor has never been clarified, and this is especially so in the case of long-term, chronic and fluctuating illness, and where patients are attending specialist clinics. Is the specialist to instruct the general practitioner in the patient's management? Several studies (Forder, Reti and Silver 1969; Blaxter 1976) have shown that his reluctance to do so has the result of keeping the general practitioner ignorant of factors he should be aware of, and sometimes leaves the GP under the impression that his responsibility for management has been taken over by the hospital. The consultants observed by Forder et al. assumed, quite wrongly, that the GP would ask for advice if he needed it; they assumed, quite wrongly, that the patient's circumstances and family would be already known by the GP; and they assumed, quite wrongly, that the GP would see himself as having a co-ordinating function, and would ensure that rehabilitative and community services swung into action. Some of the patients followed by Blaxter were being given totally incompatible advice by clinic doctors and by GPs. Specialists who had long experience in comparatively rare conditions did not appear to allow for the fact that this might be the first case that the GP had seen.

3.3 In the past rehabilitation has indeed been considered to be the responsibility of the hospital. In the absence of the specialised units recommended in the previous section, however, this has meant that the individual consultant has been expected to have expertise not only in the long-term aspects of conditions within his own speciality, but also in employment advice and knowledge of living conditions in the community. In the Aberdeen study, the few referrals to the Disablement Resettlement Officer involved hospital rather than community doctors, and some consultants had also directly contacted local authortity services on their patient's behalf. These interventions tended to produce results, but it can be questioned whether they were the best use of the time of busy specialists. And, of course, only a small minority of patients could be selected for such services.

3.4 The dilemma exists that the hospital consultant, with short-term responsibility for the patient and a limited knowledge of his life circumstances, has unlimited power to prescribe therapies, aids and appliances, and may (in a minority of cases) feel it is his responsibility to take action concerning the patient's vocational and social rehabilitation. The general practitioner, with long-term responsibility and potentially better knowledge, is unsure of his responsibilities and limited in his access to services. Following the recommendations of the BMA Working Party (1968), the GP is now permitted to prescribe a wider range of appliances, and with the development of health centres there has been some build-up of diagnostic and assessment facilities (such as radiological and physiotherapy services) available to him. The "health care team" in the community is acknowledged, ideally, to consist of at least social workers, health visitors, physiotherapists, occupational therapists, chiropodists, and nurses. Structures are evolving slowly in the community, but professional practices are lagging behind.

3.5 One doctor must have overall and long-term responsibility for the patient's future, especially during confusing periods when he may be attending several clinics or being re-admitted to hospital under the care of different consultants. Obviously many patients need, firstly, the specialised assessment and advice of the consultant and the hospital team, and the services of special rehabilitation units where they exist (these units also have an educative value, especially if the GP can be involved). For the most part and for most patients, however, rehabilitation then takes place in the community. For this purpose the general practitioner must be given better facilities, permitted more responsibility for referral to specialist therapies where they are not available in health centres, and provided with better channels through which he may obtain specialised advice. It must be clear that the long-term responsibility is his.

3.6 It is not, of course, suggested that actually co-ordinating community and health service facilities, from speech therapy to housing adaptations or home helps, is the best use of a busy doctor's time. While retaining overall responsibility, he needs to be able to delegate practical aspects, as well as the social assessments in which other professions may be more skilled than he, to another member of the community team. The Snowden Report suggested that the proper person for this role is the health visitor. Certainly it is indisputable that it should be one person, rather than (as at present) that responsibility for the initiation and provision of services should be split between hospital social workers, community social workers, health visitors, community occupational therapists, the doctors themselves, and (for special groups or in different places) many other people.

4. Community Services

4.1 The first major gap that leads to confusion and inefficiency in rehabilitation services – that between hospital medicine and community medicine – has been discussed. The second and parallel gap is that between the NHS on the one hand, and local authority and voluntary services on the other.

4.2 The welfare of the handicapped is an area where voluntary effort and local initiative have always been held to be appropriate. The result is a patchwork of services of uneven quality and immense complexity. The unvarying theme of all studies of the needs and problems experienced by handicapped people concerns lack of information, confused lines of referral for services, duplication in some services (for instance, the provision of aids) and unmet need in others (for instance, chiropody or occupational therapy services). The diagram, Annex 1, is offered as a factual representation of the sources through which a sample of disabled people in one place and at one time obtained various services and aids to assist with daily living. It cannot, of course, be generalised to other places and other times, but demonstrates a typical complexity. It is not surprising that many research studies have shown that both patients and doctors find the system difficult to deal with.

4.3 The variability of local authority services has been a subject of much criticism (eg Davies 1968; Murray and Orwell 1973; Snowden Report 1976). It can be suggested that the very fundamental problems here have never been properly faced. Within the NHS standards of care are centrally set, and most failures are visible and responsibility is clearly assignable. The nature of the organisation of local authority services fosters variability and the worst neglect is invisible. An Economist Intelligence Unit study (1973) commented:

> "No independent and critical appraisal of community services exists, nor is it likely so long as local authority 'independence' is used as a justification for not enforcing uniform minimum standards of care."

4.4 There has been a considerable body of sophisticated work of recent years which demonstrates that care in the community is economically preferable to institutional care, and to devote resources to rehabilitation services is preferable to allowing the chronically sick and handicapped to become dependent (e.g. Dunnell and Ide 1974; Wiseman and Cullis 1975; Economist Intelligence Unit 1973). The problem is, however, that the money involved comes from different sources. While the NHS must order its own priorities, nevertheless it is part of medical ideology that in the individual case cost ought not to stand in the way if "need" is established, and the responsibility for deciding whether a particular treatment can be "afforded" is largely taken off the individual doctor's shoulders by policy decisions made at higher levels. Money for local authority services, however, is perceived as coming out of the rate-payer's pocket and means-tested contributions are frequently required. Thus, these services are vulnerable to all the local and perhaps contradictory pressures: generosity towards the unfortunate versus the puritan ethic of self-help, civic pride against care with rate-payers' money, concern for children or the aged versus concern for the handicapped.

4.5 Local authorities are exhorted to offer "care in the community" for all those groups for whom "curative" medicine is inappropriate and institutional care is increasingly thought to be undesirable: the elderly, psychiatric patients, handicapped children, and the mentally handicapped. Even where provision is in principle mandatory, however, the definition of "need" and the practicable level of provision are left to local discretion. Where the services concern benefits which many of the non-disabled would also appreciate (e.g. the vexed question of the supply of telephones under the Chronically Sick and Disabled Persons Act, or the provision of modern bathrooms for local authority tenants), or where disabled and other groups of the population are in direct competition for limited resources (e.g. home-helps or meals-on-wheels for the elderly) the choices that have to be made present local authorities with almost insuperable problems of equity. Rehabilitative or "half-way" hostels for the mentally handicapped or psychiatric patients are strongly advocated at a policy level, and there is growing evidence about the benefits of care in small homes, rather than hospitals, for mentally handicapped or multiply handicapped children (Oswin 1978). Until a redistribution of funding from the NHS to community care takes place, however, and new methods are found for direct financial support to local authorities for these specific purposes, local authortity provision will inevitably be variable and inadequate.

4.6 There will obviously always be a place for voluntary effort in services for the disabled, especially in providing innovative and flexible services. The present position where local authorities rely on voluntary organisations to carry out many of their statutory duties is, however, unsatisfactory. Voluntary organisations are – as they should be – even more variable, affected by historical chance, and diverse in their definitions of "need", than local authority structures, and to use them in this way blurs the distinction between statutory rights to basic services and the extra services which the community wishes to offer voluntarily.

4.7 The position of the community social worker, outside the health service unless attached to practices, but given under the Chronically Sick and Disabled Persons Act the responsibility of filling many health-related needs, is at present unsatisfactory and misunderstood by a large proportion of the public. Better collaboration with general practitioners might utilise the special skills of social workers more effectively, particularly in providing help before crisis and the disintegration of families is reached. The day-to-day routine provision of health-related aids would, however, be much more suitably placed within the health sector than within the social work sector.

5. Aids and Appliances

5.1 The confusion between NHS, and local authority, and voluntary agency provision which has been described is a major cause of the general dissatisfaction about the aids, applicances and domestic adaptations provided for disabled people. The position concerning research and development has improved considerably since the trenchant criticism of the BMA Report of 1968, when the design of aids was described as "often empirical if not vintage Heath Robinson". The fruits of this research and development have still, however, not reached the majority of the clients. Unless fortunate enough to have access to one of the few up-to-date specialised clinics, most disabled people in the community lack advice and information about aids, struggle with makeshift adaptations and old-fashioned appliances, and leave many of the appliances they are provided with to gather dust, unused. The BMA Report considered that perhaps 30% of the wheelchairs issued proved unsuitable, and Goble and Nichols (1971) suggested that lack of utilisation of appliances was due both to the inadequacy of the equipment provided and to the inadequacy of the evaluation of the patient's real needs when assessed in an isolated hospital setting.

5.2　The BMA Report provided indisputable evidence of the failures of "an administrative procedure, haphazardly developed over the years, that combines rigidity and concentration at the centre, confusion and incomplete coverage at the point of supply and inadequate information and communication at every level between". This is still an excellent description of the system. No new enquiries about the remedies need to be instituted, for most of the comprehensive and authoritative recommendations of the BMA Working Party remain to be implemented. The greater part of these recommendations concern administrative and educational deficiencies and do not involve major allocation of resources. There is therefore little excuse for an unwillingness to make radical changes.

6.　Vocational Rehabilitation

6.1　Employment, retraining and resettlement services may be thought to be outside the sphere of health services. However, two points may be made: firstly, it is very wasteful of resources – not least in terms of professional skills – for one of society's systems to devote itself to fitting people for the resumption of work or an active community life, only to have its contribution frustrated by deficiencies in another system. The evidence is clear that many people who are capable of work do not find it, that others go back to even more unsuitable work than they may have had before, and that for very many people disablement or chronic sickness begins a slow slide into under-employment, absenteeism and finally chronic unemployment. The deficiencies of our present systems of vocational assistance and retraining have been very fully documented and discussed, not least by the consultative documents produced by the Department of Employment (Ferguson and McPhail 1954; McKenzie et al. 1962; Taylor and Fairrie 1968; Greaves 1969; Buckle 1971; Mattingly 1973; Topliss 1975; Blaxter 1976; Department of Employment 1972, 1973a, b, c, 1974; Manpower Services Commission 1978).

6.2　Secondly, vocational rehabilitation does begin within the health service, and at every point thereafter doctors are involved in making assessments and giving advice. There has been some work recently on the subject of assessment systems (Garrad and Bennett 1971; Sainsbury 1973) which should obviously be encouraged, since there is general agreement that some of the current systems of classification bear no relation to the realities of handicap and if used as a starting point in vocational guidance may actually mislead by irrelevant labelling.

6.3　Rehabilitation may begin in occupational therapy or other departments or units within a hospital, but thereafter the system is administratively fragmented and progression through it is interrupted by discontinuities at every point. Services for advice, assessment and retraining are administered by the Employment Services Agency. Sheltered employment is largely provided by "statutory/voluntary" independent agencies. "Diversionary" or "occupational" employment is offered in a network of centres – variously called occupational centres, day-centres, training centres, etc. – by local authorities and by voluntary societies. Certain voluntary societies (e.g. for spastics, or the blind) have traditionally supplied much of the training and employment service for special groups. Large employers have their own services. The Employment Medical Advisory Service within the Health and Safety Executive may also be involved.

6.4　The deficiencies of this confused system, and of the out of date policies still based on the report of the Tomlinson Committee (1943) and the Disabled Persons. (Employment) Act (1944), are well-known. There is, in summary, some agreement that the "quota" system (by which all larger employers are expected to employ disabled people as 3% of their workforce) serves little useful purpose, and that the "designation" of two low-status jobs as reserved for disabled workers merely lowers the esteem in which handicapped workers are held. It is also acknowledged that the system has problems in accommodating the older person disabled by chronic sickness who increasingly forms the major proportion of its clientele, and that the Register of disabled workers serves little useful purpose, since it is simply not known what relationship there is between those who are registered – both employed and unemployed – and those who are not. Both retraining services and sheltered employment are limited in scope, with too heavy an emphasis on industrial work, and used by only a small proportion of the people who might benefit from them. Many of the more imaginative provisions within the system, such as the possibilities of assisting people to set up their own business at home, or of providing special tools and equipment to the disabled in open employment, are very little used. Additionally, the role of the key professional worker in the resettlement service, the Disablement Resettlement Officer, is exceptionally demanding, expecting him to act simultaneously as both policeman and helper to both employees and employers.

6.5 At the conclusion of schooling, there is also concern about the point of transition to employment. There is little special provision for the disabled school-leaver, and few facilities for his vocational training. For some time, research has been demonstrating that at the point of hand-over from educational to employment services, many young people become "lost". There is a great need for careers advice, assessment, and training centres specifically for handicapped school-leavers (Jackson 1968; Tuckey et al. 1972; Morgan 1974; Department of Education and Science 1974).

6.6 The complete overhaul which the system requires (and which has been promised for some years) has been considered to be outside the boundaries of the health service. It can be suggested, however, that in the short-term the training of all doctors should at least include a knowledge of the system, so that they may help and advise their patients. It has been found (Blaxter 1976) that in fact the actions of doctors may, because of their lack of knowledge about the time-tables, requirements, and possibilities of the employment system (and similarly of the system of national insurance) actually run counter to the patient's best interests.

6.7 In the long term, there are cogent arguments for the complete removal of the employment rehabilitation services from the Employment Services Agency, who would of course retain placement and retraining services. The development of more regional hospital centres (paragraph 2.3) could lead to an expansion of vocational rehabilitation within the Health Service which would be more acceptable to the potential clients and would better integrate the medical and vocational aspects. It could be suggested that this development is particularly relevant in an economic context of relatively high rates of general unemployment. In such a situation, agencies responsible for employment cannot be expected to devote resources and priority to disabled people in preference to other, more politically urgent, groups of the population.

7. Medical Education and the Doctor's Function

7.1 Any considerable shift in medical practices and attitudes in the field of rehabilitation will, in the long term, necessitate important changes in the education of doctors. Modest changes in this area have long been advocated. The Tunbridge Report commented:

> "With few exceptions, medical schools have not followed the Piercy recommendations to include rehabilitation as an integral part of undergraduate training or of postgraduate study. Until they do, rehabilitation will never become part of the young doctor's thinking".

The Royal Commission on Medical Education (Todd Report 1968) also recommended that all medical students should receive teaching in social and behavioural sciences, so that they would become aware "of the problems for doctor, patient and family in the management of illness and handicap in the community".

7.2 Most medical schools do now provide their undergraduates with courses in behavioural sciences, and "rehabilitation" is commonly taught – in some cases in imaginative ways, involving patient contact and exposure to a "therapeutic team" approach – in departments of community medicine and general practice. On the whole, however, behavioural sciences attract little enthusiasm or priority, and rehabilitation is not considered to be one of the more interesting subjects.

7.3 It has been suggested that because of the compartmentalised structure of medical education, and the dominance of the diagnosis and treatment of acute illness, this is inevitable. To await the complete restructuring of medical education is, however, a very long-term solution, and it seems more profitable to consider the way in which education in rehabilitation should fit in current structures. Much of the problem arises because of the confusion as to whether rehabilitation is a specialised subject in its own right, an integral part of other clinical specialities, or simply a question of "the right attitudes" or "teaching the doctor to consider the whole patient". At the level of each clinical speciality, it is usually asserted that "of course" rehabilitation is taught already; at a wider level there is a tendency to talk in such vague generalities that it is hardly surprising if the subject is not taken seriously.

7.4 In fact, rehabilitation should be taught at both the specialised and the general level; within specialities it ought to be treated in a much more scientific and sophisticated way than it is at present, and – paradoxically – at the general level there is an urgent need for doctors to be taught to be receptive to non-scientific concepts of health and illness, and to ideas of sickness and disability as social as well as clinical facts. The patient is not, at the point where rehabilitation is relevant, a passive object lying in a hospital bed, but an individual who has to make choices about his activities and his future. Rehabilitation is a co-operative process, and in order to make these choices the patient has to have the best information possible not only about his present condition but also about the probable consequences for the future and the time-span of likely events. The doctor, if he is to prescribe therapy and give advice, requires this information too. It is sometimes argued that knowledge about outcomes simply does not exist, or even cannot exist because of the variation between individuals, or alternatively that it is something which every specialist knows from experience. At the level of individual specialities, it is certain that the fruits of experience require to be systematised, information about outcomes of treatment collated, therapies evaluated, and the effects of interventions monitored. The objective ought to be to teach medical students as much about outcomes of disease as about diagnosis of disease, and at as detailed, scientific and sophisticated a level. It may well be that this cannot be achieved without a considerable redirection of research effort. Only when this is possible, however, will "rehabilitation" become an exciting and important subject within the medical school.

7.5 At the more general level, all students (but especially those who will become general practitioners) should obviously have a knowledge of rehabilitation therapies and community services.

7.6 More fundamentally, if the doctor is to learn how best to collaborate with the patient in the management of long-term impairment or chronic disease, it will be necessary for medical education to undergo a basic change, so that it can accommodate lay perceptions of sickness and the sociology and social psychology of illness behaviour. At present these tend to be taught, if at all, at a trivial level, and as if they were in opposition to "medicine" instead of part of it. Rehabilitative medicine ought to include such subjects as the theories of causation which all illnesses provoke, the stratagems of toleration and normalisation in long-term conditions, and the determinants of behaviour

449

during various time-patterns of recovery, adaptation, or deterioration. The patient's own management of any progressive or fluctuating disease is complex, and various conditions have their own patterns. This part of the doctor's education should encompass not only the general literature and research findings of medical sociology and social psychology, but also the extensive literature on individual disabling conditions such as stroke, heart disease, diabetes, multiple sclerosis, rheumatoid arthritis (e.g. Hunt 1966; Davis 1973; Benoliel 1975; Strauss 1975; Wiener 1975).

8. The Longer-term

8.1 There are many trends which suggest that rehabilitation and the management of chronic conditions will inevitably become more important in the future. These include demographic changes, new patterns of disease, rising expectations about the quality of life, and the movement towards "community care". The escalating costs of high-technology institutional medicine are already raising questions about resource-use, and at the other extreme relatively cheap but dehumanising custodial care will increasingly be no longer tolerated in an advanced society. Both pressures imply an expansion of community medicine at the expense of in patient hospital medicine, or a shift of resources from the health sector (as presently delimited) to other sectors. In fact it can be argued that there would be merit in extending the boundaries of the health sector (as has been suggested in a few specific cases in this paper). Those who see dangers in "medical imperialism" might disagree, but to expand its functions might well encourage desired change within medicine itself.

8.2 Increasing demands for rehabilitation services are likely in any case to be one important factor influencing change in medical attitudes and the structures of medical care. Expansion of remedial therapies and their developing "professionalisation" (by the establishment of a stronger theoretical base, higher levels of training, and better career structures and organisational positions) seems inevitable. So does the expansion of paramedical workers, together with some revision of the role of the community doctor. Many of the tasks which at present fill his days must be delegated to ancillary workers, if he is to assume the central role envisaged.

8.3 The growing emphasis on handicap and long-term conditions has already had an influence in a new debate about our society's concepts of health and sickness, which will in time influence the provision of health care. New assessment systems are increasingly being developed, for instance, to replace the model of "success" and "failure" more appropriate to acute illness by measurements of function and the quality of life. Disability and chronic sickness are not easily conceptualised as either "health" or "illness"; they involve patient self-management and self-perception to a greater degree than does acute illness; and they highlight even more the complex chain of interaction between individuals and their physical and social environment. For all these reasons the growing importance of rehabilitation is likely to have notable effects upon the medicine of the future.

Summary

1. *General:* The field of disability and rehabilitation has been characterised, during the last 20 or 30 years, by a multiplicity of official reports of high quality. The need is not so much for the establishment of new principles, which are by now quite generally agreed, but for the sweeping away of old structures which impede the implementation of these policies.

2. *Hospital Services:* The establishment of regional hospital rehabilitation centres should be accelerated, with particular regard to geographical distribution.

Evaluative research on the remedial therapies should be strongly encouraged, and the potential contribution of clinical psychology should be actively explored and exploited.

3. *Community Doctors:* It should be formally recognised that overall responsibility for long-term chronic illness and disability for the patient living at home rests with the general practitioner.

There should be more efficient communication between GP and hospital, and the GP should have the opportunity (with the advice of specialists) to co-ordinate therapies and assessments for vocational and social help in the community.

Within the primary health-care team, practical responsibility for advice and co-ordination should rest with the health visitor.

4. *Community Services:* Local authority provision for the disabled should be mandatory, and basic minimum entitlements should be established.

Exhortations by central government that local authorities should provide community care, hostels, or sheltered housing for the various groups whose institutionalisation is deplored should be replaced by new methods of financing, to provide better geographical uniformity and ensure that policies are actually implemented.

Though certain local authority services relevant to disability will always necessarily be separate from health services, those which are most specifically health-related (such as the supply of aids and appliances) should be administered within the health sector.

5. *Aids and Appliances:* Many of the recommendations of the BMA Working Party (1968) on aids and appliances remain to be implemented.

6. *Vocational Rehabilitation:* Radical revision and simplification of the system of vocational rehabilitation and help should proceed as rapidly as possible, and the medical profession should take an active interest in this. Special services should be instituted for the training and vocational help of the handicapped school-leaver.

All rehabilitation services (as distinct from retraining and placement services) would be better placed within the health sector, within centres associated with hospitals.

7. *Medical Education:* Important changes are required in medical education, at both the post-graduate and under-graduate levels.

8. *In the Longer-term:* The increasing emphasis upon disability and rehabilitation is likely both to require quite fundamental changes in society's concepts of health and sickness, and to play an important part in the development of those changes.

Mildred Blaxter
Medical Research Council Sociologist
MRC Medical Sociology Unit
Aberdeen

May 24 1978

REFERENCES

AGERHOLM M (1972)
"Rehabilitation", *Lancet*, 2, 329

BENOLIEL J Q (1975)
"Childhood Diabetes; the commonplace in living becomes uncommon" in Strauss A L *Chronic Disease and the Quality of Life* C V Mosby Company St Louis

BLAXTER M (1976)
The Meaning of Disability Heinemann Educational Books London

BUCKLE J R (1971)
Work and Housing of Impaired Persons in Great Britain (Handicapped and Impaired in Great Britain Part II) HMSO London

BUTLER J and PEARSON M (1970)
Who Goes Home? G Bell & Sons London for the Social Administrative Research

BRITISH MEDICAL ASSOCIATION (1968)
Report on the Working Party on Aids for the Disabled

DAVIES B (1968)
Social Needs and Resources in Local Services: A Study of Variations in Standards of Provision of Personal Social Services between Local Authority Areas Michael Joseph London

DAVIS M (1973)
Living with Multiple Sclerosis Thomas Springfield Illinois

DEPARTMENT OF EDUCATION and SCIENCE (1974)
Integrating Handicapped Children HMSO London

DEPARTMENT OF EMPLOYMENT (1972)
Resettlement Policy and Services for Disabled People HMSO London

DEPARTMENT OF EMPLOYMENT (1973a)
The Quota Scheme for Disabled People HMSO London

DEPARTMENT OF EMPLOYMENT (1973b)
Sheltered Employment for Disabled People HMSO London

DEPARTMENT OF EMPLOYMENT (1973c)
Industrial Rehabilitation for Disabled People HMSO London

DEPARTMENT OF EMPLOYMENT (1974)
Vocational Training for Disabled People HMSO London

DUNNELL K and IDE L (1974)
"An Attempt to Assess the Cost of Home Care" in Lees and Shaw (eds) *Impairment Disability and Handicap* Heinemann Educational Books London for SSRC

ECONOMIST INTELLIGENCE UNIT Ltd (1973)
Care with Dignity: An Analysis of Costs of Care for the Disabled National Fund for Research into Crippling Diseases London

FERGUSON T and MacPHAIL A N (1954)
Hospital and Community OUP for the Nuffield Provincial Hospitals Trust

FORDER A RETI T and SILVER J R (1969)
"Communication in the Health Service: a case study of the rehabilitation of paraplegic patients" *Soc & Econ Admin* 33

GOBLE R E A and NICHOLS P J R (1971)
Rehabilitation of the Severely Disabled Butterworths London

GARRAD J and BARRETT A E (1971)
"A Validated Interview Schedule for Use in Population Surveys of Chronic Disease and Disability" B J Prev Soc Med 25 97

GREAVES M (1969)
Work and Disability British Council for the Rehabilitation of the Disabled London

HARRIS A (1971)
Handicapped and Impaired in Great Britain OPCS HMSO London

HEWETT S (1970)
The Family and the Handicapped Child Allen & Unwin London

HUNT P (1966)
Stigma, the Experience of Disability Geoffrey Chapman London

JACKSON R N (1968)
"Employment Adjustment of Educable Mentally Handicapped Ex-Pupils in Scotland" A J Mental Deficiency 72 6

JOHNSON G S and JOHNSON R H (1973)
"Paraplegics in Scotland: a survey of employment and facilities" B J Social Work 3 19

McKENZIE M et al (1962)
Further Studies in Hospital and Community OUP London for Nuffield Provincial Hospitals Trust

MAIR REPORT (1972)
Report of Sub-committee of the Standing Medical Advisory Committee Scottish Health Services Council on Medical Rehabilitation HMSO Edinburgh

MANPOWER SERVICES COMMISSION (1978)
Developing Employment and Training Services for Disabled People

MATTINGLY S (1973)
"Resettlement of the Disabled Worker" Update (October)

MORGAN H M (1974)
"Like other School-leavers?" in Boswell & Wingrove (eds) *The Handicapped Person in the Community* Tavistock and the Open University Press London

MURRAY J and ORWELL S (1973)
The Implementation of the Chronically Sick and Disabled Persons Act, Social Policy Research Ltd for the National Fund for Research into Crippling Diseases

MYERSON L and KERR N (1975)
Learning Theory and Rehabilitation Random House NY

McCORQUODALE REPORT (1965)
Cmnd 2867 HMSO London

OSWIN M (1978)
Children Living in Long-stay Hospitals Heinemann Medical London

PIERCY REPORT (1956)
Report of the Committee of Enquiry on the Rehabilitation Training and Resettlement of Disabled Persons Cmnd 9883 HMSO London

SAINSBURY S (1970)
Registered as Disabled G Bell & Sons London for the Social Administration Research Trust

SAINSBURY S (1973)
Measuring Disability G Bell & Sons London for the Social Administration Research Trust

SHARP REPORT (1974)
Mobility of Physically Disabled People HMSO London

SKEET M (1970)
Home from Hospital: A Study of the Home Care Needs of Recently Discharged Hospital Patients The Dan Mason Nursing Research Committee of the National Florence Nightingale Memorial Committee of Great Britain

SNOWDEN REPORT (1976)
Integrating the Disabled National Fund for Research into Crippling Diseases London

STRAUSS A L (1975)
Chronic Illness and the Quality of Life C V Mosby Company Saint Louis

TAYLOR P J and FAIRRIE A J (1968)
"Chronic disabilities and capacity for work" *B J Prev Soc Med* 22 183

TODD REPORT (1968)
Royal Commission on Medical Education HMSO London

TOMLINSON REPORT (1945)
Report of the Interdepartmental Committee on the Rehabilitation and Resettlement of Disabled Persons Cmnd 6415 HMSO London

TOPLISS E (1975)
Provisions for the Disabled Blackwell Oxford

TUCKEY L PARFIT J and TUCKEY B (1973)
Handicapped School Leavers: Their Further Education Training and Employment National Foundation for Educational Research London for the National Children's Bureau

TUNBRIDGE REPORT (1972)
Rehabilitation Report of a Sub-committee of the Standing Medical Advisory Committee HMSO London

WIENER C L (1975)
"The Burden of Rheumatoid Arthritis: Tolerating Uncertainty" *Soc Sci & Med* 9 97

WISEMAN J and CULLIS J D (1975)
"The Economics of Disability" in *Economic Policies and Social Goals: Aspects of Public Choice* Martin Robertson London

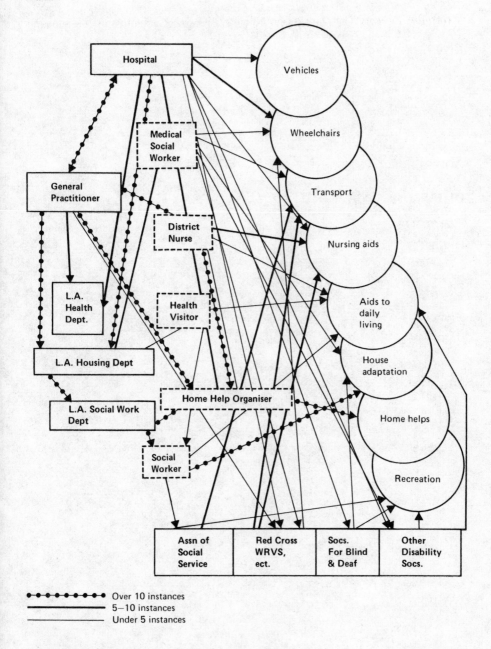

Hospital

Vehicles

Medical
Social
Worker

Wheelchairs

General
Practitioner

Transport

District
Nurse

Nursing aids

L.A.
Health
Dept.

Health
Visitor

Aids to
daily
living

L.A. Housing Dept

House
adaptation

L.A. Social Work
Dept

Home Help Organiser

Home helps

Social
Worker

Recreation

| Assn of Social Service | Red Cross WRVS, ect. | Socs. For Blind & Deaf | Other Disability Socs. |

●●●●●●●●●● Over 10 instances
━━━━━━━━━ 5–10 instances
───────── Under 5 instances

The actual weight of referrals, in one sample of 200 impaired
people, for services to help with daily living in the community.

455

Appendix H   Evidence from the Advisory Conciliation and Arbitration Service

An assessment of ACAS involvement in National Health Service Industrial Relations

GLOSSARY

ACAS	Advisory, Conciliation and Arbitration Service
AHA	Area Health Authority
ATO	Area Team of Officers
COHSE	Confederation of Health Service Employees
DA	District Administrator
DHSS	Department of Health and Social Security
DMT	District Management Team
DPO	District Personnel Officer
Grey Book	"Management Arrangements for the Re-organised Health Service" HMSO 1972
GMWU	General and Municipal Workers' Union
HSC	Health and Safety Commission
IR	Industrial Relations
JCC	Joint Consultative Committee
JNC	Joint Negotiating Committee
JSSC	Joint Shop Stewards Committee
NHS	National Health Service
NUPE	National Union of Public Employees
RHA	Regional Health Authority
TGWU	Transport and General Workers' Union
TUC	Trades Union Congress
UMA	Union Membership Agreement

INTRODUCTION

1. On the basis of ACAS contacts the general view of staff in the NHS following its creation in 1948 was that it was a unitary organisation – a family affair in which staff goodwill was expected and largely granted. By definition the main function of the NHS has always been patient care and any staff action which might have threatened patient welfare was therefore regarded as illegitimate. The majority of staff, regardless of status, supported this view and were convinced that personal interests must always be subordinated to those of the patient. It is clear from what has been said to ACAS that now many NHS workers feel, rightly or wrongly, that their goodwill has been abused in the past and that they were wrong in assuming that the NHS could ever hope to act in the best interests of staff, if the patient is always to have priority.

2. In the 1970's IR in the NHS has changed for a variety of reasons. There has been a growing awareness of the new statutory rights of workers and also of the benefits which seem to accrue from industrial action in other industries. This has been accompanied by an expansion of trade union membership and activity to which the NHS has not been able to respond adequately, having neither sufficient IR specialists and line management skills, nor the organisation. The result has been a feeling of distance between management and staff – a shift accelerated by the 1974 reorganisation which moved the operational management tier away from the hospital, up to District level.

3. Since 1975 ACAS has become increasingly involved in giving advice in the NHS, usually at the joint request of the parties, and mostly at District level and below. Our evidence to the Royal Commission is based on the in-depth work which we have conducted. This falls into three categories – eight Advisory Projects (programmes of visits to assist with a particular project or programme of work); nine Diagnostic Surveys (medium-term studies designed to identify the root causes of IR problems); and one Inquiry (similar to a diagnostic survey but a longer-term, comprehensive investigation of IR and related issues). Although all this advisory work has been carried out where it had been clear to the parties that something was wrong with IR, we have been struck by the similarities between the problems faced in the various Districts and AHAs in which we have worked. Thus, despite the fact that our evidence is not based on an examination of the NHS as a whole, we believe that general problems can be identified and that useful conclusions can be drawn from our experience.*

4. Relating particularly to joint machinery the main problems are that:

   (i) Both parties are placed in the dilemma of needing local collective bargaining and consultative machinery, where national machinery is all that is often available.

   (ii) Procedures are insufficiently clear, consistent and effective.

On the management side the problems can be summed up as being:

   (i) An organisation structure with fundamentally weak links in the chain.

   (ii) A personnel function without the authority to implement comprehensive personnel policies.

   (iii) Poor communications between NHS disciplines.

Several trade union matters are also poorly regulated, such as:

   (i) Shop steward credentials, time off, and facilities.

   (ii) Union Membership Agreements (UMAs)

   (iii) The lack of co-operation between TUC affiliated trade unions and non-affiliates in most local joint machinery.

---

*We have made a conscious decision not to identify any particular examples of our work in order to preserve the confidentiality under which they were carried out. However our conclusions have been drawn from our experience in England, Scotland and Wales.

We conclude that consideration should be given to a comprehensive overhaul of NHS personnel/IR policy, and that there is a need to train a substantial proportion of the workforce, to create a greater understanding of that policy.

5. In reaching conclusions we have had to assume that there will be no change in the organisation structure of the NHS from RHA to District level. Re-organisation of the NHS involves consideration of many factors beyond IR, but simply from an IR viewpoint we would like to emphasise that in principle a shorter organisational chain is desirable, and that there is a continuing need for a central co-ordinating function.

MANAGEMENT

IR Attitudes

6. The re-organisation of the NHS into a five tier structure*, from unit to DHSS, in the view of ACAS, has had a deleterious effect upon the progress of its IR. It permitted the development of policy at a variety of levels, but unfortunately it also provided ample opportunity for discontinuity as well as flexibility. This implies that the NHS self-imposed principle of clearly defined responsibilities and clearly allocated accountability is under threat.

7. The effect of re-organisation has been to distance staff from management. The new multi-tiered nature of the service removed much of the traditionally hospital-based authority and responsibility and placed it in the hands of District Managers – a change which after four years still has not been fully assimilated. Not only did it tend to separate staff and District Management, but also it created a certain amount of unease at lower management levels. Managers at hospital level now find their status more difficult to maintain as decisions are more frequently deferred to District Managers, and consequently some of them feel isolated. Very often the are well aware of the changing IR attitudes of their staff but are dissatisfied with the lack of support or positive reaction from District and Area Managers.

8. It is clear, on the basis of our experience, that the NHS is no longer a unitary "family" organisation but must be regarded as one which has many legitimately divergent interest groups. The problem is that many managers have yet to recognise this. Consequently the credibility of managerial authority in general is diminishing. The solution to many apparently operational problems, therefore, lies in the removal of uninformed attitudes to communications and good IR.

IR Policy

9. We detected an air of dissatisfaction amongst NHS management regarding IR and this is largely due to what they see as the lack of IR expertise in the personnel function. This, together with the deliberate concept of "consensus management" is not a recipe which inspires their confidence. Personnel Officers are often appointed from the management structure with no past experience. There is no statutory duty to appoint DPOs, and even where appointed they have no voice on their DMT other than through the DA. Consequently as DMTs tend to be non-committal on IR matters in the absence of guidance from above and lack of professional expertise to assist their deliberations, the general opinion is that management has abdicated its authority to the trade unions by default.

---

*In Scotland, responsibility for the administration of health services lies with the Secretary of State for Scotland. In Wales this responsibility lies with the Welsh Office. In both Scotland and Wales the Regional tier is absent so that AHAs in Wales and Area Health Boards in Scotland are administered directly from their respective administrative centres. In addition, throughout Great Britain there are examples of "single-District Areas" which can remove yet another tier.

10.   We conclude therefore that it is the responsibility of the AHAs and DMTs to take a lead in the formation of local IR policy, although extrapolation from our experience indicates that a consultancy, coordination and appeal role at Regional level may also be required. We suggest that consideration be given to the adoption of a policy containing two broad components:

(i)   The establishment of a clear organisation chain from top to bottom, and the delegation of responsibility for day-to-day personnel management to professional staff and line managers in the field.

(ii) The delegation of authority and responsibility for devising a comprehensive local personnel policy to the personnel officers at Area level, and its application at District level.

We examine these two components further below.

Organisation Structure

11.   The re-organised NHS structure is regarded by many staff as a bureaucracy unable to satisfy the needs of those it employs. On many occasions the prime recommendation which ACAS has made, has been to draft an organisation chart to clarify the organisation chain. From the cases we have encountered, three fundamentally weak links in that chain have emerged:

(i)   The Area/District relationship;

(ii) The IR role of DMTS;

(iii) The IR role of line managers.

Area/District Relationship

12.   This is the most obvious of these weak links. If there is to be confidence in the ATO on IR matters, then there is a need to invest it with more authority than its present co-ordinating role affords. This would permit Area Personnel Staff to co-ordinate IR at District level in a positive fashion particularly on fundamental issues such as discipline and grievance procedure, time-off for shop stewards, joint machinery, and health and safety policy. The AHA is the employer named on virtually all contracts of employment and therefore has a responsibility to ensure that all its staff are treated both uniformly and justly. Similarly the AHA has a responsibility to ensure that procedures for dealing with serious collective disputes are developed in such a way that close links are forged between Area and District. [If the NHS should be re-organised into single-District Areas, there would still be a need for a stronger second tier. This means that the stronger AHA role described above, would have to be transferred to RHAs.]

IR Role of DMTs

13.   This seems to be vague in some Districts and corporately DMTs often adopt a neutral attitude. We encountered frequently a tendency for medical professionals to consider IR as important but not primarily their concern. This attitude seems to have been carried onto the DMTs and, because of their predominantly medical composition, this attitude has become the prevailing one. Many DMTs seem neither to seek active involvement in, nor fully appreciate their corporate responsibility for, the IR decisions taken within their Districts. Such decisions should be important to the DMT because poor IR can be as detrimental to patient care as can poor medical facilities. In an organisation as large as the NHS it is essential that the policy makers should be aware of its inherent impersonality and remoteness. Above all, they must recognise that in a multi-disciplinary organisation no one discipline, particularly IR, can stand on its own.

461

IR Role of Line Managers

14. In addition to the Area/District relationship, and the IR role of DMTs, there is a third weak link in the organisation chain at the very lowest levels. Whilst the "Grey Book" states that:

"most of the responsibility for personnel management will rest with the professional staff and line managers in the field."

It seems that the NHS managers concerned have not fully recognised the fact. The nature of the organisation tends to allow IR problems to travel rapidly from their place of origin through to the next level of management. In many cases this is unnecessary and consequently a major theme in this evidence is to urge the NHS to promote more vigorously its own principle of maximum decentralisation and delegation within the District organisation but nevertheless within the framework of Area IR policy. In the experience of ACAS both unions and management would welcome a clarification of organisational relationships, in particular within the ancillary grades. At present each ancillary function has its own District organisation pyramid, sometimes without a District support services manager in a co-ordinating role. This leaves the Divisional Administrator in a difficult position if faced with multi-disciplinary industrial action at an individual hospital unit, because since re-organisation he has not had a direct line management relationship with all ancillary staff in his Division.

15. The clarification of organisational relationships and responsibilities, not only in matters of IR but also the general management of NHS activities, would be an important step toward achieving management/union co-operation, and re-establishing the more personal and direct management style of the past.

Personnel Function

16. A major cause of the often erratic development of the NHS personnel function at local level has been the Grey Book, which regards personnel work as merely an administrative task under the aegis of Regional, Area and District Administrators. Significantly, it specifies the roles of Regional and Area Personnel Officers as mandatory posts but regards DPOs as discretionary. It is also noteworthy that at no point does the Grey Book make specific mention of industrial relations. In practice the picture is less clear cut than the Grey Book envisaged. The personnel function is fragmented not only geographically, but also organisationally so that nurses often have their own separate personnel functions, most ambulancemen are administered at Area level and some Districts have no Personnel Officer at all. The anomalies and disunity which this causes have been at the root of many problems in which ACAS's assistance has been sought.

17. Criticism of the personnel function by NHS managers and shop stewards has been aimed at all levels of the organisation. Some Regional Personnel Officers claimed that neither policy and procedures nor any dispensation to take the initiative themselves were forthcoming from DHSS. Area Personnel Officers find their position even more difficult because they have no direct line relationship with District Personnel Officers. Since Districts are free to act unilaterally against ATO advice, if they choose, resulting in inter-District anomalies, it appears to us that consideration should be given to the adoption of a more positive AHA role in the delineation of IR policies for their subordinate Districts. In their turn, unless DPOs have guidance and backing from DMTs, they cannot act effectively

18. The Grey Book emphasises the responsibility of Managers in the field regarding the personnel function but neglects to provide adequately for the development of

machinery to back up those responsibilities. Whilst it details the duties of Regional and Area Personnel officers in this respect, it appears that at the vital, "shop floor" level the adaptation and application of personnel policy is left very much to chance. Local anomalies in conditions of service are a recurring subject which ACAS has encountered. Some have been caused by NHS re-organisation boundary changes, but many have been allowed to occur since that time. They occur both inter-District and within Districts.

19. We suggest for consideration, the following conclusions:

(i)   Each District in the NHS should have a District Personnel Officer.

(ii) Each DPO should be given a brief to apply a wide-ranging Area personnel policy including recruitment, selection, induction, training, joint machinery, procedures, shop steward accreditation, time off, and facilities etc.

(iii) That this brief should be formulated not only in relation to the needs of the District, but also in relation to an Area personnel policy which the APO has sufficient authority to co-ordinate.

Communications

20. The size and complexity of the NHS means that the problems raised by communications are an issue worthy of particular attention. We have already alluded to a problem of existing IR attitudes, but there are also the physical barriers presented by geographically scattered units (particlarly in the ambulance service) and shift-working. A formalised organisation structure is a pre-requisite of any good system of communications designed to overcome these barriers.

21. The importance of communications at the lower end of the organisation chain has apparently not been realised, and can perhaps best be corrected by the use of informal staff meetings. While in general, managers are keen to involve their staff in the running of their departments it seems that there is less likelihood of staff meetings being held for lower grades of staff, particularly in the ancillary or unskilled grades. In view of the fact that these are precisely the grades in which IR problems arise most frequently, we suggest that such meetings could have a beneficial effect in providing a forum for matters of general concern before they develop into matters for industrial action. Our involvement in the NHS has shown that a system of staff meetings pays particular dividends in a multi-discipline context e.g. operating theatre users committees; and could usefully be applied more widely where nursing and ancillary staff are inter-dependent.

22. In addition to informal staff meetings we have identified a need for organised and selective supplementary printed information. The overall opinion of staff is that they require concise, speedy and consistent information, and that this should complement personal briefing.

TRADE UNIONS

IR Attitudes

23. NHS staff are now generally more receptive to trade unionism and membership has increased, but they still regard care for the patient as being their first and foremost concern. Nevertheless, there is a more pragmatic side to their dedication, which means

that they feel the need to protect those rights which they previously believed could be entrusted to the guardianship of NHS management. This sense of insecurity is not limited to ancillary staff but also applies to professional staff many of whom until a few years ago would not have considered even joining a trade union, still less serving as a shop steward. Clearly the relationship between NHS management and unions has changed radically, but the NHS machinery has not been adapted accordingly. We believe that if the parties are to co-exist without conflict, then some formalisation of their new relationship is required in the form of local collective agreements. In any event, often this would only be a formal recognition of what is in fact happening already in a fragmented way.

Shop steward arrangements

24. An essential precondition of effective representation within any local IR Machinery is the formal accreditation of shop stewards. In some disciplines, particularly nursing, some senior staff leave trade union members in no doubt that their activities are unwelcome, with the result that many members are unwilling to accept union office. In others, shop steward arrangements are completely unregulated and the status of shop stewards is left open to doubt. Therefore, it is essential that management is seen to sanction officially the role of the shop steward both in principle and in practical application. The foundation of such a policy is the conclusion of District agreements on shop steward credentials, time off, and facilities (based on any guidance received from DHSS, RHA or AHA). We consider that any agreement should observe three criteria:

(i) It should apply only to unions recognised for the purposes of NHS Whitley councils.

(ii) Where possible shop stewards should be both employed in the District concerned, and also members of the group which they represent.

(iii) Shop stewards should be elected in accordance with the rule book of their trade union.

ACAS has produced a Code of Practice on Time off for Trade Union Duties and Activities which provides guidance for managers and trade unionists on how to meet the statutory obligations under the Employment Protection Act 1975.

Inter-union relationships

25. The NHS has 43 staff representative bodies recognised for the purposes of the national Whitley machinery and in many cases only one of these is appropriate to a given job. However, at present it appears that many Area and District personnel staff are divided or uncertain of what action to take regarding the local recognition of trade unions, and three main areas of uncertainty remain:

(i) Inter-union rivalry between TUC-affiliates particularly in the ancillary grades;

(ii) UMAs;

(iii) The unwillingness of TUC-affiliated unions to participate in local joint machinery where non-affiliates are also involved.

26. Friction between the ancillary staff unions occurs in almost all permutations of the four (COHSE, GMWU, NUPE, T&GWU) in some parts of the NHS. Also, for historical reasons each union has some Districts where it predominates and others where it has low membership. In one AHA, ACAS found that different unions were recognised for representational purposes in respect of identical employee groups in different Divisions of the same District. It has been the experience of some Districts that without the full agreement and goodwill of the local branches and the feasibility of an equitable

quid pro quo membership exchange, any UMA or unofficial "spheres of influence" agreement becomes inoperable and the parties quickly revert to indiscriminate recruitment. Even if at local level management and unions have jointly decided that the best way of regulating union membership questions is through a UMA, they find that there is at present no nationally agreed guidance. To assist in such circumstances, and in view of the developments on UMAs we have encountered, we believe it would lead to greater consistency if further consideration were given by management and unions at national level to the provision of joint guidance which leaves defined scope for local flexibility.

27. There still remains the need to discover some means whereby recognised independent trade unions can co-exist at District level, so that collective bargaining at this level can be carried out between management and a fully representative staff side. As far as possible the members of staff side should have the means to discuss and present a common staff side view on matters which concern them jointly e.g. UMAs; procedures; time-off for shop steward duties etc. However, in practice there are few Districts in which TUC affiliated trade unions will co-operate with non-affiliates, although this problem does not arise in the Whitley machinery. With the plethora of divergent interests which the recognised unions represent, there is a need to co-ordinate their activities in relation to local NHS management, and this could be achieved by the formation of District Joint Shop Stewards Committees.

JOINT MACHINERY

Whitley

28. The NHS is required by statute to provide for employee representation, and the system used follows the Whitley model of joint regulation of terms and conditions of employment by NHS officials and staff representatives. The system provides for eleven functional councils and one general council each operating on a purely national basis. Below this level there is no formally recognised collective bargaining machinery, and unilateral statutory policy making authority extends no lower than the AHA. In this context the remoteness and inadequacy of the Whitley regulatory processes has contributed to the dissatisfaction and increased militancy of NHS staff.

29. The Whitley machinery was reviewed in 1976 by Lord McCarthy who made important recommendations for decentralisation and local bargaining. However, his proposal for the formation of Regional Whitley Councils has not received the approval of either management or staff sides. They have officially acknowledged the need for flexibility in national agreements but have failed so far to create the machinery to handle it at local level. Our experience indicates that Regional Whitley machinery would, if anything, not have gone far enough towards decentralisation since the most troublesome IR problems occur because of the absence of machinery at District level. It is against this national backdrop that managers and shop stewards are expected to resolve joint problems arising at local level, and inevitably shop stewards turn to the consultative machinery as the only existing forum.

Consultation and Joint Regulation

30. Consultative machinery has evolved in a somewhat piecemeal fashion. Although the DHSS approves of consultation in principle, AHAs have been left very much to their own devices and some Areas, Districts and hospitals have flourishing JCCs, while others apply them to particular grades, one or two tiers, or not at all. Similarly, their impact on the local NHS organisation varies widely. Some JCCs exercise considerable

influence over major policy decisions while others are limited to the discussion of inconsequential issues and used as a rubber stamp for unilateral management decisions. If JCCs are to be credible they must perform a significant role in the decision making process, and if this is to be their purpose it is clear that the constitution of many JCCs is inadequate for the demands which unions place upon them. In the past, NHS JCCs have foundered regularly and we conclude that one reason for this has often been the unrealistic limitations on their terms of reference which fell short of employee expectations. Equally the success of JCCs depends upon the subject matter which management is prepared to put before them.

31. The system of IR which has developed in the NHS conforms in most respects with the formal/informal dichotomy of collective bargaining which the Donovan Commission identified nationally ten years ago. In the absence of formal, local collective bargaining machinery, we have found that joint consultation is already taking on a modified role in that the distinction between consultation and negotiation has been allowed to become blurred, and this could be regarded as a natural and desirable evolution.

32. By deduction we suggest that investigations are likely to reveal a need for JCCs at Regional level, but from our direct experience we suggest that consideration be given to the formation of JCC's at Area, District and in particular, Divisional level where consultation has an important role to play as the very first stage in joint machinery. This would provide a forum close to the "shop floor" so that problems can be defused as early as possible. It would also be visible and accessible for all staff and would rebuild some of the hospital unit identity which was lost in the 1974 re-organisation.

Procedures

33. One of the most common reasons for ACAS involvement with the NHS has been the inadequacy of grievance and discipline procedures. Although Whitley provides guidelines for the drafting of procedure, in many cases AHA procedures are insufficient to maintain uniformity between Districts. Some procedures are poorly drafted and implemented with little commitment to time limits, use of all procedural stages (particularly the first stage), or proper documentation. Often it is unclear which manager is designated as being responsible for the conduct of a given stage, with the result that some matters escalate rapidly while others are never properly processed. In grievance procedures a common deficiency is the lack of provision for the conduct of collective disputes as well as individual grievances, while disciplinary procedures often suffer from unclear definition of categories of offence and the disciplinary action they require. Procedures are intended to promote fairness and order in the treatment of individuals and in the conduct of IR, but in this respect many local NHS procedures have failed.

34. The recommendations which ACAS has made in several individual Districts are applicable throughout the NHS. Clear grievance and discipline procedures need to be agreed jointly at District level within the framework of AHA policy. The ACAS Code of Practice on Disciplinary Procedures deals with the whole issue in some detail. Finally, those who are to operate the procedures need to undergo training in their practical application. The lack of clarity, consistency and commitment in NHS procedures is indicative of the weakness of its IR policy making machinery and also of the gaps in collective bargaining machinery. Consequently, we see the improvement of NHS procedures as being an integral part of the reforms we have proposed.

TRAINING

The Format of IR Training

35. If NHS managers are to be expected to act as the front line in IR matters, then one significant observation which emerges from our investigations is that a considerable proportion of those managers and the shop stewards with whom they deal do not possess the skills required. This is not limited to any particular groups as examples can be found almost in every grade, in every discipline, and in every trade union. The format of a training policy should be determined by the personnel function in consultation with line management and with the trade unions where appropriate.

Management IR Training Needs

36. Some management IR training has already been undertaken by ACAS and other organisations in isolated parts of the NHS. However, we consider that the broad pattern for the future should be to establish initially the training needs for each level of management from supervisor upwards. Some officers will require only an appreciation of how all or part of the IR system works, while others may require more in-depth operating skills, but in either case systematic follow-up and evaluation is desirable. The prime management training need is in the skills of both man-management and the handling of management-union relationships, particularly at supervisor level. The aim of any training programme should be to equip each person with the skills required to operate and maintain their part of the NHS IR machinery.

Shop Steward IR Training Needs

37. The conduct of shop steward training is the responsibility of each trade union. The prime training need, which has emerged from our contacts, is in the diplomatic skills of management-union relationships. Also it is desirable that trade unions ensure that all shop stewards receive training in basic shop steward duties within a short time of taking office.

Employee IR Training Needs

38. The new employee's first real contact with the NHS is often with the unrepresentative selection of staff in the immediate work place. In our view it would be helpful if all new staff could attend some form of induction course in order to give them a slightly broader picture of their employer and also to make them aware of the basic IR machinery which they are likely to encounter. It would also be desirable if a trade union representative could be included on such courses.

CONCLUSION

39. In our view the NHS has reached the stage where it should review its IR policies and practices. Unless effective remedies are introduced urgently, we can see little prospect of avoiding continued deterioration in IR with associated frustration of management and staff, increased labour turnover, and noticeably poorer quality patient care. The involvement of ACAS in the NHS is already increasing steadily. In addition to the in-depth work described earlier we have made numerous short-term advisory visits and been involved in collective conciliation throughout the NHS. The figures show that the number of advisory visits rose from 110 in 1976, to 142 in 1977; and that the number of applications for collective conciliation rose from 36 in 1976, to 62 in 1977. In these cases it has been possible to offer constructive advice and achieve

467

tangible improvements in IR. However, this has been merely the treatment of symptoms and does not get to the root of the problem which we see as being the inadequacy of the IR policymaking process in many Areas and the widespread deficiencies in IR machinery.

40. Management-union relations throughout industry and commerce are now regulated by a considerable body of legislation, and therefore each party is under increased obligations. In addition there are the ACAS Codes of Practice on Disciplinary Practice and Procedures in Employment, Disclosure of Information to Trade Unions for Collective Bargaining Purposes, and Time-off for Trade Union Duties and Activities; as well as the HSC Code of Practice on Time off for the Training of Safety Representatives which operates from 1.10.78. ACAS conciliation services are always immediately available, and moreover, the advisory services of ACAS continue to be available to NHS managers and unions at all levels on the above and other matters including naturally the conclusions summarised below. However, we consider that our contribution to good IR in the NHS would be more productive if at least some of our resources were allocated to assisting the DHSS and RHAs to take the lead in establishing central guidelines and back up for a more comprehensive and co-ordinated IR policy. The responsibility for this must rest with the DHSS and RHAs.

SUMMARY OF CONCLUSIONS

We suggest that consideration be given to the following points:

MANAGEMENT

Organisation Structure   *Paras*

1. The NHS chain of command should be clarified and strengthened, in particular by creating a direct line relationship between Area management and District.   (11–12)

2. DMTs need to accept corporate responsibility for the general conduct of IR in their Districts in a more positive fashion, but should also ensure that the responsibility for day to day IR is placed in the hands of line managers.   (13–15)

Personnel

3. Each District should have an established DPO to support line managers in the conduct of their IR responsibilities, by providing stable and consistent machinery.   (19)
4. Each DPO should have a brief to apply a wide-ranging Area personnel policy within guidelines established by the APO. Therefore, there is also a need to provide the APO with sufficient authority to co-ordinate personnel work between Districts.   (19)

Communications

5. Managers of all grades of staff should hold regular, informal staff meetings, which would be of particular use in respect of ancillary staff and in multi-disciplinary circumstances.   (21)

468

TRADE UNIONS

Shop Steward Arrangements

6.   Agreements on shop steward accreditation, time-off, and facilities should be concluded at District level, in order to ensure effective representation in IR machinery.   (24)

Inter-Union Relationships

7.   There is a need for consideration at national level of the provision of firm guidance on UMAs.   (25–26)

8.   There is a need for the co-ordination of the divergent interests which the NHS recognised trade unions represent, and consideration should be given to the formation of joint staff bodies locally.   (27)

JOINT MACHINERY

Consultation and Joint Regulation

9.   In the absence of local collective bargaining machinery, JCCs are taking on a broader role than in the past. Thought should be given to the establishment of JCCs at Area, District and in particular Divisional level in order to satisfy the growing need of management and unions for joint regulatory machinery.   (30–32)

Procedures

10.   Clearly drafted procedure agreements should be concluded at District level within the framework of Area policy. If there is to be consistency and commitment to procedures those who operate them should be adequately trained.   (33–34)

TRAINING

The Format of IR Training

11.   The personnel function should conduct an IR training audit as the first stage in a continuing IR training policy.   (35)

Training Needs

12.   The main training needs are for: management training in man-management skills; shop steward training in basic steward duties; managers and shop stewards in management-union relations; induction of all new employees.   (36–38)

Appendix I A Revised Medical Career Structure

1. We explained in Chapter 14 our reasons for thinking that the existing hospital medical career structure was unsatisfactory. We noted that there were relatively too many doctors and dentists in the training grades below senior registrar, many of them from overseas, but that hospitals were dependent on them to maintain their services. One consequence was that in some places there were too few consultants available to supervise the work of junior doctors and dentists whose training consequently suffered. Another was that whereas in theory only consultants carried clinical responsibility for patients, in practice senior registrars and medical assistants often did also. It appeared to us that the present strategy of increasing numbers of consultant posts faster than numbers of training grade posts to bring the structure into equilibrium had not proved successful, and that a more rapid resolution of the position was needed. In the paragraphs that follow we make some suggestions.

Royal Commission on Medical Education

2. The Todd Royal Commission suggested a simplification of the career structure by amalgamation of the senior house officer and registrar grades. It further proposed that after registration there should be a period of general professional training lasting three years, with an emphasis on the breadth and generality of the training. Neither of these proposals were found acceptable: both of them seem to us sound. Entry into specifically specialist training, now commonly made within 12 or 18 months and not uncommonly immediately after registration, is too often rushed; and changes in career direction, which the Todd Commission envisaged might be made without difficulty, even at the end of the three year period of general professional training, have been made much more difficult. Even more rigidity will be built into the present situation when vocational training for general practice becomes established: the absence of a requirement for such a training has facilitated exit into general practice from hospital specialist training for those who had made a wrong or unsuccessful choice of it.

3. When it dealt with the period of higher training, the Todd Commission proposals would have complicated the present situation. It proposed two grades of specialist between the present registrar and consultant grades. The junior specialist grade itself was to be composed of two streams, one of which would be in intensive training posts comparable to the present senior registrar grade. Above the junior specialist there was to be a specialist grade, which would allow "a substantial degree of independent clinical judgment" and responsibility. The fast stream of junior specialists was expected to pass rapidly through the specialist grade to consultant.

Our suggestions for a new staffing structure

4. It seems to us that a simpler structure would be both practicable and more flexible, with the following three grades after registration: assistant physician/surgeon/psychiatrist (or other specialist), physician and consultant physician.

5. The grade of *assistant physician* would be a training grade of limited tenure, and the individual would remain in it for about four years. During this period he would have a substantial amount of specialist experience and training, and would equip himself for promotion by obtaining the appropriate higher qualification (eg MRCP). It would comprise the senior house officer and registrar grades; and some of those in the first year of the senior registrar grade. Training posts at present below senior registrar may be held only for one or two years at a time, and this imposes great strains on individual trainees who are too often having to find new jobs.

6. The next grade of *physician* would be both a training and a career grade. All aspirants to consultant rank would have to enter it and spend a period normally of at least three years in it. Entry to the grade would be following advertisement and by competition, and would require that the individual had had the necessary experience, had shown the requisite ability and normally had obtained the appropriate higher qualification. It would include the senior registrar and hospital practitioner grades; and some of those at present in the medical assistant grade might be allocated to it. It would carry clinical responsiblity for patients, matched to the individual's abilities and his seniority in the grade. Some hospital doctors would remain in this grade, but not in training posts.

7. The grade of *consultant physician* would remain essentially as at present with regard to expertise, responsibilities and criteria for appointment. Appointment would continue to be by competition for advertised posts.

8. If the physician grade were to carry clinical responsibility, the problem would arise of distinguishing its responsibility from that of the consultant. However, only those in the higher grade would have comprehensive competence and responsibility for patients at the highest level in that specialty. We think that it would be inadvisable to try to define categorically the nature and extent of consultant responsibility: its essence is sufficiently clear in practice. The broad parameters of the work of all grades should be determined by agreement between the health departments and the profession; but only the broad parameters. Those in the physician grade would normally work as members of a medical team, and the physician's clinical duties would lie within the area of recognized competence of the grade but would be determined in detail by the requirements of the particular local situation. In a medical team or unit the physician would usually have his own out-patients and in-patients, of which he would be in clinical charge; and he would have a share of the supporting staff necessary for the performance of his clinical duties. If the clinical problems confronting him proved too difficult he would, and would be expected to, consult a consultant. He would be in a hierarchical relationship to the consultant or consultants in the unit, in terms of expertise and for administrative purposes; but he would be fully clinically responsible for the patients under his charge, unless he were acting specifically as an assistant to the consultant in the investigation and management of a more complex case. It would be the responsibility of the consultant in clinical charge of the unit, in agreement with his consultant and other colleagues, to deploy the members of the team in the most appropriate and efficient manner and in accordance with each individual's contract. However close in experience, competence and responsibility those in the physician grade might come to those in the grade of consultant physician, the distinction would remain that the latter had been found fit for promotion to a higher grade by an appointments committee assisted by professional assessors.

The implications for training.

9. The new staffing structure suggested here would not interfere with the well-established arrangements for post-graduate medical education; but in association with it we would like to see introduced some greater flexibility in the arrangements for

472

training. For training purposes posts, not individuals, are approved; and the present designation of posts suitable for training would continue, in the assistant physician and physician grades. For training in the assistant physician grade the great majority of the present senior house officer and registrar posts would have the facilities required. The relatively few posts which would continue to be unsuitable would be those in very narrow specialties or without consultant supervision. There should be a limitation of tenure in this training grade, and it is suggested that a four year tenure for the whole-time occupant of such a post, and an equivalent period for part-time trainees, would be appropriate. There might be the possibility of a one-year extension on educational grounds. The trainee should not be able to re-apply for the same post: for educational reasons, he or she should move.

10. For the physician grade, certain posts would continue as at present to be approved for higher professional training by the Joint Higher Training Committees in the various specialties; and they also should be of limited tenure. The period to be spent in such a post before promotion should be related to the length and complexity of training necessary for that specialty. All specialties do not require the same length of training; and those who are in specialties which require a longer training than others should not be penalised financially.

11. It must be acknowledged that occupants of the posts designated for higher training will be more likely to become consultants. But occupation whole-time of such approved training posts (similar to the present senior registrar appointments) should not be the only possible kind of higher training and (as at present) practically the only way into a consultant appointment. It should be possible to have an appointment with both service and training sessions, the training sessions being approved for higher training. Thus an individual might hold full-time a post which included three or more training session. There would have to be a limitation of tenure on these training sessions, which in the individual case would then revert to service sessions. Such a part service/part training post might be held by an individual based in a provincial hospital who would come into a teaching hospital for his training sessions.If such arrangements were to be made the needs of the service would of course have to be safeguarded and the availability of training sessions would have to be limited and carefully controlled: but there is clearly some room for flexibility, allowing the professional and career needs of individuals to be taken into account. We would like also to see experimentation with modules of training designed with specific and limited objectives; and more educational provision made for those who want to develop a special interest rather than qualify for whole-time specialization.

12. Nothing which we have suggested would create difficulties for vocational training for general practice, two years of which will be spent in hospital posts. There is no optimum mix of such posts, a wide variety will be suitable. About half of these hospital appointments are however likely to be in planned rotational schemes of training, the pressure for more such planned schemes may be considerable, and this would build a good deal of rigidity into the educational system, whatever the career structure.

Acceptability of such a new staffing structure.

13. The introduction of a new staffing structure along the lines indicated above might permit a considerable expansion of career posts and would spread the load of clinical responsibility which is at present (at least in theory) carried by consultants alone. It is clear that any new career grade which did not carry clinical responsibility would not be acceptable. Doctors want independence, if they can have it, as soon as possible; and all their post-graduate training is a supervised exercise in assuming an ever increasing degree of responsibility. The argument must be about whether or not there can be degrees of clinical responsibility, since the individual who carries independent clinical

responsibility in cases of the full range of clinical complexity and in all situations should certainly be called a consultant. We would envisage continued expansion of the consultant grade at as near its planned rate as can be achieved. A physician post might often be more appropriate than consultant grading for a doctor who could give only a limited number of sessions to in-patient care.

14.　The acceptability of such a new career structure would be likely to depend on how far the health departments succeeded in assuring the profession that a fair balance would be struck between the two career grades and that the introduction of a new career grade would not be used to exclude properly experienced and qualified doctors from consultant rank; and on how the new structure was priced by the Doctors' and Dentists' Review Body. It may be that there should be an overlap of the salary scales of the two career grades, with the pay scale of physicians extending some way into that of the consultant grade, balancing seniority and experience in the former against the greater expectations of the latter.

Appendix J   Trent Medical Advisory Structure

See inside back cover

Index

British Broadcasting Corporation, **4**.28; **19**.29

British Dental Association,
Tattersall Committee on remuneration **9**.21–2

British National Formulary, **7**.40

budgeting *see* NHS expenditure

C

Canada,
health expenditure **3**.19
nurse practitioners **3**.19

cash benefits, **6**.26

central government,
and NHS finance **4**.28; **19**.5–6, 41; **22**.73

Central Manpower Committee, **12**.63; **14**.22, 24

Central Policy Review Staff, **6**.9

charges, **2**.12; **21**.25–9
abolition **21**.28
amenity beds **10**.32
as NHS income **21**.12, 25–6
dental **9**.6, 11, 24; **21**.25
ophthalmic **8**.18, 20; **21**.25
prescription **7**.42; **21**.12, 19, 25
to patients **4**.26; **21**.25
see also pay beds

Chief Scientist, **17**.40

child health services, **6**.49–53; **14**.58
in London and Cumbria **3**.5
see also school health services

children, **2**.12; **6**.50–4
as priority group **6**.24; **22**.15
dental health **9**.7, 10, 49–51, 61
deaf **6**.55–6

chiropodists, **8**.22–8; **15**.2; **22**.25
and NHS **8**.22, 26; **15**.2, 10
assistants **8**.27
private practice **8**.25
registration **8**.25
training **8**.25, 26, 31

chiropody services **8**.1, 22–8, 31; **22**.25
and the elderly **8**.23–4

City University Business School,
ancillary staff study **15**.44

clinical academic staff,
honorary contracts **14**.69–71; **18**.27

clinical nurse specialists, **13**.17, 41

Clothier Committee – report on dispensing
in rural areas, **8**.9

"Cogwheel" machinery, **7**.32; **12**.56; **20**.16, 29–30

collaboration,
between health visitors and social
workers **6**.54
between health and local authority
services **4**.29; **16**.2–15, 29–30; **20**.5;
22.56
PSSC document **16**.31; **22**.57
Working Party on **16**.3

Collier report – buying for the NHS,
21.47, 49

Common Services Agency, **4**.8; **15**.35

communication,
difficulties in overseas staff **6**.25
doctor-patient **10**.27–8
hospital and community services **10**.77,
89; **22**.34

community care, **6**.26–31, 61; **10**.58; **22**.16
of elderly **6**.29, 33; **16**.2
of mentally disordered **10**.58
staff **6**.27, 30
teamwork **6**.28
see also community health services

Community Health Councils, **11**.1–11, 35;
20.5; **22**.35
and complaints **11**.12–3, 25–7, 30
and health districts **20**.50
and FPCs **11**.3, 6, 9
definition **11**.2
functions **11**.3, 7–10
"patient advocates" **11**.26
staffing **4**.13
survey of **11**.6

community health services, **6**.27
and consultant services **10**.78
and hospital services **10**.75–9
doctors **14**.58–60
in inner cities **7**.52–62, 65
see also dental services
nursing care

community hospitals, **10**.45, 48, 57
and the elderly **10**.45

community medicine, **14**.50
specialists **14**.48

478

479

decision making,
  and reorganised NHS **4**.16–7; **20**.8, 11
  clinical **11**.28; **12**.40; **14**.76; **21**.53–5
  see also consensus management

demographic change, **6**.12; **22**.77

Denmark,
  listed drugs **7**.43
  nursing homes for elderly **6**.37

dental auxiliaries, **9**.6, 31, 36, 40
  see also dental therapists

Dental Estimates Board, **9**.11, 19

dental health, **9**.7–10, 15–8, 54–7, 72;
  22.26
  children's **9**.7, 10, 49–51, 61
  education **9**.67–9
  preventive **9**.16–7, 57, 66, 73
  research **9**.70–1
  total tooth loss as indicator **9**.7, 9
  see also fluoridation

dental hygienists, **9**.31, 36, 39
  in Sweden **9**.67

Dental Rates Study Group, **9**.19

dental services, **9**.1–6, 28–35, 43–53, 74
  charges **9**.6, 11, 24
  community **9**.30–1, 43, 49, 51
  complaints **9**.12–3, 20–1
  emergency **9**.25
  hospital **9**.32–5, 43
  payment for **9**.20–3
  resources distribution **9**.14
  school **9**.5, 30
  standards **9**.27
  structure **9**.43–8
  teeth extraction **3**.14

dental surgery assistants, **9**.31, 36, 38

dental technicians, **9**.31, 36, 42

dental therapists, **9**.40

dentists, **9**.3, 11–27, 37
  ancillary staff **9**.36–41
  consultant **9**.32
  education **9**.6, 34–5
  dispute **9**.13
  distribution of **9**.15, 54
  NHS contracts **9**.11, 14
  private practice **9**.11; **18**.20
  remuneration **9**.19–23

Dentists Act 1957, **12**.32

Department of Employment, **5**.28

Department of the Environment, **5**.12

Department of Health and Social Security,
  19.17–23
  and fluoridation **9**.53
  and health authorities **19**.23, 33–5
  consultative document on priorities **6**.2
  discussion document on elderly **6**.32
  functions **19**.12, 18, 19, 23
  permanent secretary **19**.15–6
  planning process **6**.15
  policy formation **19**.22
  research **17**.40
  resource allocation **6**.16–7
  review of **19**.11
  review of scientific and technical services
    15.17–19
  staffing **19**.18
  structure **19**.19–20

Department of Health and Social Services,
  6.16, 18

deputising services, **7**.9–10, 57, 64; **22**.20

dietitians, **15**.2
  numbers of **15**.2
  training **15**.10

disabled *see* physically handicapped

dispensing *see* pharmaceutical services

distinction awards, **14**.92–9

district community physicians, **14**.48

district general hospitals, **10**.42–4, 46, 86;
  20.29; **22**.31
  dental units **9**.32
  maternity units **6**.51
  optimum size **10**.47
  psychiatric units **6**.42, 44; **10**.57, 61
  services of **7**.60; **10**.44

District Management Teams,
  and consensus management **20**.12
  and functional management **20**.26
  and hospital dental service **9**.43
  and industrial relations **12**.11

district nurses, **7**.19; **22**.20
  and the elderly **6**.33
  GP attached **7**.23, 64
  numbers of **7**.21
  see also home nurses

480

doctors, **12**.41; **14**.1–103
  clinical judgments **11**.29; **12**.40; **14**.76;
    21.53–5
  demand for **14**.12, 14; **22**.49
  geographical distribution **14**.16, 20
  manpower planning **12**.61
  morale **12**.6
  numbers **14**.9–15, 18
  shortage specialties **6**.42; **14**.17, 19, 23
  shortages of **14**.17–26
  status **4**.4
  training grades **14**.45
  see also clinical academic staff
        community physicians
        consultants
        general practitioners
        geriatricians
        hospital doctors
        overseas doctors
        psychiatrists
        women doctors

Doctors' and Dentists' Review Body, **9**.19
  and industrial relations **12**.14, 18

drug,
  abuse **10**.20
  costs **7**.36
  information **7**.40; **8**.16
  limited lists **7**.43
  promotion **7**.38

Drug and Therapeutic Bulletin, **7**.40

E

economic climate,
  and the NHS, **1**.4; **4**.4; **20**.6

elderly, **2**.12; **6**.24, 32, 34; **22**.77
  and chiropody services **8**.23–4
  as priority group **6**.24, 32; **22**.15
  community care of **6**.29, 33; **16**.2
  hospital care of **6**.35; **10**.45, 49
  in London and Cumbria **3**.5
  residential care **6**.33
  specialised care **6**.36–40, 63; **22**.17
  see also geriatric services

engineers *see* works and maintenance staff

environmental health, **5**.22–4, 32; **14**.58;
  22.14

environmental health officers, **5**.16

environmental health services, **5**.22

epidemiologists, **6**.5

equipment and supplies, **21**.45–9

ethnic minorities,
  and NHS **7**.61

Expenditure Committee,
  and health services **19**.8

F

Family Practitioner Committees, **20**.2, 50,
  53–7
  abolition **20**.57, 69; **22**.70
  and CHCs **11**.3, 6, 9
  and dental services **9**.11, 43
  and deputising services **7**.10
  and GPs **7**.8, 30, 35; **20**.55
  functions **20**.54
  service committees **11**.15, 17

family practitioner services, **16**.2; **20**.53–7
  complaints procedure **11**.14–8
  expenditure **20**.56; **21**.61–4
  see also dental services
        general practice
        ophthalmic services
        pharmaceutical services

fluoridation, **5**.31; **9**.16, 53–65, 73; **22**.27

functional management, **20**.26–7

G

General Dental Council, **12**.43

general dental practitioners *see* dentists

General Medical Council, **12**.43; **17**.30

general medical practice *see* general
  practice

General Nursing Council, **13**.54

general practice, **7**.2, 7–18, 27–34, 63
  appointment systems **7**.11
  attachment schemes **7**.22–3
  continuity of care **7**.10, 13–5
  definition **7**.7
  list sizes **7**.16–7, 57, 59; **14**.7–8, 12, 15
  nurses **7**.19
  premises **7**.35, 50–1, 64
  receptionists **7**.12, 64
  record-keeping **7**.33
  research **7**.34
  sectorization **7**.5
  standards **7**.28–35
  see also deputising services
        health centres

life expectancy, **3**.19

list sizes, **7**.16–7, 57, 59; **14**.7, 8, 12, 15

local authorities,
  and environmental health services **5**.22
  priorities **16**.10–1
  relationship with NHS **4**.7; **10**.76;
    16.1–32; **21**.32; **22**.56–8

local government,
  control of NHS option **16**.16–22
  in Northern Ireland **16**.26
  reorganisation **4**.4
  Royal Commission on **16**.16
  see also local authorities

London,
  AHAs and coterminosity **20**.49
  ancillary staff shortages **15**.43
  health care problems **7**.57–63
  health centres **7**.49
  Primary Care Survey **3**.5
  RAWP formula and expenditure **7**.62
  teaching hospitals **7**.60; **17**.17–8

lotteries, **4**.25–6; **21**.30

M

McMillan Committee – report on remedial
  professions, **12**.28, 36

Manpower Advisory Committee on
  Community Medicine, **14**.22

manpower planning *see* National Health
  Service manpower

Manpower Services Commission, **19**.29

maternal deaths, **3**.19; **12**.51

maternity services, **6**.51; **10**.71
  GP **7**.8
  screening **5**.7
  see also midwives

Maude, J, **16**.16

Mayston Committee – report on local
  authority nursing service, **4**.4

meals on wheels, **16**.2

media,
  and health education **5**.21
  and NHS priorities planning **6**.7
  see also radio
      television

medical audit, **12**.51, 56; **20**.16
  and the law **12**.55
  in general practice **7**.32
  see also peer review

medical education, **17**.26–32
  and priority specialties **17**.31
  and NHS policies **17**.11
  cost sharing **17**.21–4
  post-graduate **17**.27, 33
  Royal Commission **14**.14; **17**.17, 30
  undergraduate **17**.26–8, 43; **22**.61
  see also medical schools
      teaching hospitals

medical laboratory scientific officers, **15**.30
  numbers of **15**.14

Medical Practice Committees, **14**.22
  and GP appointments **7**.17

medical records **7**.33; **12**.50

medical research *see* research

Medical Research Council, **7**.33; **17**.34;
  22.62

medical schools,
  curricula **17**.27–8, 43
  intake **14**.11, 13; **17**.32, 43

medical statisticians, **6**.5

medical students,
  clinical experience **14**.85–6, 88–9
  selection **17**.32

mental handicap hospitals, **10**.64–6
  staff shortages **6**.47

mental illness hospitals, **6**.42, 44; **10**.55–63,
  88; **20**.31–2; **22**.33

mentally handicapped, **6**.20, 24, 45–8;
  16.2; **19**.36; **22**.15, 77
  and social services **6**.45
  community care **6**.29, 45
  education **6**.45
  hospital care **6**.47; **10**.64–6
  white paper on **6**.46

mentally ill, **6**.20, 24, 41–4; **16**.2; **22**.15, 77
  community care **6**.29, 42; **10**.58
  hospital services **6**.42; **10**.55–63, 71
  white paper on **6**.2; **14**.12

midwives, **13**.1–2, 12
  community **7**.2
  functions **7**.19
  numbers of **7**.21

morale, **4**.20–2; **22**.39
of NHS workers **4**.20–2; **12**.1–6, 68;
20.67
of mental illness hospital staff **10**.59,
62–3

morbidity,
and social class **3**.10
data lack **3**.15–6

mortality, **3**.8; **5**.3, 4
and social class **3**.10
data **3**.16
in UK **3**.8
infant **3**.8
maternal **3**.19; **12**.51
perinatal **3**.8, 13, 19, 20; **6**.51

multi-disciplinary clinical teams, **12**.38–42;
17.29

N

National Development Group and Team
for the Mentally Handicapped, **6**.46
10.66; **19**.36, 38

National Health Insurance,
and NHS finance **4**.25; **19**.2; **21**.12

National Health Service (general),
administrative costs **4**.10
administrative structure **20**.1, 9, 33–4,
52, 65–6, 69
central government control **19**.1–7,
12–24
decision-making **4**.16–7; **20**.8, 11
efficiency **3**.21–2
geographical equality **2**.11; **3**.7–9;
22.11, 74
objectives **2**.1–17; **22**.10
parliamentary influence and **19**.8–11
planning system **4**.5; **6**.14–9, 22; **22**.16
priorities **4**.23; **6**.1–65
relationship with personal social services
6.27; **10**.76; **16**.1–4, 8
reorganisation 1974 **1**.4; **4**.3, 5, 15, 16,
30; **20**.3–5
social equality and **2**.8; **3**.10–2; **22**.11
standards **2**.10; **7**.28–35; **12**.44–56;
19.36–40
see also NHS expenditure
NHS finance
NHS management
NHS manpower

National Health Service Act 1977, **2**.4

National Health Service expenditure, **6**.16;
12.17; **21**.3–11, 70

and budgeting **21**.50–60
and GDP **3**.18; **21**.3
and hypothecated taxes **21**.33–4
capital **6**.20, 27; **21**.3, 65–9
discretionary **6**.21
family practitioner services **21**.61–4
hospitals **21**.36
research **17**.40
revenue **21**.45–9, 65
see also NHS finance

National Health Service finance, **2**.17;
4.24–6; **21**.1–74; **22**.66, 71–5
alternative sources **4**.25–7; **21**.30–4, 72;
22.73
and GNP **4**.24
capital funds **6**.20; **21**.66–9
government control **4**.28; **19**.2, 15–6;
22.73
health commission option **4**.28; **19**.30
international comparisons **21**.6, 9, 20
joint financing **16**.4–5, 12, 14, 19; **21**.64
methods of financing **19**.2; **21**.12–29
revenue funds **6**.20; **21**.38
see also NHS expenditure

National Health Service management,
20.10
advisory committees **20**.16–20
consensus **20**.3, 5, 12–5
financial **4**.19; **19**.41; **21**.44–69, 74;
22.75
functional **20**.6–7
health authorities option **19**.33–5
health commission option **19**.28–32
local government option **16**.16–22; **19**.27
social services absorption option **16**.23–4
tiers **4**.6–9; **20**.5, 8, 33–44; **22**.70
see also AHAs
DHSS
DMTs
NHS finance
RHAs

National Health Service manpower, **3**.22;
12.1–74; **22**.83
flexibility **12**.26–35; **22**.43
in inner cities **7**.54, 61
morale **4**.20–2; **12**.1–6, 68; **22**.39
numbers **12**.57
occupational health service for **12**.66–7,
73; **22**.44
pay and conditions **12**.14; **22**.41, 42
performance **12**.51–6
planning **12**.57–65; **13**.24–31
professionalism **12**.29, 42
unionisation **12**.10; **20**.6
unqualified **12**.36–7
see also individual groups of workers

485

National Health Service (Vocational Training) Act 1976, 7.29; **14**.45

National Quality Control Scheme, **12**.54

National Staff Committees, **12**.62; **15**.46

needs,
and resource allocation **6**.3–4
individual health **6**.5; **22**.8
local health **2**.15
measuring **6**.3

Netherlands,
health expenditure **3**.19

New Zealand,
drug prescribing **7**.43, 45
election of health authorities **20**.63

noise pollution, **5**.23

Normansfield Hospital, **19**.37

Northern Ireland, **1**.4
ambulance service **15**.35
doctors **14**.10
family practitioner services **20**.53
health and personal social services **6**.18; **16**.26–8; **22**.40
health centres **7**.48, 49, 50
Labour Relations Agency **12**.12
local government **16**.26
needs of elderly **6**.32
private health care **18**.4
resources distribution **3**.9; **21**.39
teaching hospitals administration **17**.6

Nuffield Committee of Enquiry into Dental Education, **9**.2; **22**.28

Nuffield Nursing Homes Trust, **18**.6

nurse learners, **13**.47–9

nurse practitioners, **13**.19

nurses, **4**.4; **13**.1–2, 13, 58–60
administrative grades **4**.11–2; **22**.12, 47
clinical career structure **13**.32–44; **22**.47
education **13**.10, 45–55, 61; **22**.48
geographical distribution **13**.28
legal liability **13**.22
manpower planning **13**.24–31
numbers of **13**.8
role of **13**.9–23
shortages **13**.26–8
specialisation **13**.10, 17, 41–2
unqualified **13**.29

see also clinical nurse specialists
community nurses
home nurses
nurse learners
nurse practitioners
nurse teachers
nursing aides
nursing auxiliaries

Nurses, Midwives and Health Visitors Act 1979, **13**.45, 59; **22**.46

nurse teachers, **13**.53–5; **22**.46

nursing aides, **12**.36–7

nursing auxiliaries, **12**.36

nursing care,
in hospitals **13**.5
in the community **7**.2, 21–6; **13**.5
of elderly **6**.36–7
research **7**.27; **13**.56–7
standards **13**.5–7; **22**.45

nursing homes, **10**.49, 86
abortion facilities **18**.11
for elderly **6**.37; **18**.7, 41; **22**.31, 63
private **18**.4–10; **22**.63

nursing officers, **13**.38–40

nutrition, **5**.3, 5

O

occupational health, **5**.25–9, 33

occupational health services,
and NHS **5**.26–9; **22**.14
for NHS staff **5**.25; **12**.66–7, 73

occupational therapists **15**.2
helpers **15**.9
numbers of **15**.2
shortages **15**.9
training **15**.10, 11

old people *see* elderly

ophthalmic services, **8**.17–21
spectacle frames **8**.18, 20, 30; **22**.24

opticians, **8**.17–21
NHS work **8**.19
numbers of **8**.17
private practice **8**.17

orthoptists, **15**.2
numbers of **15**.2
training **15**.10

overseas doctors, **14**.31–42; **22**.50
and hospital services **14**.37, 87, 91
and hospital specialties **14**.35
numbers of **14**.34
proportion of **10**.23; **14**.35
training deficiencies **14**.39–40

P

panel of assessors for district nursing, **13**.51

parliament, **19**.2
influence on NHS **6**.4, 61; **19**.8–11
MPs' questions **19**.8–9
see also Public Accounts Committee

PARR formula, **16**.27

Pater formula, **17**.22

pathologists, **15**.25
and laboratory management **15**.23, 28

patient advocates, **11**.26

patient committees, **11**.34, 37; **22**.37

patients, **1**.7–9
attitudes **9**.15
day-patients **6**.29; **10**.19
freedom of choice **2**.13; **7**.5; **18**.10
information **10**.26–9; **22**.29
in-patients **3**.4; **6**.29; **10**.3-4, 25
out-patients **6**.29; **10**.14–9
privacy **10**.30–5
private **18**.21, 37
views **3**.3–5; **11**.35
wakening times **10**.36–8, 84; **22**.29

pay beds, **1**.4; **4**.4; **18**.14, 31–40
and consultants **18**.14, 36
charges **18**.37
numbers **18**.14, 32
revocation **18**.34–5

pay disputes *see* industrial disputes

peer review, **12**.52, 56

peripheral hospitals *see* acute hospitals

permanent secretary, **19**.15–6; **22**.66

personal social services, **4**.29; **6**.6, 27; **10**.58; **22**.58
in Northern Ireland **16**.26–8
NHS liaison officers **16**.8
NHS transfer option **16**.23–4, 32
planning **6**.15
relationship with NHS **6**.27; **10**.76; **16**.1–4, 8

personnel officers, **12**.11; **20**.6

pharmaceutical services, **8**.3–16, 29; **22**.23
see also pharmacies

pharmacies, **8**.4–11, 15; **22**.23
costs **8**.6
distribution **8**.7, 10–1
in health centres **8**.15
numbers of **8**.4

pharmacists, **8**.12–6
as consumer advisers **5**.19; **8**.13–4; **22**.23
numbers of **8**.16
training **8**.12

physically handicapped, **2**.12; **10**.82; **16**.2

physiotherapists, **15**.2, 12
and remedial gymnasts **12**.28; **15**.7, 11
helpers **15**.9
numbers **15**.2
shortages **15**.9
training **15**.11

poliomyelitis, **5**.4

political influences,
on NHS **2**.5; **4**.27; **19**.10, 13, 21–24, 72
of pressure groups **6**.9, 61
on priorities **6**.9, 61
see also parliament

Post Office, **19**.29

Prescribers Journal, **7**.40

prescribing,
costs **7**.36
GP **7**.36–41, 46, 65; **22**.21
generic **7**.44
limited period **7**.45
over **7**.41

pressure groups, **6**.9, 61

preventive medicine, **5**.2–12, 31; **22**.14
and NHS costs **5**.11–2
and personal freedom **5**.8–9
see also dental health

primary care services, **7**.1–26, 46–62; **9**.28; **20**.20–2
see also community health services
family practitioner services

primary health care teams, **6**.33, 41, 54; **7**.4, 64; **14**.8; **22**.20

remuneration, **12**.14; **20**.6; **21**.1, 62
  dentists **9**.19–23
  NHS workers **21**.1

research, **17**.34–40, 44; **22**.62
  administration **17**.34
  and private practice **18**.27
  clinical **17**.36
  expenditure **17**.40
  general practice **7**.34
  health care institutes **12**.65; **17**.39
  health services **7**.64; **10**.19; **17**.2, 37–8;
    22.62

mental handicap **6**.46
  nursing **7**.27; **13**.56–7
  on NHS **1**.13

residential care, **6**.49
  for elderly **6**.33
  for mentally disordered **6**.42, 45

Resource Allocation Working Party, **3**.9;
    10.54; **14**.24, 26; **17**.4; **21**.38
  formula **7**.63; **19**.22; **21**.40–3
  Service Increment for Teaching **9**.34–5;
    17.14; **21**.38

resources, **1**.5; **3**.8; **21**.3
  allocation **6**.3, 17; **21**.36–43
  and priorities **6**.3, 9; **19**.39–40; **21**.5
  dental **9**.14
  distribution **3**.9, 20; **21**.35–43
  international comparisons **3**.18–9;
    21.6, 9
  see also NHS finance
    NHS manpower

retirement schemes,
  for GPs **7**.18

road accidents, **5**.5, 31
  cost to NHS **5**.12

Royal College of General Practitioners,
    7.6; **14**.6

Royal College of Midwives, **12**.43

Royal College of Nursing, **12**.43; **13**.56;
    22.45

Royal College of Physicians,
  Faculty of Community Medicine **14**.50

rural areas,
  dispensing **8**.4–5, 9
  health care problems **7**.52

S

Salmon Committee – report on senior
    nursing structure, **4**.4, 11, 12; **20**.6, 28

school health services, **6**.53–4

schools,
  and health education **5**.15
  dental services **9**.5, 30
  nurses **6**.53; **7**.19

scientific advances, **22**.79

scientific and technical staff, **15**.14–32, 55;
    22.53
  national body **15**.22, 55
  numbers of **15**.14
  staffing arrangements **15**.20
  see also medical laboratory scientific
      officers
      psychologists

scientists, **15**.23–32

Scotland,
  ambulance service **15**.35
  child dental service **9**.52
  dental teaching costs **9**.34
  family practitioner services **20**.53, 69;
    22.70
  health boards and local authorities **16**.9
  health centres **7**.48, 50
  Health Education Unit **5**.17, 21
  health expenditure **14**.25
  Hospital Advisory Service **12**.53
  NHS planning system **6**.19
  needs of elderly **16**.31
  number of doctors **14**.10, 25
  private health care **18**.4
  resources distribution **3**.9; **6**.7; **21**.38
  rural health care **7**.52
  teaching hospital administration **17**.6;
    22.60

Scottish Advisory Committee on Hospital
    Medical Establishments, **14**.24

Scottish Advisory Council on Social Work,
    6.32

Scottish Health Services Planning Council,
    6.19
  and needs of elderly **6**.32

screening, **5**.7; **6**.57; **7**.3

seat belts, **5**.5, 12

Secretary of State for Social Services,
    12.23; **15**.17; **19**.12–4
  and priorities **6**.4, 15
  functions **2**.4; **19**.21

self-care, **5**.16, 19

self-help groups, **11**.32

sheltered workshops,
  for mentally ill **6**.42

SIFT *see* Resource Allocation Working
  Party

single district areas, **20**.5, 43, 46, 69; **22**.70

smoking, **5**.5, 6, 14, 23, 31

social attitudes, **5**.14–5; **22**.78

social policy, **6**.10

social problems, **5**.5; **7**.52; **10**.20

social security,
  and DHSS role **19**.18

social services *see* personal social services

social work,
  in the health services **16**.4, 8
  local authority **4**.7, 29; **6**.42; **16**.2, 24

social workers, **10**.76; **12**.38, 40; **16**.4
  see also community workers

Solihull, **20**.14

speech therapists, **15**.2
  training **15**.10

Strathclyde,
  health liaison committee **20**.49

supra-regional assay services, **15**.21

surveyors *see* works and maintenance staff

Sweden,
  dental health education **9**.67
  health expenditure **3**.19

T

taxation,
  and NHS finance **4**.25; **19**.2; **21**.12, 20
  GPs **14**.77
  see also hypothecation

teachers,
  and health education **5**.15
  for mentally handicapped **6**.45, 47

teaching hospitals,
  administration **17**.4–6
  and primary care services **7**.60
  and RAWP formula **17**.14, 18; **21**.42
  as "centres of excellence" **17**.15–6; **21**.42
  costs **17**.14; **21**.42
  finance **17**.13, 19, 42; **22**.60
  London **17**.17–8

technological development, **15**.21; **22**.80
  and NHS costs **22**.82
  see also computers

television, **5**.21; **6**.7; **22**.14

Temporary Registration Assessment
  Board, **14**.36

Todd Commission – report on medical
  education, **14**.14; **17**.17, 30

trade unions, **12**.10, 11
  and health authority membership **20**.62
  TUC **12**.23–4, 71

training, **17**.1–2
  ancillary staff **15**.45, 46–7, 56; **22**.54
  joint **7**.4
  nurses **13**.10, 45–55
  PSMs **15**.10–1
  receptionists **7**.12, 63
  social workers **16**.4
  see also medical education

training centres,
  for mentally handicapped **6**.45

Tunbridge Committee – report on care of
  health of hospital staff, **12**.66–7

U

United Kingdom Central Council for
  Nursing, Midwifery and Health
  Visiting, **13**.10, 45, 50, 61; **22**.48

United States of America,
  "defensive medicine" **12**.55
  health **3**.19
  insurance schemes **4**.26; **21**.14
  nurse practitioners **13**.19
  patient advocates **11**.26

universities,
  and medical education **17**.11, 26–35, 43
  clinical academic staff **14**.69–71
  cost-sharing **17**.20–4
  departments of community medicine
    14.57
  finance **19**.5
  liaison committees **17**.7, 10
  relationship with NHS **17**.3, 7–12, 41;
    22.59
  research **17**.2, 34–40

University Grants Committee **19**.5, 29
  liaison with health departments **17**.11–2

University of London,
  working party on London medical and
    dental schools **17**.17

urban areas, **7**.1
  deputising services **7**.9
  health care **7**.53–63, 66; **22**.22
  health centres **7**.49
  health workers shortage **7**.55, 62
  white paper on **7**.53

V

vaccination, **5**.12

voluntary organisations, **5**.18; **11**.31; **22**.37
  and NHS funding **21**.31
  see also self-help groups

volunteers,
  in NHS **11**.31–2; **22**.37

W

waiting lists, **10**.5–13, 85
  and private practice **18**.38
  geographical differences **10**.11
  hospital **10**.6–10

wakening times, **10**.36–8, 84

Wales,
  GP prescribing costs **7**.35
  health centres **7**.48
  NHS planning system **6**.18
  number of doctors **14**.10
  patient committees **11**.33
  private nursing homes **18**.4, 7
  resources distribution **3**.9
  structure of NHS **19**.25

Warnock Committee – report on special
  education, **13**.46

West Germany,
  health **3**.19

Whitley Councils, **12**.14–9, 70; **13**.30;
  22.41
  and industrial relations **12**.11, 23
  agreements **12**.15, 27, 43
  McCarthy review **12**.19; **22**.41
  see also General Whitley Council

Willink Committee – report on medical
  practitioners and students, **14**.14

Women doctors, **14**.43–7, 91; **22**.50
  part-time work **14**.46
  proportion of **14**.43
  training difficulties **14**.44, 47

women doctors' retainer scheme, **14**.46

works and maintenance staff, **15**.48–53
  career structure for craftsmen **15**.52
  numbers of **15**.48
  shortages **15**.51
  see also works officers

works officers, **15**.49–50, 56; **22**.54

World Health Organisation,
  and fluoridation **9**.53
  dental services report **9**.50

Z

Zuckerman Committee – report on
  hospital scientific and technical
  services, **15**.15, 16, 18, 22, 55; **22**.53,
  55

Printed in England for Her Majesty's Stationery Office by Commercial Colour Press,London E.7.
Dd.626753 K40 7/79 CCP